Career Counseling

Applied Concepts of Life Planning

Titles of Related Interest

Clarke G. Carney & Linda Field Wells
  Discover the Career Within You, Fourth Edition

Gary Lynn Harr
  Career Guide: Road Maps to Meaning in the World of Work

Robert D. Lock
  Taking Charge of Your Career Direction, Third Edition
  Job Search, Third Edition
  Student Activities for Taking Charge of Your Career Direction, Third Edition
    and Job Search, Third Edition

Gary W. Peterson, James P. Sampson, Jr., & Robert C. Reardon
  Career Development and Services: A Cognitive Approach

Lola Sikula
  Changing Careers: Steps to Success

Richard S. Sharf
  Applying Career Development Theory to Counseling, Second Edition
  Occupational Information Overview

Vernon G. Zunker & Debra Norris
  Using Assessment Results for Career Development, Fifth Edition

FIFTH EDITION

Career Counseling

Applied Concepts of Life Planning

Vernon G. Zunker

Southwest Texas State University

Brooks/Cole Publishing Company

I(T)P® An International Thomson Publishing Company

Pacific Grove • Albany • Belmont • Bonn • Boston • Cincinnati • Detroit • Johannesburg
London • Madrid • Melbourne • Mexico City • New York • Paris • Singapore
Tokyo • Toronto • Washington

Sponsoring Editor: *Eileen Murphy*
Marketing Team: *Jean Thompson,*
   Romy Taormina, Deanne Brown
Editorial Assistant: *Lisa Blanton, Susan Carlson*
Production Editor: *Nancy L. Shammas*
Manuscript Editor: *Barbara Kimmel*
Permissions Editor: *Fiorella Ljundgren*
Design Coordinator: *E. Kelly Shoemaker*

Interior and Cover Design: *Lisa Thompson*
Interior Illustration: *Laurie Albrecht*
Cover Illustration: *Harry Briggs*
Art Editor: *Jennifer Mackres*
Typesetting: *Thompson Type*
Cover Printing: *Phoenix Color Corporation*
Printing and Binding: *The Maple-Vail Book*
   Manufacturing Group, Inc.

For more information, contact:

BROOKS/COLE PUBLISHING COMPANY
511 Forest Lodge Road
Pacific Grove, CA 93950

International Thomson Publishing Europe
Berkshire House 168-173
High Holborn
London WCIV 7AA
England

Thomas Nelson Australia
102 Dodds Street
South Melbourne, 3205
Victoria, Australia

Nelson Canada
1120 Birchmount Road
Scarborough, Ontario
Canada, M1K 5G4

International Thomson Editores
Seneca 53
Col. Polanco
11560 México, D. F., México

International Thomson Publishing GmbH
Königswinterer Strasse 418
53227 Bonn
Germany

International Thomson Publishing Asia
221 Henderson Road
#05-10 Henderson Building
Singapore 0315

International Thomson Publishing Japan
Hirakawacho Kyowa Building, 3F
2-2-1 Hirakawacho
Chiyoda-ku, Tokyo 102
Japan

Printed in the United States of America

10   9   8   7   6   5   4   3   2

Library of Congress Cataloging-in-Publication Data
Zunker, Vernon G., [date]
   Career counseling : applied concepts of life planning / Vernon G. Zunker. — 5th ed.
      p.   cm.
   Includes bibliographical references and index.
   ISBN 0-534-34668-5
   1. Vocational guidance.   I. Title.
HF5381.Z86 1997   97-11166
371.4'25—dc21   CIP

To Rosalie

For years of love, trust, and devotion

CONTENTS

CHAPTER THREE

Theories of Career Development—II: New Evolving Theories   70

CHAPTER FOUR

Career Life Planning   91

CHAPTER FIVE

The *Dictionary of Occuptional Titles,* the *Occupational Outlook Handbook,* and Career Clusters   109

This book has been a significant part of my professional life since the 1970s. It represents an important part of my work role. As such, it has touched most other aspects of my lifestyle, including all life roles. Among my friends and family, it has been labeled "the book" and was often the focus of discussion. In this sense, it has provided me with a living example of how pervasive work is and has become. At times "the book" became very intrusive and limited social events and time that could have been well spent just relaxing. But in retrospect, as one looks back over a lifetime of work, the rewards of dedication to worthwhile projects far outweigh the negative factors.

As I complete the last pages of this edition of "the book," I hope it is not presumptuous of me to suggest that readers will be at least somewhat inspired to experience a lifetime of rewarding work as I did. The time for the recognition of the importance of career counseling has certainly arrived. In fact, a new era seems to be fast approaching in which career counseling will converge with other disciplines into an integrative counseling approach designed to give equal consideration to all life roles. The focus of counseling procedures in the 21st century will surely include changing goals and directions to meet the challenges of changes in the future workplace. New techniques should develop that will provide a future sense of direction for the counseling profession.

Among recent sweeping changes, the approach to working per se may change into what I have labeled "the personal agency person"—one who takes full responsibility for his or her own career development. Historians have documented the amazing adaptive nature of the human being; and so, in our time, men and women will also adapt to changing work roles and their influence on all life roles. As a member of the counseling profession, you too will have the opportunity to find many rewarding experiences in your work role. As Shakespeare stated, "Do well your part, there lies the glory." Good luck!

The fifth edition of *Career Counseling: Applied Concepts & Life Planning* contains two new chapters. One chapter covers emerging career development theories that have surfaced since the 1990s. The other contains two parts: first, a description of the family as a system that influences career development, and second, conflicts in dual-career marriages. In addition, every chapter has been revised or updated with recent research and current programs. A greater emphasis has been given to the changing workplace and subsequent changing work role.

A companion text, *Using Assessment Results in Career Development*, Fifth Edition, has been developed as a supplement to this book. The purpose of this ancillary text is to illustrate how assessment results can be used to increase self-awareness and rational choices. Readers will find that this text provides detailed information on applying knowledge of tests and measurements in counseling encounters and using assessment results in a wide variety of counseling situations.

This book is divided into five parts. Part One, Foundations and Resources, covers career counseling today, historical developments, career development theories, career life-planning procedures, and career counseling resources. The first chapter provides a perspective of developing challenges to the career counseling profession and its historical development. Chapters 2 and 3 provide career counselors with a philosophical frame of reference. The third chapter covers several counseling programs promoting career life planning as a lifelong process. Chapter 5 discusses the use of occupational classification systems and provides the counselor with an understanding of occupational titles and job information systems. Interactive and information-oriented computer programs designed to enhance the career counseling process are the focus of Chapter 6. Chapter 7 discusses assessment techniques that emphasize the use of tests and inventories in career counseling. Chapter 8 provides a detailed discussion of career resource centers, including organizational structures and operational procedures, as well as comprehensive descriptions of career information components and materials.

Part Two, Career Guidance Programs in Educational Institutions, provides innovative counseling models and programs for elementary through senior high school and for postsecondary institutions of higher learning. Chapter 9 presents implications of human development and relevant research for career guidance programs in schools. Chapter 10 explores a variety of approaches to career counseling for elementary, junior high, and senior high schools. The characteristics of individuals in college and the development of career guidance programs to help meet their varied needs are the subjects of Chapter 11.

Part Three, Career Guidance Programs for Adults in Transition, is intended to build an understanding of adults' career development in new and developing organizations, changes in work requirements and in workplace environments, stages and transitions in adult development, and career counseling programs designed to meet their needs. Chapter 12 discusses several work-related issues, the personal agency person, and how these factors relate to individual functioning in organizations. Chapter 13 covers a national survey of working America, major themes in human development, and counseling components for adults in career transition.

Changing organizational structures and operational procedures plus new concepts in career development in organizations are discussed in Chapter 14.

Part Four, Career Guidance Programs for Special Populations, includes a discussion of innovative counseling models and career counseling programs for special populations. The special needs of women are identified and discussed in Chapter 15. Chapter 16 reviews the socialization process that has shaped men's lives, influencing their perspectives of appropriate masculine roles. Career counseling procedures designed to help men meet the needs of their career life roles in a changing society are also discussed. The family's influence on career development and the issues facing dual-career marriages are covered in Chapter 17. A new theory for multicultural counseling and career counseling programs for culturally diverse populations is presented in Chapter 18. Special counseling components for meeting the unique needs of persons with disabilities are discussed in Chapter 19.

In Part Five, Techniques for the Career Counseling Intake Interview, Chapter 20 includes the rationale for a career counseling intake interview and some techniques for conducting the interview. A section of this chapter contains a supplement to the interview that covers problems that interfere with career development, such as behaviors that may lead to work maladjustment and a lack of cognitive clarity. Chapter 21 includes case studies that illustrate the use of the career counseling interview.

I am indebted to many individuals who assisted and encouraged me through these five editions. Without listing names for fear of leaving someone out, I wish to thank everyone, including those who read and offered suggestions and those who offered words of encouragement and understanding. I am most appreciative.

I owe a special thanks to Debra Norris and Robert Reardon of Florida State University, Howard Splete of Oakland University, and Rich Feller of Colorado State University. They made significant suggestions for improving this text and provided me with resources that made this edition possible.

I am also indebted to Eileen Murphy and Lisa Blanton of Brooks/Cole for their assistance, especially for the resources they provided. I also wish to acknowledge the help of Nancy Shammas and Kelly Shoemaker, also from Brooks/Cole, and Barbara Kimmel, manuscript editor. I want to acknowledge the help of my typist, Carolynn Thornton, who put the references in final form. Finally, I dedicate this book to my wife, who has stood by me and supported me through all five editions. And so as a friend in Mexico once told me, there is only one way to speak of the one who is most dear—*mi vida*.

Vernon G. Zunker

Career Counseling
Applied Concepts of Life Planning

Foundations and Resources

Career Counseling Today and Its Historical Development

The review of current literature on the subject of career development suggests that we are at a crossroads in the career counseling movement. Career counseling increasingly is being challenged to meet the needs of a society that is experiencing vast changes in the workplace. There is a call for career counseling to unite its efforts with the entire counseling profession and other mental health workers and to clarify its role for future direction. This movement is precipitated by the fact that the role and scope of career counseling has expanded to include clients' mental health concerns. Some of these concerns involve dysfunctional workers (Lowman, 1993), linking career counseling to personality disorders (Kjos, 1996), and addressing faulty cognitions (Krumboltz, 1991; Doyle, 1992).

Some researchers have suggested that career counseling take an integrative approach (Gysbers, 1996; Hansen, 1996), whereas others argue that career counseling cannot be separated from other life roles in the counseling process (Burlew, 1996; Super, Savickas, & Super, 1996). These examples represent a growing list of issues that will confront the career counseling profession well into the 21st century.

The first section of this chapter, "Career Counseling Today," addresses some current issues facing the profession. The second part of this chapter covers the historical development of career counseling.

Career Counseling Today

As the introduction to this chapter suggests, the career counseling profession is faced with some major challenges. A changing work force and changing workplace have created a number of relevant needs for our society today that will extend well into the 21st century. Since 1979, 43 million jobs have been lost (Uchitelle & Klein-field, 1996), many in higher-paying, white-collar professions. Ironically, more jobs have been created than lost, but the new jobs pay less than those they've replaced. Sad but true, many workers in the United States have lost the old certainties of job security. Getting a lifetime job unfortunately is not very probable in today's work environment.

The workplace will become more diverse in the 21st century. More women will find their way into the workplace, and the work force will become more culturally diverse. Working relationships are being tested in a changing work environment that will grow even more diverse in the future (see Chapter 12).

Industrial organizations in the United States are competing in a global economy that has necessitated changes in strategies and operating procedures. Many organizations have significantly reduced their work force and are retraining workers for different jobs that fit into different work environments. Changes in the workplace have changed the "American dream" of job, security, home, and family. The typical worker of tomorrow faces a different set of circumstances; for instance, the work done today may change tomorrow or be whisked off to another site, possibly overseas. "Be flexible and adaptable" is the message relayed to the worker, and most important, "use personal agency (take responsibility for your own career development) to keep abreast with changing times." Today's worker is to be a team player; interpersonal skills are highly valued.

What we are discussing here touches practically every U.S. family; one's work or career is so pervasive in U.S. lifestyles. Our career determines where we live, how we live, and, to a great extent, with whom we associate. Americans have long believed that their freedom to choose work is a sacred privilege, and the patterns of work—such as joining an organization that will provide security for a lifetime—were deeply embedded in our society in previous decades. In many ways, the very foundations of our society will be tested by the changes we have only briefly discussed.

A number of academic disciplines, including sociology and developmental psychology, have addressed the subject of work. There is a need to combine the efforts of all academic disciplines in an attempt to converge strategies to assist individuals who have work-related problems. Some specific work-related problems to be discussed in this text are:

stress at work	the fired worker
career burnout	the unsatisfied worker
occupational insecurity	workers with disabilities
coping with joblessness	multicultural workers
developing work roles	the depressed worker
changing workplaces	the schizophrenic worker
work overload	workers with personality disorders
work commitment	how work affects other life roles
work dysfunctions or impairment	

There are more topics to add to this list, but what we have so far illustrates the pervasive nature of work and the implications of the psychological constructs that accompany it. These are problems career counselors face that require a working knowledge not only of career counseling techniques but also of many different counseling strategies and interventions. An integrated approach to career counseling means that career counselors will need a wide background of counseling skills to meet the needs of their clients.

Other mental health workers also will need a knowledge of career-related problems and subsequent solutions. For instance, career counselors will come face-to-face with marital conflicts in dual-earner homes, and marriage counselors may need to assess some clients' work-related problems. Moreover, for the depressed client who seeks a job change, counselors will need to determine whether the work is responsible for the depression or whether the depression has caused the poor work habits.

The Case of the Depressed Worker

Alma, a worker in her late thirties, told her career counselor that she wanted to change jobs. She was currently doing secretarial work in a large firm, a job she had held for two years. Her reasons for seeking a change were somewhat vague, as she stated, "I just don't like it there any more." And she added, "I'm very depressed."

Depression can come from a variety of sources, and it can be work-related, non-work-related, or both. But as Lowman (1993) points out, depression can both lower work performance and affect nonwork factors. In Alma's case, work seems to be at the center of her problem. Many aspects of work have been found to influence depression, such as problems with supervision, overly demanding work, ambiguity of authority, lack of social support, and corporate instability (Golding, 1989; Firth & Britton, 1989, cited in Lowman, 1993). The source of Alma's depression seems to be the work climate.

The career counselor was able to determine that Alma's perception of her problems had to do with a poor relationship with her immediate supervisor. Alma also perceived that her work was demanding and that she received little in the way of feedback support. When clients present signs of depression, there are many questions to be answered. For instance: What are possible sources of stress in the workplace? in the home? Is this client predisposed to depression? How do we decrease depression or anxiety?

Such cases may follow several pathways. If the counselor determines that the client is suffering from work-related depression, the choices are usually either to change the job situation or to change the individual—or both. When job change is the best choice, the client must reevaluate goals, changing values, and developed abilities. A person-environment fit suggests congruence between the individual's needs and abilities and the requirements of a work environment.

The choice to change the person could involve stress reduction exercises, drug therapy, physical activity programs, and interpersonal skills training, among others. Combinations of such programs are often used. More than likely, Alma's career counselor would suggest programs of stress reduction to accompany the process of choosing a different occupation.

In this brief review of a case study, a number of counseling skills were suggested and implied: for example, skills in diagnosing symptoms of depression, skills of interviewing, skills in anxiety reduction programs, and skills in career decision-making procedures. A more integrative approach to counseling recognizes that an individual's total development includes a broad spectrum of domains; we are not just career counselors, we counsel individuals. As always, counselors must recognize their limitations and refer clients when it is in their clients' best interest.

Other Current Career Counseling Programs

Career counselors do offer a large number of career-related programs. For example, in many schools, K–12, students are provided with comprehensive counseling programs that require written career and life plans beginning in middle school, and school-to-work programs focus on preparing students for work through experiential activities in communities. Colleges and universities have career centers that offer placement or employment services. In organizations, career planning specialists offer workers a variety of services.

A large volume of career-related background information has developed, some of which is included in most career counseling courses. For instance, theories of career development suggest how and why people chose certain career paths. What factors influence individuals in the career decision-making process are debated and have been empirically evaluated. How theories translate into practical application has recently been accomplished by most theorists. Some established theories have a long history, whereas other theories are new and emerging. How they mesh with sociological and developmental psychological perspectives is yet to be determined, but some beginnings have been made (see Chapters 2 and 3).

The use of assessment results has had a long association with career counseling. Not only have interest inventories been refined, but new and different tests are being used with other information in the counseling process to assess variables considered important. The almost immediate availability of assessment results via the computer enhances their use (see Chapter 7).

The issue of special populations is an ongoing process of discovery. For example, more women are working full time, and many are working by choice. The special needs of women in the work force continue to be viable topics in career couseling. The growing cultural diversity in the population has also created special needs that require the attention of the entire counseling profession. A recently developed theory, published in 1996 and reported in Chapter 18, presents some intriguing perspectives for multicultural counseling: the multicultural cultural theory (MCT) suggests that couselors become aware of their own cultural values and biases, develop an awareness of the client's worldview, and develop a repertoire of culturally appropriate intervention strategies. Individuals with disabilities, often ignored, have counseling needs that must continue to receive our attention.

Finally, technological advances have provided counseling tools that have gone far beyond the expectations of most career counselors. It has been suggested that today's technology is only in its infancy. In the meantime, the increase in number of users of computer-based tools to help in the career search has been phenomenal; in 1994, more than 9 million individuals at 20,000 different sites used career information delivery systems (Mariani, 1995-96). There seems to be no end to the potential use of computer-based tools. For instance, consider the global webs of career information that are being developed. If you wish to move to Bangkok, job openings will be available on global webs right in your own living room. (For more information on the use of computers, see Chapter 6.)

As you read the following pages, become more aware of the changing roles of career counselors. The time has passed—though it never really existed—when all counselors had to do was test clients, tell them the results, find job openings, and move on "in a cloud of dust."

The Historical Development of Career Counseling

The career guidance movement is a product of our development as a nation. It is the story of human progress in a nation founded on the principle of human rights. It touches all aspects of human life, for it has involved political, economic, educational, philosophical, and social progress and change. To think of the career guidance movement as merely another educational event is a gross misinterpretation of its broader significance for social progress. It is, in fact, a movement that has had and will have a tremendous impact on the working lives of many individuals. Knowledge of the historical perspectives of this movement will provide a greater insight into the development of the career counselor's role in career guidance.

Many terms will be introduced and defined throughout this book. Some of the terminology that is briefly described in this chapter to clarify the theoretical concepts discussed will be explained in greater detail in succeeding chapters, within the context of the program descriptions and practical illustrations.

Career development as defined by the American Counseling Association "is the total constellation of psychological, sociological, educational, physical, economic, and chance factors that combine to influence the nature and significance of work in the total life span of any given individual" (Engels, 1994, p. 2). Specifically, the term reflects individually developed needs and goals associated with stages of life and with tasks that affect career choices and subsequent fulfillment of purpose.

The terms *vocation, occupation,* and *job* are used interchangeably to indicate activities and positions of employment. *Career* refers to the activities and positions involved in vocations, occupations, and jobs as well as to related activities associated with an individual's lifetime of work.

Career counseling includes all counseling activities associated with career choices over a life span. In the career counseling process, all aspects of individual needs (including family, work, and leisure) are recognized as integral parts of career decision making and planning. *Career guidance* encompasses all components of services and activities in educational institutions, agencies, and other organizations that offer counseling and career-related educational programs.

The Birth of the Career Guidance Movement

The discussion of the career guidance movement during the period from 1850 to 1940 includes the following events: (1) the Industrial Revolution, (2) the study of individual differences, (3) World War I, (4) the National Conference on Vocational Guidance, (5) the measurement movement, and (6) significant federal acts. Individuals who made significant contributions during this period include: Francis Galton, Wilheim Wundt, James Cattell, Alfred Binet, Frank Parsons, Robert Yerkes, and E. K. Strong.

THE RISE OF INDUSTRIALISM

The rise of industrialism in the late 1800s dramatically changed work environments and living conditions. Urban areas grew at tremendous rates, largely through immigration. In addition, the rapid growth and centralization of industry attracted many from rural areas who were in need of work. Many people found the long hours required by industrial establishments and the harsh and crowded living conditions in tenement houses to be undesirable. Perhaps even more significant was a loss of identity many experienced in these crowded work and living environments. A spirit of reform emerged in reaction to the impersonal industrial systems and chaotic conditions of urban life in the United States and in Europe. As if in response to deteriorating social conditions, several outstanding scientists turned their attention to human behavior and to the study of individual differences.

The study of human abilities.   Francis Galton of England published his first and second books devoted to the origins of human abilities in 1874 and 1883. In 1879, Wilheim Wundt established an experimental laboratory in Leipzig, Germany, to study human behavior. In France, Alfred Binet and V. Henri published an article in 1896 describing mental measurement concepts (Borow, 1964). These studies of human differences turned our attention to the conditions of life and work in a society changed by the Industrial Revolution.

In the United States, G. Stanley Hall founded a psychological laboratory in 1883 to study and measure physical and mental characteristics of children. In 1890, James Cattell published an article in which he referred to mental tests as measures of individual differences. John Dewey called for a reform of the lockstep method of education to one in which more attention was given to individual motivations, interests, and development. The case for the individual was being carefully formulated.

EARLY PROGRAMS OF CAREER GUIDANCE

Near the turn of the century, public schools established isolated programs of career guidance. In San Francisco, George A. Merrill developed a plan for students to explore industrial arts courses. Brewer (1918) credits Merrill as being a forerunner of vocational guidance, but Merrill's primary interests were in vocational education

(Picchioni & Bonk, 1983). Many of his innovations resemble the career education movement of the 1970s (see Chapter 10).

In Central High School in Detroit, Jesse B. Davis served as counselor for 11th-grade students from 1898 to 1907 (Brewer, 1918). His major duties involved educational and vocational counseling. Later, as principal of the school, he required all 7th-grade students to write a weekly report on occupational interests for their English class. Davis emphasized the moral value of hard work as well as the benefits of occupational information.

These guidance activities and others were indeed innovative, but a logical and straightforward conceptualization of career guidance was needed to make it a viable movement. In the early 1900s, Frank Parsons provided a systematic plan for career guidance that has endured, with some modifications, to the present time. According to his philosophical orientation to social reform, there was to be equality and opportunity for all. The procedures he outlined for helping individuals select an occupation were to be based primarily on people's interests and aptitudes and on occupational information.

FRANK PARSONS

The social reform movements and civic developments of the late 1800s captured the interest of young Frank Parsons, who had been educated as an engineer at Cornell University. He wrote several books on social reform movements and articles on such topics as women's suffrage, taxation, and education for all. Parsons taught history, math, and French in public schools, worked as a railroad engineer, and passed the state bar examination for lawyers in Massachusetts in 1881 (Picchioni & Bonk, 1983). He also taught at Boston University's law school and at Kansas State Agricultural College, and he was academic dean of the extension division of Ruskin College in Trenton, Missouri. However, his real interests appeared to lie in social reform and in helping individuals make occupational choices. These interests surfaced when Parsons returned to Boston in the early 1900s.

In 1901, the Civic Service-House had been established in Boston for the purpose of providing educational programs for immigrants and young persons seeking work. In 1905, Parsons was named director of the Breadwinner's Institute, which was one of the Civic Service-House programs. Eventually, through Parsons's leadership, the Vocation Bureau of Boston was established on January 13, 1908.

On May 1, 1908, Parsons presented a lecture that had a tremendous impact on the career guidance movement. His report described systematic guidance procedures used to counsel 80 men and women who had come to the vocational bureau for help. Parsons's major work, *Choosing a Vocation,* was posthumously published in May 1909. Frank Parsons died on September 26, 1908 (Picchioni & Bonk, 1983).

One of Parsons's important contributions to the career guidance movement was his conceptual framework for helping an individual select a career. Parsons defined his three-part formulation as follows.

> First, a clear understanding of yourself, aptitudes, abilities, interests, resources, limitations, and other qualities.

Second, a knowledge of the requirements and conditions of success, advantages
and disadvantages, compensations, opportunities, and prospects in different
lines of work.

Third, true reasoning on the relations of these two groups of facts. (Parsons,
1909, p. 5)

Edmund G. Williamson (1965) pointed out that, with some modification, Parsons's
three-part formulation greatly influenced the procedures used in career counseling
over a significant period of time. Parts of Parsons's three-part formulation are practices used in many career counseling programs today. Moreover, Parsons's conceptual framework ignited a national interest in career guidance.

FIRST NATIONAL CONFERENCE ON VOCATIONAL GUIDANCE

In 1910, the First National Conference on Vocational Guidance was held in Boston.
Several speakers, including Charles W. Elliott, president of Harvard, emphasized
the need for school guidance personnel. Other speakers, including the superintendent of schools in Boston, strongly suggested that methods for determining each
student's potential be an objective of future scientific investigations. Understandably, the spread of organized guidance in other cities was greatly influenced by
this conference and by the second national conference in New York City in 1912.
At the third national conference in Grand Rapids, Michigan, in October 1913, the
National Vocational Guidance Association, Incorporated, was founded. This organization, now called the National Career Development Association (NCDA), was
most instrumental in providing the leadership to advance the career guidance
movement.

Industrial psychology.   An important related development that influenced the
career guidance movement was the work of the German psychologist Hugo Mus-
terberg. He joined the Harvard faculty in 1897 and introduced several methods of
determining aptitudes and characteristics of men successfully employed in certain
occupations in Germany. In his 1912 book, *Psychology and Industrial Efficiency,*
Munsterberg reported several studies of occupational choice and worker performance. In this publication and in others, Munsterberg pointed out the utility of
psychological testing instruments and techniques for selection of industrial employees. Munsterberg was influential in establishing industrial psychology as a
relevant field of applied psychology.

THE MEASUREMENT MOVEMENT, 1900–1940

In many respects, the measurement and guidance movements coincided in development and shared many of the same roots. One of the early, influential individuals
was Wilheim Wundt of Leipzig, Germany, who had established the first experimental laboratory in psychology. His work in measurement was confined to evaluation
of reaction times to certain stimuli. However, Kraepelin and Ebbinghaus, two other
German psychologists who were influenced by Wundt's work, became directly

involved in constructing measuring devices and were among the pioneers of the measurement movement (Ross & Stanley, 1954). Wundt also contributed directly to the measurement movement by his standardization of procedures that became models for developing standardized tests.

James M. Cattell, who studied at Wundt's laboratory in Germany, became interested in individual differences. When Cattell returned to the United States, he became active in the measurement movement and first used the term *mental test* in an article written in 1890. He also studied the work of Galton, another pioneering force in the measurement movement, who had devised sensory discrimination tests as measures of judgment and intelligence.

The credit for constructing the first intelligence test is generally given to Alfred Binet and Theophile Simon of France. This test, published in 1905, is administered individually and is known as the Binet-Simon scale, or simply the 1905 scale. In 1916, under the direction of L. M. Termen of Stanford University, the revised Binet-Simon scales were published as the Stanford-Binet. The introduction of the term *intelligence quotient* contributed to the popularity of this test and of tests in general.

The need for testing the abilities of large groups became apparent at the beginning of World War I. Close to 1.5 million people needed classification and subsequent training for the armed services. Under the direction of Robert M. Yerkes, the first group intelligence tests were developed. Arthur S. Otis, who had constructed (but not published) an objective item test for group administration, contributed his work to the cause. The tests developed for the army became known as the Army Alpha and Beta Tests. Unlike the more typical verbal Alpha Test, the Beta Test contained a nonlanguage scale for illiterate and foreign recruits. After the war, these tests were made available to counselors of the general public.

The testing movement made rapid advances during the next two decades. Special aptitude tests were developed; Clark L. Hull published *Aptitude Testing* in 1928. This publication was devoted to the use of aptitude-test batteries in vocational guidance and emphasized his concept of matching human traits with job requirements. The idea of forecasting job satisfaction and success from standardized measures of aptitude succinctly linked the measurement and guidance movements.

Another direct link between the measurement and guidance movements was the development of interest assessment. In 1927, Edward K. Strong, Jr., of Stanford University published the first edition of an interest inventory, *The Strong Vocational Interest Blank*. This measure of interest, constructed from the responses of individuals in certain occupations, provided career counselors with a most important tool for linking assessment results with certain occupations.

Achievement testing in public schools made rapid progress during the 1920s. Personality testing began during World War I but was much slower in development. However, the testing movement also had its pitfalls for many career counselors. Too much reliance was placed on assessment results in the career-decision process; excessive dependence on testing provided little opportunity for considering many other aspects of human development and experience. Nevertheless, the testing tools developed during this period for measuring individual differences provided the much-needed standardized support materials for the career guidance movement.

SIGNIFICANT FEDERAL ACTS AND CONTRIBUTIONS FROM THE PRIVATE SECTOR

The federal government has played a significant role in the career guidance movement. Relevant national legislative acts passed from 1917 to 1940 are summarized in this section, and other significant national legislation is reported in subsequent sections of this chapter.

In 1917, the Smith-Hughes Act established federal grants for support of a nationwide vocational educational program. This act was also influential in supporting the establishment of counselor-training departments at major universities. The George-Dean Act of 1936 continued the support of the vocational education movement. In response to the Great Depression, the Wagner-Peyser Act of 1933 established the U.S. Employment Service. The Civilian Conservation Corps was created in 1933, and the Works Progress Administration was established in 1935. All of these legislative acts were designed to provide employment for the masses who could not find jobs during this period. In 1939, the first edition of the *Dictionary of Occupational Titles* was published by the U.S. Employment Service.

In the private sector, the B'nai B'rith Vocational Service Bureau was established in 1938. Its purpose was to offer group vocational guidance programs in metropolitan areas. In 1939, the Jewish Occupational Council was established to conduct counseling, placement, and rehabilitation services for Jewish immigrants through the B'nai B'rith, other offices, and sheltered workshops. The efforts of the Jewish Occupational Council established models for delivery of career guidance programs.

Growth of the Career Guidance Movement: 1940 to the Present

Significant events covered during the period from 1940 to the present are as follows: (1) the appearance of major counseling publications, (2) World War II, (3) significant federal programs, (4) the formulation of theories of career development, (5) the development of career education, (6) the professionalism movement, and (7) the advances of technology. Individuals who made significant contributions to the career guidance movement during this period are E. G. Williamson, Carl Rogers, Eli Ginzberg, Ann Roe, Donald Super, John Holland, David Tiedeman, and H. B. Gelatt.

EDMUND G. WILLIAMSON'S DIRECTIVE COUNSELING

During the early 1940s, E. G. Williamson's publication, *How to Counsel Students* (1939), made a tremendous impact on the career guidance movement. This comprehensive work was, in many respects, an extension of Parsons's formulations.

However, Williamson's straightforward approach to counseling was thoroughly illustrated and contained six sequential steps: analysis, synthesis, diagnosis, prognosis, counseling, and follow-up. Williamson's approach to counseling became known as *directive counseling*. Williamson was one of the members of the Minnesota Employment Stability Research Institute who were influential in the development of vocational psychology at the University of Minnesota. This group was later identified with trait-and-factor approaches to career guidance as discussed in the next chapter.

CARL R. ROGERS'S NONDIRECTIVE COUNSELING

In 1942, Carl R. Rogers's influential book, *Counseling and Psychotherapy*, was published. Although as a therapist Rogers had worked primarily with emotionally distressed clients, his method of *nondirective counseling* or *client-centered counseling* caused a complete reexamination of the early established assumptions in career counseling. The Rogerians attacked directive counseling procedures and philosophical orientation in numerous articles and debates. First, according to opponents of directive counseling, the relatively straightforward concept of matching human traits with job requirements had to be revamped. The concepts of affective and motivational behavior were among other considerations to be included in the counseling process. Second, client self-acceptance and self-understanding were primary goals. Third, more attention was to be given to client-counselor interactions and to the verbalization of clients in the counseling process. In essence, the counseling relationship was to be one of mutual respect, directed toward the client's gaining an understanding of self and taking steps to control his or her destiny. The center of attention shifted to the client and to counseling techniques, with less emphasis given to testing, cumulative records, and the counselor as an authority figure.

Rogerian theory was responsible for the first major breach from Parsons's straightforward approach. Many Rogerian concepts were later endorsed and integrated into directive counseling, resulting in an approach to career guidance that included a broader perspective of human development and life experience. However, the psychotherapy movement and the growing interest in expanding the professional role of counselors had to wait until after World War II.

WORLD WAR II AND FEDERAL PROGRAMS

During World War II, the armed services were once again in need of testing procedures to classify recruits. In response to these needs, the army created a personnel and testing division in 1939. The Army General Classification Test (AGCT) was produced in 1940, and this instrument became the principal general-ability test used by the armed services during the World War II years. The points of influence here were the counseling programs established by the military. These programs were designed to maximize individual potential as measured by assessment results when placing recruits in various components of the armed services.

At the end of World War II, the armed services established separation counseling programs. The major goal of these programs was to assist veterans returning to civilian life; counseling procedures introduced various options to veterans, including future educational and vocational planning suggestions. In 1944, the Veterans Administration established centers throughout the country for career guidance and other services. Many were established on college and university campuses; these counseling services became models for development of career guidance programs at many institutions of higher learning.

In recognition of the general need for more guidance services, Congress passed the George-Barden Act in 1946. This act provided funds for establishing academic counselor-training programs and provided a more liberal method of distributing funds to states for maintaining vocational guidance programs.

THE TESTING MOVEMENT AFTER WORLD WAR II

The growth of applied psychology after World War II contributed significantly to the growth of the measurement movement. Such branches of psychology as industrial psychology, counseling psychology, educational psychology, and school psychology were incorporated into formal training programs at many institutions of higher learning. Courses in testing principles and practices were major components of these training programs. A renewed interest in the use of tests in all branches of applied psychology had direct links with career guidance practices. For example, the use of tests in counseling individuals for various life roles, including the work role, was recognized as a viable component of applied psychology. Moreover, the increased emphasis on the applied use of assessment results created a need to develop instruments that could be used as counseling support tools. This applied emphasis continues to motivate the development of instruments that are designed for use with individuals of both sexes and all age groups, ethnic minorities, and special populations. The use of assessment results in career counseling is discussed in Chapter 7.

After World War II, there was a significant increase in enrollment at colleges and universities. This increased enrollment and subsequent need for educational planning created a wider use of the College Entrance Examination Boards and the American College Testing Program (ACT). These tests, designed to predict success at the college level, are also used as one means for helping individuals select academic majors and/or careers. The ACT also contains an interest inventory report that is directly related to jobs and college majors.

The passage of the National Defense Educational Act in 1958 greatly influenced the career guidance movement in general and had special impact on the testing movement. In fact, this act endorsed the close relationship between testing and the career guidance movement. The primary purpose of this act was to identify students of outstanding aptitude and ability early in their public secondary schooling and to provide them with counseling programs designed to help them make the best use of their talents. The specific use of tests mandated by this act significantly increased the opportunity to incorporate tests in public school counseling programs through federal funds that were made available to state departments of education.

Shortly before World War II, and especially after the war, a significant number of books on the subject of testing were published. For example, the first *Mental Measurements Yearbook* was published in 1938 and has been followed by several editions. Books by F. B. Davis (1947), D. C. Adkins (1947), L. J. Cronbach (1949), F. L. Goodenough (1949), W. Stephenson (1949), D. E. Super (1949), R. L. Thorndike (1949), H. Gulliksen (1950), and A. Anastasi (1954) are other examples of significant publications on testing that appeared following World War II.

Two recent publications that limit their discussion of assessment instruments to career development are *A Counselor's Guide to Assessment Instruments,* 3rd edition, by J. T. Kapes, M. M. Mastie, and E. A. Whitfield (1994), and *Using Assessment Results for Career Development,* 4th edition, by V. G. Zunker (1994).

During the rapid growth of testing after 1945, there was a move toward centralizing the publication of tests. The Educational Testing Service was formed in 1948 by combining a number of specialized testing programs. The American College Testing Program was founded in 1959. Other commercial publishers merged into larger companies and corporations. The primary reason for these mergers was the need for financial and technical commitments to develop and maintain the variety of testing programs on the market today (Cronbach, 1984). Currently, the design, construction, and updating of tests requires sophisticated technical support systems.

The advances in technology that have led to rapid scoring procedures have made testing more attractive to career guidance personnel. Computerized printouts of scores and narrative descriptions of assessment results have increased their utilization in career guidance. This immediate access to assessment results for career counselors and their counselees affords the use of a greater variety of testing instruments in the career counseling process.

No doubt, the future use of assessment results in career counseling will be greatly influenced by advancements in technology. However, the use of assessment results in career counseling must be kept in perspective; assessment results should not dominate the decision-making process in career guidance. Skills developed through work and leisure experiences are examples of other considerations that are as important as assessment results are in career decision making.

THEORIES OF CAREER DEVELOPMENT

In the early 1950s, Ginzberg, Ginsburg, Axelrad, and Herma (1951), Roe (1956), and Super (1957) published career development and occupational choice theories that have become landmarks in the development of the career guidance movement. Understandably, these publications were instrumental in creating a greater interest in career guidance practices and support materials used by practitioners. Their formulations have led to numerous research projects and subsequent methods for delivering career guidance programs. (Other theorists who followed and have significantly contributed to the career development process are discussed in Chapters 2 and 3.) Theories of career development and choice have become enduring issues the counseling profession addresses in important publications and professional meetings.

Theoretical perspectives on career development have contributed a great deal to career guidance programs by providing insights into developmental stages and tasks associated with transitions between stages, identification of personality types and corresponding work environments, and decision-making techniques. In addition, these theories have delineated the effects of sex-role stereotyping, provided special insights into the career development of women, ethnic minorities, and other groups, and clarified aspects of social learning theory and its relationship to career development. For each new practitioner, theories serve as a starting point from which new ideas and practices can be generated and validated (Zunker, 1987).

THE CAREER GUIDANCE MOVEMENT FROM THE 1960s

At this point in our discussion, we have covered a period of over 100 years in which the career guidance movement made giant strides of progress. The counseling profession was provided with leadership through national and local organizations. Child labor laws prohibited the exploitation of the very young, and working conditions for most Americans generally improved. There was a growing interest in increasing and improving social services for all citizens at all age levels. At the end of the 1950s, the career guidance movement had strong, organized leadership, but the 1960s were not destined to be peaceful times for the United States.

The turbulent 1960s have been described as a period of unrest that was precipitated by an awakened social conscience and the loss of a sense of meaning among the young. Several descriptions have been used to characterize the youth of the 1960s, including rebellious, militant, restless, and hippie. A questioning of all aspects of the U.S. way of life erupted into overt acts of militant rioting in cities, protest marches on college campuses, and a general rebellion against many established social values. With these events came further challenges for the counseling profession in general and for career guidance specifically. For example, the role and meaning of work in society was seen as a major issue in the 1960s and 1970s. Other issues, such as the women's movement and guidance for older people were dominant forces in shaping the career guidance movement.

In the last 20 years, the career guidance movement has broadened its role and scope. There is a trend toward greater emphasis on a humanistic, existential orientation (Picchioni & Bonk, 1983). The humanistic approach, designed to expand one's awareness of life, brings greater meaning to all aspects of lifestyle. The philosophical rationale of an existential approach provides a greater recognition of individual significance in society. In essence, the more an individual is aware of his or her potential and experience, the greater the likelihood of self-assertion and direction. These philosophical orientations have set the patterns for career guidance models now in vogue.

The federal government continued its support of programs that directly and indirectly affected career guidance. During the early 1960s, Congress passed manpower legislation designed to create new jobs through occupational training programs. In addition, funds were made available for placement counseling in a variety of settings, including the establishment of agencies in communities. Other legislation under the Economic Opportunity Act funded such projects as Head

Start, Job Corps, Neighborhood Youth Corps, and Community Action Programs. Many of these programs involved special counseling services like the Job Training Partnership Act (JTPA).

The Vocational Educational Act of 1963 deserves special recognition for its influence on the career guidance movement. According to Picchioni and Bonk (1983), this act "provided individual job seekers the formal preparation through guidance and training necessary for occupational adjustment in an increasingly technical and sophisticated economy" (p. 81). Later amendments to the act provided funds for guidance services in elementary and secondary schools, public community colleges, and technical institutes.

Career education.   A new concept of education emerged in the early 1970s in reaction to the charge that current educational systems were not adequately preparing youth for work. In 1971, Commissioner of Education Sidney P. Marland proposed a plan that would specifically address career development, attitudes, and values in addition to traditional learning. This new educational philosophy—career education—was considered integral to the education process, from kindergarten through adulthood. The career education programs that evolved during the 1970s have centered on such topics as career awareness, career exploration, value clarification, decision-making skills, career orientation, and career preparation. Understandably, career education programs have focused more attention on the career guidance movement. The concept of career education is discussed in Chapter 10, and the career counselor's role in delivering various components of career education programs is also explored.

Vocational-technical education changes.   In the last decade, there have been significant changes in vocational education as we once knew it. The major thrust of current programs is centered around the goal of teaching students employable skills needed in the changing technological workplace. Students now face new technologies and business management systems that require high-level worker skills. As the result of vast technological changes, vocational education focuses more on technology than on vocational educational perspectives. The growing interest in integrating academic and vocational education has primarily evolved from a need to encourage vocational education students to take more rigorous academic courses. In fact, "Tech-Prep" programs are designed to offer vocational education students more advanced academic courses that meet the admission requirements at some institutions of higher education. More information about the changing role of vocational education can be found in Chapter 10.

THE NATIONAL OCCUPATIONAL INFORMATION COORDINATING COMMITTEE (NOICC)

In 1976, the National Occupational Information Coordinating Committee was established by an act of Congress. This committee is supported by four federal agencies: the Bureau of Labor Statistics, the Employment and Training Administration, the Office of Vocational and Adult Education, and the National Center for Educational Statistics. The NOICC has defined four basic functions: (1) to develop an occupational information system that provides information on employment and training programs at federal, state, and local levels; (2) to assist in the organization and operation of state committees, referred to as State Occupational Information Coordinating Committees (SOICCs); (3) to assist all users of occupational information in sharing information; and (4) to provide labor market information for the needs of youth (Flanders, 1980).

More recently, NOICC has sponsored a project to establish national career counseling and development guidelines. The major purpose of the guidelines is to encourage the development of career guidance standards at the state and local levels. Specifically, the guidelines are to be used to develop standards of client competencies, counselor competencies, and institutional capabilities at all educational levels. Likewise, standards are to be developed for young adult and older adult career guidance programming. The effectiveness of these programs will be evaluated in order to encourage program improvement.

The implementation of national guidelines by states and local communities should facilitate: (1) achievement of career development competencies by all students; (2) improved career guidance and counseling programs that are comprehensive and integrated within the total guidance and counseling program; (3) clearly defined staff roles, increased teaming with teachers and other school and district staff, and improved counselor expertise; (4) greater program accountability; and (5) improved articulation of career-related programs across educational levels (NOICC, 1989, p. 30).

The steps for implementing national guidelines include developing a needs analysis, establishing local career development standards, securing the resources and staff, conducting staff development, and designing and conducting program evaluations.

In 1992, NOICC established the National Career Development Training Institute (NCDTI) to design career development training programs for states to use in training personnel who help students and adults acquire career planning skills and make career decisions. Current plans call for this institute to be coordinated through the University of South Carolina, the Wisconsin Center on Education and Work at the University of Wisconsin at Madison, and the Continuum Center and Adult Career Counseling Center at Oakland University in Rochester, Michigan. All 56 SOICCs assisted the institute in designing and implementing the National Career Development Training agenda.

Professionalism.   The focus of attention in the early 1970s shifted to standards of counselor preparation and to the general advancement of the counseling profession. In 1972, standards for entry preparation of counselors were approved by the Board of Directors of the American Personnel and Guidance Association (APGA). In 1977, APGA established guidelines for doctoral training programs in counselor education (Picchioni & Bonk, 1983). These actions were followed by the APGA's declared interest in state licensure of professionals. The APGA (now the American Counseling Association, or ACA) has enhanced public recognition of all counseling efforts and has added support to counseling as a distinct social service. In 1984, the National Career Development Association set up procedures for the credentialing of career counselors, referred to as the National Board of Certified Counselors (NBCC). Currently, career counselors must meet minimum educational course work requirements, meet experience requirements, and pass an exam to reach the level of a National Certified Career Counselor (NCCC).

A Glance into the Past and a Look into the Future

In the beginning of this discussion, several references were made to events and social conditions that determined the course of the career guidance movement. The chronology of the career guidance movement reflects the continuous influence of social, political, economic, and other changes in our nation. In the political arena, the career guidance movement has found support. Federal legislation has provided funds for underwriting several career counseling programs and training programs for counselors. The fact is that the federal government has played a significant role in the career guidance movement.

We cannot overlook the foresight, dedication, and pioneering efforts of many individuals. Those who came forth with conceptualizations of career guidance that have endured for many decades provided the guidelines for contemporary practices. Other individuals concentrating on basic research in human development also contributed immeasurably to the career guidance movement. The leaders in related branches of applied psychology and contributors to technological advancements all played a part in developing what has become the mainstream of this movement.

Career guidance was founded to help people choose vocations. The early, straightforward procedures used in helping individuals choose occupations have evolved into diverse strategies, incorporating career decision making and life planning. The development of career guidance programs has been largely dictated by societal changes and subsequent needs of the society, and the future will no doubt provide changes and issues that we cannot fully anticipate at this time. It should be clear that career guidance is not a drab, static profession, but on the contrary provides vast opportunities for future leaders. The career counselors of today and tomorrow will become catalysts for an expanded guidance movement in this country.

Summary

1. The changing workplace and changing work force has challenged the career counseling profession. Since 1979, 43 million jobs have been lost, and many newly created jobs pay less.

2. The work force will become more diverse in the 21st century. More women and a more culturally diverse group of workers will enter the work force.

3. Organizations that have reduced their work force are retraining workers to fit different work environments.

4. Work in the United States is very pervasive in our society; it determines to a great extent how we live, where we live, and whom we associate with.

5. Work-related problems will continue to be a key focus of the career counselor.

6. An integrated approach to career counseling suggests that counselors must have a wide background of skills to meet clients' needs. A more integrative approach recognizes that an individual's total development includes a broad spectrum of domains.

7. Career counselors are involved in a large number of career-related programs. In schools, comprehensive counseling programs require that each student have a written plan. School-to-work programs focus on preparing students for work via cooperating workplaces in the community used as experiential sites.

8. Colleges and universities have active career centers for their students, and some offer their services to the community.

9. Theories of career development have received more attention with the aim of merging them with knowledge of career development from other academic disciplines.

10. Special issues of special populations are an ongoing process of discovery. Special needs of women, culturally diverse groups, and individuals with disabilities must continue to receive attention.

11. Technological advances have provided counseling tools that have gone far beyond the expectations of most career counselors. In 1994, 9 million individuals used computerized career information delivery systems.

12. The rise of industrialism in the late 1800s dramatically changed work environments and living conditions for many Americans. A spirit of reform emerged in reaction to the impersonal industrial systems and chaotic conditions of urban life in the United States and in Europe.

13. Several outstanding scientists turned their attention to human behavior and to the study of individual differences. Francis Galton of England, Wilheim Wundt of Germany, and Alfred Binet and V. Henri of France published studies of human abilities and human differences.

14. In the United States, G. Stanley Hall became interested in mental characteristics of children, James Cattell published an article referring to mental tests, and John Dewey called for reforms in our educational system.

15. Frank Parsons developed a vocational bureau in Boston, in which he provided systematic guidance to 80 men and women. Parsons's major work, *Choosing a Vocation*, was posthumously published in May 1909. His three-part formulation of career guidance provided the foundation for early career counseling procedures.

16. In 1910, the First National Conference on Vocational Guidance was held in Boston.

17. The measurement and guidance movements coincided in development and shared many of the same roots. In France, the first intelligence test was published in 1905. The Army Alpha and Beta Tests were made available to the public shortly after World War I. The first edition of *The Strong Vocational Interest Blank* was published in 1927.

18. The federal government played a major role in the career guidance movement by passing significant national legislation between 1917 and 1940. These acts

included the Smith-Hughes Act, George-Dean Act, Wagner-Peyser Act, Civilian Conservation Corps, and Works Progress Administration. The first edition of the *Dictionary of Occupational Titles* was published in 1939.

19. The private sector, through the Jewish Occupational Council, established counseling, placement, and rehabilitation services for Jewish immigrants.

20. Two books had a dramatic impact on the career counseling movement: Williamson's book *How to Counsel Students* was published in 1939, and Rogers's influential *Counseling and Psychotherapy* was published in 1942. Rogerian theory was responsible for the first major break from Parsons's straightforward approach to career counseling.

21. At the end of World War II, the armed services established separation counseling programs. The testing movement made rapid advances, and a number of significant books were published on testing.

22. In the early 1950s, career development and occupational choice theories were developed. The theories of career development and choice have become enduring issues addressed by the counseling profession, major publications, and professional meetings.

23. In the last 20 years, the career guidance movement has broadened its role and scope. There is a trend toward greater emphasis on a humanistic and existential orientation.

24. Other developments that have influenced the career guidance movement are the development of career education, the focus on professionalism, advances in technology, and the NOICC.

Supplementary Learning Exercises

1. Write a summary of the relevant issues facing career counselors in the 21st century. Share it with your class.
2. What does an integrative approach to counseling suggest in terms of career counseling procedures and strategies? Defend your conclusions with examples.
3. Give an example of how a career counselor and another mental health worker could work together to meet a client's needs.
4. Should the training of most counselors include a course in career counseling? Defend your conclusions.
5. Compare Parsons's three-part formulation of counseling procedures with Williamson's six sequential steps. Describe similarities and differences.
6. Describe how the development of industrial psychology has aided the career guidance movement.
7. Defend or criticize the following statement: The federal government should take an active role in supporting career guidance activities in this country.
8. Choose either directive or nondirective methods of counseling as being the most influential to the career guidance movement. Defend your choice in a debate or in writing.
9. Write to one of the National Career Training Institutes established by the NOICC and share with the class their plans for training.
10. Should a career counselor have courses in marriage counseling? Defend your conclusion with examples.

CHAPTER TWO

Theories of Career Development—I

In the beginning of any study, someone usually forms the shape, provides the model, establishes the pattern, and introduces the basic concepts. The theories discussed in this chapter have been most instrumental in providing the foundation for research in vocational behavior. To comprehend these theories is to understand the priorities in career counseling today. The conceptual shifts in career counseling, test format, work satisfaction studies, and classification systems of occupations have primarily evolved from theories. Understandably, the study of career counseling should begin with them.

This chapter includes a brief discussion of several established and historically significant theories and provides references for greater in-depth study of these theories. It serves as an introduction to trait-and-factor theory, the theory of work adjustment and person-environment-correspondence counseling theory, several developmental theories, a needs-theory approach, a typology approach theory, a learning theory of career choice and counseling, and a sociological perspective on work and career development. The renewed interest in career development theories in the last two decades has led to the development of several evolving theories that have been added to this edition. In Chapter 3, Theories of Career Development—II, five emerging theories will be introduced. References to the information contained in both Chapters 2 and 3 will be made throughout the book.

Trait-and-Factor Theory

Among early theorists on vocational counseling, Parsons (1909) maintained that vocational guidance is accomplished first by studying the individual, second by surveying occupations, and finally by matching the individual with the occupation. This process, called trait-and-factor theory, became the foundation of many vocational counseling programs such as those of the Veterans Administration, the YMCA, the Jewish vocational services, and colleges and universities (Super, 1972.)

The trait-and-factor approach has been the most durable of all theories of career guidance. Simply stated, it means matching the individual's traits with requirements of a specific occupation, subsequently solving the career-search problem. The trait-and-factor theory evolved from early studies of individual differences and developed closely with the testing, or *psychometric*, movement. This theory greatly influenced the study of job descriptions and job requirements in an attempt to predict future job success by measuring job-related traits. The key characteristic of this theory is the assumption that individuals have unique patterns of ability or traits that can be objectively measured and correlated with the requirements of various types of jobs.

The development of assessment instruments and refinement of occupational information are closely associated with the trait-and-factor theory. The study of aptitudes in relation to job success has been an ongoing process. Occupational interests occupy no small part of the research literature on career development. The development of individual values in the career decision-making process is also a significant factor.

Through the efforts of Parsons (1909) and Williamson (1939, 1965), components of the trait-and-factor theory were developed into step-by-step procedures designed to help clients make wise career decisions. Parsons's three-step procedures—studying the individual, surveying occupations, and finally matching the individual with an occupation—may at first glance be judged to be completely dominated by test results. But, on the contrary, Parsons's first step suggests that evaluating each individual's background is an important part of his counseling paradigm.

Williamson (1939, 1949) was a prominent advocate of trait-and-factor counseling. Williamson's counseling procedures maintained the early impetus of the trait-and-factor approach that evolved from the work of Parsons. Even when integrated into other theories of career guidance, the trait-and-factor approach plays a very vital role. Its impact and influence on the development of assessment techniques and the utilization of career information have been of inestimable value.

Brown, Brooks, and Associates (1990) argued that trait-and-factor theory has never been fully understood. They suggested that advocates of trait-and-factor approaches never approved of excessive use of testing in career counseling. For example, Williamson (1939) suggested that test results are but one means of evaluating individual differences. Other data, such as work experience and general background, are as important in the career counseling process.

Recently, Sharf (1996) summarized the advantages and disadvantages of trait-and-factor theory and suggested that it is a static theory rather than a developmental one. Furthermore, it focuses on identifying individual traits and factors but does not account for how interests, values, aptitudes, achievement, and personalities grow and change. The major point is that clients can benefit from dialogue that is directed toward continually evolving personal traits and how changes affect career decision making.

The following assumptions of the trait-and-factor approach also raise concerns about this theory: (1) there is a single career goal for everyone, and (2) career decisions are primarily based on measured abilities (Herr & Cramer, 1996). These assumptions severely restrict the range of factors that can be considered in the career development process. In essence, the trait-and-factor approach is far too narrow in scope to be considered a major theory of career development. However, we should recognize that standardized assessment and occupational analysis procedures stressed in trait-and-factor approaches are useful in career counseling.

In fact, assessment instruments designed primarily to assist in career decision making continue to be developed and refined. The same may be said about occupational information, as growing numbers of research projects have focused on optimal use of job descriptions and requirements, work environments, and job satisfaction studies. Bridging the gap between assessment scores and work environments is a huge challenge facing career counselors now, as in the past (Prediger, 1995).

Of related interest is the theory of work adjustment and person-environment-correspondence counseling (Dawis, 1996), discussed more fully in the next section of this chapter. This theory involves workplace reinforcers that can lead to job satisfaction. But more relevant to our discussion here is the profound emphasis on "satisfactoriness" that is predicted from correspondence between the work environment and several variables, including the individual's *measured* abilities and values (Dawis, 1996). This theory is a good example of how trait-and-factor theory has been integrated into an evolving theory of career development.

Other person-environment fit models are discussed by Chartrand (1991), who concludes that trait-and-factor approaches have evolved into contemporary career development models. These counseling procedures include acquiring and compiling information—*some by standardized testing instruments*—in a structured, systematic manner. The client's "best fit" in a work environment—that is, one that matches such human factors as ability, achievement, interests, personality, values, and other characteristics—will more than likely continue to be a major focus of career counseling objectives in the future.

Will trait-and-factor theory be revitalized for the 21st century? Prediger (1995) suggests that person-environment fit theory has indeed enhanced the potential for a closer relationship between assessment and career counseling; assessment information can provide the basis for developing career possibilities into realities. For example, assessment results along with other information can provide a pathway for growth and how it can be accomplished. Prediger suggested a *similarity model,* designed not to predict success or to find the "ideal career" but to provide a means of evaluating occupations that "are similar to you in important ways" (Prediger, 1995, p. 2).

Trait-and-factor theory as part of a similarity model is buttressed by recent research suggesting that observed differences among career groups is of sufficient magnitude to provide focus to career exploration (Rounds & Tracey, 1990; Zytowski, 1994). The relevant message here is that trait-and-factor theory has an important future role in career development theory.

Summary of Practical Applications

1. One of the major career counseling roles of early trait-and-factor approaches was that of diagnosis. In this context, diagnosis was the process of analyzing data collected through a variety of tests. Individual strengths and weaknesses were evaluated with the primary purpose of finding a job that matched measured abilities and achievements. The primary goal of using assessment data was to predict job satisfaction and success.

2. Contemporary career counseling practices are expanding the use of test data. One example is the study of the relationship between human factors and work environment variables. The results of this research are used to find congruences between individual human factors and reinforcers that exist in work environments.

3. Instead of predicting the possibility of success in a particular career on the basis of actuarial information, the counselor interprets test data and informs the client of observed similarities to current workers in a career field. Clients use this information along with other data in the career decision process. Assessment data are considered to be *one source* of information that can be most effectively used in conjunction with other data.

Person-Environment-Correspondence Counseling

This theory's development has a long history, and as late as the early 1990s it was referred to as the theory of work adjustment (TWA). In 1991, it was once again revised to include descriptions of the differences between personality structure and personality style and between personality style and adjustment style. The theory at that point had become more inclusive to embrace how individuals interact in their everyday lives as well as how they interact in the work environment. The broader label of person-environment-correspondence (PEC) was added in 1991 (Lofquist & Dawis, 1991).

This theory has always emphasized that work is more than step-by-step task-oriented procedures. Work includes human interaction and sources of satisfaction, dissatisfaction, rewards, stress, and many other psychological variables. The basic assumption is that individuals seek to achieve and maintain a positive relationship with their work environment. According to Dawis and Lofquist, individuals bring their requirements to a work environment, and the work environment makes its requirements of individuals. To survive, the individual and the work environment must achieve some degree of congruence (correspondence).

To achieve this consonance, or agreement, the individual must successfully meet the job requirements, and the work environment must fulfill the requirements of the individual. Stability on the job, which can lead to tenure, is a function of correspondence between the individual and the work environment. The process of achieving and maintaining correspondence with a work environment is referred to as *work adjustment*.

Four key points of Dawis and Lofquist's theory are summarized as follows: (1) work personality and work environment should be amenable, (2) individual needs are most important in determining an individual's fit into the work environment, (3) individual needs and the reinforcer system that characterizes the work setting are important aspects of stability and tenure, and (4) job placement is best accomplished through a match of worker traits with the requirements of a work environment.

Dawis and Lofquist (1984) have identified occupational reinforcers found in the work environment that are vital to an individual's work adjustment. They evaluated work settings to derive potential reinforcers of individual behavior. In the career counseling process, individual needs are matched with occupational reinforcers to determine an individual's fit into a work environment. Some examples of occupational reinforcers are achievement, advancement, authority, co-workers, activity, security, social service, social status, and variety.

In related research, Lofquist and Dawis (1984) found a strong relationship between job satisfaction and work adjustment. Job satisfaction was evaluated from outcomes (results or consequences) of work experience, such as tenure, job involvement, productivity, work alienation, and morale. They found that satisfaction is negatively related to job turnover, withdrawal behavior (such as absenteeism and lateness), and worker alienation. On the other hand, satisfaction is positively related to job involvement, morale, and overall life situations, or nonwork satisfaction. In general, satisfaction is only minimally correlated with job performance and productivity (pp. 228–229).

The research reviewed by Lofquist and Dawis (1984) strongly suggests that job satisfaction is a significant indicator of work adjustment. For example, job satisfaction is an indicator of the individual's perception of work and the work environment and is highly related to tenure in a work situation. The theory of work adjustment has the following implications for career counselors:

1. Job satisfaction should be evaluated according to several factors, including satisfaction with co-workers and supervisors, type of work, autonomy, responsibility, and opportunities for self-expression of ability and for serving others.
2. Job satisfaction is an important career counseling concern but does not alone measure work adjustment. Work adjustment includes other variables, such as the individual's ability to perform tasks required of work.
3. Job satisfaction is an important predictor of job tenure, and the factors associated with job satisfaction should be recognized in career counseling. An individual's abilities and how they relate to work requirements are not the only career counseling components of work adjustment.
4. Individual needs and values are significant components of job satisfaction. These factors should be delineated in career counseling programs designed to enhance work adjustment.
5. Individuals differ significantly in terms of specific reinforcers of career satisfaction. Therefore, career counseling must be individualized when exploring interests, values, and needs.
6. Career counselors should consider the reinforcers available in work environments and compare them to the individual needs of clients.

In this conceptual framework, career counselors should consider clients' job satisfaction needs in order to help them find an amenable work environment. Job satisfaction is a significant variable in determining productivity, job involvement, and career tenure. Career counselors should use occupational information to assist clients in matching individual needs, interests, and abilities with patterns and levels of different reinforcers in the work environment. For example, the reinforcer of "achievement" is related to experiences of accomplishment in the work situation. Social service is related to the opportunities that a work situation offers for performing tasks that will help other people.

Lofquist and Dawis warned that career counselors may have difficulty identifying occupational reinforcers because of the lack of relevant research, the vast variety of jobs in the current labor force, and emerging jobs in the future. Meanwhile, the theory of work adjustment has focused more attention on the importance of worker satisfaction. In the future, workers may have to adjust to finding satisfaction in a variety of jobs that use their individual skills, rather than in one job setting.

More recently, Dawis (1996) identified *personality structure* as stable characteristics of personality that consist primarily of abilities and values. Personality style is seen as "typical temporal characteristics" of an individual's interaction with the environment. *Ability* dimensions are used to estimate the individual's probable levels of work skills or abilities. *Values* are viewed as work needs and are identified primarily through the *Minnesota Importance Questionnaire* (University of Minnesota, 1984).

Work needs are considered to be very similar to "ordinary psychological needs," for many needs that may develop outside the work environment also apply to the work setting—recognition and need achievement, for example. Both abilities (work skills) and values (work needs) are considered to be rather stable.

Environmental structure is identified as the characteristics of abilities and values of individuals who inhabit the environment. Therefore, the matching model of person-environment-correspondence can be readily applied.

Work adjustment is an ideal when person and environment have matching work needs and work skills, but vast changes in both can lead to worker dissatisfaction. A worker's attempt to improve his or her fit within the work environment is referred to as *work adjustment,* and adjustments follow one of two modes: active and reactive. In the active mode, the worker makes an attempt to change the work environment, whereas in the reactive mode, the worker attempts to become more correspondent to the work environment.

Important to the career counselor here is that work adjustment is closely related to personality style, although they are considered to be distinct concepts. Adjustment behavior—that is, degrees of flexibility, activeness, reactiveness, perseverance, and personality style—can be used in career planning and, in particular, to find the best person-environment fit.

EMPIRICAL SUPPORT FOR THE PERSON-ENVIRONMENT-CORRESPONDENCE THEORY

For person-environment-correspondence, see Holland (1992) and Spokane (1985). For prediction of satisfactoriness, see Hunter and Hunter (1984). For prediction of satisfaction, that is, worker satisfaction from need-reinforcer correspondence, see

Dawis (1991). For other studies that offer information about various propositions of the theory, see Rounds (1990) and Bretz and Judge (1994).

Summary of Practical Applications

1. The person-environment-correspondence theory is heavily dependent on client assessment, for its major objective is to identify groups of occupations that hold the greatest potential for a client's satisfaction in a work environment and, conversely, those that will be less likely to meet the criteria for satisfaction. Of major concern are a client's abilities (work skills) and values (work needs).

The U.S. Employment Service's *General Aptitude Test Battery* (U.S. Department of Labor, 1970a) is recommended for measuring abilities, whereas the *Minnesota Importance Questionnaire* (University of Minnesota, 1984) is used to assess values. Personality style is to be evaluated by the counselor in an interview.

The *Minnesota Occupational Classification System III* (Dawis, Dohm, Lofquist, Chartrand, & Due, 1987) provides an index for level and patterns of abilities and reinforcers that different occupations provide. This index is used for matching work skills to requirements of occupations and as a means of determining reinforcers available by occupation.

Presentation of assessment information should be tailored to the client's abilities, values, and style. The highly verbal client would probably prefer a verbal presentation with time allowed for discussion. A client high in spatial ability would most likely prefer a graphic presentation. The point here is that the counselor should present the information in the most meaningful way for a broad category of clients.

2. Career planning should be conceptualized to be most meaningful to the client by determining whether the client is more achievement- (satisfactoriness) oriented or more self-fulfilled- (satisfaction) oriented. The rationale here is that the counselor should ascertain client orientation to determine which prediction system to stress in the career planning process.

Work adjustment counseling has taken on a different perspective in today's society, where clients are faced with constantly changing work environments. Assisting clients to learn new skills and develop appropriate work habits that match the needs of changing work environments are relevant counseling strategies for the 1990s and the 21st century (Dawis, 1996).

Developmental Theories

The developmental theories discussed in this section are based on assumptions similar to those of the trait-and-factor approach, but the primary assumption is that career development is a process that takes place over the life span. Because career development is viewed as a lifelong process, career guidance programs should be designed to meet the needs of individuals at all stages of life. Thus, stages of career development are important points of reference for the career development theorists. Indeed, among other points of reference, the theorists have focused on developmental stages that are somewhat related to age: the process of career maturity, the development of self-concept as it relates to a career, and the development of sex-role orientation. Adult developmental models have received particular attention in the last two decades.

Ginzberg and Associates

Ginzberg, Ginsburg, Axelrad, and Herma (1951) are generally considered to be the first to approach a theory of occupational choice from a developmental standpoint. This team, consisting of an economist, a psychiatrist, a sociologist, and a psychologist, set out to develop and test a theory of occupational choice. Their original study was part of a more comprehensive study of the world of work.

In developing their theory, Ginzberg and associates undertook an empirical investigation of a carefully selected sample of individuals who would have reasonable freedom of choice in selecting an occupation. Their sample comprised males from upper-middle-class, urban, Protestant or Catholic families of Anglo-Saxon origin, whose educational level ranged from sixth grade to graduate school. Because of the highly selective nature of the sample, the conclusions of the study have limited application (Osipow, 1983). Specifically, female and ethnic minority career developmental patterns were not considered, nor were those of the rural or urban poor. Therefore, be aware that the conclusions this study reached do not necessarily apply to other than the identified sample.

The Ginzberg group concluded that occupational choice is indeed a developmental process, which generally covers a period of six to ten years, beginning around age 11 and ending shortly after age 17 or in young adulthood. There are three distinct periods or stages in the occupational choice process entitled *fantasy*, *tentative,* and *realistic.* Table 2-1 outlines these steps.

TABLE 2-1
Stages or Periods in the Ginzberg Study

Period	Age	Characteristics
Fantasy	Childhood (before age 11)	Purely play orientation in the initial stage; near end of this stage, play becomes work-oriented
Tentative	Early adolescence (ages 11–17)	Transitional process marked by gradual recognition of work requirements; recognition of interests, abilities, work rewards, values, and time perspectives
Realistic	Middle adolescence (ages 17 to young adult)	Integration of capacities and interests; further development of values; specification of occupational choice; crystallization of occupational patterns

According to Ginzberg and associates, during the fantasy period play gradually becomes work-oriented and reflects initial preferences for certain kinds of activities. Various occupational roles are assumed in play, resulting in initial value judgments on the world of work.

The tentative period is divided into four stages. First is the *interest* stage, during which the individual makes more definite decisions concerning likes and dislikes. Next is the *capacity* stage of becoming aware of one's ability as related to vocational aspirations. Third is the *value* stage, a time when clearer perceptions of occupational styles emerge. During the final *transition* stage, the individual becomes aware of the decision for vocational choice and the subsequent responsibilities accompanying a career choice.

The realistic period is divided into three stages. The first stage is the *exploration* stage, which, for the group studied by Ginzberg and associates, centered on college entrance. During this stage, the individual narrows the career choice to two or three possibilities but is generally in a stage of ambivalence and indecisiveness. However, the career focus is much narrower in scope. The second stage, *crystallization,* is when the commitment to a specific career field is made. Change of direction for some—even at this stage—is referred to as pseudo-crystallization. The final stage, *specification,* is when the individual selects a job or professional training for a specific career.

The Ginzberg group recognized individual variations in the career decision process. Individual patterns of career development that lacked conformity with age-mates were identified as deviant—that is, deviant from the highly selected sample that comprised white males from upper-middle-class, urban families. Two primary causes for individual variations in career development were suggested: (1) early, well-developed occupational skills often result in early career patterns, deviant from the normal development; and (2) timing of the realistic stage of development may be significantly delayed due to such variables as emotional instability, various personal problems, and financial affluence.

From this study emerged a distinctive, systematic process based primarily on adolescent adjustment patterns that lead individuals to occupational choice. More specifically, the occupational choice process was the gradually developed precept of occupations subjectively appraised by the individual in the sociocultural milieu from childhood to early adulthood. As one progresses through the stages outlined by this study, vocational choice is being formulated. As tentative occupational decisions are made, other potential choices are eliminated.

In the original study, Ginzberg and associates stated that the developmental process of occupational decision making was irreversible in that the individual could not return chronologically or psychologically to the point where earlier decisions could be repeated. This conclusion was later modified to refute the earlier stand that occupational decision making is an irreversible process; however, Ginzberg (1972) continued to stress the importance of early choices in the career decision process. The work of Ginzberg and associates has greatly influenced occupational research, particularly in dealing with developmental tasks as related to career development.

In a later review of his theory, Ginzberg (1984) reemphasized that occupational choice is lifelong and coextensive with a person's working life:

> Occupational choice is a lifelong process of decision making for those who seek major satisfaction from their work. This leads them to reassess repeatedly how they can improve the fit between their changing career goals and the realities of the world of work. (p. 180)

Some evidence has supported the major theoretical tenets of this theory. O'Hara and Tiedeman (1959) investigated the four stages of the tentative period (interests, capacity, value, and transition) and found that they do occur in the order theorized, but at earlier ages. Studies by Davis, Hagan, and Strouf (1962) and Hollender (1967) tend to support the concepts of vocational development postulated, although the timing and sequence of the stages have not been completely supported.

The developmental conceptualization of the process of career decision making is quite a departure from the trait-and-factor approach. Although not fully tested, the theory provides a description of a developmental process for normal and deviant patterns of vocational development. The theory is more descriptive than explanatory in that it does not provide either strategies for facilitating career development or explanations of the developmental process. It appears that the major usefulness of this theory is in providing a framework for the study of career development (Osipow, 1983).

The Life-Span, Life-Space Approach to Careers

Donald Super (1972) thought that he had often been mislabeled as a theorist. In fact, Super did not believe that he had developed a theory that could be labeled specifically at that time. On the contrary, he looked on his work as the development of segments of possible theories of the future. He indicated that if he is to carry a label, it should be broad, such as differential-developmental-social-phenomenological psychologist. His multiple approach to career development is reflected first of all in his interest in differential psychology or the trait-and-factor theory as a medium through which testing instruments and subsequent norms for assessment are developed. He thought that differential psychology is of utmost importance in the continuing attempt to furnish data on occupational differences related to personality, aptitude, and interests. This he viewed as an ongoing process as we learn more about the world of work.

Self-concept theory is a very vital part of Super's approach to vocational behavior. This approach has generated a number of research projects aimed at determining how the self-concept is implemented in vocational behavior (Norrell & Grater, 1960; Englander, 1960; Stephenson, 1961; Kibrick & Tiedeman, 1961; Schutz & Blocher, 1961; Anderson & Olsen, 1965). The research projects have focused more attention on the significance of self-concept in the career development process. Specifically, the research has indicated that the vocational self-concept develops through physical and mental growth, observations of work, identification with working adults, general environment, and general experiences. Ultimately, differences and similarities between self and others are assimilated. As experiences become broader in relation to awareness of the world of work, the more sophisticated vocational self-concept is formed. Although the vocational self-concept is only a part of the total self-concept, it is the driving force that establishes a career pattern one will follow throughout life. Thus, individuals implement their self-concepts into careers that will provide the most efficient means of self-expression.

Another of Super's important contributions has been his formalization of vocational developmental stages. These stages are as follows:

1. *Growth* (birth–age 14 or 15), characterized by development of capacity, attitudes, interests, and needs associated with self-concepts;
2. *Exploratory* (ages 15–24), characterized by a tentative phase in which choices are narrowed but not finalized;
3. *Establishment* (ages 25–44), characterized by trial and stabilization through work experiences;
4. *Maintenance* (ages 45–64), characterized by a continual adjustment process to improve working position and situation; and
5. *Decline* (ages 65+), characterized by preretirement considerations, reduced work output, and eventual retirement. (Issacson, 1985, pp. 51–53)

These stages of vocational development provide the framework for vocational behavior and attitudes, which are evidenced through five activities known as vocational developmental tasks. These five developmental tasks are shown in Table 2-2, delineated by typical age ranges (tasks *can* occur at other age levels) and by their general characteristics.

The *crystallization* task is the forming of a preferred career plan and considering how it might be implemented. Pertinent information is studied with the goal of becoming more aware of the preferred choice and the wisdom of the prefer-

TABLE 2-2
Super's Vocational Developmental Tasks

Vocational developmental tasks	Ages	General characteristics
Crystallization	14–18	A cognitive process period of formulating a general vocational goal through awareness of resources, contingencies, interests, values, and planning for the preferred occupation
Specification	18–21	A period of moving from tentative vocational preferences toward a specific vocational preference
Implementation	21–24	A period of completing training for vocational preference and entering employment
Stabilization	24–35	A period of confirming a preferred career by actual work experience and use of talents to demonstrate career choice as an appropriate one
Consolidation	35+	A period of establishment in a career by advancement, status, and seniority

ence. The *specification* task follows, in which the individual feels the need to specify the career plan through more specific resources and explicit awareness of cogent variables of the preferred choice. The *implementation* task is accomplished by the completion of training and entry into the career. The *stabilization* task is reached when the individual is firmly established in a career and develops a feeling of security in the career position. Finally, the *consolidation* task follows with advancement and seniority in a career (Super, Starishesky, Matlin, & Jordaan, 1963).

More recently, Super (1990) modified developmental tasks through the life span, as shown in Table 2-3. He uses the terms *cycling* and *recycling* through developmental tasks. This formulation clarifies Super's position, which may have been misunderstood in the past; that is, he views ages and transitions as very flexible and as not occurring in a well-ordered sequence. A person can recycle through one or more stages, which refers to a *minicycle*. For example, an individual who experiences disestablishment in a particular job may undergo new growth and become ready to change occupations. In this instance, the individual has reached the point of maintenance but now recycles through exploration in search of a new and different position.

TABLE 2-3
The Cycling and Recycling of Developmental Tasks through the Life Span

Life stage	Age			
	Adolescence 14–25	*Early adulthood 25–45*	*Middle adulthood 45–65*	*Late adulthood over 65*
Decline	Giving less time to hobbies	Reducing sports participation	Focusing on essential activities	Reducing working hours
Maintenance	Verifying current occupational choice	Making occupational position secure	Holding own against competition	Keeping up what is still enjoyed
Establishment	Getting started in a chosen field	Settling down in a permanent position	Developing new skills	Doing things one has always wanted to do
Exploration	Learning more about more opportunities	Finding opportunity to do desired work	Identifying new problems to work on	Finding a good retirement spot
Growth	Developing a realistic self-concept	Learning to relate to others	Accepting one's limitations	Developing nonoccupational roles

SOURCE: From "A Life-Span, Life-Space Approach to Career Development," by D. E. Super. In *Career Choice and Development: Applying Contemporary Theories to Practice,* 2nd ed., by D. Brown, L. Brooks, and Associates, p. 206. © 1990 by Jossey-Bass, Inc., Publishers. Reprinted by permission.

The concept of career patterns was an early interest of Super (1957) and his colleagues. He was particularly interested in the determinants of career patterns revealed by the research of Davidson and Anderson (1937) and Miller and Form (1951). He modified the six classifications used by Miller and Form in their study of career patterns for men into four classifications, which are outlined in Table 2-4.

Super also classified career patterns for women into seven categories ranging from a stable homemaking career pattern to a multiple-trial career pattern. Recently, he suggested that these classifications were no longer valid for women in modern society and has applied the principles of his theory to both genders (Super, 1990).

One of Super's best-known studies, launched in 1951, was designed to follow the vocational development of ninth-grade boys in Middletown, New York (Super & Overstreet, 1960). One of the major considerations of this study was to identify and validate the vocational developmental tasks relevant to each stage of development. Super thought that the completion of the appropriate tasks at each level was an indication of what he termed *vocational maturity*. The findings suggest that the ninth-grade boys in this study had not reached a level of understanding of the world of work or of themselves sufficient to make adequate career decisions. Vocational maturity seemed to be related more to intelligence than to age.

Various traits of vocational maturity (such as planning, accepting responsibility, and awareness of various aspects of a preferred vocation) proved to be irregular and unstable during a three-year period in high school. However, those individuals who were seen as vocationally mature in the ninth grade (based on their knowledge of an occupation, planning, and interest) were significantly more successful as young adults. This suggests that there is a relationship between career maturity and adolescent achievement of a significant degree of self-awareness, knowledge of occupations, and developed planning capability. Thus, ninth-grade vocational behavior does have some predictive validity for the future. In other words, boys who successfully accomplish developmental tasks at periodic stages tend to achieve greater maturity later in life.

TABLE 2-4
Super's Career Patterns for Men

Classification of pattern	Classification of typical career	Characteristics
Stable career pattern	Professional, managerial, skilled workers	Early entry into career with little or no trial work period
Conventional career pattern	Managerial, skilled workers, clerical workers	Trial work periods followed by entry into a stable pattern
Unstable career pattern	Semiskilled workers, clerical and domestic workers	A number of trial jobs that may lead to temporary stable jobs, followed by further trial jobs
Multiple-trial career pattern	Domestic workers and semiskilled workers	Nonestablishment of career marked by continual change of employment

The career maturity concepts developed by Super have far-reaching implications for career education and career counseling programs. The critical phases of career maturity development provide points of reference from which the desired attitudes and competencies related to effective career growth can be identified and subsequently assessed. Moreover, the delineation of desired attitudes and competencies within each stage affords the specification of objectives for instructional and counseling projects designed to foster career maturity development. Super (1974, p. 13) identified six dimensions that he thought were relevant and appropriate for adolescents:

1. *Orientation to vocational choice* (an attitudinal dimension determining whether the individual is concerned with the eventual vocational choice to be made);
2. *Information and planning* (a competence dimension concerning specificity of information individuals have concerning future career decisions and past planning accomplished);
3. *Consistency of vocational preferences* (individuals' consistencies of preferences);
4. *Crystallization of traits* (individual progress toward forming a self-concept);
5. *Vocational independence* (independence of work experience); and
6. *Wisdom of vocational preferences* (dimension concerned with individual's ability to make realistic preferences consistent with personal tasks).

The translation of these dimensions into occupational terms provides clarity for program considerations. For example, the attitudinal dimension of orientation to vocational choice may translate for one individual to mean "I don't know what I'm going to do and haven't thought about it" and for another to mean "I really want to decide, but I don't know how to go about it." The difference in levels of career maturity development are apparent from these remarks, providing clues from which the counselor may stimulate the growth of both individuals.

The dimensions of career maturity developed by Super support the concept that education and counseling can provide the stimulus for career development. The index of career maturity may be assessed by standardized inventories, which are discussed in Chapter 7. Career maturity is concerned not only with individually accomplished developmental tasks but also with the behavior manifested in coping with the tasks of a given period of development. The readiness of individuals to enter certain career-related activities is of inestimable value in the career counseling process.

The phenomenology of decision making and career development, according to Super, is indeed the combined complexities and variables of differential psychology, self-concept theory, developmental tasks, and sociology of life stages. Primarily, Super took a multisided approach to the career development process. His theory of vocational development is considered the most comprehensive of all developmental theories (Bailey & Stadt, 1973, p. 88) and offers valid explanations of developmental concepts that have been generally supported by numerous research projects (Osipow, 1983). The theory is highly systematic and is useful for developing objectives and strategies for career counseling and career education programs. The developmental aspects of Super's theory provide explanations of the various factors that influence the career choice process. The following two major tenets of his theory give credence to developmental theories in general: (1) career development is a lifelong process occurring through defined developmental periods, and (2) the self-concept is being shaped as each phase of life exerts its influence on human behavior. More recently, Super (1984) clarified his position on self-concept theory as "essentially a matching theory in which individuals consider both their own attributes and the attributes required by an occupation" (p. 208). Super saw self-concept theory as divided into two components: (1) personal or psychological, which focuses on how individuals choose and adapt to their choices; and (2) social, which focuses on the personal assessment individuals make of their socioeconomic situations and current social structure in which they work and live. The relationship of self-concept to career development is one of the major contributions of Super's theory.

Super's concept of vocational maturity should also be considered a major contribution to career developmental theories. Conceptually, career maturity is acquired through successfully accomplishing developmental tasks within a continuous series of life stages. Career maturity on this continuum is described in terms of attitudinal and competence dimensions. Points of reference from this continuum provide relevant information for career counseling and career education objectives and strategies.

In a more recent classification of stage transitions, Super (1990) illustrated a life-stage model by using a "life rainbow." This two-dimensional graphic schema presents a longitudinal dimension of the life span, referred to as a "maxicycle," and corresponding major life stages, labeled "minicycles." A second dimension is "life space," or the roles played by individuals as they progress through developmental stages, such as child, student, "leisurite," citizen, worker, spouse, homemaker, parent, and pensioner. These roles are experienced in the following theaters: home, community, school (college and university), and workplace. This conceptual model leads to some interesting observations: (1) because people are involved in several roles simultaneously within several theaters, success in one role facilitates success in another; and (2) all roles affect one another in the various theaters.

In the early 1990s, Super created an "archway model" to delineate the changing diversity of life roles experienced by individuals over the life span. This model is used to clarify how biographical, psychological, and socioeconomic determinants influence career development. Figure 2-1 illustrates the archway model. One base stone in the arch supports the person and his or her psychological characteristics, and the other base stone supports societal aspects such as economic resources, community, school, family, and so on. The point is that societal factors interact with the person's biological and psychological characteristics as he or she functions and grows.

The column that extends from the biological base encompasses the person's needs, intelligence, values, aptitudes, and interests—those factors that constitute personality variables and lead to achievement. The column rising from the geo-

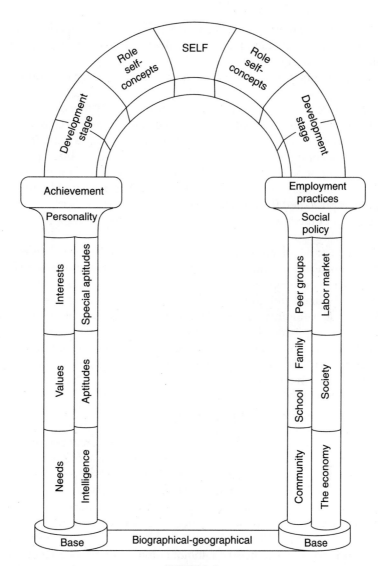

FIGURE 2-1

A segmental model of career development

SOURCE: From "A Life-Span, Life-Space Approach to Career Development" by D. E. Super in *Career Choice and Development: Applying Contemporary Theories to Practice,* 2nd ed., by D. Brown, L. Brooks, and Associates, pp. 206–208. © 1990 by Jossey-Bass, Inc., Publishers. Reprinted by permission.

graphical base stone includes environmental influences such as family, school, peer group, and labor markets—factors that affect social policy and employment practices.

The arch joining the columns is made up of conceptual components, including developmental stages from childhood to adulthood and developed role self-concepts.

The keystone of the archway is the self or person who has experienced the personal and social forces that are major determinants of self-concept formation and active life roles in society.

In essence, interactive learning is the fundamental concept that forms the keystone (self) of the archway as the individual encounters people, ideas, facts, and objects in personal development. The relationship of all the model's segments highlights the profound interactional influences in the career development process. The integration of life activities and developmental stages is a prime example of perceiving career development as a pervasive part of life. Career guidance programs that incorporate developmental concepts must address a broad range of counseling techniques and intervention strategies. This seems to be the message that Super has promoted for several decades.

Donald Super died in 1994, and in a recent publication his theory was labeled "the life-span, life-space approach to careers" (Super, Savickas, & Super, 1996). Because this theory evolved over a period of 60 years of research, it is no wonder that it stands out as one of the most comprehensive vocational development models in the career counseling profession. Over this 60-year period, Super's theory was constantly refined and updated, once being labeled "career development theory" and later "developmental self-concept theory." The recent name change reflects contemporary issues related to life-span needs and Super's most recent research of life roles. In this broad-based approach, gender and cultural differences are also addressed; the needs of cultural and ethnic minorities are considered important variables in the career counseling process.

EMPIRICAL EVALUATIONS OF SUPER'S THEORY

Recent evaluations of Super's theory have been predominantly positive, although empirical research has been difficult to accomplish because of the theory's broad scope (Brown, Brooks, & Associates, 1990). Swanson (1992) has suggested that more segments of the theory be empirically evaluated, especially the life space of adolescents and young adults and the life-span research of adults.

In a very provocative article that traces the development of Super's theory, Salomone (1996) suggested that Super has not offered testable hypotheses for various propositions of his theory. Salomone argued that Super failed to consistently define hypothetical constructs that are operational and that lend themselves to quantitative measures that support his statements. In Salomone's opinion, such constructs as work satisfaction, career maturity, and vocational development are not readily measurable, either because they are rather vague in concept or instruments at a given point in time were not available to measure them. Perhaps Salomone's criticism of Super's concepts can best be explained with the example of Super's definition of career. Salomone contended that Super expanded the concept of career (child, leisurite, and citizen) to be too inclusive for "three ingredients of good definitions—clarity, specificity, and exclusivity"; thus, when concepts are vague and nonspecific, they lose their usefulness. In this respect, Super's theory is very elusive; the relationship between theoretical propositions and empirical findings is not clearly delineated. However, despite the limitations of Super's theory as outlined in his article, Salomone did recognize that Super has had a monumental impact on career development.

Finally, Osipow and Fitzgerald (1996) and Hackett, Lent, and Greenhaus (1991) support Super's theory in general, and specifically as one that provides a description of the process of vocational development and one that will provide the mainstream of research for developmental psychology in the future.

SUMMARY OF PRACTICAL APPLICATIONS

When observing Super's suggestions for practical applications, it must be kept in mind that he remained dedicated to the roles of developmental stages within three major segments of his theory—life space, life span, and self-concepts. He and his colleagues developed numerous assessment instruments designed to measure developmental tasks over the life span that are currently used in the career counseling process. Following are summaries of the counseling steps.

1. *Assessment:* A career development assessment and counseling model (C-DAC) was developed to measure constructs from the basic life-span, life-space theory in four phases: (1) life structure and work-role salience; (2) career development status and resources; (3) vocational identity with its work values, occupational interests, and vocational abilities; and (4) occupational self-concepts and life themes. The counselor begins with an intake interview, encouraging the client to express career concerns. Background information is gathered from school records and other sources. After comparing background information with the client's career concerns in the first interview, the counselor begins a four-step procedure to complete the assessment component.

    a. The first step focuses on the client's life structure (social elements that constitute an individual's life) and work-role salience. If the client considers the work role to be important, further assessment will be more meaningful. If not, career orientation programs are recommended. The *Salience Inventory* (Nevill & Super, 1986) is used to determine the client's life space (participation and commitment to five life roles for school, work, family, community, and leisure). Scores for the client's life structure are also obtained from the constellation of 15 scores from the inventory, and they provide clues to the pattern of the client's activity in and hopes for five major life roles.

    b. The second assessment phase measures the client's perception of the work role, referred to as the client's *career stage* (vocational developmental tasks that concern the client) and *career concerns* (the amount of concern the client has with exploration, establishment, maintenance, and disengagement). The *Adult Career Concerns Inventory* (ACCI) (Super, Thompson, & Lindeman, 1988) provides a measure of career stage and career concerns, or they can be obtained through an interview.

        In addition, assessment within this step includes a measure of the client's resources for choosing or coping with tasks when making decisions. The *Career Development Inventory* (Thompson, Lindeman, Super, Jordaan, & Myers, 1984; Savickas, 1990) is used to measure the variables of career planning, career exploration, information about work, and knowledge of occupations. Finally, an assessment is made of the client's resources of adapting through use of the *Career Mastery Inventory* (Crites, in press).

    c. The third phase includes measures of abilities, interests, and values. Interest inventories that provide estimates of RIASEC types (Holland, 1992) are recommended. The *Differential Aptitude Test* (Bennett, Seashore, & Wesman, 1974) is recommended to measure aptitudes, and the *Values Inventory (Nevill & Super, 1986) or the Work Value Inventory* (Super, 1970) are recommended to measure values.

    d. The fourth phase includes assessment of self-concepts and life themes by using adjective checklists, card sorts, or a repertory grid technique to assess the client's self-schema in world space.

2. *Data integration and narrative interpretation:* After assessment has been accomplished, the counselor interprets the data to the client. The interpretation process is referred to as *integrative interpretation,* in which the client's life story unfolds.

3. *Counseling goals:* In the process of setting goals, the counselor attempts to assist the client to develop an accurate picture of his or her self and life roles. Choices are to be based on implementing the self-concept into the work world in a realistic manner.

4. *Procedures:* Career development counseling procedures pertinent to career development tasks such as exploration, establishment, maintenance, and disengagement are recommended. A variety of techniques may be used that incorporate the use of life stages and developmental tasks.

5. *Processes:* Counseling to promote career development may use coaching, educating, mentoring, modifying, or restructuring during an interview. Super also recommends cyclical counseling, in which the counseling interviews may at times be directive and at other times be nondirective. For example, directive approaches may be used to provide confrontations with reality, whereas nondirective approaches assist the client with interpreting the meanings associated with confrontations.

Life-span, life-space theory is indeed a comprehensive framework from which career development counseling has emerged. The counseling procedures developed from this theory are designed to foster maximal development (Super, Savickas, & Super, 1996).

David Tiedeman

The key concept of Tiedeman's approach to career development is self-development in the broadest sense (Tiedeman & O'Hara, 1963). The total cognitive development of the individual and the subsequent process of decision making have been its main focus. According to Tiedeman, career development unfolds within the general process of cognitive development as one resolves ego-relevant crises. He believed the evolving ego identity is of central importance in the career development process. He referred to the evolving self-in-situation from the earliest awareness of self to the point at which the individual becomes capable of evaluating experiences, anticipating and imagining future goals, and storing experiences in memory for future reference.

Within this context, the path of career development parallels stages of development drawn from the theoretical orientation of Erikson's (1950) eight psychosocial crises, as follows: (1) trust, (2) autonomy, (3) initiative, (4) industry, (5) identity, (6) intimacy, (7) generativity, and (8) ego integrity. Self-in-situation, self-in-world, and the orientation of work evolve as one resolves the psychosocial crises of life. As the ego identity develops, career-relevant decision-making possibilities also develop; one can contemplate broad career fields and specific occupations, taking all possible situations into consideration.

Eventually in career decision making, one reaches the point that Tiedeman referred to as *differentiation and integration.* Differentiation is the process of evaluating self or self-in-world through identification and study of various aspects of occupations. The process is complex and yet unique for each individual, depending on biological potential and the social structure of the individual's milieu. Influences are both internally and externally generated. As the individual's cognitive structure develops, impetus for differentiation may be internally provided either physiologically or psychologically. Activities within the individual's environment, including formal education, provide external stimulation.

One of the major goals of differentiation is to resolve the trust-mistrust crisis (Erikson, 1950) as it relates to the world of work. Tiedeman and O'Hara (1963) postulated that society and the individual continually strive toward a common goal: to establish what meaning each has for the other. In essence, the individual is striving to integrate within society—more specifically, within a career—searching for acceptance by members of a career field yet retaining some individuality. If the uniqueness of the individual finds congruency with the uniqueness of the world of work, integration, synthesis, success, and satisfaction will follow. According to Tiedeman, theories of occupational choice and vocational development have not explored how the evolutionary process of differentiation and integration could apply to career development. He has, therefore, conceptualized a pattern or paradigm of problem solving as the mechanism of career decision making. His paradigm covers four aspects of *anticipation* or *preoccupation* (exploration, crystallization, choice, and clarification) and three aspects of *implementation* or *adjustment* (induction, reformation, and integration), which are summarized in Table 2-5.

Tiedeman viewed decision making as a continuous process in which individuals will change their courses of career action, generally by leaving a particular setting or environment. The departure from a particular setting may be caused by external forces (such as the call of the armed service, an economic crisis, the work setting itself) or by broad internal psychological drives (such as unmet needs, changing aspirations, role diffusion). A new decision unfolds and must be made according to the prescribed sequence, beginning with exploration and eventually reaching integration. If integration is not reached once again, the individual may adapt to a career environment or may simply withdraw and begin a new search for eventual integration.

TABLE 2-5
Aspects of Anticipation, Preoccupation, Implementation, and Adjustment

Aspects of anticipation or preoccupation	Characteristics	Aspects of implementation or adjustment	Characteristics
Exploration	1. Thinking is rather temporary and evanescent in nature. 2. There is consideration and reconsideration of possible courses of action. 3. Through imagination, one experiences numerous activities by relating feelings of self within certain structures or premises. 4. There is searching through projection into tentative goals. 5. There is a focus on future behavior with alternative courses of action. 6. There is reflection upon aspirations, abilities, interests, and future societal implications related to career choice.	Induction	1. This period begins the social interaction experience with career identification. 2. There is a further identification of self and defense of self within the career social system. 3. As acceptance is experienced within the career, part of self is merged with the accepting group. 4. There is further progression of the individualized goal but within the framework of the totality of a career concerning social purpose.
Crystallization	1. There is a continued assessment of alternatives. 2. Fewer alternatives are under consideration. 3. There is an emergence of tentative choices. 4. Tentative choices may be reevaluated in the process of valuing and ordering. 5. Goals become more definite and formed but are not irreversible. 6. There is a definite move toward stability of thought.	Reformation	1. The career group offers acknowledgment of acceptance as a group member. 2. There is assertive action on the part of the individual within the career group and outside the career group, spawned by the newfound conditions. 3. Assertive action takes the form of convincing others to conform to the self-view held by the individual and toward greater acceptance of modified goals.

TABLE 2-5   *(continued)*

Aspects of anticipation or preoccupation	Characteristics	Aspects of implementation or adjustment	Characteristics
Choice	1. A definite goal is chosen. 2. There is focus on the particular behavior necessary to reach the chosen goal.	Integration	1. A compromise of intentions of goals is achieved by the individual as he or she interacts with the career group. 2. Objectivity of self and the career group is attained. 3. Identification of a working member within the total system of the career field emerges. 4. Satisfaction of a committed cause or action is at least temporarily attained.
Clarification	1. This period is marked by further clarification of self in the chosen position. 2. Further consideration of the anticipated position lessens the doubts of the career decision. 3. A stronger conviction about the career decision is developed. 4. This ends the anticipatory or preoccupational stage.		

SOURCE: Adapted from Tiedeman and O'Hara, 1963.

The duration and timing of developmental stages is of major importance in career development, according to Tiedeman. The individual's self-awareness and total combined activities make up a part of the time that must be spent in career decision making. But how much of the individual's time, awareness, and activities are concerned with considerations of the world of work? Is there a time-occupancy framework pertinent to work per se within personal development patterns?

Tiedeman suggested that time occupancy is preempted by biological requirements (such as sleeping and eating), expectations of independence (at work, in the community, and so on), and the quest for identity (as a citizen, parent, worker, and other roles). These particular aspects of human time commitment are assigned stages of timing within the overall pattern of human development. As individuals fit their careers into life plans, the study of the time invested in this activity as well as its particular time staging may yield information of inestimable value for the study of career development patterns as well as personal development patterns.

Tiedeman and others (Dudley & Tiedeman, 1977; Peatling & Tiedeman, 1977; Miller-Tiedeman & Tiedeman, 1990) have recently focused on ego development as a major component for the career decision process. Their position was that each person has I-power, or potential for self-improvement. Clarifying one's current status and projecting oneself into anticipated career environments are examples of self-development. Understanding of one's belief system is a product of the decision-making process and allows one to live a decision-guided life. Moreover, in viewing life as a career, individuals should be guided to become more self-directed. As Miller-Tiedeman (1988) stated, "One is essentially a scientist applying and observing the results of moving to one's own inner wisdom" (p. 34). Whereas theorists have generally focused on the decision-making process itself, Tiedeman and Miller-Tiedeman have researched individual processes in decision making. Individual experiences and understanding of the decision-making process are important outcomes for career development and selection.

In sum, Tiedeman conceptualized career development within a framework of time stages. The process is one of continuously differentiating one's ego identity, processing developmental tasks, and resolving psychosocial crises. Career decisions are reached through a systematic problem-solving pattern requiring the individual's total cognitive abilities, and combining both the uniqueness of the individual and the uniqueness of the world of work.

Miller-Tiedeman and Tiedeman (1990) currently advocate a "lifecareer theory." Based on self-organizing systems, process, and decision theory, lifecareer theory views career choices as a "shift and focus to one's internal frame of reference" (p. 31). Following this logic, one searches from within to find career direction and then applies the strategies of career development for a career decision. However, to find career direction, one must view life as a learning process, recognizing that one should be flexible in using various methods to solve problems and meeting one's needs as life unfolds. In reviewing the theory, Wrenn (1988) observed: "Don't push life in *your* direction (or what you assume this direction to be), life has a direction for you to learn; learn from life, and let life teach you" (p. 340).

A major contribution of Tiedeman's and O'Hara's (1963) theory is the focus on increased self-awareness as important and necessary in the decision-making process. Attention is directed toward effecting change and growth through adjustment to the mores of existing career social systems. Adaptation to a working environment for meaningful peer group affiliation and work performance is stressed. Although this theory has had an important impact on the career decision process, it is limited by lack of empirical data. It was theoretically formulated in accord with Erikson's stages on the basis of the vocationally relevant experiences of five white males.

SUMMARY OF PRACTICAL APPLICATIONS

The authors of this theory have more recently concentrated on developing a specific design of personal use of decision making (Miller-Tiedeman & Tiedeman, 1990). The major element of their model is one of self-constructionism within which the individual views career and the process of career development as a whole, particularly along with one's ego development and value level. The objective of the model is to guide clients in selecting experiences that are potentially growth promoting and that are designed to build ego development from which priorities in the value structure are defined and rearranged. This model has been used to develop a curriculum in a variety of classroom settings, ranging from classes for students with learning disabilities to humanities classes. The learning objectives are paraphrased as follows.

Learning Objective 1: Identify and define several levels of ego development.

Learning Objective 2: Identify and define nine decision-making strategies.

Learning Objective 3: Identify some examples of experience that illustrate stages of ego development and decision-making strategies.

Learning Objective 4: Compare stages of ego development with decision-making strategies.

Learning Objective 5: Point out the importance of ego development and decision making in life situations.

Learning Objective 6: Have students teach a class on the ego development model.

Learning Objective 7: Have each student help another student with a career planning unit. While helping students to achieve an understanding of their own career development vis-à-vis ego development and value structure, each student is encouraged to pursue a holistical life. Ideally, students advance to a level of self-awareness that releases them to make wise decisions (Miller-Tiedeman, 1990).

Circumscription and Compromise: A Developmental Theory of Occupational Aspirations

The development of occupational aspirations is the main theme of Gottfredson's (1981) theory. Incorporating a developmental approach similar to Super's developmental stages, her theory describes how people become attracted to certain occupations. Self-concept in vocational development is a key factor to career selection, according to Gottfredson, because people want jobs that are compatible with their self-images. Yet self-concept development in terms of vocational choice theory needs further definition, argued Gottfredson: key determinants of self-concept development are one's social class, level of intelligence, and experiences with sex-typing. According to Gottfredson, individual development progresses through four stages:

1. *Orientation to size and power (ages 3–5):* Thought process is concrete; children develop some sense of what it means to be an adult.
2. *Orientation to sex roles (ages 6–8):* Self-concept is influenced by gender development.
3. *Orientation to social valuation (ages 9–13):* Development of concepts of social class contributes to the awareness of self-in-situation. Preferences for level of work develop.
4. *Orientation to the internal, unique self (beginning at age 14):* Introspective thinking promotes greater self-awareness and perceptions of others. Individual achieves greater perception of vocational aspirations in the context of self, sex-role, and social class.

In this model of development, occupational preferences emerge within the complexities that accompany physical and mental growth. A major determinant of occupational preferences is the progressive circumscription of aspirations during self-concept development; that is, from the rather simplistic and concrete view of life as a child to the more comprehensive, complex, abstract thinking of the adolescent and adult. For example, in stage 1, the child has a positive view of occupations based on concrete thinking. In stage 2, the child makes more critical assessments of preferences, some of which are based on sex-typing. In stage 3, the child adds more criteria to evaluate preferences. In stage 4, the adolescent develops greater awareness of self, sex-typing, and social class, all of which are used with other criteria in evaluating occupational preferences.

Gottfredson suggested that socioeconomic background and intellectual level greatly influence individuals' self-concept in the dominant society. As people project into the work world, they choose occupations that are appropriate to their "social space," intellectual level, and sex-typing. In the Gottfredson model, social class and intelligence are incorporated in the self-concept theory of vocational choice.

Another unique factor in this theory is the concept of compromise in decision making. According to Gottfredson, compromises are based primarily on generalizations formed about occupations or "cognitive maps" of occupations. Although each person develops a unique map, each uses common methods of evaluating similarities and differences, namely through sex-typing, level of work, and field of work. In this way, individuals create boundaries or tolerable limits of acceptable jobs. Gottfredson suggested that people may compromise their occupational choices because of the accessibility of an occupation or even give up vocational interests to take a job that has an appropriate level of prestige and is an appropriate sex-typing. In general, individuals are less willing to compromise job level and sex-type because these factors are more closely associated with self-concept and social identity.

This theory has a strong sociological perspective. The external barriers that limit individual goals and opportunities are of major concern for Gottfredson, and her theory differs from other theories in four major ways. First, in career development, there is an attempt to implement the social self and, secondarily, the psychological self. Gottfredson places much more emphasis on the idea that individuals establish social identities through work. Second, how cognitions of self and occupations develop from early childhood is a major focus of the theory. Third, the theory prescribes to the premise that career choice is a process of eliminating options, thus narrowing one's choices. Fourth, the theory attempts to answer how individuals compromise their goals as they try to implement their aspirations. In Gottfredson's view, career choice proceeds by eliminating the negative rather than by selecting the most positive.

Although these differences make this theory distinctive, the theory also shares some of the fundamental assumptions of other theories. For example, career choice is a developmental process from early childhood. Second, individuals attempt to implement their self-concepts into career choice selections. Finally, satisfaction of career choice is largely determined by a "good fit" between the choice and the self-concept.

MAJOR CONCEPTS OF GOTTFREDSON'S THEORY

Self-concept. Following Super and associates (1963), Gottfredson defines *self-concept* as one's view of self that has many elements, such as one's appearance, abilities, personality, gender, values, and place in society.

Images of occupations. Images of occupations refer to occupational stereotypes (Holland, 1992) that include personalities of people in different occupations, the work that is done, and the appropriateness of that work for different types of people.

Cognitive maps of occupations. These cognitive maps constitute how adolescents and adults distinguish occupations into major dimensions, specifically, masculinity/femininity, occupational prestige level, and field of work. A two-dimensional map of sextype (Holland's term) and prestige level has been constructed to portray certain occupations by these two dimensions, and Holland's typology is used to indicate field of work. For example, an accountant (field of work), has above-average prestige level, and sextype is rated as more masculine than female. This map is primarily used to locate "areas" of society that different occupations offer.

Individuals use images of themselves to assess their compatibility with different occupations. Some refer to this process as congruence, or person-environment fit. If the core elements of self-concept conflict with an occupation, that occupation is rejected in Gottfredson's scheme.

Social space. This term refers to the zone of acceptable alternatives in each person's cognitive map of occupations, or each person's view of where he or she fits or would want to fit into society. Gottfredson suggests that career decision making should center around points of reference as "territories," either measured or contemplated, rather than specific points of reference to a single occupation.

Circumscription.   Circumscription reflects the process by which an individual narrows his or her territory when making a decision about social space or acceptable alternatives. The stages of circumscription have been outlined earlier.

Compromise.   This term is a very significant process in Gottfredson's theory. As she puts it, "Individuals often discover, when the time comes, that they will be unable to implement their most preferred choices" (Gottfredson, 1996, p. 187). Within this process, individuals will settle for a "good" choice but not the best possible one. Compromise is the process of adjusting aspirations to accommodate external reality, such as local availability of educational programs and employment, hiring practices, and family obligations. According to Gottfredson, individuals will not compromise their field of interest by prestige or sex type when there are small discrepancies. When there are moderate trade-offs within the process of compromise, people avoid abandoning prestige rather than sex type. In major trade-offs, people will sacrifice interests rather than prestige or sex type (Gottfredson, 1996).

EMPIRICAL SUPPORT

Lapan and Jingeleski (1992) found some agreement with the concept of social space in that individuals did assess compatibility with regard to zones of alternatives within the broad scope of the occupational world. Sastre and Mullet (1992) confirmed that gender, social class, and intelligence are related to work field and level of occupational aspirations. Leung, Conoley, and Scheel (1994) studied 149 immigrant and native-born Asian American college students to determine whether the boundaries of social space are set by age 13 (stage 3). They concluded that social space increased in size from age 8 through 17, disconfirming the theory's predictions. Although this one study should not negate Gottfredson's individual development through four stages, there remains the possibility that some students widen their range of career exploration during high school.

SUMMARY OF PRACTICAL APPLICATIONS

Gottfredson directs career counselors to what she refers to as underappreciated problems and possibilities in career development. Counselors are to encourage clients to be as realistic as possible when exploring potential occupational goals. She concludes that reality is either ignored, or the client fails to deal effectively with it. She recommends five developmental criteria to aid the counselee in dealing with reality.

   1. *The counselee is able to name one or more occupational alternatives.* If not, then the counselor is to determine whether indecision reflects the inability to choose among high-quality alternatives or whether there is an unwillingness to

attempt to choose. Some questions to be answered are: Is there a lack of self-confidence? Are there internal or external conflicts in goals? Is there impaired judgment?

2. *The counselee's interests and abilities are adequate for occupations chosen.* If not, is this the result of misperceptions about self? Are there external pressures from parents or other important adults?

3. *The counselee is satisfied with the alternatives he or she has identified.* If dissatisfied, does the counselee consider the selected alternatives as an unacceptable compromise of interests, sex type, prestige or family concerns, or other concerns? Attempt to determine internal or external constraints.

4. *The counselee has not unnecessarily restricted his or her alternatives.* Did the counselee consider suitable and accessible alternatives? Has there been a lack of exposure to compatible alternatives? Does the counselee have an adequate knowledge of his or her own abilities?

5. *The counselee is aware of opportunities and is realistic about obstacles for implementing the chosen occupation.* What are the reasons the counselee has not been realistic about obstacles? Is there wishful thinking or a lack of information or planning? Information to seek during the counseling interview includes why certain options seem to be rejected and why some compromises are more acceptable than others. Use the following questions: What is the preferred self, in terms of both sociability and personality type? Are the perceptions of boundaries in social space adequate? Who are the primary reference groups, and what family circumstances influence the counselee?

Finally, Gottfredson suggests that information that provides compatibility and accessibility are essential. One may do this through exploration of social space that includes aptitude requirements of occupations, arrays of occupational clusters, and the counselee's perceptions of sex type and prestige. Occupational clusters depicted on a map are to be used to focus attention on compatible clusters. As the counselee selects more specific occupations, the characteristics of the occupation and the availability of training should be discussed. Eventually, as the client reaches the realm of constructive realism, a subset of best choices can be realistically made and, subsequently, one best choice with a list of alternatives.

Ann Roe: A Needs Approach

Early relations within the family and their subsequent effects on career direction have been the main focus of Ann Roe's work (1956). The analysis of differences in personality, aptitude, intelligence, and background as related to career choice was the main thrust of her research. She studied several outstanding physical, biological, and social scientists to determine whether vocational direction was highly related to early personality development.

Roe (1956) emphasized that early childhood experiences play an important role in finding satisfaction in one's chosen field. Her research led her to investigate how parental styles affect need hierarchy and the relationships of these needs to later adult lifestyles. She drew heavily from Maslow's hierarchy of needs in the development of her theory. The need structure of the individual, according to Roe, would be greatly influenced by early childhood frustrations and satisfactions. For example, individuals who desire to work in contact with people are primarily drawn in this direction because of their strong needs for affection and belonging-ness. Those who choose the nonperson-type jobs would be meeting lower-level needs for safety and security. Roe hypothesized that individuals who enjoy work-ing with people were reared by warm and accepting parents and those who avoid contact with others were reared by cold or rejecting parents.

Roe (1956) classified occupations into two major categories: *person-oriented* and *nonperson-oriented*. Examples of person-oriented occupations are: (1) service (concerned with service to other people); (2) business contact (person-to-person contact, primarily in sales); (3) managerial (management in business, industry, and government); (4) general culture (teaching, ministry, and journalism); and (5) arts and entertainment (performing in creative arts). Examples of nonperson-oriented jobs are in the arenas of: (1) technology (production, maintenance, and transpor-tation); (2) the outdoors (agriculture, forestry, mining, and so on); and (3) science (scientific theory and application).

Within each occupational classification are progressively higher levels of func-tioning. Roe (1956) contended that the selection of an occupational category was primarily a function of the individual's need structure but that the level of attain-ment within the category was more dependent on the individual's level of ability and socioeconomic background. The climate of the relationship between child and parent was the main generating force of needs, interests, and attitudes that were later reflected in vocational choice.

When thinking back on how she developed the classification system, Roe says she was greatly influenced by research on interests and the development of interest inventories (Roe & Lunneborg, 1990). Nevertheless, six studies reported by Roe and Lunneborg (1990) support the validity of the classification system in that ap-proximately two-thirds of job changes by the individuals studied occurred within the same occupational classification group.

Roe modified her theory after several studies refuted her claim that different parent-child interactions result in different vocational choices (Powell, 1957; Green & Parker, 1965). She currently takes the position that the early orientation of an individual is related to later major decisions—particularly in occupational choice—but that other variables not accounted for in her theory are also important factors. The following statements by Roe (1972) express her own viewpoint on career development:

1. The life history of any man and many women, written in terms of or around the occupational history, can give the essence of the person more fully than can any other approach.

2. Situations relevant to this history begin with the birth of the individual into a particular family at a particular place and time and continue throughout his or her life.

3. There may be differences in the relative weights carried by different factors, but the process of vocational decision and behavior do not differ in essence from any others.

4. The extent to which vocational decisions and behaviors are under the voluntary control of the individual is variable, but it could be more than it sometimes seems to be. Deliberate consideration of the factors involved seems to be rare.

5. The occupational life affects all other aspects of the life pattern.

6. An appropriate and satisfying vocation can be a bulwark against neurotic ills or a refuge from them. An inappropriate or unsatisfying vocation can be sharply deleterious.

7. Because the goodness of life in any social group is compounded of and also determines that of its individual members, the efforts of any society to maintain stability and at the same time advance in desired ways can perhaps be most usefully directed toward developing satisfying vocational situations for its members. But unless the vocation is adequately integrated into the total life pattern, it cannot help much.

8. There is no single specific occupational slot that is a one-and-only perfect one for any individual. Conversely, there is no single person who is the only one for a particular occupational slot. Within any occupation, there is a considerable range in a number of variables specifying the requirements.

Roe's theory is usually referred to as a *needs-theory approach* to career choice (Zaccaria, 1970; Bailey & Stadt, 1973). According to Roe, combinations of early parent-child relations, environmental experiences, and genetic features determine the development of a need structure. The individual then learns to satisfy these developed needs primarily through interactions with people or through activities that do not involve people. Thus, Roe postulated that occupational choice primarily involves choosing occupations that are person-oriented, such as service occupations, or nonperson-oriented, such as scientific occupations. The intensity of needs is the major determinant that motivates the individual to the level hierarchy within an occupational structure (Zaccaria, 1970).

There have been several practical applications of Roe's classification system (Lunneborg, 1984). For example, both dimensions of the system were used to construct the *Occupational Preference Inventory* (Knapp & Knapp, 1977), the *Vocational Interest Inventory* (Lunneborg, 1981), and an interest inventory used in the fourth edition of the *Dictionary of Occupational Titles* (U.S. Department of Labor, 1977).

Roe's theory has generated considerable research but little support for her theoretical model (Osipow, 1983). Roe's postulated effect of the parent-child interactions on later vocational choices is difficult to validate. Differing parental attitudes and subsequent interactions within families present such an overwhelming number of variables that no study could be sufficiently controlled to be considered empirical. The longitudinal requirements necessary to validate the theory present another deterring factor. Notwithstanding, Roe made a great contribution to career counseling in having directed considerable attention to the developmental period of early childhood.

Summary of Practical Applications

1. Roe and Lunneborg (1990) did not present step-by-step career counseling procedures, but they did include examples of the use of Roe's two-way occupational classification system in a variety of career-related programs that have existed in several states.

2. Roe's theory has been applied to career exploration programs and career choice measures based on the two-way occupational classification system.

3. Anyone familiar with Roe's views concerning counseling applications of her work will not be surprised that she has not constructed a counseling program per se, for as she puts it, "Osipow's (1983) major objection throughout seems to be that the theory is not specifically adapted to or drawn up for the counseling situation. I can only remark that it was not devised to be" (Roe & Lunneborg, 1990, p. 80).

4. Three examples of the use of Roe's theory have been selected to illustrate the practical application of her work in interest measurement and in career guidance programs. For example, the *Career Occupational Preference System (COPS) Interest Inventory* (Knapp & Knapp, 1984, 1985) was based on Roe's two-way classification system. The major purpose was to foster greater career awareness through a two-dimensional perspective of careers.

5. In a career development program developed by Miller (1986), clients organize vocational card sorts according to Roe's eight interest groups. One of the first decisions made is between two major groups; occupations oriented toward people or occupations oriented away from people. Discussions follow with the purpose of narrowing choices to fields of work and, if possible, to specific occupations.

6. Educational and vocations decisions are the major focus of a guidance program sponsored by colleges in Washington state. Interest feedback is given to students through Roe's two-way classification system, and a guide uses Roe's framework to project employment opportunities in Washington, Idaho, Montana, Oregon, and Alaska (Roe & Lunneborg, 1990).

John Holland: A Typology Approach

According to John Holland (1992), individuals are attracted to a given career by their particular personalities and numerous variables that constitute their backgrounds. First of all, career choice is an expression of, or an extension of, personality into the world of work followed by subsequent identification with specific occupational stereotypes. A comparison of self with the perception of an occupation and subsequent acceptance or rejection is a major determinant in career choice. Congruence of one's view of self with occupational preference establishes what Holland refers to as the *modal personal style.*

Modal personal orientation is a developmental process established through heredity and the individual's life history of reacting to environmental demands. Central to Holland's theory is the concept that one chooses a career to satisfy one's preferred modal personal orientation. If the individual has developed a strong dominant orientation, satisfaction is probable in a corresponding occupational environment. If, however, the orientation is one of indecision, the likelihood of satisfaction diminishes. The strength or dominance of the developed modal personal orientation as compared to career environments will be critical to the individual's selection of a preferred lifestyle. Again, the key concept behind Holland's environmental models and environmental influences is that individuals are attracted to a particular role demand of an occupational environment that meets their personal needs and provides them with satisfaction.

For example, a socially oriented individual prefers to work in an environment that provides interaction with others, such as a teaching position. On the other hand, a mechanically inclined individual would seek out an environment where trade could be quietly practiced and would avoid socializing to a great extent. Occupational homogeneity provides the best route to self-fulfillment and a consistent career pattern. Individuals out of their element who have conflicting occupational environmental roles and goals will have inconsistent and divergent career patterns. Holland stressed the importance of self-knowledge in the search for vocational satisfaction and stability.

From this frame of reference, Holland proposed six kinds of modal occupational environments and six matching modal personal orientations. These are summarized in Table 2-6, which also offers representative examples of occupations and themes associated with each personal style.

Holland proposed that personality types can be arranged in a coded system following his modal-personal-orientation themes such as R (realistic occupation), I (investigative), A (artistic), S (social), E (enterprising), and C (conventional). In this way, personality types can be arranged according to dominant combinations. For example, a code of CRI would mean that an individual is very much like people in conventional occupations, and somewhat like those in realistic and investigative occupations. Holland's Occupational Classification (HOC) system has corresponding *Dictionary of Occupational Titles (DOT)* numbers for cross-reference purposes.

The four basic assumptions underlying Holland's (1992) theory are as follows:

1. In our culture, most persons can be categorized as one of six types: realistic, investigative, artistic, social, enterprising, or conventional (p. 2).
2. There are six kinds of environments: realistic, investigative, artistic, social, enterprising, or conventional (p. 3).
3. People search for environments that will let them exercise their skills and abilities, express their attitudes and values, and take on agreeable problems and roles (p. 4).
4. A person's behavior is determined by an interaction between his personality and the characteristics of his environment (p. 4).

The relationships between Holland's personality types are illustrated in Figure 2-2. The hexagonal model provides a visual presentation of the inner relationship of personality styles and occupational environment coefficients of correlation. For example, adjacent categories on the hexagon such as realistic and investigative are most alike, but opposites such as artistic and conventional are most unlike.

TABLE 2-6
Holland's Modal Personal Styles and Occupational Environments

Personal styles	Themes	Occupational environments
May lack social skills; prefers concrete vs. abstract work tasks; may seem frank, materialistic, and inflexible; usually has mechanical abilities.	Realistic	Skilled trades such as plumber, electrician, and machine operator; technician skills such as airplane mechanic, photographer, draftsperson, and some service occupations
Very task-oriented; is interested in math and science; may be described as independent, analytical, and intellectual; may be reserved and defers leadership to others.	Investigative	Scientific such as chemist, physicist, and mathematician; technician such as laboratory technician, computer programmer, and electronics worker
Prefers self-expression through the arts; may be described as imaginative, introspective, and independent; values aesthetics and creation of art forms.	Artistic	Artistic such as sculptor, artist, and designer; musical such as music teacher, orchestra leader, and musician; literary such as editor, writer, and critic
Prefers social interaction and has good communication skills; is concerned with social problems, and is community-service-oriented; has interest in educational activities.	Social	Educational such as teacher, educational administrator, and college professor; social welfare such as social worker, sociologist, rehabilitation counselor, and professional nurse
Prefers leadership roles; may be described as domineering, ambitious, and persuasive; makes use of good verbal skills.	Enterprising	Managerial such as personnel, production, and sales manager; various sales positions, such as life insurance, real estate, and car salesperson
May be described as practical, well-controlled, sociable, and rather conservative; prefers structured tasks such as systematizing and manipulation of data and word processing.	Conventional	Office and clerical worker such as timekeeper, file clerk, teller, accountant, keypunch operator, secretary, bookkeeper, receptionist, and credit manager

SOURCE: Adapted from Holland, 1985a, 1992.

Those of intermediate distance such as realistic and enterprising are somewhat unlike.

According to Holland, the hexagonal model introduces five key concepts. The first, *consistency,* relates to personality as well as to environment. Some of the types have more in common than others; for instance, artistic and social types have more in common than do investigative and enterprising types. The closer the types are on the hexagon, the more consistent the individual will be. Therefore, high consistency is seen when an individual expresses a preference for adjoining codes such as ESA or RIC. Less consistency would be indicated by codes RAE or CAS.

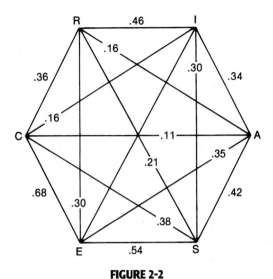

FIGURE 2-2

Holland's model of personality types and occupational environments

SOURCE: From *An Empirical Occupational Classification Derived from a Theory of Personality and Intended for Practice and Research,* by J. L. Holland, D. R. Whitney, N. S. Cole, and J. M. Richards, Jr., ACT Research Report No. 29, The American College Testing Program, 1969. Copyright 1969 by the American College Testing Program.

The second concept is *differentiation.* Individuals who fit a pure personality type will express little resemblance to other types. Conversely, those individuals who fit several personality types have poorly defined personality styles and are considered undifferentiated or poorly defined.

Identity, the third concept describes those individuals who have a clear and stable picture of their goals, interests, and talents. In the case of environments, identity refers to the degree to which a workplace has clarity, stability, and integration of goals, tasks, and rewards. For example, individuals who have many occupational goals, as opposed to a few, have low identity.

The fourth concept, *congruence,* occurs when an individual's personality type matches the work environment. Social personality types, for example, prefer environments that provide social interaction, concerns with social problems, and interest in educational activities. In reviewing the major studies investigating this concept, Spokane (1985) concluded that the research did support the theory that congruence is highly related to academic performance and persistence, job satisfaction, and stability of choice.

Finally, Holland's model provides a calculus for his theory. Holland proposed that the theoretical relationships between types of occupational environments lend themselves to empirical research techniques. The practical application of further research will provide counselors and clients with a better understanding of Holland's theory.

As important as the individual's self-knowledge is occupational knowledge. Holland believed critical career judgments are partially drawn from the individual's occupational information. The importance of identification with an occupational environment underscores the significance of occupational knowledge in the process of appropriate career choice. Knowledge of both occupational environment and corresponding modal personal orientations is, according to Holland, critical to appropriate career decision making.

In the process of career decision making, Holland postulated that the level hierarchy or level of attainment in a career is determined primarily by individual self-evaluations. Intelligence is considered less important than personality and interest (Holland, 1966). Furthermore, the factor of intelligence is subsumed in the classification of personality types; for example, individuals who resemble the investigative type of modal personal orientation are generally intelligent and naturally have skills such as analytical and abstract reasoning.

According to Holland, the stability of career choice depends primarily on the dominance of personal orientation. Putting it another way, individuals are products of their environment, which greatly influences their personal orientations and eventual career choices. Personality development is a primary consideration in Holland's career-typology theory of vocational behavior.

Holland's theory is primarily descriptive, with little emphasis on explaining the causes and the timing of the development of hierarchies of the personal modal styles. He concentrated on the factors that influence career choice rather than on the developmental process that leads to career choice. Holland's early theory was developed from observations made on a population of National Merit Scholarship finalists. He later expanded the database to include a wider sample of the general population. His research has been extensive and longitudinal. Recently, Holland (1987a) compared his theories with developmental positions:

> I find experience for a learning theory perspective to be more persuasive (than developmental views). In my scheme, different types are the outcomes of different learning histories. Stability of type is a common occurrence because career (types) tend to snowball over the life course. The reciprocal interaction of person and successive jobs usually leads to a series of success and satisfaction cycles. (p. 26)

There is some evidence to suggest that Holland's theory is applicable to male and female nonprofessional workers (Salomone & Slaney, 1978). However, the widely used *Self-Directed Search (SDS)* and Holland's theory in general have been attacked as being gender-biased. The major criticism has centered on the claim that the *SDS* limits the career considerations for women and that most females tend to score in three personality types (artistic, social, and conventional) (Weinrach, 1984, p. 69). In defense of the *SDS*, Holland suggested that in our sexist society, females will display a greater interest in female-dominated occupations.

Holland's theory places emphasis on the accuracy of self-knowledge and career information necessary for career decision making. It has had a tremendous impact on interest assessment and career counseling procedures; a number of interest inventories present results using the Holland classification format. Its implications for counseling are apparent; a major counseling objective would be to develop strategies to enhance knowledge of self, occupational requirements, and differing occupational environments.

In sum, Holland's theory has proved to be of more practical usefulness than any of the other theories discussed in this text. In addition, most of his propositions have been clearly defined, and they lend themselves to empirical evaluations. The impact of his scholarly approach to RIASEC theory has had and will continue to exert tremendous influence on career development research and procedures.

Empirical Support for Holland's Theory

Extensive testing of Holland's theory suggests that his constructs are valid, and in fact the body of evidence is extremely large and almost overwhelming. Recent research is reviewed by Spokane (1996), whereas Osipow and Fitzgerald (1996), Holland, Fritzsche, and Powell (1994), Holland, Powell, and Fritzsche (1994), and Weinrach and Srebalus (1990) have reported more extensive reviews. Examples of other research topics include the interplay between personality and interests by Gottfredson, Jones, and Holland (1993) and Carson and Mowesian (1993); the studies of the hexagon by Rounds and Tracy (1993); person-environment congruence and interaction by Spokane (1985) and Meir, Esfromes, and Friedland (1994). The best current statements about exploring careers with a typology are by Holland (1996). The original documents should be read for more details of current research projects.

Summary of Practical Applications

Applying Holland's theory in career counseling requires a working knowledge of several inventories and diagnostic measures. Some of these instruments will only be introduced here, as more information is given about some of them in Chapter 7.

1. The *Vocational Preference Inventory* (Holland, 1985b) has undergone eight revisions.
2. *My Vocational Situation* (Holland, Daiger, & Power, 1980) and *Vocational Identity Scale* (Holland, Johnston, & Asama, 1993) provide information about goals, interests, and talents.
3. The *Position Classification Inventory* (Gottfredson & Holland, 1991) is a job analysis measure of RIASEC environmental codes.
4. The *Career Attitudes and Strategies Inventory* (Gottfredson & Holland, 1994) measures work environment variables.
5. The *Self-Directed Search* (SDS) (Form R) (Holland, 1994a) is one of the most widely used interest inventories, has over 20 foreign language versions, can be administered by computer, and includes computer-based reports. It has been revised four times, the latest being in 1994. Accompanying the assessment booklet are several companion materials: the *Educational Occupations Finder* (Rosen, Holmberg, & Holland, 1994b), the *Dictionary of Educational Opportunities* (Rosen, Holmberg, & Holland, 1994a), the *You and Your Career Booklet* (Holland, 1994c), a *Leisure Activities Finder*

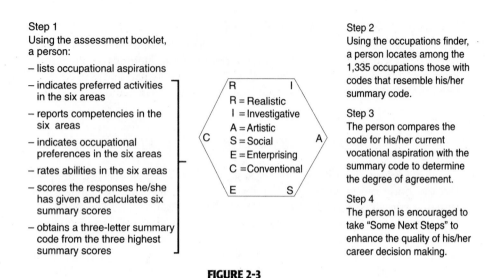

Step 1
Using the assessment booklet,
a person:

- lists occupational aspirations
- indicates preferred activities
  in the six areas
- reports competencies in the
  six areas
- indicates occupational
  preferences in the six areas
- rates abilities in the six areas
- scores the responses he/she
  has given and calculates six
  summary scores
- obtains a three-letter summary
  code from the three highest
  summary scores

R
I
R = Realistic
I = Investigative
A = Artistic
C
S = Social
A
E = Enterprising
C = Conventional
E
S

Step 2
Using the occupations finder,
a person locates among the
1,335 occupations those with
codes that resemble his/her
summary code.

Step 3
The person compares the
code for his/her current
vocational aspiration with the
summary code to determine
the degree of agreement.

Step 4
The person is encouraged to
take "Some Next Steps" to
enhance the quality of his/her
career decision making.

FIGURE 2-3

Steps in using the SDS

SOURCE: Adapted and Reproduced by special permission of the Publisher, Psychological Assessment Resources, Inc., Odessa, FL 33556, from the *Self-Directed Search Professional User's Guide,* by J. Holland, A. Powell, and B. Fritzsche. Copyright 1985, 1987, 1994 by PAR, Inc. Further reproduction is prohibited without permission from PAR, Inc.

(Holmberg, Rosen, & Holland, 1990), and a *Dictionary of Holland Occupational Codes* (Gottfredson & Holland, 1989).

Figure 2-3 presents the steps for using the SDS assessment booklet and the *Educational Occupations Finder.*

Krumboltz's Learning Theory of Career Counseling

A social-learning theory approach to career decision making was first proposed by Krumboltz, Mitchell, and Gelatt (1975), and then several years later by Mitchell and Krumboltz (1990). More recently, Mitchell and Krumboltz (1996) have extended the earlier social-learning theory approach to include Krumboltz's learning theory of career counseling, and they now suggest that the entire theory be referred to as learning theory of career counseling (LTCC). In this review of the two parts of the theory, part one will explain the origins of career choice, and part two will address the important question of what career counselors can do to help solve career-related problems.

The theory is an attempt to simplify the process of career selection and is based primarily on life events that are influential in determining career selection. In this theory, the process of career development involves four factors: (1) genetic endowments and special abilities, (2) environmental conditions and events, (3) learning experiences, and (4) task approach skills.

Genetic endowments and special abilities include inherited qualities that may set limits on the individual's career opportunities. The authors do not attempt to explain the interaction of the genetic characteristics and special abilities but emphasize that these factors should be recognized as influences in the career decision-making process.

Environmental conditions and events are factors of influence that are often beyond the individual's control. What is emphasized here is that certain events and circumstances in the individual's environment influence skills development, activities, and career preferences. For example, government policies regulating certain occupations and the availability of certain natural resources in the individual's environment may determine to a large extent the opportunities and experiences available. Natural disasters, such as droughts and floods, that affect economic conditions are further examples of influences beyond the control of the individuals affected.

The third factor, *learning experiences*, includes instrumental learning experiences and associative learning experiences. *Instrumental learning experiences* are those the individual learns through reactions to consequences, through direct observable results of actions, and through the reactions of others. The consequences of learning activities and their later influence on career planning and development are primarily determined by the reinforcement or nonreinforcement of the activity, the genetic endowment of the individual, special abilities and skills, and the task itself.

Associative learning experiences include negative and positive reactions to pairs of previously neutral situations. For example, the statements "all politicians are dishonest" and "all bankers are rich" influence the individual's perceptions of these occupations. These associations may also be learned through observations, written materials, and films.

The fourth factor, *task approach skills*, includes the sets of skills the individual has developed, such as problem-solving skills, work habits, mental sets, emotional responses, and cognitive responses. These sets of developed skills to a large extent determine the outcome of problems and tasks the individual faces.

Task approach skills are often modified as a result of desirable or undesirable experiences. For example, Sue, a high school senior, occasionally takes and studies class notes. Although she was able to make good grades in high school, she may find that this same practice in college may result in failure, thus causing her to modify note-taking practices and study habits.

Krumboltz and associates stressed that each individual's unique learning experiences over the life span develop the primary influences that lead to career choice. These influences include (1) generalization of self derived from experiences and performance in relation to learned standards, (2) sets of developed skills used in coping with the environment, and (3) career-entry behavior such as applying for a job or selecting an educational or training institution.

The social-learning model emphasizes the importance of learning experiences and their effect on occupational selection. Genetic endowment is considered primarily as a factor that may limit learning experiences and subsequent career choice. Career decision making is considered to be a lifelong process and a very important skill to be taught in education and career counseling programs. In teaching decision-making skills, it is recommended that the identified factors that influence career choice be stressed.

The factors that influence preferences in the social-learning model are composed of numerous cognitive processes, interactions in the environment, and inherited personal characteristics and traits. For example, educational and occupational preferences are a direct, observable result of actions (referred to as self-observation generalizations) and of learning experiences involved with career tasks. If an individual has been positively reinforced while engaging in the activities of a course of study or occupation, the individual is more likely to express a preference for the course of study or the field of work. In this way, the consequence of each learning experience, in school or on a job, increases the probability that the individual will have a similar learning experience in the future. However, an individual can become proficient in a field of work by developing skills, but even this fact does not ensure that an individual will remain in the field of work over a life span. An economic crisis or negative feedback may initiate a change of career direction.

Genetic and environmental factors are also involved in the development of preferences. For example, a basketball coach might reinforce his players for their skills, but the coach will more likely reinforce tall players than ones smaller in stature.

Other positive factors influencing preferences are valued models who advocate engaging in a field of work or an educational course, or who are observed doing so. Finally, positive words and images, such as a booklet describing an occupation in glamorous terms, will lead to positive reactions to that occupation. In social-learning theory, learning takes place through observations as well as through direct experiences.

The determination of an individual's problematic beliefs and generalizations is of major importance in the social-learning model (Mitchell & Krumboltz, 1984). For example, the identification of content from which certain beliefs and generalizations have evolved is a key ingredient for developing counseling strategies for individuals who have career decision-making problems. The counselor's role is to probe assumptions and presuppositions of expressed beliefs and to explore alternative beliefs and courses of action. Assisting individuals to fully understand the validity of their beliefs is a major component of the social-learning model. Specifically, the counselor should address the following problems (Krumboltz, 1983).

1. Persons may fail to recognize that a remediable problem exists (individuals assume that most problems are a normal part of life and cannot be altered).
2. Persons may fail to exert the effort needed to make a decision or solve a problem (individuals exert little effort to explore alternatives; they take the familiar way out).
3. Persons may eliminate a potentially satisfying alternative for inappropriate reasons (individuals overgeneralize from false assumptions and overlook potentially worthwhile alternatives).

4. Persons may choose poor alternatives for inappropriate reasons (the individuals are unable to realistically evaluate potential careers because of false beliefs and unrealistic expectations).
5. Persons may suffer anguish and anxiety over perceived inability to achieve goals (individual goals may be unrealistic or in conflict with other goals).

This theory is both descriptive and explanatory: the process of career choice is described and examples of factors that influence choice are given. Although the authors have attempted to simplify the process of career development and career choice, the many variables introduced in this theory make the process of validation extremely complex. Meanwhile, the authors should be commended for specifying counseling objectives based on this theory and for providing strategies designed to accomplish these objectives. They also provided several observations for career counseling (Krumboltz, Mitchell, & Gelatt, 1975, pp. 11–13):

1. Career decision making is a learned skill.
2. Persons who claim to have made a career choice need help too (career choice may have been made from inaccurate information and faulty alternatives).
3. Success is measured by students' demonstrated skill in decision making (evaluations of decision-making skills are needed).
4. Clients come from a wide array of groups.
5. Clients need not feel guilty if they are not sure of a career to enter.
6. No one occupation is seen as the best for any one individual.

Empirical Support for Krumboltz's Learning Theory

The learning theory of career counseling has been developed only recently, and therefore relevant research has yet to be accomplished. The original theory, social-learning theory of career decision making, claimed validity from the development of educational and occupational preferences, the development of task approach skills and factors that cause people to take action, and from an extensive database on general social-learning theory of behavior. More information about the validity of this theory can be obtained from Mitchell and Krumboltz (1996).

Summary of Practical Applications

According to Mitchell and Krumboltz (1996), when people in modern society make career choices, they must cope with four fundamental trends. Career counselors must recognize these trends and be prepared to help.

1. *People need to expand their capabilities and interests, not base decisions on existing characteristics only.* This first trend centers around the use of interest inventories. Because many individuals have limited experiences with the vast

number of activities that interest inventories measure, people may become indifferent to many activities they have not had the chance to experience personally. The point here is that career counselors should assist individuals in exploring new activities, rather than routinely directing them to career decision making based on measured interests that reflect limited past experiences.

2. *People need to prepare for changing work tasks, not assume that occupations will remain stable.* The changing role of job requirements and workplace environments in our current society suggests that career counselors must be prepared to help individuals learn new skills and attitudes in order to meet the demands of international competition. The radical restructuring of the work force and the disruptions of expectations can be very stressful. Therefore, career counselors also should be prepared to help individuals cope with stress as they learn to develop new skills on an ongoing basis.

3. *People need to be empowered to take action, not merely given a diagnosis.* Many issues about career decisions are often overlooked, including a lack of information about working per se, families' reaction to a member's taking a particular job, and how to go about getting a job. These issues and others, such as restructuring of the workplace, could cause fear of the decision-making process itself, referred to as *zeteophobia,* or cause procrastination about making a decision. Career counselors are directed to help individuals find answers to these questions and others while providing effective support during the exploration process.

4. *Career counselors need to play a major role in dealing with all career problems, not just with occupational selection.* Krumboltz (1993), Richardson (1993), and Zunker (1994), among others, have suggested that career and personal counseling should be integrated. Such issues as burnout, career change, peer affiliate relationships, obstacles to career development, and the work role and its effect on other life roles are examples of potential problems that call for interventions by the career counselor.

Other suggestions

1. The role of career counselors and the goals of career counseling need to be reevaluated. Counselors need to continue to promote client learning, but perhaps in a different way. Counselors may have to become coaches and mentors to help individuals meet the changes in work force requirements.

2. Learning experiences should be used to increase the range of opportunities that can be considered in career exploration. Counselors should attempt to discover unlimited experiences among clients and offer proper learning solutions.

3. Assessment results can be used to create new learning experiences. For instance, aptitude test results can be used to focus on new learning. Key interests identified through interest inventories need to be developed. Assessment results can be starting points for establishing new learning experiences.

4. Intervention strategies suggested by Mitchell and Krumboltz include the use of job clubs. Individuals can offer support to each other in the job search process. A wide range of media should be made available to clients, and local employers should offer high school students structured work-based learning experiences.

5. Career counselors should become adept at using cognitive restructuring. For the youngster who is to report to work with fear of doing a poor job, the counselor can suggest another perspective. Cognitive restructuring suggests to such a client that he or she should report to the new job as a chance to impress the boss and fellow workers with enthusiasm. "Reframing" the perspective for this client should be helpful in making the first day on a job a satisfactory one.

6. Career counselors should also use behavioral counseling techniques, including role playing or trying new behaviors, desensitization when dealing with phobias, and paradoxical intention. The latter technique suggests that a client engage in the types of behavior that have created a problem (Mitchell & Krumboltz, 1996).

Sociological Perspective of Work and Career Development

This theory was built around a sociological perspective of work by Blau, Gustad, Jessor, Parnes, and Wilcox (1956) that included relationships of choice and process of selection. That is, they suggested that the effects of social institutions on career choice and development emphasized the interrelationship of psychological, economic, and sociological determinants of occupational choice and development. Also, the authors suggested that individual characteristics that are responsible for choice are biologically determined and socially conditioned through family influences, social position and relations, and developed social-role characteristics. Eventually, the individual reaches a preference hierarchy from which choices are made.

In a more comprehensive approach to the sociological perspective of work and its relationship to career development, Hotchkiss and Borow (1996) provide a general background for the development of a model that includes recommendations for career counseling in the career decision-making process. In the sociological perspective, it must be remembered that sociologists view occupational choice as part of a broad system of social stratification, as outlined in the introductory paragraphs to this model.

The differences between the sociological perspective of work and the psychology of career development provides the counselor with key perspectives from which to better understand the sociological effects on the individual during the career decision-making process.

Work per se is viewed as much more inclusive from a sociologist's point of view than generally perceived; the status hierarchy of occupational structure, power and authority in the workplace, work socialization processes, labor unions and collective bargaining, the operation of the labor market, and sociology of professions are examples. Second, career development theories assume that individuals have at least a moderate degree of control in the process of making career decisions. In contrast, sociological theory strongly suggests that institutional and impersonal market forces constrain decision making and greatly impede satisfaction of career aspirations. Third, there has been much more significantly relevant research and interest on the part of sociologists than by career development theorists on institutional factors that determine and shape workplace environments. According to sociologists, forces such as formal rules and supply and demand determine the nature and scope of work activities. Although there is an appreciation of the constellation of personal attributes that influence job performance and satisfaction, sociological research has been directed to other determinants of career development that should be of major concern to the career counselor. The following topics are used to represent sociological perspectives of work and career development.

Status attainment theory.   The hypothesis of this theory is that parental status greatly affects the occupational level offspring attain. More fully, parental status influences attitudes concerning appropriate levels of education and the career plans (including educational level) of their children.

Sociology of labor markets.   In taking this position, sociologists argue that institutional practices shape career outcomes rather than individual career aspirations. For example, in the structure of organizations, a satisfying career is not necessarily one that has been planned but is more a matter of obtaining a preferred position when the opportunity presents itself. In a much broader sense, individuals are assigned to job slots or work positions, rather than obtaining them from personal planned choices.

The structure of some business and government organizations is characterized by the institutional career ladder of promotions. Some of the ways institutional policies of management effect career development are as follows: (1) those who work in the core sector of an industry make higher wages than do those in the periphery sector; (2) level of education and experience have a greater influence on wages in the core sector than in the periphery, and (3) minorities and women have limited access to jobs in the core sector.

Race and gender effects.   Ongoing research indicates that minorities are concentrated in low-status occupations and earn less than whites do (Saunders, 1995). Some evidence suggests that there is a decline in gender segregation of jobs (Roos & Jones, 1993), but women tend to be concentrated in a narrow band of occupations that pay less than men earn (Reskin, 1993). Interestingly, men and women both earn less in jobs that are culturally defined as "women's work."

School processes.   Ability grouping and tracking students in school have been attacked as two methods that mirror the dominant larger social system; ascribed status and adult achievement (educational, vocational, and economic achievement) influence standardized measures, which perpetuate the earlier suggestion that family status is a major determinant of educational achievement and subsequent job opportunities.

Youth competence and outcomes of youth work.   *Developed planning ability of planfulness* is a term used by Super (1990) that was also used by Clausen

(1991) in a research project aimed at proving that adolescent planful competence emerges from environmental states, family status, and parental socialization processes. In addition, Clausen hypothesized that adolescent competence regarding mastery of behavior during high school years greatly influenced later educational attainment, career stability, and marital status. The results of this research suggest that adolescent competence is a very powerful predictor of adult outcomes concerning occupational attainment and marriage stability.

It was estimated in the late 1980s that 90% of 11th- and 12th-graders held part-time jobs during the school year. Research in the 1980s also indicated that part-time work did not provide an environment for psychological growth and development, nor did it forge links to full-time career objectives (Greenberger & Steinberg, 1986).

A more positive report was given by Marsh (1991), who indicated that summer jobs do not conflict with schoolwork and therefore are not associated with negative factors, as reported earlier. In fact, there were indications that summer employment enhanced adolescents' self-esteem.

Family effects.   The question here is, What role does the family play in shaping career choices and development of individuals? We have previously discussed how parental work and occupational status affects their children's future career attainment. The interest in family effects centers around how family structure and maternal work outside the home influence the choices and attitudes of youth. Because the numerically dominant family type is now a dual-work or dual-career one, research has now focused on a different kind of family-work relationship. In a study by Parcel and Menaghan (1994), no relationship was found between maternal employment and the child's social behavior. However, the most far-reaching finding indicated that a working mother's ability to transmit behavior norms to children is not diminished by her working.

Work commitment.   Sociologists view work commitment as rather transient and as being greatly affected by current social structures on the job. Research by Halaby and Weakliem (1989) proved three significant hypotheses: (1) if jobs have an intrinsically rewarding nature, the stronger will be the worker's attachment to the organization; (2) the closer the job match to the worker's abilities, the stronger is the commitment to the job; and (3) workers who have greater opportunity for alternative employment have a weaker attachment to the organization. Not surprisingly, the greatest strengthening bond of the three hypotheses was the matching of job requirements and worker's abilities.

Summary of Practical Applications

1. Career counselors need to be aware of sociological research that informs them of how individuals choose and are selected for work roles. In the career choice process, the sociologist stresses that choice is restricted by a number of variables, including status of parents, labor market demands, and structures in

organizations. Thus, counseling strategies need to be developed to assist clients to cope with the social environment they encounter.

2. Career counselors should inform clients about the complexities of the world of work and the difficulties they may experience when they encounter the labor market. Counselors need to develop strategies to enhance realism about the work world.

3. Career counselors need to assist clients in combating gender stereotyping, which limits career options.

4. Minority groups can be assisted in career planning by improving their chances for completing educational programs, enhancing attitudes about work, providing career information, and developing skills. Finally, clients should be offered assistance in using community resources.

5. Career counselors should provide assistance for raising educational aspirations. Counselors can display evidence of the close relationship between years of schooling and status level of parents and between years of schooling and success at work (Hotchkiss & Borow, 1996).

Implications for Career Guidance

Theories of career development are conceptual systems designed to delineate apparent relationships between a concomitance of events that lead to causes and effects. Although the theories described in this chapter have a variety of labels, all emphasize the relationships between the unique traits of individuals and the characteristics of society in which development occurs. The major difference among the theories is the nature of the influential factors involved in the career decision process, but all the theories have common implications for career guidance.

1. Career development takes place in stages that are somewhat related to age but are influenced by many factors in the sociocultural milieu. Because career development is a lifelong process, career guidance programs must be designed to meet the needs of individuals over the life span.

2. The tasks associated with stages of career development involve transitions requiring individuals to cope with each stage of life. Helping individuals cope with transitions is a key concept to remember while promoting development.

3. Career maturity is acquired through successfully accomplishing developmental tasks within a continuous series of life stages. Points of reference from this continuum provide relevant information for career guidance program development.

4. Each person should be considered unique. This uniqueness is a product of many sources, including sociocultural background, genetic endowment, personal and educational experiences, family relationships, and community resources. In this context, values, interests, abilities, and behavioral tendencies are important in shaping career development.

5. Self-concept affects career decisions. Self-concept is not a static phenomenon but rather is an ongoing process that may gradually or abruptly change as people and situations change. Accurate self-concepts contribute to career maturity.

6. The stability of career choice depends primarily on the strength and dominance of one's personal orientation of personality characteristics, preferences,

abilities, and traits. Work environments that match personal orientations provide appropriate outlets for personal and work satisfaction. Finding congruence between personality traits and work environments is a key objective of career development.

7. Individual characteristics and traits can be assessed through standardized assessment instruments. Identified traits are used to predict future outcomes of probable adjustments. Matching job requirements with personal characteristics may not dominate career-counseling strategies but remains a viable part of some programs.

8. Social learning emphasizes the importance of learning experiences and their effect on occupational selection. Learning takes place through observations as well as through direct experiences. Identifying the content of individual beliefs and generalizations is a key ingredient in developing counseling strategies.

9. Introducing occupational information resources and developing skills for their proper use is a relevant goal for all educational institutions. Moreover, this need persists over the life span.

10. Career development involves a lifelong series of choices. Assistance in making appropriate choices is accomplished through the teaching of decision-making and problem-solving skills. Understanding individual processes involved in choices enables counselors to be of better assistance during the decision-making process.

11. The concept of human freedom is implied in all career development theories. This concept implies that career counselors should provide avenues of freedom for individuals to explore options within the social, political, and economic milieu. The limits of personal freedom are often external (for example, economic conditions, discrimination, and environmental conditions), but freedom may also be constrained from such internal sources as fear, lack of confidence, faulty attitudes, poor self-concept development, and behavioral deficits. Within this context, the career counselor should be concerned not only with career development but with all facets of human development. Counseling strategies must be designed to meet a wide range of needs.

12. The importance of cognitive development and its relationship to self-concept and subsequent occupational aspirations are receiving greater attention. This focus is concerned primarily with the role of cognitive development in terms of appropriate gender roles, occupational roles, and other generalizations that directly affect career development. This fine-tuning of relationships between human and career development implies that counselors must develop a greater sensitivity to both.

Summary

1. The trait-and-factor theory evolved from early studies of individual differences and developed closely with the psychometric movement. The key characteristic of the trait-and-factor theory is the assumption that individuals have unique patterns of ability or traits that can be objectively measured and subsequently matched with requirements of jobs.

2. The theory of work adjustment emphasizes that work is more than a step-by-step procedure; it includes human interaction, sources of satisfaction and dissatisfaction, rewards, stress, and many other psychological reinforcements. The basic assumption is that an individual seeks to achieve and maintain a positive relationship within his or her work environment.

3. Ginzberg, Ginsburg, Axelrad, and Herma are considered to be the first to approach a theory of occupational choice from a developmental standpoint. They suggested that occupational choice is a developmental process that generally covers a period of six to ten years, beginning at around the age of 11 and ending shortly after age 17. The three periods or stages of development are called fantasy, tentative, and realistic.

4. Super has made many contributions to the study of vocational behavior, including his formalization of developmental stages: growth, exploratory, establishment, maintenance, and decline. Super considered self-concept as the vital force that establishes a career pattern one will follow throughout life. In 1951 he designed a study to follow the vocational development of ninth-grade boys in Middletown, New York. Those individuals who were seen as vocationally mature in the ninth grade (based on their knowledge of occupations, planning, and interests) were significantly more successful as young adults. His conclusions suggest that there is a relationship between career maturity and adolescent achievement of a significant degree of self-awareness, knowledge of occupations, and developed planning ability. Super's theory on the career development process takes a primarily multisided approach.

5. Tiedeman conceptualized career development as a process of continuously differentiating one's ego identity, processing developmental tasks, and resolving psychosocial crises. These ongoing activities are perceived within a framework of time stages. According to Tiedeman, career decisions are reached through a systematic problem-solving pattern that includes seven steps: (a) exploration, (b) crystallization, (c) choice, (d) clarification, (e) induction, (f) reformation, and (g) integration.

6. In Gottfredson's model, occupational preferences emerge from the complexities that accompany physical and mental growth. A major determinant of occupational preferences is the progressive circumscription of aspirations during self-concept development. Gottfredson suggested that socioeconomic background and intellectual level greatly influence self-concept development.

7. Roe's theory focuses on early relations within the family and their subsequent effects on career direction. Roe emphasized that early childhood experiences were important factors in the satisfaction of one's chosen occupation. She classified occupations into two major categories: person-oriented and nonperson-oriented.

8. Holland considered career choice as an expression or extension of personality into the world of work, followed by subsequent identification with specific occupational stereotypes. Holland considered modal personal orientation as the key to individual occupational choice. Central to Holland's theory is the concept that individuals choose careers to satisfy their developed preferred personal modal orientations. Holland developed six modal personal styles and six match-

ing work environments: realistic, investigative, artistic, social, enterprising, and conventional.

9. Krumboltz, Mitchell, and Gelatt postulated that career selection is significantly influenced by life events. Four such factors are (a) genetic endowments and special abilities, (b) environmental conditions and events, (c) learning experiences, and (d) task approach skills. Decision making is considered to be a continuous process extending over the life span.

10. Sociologists view occupational choice as a part of a broad system of social stratification. Sociological theory suggests that institutional and impersonal market forces greatly impede satisfaction of career aspirations. Counseling strategies need to assist clients to cope with the social environment they encounter.

Supplementary Learning Exercises

1. Why is the trait-and-factor approach considered the most durable theory? Give examples of the use of the trait-and-factor theory in current career-counseling programs.
2. Defend the statement: Career development is a continuous process.
3. Write your own definition of career development and career counseling.
4. Using the following reference, write a comprehensive report on Super's Career Pattern Study conducted in Middletown, New York. Identify the dimensions of vocational maturity used, the procedures, and the conclusions.

   Brown, D., Brooks, L., and Associates (1990). *Career choice and development* (2nd ed.). San Francisco: Jossey-Bass Publishers.

5. Compare Holland's approach to career development with Roe's. Summarize the similarities and differences.
6. Using the following reference, explain the principles behind Holland's theory of vocational choice. Defend or criticize his thesis that vocational interests are not independent of personality.

   Holland, J. L. (1992). *Making vocational choices* (2nd ed.). Odessa, FL: Psychological Assessment Resources.

7. Compare Tiedeman's aspects of anticipation and preoccupation with those he outlines for implementation and adjustment. What are the major counseling considerations for both sets of aspects?
8. Apply a career development theory to your own career development. Using Super's developmental stages, identify your current stage of development and the ages at which you accomplished other stages.
9. Outline the factor that you consider most important in the career development of an adult you know or one you interview.
10. Develop your own theory of career development. Identify the components of other theories you agree with and why you agree with them.

CHAPTER THREE

Theories of Career Development—II: New Evolving Theories

This chapter is a continuation of Chapter 2, however, this chapter will introduce five evolving career development theories that have emerged in the 1990s. These theories show promise for future development, and should their constructs become more carefully defined through further research and assigned levels of importance, they will become more meaningful to the career counseling profession (Brown, Brooks, & Associates, 1996).

As you read each theory, you will find that increasingly more attention is being given to women and ethnic minorities. There is also an endeavor among some to develop practical applications to what they have theorized. There also appears to be a recognition of the necessity to carefully explain various components of each theory. As the interest in career development theories continues to expand—especially to other disciplines—we should not be surprised to find other theories in the professional literature emerging well into the 21st century.

The five evolving theories introduced in this chapter include (1) a cognitive information processing approach to career problem solving; (2) career development from a social cognitive perspective; (3) a values-based, holistic model of career and life-role choices and satisfaction; (4) a contextual explanation of career; and (5) a summary of a self-efficacy model. In addition, a section is devoted to how career theories may be converging.

Career Development from a Cognitive Information Processing Perspective

This career development theory is based on the cognitive information processing (CIP) theory and was developed by Peterson, Sampson, and Reardon (1991). CIP theory is applied to career development in terms of how individuals make a career decision and use information in career problem solving and decision making. CIP's major premise is based on the ten assumptions shown in Table 3-1. Using these assumptions as a focal point, the major strategy of career intervention is to provide learning events that are designed to develop the individual's processing abilities.

TABLE 3-1

Assumptions Underlying the Cognitive Information Processing (CIP) Perspective of Career Development

Assumption	*Explanation*
1. Career choice results from an interaction of cognitive and affective processes.	CIP emphasizes the cognitive domain in career decision making; but it also acknowledges the presence of an affective source of information in the process (Heppner & Krauskopf, 1987; Zajonc, 1980). Ultimately, commitment to a career goal involves an interaction between affective and cognitive processes.
2. Making career choices is a problem-solving activity.	Individuals can learn to solve career problems (that is, to choose careers) just as they can learn to solve math, physics, or chemistry problems. The major differences between career problems and math or science problems lie in the complexity and ambiguity of the stimulus and the greater uncertainty as to the correctness of the solution.
3. The capabilities of career problem solvers depend on the availability of cognitive operations as well as knowledge.	One's capability as a career problem solver depends on one's self-knowledge and on one's knowledge of occupations. It also depends on the cognitive operations one can draw on to derive relationships between these two domains.
4. Career problem solving is a high-memory-load task.	The realm of self-knowledge is complex; so is the world of work. The drawing of relationships between these two domains entails attending to both domains simultaneously. Such a task may easily overload the working memory store.
5. Motivation	The motivation to become a better career problem solver stems from the desire to make satisfying career choices through a better understanding of oneself and the occupational world.

(continued)

TABLE 3-1
**Assumptions Underlying the Cognitive Information
Processing (CIP) Perspective of Career Development**   *(continued)*

Assumption	*Explanation*
6. Career development involves continual growth and change in knowledge structures.	Self-knowledge and occupational knowledge consist of sets of organized memory structures called *schemata* that evolve over the person's life span. Both the occupational world and we ourselves are ever-changing. Thus, the need to develop and integrate these domains never ceases.
7. Career identity depends on self-knowledge.	In CIP terms, career identity is defined as the level of development of self-knowledge memory structures. Career identity is a function of the complexity, integration, and stability of the schemata constituting the self-knowledge domain.
8. Career maturity depends on one's ability to solve career problems.	From a CIP perspective, career maturity is defined as the ability to make independent and responsible career decisions based on the thoughtful integration of the best information available about oneself and the occupational world.
9. The ultimate goal of career counseling is achieved by facilitating the growth of information-processing skills.	From a CIP perspective, the goal of career counseling is therefore to provide the conditions of learning that facilitate the growth of memory structures and cognitive skills so as to improve the client's capacity for processing information.
10. The ultimate aim of career counseling is to enhance the client's capabilities as a career problem solver and a decision maker.	From a CIP perspective, the aim of career counseling is to enhance the client's career decision-making capabilities through the development of information processing skills.

SOURCE: Career Development and Services: A Cognitive Approach, by G. Peterson, J. Sampson, and R. Reardon, pp. 7–9. Copyright 1991 by Brooks/Cole Publishing Company, a division of International Thomson Publishing Inc.

In this way, clients develop capabilities as career problem solvers to meet immediate as well as future problems.

The stages of processing information begin with screening, translating, and encoding input in short-term memory; then storing it in long-term memory; and later activating, retrieving, and transforming the input into working memory to arrive at a solution. The principle function of the counselor in CIP theory is to identify the client's needs and develop interventions to help the client acquire the knowledge and skills to address those needs.

The authors stress that career problem solving is primarily a cognitive process that can be improved through a sequential procedure known as CASVE, which includes the following generic processing skills: communication (receiving, encoding, and sending out queries), analysis (identifying and placing problems in a conceptual framework), synthesis (formulating courses of action), valuing (judging each action as to its likelihood of success and failure and its impact on others), and execution (implementing strategies to carry out plans). Table 3-2 describes the CASVE cycle in terms of its phases by using career information and media.

This model emphasizes the notion that career information counseling is a learning event. This is consistent with other theories that make this same assumption and present procedures for developing decision-making skills. However, one major difference between CIP theory and other theories discussed in this chapter is the role of cognition as a mediating force that leads individuals to greater power and control in determining their own destiny. As we learn more about CIP theory, the CASVE approach will be further delineated for the counseling profession.

Empirical Support for the CIP Perspective

For a discussion of metacognitions or executive processing domain, see Helwig (1992). For information about the *Career Thoughts Inventory,* see Peterson, Sampson, and Reardon (1991) and Sampson, Peterson, Lenz, Reardon, and Saunders (1996a). Major strengths of theory are covered in Krumboltz (1992).

TABLE 3-2
Career Information and the CASVE Cycle

Phase of the CASVE cycle	*Example of career information and media*
Communication (identifying a need)	A description of the personal and family issues that women typically face in returning to work (information) in a videotaped interview of currently employed women (medium)
Analysis (interrelating problem components)	Explanations of the basic education requirements for degree programs (information) in community college catalogues (medium)
Synthesis (creating likely alternatives)	A presentation of emerging nontraditional career options for women (information) at a seminar on career development for women (medium)
Valuing (prioritizing alternatives)	An exploration of how the roles of parent, spouse, citizen, "leisurite," and homemaker would be affected by the assumption of the worker role (information) in an adult version of a computer-assisted career guidance system (medium)
Execution (forming means-ends strategies)	A description of a functional résumé emphasizing transferable skills, followed by the creation of a résumé (information) presented on a computer-assisted employability skills system (medium)

SOURCE: From *Career Development and Services: A Cognitive Approach,* by G. Peterson, J. Sampson, and R. Reardon, p. 200. Copyright 1991 by Brooks/Cole Publishing Company, a division of International Thomson Publishing Inc.

Summary of Practical Applications

Peterson, Sampson, Reardon, and Lenz (1996), the developers of this theory, have also proposed a seven-step sequence for career delivery service, as shown in Figure 3-1. This sequence can be used as a delivery option for both problem solving and decision making, and it can be used for individual, group, self-directed, and curricular programs. Group counseling requires that the counselor do prescreening in Steps 1 and 2. The following list presents the seven-step sequence in a paraphrased format (pp. 450–457).

Step 1: Initial interview. The major purpose of the interview is twofold. The counselor seeks information about the client's career problems and establishes a trusting relationship. More specifically, the counselor attends to both the emotional and cognitive components of the client's problems. The counselor recognizes that an effective relationship enhances client self-efficacy and fosters learning.

Step 2: Preliminary assessment. To determine the client's readiness for problem solving and decision making, the *Career Thoughts Inventory* (CTI) (Sampson et al., 1996a) is administered. This inventory is used as a screening and as a needs assessment; as such, it will identify client's who could experience difficulty in the career choice process as a result of dysfunctional thinking.

Step 3: Define problem and analyze causes. In this step, the counselor and the client agree on a preliminary understanding of the client's problem(s). For example, the problem may be defined as a "gap" between the state of the client's indecision and the ideal state of "career decidedness." A word of caution: the

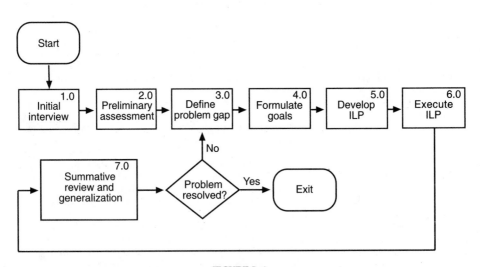

FIGURE 3-1

A career counseling sequence for individuals

SOURCE: From *Career Development and Services: A Cognitive Approach,* by G. Peterson, J. Sampson, and R. Reardon, p. 231. Copyright 1991 Brooks/Cole Publishing Company, a division of International Thomson Publishing Inc.

client's problems should be explained and stated in neutral, rather than judgmental terms.

Step 4: Formulate goals. The formulation of goals is a collaborative effort between counselor and client. Goals are put in writing on an Individual Learning Plan (ILP), shown in Figure 3-2.

Step 5: Develop individual learning plan. Again, the counselor and the client collaborate when developing the ILP, which provides a sequence of resources and activities that will assist the client in meeting needs or goals established earlier. These are very evident on the written ILP. The ILP also serves as a contract between client and counselor.

Step 6: Execute individual learning plan. This step requires that the client take the initiative in proceeding with the agreed-upon plan. The counselor encourages and directs the progress and may provide more information, clarification, or reinforcement of the client's progress and may offer planning for future experiences. With dysfunctional clients, a workbook is used as a supplement to learning about the results of the *Career Thoughts Inventory* administered in Step 2. This workbook, entitled *Improving Your Career Thoughts: A Workbook for the Career Thoughts Inventory* (Sampson, Petersen, Lenz, Reardon, & Saunders, 1996b) is used for cognitive restructuring, within which the client uses a four-step procedure (identify, challenge, alter, and take action).

Selected strategies for enhancing career problem solving and decision making are summarized as follows: for discovering self-trace, the development of your interests, write an autobiography and prepare a vocational history; for life experiences, write a description in the third person and analyze emergent themes. Take an interest inventory and relate the results to real-life events.

Step 7: Summative review and generalization. Progress in solving the gap that may have motivated the client to seek counseling is reviewed in this last step. A determination is also made about how effective the progress has been in terms of following through with the ILP. The focus through all steps is on the client's career decision-making status. Finally, the lessons learned within the preceding six steps are generalized as skills learned to solve future career and personal problems.

Career Development from a Social Cognitive Perspective

The study of cognitive variables and processes has become a popular topic for researchers who apply what is often referred to as the "cognitive revolution" to the study of career development. This theory has indeed followed such a script by offering a social cognitive career theory (SCCT) to complement existing theories and to build connecting bridges to other theories of career development.

According to Lent, Brown, and Hackett (1996), the authors of this theory, there are three ways to translate and share knowledge with existing theories and emerging ones. The first is to agree on a common meaning for conceptually related concepts, such as self-concept and self-efficacy. Betz (1992b, p. 24) defines career

Individual Learning Plan

Career Resource Center
Central Community College—110 Social Science Building

Goal(s) 1. Understand personal barriers to decision making.

2. Clarify self-knowledge and occupational knowledge.

3. Improve decision-making skills.

4. _____

Goal	Priority	Activity	Purpose/Outcome
1, 2 & 3	1	Individual Counseling	Clarify issues and obtain information
1	2	Modules EP∅ and EP2 and cognitive exercise	Explore Self-Talk
1	3	monitor thoughts related to a real decision	monitor Self-Talk
3	4	Module IP∅	Clarify decision-making knowledge
2	5	OCC-U-SORT & Module SK∅	Self knowledge and generate options
2	6	SDS: CV	" "
2	7	Written Summary of Self-Knowledge	" "
2	8	Career Key & module OK∅	Identify resources & obtain occ. info.
2	9	CHOICES	Narrow options
2	10	video tapes, information interviews and shadowing	" "
2	11	Print Materials	" "

Joe Williams   Marilyn Abbey   3/12/90
Client   Career Counselor   Date

FIGURE 3-2

Individual learning plan

SOURCE: From *Career Development and Services: A Cognitive Approach,* by G. Peterson, J. Sampson, and R. Reardon, p. 231. Copyright 1991 by Brooks/Cole Publishing Company, a division of International Thomson Publishing Inc.

self-efficacy as "the possibility that low expectations of efficacy with respect to some aspect of career behavior may serve as a detriment to optimal career choice and the development of the individual." Further delineation of this theory involves Betz's reference to career-choice content (content domains such as math, science, or writing) and career-choice process (behavioral domains that enhance the implementation of a career). From this frame of reference, an individual may avoid areas of course work surrounding a career because of low self-efficacy. Likewise, self-efficacy deficits may lead to procrastination in or avoidance of a career decision.

Hackett and Betz (1981) suggest that social beliefs and expectations are the mechanisms through which self-efficacy deficits are developed, particularly for women. They cite a restricted range of options and underutilization of abilities as important factors hindering women's career development. Using this logic, women's vocational behavior can be at least partially explained.

The second way to translate and share knowledge about existing theories and emerging ones is to fully describe and define common outcomes such as satisfaction and stability, found in a number of theories. Finally, a third way is to fully explain the relationships among such diverse constructs as interests, self-efficacy, abilities, and needs. Clearly, the plea is to find a common ground for communicating a conceptual order to the vast number of variables found in career-related literature.

The underlying assumptions and constructs of this theory are embedded in general social cognitive theory (Bandura, 1986), which blends cognitive, self-regulatory, and motivational processes into a lifelong phenomenon. More specifically, SCCT's major goals are to find methods of defining specific mediators from which learning experiences shape and subsequently influence career behavior. Furthermore, the aim is to explain how variables such as interests, abilities, and values interrelate and, most important, how all variables influence individual growth and the contextual factors (environmental influences) that lead to career outcomes. Also emphasized in this theory is the term *personal agency,* which reflects how and why individuals exert power to either achieve a solution, such as a career outcome, or adapt to career changes. To identify and conceptualize the causal influences interacting between individuals and their environment, SCCT subscribes to Bandura's (1986) model of causality known as the *triadic reciprocal.* Within this bidirectional model, there are three variables: (1) personal and physical attributes, (2) external environmental factors, and (3) overt behavior. All three interact to the point of affecting one another as causal influences of an individual's development. Using this logic, SCCT conceptualizes the interacting influences among individuals, their behavior, and their environments to describe how individuals influence situations that ultimately affect their own thoughts and behavior.

What we have here is a complex, interacting system that is bidirectional and within which behavior, as one factor, and situations in the environment, as another, act as co-determinants in shaping personal thoughts and behaviors and external environmental factors. In essence, it is a person-behavior-situation interaction.

Key Theoretical Constructs

The personal determinants of career development have been conceptualized as self-efficacy, outcome expectations, and personal goals. The "big three" are considered to be building blocks within the triadic causal system that determine the course of career development and its outcome. Self-efficacy is not viewed as a unitary or fixed trait but rather as a set of beliefs about a specific performance domain. Self-efficacy is developed through four types of learning experiences (Lent, Brown, & Hackett, 1996): "(1) personal performance accomplishments, (2) vicarious learning, (3) social persuasion, and (4) physiological states and reactions" (p. 380). Self-efficacy is strengthened when success is experienced within a performance domain, whereas it is weakened when there are repeated failures.

Outcome expectations are also regarded as personal beliefs about expectations or consequences of behavioral activities. Some individuals may be motivated by extrinsic reinforcement, such as receiving an award; others by self-directed activities, such as pride in oneself; and yet others by the actual process of performing an activity. Outcome expectations are shaped by learning activities similar to those of self-efficacy.

One of most important reasons for personal goals in this theory is that they are considered to be guides that sustain behavior. While processing personal goals, individuals generate *personal agency* that interacts with the three building blocks, which in effect shapes self-directed behavior.

Interest Developmental Model

Individuals develop interests through activities in which they view themselves as competent and generally expect valued outcomes. Interests fail to develop when self-efficacy is perceived as weak and negative outcomes are expected from an activity. Activities that produce valued outcomes and that have been developed as personal interests are sustained by individuals through the development of goals that ensure their involvement in those activities. Following this logic, activity practice tends to solidify interests and reshape and reinforce self-efficacy.

Attitudes and Values

Within the framework of SCCT, values are subsumed in the concept of outcome expectation. In effect, values are preferences for particular reinforcers such as money, status, or autonomy. This theory stresses that outcome expectations are influenced by value systems that are positively reinforced when involved with a particular activity.

Gender and Race/Ethnicity

It is most important in this theory to focus on how career development was influenced from personal reactions to the social and cultural environment. Thus, the individual's socially constructed world, not the inherited biological traits, are the focus of gender and race in the SCCT.

It is therefore not surprising that this theory calls attention to the social, cultural, and economic conditions that shaped learning opportunities to which individuals were exposed, interpersonal reactions experienced for performing certain activities, and the future outcomes that have been generated. In sum, the effects of gender and ethnicity on career interests, choice, and performance are associated primarily with differential learning experiences that influenced and subsequently shaped self-efficacy and outcome expectations.

Choice Model

The choice process is divided into three components: (1) establishing a goal; (2) taking action (by enrolling in a training or school program) to implement a choice; and (3) attaining a level of performance (successes or failures) that determines the direction of future career behavior. One's personal agency is seen as a most important variable in determining the degree of progression in the choice process.

The pathways to career choice in SCCT are as follows: (1) self-efficacy and outcome expectations promote career-related interests; (2) interests in turn influence goals; (3) goal-related actions lead to performance experiences; (4) the outcome serves to determine future paths (determined by whether self-efficacy is strengthened or weakened); and (5) finally, one establishes a career decision or redirects goals.

One of the major hurdles in the choice model has to do with contextual or environmental influences. The rationale is based on opportunity structure experienced in the environment. For instance, individuals who experience support and other beneficial environmental conditions readily take their goals into actions more so than do those who experience the opposite from their environment.

Performance Model

The SCCT contains a performance model that appears to be a summary description of this theory. Its purpose is twofold: (1) it illustrates concern for the level and quality of an individual's accomplishments and for the personal agency involvement in career-related pursuits; and (2) it points out the interplay of ability, self-efficacy, outcome expectations, and the establishment of goals for judging performance. This model can also serve as a method of determining points of reference for implementing effective intervention strategies.

Empirical Support

Selected references on career self-efficacy include Hackett (1995), Hackett and Lent (1992), Betz and Hackett (1986), Zimmerman (1995), and Schunk (1995). For relevant findings to SCCT's major hypotheses, see Coon-Carty (1995), Multon, Brown, and Lent (1991), and Sadri and Robertson (1993).

Summary of Practical Applications

1. Suggestions for expanding interests and facilitating choice include the recommendation that educational programs in schools should not only concentrate on developing interests, values, and talents but should also focus on the cognitive basis for linking with these variables.

2. It is suggested that individuals who are experiencing great difficulty with career choice or change should be presented with an array of occupations that correspond with their abilities and values, but not necessarily with their interests. The authors of this theory argue that individuals will not consider some occupations because of false impressions of their abilities and, subsequently, will respond indifferently to such occupations on interest inventories. For example, the individual who does not indicate an interest in nursing may have been told that "you will have to take a lot of science courses." And because he views his ability to pass science courses as poor, he reacts negatively to nursing when in fact his past performance and ability scores indicate he has a better than average chance of being successful in a nursing program.

3. A strategy used to combat perceived weaknesses includes the use of occupational card sorts. The individual is asked to sort occupational titles into categories of "might choose," "in question," and "would not choose." The client is then asked to further sort cards from "in question" and "would not choose" into subcategories by self-efficacy beliefs ("if I had the skills I might choose"), outcome expectations ("might choose if they matched my values") and definite lack of interest ("not considered a possible choice"), and other. Clearly, the purpose of this procedure is to assist the client in fully understanding the interacting forces that determine self-appraisals in the career decision process. Individuals who have developed false notions about their abilities and values may indeed become indifferent toward certain occupations.

4. Overcoming barriers to choice and success is a significant goal for career counseling in SCCT. The rationale here is that individuals who perceive insurmountable barriers to career entry will be unwilling to pursue occupational interests in the career choice process. A decisional balance sheet is used to assist clients in evaluating perceived barriers. Each client is asked to generate a list of both positive and negative consequences for each career alternative he or she has selected. Each individual is then asked to develop strategies designed to overcome barriers that interfere with choice implementation.

5. School-to-work initiatives suggested by SCCT include designing skill programs that provide for self-efficacy enhancement, realistic outcome expectations, and goal-setting skills (Lent, Brown, & Hackett, 1996).

Brown's Values-Based, Holistic Model of Career and Life-Role Choices and Satisfaction

Brown's (1996) values-based approach to career development assumes that human functioning is greatly influenced and shaped by a person's value orientation. Certain established standards of behavior are considered important in the developmental process, are also value-based, and become the rules by which individuals judge their own actions and the actions of others. Unlike many other theories, interests play a more minor role in career decision making in this theory. For example, interests are indications of developed likes and dislikes that grow out of values, but they are not as dominant in shaping behavior as values are simply because interests do not serve as benchmarks for standards of behavior. Thus, values are most important in career decision-making processes, as they provide the direction to a desired end state and as such have a central role in setting goals.

Values are also seen as strong determinants in rationalizing behavior roles. For example, a strong value for social service would point an individual toward seeking an occupation that helps others, whereas a dominant value toward independence would direct an individual toward searching for work environments that allow freedom of action with few controls. Using these assumptions, Brown has developed a values-based model for life-role decision making.

How Values Are Developed

Brown suggests that values are generally developed through the interaction of inheritance characteristics and experience. He relies on a study by Keller, Bouchard, Arvey, Segal, and Dawis (1992) that supports his position. In their conclusions, genetics accounted for 40% of variance associated with the development of work values, while the remaining 60% was environmentally influenced or was error variance. Brown further supports his assumption by observing that children are exposed to thousands of "values-laden messages" from parents, siblings, other children, many adults, and the media. He suggests that, as children assimilate values-laden messages, values are developed in "bits and pieces" and later form the core of what shapes individual cognitive, affective, and behavioral patterns.

However, some values-laden information may contain contradictory messages, and some developed values may conflict with others. In this way, some values are weakened and may cause ambivalent cognitions and subsequent contradictory behavior patterns. Finally, Brown concludes that values are prioritized and crystallized at any given time in their development, but the processing of values may be greatly affected by an individual's cognitive clarity.

Brown makes it clear that he believes that values have the dominant role in human development. He suggests that values influence all aspects of human functioning but particularly the processing of data one experiences in daily life;

although Brown concludes that some values have little effect on cognition because they are not crystallized. He explains that a value becomes crystallized when individuals are able to use that value to explain their behavior: "I am planning to be a social worker because I want to help people."

Values are prioritized by their importance as guides to behavior in one's environment. For instance, when congruence is found in the environment, such as between certain desirable actions and behaviors, values associated with these behaviors are crystallized and subsequently prioritized. However, environmental barriers can block individuals from acting on their value orientation because of their perception of the circumstances that discourage actions. For example, a worker desires to put forth more time, energy, and concentration to finish an assignment, but his fellow workers—the power group in this particular work environment—frown on such behavior.

The value systems of environments is an interesting concept of Brown's theory. He sees Holland's theory as a system that identifies the personality of people in an environment, but he reflects that this is useful only when there are well-defined boundaries. In complex environments, such as large industrial organizations, the dominant values are established by the "power elite," and their values become the greatest single determinant in shaping the actions and reactions between individuals and the environment. Thus, complex environments require careful scrutiny when studying individual behavioral patterns within them.

The Values-Based Model of Career Choice

The six basic propositions for this values-based model are presented here in abridged form.

1. There are only a small number of values that individuals prioritize.
2. Highly prioritized values are the most important determinants of life-role choices if they meet the following criteria:
   a. One option must be available to satisfy the life-role value.
   b. Options to implement life-role values are clearly delineated.
   c. The difficulty level of implementing each option is the same.
3. Values are acquired through learning from values-laden information in the environment. This information is cognitively processed while interacting with the individual's inherited characteristics. Other factors that influence social interactions and opportunities are cultural background, gender, and socioeconomic level. According to Brown, these factors subsequently influence choice of careers and other life roles.
4. Life satisfaction is dependent on life roles that satisfy all essential values.
5. A role's salience is directly related to the degree of satisfaction of essential values within roles.
6. Success in a life role is dependent on many factors, some of which are learned skills and some of which are cognitive, affective, and physical aptitudes.

Empirical Support

For general information on values, see Rokeach (1973), Crace and Brown (1996), Locke and Latham (1990), and Judge and Bretz (1992). For more on how values are developed, see Stimpson, Jensen, and Neff (1992), Leong (1991), and de Vaus and McCallister (1991).

More on life-role satisfaction and position can be found in Super (1990), Watson and Ager (1991), and O'Driscoll, Ilgen, and Hildreth (1992). For salience of role and satisfaction, see Brown and Crace (1995), Chusmir and Parker (1991), Flannelly (1995), and Posner (1992).

Summary of Practical Applications

Brown suggests that all career counselors answer the following questions about their clients: Are there mood problems that will interfere with decision making? Are the relationships between career and life roles clear to the client? Is there evidence that values have been crystallized and prioritized?

1. In an interview, mood problems are to be carefully scrutinized. Mood problems are anxiety, depression, and other mental health problems (discussed in the final two chapters of this book).
2. Values are to be assessed by qualitative and quantitative methods. Qualitative methods include card sorts and guided fantasies (Brown, Brooks, & Associates, 1990). Quantitative measures include value inventories and value scales (reviewed in Chapter 7).
3. The discussion of inventory results can also be considered as intervention. Individuals are to be confronted with the question of why—for instance, "Why do you believe this?" and so on. The "why technique" is designed to frustrate the client in order to raise the level of introspection that will lead to conclusions about values.
4. The counselor is to link values with careers with the use of the *Enhanced Guide for Occupational Exploration* (JIST, 1993) and through computerized career exploration programs.

A Contextual Explanation of Career

Contextualism is a proposed method to establish a contextual action explanation of career research and career counseling. Contextualism is based on the philosophical position known as *constructivism* (Brown, Brooks, & Associates, 1996). According to Sharf (1996), the constructivist position suggests "that individuals construct their own way of organizing information and that truth or reality is a matter of perception" (p. 405). Understanding how clients construct personal meanings from present actions and subsequent experiences touches the central core of this theory.

The contextual model for human development is an ever-changing, ongoing interplay of forces. The major focus is on the relationship between person and environment, because they are considered to be inseparable and are looked on as a unit. As people and the environment interact, development can proceed along many different pathways, depending upon how one influences the other (Sigelman & Shaffer, 1995).

Young, Valach, and Collin (1996) propose that one way to understand a contextualist explanation of career counseling is by action theory. Action, in this sense, focuses on the whole in the context in which action is taken. For example, a career counselor, client, and a worker in the field the client is currently interested in have a discussion about the work, peer affiliates, and work environment. The total action of all three people is the context in which this particular counseling took place, and their actions form the basis for constructing personal meaning. To break the process into parts would be similar to unraveling an event into meaningless fragmentation. Thus, it is the wholeness of an event and the succession of changes that result from interaction with others and their contexts that is the contextualist perspective. In essence, contextualists support the idea that events take shape as people engage in them, and only then is an analysis of actions and events practical.

The study of actions is the major focus of the contextual viewpoint. Actions are conceptualized as being cognitively and socially directed and as reflecting everyday experiences; they are social processes and, as such, reflect each individual's social and cultural world. Actions are viewed from three perspectives: they manifest behavior, for example, taking notes of a lecture; they are internal processes, like feeling nervous about an examination; and they have social meaning, such as being successful in a career.

Action systems are composed of joint and individual actions and two terms referred to as *project* and *career. Joint actions* simply means that many career-related actions occur among people. According to the contextualist point of view, career values, interests, identity, and behaviors are constructed largely through language in conversation with others. Instead of evaluating the discussions individually between client and counselor, the contextualist conceptualizes joint action as a unit between client and counselor. The major focus here is on the action of the dyad.

Project refers to an agreement of actions between two or more people. For example, a single parent and adolescent child form an agreement of household responsibilities so that both may work. Because of changing work conditions and working hours, parent and child renegotiate responsibilities. In this example, individual and joint actions—including manifest actions—internal processes, and social meaning contribute to the project. The parent's and the child's behavior can be interpreted individually and jointly by this project.

The term *career,* as used in this theory, is similar to the term *project*. It can also be used to construct connections among actions and to evaluate plans, goals, emotions, and internal cognitions. The major difference between project and career is that career extends over a longer period of time and subsequently involves more actions. The actions can become complex and include greater social meaning. In this way, career approximates the idea of vocation.

The authors of this theory have developed an aspects-of-action theory to illustrate action systems, perspectives on action, and levels of action organization. Levels of action organization include elements, functional steps, and goals.

Elements refer to physical and verbal behavior, such as words, movements, and environmental structures. *Functional steps* refer to higher-level actions than elements—for example, pleading and reminding can be used to convey a desired action. *Goals,* the highest level of action, usually represent the general intention of the individual or group.

The major purpose of defining actions in this manner is to organize the interpretation of human actions. Interpretation within this script offers a systematic method of evaluating and interpreting actions and the context in which they happen—what the counselor and client are doing together.

Empirical Support

For more on action theory, see Polkinghorne (1990) and von Cranach and Harre (1982). For discussions on context and environment, see Holland (1992) and Krumboltz and Nichols (1990). For more on this theory in general, see Valach (1990), Young and Valach (1996), Shotter (1993), Richardson (1993), and Hermans (1992).

Summary of Practical Applications

1. Counselors must be aware of clients' conceptualizations, concepts, and constructs during the interview process and other discussions.
2. Counselors should help clients become aware of their constructs by offering support. Although it is not clear, support could come by discussing identified constructs.
3. Clients should also be assisted in constructing a narrative, which may have the theme of frequently mentioned topics. Client and counselor are to discuss the narrative with the goal of discovering the context of their lives (Young, Valach, & Collin, 1996).
4. Through joint action activities, client and counselor develop joint goals that emerge from the joint activities.

Self-Efficacy Theory

Most of the early career development theories were devoted to explaining the career development of men. Only recently has there been an attempt to explain gender differences. Some research has noted that women underutilize abilities and talents, whereas other research has pointed out differences in the developmental processes of women and men (Betz & Fitzgerald, 1987). But currently we do not have a definitive career development theory for women.

One of the most promising theories that may lend itself to addressing gender differences is Hackett and Betz's (1981) self-efficacy theory that is based primarily on Bandura's (1977, 1986) social learning theory. The brief explanation that follows identifies only some major constructs of these theories. More information on self-efficacy theory can be found in Hackett and Betz (1981) and in this chapter's previous section on career development from a social cognitive perspective.

Bandura's social learning theory emphasizes that self-efficacy involves an individual's thoughts and images that influence psychological functioning. For example, an individual's belief in his or her ability to perform certain tasks determines whether the individual will attempt those tasks and how well he or she will perform. Self-efficacy also determines the intensity of an individual's effort, as explained by Bandura (1989):

> Those who have a high sense of efficacy visualize success scenarios that provide positive guides for performance and they cognitively rehearse good solutions to potential problems. Those who judge themselves as inefficacious are more inclined to visualize failure scenarios and to dwell on how things will go wrong. Such inefficacious thinking weakens motivation and undermines performance (p. 729).

Hackett and Betz (1981) suggest that women who believe they are incapable of performing certain tasks (low self-efficacy) limit their career mobility and restrict their career options. Also, women are hindered in developing self-efficacy when they find themselves in work environments that are less responsive to women than to men and that do not equally reward their accomplishments. Furthermore, self-efficacy is affected by a history of restricted options and underutilization of abilities. Thus, women who judge their efficacy to be low tend to give up, procrastinate, and avoid career decisions. This theory, as with many of the others mentioned in this chapter, will undoubtedly be further developed as guidelines for career development counseling and intervention strategies to meet the needs of clientele.

Convergence of Career Development Theories

There has been an increasingly growing movement, particularly among vocational psychologists, to unify existing theories of career development. This movement has many roots, but the main driving force appears to be a recognition of an increasing interest in career development theories per se and the desire to bring vocational psychology out of isolation from other psychological disciplines—namely, developmental, social, cross-cultural, personality, and issues involving gender studies. Moreover, practitioners have long complained that career development theories have added little to their knowledge of how to produce beneficial results in clients, with the exception of Sharf (1996) and Jepsen (1986), who have demonstrated how theories have addressed counseling practice (Savickas, 1995).

Savickas (1995) has also pointed out two other schisms that have heated the debate of convergence among researchers and practitioners. First, many psychologists continue to view career counseling as a subdiscipline of psychotherapy (Blustein, 1990). Some psychotherapists have argued that career counselors should adopt models or methods from psychotherapy. Second, prominent researchers in career development theory have not operationally defined constructs in the same way; instead, they have taken a developmental, differential, or decisional perspective pathway to explore vocational behavior. Furthermore, current approaches to career development theory use different operational definitions, which have contributed to the problems of research integration.

There seems to be some current justification for encouragement among career development theorists and researchers from other disciplines that theory convergence is moving ahead (Staats, 1981). Although the past emphasis on the uniqueness of theoretical approaches has created diversity through disparate views, Krumboltz and Nichols (1990) have proposed methods of bridging theories and reducing redundancy. For instance, they propose a cross-theoretical framework in which theories' major aspects can be examined and the contributing theorists can be free to maintain their particular interests. Thus, both convergence and individual initiative can be maintained.

In 1992, a career intervention special-interest group of the Counseling Psychology Division in the American Psychological Association met to discuss issues and merits of unifying the theories of career choice and development. According to Savickas (1995), although most researchers saw more disadvantages than advantages in a unification project, most did agree on theory "renovation" to clarify the constructs and purpose of theories. The major disadvantages of theory unification presented at the above-mentioned meeting were as follows (Savickas, 1995, pp. 9–10).

1. Unification may discourage creativity of counselors in forming their own theories.
2. Unification efforts may be premature because unification requires a larger empirical base than is now available.
3. Convergence and unification should be empirical questions, not literary projects.
4. Quick integration may lead to ambiguous constructs drawn from different theories.
5. Constructive, piecemeal theory building is better.
6. A unification project may force a political agenda on theorists.
7. Committees cannot construct theories.
8. The most that a unification project could achieve would be convergence in terminology, not in philosophy or theory.
9. Postmodern approaches to science are moving toward pluralism, not unity.
10. In emphasizing convergence, researchers may ignore interesting aspects of each theory.

Of significant concern to career counselors was the proposal that the *concept of career may not have a future* (Collin, 1994). The argument supporting the death of "career" as a concept centers around (1) the current restructuring of the work force and changing operational procedures in large organizations, and (2) the fact that large bureaucratic organizations that lend support to current concepts of career, such as career ladders, are disappearing (Reich, 1991; Meister, 1994; Hammer & Champy, 1993).

According to Collin (1994), organizations are changing to become more flexible, elastic, and adaptive. To survive, organizations must change slow-paced operating procedures to meet the needs of the 21st-century information age; they must be able to react more quickly than the bureaucratic organization does and must adapt to changing environments. There is a need for what is referred to as "elastic" employment contracts to respond to changing demands. For example, workers would be summoned when needed, but in the meantime they would be a reserve army of labor. The new metaphor for career will be the worker's portfolio of developed skills, rather than the individual's position on the career ladder and the passage through stages within bureaucratic organizations.

The debate on the procedures career development researchers are to follow will continue. To more fully understand the components of the debate, read the references cited in this discussion. In the meantime, researchers have followed the recommendations of Walsh, Craik, and Price (1992), Walsh and Chatrand (1994), and Rychlak (1993), using the framework provided by theories of action discussed previously in this chapter.

Savickas (1995) suggests that the framework that theories of action provide should offer interpretative potential for vocational psychology and research. In sum, the theory of action addresses personal traits that may influence the career choice process. Second, research would focus on the external environment; social learning and social cognitive models of vocation behavior would be delineated. The third dimension includes person-environment transaction theories, in particular, the fit between individual and environment. Finally, research efforts would include developmental contextualism that emphasizes the person and the context as coexisting and as continually defining each other.

Implications for Career Guidance

A clearer understanding of the decision-making process is a major goal of cognitive theory. An understanding of self-knowledge, occupational knowledge, information processing skills, and metacognitions no doubt will provide the career counselor with valuable information to use in educational programs as well as for intervention strategies.

Career counselors must also consider sociological variables as being important information in the counseling process. Social class, for example, has been used as an important variable that influences career choice. Environmental influences and personal agency are key concepts that act as interacting influences that shape behavior.

Values should be given a greater role in the career development process. How values are developed should be a growing concern of the career guidance profession. Values as a dominating role in influencing human development will provide clues as to why and how decisions are made.

A clearer understanding of the relationship between person and environment should subsequently lead to clearer understanding of perceptions an individual has learned from his or her environment. One way to understand this process is to observe the actions of people in context. The pathways one follows to construct personal meaning from interacting with people in an environment will provide guidelines for counseling intervention.

The proposition of self-efficacy is a means of judging the nature of career development for women. Those career behaviors that limit career choice for women are significant factors for developing educational and counseling programs for both sexes.

Finally, an agreement among theorists and researchers of terms and constructs used in the development of theories should provide more guidelines for building practical applications of both established and evolving theories. Furthermore, other academic disciplines will have greater accessibility to contributing to the career counseling profession. As the pervasive nature of career counseling is recognized, it should rightfully be given equal status with other counseling endeavors.

Summary

1. Cognitive information theory has been applied to career development in terms of how one makes a career decision. A sequential procedure has been developed to help individuals process information in order to make career decisions in their own best interests.

2. Career development from a social cognitive perspective is embedded in general social cognitive theory, which blends cognitive, self-regulatory, and motivational processes into lifelong phenomena. This theory seeks (a) to find definitions of specific mediators from which learning experiences shape career behavior; (b) to explain how interests, abilities, and values interrelate; and (c) to determine the contextual factors that lead to outcomes. Social beliefs and expectations are the mechanism through which self-efficacy deficits are developed, particularly for women.

3. A values-based approach to career development assumes that one's functioning is greatly influenced and shaped by one's value orientation. Several other assumptions of this theory are that (a) values are most important in career decision-making processes, as they provide the direction to setting goals; (b) values are strong determinants in rationalizing behavior roles; and (c) values are developed through the interaction of inherited characteristics and experiences.

4. The contextual model for human development is an ever-changing and ongoing interplay of forces. The major focus is on the relationship between person and environment, both of which are looked on as a unit. The study of actions is the major focus of the contextual viewpoint. Actions are viewed from three perspectives: they manifest behavior, they are internal processes, and they have social meaning.

5. There is a growing movement to unify existing theories of career development. One of the driving forces behind this movement is to bring vocational psychology out of isolation from other psychological disciplines. Most researchers of career development theories have resisted theory unification but have agreed to renovate theories to clarify their constructs and purpose.

Supplementary Learning Exercises

1. Compare one evolving theory with an established one. What are your conclusions?
2. List differences and agreements between a social cognitive perspective of career development and Krumboltz's learning theory of career choice and counseling (Chapter 2).
3. Are values more important than interests in career choice? State reasons for your position.
4. Follow the example for the Individual Learning Plan found in the cognitive information processing conceptual perspective and develop one for yourself. Explain the counseling interventions.
5. Develop a script for three individuals who are exchanging career information. Use a contextual explanation of career as a model to describe how actions influence the three individuals in the script.
6. Compare two theories with the goal of determining likes and differences. What are your conclusions?
7. Should career development theories converge? Debate as teams or individually.
8. If you agree that self-efficacy influences career decisions, which sex does it affect most? Give your reasons.
9. Draw up a list of values that have greatly influenced your life. Use the results of an interest inventory to determine your interests. Can you explain how the values you listed influenced your measured interests?
10. Debate the pros and cons of the following statement: Career development theories lead to nowhere.

CHAPTER FOUR

Career Life Planning

Throughout this book, constant references will be made to individual needs associated with work, leisure, and home. Individual lifestyle will be the focal point of our discussion whenever career counseling programs are considered. We will segregate individual needs only when considering how each facet of individuality contributes to the concept of the *total person;* we have the total person in mind as we counsel, offer guidance, and provide direction toward career life planning. What will be communicated is that career counseling is a vital part of life planning. We will not consider an individual's work in isolation; rather, work is conceptualized as a major commitment in life planning that must be integrated into an individual's style of life. Because career life planning can affect individual lifestyle tremendously, it should be considered an ongoing process that must allow for change of individual needs or situational circumstances. We cannot imply that career utopia is possible for everyone, but we can stress that those career counseling programs that emphasize career life-planning concepts and cope with change provide the best avenues to fulfillment in life.

In this chapter, we will consider several counseling programs designed to promote career life planning as a lifelong process. Each program considers career life planning as a developmental process that must encompass needs generated from work, family, home, and leisure. Each program focuses on strategies that assist individuals in meeting these needs and adjusting to changes that are both internally and externally caused. The first program is a life-planning workshop using step-by-step procedures. A discussion of other prominent career life-planning programs includes a description of a popular job-hunter's manual used for planning and a program developed by the *National Consortium of State Career Guidance Supervisors* that links with comprehensive school guidance programs. The next program is designed to present career life planning as a promotion of personal competence, introducing skills that are helpful in meeting future events. This is followed by a program that introduces methods of identifying dimensions of lifestyle associated with work, family, home, and leisure. More specifically, this program focuses on such factors as place of residence, marital status, levels of education and income, leisure-time activities, family status, leadership needs, social opportunities, and major goals in life. Lifestyle dimensions are compared with potential career choices in an attempt to determine lifestyle congruence with certain careers. Clarification of lifestyle dimensions can be accomplished through group or individual counseling. First, we will review some dimensions of career life planning.

Dimensions of Career Life Planning

In the process of career life planning, the individual uses a variety of skills. One of the primary purposes of career life planning is to develop skills through which individuals learn to control their futures. For example, we learn to identify our skills and plan how we can continue to upgrade them through life-learning programs. We learn how to develop options and alternatives and effectively decide which to follow. We learn to identify our personal needs and the needs of our closest associates and how to integrate those needs into our life plans. We learn to make plans that we can change and revise as we ourselves change or as circumstances necessitate change. Thus, our planning must be flexible and include realistic options from which effective decisions can be made to promote a fuller and more satisfying life.

Humanity has long searched for fulfillment and satisfaction. Recent generations are no exception. In fact, their search has been perhaps as intense as any ever experienced in American society. Many traditional beliefs have recently been challenged; even our working role and the organizations in which we work have been questioned (McDaniels, 1990). The prevailing question of the current generation is, "How do I find fulfillment in life?" We have stressed that fulfillment or satisfaction with what we do and how we live changes as we ourselves change. Thus, the fulfillment we seek is an ongoing challenge all of us must face as we work and live. As we pass through various stages of life and as situational changes occur, we set goals, choose from options and alternatives, and make decisions. For many, the process of change is difficult and threatening, particularly for those who haphazardly chart their course only to find frustration and dissatisfaction. Through career life planning, we learn to center our attention on carefully laid plans and on those variables over which we have some control.

There are many variables to be considered in career life-planning programs. One is how we judge success. This is a crucial decision consciously or subconsciously faced by everyone. As career counselors, our concerns are centered on the success criteria with which we evaluate our lives and others evaluate us. These success criteria are based, to a great extent, on the kind or quality of work we do.

What motivates us to work is a key question. According to McClelland (1961), people have a driving need for achievement and subsequent power over others. Other work motivators are the security and symbols of success that come from earning money, identification with prestigious organizations or peer affiliates, and status associated with certain occupations and professions (O'Toole, 1981). Central to our concerns, however, are the intrinsic satisfactions from which individuals judge their success in life and work. We should recognize that these judgments may change as individuals' needs change over their life spans. We should set a goal of providing flexible career life planning that can help individuals identify their changing needs and set realistic goals to meet them.

Super (1990), among others, has suggested an integrative approach to career counseling that focuses on the development of life roles over the life span with emphasis on interrole congruence. Hansen's (1996) integrative life-planning model incorporates career development, life transitions, gender-role socialization, and social change. These integrative approaches recognize a broad spectrum of domains that must be considered in career life planning. The comprehensive career life plan considers all life roles, including relationships, as a major comprehensive view of development.

Obsolescence is insidious to us all, and it not only threatens our ability to perform in our chosen occupation but also can hinder our effectiveness and the subsequent satisfaction that comes from staying up to date in what we do. A number of authors have suggested that educational programs should be developed to support the ongoing life-learning needs of today's individuals (Drucker, 1992; Bolles, 1993). More and more educational institutions offer flexible, continuing education programs (Cetron & Gayle, 1991), and career development programs are also sponsored by organizations. Through career life-planning programs, we not only provide sources of education and training, but we assist individuals in determining their needs for programs and in understanding the reasons for adopting a life-learning concept.

As we project into the future, our major effort should be to identify those variables in our lives over which we can exert some control. Our lives can be charted more effectively through the maze of changes that we experience, both individually and situationally, by planning programs that place these variables in perspective.

Career Choice

Career life planning focuses on a significant number of factors that influence career choice. Setting priorities and goals for career life planning, developing ultimate life designs, and setting long-range and short-term goals are major choice objectives. In career life planning, values, interests, abilities, achievement, and work-life experiences are viable factors to discuss, evaluate, and clarify when making career life-planning determinations. Decision-making models also provide a framework from which career-choice counseling objectives are derived (Gelatt, 1989). Clearly defined steps in decision-making strategies provide sequences designed to assist individuals in making a career choice.

One problem-solving approach for career choice was suggested by Tiedeman and O'Hara (1963). Career choice involves processing developmental tasks and resolving psychosocial crises. All theories, systems, and strategies underscore the inclusive and complex nature of the career-choice process. Because individuals experience periods of indecision and indiscriminateness, career choice is not considered wholly continuous (Super, 1990).

Super (1990) also considered indecisiveness as a period in the developmental process when interests have not been fully crystallized. Uncertainty about future career goals may lead some individuals to make indiscriminate choices of two or more occupational objectives. As individuals become more aware of the developing character of the career process itself, they are more willing to make changes and to alter or redefine a decision (Miller-Tiedeman & Tiedeman, 1990; Healy, 1982). The process of deciding is complex and unique for each individual, depending on cognitive factors and the social structure of the individual's milieu. In essence, individuals evaluate their choices internally by considering values, interest, achievement, and experiences and externally by seeking acceptance and approval within the working environment.

In career life-planning programs, career choices are tentative from the standpoint that practically every choice involves some doubt about the credibility of the chosen career and the possibility that it can be successfully carried out over a lifetime. The individual's uncertainty is compounded by the career possibilities that have disappeared because of changing economic conditions and the career uncertainties and unknowns forecast by vast imminent technological changes. Moreover, career choice is a process in which one not only chooses but also eliminates and consequently stifles some interests and talents. Parts of us are left to go to seed when a career choice is made, because eventually we must give up a chance to develop talents and interests as we limit ourselves on the narrow pathway leading to a career. Career choice is also clouded by the search all of us experience for self-identity and meaning in a world society that is drawing closer together. Fortunately, career life-planning programs provide for a regular reevaluation of where we have been and where we are going. Opportunities are available to reconsider choices of the past and to realign them with new values, interests, and changing workplaces. Those talents and interests that have remained latent can be nurtured and developed in career life-planning programs.

Life-Planning Workshops

Life-planning workshops for college students were conducted at Colorado State University for several years. These workshops were designed primarily to actively involve individuals in developing life plans through a highly structured step-by-step program. One of the major goals of these workshops is to promote self-awareness and the recognition that each individual has certain responsibilities in the development of his or her future. Even though these programs were developed for college students, the format could easily be adapted for other groups, including adults who have finished or dropped out of college.

The life-planning workshops are usually conducted in one-day sessions lasting approximately seven hours. Groups of four persons are formed with a facilitator for each group. The program is highly structured, but each group may progress at its own pace. Because the structure of the program is set, facilitators need only minimal training. Group members remain together through the session.

The workshop format consists of eight structured exercises, as follows. Each exercise is shared in the group, and interaction is strongly emphasized. The first exercise, *life line*, requires that an individual draw a line from birth to death (life line) and indicate on it key life experiences and present position. These exercises are designed to involve the participants actively in concentrating on future tasks and life planning.

Exercise	*Purpose*
1. Life line	To identify past and current situations in life
2. Identifying and stripping of roles	To identify individual roles in life and share individual feelings as one strips roles
3. Fantasy time	To develop more self-awareness when free of identified roles
4. Typical day and a special day of the future	To further crystallize self-awareness and individual needs for the future when free of identified roles
5. Life inventory	To identify specific needs and goals with emphasis on identification of each individual's positive characteristics
6. News release	To further clarify specific interests and future accomplishments desired
7. Reassume roles	To clarify or reformulate goals while reassuming originally identified roles
8. Goal setting	To set realistic short-term and long-term goals

Identifying and stripping of roles, the second exercise, requires that each individual identify and rank in importance five different roles currently occupying his or her life. Each participant is encouraged to identify positive as well as negative roles. The next step is to start with the least important role and "strip" that role (no longer assume the role) and express feelings associated with freedom from that role. In this manner, each role is stripped until the person is role-free and subsequently able to express "freely" personal life-planning needs.

The third exercise, *fantasy time*, is a continuation of the second exercise, in which the individual is encouraged toward further introspection while being role-free. More specifically, the individual considers the influence of roles when developing future plans.

Once roles have been stripped, the individual in the fourth exercise is to outline a *typical day and a special day of the future.* Now that the individual is able to visualize his or her life without the restrictions of roles, he or she can subsequently better consider ideal circumstances. This exercise is designed to provide an opportunity to consider how identified roles influence or actually block present and future need fulfillment.

The fifth exercise requires that each individual fill out a *life inventory,* which includes questions asking for greatest experiences, things done well and poorly, and desired future accomplishments. Each individual is directed toward developing specific needs and values while focusing attention on desired changes in the future. This exercise is designed to be a rebuilding process through identification of specific needs.

During the sixth exercise, *news release,* each individual considers his or her life line, as drawn in an earlier exercise, in relation to what the future should be. Each person writes a sketch of his or her life, projecting into the future while focusing on accomplishment and predominant roles. The major purpose is to promote the development of realistic future needs.

In the seventh exercise, *reassume roles,* the focus is on reassuming the roles that were stripped in earlier exercises. Each individual now must decide which roles should be kept and which should be discarded in order to reach his or her life goals. Reassumed roles may be rearranged in priority or replaced with new roles that provide greater opportunity for meeting goals. The emphasis is on the factors that can be changed in order to gain greater control of future life planning.

The final exercise, *goal setting,* requires that each individual describe specific behaviors that can bring about desired changes in his or her life. Again, the emphasis is on the individual's ability to make changes in order to meet life-planning goals.

An Example of Life-Planning Workshop Exercises

The following illustration demonstrates the more specific activities involved in this program. Liang has been married for six years, has two children, and is currently employed as a high school biology teacher. Her family life has been stable for most of her marriage, but she has recently felt a need to change her career and life direction. As she stated to her counselor, "I'm not sure of what's happened—I just feel frustrated. I love my husband and children, but I am unhappy." After several counseling sessions, the counselor recommended that Liang participate in a life-planning workshop.

After being introduced to staff and members of the group, she heard an explanation of the purpose and goals of the exercises. The first exercise required that Liang construct a life line in which she included the results of important decisions and events, such as the birth of her brother, death of her father, meeting her husband, marriage, the birth of her children, and so on. She jotted down her age at the time of each event and drew an arrow next to the more significant decisions. Valleys and peaks indicated the ups and downs of life.

Then Liang shared her life line with Chris, another participant.

Liang: We have some similar experiences, I see.
Chris: Yes, but you have more work experiences than I have. I wish I had more experiences so I could figure out what to do.
Liang: I have worked since I was married and before, and yet I am confused. Come to think of it, I guess working helps you figure out some things.
Chris: Yeah, I would hope so.
Liang: Mainly, what you learn is what you don't want to do.
Chris: Oh look, the major events in your life line are like mine; they center around family.

A general discussion of the purpose of a life line was led by the group leader. Her major focus was the value of previous experience in determining future goals.

The next exercise, identifying and stripping of roles, created considerable tension for Liang because she was not prepared to strip her roles as parent, spouse, teacher, homemaker, and friend.

Liang: I don't want to dump my husband and children—it's hard for me to think of myself without them.
Chris: I know, but remember, this is make-believe.
Liang: That's so, but I still feel it is difficult.
Chris: Go on, tell me what you would do.
Liang: Well, I've always wanted a higher degree, but with the children, I don't have time for college.
Chris: Go on. I bet you would like a different job too!
Liang: This sounds like bragging, but my college profs encouraged me to consider college teaching.

As Liang and Chris continued to strip away roles, they recognized the ambiguities associated with the exercise as well as the benefits of imagined freedom.

Liang: I've wound up with quite a different lifestyle, and you have too.
Chris: If only I could do it. How many jobs do you have listed?
Liang: Let me see. College professor, model, business owner, chief executive officer. Oh yeah, I want to live on the West Coast! But really, how could I realistically accomplish any of these?

After the third exercise, fantasy time, Liang outlined a "typical day" and a "special day" in the future.

Typical day
    Breakfast between 8:00 and 9:00
    Go to campus for class preparation 9–11
    Teach classes 11–12
    Have lunch at faculty lounge 12–1:30
    Office hours 2–3
    Play tennis 3–5
    Shop 5–6

Dinner 7–8
Attend play 8–10
Bedtime
Special day (no time commitments)
Wake up whenever I want in a plush room in a resort hotel
Breakfast in bed
Hike in the mountains
Go skiing
Meet friends around the fireplace at Happy Hour
Dine and dance

As Liang fantasized a role-free lifestyle, she also recognized the meaningful-ness of her current roles. She deeply cared for her husband and children and did not want to give them up under any circumstances, but she also came to the conclusion that something was missing from her life. Perhaps, she thought, it was the desire for more freedom with fewer time commitments. But everyone likes that, she mused, so what's new?

As she filled out the life inventory for Exercise 5, she was now faced with having to make significant decisions about the future. As she listed her greatest experiences and things she had done well and poorly, the items seemed to center around academic achievements and her family. Surprisingly, after considerable thought, Liang listed some of her teaching activities under tasks done poorly. "This is awful," she almost stated out loud, but it was true. She had to face it. Her heart had not been in it. What a mess—she loved her students, and yet, she was not giving them her best.

When Liang focused on changes for the future, she came to the conclusion that a career change was necessary, but accompanying this thought was the chill-ing reality of what this would mean. Her entire lifestyle and routine would have to be changed, she concluded. Is it worth it? How would her husband react? Liang's list of specific needs included the following:

- a greater commitment to my work;
- a change to pursue my interest of more academic training;
- a higher-level job in education; and
- more and better communication with my family—let my family know how *I* feel

During this exercise, Liang heard the following exchange in her group.

Dante: What's the sense of all this? These needs I have would disrupt my current lifestyle tremendously.
Jim: It might take that, Dante.
Ted: It's not that simple. I would like to follow through on my needs, but I have to consider the needs of my family too. I think we gotta negotiate.

As Liang listened to the members discuss the problems of implementing their needs list, she realized that she was not the only one experiencing frustration. It was comforting to know she was not alone in wanting something different, but she also realized that different personal situations required personal solutions. The conversation in the group continued.

Jean: I never thought of getting older as an advantage, but my perspective of the future has fewer complications since my children left home.

Liang: Would you follow through on your need list if your children still lived at home?

Jean: Yes, I think so; in fact, I know I would, but everyone's situation is different.

Liang performed the sixth exercise, news release, while observing her life line. By looking at her life as a series of peaks and valleys, she realized that it was more important now to live a more directed life with a balance between life roles. She recognized that it was her choice to devote the major part of life to her family, but she also wanted more out of life at this point. Perhaps, she thought, there would be fewer valleys and more peaks in the future for everyone in the family.

As the group continued this discussion, Jean made another point.

Jean: Being older also makes you realize that life goes by quickly. Just look at your life line—if it tells you anything at all, it is that opportunities are there for the taking. But if you don't, well, the line just keeps on moving.

As Liang began Exercise 7, she felt no aversion to reassuming roles, and in fact, realized that she wanted to retain her current life roles.

Liang: There is no way I would give up my family. Through all of this, they still come first.

Jean: I don't see that as a negative; in fact, I think it's great.

In the final exercise, goal setting, Liang felt that she had gained the confidence to follow through on some specific goals. It would take courage, she thought, to change career direction. It would disrupt everyone's lifestyles to do it, but the chances were that it would be worth it in the future. She would use negotiation as a means of restructuring family life while she attended the university. Putting some money aside each month for the next year would help finance graduate school, and meanwhile she could attend evening classes.

Liang: I have decided that going back to the university is best for me and my family!

Dante: That's not good enough, Liang. You're supposed to give specific behaviors to change things.

Jean: Yes, that's too general.

Liang: OK, let me see. I will have a meeting with my husband on Monday at 6:30. We will discuss the following topics: advantages of going to graduate school, financial arrangements, family arrangements, sharing household duties, and options for time of enrollment.

Liang's case points out the value of delineating and specifying the consequences of life roles. Individuals may become so involved in fulfillment of a particular role that other roles are ignored, and frustrations and stressful conditions that evolve are often left unidentified and unresolved. The interaction of group members often provides support for individuals to discover their own needs for career development.

Other Prominent Career Life-Planning Programs

A very well-received job-hunter's manual, *What Color Is Your Parachute?* by Richard Bolles (1993), was first published in 1978 and has been revised annually. The informal and straightforward writing style and clever illustrations have made this manual a phenomenal success. Bolles's publications have removed much of the drabness and boredom associated with career exploration and have turned it into an exciting adventure—a process he visualized as not only continuous and complex but also interesting and challenging.

In *What Color Is Your Parachute?* Bolles attacked current methods of job hunting and suggested steps he found more effective. Examples of useful methods of locating job openings and the advantages and disadvantages of each are given. A list of resources for career counseling help is also provided. The process of deciding on a career is approached from a career- and life-planning perspective; that is, while he considered decisions that meet immediate needs, he also pointed out how planning should include long-term future goals. He suggested that life-planning programs consider the possibility of several careers. His prescription for successful planning includes the following objectives: (1) establish goals, (2) identify skills, (3) establish time lines (when goals are to be accomplished), and (4) establish who's in control (the individual should take control of his or her own life).

In the book's final section, Bolles provided information on the job market and offered practical suggestions for finding job openings. He suggested that deciding where one wants to work is a key factor in the career decision process. More specifically, he advised that each individual consider geographical location, work climate, organizational structure, and the purpose of each organization as relevant to career/work planning.

Practical exercises are offered throughout the manual on such subjects as résumé preparation, interview skills development, skills identification, achievement identification, and the process of finding occupations of interest. The Quick Job-Hunting Map (Bolles, 1993), adapted from Holland's (1992) six modal personal styles and matching work environments, is a basic tool for career decision making.

In the late 1980s, Gysbers and Henderson (1988) introduced a comprehensive school guidance program that has grown in popularity. One of the features of this program is life career planning. Gysbers and Henderson stressed decision making and planning as a need for all students in schools, and as a result many schools require that students develop a written life plan.

Many of the concepts of career life planning discussed in this section, such as identifying variables in one's life that can be controlled, are strategies used in this program. Moreover, career plans are developed to be flexible in order to meet the ever-changing job requirements and workplace changes. (More about this program is reported in Chapter 10.)

A related program that connects with the comprehensive school guidance programs is *Planning for Life* (National Consortium of State Career Guidance Supervisors, 1996). Its major emphasis is on career life planning for grades K–12 and postsecondary institutions. This is another program that has received national recognition.

The contents of a career life plan are carefully spelled out in guidelines for schools to follow. For example, the information needed for a life career plan is as follows:

Demographic data about the individual
School and activity preferences
Goals
Desired lifestyle
Current career choices, including reasons for those choices
Assessment results
Work experiences
Implications of above information

Each student's plan is used to select courses and is reviewed each year. New information about each student is placed in his or her planning package as it becomes available, and discussions about life plans are held periodically throughout the school year. Career life plans are the focus of exit interviews with students who drop out, transfer, or graduate.

Career Life Planning as a Promotion of Personal Competence

The concept of career life planning as discussed in this chapter suggests that career programs should be constructed from a broad-based framework of life events, conditions, and situations over the life span. The major goal of career life planning is to help individuals cope with changing events and accomplish the tasks and transitions of developmental stages successfully.

Although the experiences of life teach us how to cope with certain events, the future is always challenging and unpredictable. Lazarus (1980) suggested that past experiences, however, can help one cope with future events. Calling this process "anticipatory coping," he proposed that the skills learned through successfully coping with experiences can help when encountering future events, and unsuccessful experiences can provide a basis for identifying behaviors that should be modified. Though all experiences are useful for future encounters, successful experiences tend to have a snowball effect by providing indexes to appropriate behaviors. The purpose of career life planning is to provide skills that may be applied in coping effectively with a variety of future events. Teaching skills that are helpful in meeting future events is one of the developmental goals of career life planning.

The model in *Life-Development Intervention* (Danish & D'Augelli, 1983) provided a framework for teaching skills for career life planning:

1. Identify levels of skill development
   a. problem-solving skills
   b. decision-making skills
   c. planning skills
   d. goal-setting procedures
   e. career resources and how to use them
2. Decision-making skills
   a. knowledge of personal characteristics
   b. steps in decision making and applying them to a variety of life encounters
3. Identifying assistance systems
   a. public and private career counseling locations
   b. sources of career counseling in organizations and institutions
   c. educational and training assistance programs
   d. social support systems
4. Identifying and using job market projections
   a. sources and use of job market projections
   b. potential future work roles
5. Identifying career and life-coping skills
   a. job satisfaction variables
   b. sources of stress
   c. methods of modifying behavior
   d. coping skill in work and life

The first step requires a careful analysis of individual skills in specific areas related to problem solving, decision making, goal setting, and using resources. From this baseline, individual needs determine the objectives for developing skills in these vital areas. Danish (1977) suggested a method of teaching skills as follows: (1) skills are defined in behavioral terms, (2) the purpose for learning a skill is presented, (3) a criterion for measuring skill attainment is discussed, (4) a model of effective and ineffective skills is presented, (5) skills are practiced and supervised, (6) skills are practiced in assigned sites, and (7) skill levels are evaluated.

The second component recommends that individual skills be assessed and projected into work environments. The rationale for decision making is presented in terms of its use in both career decisions and other life decisions, such as purchasing a home or automobile. The second component reinforces the skills learned in the first component while emphasizing the probable necessity of making several career decisions over the life span. Coping with increasing family obligations and changing values and interests is also stressed.

The third component is designed to assist individuals in locating support systems that may be helpful in the future. Although every community is different in this regard, the skills learned in locating systems in one community should help in locating systems in others.

The evidence suggests that major shifts will occur in the labor market, as well as in the creation of new occupations (Cetron & Davies, 1988). Individuals will have to cope with these changes, probably through retraining. Coping with career changes and refocusing training efforts can be assisted by anticipating and planning such changes through appropriate interpretations of future projections.

The final component focuses on developing personal competencies and methods of modifying behavior to cope with stress. By building individual strengths and increasing learning skills, supplemented by assistance systems, individuals are better able to adjust to adverse circumstances that may be encountered in the future. This component focuses on preventing stress through the development of coping skills that may be transferred to other life situations.

The next section describes a method of helping college students project into future lifestyle dimensions by exploring the variety of choices available through career life planning.

Dimensions of Lifestyle Orientation

The emergence of career life-planning programs and their subsequent popularity clearly established the need for career counseling programs that clarify the individual's lifestyle orientation (Super, 1990). Programs that incorporate dimensions of lifestyle address important career planning factors that might otherwise be ignored. For example, the individual's orientation toward such factors as job, leisure, membership in organizations, home, and family is an important consideration in career life planning. In addition, attention must be directed to choices of residence and work locations as well as to other individual lifestyle aspirations. More specifically, individual aspirations for social status, a particular work climate, education, mobility, and financial security are key factors in determining life plans.

A Dimensions of Life-Style Orientation Survey (DLOS) (Zunker, 1994), still in an experimental stage, was incorporated into ongoing career counseling programs at Southwest Texas State University. The survey is designed to assist students in determining individual lifestyle dimensions. From a list of 80 phrases, students are asked to select those phrases that they feel are important to their lifestyles. They are also asked to answer several questions concerning desired geographical location, and given the option to write an essay. Part I, the phrase selection component of the survey, is outlined below.

> *Directions:* This is not a test but an inventory to help you think in terms of lifestyle after graduation from college. Your lifestyle preferences are important to consider when making future decisions about your life. In this first part of the inventory you are asked to rate your preferences from a list of statements concerning such matters as job style, leisure style, membership style, home style, and family style.
> Examples of the phrase-selection part are as follows:

> 43. Be comfortable, but not rich
> 48. Strive to be outstanding in my work
> 68. Have a job from 8–5, five days a week
> 82. Be a recognized authority in my field

To complete the DLOS, students are asked to select those phrases that are "unimportant," "moderately important," or "of greatest importance" to their lifestyle. The student assigns a value on a three-point scale to each phrase to indicate its importance.

In Part II, the individual chooses a place of residence, indicating preference for a community, state, or foreign country from lists provided. In each case, the individual can indicate "undecided" or "no preference." The counselor may also opt to have the student write an essay envisioning his or her lifestyle in ten years, from a list of ten selected topics.

The DLOS was designed primarily as a counseling tool for assisting individuals in determining their lifestyle orientations and preferences in regard to career, family, leisure, place of residence, work climate, and overall style of life. The survey may be used for a variety of counseling programs, but it is most useful as a facilitator for discussion in groups or individual counseling programs where important decisions for career life planning are determined.

Individual items marked "of greatest importance" provide relevant materials for discussion. For example, lifestyle preferences such as "Like to live in different parts of the country" or "Have a job that is easygoing with little or no pressure" can be clarified and considered in the decision-making process. Likewise, other items provide stimulus for discussion groups and assist individuals in clarifying their individual needs through group interaction.

A varimax factor analysis of the 80 items extracted 11 dimensions common to males and females. The scores are reported on a profile that shows the degree of importance the student has rated each dimension as compared to students in the normative sample. The 11 dimensions of lifestyle are identified as follows:

1. *Financial Orientation*—an orientation toward financial independence and social prominence.
2. *Community-Involvement Orientation*—an orientation toward participation in community activities and community services.
3. *Family Orientation*—an orientation toward family life.
4. *Work-Achievement Orientation*—an orientation toward career development and commitment.
5. *Work-Leadership Orientation*—an orientation toward a leadership role in the workplace.
6. *Educational Orientation*—an orientation toward self-improvement through educational attainment.
7. *Structured Work-Environment Orientation*—an orientation toward regularly scheduled work hours.
8. *Leisure Orientation*—an orientation toward leisure activities.
9. *Mobility Orientation*—an orientation toward diversification and change.
10. *Moderate-Secure Orientation*—an orientation toward moderation.
11. *Outdoor-Work-Leisure Orientation*—an orientation toward work and leisure activities in the out-of-doors.

As mentioned, the dimensional factors can be used as a stimulus for discussion in either group or individual counseling programs. Take, for example, a strong orientation toward factor 1, the financial dimension. In the clarification process, the individual considers this need with potential financial compensation from identified careers. If there are significant differences between individual financial needs and potential careers under consideration, the individual is required to prioritize preferences for lifestyle. For one individual, need fulfillment associated with a career may be more important than the financial potential. For another individual, the opposite may be true. Through this process priorities are clarified, and realistic alternatives and options are developed for future planning.

A summary of lifestyle dimensions also provides an index to overall lifestyle preferences that focuses on important considerations in career life planning. A comparison of lifestyle factors with other individual characteristics, such as skills identification and interests, can point up congruences or striking differences. For example, if an individual has strong orientations toward factor 3, the family dimension, and factor 8, the leisure dimension, but is considering careers that are highly pressured and require long hours and considerable dedication, these differences are identified and discussed. The approach is not to discourage any of the identified needs associated with lifestyle or career, but to promote an understanding of current potential conflicts that could cause serious future problems. When striking conflicts are evident, further clarification of lifestyle orientations and career interests is encouraged. Thus lifestyle factors assist in the setting of priorities and goals for career life planning.

Role of Leisure in Career Life Planning

The role of leisure in career life planning can easily be overlooked because leisure activities are often taken for granted. However, in recent decades, the role of leisure has taken on new meaning in terms of self-expression (Kelly, 1981) and counseling responsibility (McDaniels, 1984).

According to McDaniels (1990), who has written extensively on leisure as a counseling objective, career planning involves a work-leisure connection. In this conceptualization of a career, work and leisure are seen as inseparable counseling objectives that should be addressed in a holistic framework. Wilson (1981) suggested that leisure should not be viewed as an activity that one does if and when time permits, but instead as an endeavor that requires active planning and definite time commitments. In this framework, leisure is considered an essential ingredient in life. In essence, career life planning must include planning for leisure activities that provide for relaxation with family and friends.

Career Life Planning in Perspective

In this chapter, we have emphasized numerous components of career life planning that, when integrated into future plans, can effectively pinpoint and meet individual needs. We have discovered that career life planning includes continuous learning; that is, some education or training will more than likely be necessary throughout the life span. Critical to career life planning are decision-making techniques that are useful in making not only an initial choice but many subsequent decisions as well. Career life-planning programs give significant consideration to dimensions of lifestyle preference; a major goal of career life planning is to identify those dimensions that provide meaning and purpose and that sustain our efforts toward self-fulfillment.

Some have labeled our current conditions as career transitions in turbulent times (Feller & Walz, 1996). What is being referred to are the vast changes in work environments and in work requirements that will be discussed more fully in the chapters that follow. But in the context of career life planning, the downsizing of organizations, the significant changes in career development in organizations and in operating procedures, and the lack of assurances and guarantees of lifetime employment from employers may require adjustments in career life-planning dimensions.

In an environment where employers make few future commitments to their employees, individuals will be required to be more assertive in personal agency (see description of the personal agency person in Chapter 12). For instance, career development is more self-directed. "Turbulent times" suggest that more changes will evolve, and one must be prepared to adjust and adapt to them. The uncertainty of the future calls for adopting the philosophy of planning for change that will surely come.

Planning for change suggests that one must be very alert to career opportunities as they evolve. In this perspective, one must be willing to shift views and develop new skills and interests while cultivating self-reliance. Planning to stay focused on what you want in changing times requires flexibility of thinking and the courage to learn something new.

Finally, it is the individual who must chart his or her life course and decide on the direction that course will take in this ever-changing society. A positive outlook on life and the realization that factors important to career and life success can be controlled are good attitudes to cultivate. Our challenge is to help others and ourselves by remaining optimistic throughout various changes we experience individually and situationally. We must recognize that there are options to pursue if we learn to plan effectively and keep our alternatives in proper perspective. Ideally, through career life planning we become better prepared to meet life's challenges. Ultimately, we hope to be as confident of our choices and actions as was expressed so succinctly over 400 years ago: "If I knew the world was coming to an end tomorrow, I would pay my debts and plant the apple tree" (attributed to Martin Luther [1483–1546] in a speech by Martin L. Cole, 1963).

Summary

1. Career life planning is an ongoing process that allows for change of direction as individuals' needs change or as situational circumstances cause change. Career life planning provides the means to manage changes and thus allows

greater opportunity for fulfillment in life. Career life planning is a developmental process encompassing needs generated from work, family, home, and leisure.

2. One of the main purposes of career life planning is to develop skills with which individuals can learn to control their futures. Through career life planning, individuals learn to center their attention on carefully laid plans and on those variables over which they have control.

3. There is a need for career life planning and career counseling programs that clarify individuals' lifestyle orientations. Programs that incorporate dimensions of lifestyle address important career planning factors.

4. Life-planning workshops for college students have been conducted at Colorado State University for several years. The workshops are designed primarily to help students develop a life plan. Life-planning workshops (usually one-day sessions) consist of highly structured, step-by-step exercises.

5. Richard Bolles attacked commonly advocated methods of job hunting in his book *What Color Is Your Parachute?* Practical exercises are also offered on such topics as résumé preparation, interview-skills development, skills identification, achievement, and the location of occupations of interest.

6. Planning-for-life programs were developed to mesh with current comprehensive school guidance programs for grades K–12 and in postsecondary institutions.

7. Career life planning as a promotion of personal competence suggests that skills learned through coping with experiences help individuals encounter future events.

8. Career life-planning programs that incorporate dimensions of lifestyle orientation address important factors that might otherwise be ignored. Examples of such dimensions are social status, work climate, mobility, and financial security.

Supplementary Learning Exercises

Using the DLOS (Dimensions of Life-Style Orientation Survey), answer the following questions and complete the projects listed below.

1. Select the dimensions of lifestyle that describe you. How can these dimensions be incorporated into your career life plans?
2. Select three lifestyle dimensions and develop a list of careers that correspond to each.
3. Select two lifestyle dimensions and write a description of each, projecting future family, leisure, and career orientations.
4. Form a discussion group and have each member select a different lifestyle dimension. Discuss careers, family, leisure, and place of residence associated with each lifestyle dimension.

Using the description on pages 94–99 of the Life-Planning Workshops developed at Colorado State University, answer questions 5, 6, and 7.

5. Complete Exercises 1 and 2 and describe their significance for career life planning.
6. Form a group and complete Exercises 2, 3, and 4. What is the significance of being free of roles in career life planning?

7. Describe what you consider to be the major advantages of life-planning workshops.
8. Interview a school counselor and determine whether career life planning is a part of his or her guidance program. Report your findings.
9. Define *career choice*. Write an essay on the subject of career choice and its relationship to lifestyle preferences.
10. What do you consider to be the major goals of career life planning? Describe the major principles and components that you believe should be integral to career life-planning programs.

CHAPTER FIVE

The *Dictionary of Occupational Titles,* the *Occupational Outlook Handbook,* and Career Clusters

The U.S. Department of Labor generates and publishes a vast amount of career-related information that is used primarily by a number of federal and state agencies for research, job placement, and career counseling programs. Many of the career-related materials are free, and others may be purchased for a nominal fee. Of all career-related materials published by the Department of Labor, the *Dictionary of Occupational Titles (DOT),* now in its revised fourth edition, is as widely known as any and has been in use for over 40 years. The *DOT* is an occupational classification system developed by the Department of Labor. The format used in describing occupations is highly technical. Because of this technical style, the voluminous amounts of information, and the complexity of accessing the information, career counselors have had difficulty making the most effective use of the *DOT* in career counseling programs.

In the first part of this chapter, we briefly discuss the development of the *DOT,* explain its numerical classification system, and emphasize the usefulness of these volumes in career counseling programs. Then the O*NET, an automated replacement for the *DOT,* is described. The *Guide for Occupational Exploration (GOE)* is highlighted next as providing a career counseling approach to the occupational information in the *DOT* and other related publications.

In the second section of this chapter, the *Occupational Outlook Handbook (OOH)* is reviewed. This is another Department of Labor publication, written in a nontechnical, narrative style. In contrast to the *DOT,* the *OOH's* format is straightforward, and the occupational information is easily accessed. The major sections of the *OOH* are described and the usefulness of this volume for career counseling programs is emphasized.

The third section of the chapter consists of a discussion of career clusters and other career classification systems, including two-dimensional ones.

The Importance of Labor Market Information

To assist in the career decision-making process, the counselor should be alert to the most relevant labor market information available. The availability of resources has grown tremendously in the last 20 years. Thus, counselors must assist clients in sorting out the most relevant information, monitoring the process of collection, and eventually integrating the information with other resources such as test data. Among other purposes, labor market information is most helpful in evaluating how certain careers can meet the individual client's needs, discovering available options, and considering occupational alternatives.

Throughout this text, references will be made to the changing workplace, economics, downsizing of organizations, the internationalization of workplaces, and the changing job market. Current labor market information is therefore a viable part of each client's career search. Our goal as counselors should be to help clients understand and effectively use the occupational information available. An impressive program for integrating occupational information and guidance was compiled by Ettinger (1991), with the assistance of several contributing authors and resource groups. The Improved Career Decision-Making Program (ICDM) was developed to train career development facilitators to help students and clients (1) understand labor market information, (2) use information to make career decisions, (3) improve decision-making skills, and (4) develop an action plan to make more effective use of information in career decision making. To accomplish these goals, ten modules were developed for clients, and training materials were prepared for counselors.

A good example is module 3, "Demographic Trends that Impact Career Decision Making." Demographic trends point out the maturation of America and the effects this trend will have on the labor market. For example, there will be a greater need for training and retraining entry-level workers from new sources. A second trend is the predicted increased diversity of our population and the special programs that will be needed to fully utilize ethnic minorities in the workplace. These are national trends, but they could differ significantly in local situations. Nevertheless, the ICDM helps the informed client interpret this information in terms of entrepreneurial opportunities or the impact on tentative career choices. Relating available opportunities in the world of work to self-knowledge in the career decision-making process is an important step to understanding the significance of the changing world of work. The resources discussed in this chapter are only examples of career information and labor market information projections. Computer-assisted career guidance programs are discussed in Chapter 6, and a career resource center is covered in Chapter 8.

The *Dictionary of Occupational Titles (DOT)*

The first edition of the *DOT* was published in 1939. It contained 17,500 alphabetical listings of occupational titles and coded each definition according to an occupational classification system developed for this volume. Each occupation was assigned a five- or six-digit code, according to 550 occupational groups. In addition, each occupation was classified as skilled, semiskilled, or unskilled.

The *DOT* was updated in 1949 when the second edition was published. This edition combined the material in the first edition and the supplements published between 1939 and 1945 into one volume. More than 6,100 new occupations were added to the second edition, which reflected the newly created occupations of the World War II era. Several new manufacturing industries developed during this period, and subsequent occupations were added to the second edition.

Rapid changes in technology accompanied by new and different occupations brought forth the third edition of the *DOT* in 1965. This edition reflects the industrial development and occupational changes experienced during the 1960s and earlier. Volume I of the third edition, like the earlier editions, contains an alphabetical listing of occupations consisting of 21,741 separate occupations and 13,809 alternate titles.

Volume II of the third edition (also published in 1965) groups the occupations contained in Volume I. The groupings were determined by code numbers assigned to each occupation in Volume I. A six-digit coding arrangement was devised for each occupation in this volume. The first digit specifies the occupational category, the second digit the occupational division, and the third digit the occupational group. The last three digits provide information concerning the activities involved in each occupation according to worker-function arrangements. More specifically, the last three digits express the relationship the worker would have with data, people, and things. The worker-function hierarchy of data, people, and things will be discussed later in this chapter.

Two supplements were added to Volumes I and II, and the complete *DOT* system before 1977 consisted of four publications:

- *Volume I, Definitions of Titles*
- *Volume II, Occupational Classifications*
- *A Supplement to the DOT, Selected Characteristics of Occupations*
- *Supplement 2 to the DOT, Selected Characteristics of Occupations by Worker Traits and Physical Strength*

These publications have made a significant contribution to the job information system developed by the Department of Labor. However, rapid changes of industrial technology since the 1960s and subsequent changes in occupational requirements brought about a need for the *DOT* fourth edition, published in 1977.

The DOT *Fourth Edition*

During the years from 1965 to the mid-1970s, the Department of Labor State Occupational Analysis Field Center staffs conducted 75,000 on-site analyses of a variety of jobs in numerous industries. The major purpose of these on-site visitations was to provide an up-to-date definition of occupations and to identify new ones. This study resulted not only in identifying 2,100 new occupational definitions but also in deleting 3,500 that were in the third edition.

One of the major changes in the fourth edition is in the listing and definitions of occupational titles. In the previous editions, occupational titles were listed in alphabetical order; but in the fourth edition, occupational titles are listed in ascending order according to their assigned nine-digit code numbers. However, an alphabetical index of occupational titles with their respective industrial designation and occupational codes is provided. This change is significant because it focuses more attention on the occupational codes.

The DOT *Fourth Edition Revised*

The fourth edition of the *DOT* was revised in 1991 and is contained in two volumes. The occupational definitions in the 1982 and 1986 supplements were incorporated in this edition, which contains three different arrangements of occupational titles: (1) occupational group arrangement (occupations listed in ascending order by nine-digit code numbers), (2) alphabetical order of titles (an alphabetical list of titles followed by the nine-digit code numbers and industry designations), and (3) occupational titles arranged by industry designation. Table 5-1 summarizes the uses of these three arrangements.

The nine-digit occupational code incorporated in the revised fourth edition warrants special consideration. Each digit in the code has important occupational meaning. An example of an actual occupational code for an automobile upholsterer, 780.381-010, will be used to illustrate the code structure. The nine digits will be divided into three groups to make it easier to identify the significance of each digit in the occupational code structure.

In this example, the first three digits of the occupational code are identified. The first digit identifies the occupational category from nine divisions used in the *DOT*. The second digit is used to identify one of 97 occupational divisions. The third digit specifies the location of the occupational group within an occupational division.

TABLE 5-1
Arrangements of Occupational Titles in the *DOT*, Fourth Edition

Use . . .	*If you . . .*
The Occupational Group Arrangement	have sufficient information about the job tasks.
	want to know about other closely related occupations.
	want to be sure you have chosen the most appropriate classification using the other arrangements.
Occupational Titles Arranged by Industry Designation	know only the industry in which the job is located.
	want to know about other jobs in an industry.
	want to work in a specific industry.
The Alphabetical Index of Occupational Titles	know only the job title and cannot obtain better information.

SOURCE: U.S. Department of Labor, 1991a, p. xxvii.

7—Occupational Category
This category is based on nine broad categories as follows:

0/1. Professional, Technical, and Managerial Occupations
  2. Clerical and Sales Occupations
  3. Service Occupations
  4. Agricultural, Fishery, Forestry, and Related Occupations
  5. Processing Occupations
  6. Machine Trade Occupations
  7. Bench Work Occupations
  8. Structural Work Occupations
  9. Miscellaneous Occupations

8—Occupational Division
There are 97 occupational divisions listed in the *DOT.* This particular code is within the Bench Work occupational category and in the occupational division of occupations in fabrication and repair of textile, leather, and related products.

0—Occupational Group
The third digit specifies the location of the occupation within the occupational division. In this case, the occupational group is occupations in upholstering and in fabrication and repair of stuffed furniture, mattresses, and related products.

Thus, for the automobile upholsterer the *occupational category* (7) is Bench Work. The *occupational division* (78) is occupations in fabrication and repair of textile, leather, and related products. The *occupational group* (780) is occupations in upholstering and in fabrication and repair of stuffed furniture, mattresses, and related products.

The middle three digits (381) of the nine-digit system are used to identify the relationship the worker has with three worker-function groupings of data, people, and things. The following worker functions form a hierarchical structure, in that the functions become progressively more complex as one ascends the scale. For example, under the data/worker function, *comparing* is less demanding in nature and worker performance than *copying, computing,* and others on the scale. Conversely, *mentoring* under the people/worker function is at the highest level of complexity for that group. The definitions of all the worker function terms are provided in Appendix A (pp. 529–531).

3—Data	*8—People*	*1—Things*
0 Synthesizing	0 Mentoring	0 Setting-Up
1 Coordination	1 Negotiating	1 Precision Work
2 Analyzing	2 Instructing	2 Operating/Controlling
3 Compiling	3 Supervising	3 Driving/Operating
4 Computing	4 Diverting	4 Manipulating
5 Copying	5 Persuading	5 Tending
6 Comparing	6 Speaking/Signaling	6 Feeding/Offbearing
	7 Serving	7 Handling
	8 Taking Instructions/ Helping	

The automobile upholsterer is near the top of the scale for things/worker function, having to do precision work to accomplish the job. The work is somewhat less demanding in the data/worker function, which requires compiling, and significantly less complex in the people/worker function of taking instructions/helping. The worker-function scheme provides a means of analyzing each occupation from the basis of a hierarchical structure that may be used to determine specific demands of a job from three distinct dimensions. In the case of the automobile upholsterer, it is essential that the individual be able to work well with his or her hands, use tools or work aids, and follow established standards. The other worker functions are of less importance.

The last three digits (010) of the occupational code are used to further identify a particular occupation within an occupational group. For example, some occupations have the same first six digits; therefore, the last three digits are used to differentiate these occupations. Thus, one can expect to find occupations in the *DOT* with the same first six digits, but none will have the same nine digits. The distinction between similar occupations is determined by alphabetical position within occupational groups. In the example of the automobile upholsterer, this occupation takes the first position within its occupational group and is assigned the digits 010. Each occupation in the group thereafter is assigned a different number by adding 4. More specifically, each occupational group begins with 010 and continues with 014, 018, 022, and so on. The example that follows illustrates this format (U.S. Department of Labor, 1991a, p. 808):

> 780.381-010 Automobile Upholsterer
> 014 Automobile Upholsterer Apprentice
> 018 Furniture Upholsterer
> 022 Furniture Upholsterer Apprentice
> 026 Hearse Upholsterer
> 030 Pad Hand
> 034 Slipcover Cutter

Automobile upholsterer appears in the *DOT* (U.S. Department of Labor, 1991a, p. 808) as follows:

780.381-010   AUTOMOBILE UPHOLSTERER (automotive ser.)
     Repairs or replaces upholstery in automobiles, buses, and trucks: Removes old upholstery from seats and door panels of vehicle. Measures new padding and covering materials, and cuts them to required dimensions, using knife or shears. Adjusts or replaces seat springs and ties them in place. Sews covering material together, using sewing machine. Fits covering to seat frame and secures it with glue and tacks. Repairs or replaces convertible tops. Refurbishes interiors of streetcars and buses by replacing cushions, drapes, and floor coverings. May be designated according to specialty as Body Trimmer (automotive ser.); Bus Upholsterer (automotive ser.); Top Installer (automotive ser.).
     GOE: 05.05.15 STRENGTH: M GED: R3 M2 L3 SVP: 6 DLU: 77

Of particular interest to the counselor are the so-called components of the definition trailer found immediately following the description of the occupation:

- *GOE* is the *Guide for Occupational Exploration* (U.S. Department of Labor, 1979a), which is discussed in the following pages.
- The code assigned to occupations provides an index to interests, aptitudes, adaptability requirements, and other descriptors found in the *GOE*.
- The strength rating is expressed in five categories—Sedentary, Light, Medium, Heavy, and Very Heavy—and is defined in Appendix C of Volume II of the *DOT*.
- GED (General Education Development) ratings are made within six levels (1–6) and explained by reasoning, mathematical, and language development in Appendix C of Volume II of the *DOT*.
- SPV (Specific Vocational) is the amount of time required to learn an occupation's techniques and requirements. For the automobile upholsterer, the number 6 suggests that the preparation time is over one year and up to and including two years.
- DLU (Date of Last Update) indicates the last year in which the descriptive material was obtained.

Using the DOT

Many counselors have found the overwhelming amount of information contained in the *DOT* system insurmountable and too difficult to manage for practical use. Before the fourth edition, two volumes and two supplements were used conjointly, which contributed to the apprehension of critics. The revised fourth edition combines the information contained in previous publications into two volumes to provide easier access to useful information for the career counselor. This section will provide suggestions for making this publication useful for career counseling.

Knowledge of occupations.   The *DOT* is most useful in providing relevant information on a majority of occupations found in the U.S. economy. Each occupation is thoroughly defined, providing the counselor and client a resource for learning facts about occupations to incorporate in the counseling process. Let us return to the example of the automobile upholsterer to make this point clear.

During the process of career exploration, specific information about an occupation becomes relevant. Certain questions are usually considered in the information-seeking sequence. Examples of key questions and answers found in the *DOT* revised fourth edition are as follows:

Question	*Answer*
1. What are the typical work activities performed on this job?	1. Repair, replace, remove, measure, cut, and tack upholstery. Adjust and replace seat springs. Refurbish interiors of streetcars and buses.
2. What are the specific skills needed to perform the required work?	2. Use body members, tools, and work aids. Measure according to required dimensions. Use knife or shears. Sew covering material together.

Question	Answer
3. What is the typical industry(s) in which the job is performed?	3. Automobile service.
4. What are the work aids typically used on this job?	4. Knife, shears, hammer, and sewing machine.

In summary, the *DOT* system can be used most effectively to determine the following: (1) the specific tasks and skills required of occupations; (2) the purpose of the occupation; (3) the machine, tools, equipment, or work aids used; (4) the service, products, materials, and academic subject matter included; (5) the industries with which the occupation is typically identified; (6) the worker/function requirements; and (7) the location (indoors, outdoors, water, and so on) of work for each occupation.

O*NET: The Automated Replacement for the *DOT*

The increasing need for up-to-date occupational information has resulted in a new automated replacement of the *DOT*. O*NET's database was designed to be user-friendly and to help people find jobs and help businesses find employees. It will be used in one-stop career centers (see Chapter 6) established through government funds, in highly visible locations in major cities, and by state employment service offices and anyone who has access to a computer.

To make this system more effective, O*NET will serve as a common language benchmark for identifying and defining worker requirements and characteristics, experience requirements, and occupational requirements and characteristics. The goals of O*NET are to provide comprehensive information about work and workers in a common language that will be useful to students, educators, employers, and workers. O*NET content descriptors are shown in Figure 5-1. O*NET can be accessed as follows: URL: http://www.doleta.gov/programs/onet/onet-hp.htm

Using the Military Career Guide with the DOT

The *Military Career Guide* (1989), covering all branches of the armed forces (army, navy, air force, marine corps, and coast guard), describes military career paths for enlisted personnel and officers. The enlisted and officer occupations are grouped in clusters. For example, the enlisted category of "Transportation and Material Handling Occupation" includes air crew members, air craft launch and recovery specialists, boat operators, cargo specialists, construction equipment operators, flight engineers, petroleum supply specialists, quartermasters, seamen, and truck drivers.

Each military occupation is described by eight factors: (1) function, (2) special qualifications, (3) helpful attributes, (4) physical demands, (5) training provided, (6) work environment, (7) civilian counterparts, and (8) opportunities. Under the civilian counterpart subheading, comparable civilian occupations are listed. For

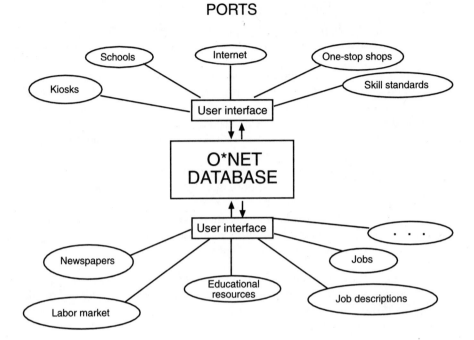

FIGURE 5-1

O*NET content descriptors

SOURCE: DOL/Office of Policy and Research, Division of Skills Assessment and Analysis. Washington, DC 20210.

example, under Flight Operations Specialist for enlisted personnel, the civilian counterparts section states: "Civilian career operations specialists work for commercial and private airlines and air transport companies. They perform duties similar to military flight operations specialist" (*Military Career Guide,* 1989, p. 103). The reader is then referred to a *DOT* index by occupations. Under the Flight Operations Specialist, the following is listed:

> *DOT* #248.367-010 Airplane Dispatch Clerk
> 248.387-010 Flight Operations Specialist
> 912.367-010 Flight-Information Expediter

Using the *DOT* codes, the reader can find more specific information on related civilian occupations in the *DOT* and the *OOH*.

Another interesting feature is the use of the *Armed Services Vocational Aptitude Battery* (U.S. Department of Defense, 1978; see Chapter 7). The results of the test battery are used to help individuals identify military and civilian occupations. By using the score report, individuals are directed to consider occupations on the basis of scores and experience for both military and civilian occupations.

Definitions of Interests:
The *Guide for Occupational Exploration*

A supplement to the *DOT* is entitled *Guide for Occupational Exploration (GOE)*. It was designed primarily to be used by career counselors and by individuals working on their own career exploration. The *GOE* is to be used with a recently developed United States Employment Service (USES) interest inventory and a revised interest checklist. In fact, the data in the *GOE* (all jobs in the United States) are organized to coincide with the twelve interest areas measured by the USES inventory. The USES interest areas in turn are arranged to coincide with Holland's (1992) six modal personal styles and corresponding work environments as shown in Table 5-2 (U.S. Department of Labor, 1979a, appendix).

The *GOE* data are keyed to the interest areas as shown in Table 5-2. An interest area is identified by a two-digit code number accompanied by a brief description as follows (U.S. Department of Labor, 1979a).

1. *Artistic*—Interest in creative expression of feelings or ideas.
2. *Scientific*—Interest in discovering, collecting, and analyzing information about the natural world and in applying scientific research findings to problems in medicine, life sciences, and natural sciences.

TABLE 5-2
Holland and the USES Interest Areas

Holland occupational categories	*USES occupational interest areas*
Artistic	Artistic
Investigative	Scientific
Realistic	Plants and Animals Protective Mechanical Industrial
Conventional	Business Detail
Enterprising	Selling
Social	Accommodating[1] Humanitarian Leading-Influencing[2] Physical Performing

[1] This is a relatively narrow area, but it includes a few occupations covered by Holland's enterprising and realistic categories in addition to those covered by the social category.
[2] This is a broad area. It includes, in addition to those covered by the Holland social category, business management and law/politics occupations covered by the enterprising category, and social science occupations covered by the investigating category.

SOURCE: Adapted from *Guide for Occupational Exploration,* Appendix. U.S. Department of Labor, 1979a.

3. *Plants and Animals*—Interest in activities involving plants and animals, usually in an outdoor setting.
4. *Protective*—Interest in using authority to protect people and property.
5. *Mechanical*—Interest in applying mechanical principles to practical situations, using machines, hand tools, or instruments.
6. *Industrial*—Interest in repetitive, concrete, organized activities in a factory setting.
7. *Business Detail*—Interest in organized, clearly defined activities requiring accuracy and attention to details, primarily in an office setting.
8. *Selling*—Interest in bringing others to a point of view through personal persuasion, using sales and promotion techniques.
9. *Accommodating*—Interest in catering to and serving the desires of others, usually on a one-to-one basis.
10. *Humanitarian*—Interest in helping others with their mental, spiritual, social, physical, or vocational goals.
11. *Leading-Influencing*—Interest in leading and influencing others through activities involving high-level verbal or numerical ability.
12. *Physical Performing*—Interest in physical activities performed before an audience. (p. 8)

General Educational Development Work Groups were allocated to each of the 12 interest areas, primarily based on capabilities (levels, skills, physical requirements, job knowledge) and adaptability (tolerance of work-group situations) required of workers as judged by a group of occupational analysts. A four-digit code and title are assigned to each work group. Each work group is further divided into subgroups that are assigned six-digit codes and titles accompanied by the nine-digit *DOT* codes. The following example illustrates the six-digit code and the title arrangement:

01 Artistic
01.01 Literary Arts
01.01–01 Editing
01.02–02 Creative Writing
01.03–03 Critiquing

Each work group is described in a nontechnical narrative form accompanied by lists of jobs and profiles of worker requirements. The nontechnical approach was adopted to provide a more useful guide for career counseling programs. For example, specific suggestions are given in the guide for (1) identifying occupational areas to be considered, (2) exploring work groups, (3) exploring subgroups and specific occupations, (4) selecting occupational goals, (5) developing a plan for attaining the selected goals, and (6) assigning appropriate occupational classifications.

Using the Guide for Occupational Exploration (GOE)

The *GOE* primarily provides a counseling approach for aiding individuals in determining occupational goals and accessing the vast data bank of occupational information compiled by the U.S. Department of Labor. In other words, it can be used both as a counseling tool and as a reference tool. The career counseling program evolving from USES through the *GOE* will be welcomed by career counselors and should provide guidelines for greater use of related government publications and assessment instruments.

The *GOE* describes career exploration in five steps. The first of these steps has the individual *relate interests to job titles*. For example, if one is interested in 01 Artistic, as shown in the preceding example, all job titles under that work group would be evaluated.

Step 2, *select one or more work groups to explore,* directs the individual to investigate each work group selected in Step 1, evaluating specific job titles by level of skills, training, and work requirements. In most cases, work groups that require the most education, training, and experience are listed first. For example, under the fifth work group, 01 Industrial Supervision and Instruction and Production Technology, 06.01-01, requires more training and experience than Wrapping and Packing, 06.04-38. An overview of a complete work group also provides a career-ladder approach to evaluating related occupational opportunities.

In Step 3, *explore the work group selected,* the individual is directed toward the *GOE* section providing a description of each work group. For example, Medical Services (U.S. Department of Labor, 1991a), 02.03 is described as follows:

02.03 Medical Services

Workers in this group are involved in the prevention, diagnosis, and treatment of human and animal diseases, disorders, or injuries. It is common to specialize in specific kinds of illnesses, or special areas or organs of the body. Workers who prefer to be more general may become general practitioners, family practitioners, or may learn to deal with groups of related medical problems. A wide variety of work environments is available to medical workers ranging from large city hospitals and clinics, to home offices in rural areas, to field clinics in the military or in underdeveloped countries.

What kind of work would you do?

Your work activities would depend upon your specific job. For example, you might:

- perform surgery to correct deformities, repair injuries, or remove diseased organs
- diagnose and treat diseases of the ear, nose, and throat
- diagnose and treat mental illnesses
- remove teeth and perform other mouth surgery
- examine patients to determine causes of speech defects
- oversee all medical activities of a hospital
- examine and treat patients for all physical problems, referring them to specialists when necessary

What skills and abilities do you need for this kind of work?

To do this kind of work, you must be able to:

- use logic and scientific thinking to diagnose and treat human or animal injuries and illnesses

- deal with people or animals when they are in pain or under stress
- stay calm and keep your head in emergencies
- use eyes, hands, and fingers with great skill and accuracy
- deal both with things that are known and obvious and with things which frequently are not easy to recognize or understand
- make important decisions using your own judgment
- make decisions based on information you can measure or verify

How do you know if you would like to or could learn to do this kind of work?

The following questions may give you clues about yourself as you consider this group of jobs.

- Have you taken courses in biology, physiology, or anatomy? Can you understand scientific concepts?
- Have you had any training in first-aid techniques? Have you treated an accident victim? Can you work well with people in emotionally upsetting situations?
- Have you dissected an animal? Can you skillfully handle small instruments such as scalpels, syringes, or tweezers?
- Have you watched medical shows on television? Do you enjoy these programs? Can you understand the technical terms used?
- Have you been a medical corpsman in the armed services? Did you learn techniques and terminology that would be helpful in medical school?

How can you prepare for and enter this kind of work?

Occupations in this group usually require education and/or training extending from four years to over ten years, depending upon the specific kind of work. Academic courses helpful in preparing for the medical sciences are: algebra, geometry, advanced math, chemistry, biological sciences, English, and Latin. Two to four years of undergraduate study followed by four years of advanced study is considered the minimum preparation. Most doctors serve a one- or two-year internship in an approved hospital after graduation from medical school.

Some physicians spend several additional years in study and training as a resident or intern to specialize. Dentists who specialize, teach, or perform research must have post-graduate courses or complete a residency in a hospital or clinic. Medical doctors, dentists, and veterinarians must have a license to practice.

What else should you consider about these jobs?

The training time and cost involved are significant. Workers must adjust to irregular hours, weekend and holiday work, and 24-hour on-call duties.

Workers should update their knowledge and professional skills through periodic courses and continuous study.

If you think you would like to do this kind of work, look at the job titles listed on the following pages. Select those that interest you, and read their definitions in the *Dictionary of Occupational Titles*. (pp. 43–44)

The work-group descriptions and questions provided in the *GOE* offer rich sources of counseling material. The working situation requirements, skills, and training of each work group are potential sources of discussion for further exploration. Interests, aptitudes, skills, traits, and occupationally significant information provide a basis for integrating relevant material and personal characteristics into career exploration.

Step 4, *explore subgroups in specific occupations,* refers the individual to the *DOT.* Specific occupations in each work group are given a *DOT* code (such as Veterinary Meat-Inspector GOV, SER.   073.264-010) that is easily referenced in the *DOT.*

In Step 5, *get it all together,* the individual establishes goals and plans, selecting specific occupations to be evaluated for immediate employment or training required. The requirements for upward movement in a work group are concisely illustrated in the *GOE* steps for career exploration.

The *Occupational Outlook Handbook (OOH)*

The *OOH* is prepared by the Bureau of Labor Statistics, Division of Occupational Outlook, of the U.S. Department of Labor and is published every two years. The 1994-1995 handbook contains employment projections, 250 occupational descriptions grouped in 13 clusters, 125 additional occupational classifications, *DOT* codes, and information on how employment projections are made. Explicit instructions for using this handbook are provided in the introductory section.

A major section of the *OOH* covers employment trends and projections. Because the current job market is so competitive, many individuals turn immediately to this section—particularly readers who will soon be entering the labor force. The 1994-1995 edition provides several interesting graphs of employment shifts and projections, such as those shown in Figure 5-2. Other graphs in this section project total labor force growth, percentage of employment in certain occupations, and so on.

Detailed descriptions of the 250 occupations are also provided. Each occupation is assigned to one of the following 13 occupational clusters:

> Executive, Administrative, and Managerial Occupations
> Professional Specialty Occupations
> Technicians and Related Support Occupations
> Marketing and Sales Occupations
> Administrative Support Occupations, Including Clerical
> Service Occupations
> Agriculture, Forestry, Fishing, and Related Occupations
> Mechanics, Installers, and Repairers
> Construction Trades and Extractive Occupations
> Production Occupations
> Transportation and Material Moving Occupations
> Handlers, Equipment Cleaners, Helpers, and Laborers
> Job Opportunities in the Armed Forces

Each occupation is described in concise, straightforward, nontechnical language, covering the following information: (1) nature of work, (2) working conditions, (3) employment, (4) training and other qualifications and advancement, (5) job outlook, (6) earnings, (7) related occupations, and (8) sources of additional information. The *DOT* code is also listed.

The value of the *OOH* for the career counselor is apparent. Its nontechnical format makes the *OOH* attractive to many readers. The overview of national job

The age distribution of the labor force will continue to shift.

Percent distribution by age of the civilian labor force

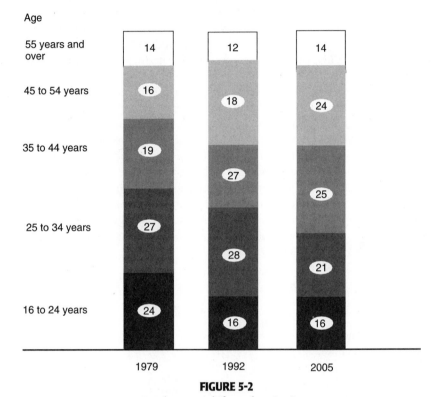

FIGURE 5-2
Employment shifts and projections
SOURCE: U.S. Department of Labor, 1994–1996, p. 13.

prospects and the long-term job outlooks are important resources and are receiving increasing attention from individuals who are planning their education and career. The *OOH* can be assessed on the Internet as follows: URL:http://stats.bls.gov/ocohome.htm

Another government publication, the *Standard Occupational Classification Manual* (U.S. Executive Office of the President, 1977), was created to develop a classification system that standardized occupational data collection. The format and structure of this manual are included in the appendix.

Career Clusters

The idea of career clusters is not new to the field of career counseling. On the contrary, one may consider the *DOT* system and the census classification system as career clusters. For our discussion, let us consider *career clusters* as a method of grouping occupations according to commonalities. As our discussion of career clusters progresses, we will develop the rationale for a variety of cluster systems, emphasizing their usefulness for career-related instructional programs and career guidance.

The attraction of a career cluster arrangement is the provision of a broad overview of occupational fields from which the commonalities of specific and related occupations within the field may be explored. For example, the common training, experience, and other requirements associated with the career cluster are easily identified. Specifically, career cluster systems provide for (1) information concerning methods and levels of entry into an occupational field, (2) related job skills, (3) information concerning commonalities of work requirements and worker functions, and (4) information concerning training requirements for mobility within the occupational field. In this section, we will first consider several forms of cluster organizations to better understand the patterns and structure of cluster systems. In addition, two cluster systems will be presented and discussed.

The first format to be considered is clustering occupations by their products. In this format, the center of attention is on the production aspect of an occupational field and the occupations that form productive units. The illustration that follows is taken from an agricultural component developed by the Maryland State Department of Education (Maley, 1975, p. 87).

Agricultural production:
Animal science
Plant science
Farm mechanics
Farm business management

Agricultural supply and service:
Agricultural chemicals
Feeds
Seeds
Fertilizers

Agricultural mechanical services:
Agricultural power and machinery
Agricultural structures and conveniences
Soil management
Water management
Agricultural mechanics skills
Agricultural construction and maintenance
Agricultural electrification

This form of clustering is most helpful for an individual who wants to evaluate specific jobs based on products of an occupational field. The format would also be useful to the individual who is interested in the field of agriculture but is not sure about the specific jobs available. Clustering jobs by their products provides a unique and interesting way of considering an occupational field.

In most discussions concerning career cluster systems, the term *ladder approach* is used. As the term implies, occupations are placed in ascending order within a cluster, usually by level of training or skills necessary to qualify for a particular occupation. The rationale of this approach is that as individuals are exposed to a career field, they are also exposed to the hierarchy of occupations within the field. Table 5-3 illustrates this concept. A major argument for using this format is that occupational exploration of a career field is greatly enhanced when the skills and other requirements of upward mobility are identified. In addition, the individual is much better prepared to make career decisions when exposed to the commonalities of a career field.

TABLE 5-3
Transportation Clusters

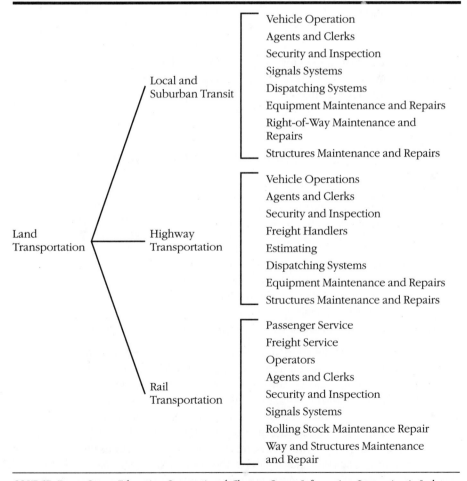

SOURCE: From *Career Education Occupational Clusters,* Career Information Center, Austin Independent School District, Austin, Texas, 1979. Reprinted by permission.

U.S. Office of Education (USOE) Career Clusters

The USOE has prepared 15 occupational clusters to illustrate for students and teachers the career opportunities available in the United States and also to provide a standard method for classifying occupations in career education programs. This system is designed primarily to provide a national format for career-related instructional projects and career guidance programs. By using one classification system, the USOE hopes to provide a basis for designing career-related materials in most educational institutions.

The USOE clusters have a career ladder format, which emphasizes possibilities of upward mobility within each cluster. Each of the clusters is broken down into occupational fields similar to the transportation cluster shown in Table 5-3. The 15 USOE major occupational clusters are as follows:

Agribusiness and Natural Resources	Hospitality and Recreation
Business and Office	Manufacturing
Communications and Media	Marketing and Distribution
Construction	Marine Science
Consumer and Homemaking	Personal Service
Environmental	Public Service
Fine Arts and Humanities	Transportation
Health	

Holland Occupational Classification System (HOC)

Holland's six modal personal styles and corresponding work environments (discussed in Chapter 2) form the structure for the HOC (Holland, 1992). Holland's cluster system is divided into six broad occupational areas:

R—*Realistic* (skilled trades; technical and service occupations)
I—*Investigative* (scientific and some technical occupations)
A—*Artistic* (artistic, musical, and literary occupations)
S—*Social* (educational and social-welfare occupations)
E—*Enterprising* (managerial and sales occupations)
C—*Conventional* (office and clerical occupations)

The use of the classification system is illustrated with the *Self-Directed Search (SDS)* (Holland, 1987b), a self-administered and self-interpreted instrument designed for educational and vocational planning. For example, the results of the *SDS* provide the three most dominant modal personal styles within the HOC. These three dominant styles form a combination of code letters (primary, secondary, and tertiary) for which occupations are provided in the *Occupations Finder* (Holland, 1987c). In the example that follows, several combinations of codes illustrate cluster groups used in this system. In addition to the specific occupations listed, the third edition *DOT* codes and the general educational level for each occupation are provided (Holland, 1987c, pp. 3–5).

Code: RIA	*ED*
Landscape Architect (019.081)	5
Architectural Drafter (017.281)	4
Dental Technician (712.381)	4
All-Around Darkroom Technician (976.381)	4

Code: IAS	*ED*
Economist (050.088)	6
Mathematician, Statistician (020.088)	6
Marketing Research Worker (050.088)	5

Code: ASE	*ED*
Drama Coach (150.028)	5
English Teacher (091.228)	5
Journalist/Reporter (132.268)	5
Drama Teacher (150.028)	5
Dancing Teacher (151.028)	5
Foreign Language Interpreter (137.268)	5

This system has the distinction of being derived from a research base of personality styles and corresponding work environments. The specific occupations suggested in each cluster are based on a number of factors, including values, personality traits, role preferences, and preferred activities. The clusters' emphasis is on the congruence of one's personality type with the suggested work environment. It is quite likely that other classification systems developed in the future will be derived from a research base.

Two-Dimensional Classifications

In our consideration of the form and structure of career clusters, the vertical dimension (*ladder concept*) of upward mobility was emphasized. You will recall that the vertical dimension provides information on requirements, background, and experience necessary to move up the occupational ladder. Let us now consider a two-dimensional system that employs a horizontal *activity dimension* as well. The two-dimensional system simplifies career exploration by combining occupational groups with their primary activities. The two-dimensional system designed by Roe (1956) is an excellent example.

The first dimension of Roe's system (the horizontal dimension) provides a classification of occupations by field as follows: (1) service, (2) business contact, (3) organization, (4) technology, (5) outdoor, (6) science, (7) general culture, and (8) arts and entertainment. The second dimension describes occupations within the field according to the following levels: (1) professional and management—independent responsibility, (2) professional and managerial—other, (3) semiprofessional and small business, (4) skilled, (5) semiskilled, and (6) unskilled. Thus for each of the occupational groups, a hierarchy of occupations is provided. For example, a skilled job in the science occupational group could be technical assistant, whereas the professional and managerial positions in the same occupational group may include scientists, nurses, pharmacists, and veterinarians.

One can readily see the advantage of a two-dimensional classification for both the counselor and the counselee. We live in a world consisting of an overwhelming number of possible job opportunities. Adolescents and adults both are often confused and sometimes frustrated when attempting to find their way through the maze of occupational structure and the vast amount of career-related material available today. By combining occupational groups with training, skills, and other job function demands, the career exploration process is simplified. Finally, the major value of the two-dimensional classification system is that it succinctly illustrates the relationship of educational training and occupational mobility.

A more recent two-dimensional classification system, the World-of-Work Map, was developed by the American College Testing Program (ACT). This system is used in conjunction with the ACT national testing program, the ACT Career-Planning Program, and the computerized career information system, DISCOVER. Most of the occupations used in this system require postsecondary training, as the ACT program is designed for students seeking admission to postsecondary institutions.

The first dimension of this system is the 12 regions of work that represent general areas of work or job families. The second dimension is derived from bipolar work dimensions—data/ideas and people/things. These dimensions provide information on the required work tasks associated with the job family. For example, Region 7 is designated as engineering and other applied technologies and consists of major tasks involved with things (machines/materials).

The usefulness of this system, as in Roe's two-dimensional system, stems from the presentation of broad occupational areas along with corresponding work tasks. In the ACT system, however, the work dimensions are given in terms of data/ideas and people/things. Thus, the individual is not provided only with a system of exploring an occupation within a job family structure but also with the work tasks and the work dimensions associated with that job family.

Summary

1. The *DOT* is an occupational classification system developed by the U.S. Department of Labor. The complete *DOT* consists of the following publications: Volume I—*Definitions of Titles,* Volume II—*Occupational Classifications,* Supplement 1—*Selected Characteristics of Occupations,* Supplement 2—*Selected Characteristics of Occupations by Worker Traits and Physical Strength,* the *DOT* fourth edition, fourth edition revised, and the supplement to the *DOT* fourth edition— *Guide for Occupational Exploration (GOE).*

2. The *DOT* is most useful in providing information on the majority of occupations found in the United States. Each occupation is defined and described by the typical industry in which the job is performed, and the specific skills needed to perform the required work are delineated. The O*NET is the automated replacement for the *DOT.*

3. The supplement to the *DOT* fourth edition, the *GOE,* is designed to be used primarily by career counselors and individuals in career exploration. All jobs in the U.S. economy are organized to coincide with 12 interest areas used in the USES interest inventory. The *GOE* provides a counseling approach for determining occupational goals and accessing the vast data bank of occupational information compiled by the U.S. Department of Labor.

4. The *Military Career Guide* describes career paths for all branches of the armed forces and references the *DOT* codes and comparable civilian occupations.

5. The *OOH* is also prepared by the Department of Labor and is published every two years. The handbook contains employment projections, occupational descriptions, industrial briefs, and an index of job titles by *DOT* code. An overview of national job prospects and long-term job outlooks contained in the *OOH* makes this publication a valuable resource for career counseling programs.

6. Clustering or grouping occupations according to some scheme, such as commonalities of work content, is another method of classifying occupations. The primary attraction of the career cluster arrangement is the provision of a broad overview of occupational fields from which the commonalities of specific and related occupations within the field may be explored.

7. The USOE has prepared 15 occupational clusters to illustrate to students and teachers the career opportunities available in the United States. This system provides a standardized method of classifying occupations for career education programs.

8. Holland's Occupational Classification System is based on six modal personal styles and corresponding work environments. The specific occupations suggested in each cluster are based on a number of factors, including values, personality traits, role preferences, and preferred activities.

9. Two-dimensional classification systems are designed to simplify career exploration by combining occupational groups with their primary activities. Roe's two-dimensional classification of occupations is a good example. More recently, the American College Testing Program developed a two-dimensional classification system combining occupational groups with their primary activities.

Supplementary Learning Exercises

1. Identify the hierarchical components of the worker-functions data, people, and things as described in the *DOT.* List ten separate jobs and describe each job in terms of the coded worker functions of the *DOT.*
2. List and describe at least five ways a counselor can use the *DOT* publications in career counseling programs. Document your suggestions with examples.
3. Using the list of occupations below, choose two or more and do the following:
   a. Define the occupation according to the *DOT.*
   b. Describe the worker-function traits and qualifications.
   c. Identify the industry in which the occupation is found.
      1. Podiatrist   3. Industrial traffic manager
      2. Surveyor   4. Chemist

5. Commercial artist	13. Lather
6. Newspaper reporter	14. Blacksmith or farrier
7. Librarian	15. Furniture upholsterer
8. Civil engineer	16. Brakeman
9. Architect	17. Bank teller
10. Pharmacist	18. Ovenman
11. Printing-press operator	19. Pipe-layer helper
12. Over-the-road truckdrivers	20. Welding-machine operator

4. Choose two or more of the occupations listed and consult the *OOH*. Write a review of each occupation. Include the nature of the work, places of employment, training, employment outlook, earnings, and work conditions.

5. Consult the section of the *OOH* that reviews the outlook for industries. Choose two or more industries and summarize the nature of the industry, occupations in the industry, and the employment outlook.

6. Using the "Additional Sources of Information" section for any occupation described in the *OOH,* write to one of the recommended resources for additional information. Compare the information obtained with that included in the *OOH.* Summarize the similarities and differences.

7. Using the *DOT* section "Occupations in Fabrication and Repair of Musical Instruments," locate and describe three occupations associated with a piano.

8. An individual who has had some experience in working with jewelry is interested in reviewing related jobs. Locate the occupational category in the *DOT* and compile a list of jobs with *DOT* titles for review.

9. Describe the advantages of a two-dimensional classification system. Describe how this type of classification system will aid students in career exploration.

10. Develop a list of advantages and disadvantages of using cluster systems in career counseling programs for junior and senior high school students and college juniors and seniors.

CHAPTER SIX

Using Computers for Career Counseling

New technology, automation, computer science, and increased specialization have brought about numerous changes in occupational structure and job demand in the last three decades. The pace of change is ever-increasing; jobs that existed a few years ago no longer exist. The career counselor has traditionally been faced with an overwhelming amount of career information that must be organized to be useful—always requiring an enormous time commitment. An attempt to keep abreast with basic occupational information itself is very time-consuming. In addition, career counseling has broadened in scope as more emphasis is focused on the variables involved in career life planning. The traditional primary role of occupational information provider is now only part of most career counseling programs. By necessity, the time once allocated to organizing, editing, and classifying occupational information has been reduced by the increasing demand for the development of broad-scope career-related programs. Nevertheless, the effective career counselor must be provided with current occupational information and resources reflecting the ever-changing labor market.

Today's sophisticated student demands up-to-date projections on the work force and uses this information as a major factor in making career decisions. Current job search strategies must include projections of the labor market as well as current job descriptions. Therefore, keeping abreast with changing occupational trends remains a very important part of the career counseling program.

It is not surprising that the career counseling profession has for the most part emphatically endorsed the development of computer-assisted career guidance systems. The fast-paced development of both hardware and software systems has created very attractively designed programs for different populations and for different purposes. The easily accessible up-to-date career information on computer-based programs has given the career counselor a very powerful tool to help meet the needs of our society in the current job market. Other developments such as on-line assessment and interactive career guidance software systems have greatly added to the flexibility of programming. Clearly, career counselors will periodically need easily accessible information to stay abreast with future developments.

The first part of this chapter contains some relevant research about computer-assisted career guidance systems, including a brief discussion of the disadvantages and advantages of using these systems. This discussion is followed by a section that describes system components. The third section covers the development of Career Information Delivery Systems (CIDS), and the fourth section illustrates how DISCOVER (the college and adult version) might be used to counsel a college student. The fifth section provides some sources of labor market and job information on the Internet. Finally, the last section describes how to use and implement a computer-assisted career guidance system.

Some Implications of Research

Evaluating the effectiveness of computer-assisted career guidance systems is an ongoing process undertaken by many counseling professionals, including the Center for the Study of Technology in Counseling and Career Development at Florida State University. The purpose of this center is to provide continuing support for the improved professional use of computer applications in counseling and career guidance. In recent years, the center has contributed a great deal of research for this effort.

In a study comparing the effectiveness of three computer-assisted career guidance systems, DISCOVER (American College Testing Program, 1984), System of Interactive Guidance and Information (SIGI) (Katz, 1975), and SIGI PLUS, the center found that clients who used these systems responded favorably to the career options generated (Peterson, Ryan-Jones, Sampson, Reardon, & Shahnasarian, 1987). In a related study, Kapes, Borman, Garcia, and Compton (1985) compared user reactions to DISCOVER and SIGI. Specifically, they evaluated the reactions (ease of use, quality of information provided, and total effectiveness) of undergraduate and graduate students and found no significant differences among the ratings of the two systems. Perhaps more important, both systems were rated as highly useful.

In a study of general satisfaction of computer-assisted career guidance among undergraduate students at a medium-size Southern university, Miller and Springer (1986) found that students rated DISCOVER as a worthwhile counseling intervention that helped them meet their career exploration needs. In another study analyzing the effectiveness of SIGI, Maze and Cummings (1982) found that the users needed very little assistance with various components. Splete, Elliott, and Borders (1985) have successfully used DISCOVER II and SIGI in their Adult Career Counseling Center at Oakland University.

A study by Roselle and Hummel (1988) compared the effectiveness of using DISCOVER II with two groups of college students, who were separated according to levels (high versus low) of intellectual development as measured by a standardized instrument. To evaluate how effectively they used the system, the students were observed and audiotaped as they interacted with DISCOVER II. The evaluation criteria included how well they learned about career possibilities, integrated career information, reached a career decision, and took appropriate action. The results supported the hypothesis that effective interaction with DISCOVER II is related to intellectual development. These results may not be surprising, but they did suggest that students with low intellectual development need more structure and opportunities for discussion with a counselor during and after their interaction with computer-assisted career guidance systems.

In a related study, Kivlighan, Johnston, Hogan, and Mauer (1994) posed the question, Who benefits most from computer-assisted career guidance systems? This group of researchers used vocational identity to evaluate the effects of SIGI PLUS on 54 college students. They discovered that those students who had a sense of direction and purpose benefited most when exposed to a computer-based career program. These results suggest that strategies used to address clients' purpose and direction are productive methods of assisting them to gain maximum benefits from computer-assisted career guidance systems.

In general, these studies indicate that users react positively to computer-assisted career guidance systems. Moreover, the results suggest that these systems are worthwhile counseling tools that can help clients meet career exploration needs. Therefore, career counselors should be computer literate in terms of understanding the development, rationale, and purpose of computer-assisted career guidance systems and being able to use them on a daily basis.

Disadvantages of Computer-Assisted Career Guidance Systems

Some disadvantages of computer-assisted career guidance systems have also emerged from the research. Maze (1985) pointed out that hardware and software equipment can be very expensive and may require personnel commitments, calling into question the feasibility or even necessity of computerized systems, since career guidance can be accomplished in more traditional ways.

A more serious concern is that of confidentiality (Sampson, 1983). Confidentiality abuses are more likely with electronic data storage systems than with traditional approaches. Velasquez and Lynch (1981) maintained that this problem can be solved with identification codes, passwords, and general restrictions on individuals who may access client information, but career counselors must assure each client of the specific methods used to maintain confidentiality.

The fear among some career counseling professionals is that computerized systems will be the sole source of career guidance programming. Computer-assisted career guidance systems should supplement, but not replace, the counselor. Although software programs are becoming more user-friendly, the career counselor must structure and sustain the client throughout the career guidance sequence. Computers do allow for independent and individualized courses of action but do not remove the career counselor's responsibility for direction and structure.

Finally, the counselor must address the problem of user anxiety. Inadequately prepared users may easily become discouraged with computerized systems. Personnel must be available to instruct the user during the initial stages, assist users through various phases of the system, and follow up on users who have experienced the system (Sampson & Pyle, 1983).

Advantages of Computer-Assisted Career Guidance Systems

The interactive capability of computerized systems allows users to become more actively involved in the career guidance process. It is hoped that this active involvement will encourage users to ask more questions of the process itself. Second, user motivation is sustained through the unique use of immediate feedback. Third, the opportunity to individualize the career exploration process provides opportunities to personalize career search strategies. Fourth, computer-assisted career guidance systems provide systematic career exploration and career decision programs that may be accessed at any given time. Finally, access to large databases of up-to-date information for local, state, national, and international locations is immediately available.

Types of Computer-Assisted Career Guidance Systems

The most common types of computer-assisted career guidance systems are information systems and guidance systems. Information systems provide users with direct access to large databases on such subject areas as occupational characteristics (work tasks, required abilities, work settings, salary) and lists of occupations, educational and training institutions, military information, and financial aid.

Guidance systems are typically much broader in scope. They contain a variety of available modules, such as instruction in the career decision process, assessment, prediction of future success, assistance with planning, and development of strategies for future plans. Many computer-assisted career guidance systems contain an information system as well as a guidance system. Many systems are directed toward certain populations, such as students in junior high school, high school, and college; some systems are for people who work in organizations; and some address the needs of retirees.

Computer-assisted career guidance systems have undergone vast changes in the last decade. Future modifications could come even more quickly as these systems are designed to meet the needs of an ever-changing work environment and the skills associated with rapid technical change.

Understandably, many of the computer-assisted career guidance systems have similar components and are accessed through menus that provide some flexibility for individual needs. The following components are found in most systems:

1. Occupational information
2. Armed service information

3. Information about postsecondary institutions of higher learning
4. Information on technical and specialized schools
5. Financial aid information
6. Interest inventories
7. Decision-making skills

Other common components include:

1. Local job information files
2. Ability measures
3. Value inventories
4. Prediction of success in college
5. Job search strategies
6. How to prepare a résumé
7. Information on job interviews
8. Components for adults

The Development of Career Information Delivery Systems

The growth of the Career Information Delivery Systems (CIDS) was a direct result of funding from the National Occupational Information Coordinating Committee (NOICC) through its State Occupational Information Coordinating Committees (SOICCs). Improved microcomputer technology in the 1980s resulted in a movement away from mainframe delivery systems and significantly reduced the cost of implementing a system. Career information is organized in most systems on a national and state basis. Some of the national commercial systems include options to develop state and local information (McCormac, 1988).

Since its beginning in the late 1980s, CIDS has become a very popular tool that has been used effectively within comprehensive counseling programs in schools, colleges, and by adults seeking further training or education or different jobs. It is estimated that in 1994 more than 40 states had CIDS users as official state systems, and more than 9 million people used them at about 20,000 different sites (Mariani, 1995-96).

The four components common to most CIDS are assessment, occupational search, occupational information, and educational information. On-line assessment includes the use of instruments that measure values, interests, skills, aptitudes, or experiences as they relate to career choice. Many systems will accept results from additional assessment instruments, such as the *Self-Directed Search, ASVAB, Strong Interest Inventory,* and *GATB* (referenced and discussed in Chapter 7).

Skills assessment is a relatively new tool to help students and experienced workers identify skills desired and needed in the current work force. The American College Testing Program's *Work Keys System* is designed to help learners make transitions from school to work or from job to job. It assesses the skills individuals possess, determines the skills that jobs require, and provides instructional support to help learners improve their skills. The process includes a comparison of skill levels required for particular jobs with learners' skill levels (American College Testing Program, 1996a).

The CIDS occupational search is very innovative. Users can generate lists of occupations from assessment results. Second, as users choose search variables from a list, the level of congruence the user gives to each variable is used by the computer to generate lists of occupations. If a user is not satisfied and wishes to explore other occupations, systems allow users to change the criteria used in the original search. Finally, a user may simply select an occupation for review.

The occupational information component contains key information about a large number of occupations, such as the nature of the work, working conditions, numbers employed, job outlook, education and training requirements, recommended school courses, earnings, related occupations, physical demands, common career ladders, and sources for more information. Many CIDS programs include state and local information about occupations.

The educational component includes information on vocational and technical schools, two- and four-year colleges, and, in some systems, graduate schools. Included in this component are admission requirements, programs of study, types of degrees offered, school affiliation, community setting, tuition and fees, financial aid information, total enrollment, housing information, athletic programs and other student activities, student body characteristics, military training opportunities, special programs, and sources for more information (Mariani, 1995-96).

Career development programs in schools use CIDS in many innovative ways. For example, counselors use printouts of occupational descriptions in grades 3 and 4 to illustrate the kind of information that can be found in their local CIDS.

In a related type of program, students in elementary schools are asked to make a list of occupations that interest them. The counselor then provides printed descriptions of the requested occupations. Both programs are used as an introduction to CIDS that primes the students to use the career exploration program individually when it is available to them.

The extent of the use of CIDS in secondary schools is often dependent on the number of staff or computers available. In some schools, peer counselors or adult volunteers are used to introduce students to CIDS.

CIDS is also integrated into the curriculum in some junior and senior high schools. Some schools offer career exploration programs that include the use of CIDS. Others infuse career exploration into existing courses, such as a major writing project in a English class on one's career choice.

Universities and colleges usually incorporate CIDS in their career center as a part of a total career exploration system. Credit courses in career exploration are also offered at some postsecondary institutions. Some instructors require that students do a career search as a part of a course requirement, or they assign projects that include the use of CIDS.

CIDS are also used at other sites, such as employment and training offices, vocational rehabilitation offices, state job services, public libraries, prisons, and public businesses. There is a movement by the federal government to set up one-stop career centers in several states. As Mariani (1995-96, p. 22) put it, "Some people may find themselves choosing a career, getting a job, and buying a new wardrobe all at the local mall."

More information can be obtained from state CIDS directors and from the following sources.

National Occupational Coordinating Committee
2100 M Street NW., Suite 156
Washington, DC 20037
202-653-5665

Association of Computer-Based Systems for Career Information
c/o National Career Development Association
5999 Stevenson Avenue
Alexandria, VA 22304-3300
703-823-9800, ext. 309

National Career Development Association
5999 Stevenson Avenue
Alexandria, VA 22304-3300
703-823-9800

Center for the Study of Technology in Counseling and Career Development
Florida State University Career Center
5408 University Center, 4th Level
Tallahassee, FL 32306-1035
904-644-6431

Using DISCOVER

The original DISCOVER system was designed to assist high school and college students in making career choices. DISCOVER for colleges and adults, published by the American College Testing Program (1987), contains the following modules:

1. Beginning the career journey
2. Learning about the world of work
3. Learning about yourself
4. Finding occupations
5. Learning about occupations
6. Making educational choices
7. Planning next steps
8. Planning your career
9. Making transitions

Although users are advised to proceed through the modules in a sequential order, certain modules can be accessed on demand. For example, an individual seeking information about educational institutions can access two-year or four-year college lists. In the example of Yasmin, a freshman who is undecided about a major or a career, the sequential order is most desirable.

Yasmin: In high school, I never gave too much thought to a career, even though my parents tried to persuade me to make up my mind. I guess I just didn't get around to it. I hope you can help me decide.

Counselor: We have several ways to help you. First I'll explain the various materials we have, the usual sequence students go through, and the time involved.

After the counselor informed Yasmin of the career guidance programs, he obtained a time commitment from her.

Counselor: I want you to understand that you will have to spend considerable effort and time to find the answers to your questions. If you agree to that, I believe we can help you make a good decision about your future.

Yasmin chose the DISCOVER program from the range of options offered by the counselor.

Yasmin: I actually like to work with computers. In high school, we used computers in several of our courses.

The counselor informed Yasmin of the various components of DISCOVER, their purpose, and how to access them. Yasmin began with Module I. She was asked to respond to questions as follows:

3 = I already know this
2 = I know something about this, but not enough
1 = I don't know this at all[1]

The first group of questions concerned the world of work. For example, Yasmin was asked whether she knew that academic majors can be grouped in a logical way, and how choices of academic majors are related to occupations. In the second group of questions, she was asked about herself; that is, if she had knowledge about her abilities, interests, or work-related values. In the third section, she was asked to explore occupations in terms of how they related to her interests, abilities, values, and experiences. Other questions dealt with learning about occupations, making decisions about education, planning next steps, planning a career, and coping with transitions.

After Yasmin completed these questions and the computer compiled the information, the counselor requested a printout to determine what direction Yasmin should take. In Yasmin's case, the greatest needs seemed to involve knowing about the world of work, herself, and which occupations to explore. From this list, the counselor and Yasmin decided that she would take the ability, interest, and value inventory offered in the system.

[1]This and the following computerized material in this section are from the DISCOVER programs, college and adult version. American College Testing Program, Iowa City, Iowa. Reprinted by permission.

Yasmin began with the interest inventory offered in Career Planning Task Two. She received the following instructions: Consider whether you would like or dislike doing each of the activities listed, not your ability to do it. For each of the 90 activities, use the following key. Circle your choice.

L = If you LIKE the activity
I = If you are INDIFFERENT (don't care one way or the other about the activity)
D = If you DISLIKE the activity

Then Yasmin moved on to the abilities inventory, where she was asked to rate herself in comparison to other persons her own age. She was instructed to use the following scale:

5 = High (top 10% of persons my age)
4 = Above average (upper 25%)
3 = Average (middle 50%)
2 = Below average (lower 25%)
1 = Low (bottom 10%)

Yasmin was asked to rate her ability in meeting people and helping others; that is, whether she was good in sales, leadership, organization, and clerical or mechanical tasks. She was asked about her manual dexterity and her numerical, scientific, creative/artistic, creative/literary, reading, language usage, and spatial abilities.

On the values inventory, she was instructed to read each value carefully, mark one of the choices provided, and rank-order the values from 1 through 9. An example of one value is listed below.

Priority   *Value*

☐   *1. Creativity in a job means:*
        • discovering, designing, or developing new things, and/or
        • being inventive in your job, and/or
        • finding new ways to make or do things

        What opportunity for creativity do you want in a job?
        4 = High
        3 = Medium to high
        2 = Medium
        1 = Skip this value

After completing this module, Yasmin made an appointment to see the counselor.

Meanwhile, Yasmin could investigate science careers on her own. The combination of her scores on the inventories suggested that she was interested in ideas and things, as opposed to people and data. (The DISCOVER World-of-Work Map depicts 12 regions of work represented by general areas of work or job families, and a second dimension of work by Data/Ideas and People/Things. A third dimension refers users to Business Contact, Business Operations, Technical, Science,

Arts, or Social Services.) Yasmin was directed toward Region 9, Natural Science and Mathematics, and Region 8, Medical Specialties, Technologies, Engineering, and Related Techniques. Her second dimension was Ideas and Things, and the third dimension was in Science. At the next counseling session, the following exchange took place.

Counselor: · You seem to have a definite interest in the sciences and medical specialties, Yasmin. What do you think?

Yasmin: All I can say is, I did well in biology, chemistry, and math in school. Maybe that's the reason I ended up in this area.

As the conversation continued, it became clear that Yasmin needed more information about occupations, since her work experience was very limited. She decided to go to Career Planning Task 6: Selecting Occupations. In this module, she was asked to select desirable characteristics of occupations. For example, in selection of a work setting she responded to the following:

Work Setting (where you'd work)—I want to work:

   a. Indoors in an office
   b. Indoors other than in an office
   c. Outdoors
   d. Combination of indoors and outdoors

Other characteristics Yasmin evaluated were "employment outlook," "work hours," "supervision of others," "travel required," "unusual pressure," "beginning income," and "educational level."

Yasmin wanted a job projected to have openings by 1999. She also preferred working indoors as opposed to outdoors and wanted a regular shift of seven to eight hours a day. Yasmin also indicated that she would be willing to earn a bachelor's degree or continue with graduate work, if necessary, to meet her goal. She was interested in a starting salary of about $30,000 per year.

After providing the program with a measure of interests, abilities, values, and characteristics of desired occupations, Yasmin was presented with a list of occupations for consideration. She asked the counselor to assist her in evaluating these findings.

Yasmin: I have a long list of occupations here, and I'm not sure what to do with all of them.

Counselor: Well, follow the instructions and you can get more information about each of them. Perhaps you might want to think about or explore several of them further. Remember, you can get a printout for the ones you select.

Yasmin then selected some occupations from the list. One of her selections was Medical Technologist. She requested a detailed printout that included a description of the work tasks, work settings, tools and materials used, related civilian occupations, related military occupations, education or training possibilities, special requirements, personal qualities needed, the career ladder, salary potential, projected demand for new workers, the advantages and disadvantages, and where to get more information. In addition, the code for the *Dictionary of Occupational Titles* was given along with the code for the *Standard Occupational Classification* and the *Guide for Occupational Exploration.*

In subsequent counseling sessions, Yasmin concluded that medical technology was of great interest, and she decided to further explore this field. To gain more information, she visited a local hospital where medical technologists were employed. In the course of considering this career, Yasmin discovered that medical technology matched her interests, values, abilities, work tasks, and desired work setting. She was also pleased to discover that the starting salaries for medical technologists generally met her financial requirements. Yasmin later returned to the computer for more information concerning training sites and financial aid.

DISCOVER provided meaningful interactive tasks and information modules to help Yasmin make a career decision. The on-line assessment program provided an effective method of evaluating interests, abilities, and values. The flexibility of this program made it possible to access relevant tasks and data as needed, such as job descriptions and education-training information. Using the job description, the counselor encouraged Yasmin to seek more information from other materials and from an on-site visit.

Finally, the counselor should be aware that computer-based programs are changing rapidly. DISCOVER is an on-line program that is very script-driven and may be replaced with more interactive programs. In the meantime, the counseling sessions with Yasmin provide a good introduction to currently used computer-based career programs.

DISCOVER Multimedia

DISCOVER Multimedia has recently been introduced as a new version of DISCOVER in compact disc-interactive (CD-i) format. It should not be confused with CD-ROM. This new system does not require a computer, as it can be used on a color TV and a disc player.

DISCOVER Multimedia consists of three discs. Disc 1 is entitled "Learning about Yourself" and includes the opportunity of visually identifying occupations that match specific interests and abilities. Six video sequences that illustrate the World-of-Work Map are also available.

Disc 2 contains detailed information of approximately 500 different occupations through the use of a slide show that enhances the text for each occupation. There is a 15- to 20-second narrative for each occupation, accompanied by color photographs.

Disc 3 contains a two-year and four-year college search sequence. A narrative is accompanied by two photographs of most four-year institutions.

The publishers of this program suggest that DISCOVER Multimedia will encourage young people, especially those who are accustomed to playing video games, to learn more about career information. The major rationale for this new program is that photographs and full-motion video will make career planning not only more enjoyable but also more realistic.

Steps in Using Computer-Assisted Career Guidance Programs

Throughout this chapter, several direct references have been made to the use of computer-assisted career guidance programs. The primary purpose has been to emphasize the computer's role in meeting the career exploration needs of individuals and groups. Structured procedures that utilize components of computerized programs as a career counseling assistant are a major advantage. Computer-assisted career guidance programs are one of the major components of a total career guidance program. As such, they are coordinated with other components, materials, and procedures; they are not the *sole* delivery system. Individual needs may dictate the use of several components including computerized systems; or in some cases, computerized systems alone may meet client needs. Within this framework, the following steps for using computer-assisted career guidance programs are offered.

1. *Assessment of needs.* Individualized needs of each student should determine the direction of program use and the components accessed. For example, one student may need only information on financial aid programs. A student moving to a distant state may be seeking information on two-year and four-year colleges within driving distance of his or her future residence. Others, like Yasmin, can be helped in determining their career direction.

2. *Orientation.* Each student or group of students should be given a thorough orientation on the purpose, goals, and demonstrated use of computerized systems.

3. *Individualized programs.* Each individual should follow a preconceived plan based on needs. This plan can be modified as needed; the flexibility of computerized programs can be a distinct advantage when plans change.

4. *Counselor intervention.* The individualized plan should provide for counselor intervention. For example, an appropriate point may be a discussion of the results of one of the inventories. Providing sources of additional occupational information and discussing tentative occupational choices are good strategies in the career exploration process. The point is that individuals should not be "turned over to the computer" without any planned intervention from a counselor.

5. *On-line assistance.* Provisions should be made to assist individuals in various stages of career exploration. How to return to the main menu or how to access various components can be frustrating experiences for the computer novice. Questions that can be anticipated are: "How can I get this printed?" "I need to stop now and go to class—what should I do?" "I hit the wrong key, can you help me?"

6. *Follow-up.* As in all phases of career exploration, individual progress should be monitored. Career counselors should help individuals sustain their motivation, evaluate their progress, and evaluate the effectiveness of programs.

These activities are designed to develop the individual's decision-making skills. The counselor should assist the student at various stages, including helping the student and accessing different areas of the system. Most important, the counselor should make use of the information obtained from the computer for more effective career counseling.

Career Information on the Internet

The Internet may be described as a proverbial sleeping giant that has enormous potential for the career counseling profession. We are beginning to tap the resources that are available now, but the future use of Internet will be an important subject of the career counseling profession in the generations to come. For the present, information that can be obtained from Internet includes economic, labor market, job search, and career development resources.

In this section, we will briefly review some of the information available on the Internet. For more information, see the March 1996 issue of the *WORKFORCE* journal. You may also want to access information from the National Occupational Information Coordinating Committee (NOICC) at http://www.profiles.iastate.edu/ided/ncdc/noicc.htm. Following are some current programs.

America's Job Bank
URL: http://www.ajb.dni.us

> A computerized network that links 1,800 state employment offices and contains a national pool of active job opportunities. This is currently one of the most widely used sites.

America's Labor Market Information System (ALMIS)
URL: http://www.ecu.edu/-lmi.html

> This site provides information about various projects, such as the latest developments on job banks and technology resource centers.

U.S. Department of Education
URL: http://www.ed.gov

> This site is designed to help parents, teachers, and students. Information on such topics as financial aid, grants, and educational software packages can be reviewed, and some of it can be downloaded.

Training Technology Resource Center (TTRC)
URL: http://www.ttrc.doleta.gov

> This site offers information on federal and state employment and training activities. Information about state agencies, including CIDS programs, can be obtained from this site. (See Chapter 5 for information on O*NET.)

Be aware that there are many other public and commercial sites available for career-related information. Some sites include lists of employers, colleges, and government job sources. Others include career-related associations and organizations as well as career libraries. Still others include job listings from city newspapers and the international job market. You may also submit your résumé to a database, or you may want to participate in an on-line job fair.

This brief introduction to the Internet suggests that computerized career-related programming has only begun to surface. We can expect to see a growing list of innovative ideas that will build to a comprehensive linked system of the future. One of the goals of the Internet is to build a nationwide talent bank to help employers and prospective employees make initial contacts (Woods & Ollis, 1996). The unique career-related programs developed at this time should serve as the foundation for the continuing evolution of computerized career-related programming.

Implementing a Computer-Based Program

It has often been said that the first steps in implementing a new program are the most important ones. This cliché certainly applies to implementing a computer-assisted system for career guidance. Systematic planning for computer-assisted systems is highly related to their effectiveness and acceptance by students, faculty, and community (Sampson, 1994). In this section, we will review an implementation model, but first we will discuss implementation problems.

The information contained in Box 6-1 identifies problems associated with implementing a computer-assisted career guidance (CACG) program. Some of these identified problems suggest a lack of effective planning, whereas others are associated with inadequate staff training and a lack of integration with other career services. For instance, staff must be aware that CACG does not take the place of counselor intervention with clients and that clients need assistance with linking information found on CACG to their career search and other assistance. The significant danger here is the false assumption that CACG is the sole career service component!

Sampson (1994) makes a very important point that implementation problems could very easily limit CACG's long-term effectiveness. Furthermore, all parties must be educated to the effective use of CACG *before* it is selected and put on-line. Proper implementation suggests that CACG is an important component of career services.

The process of implementing CACG includes the following seven-step implementation model developed by Sampson (1994).

1. Begin with a program evaluation to determine how well current guidance services meet clients' needs. If the evaluation discloses unmet needs, the staff should highlight the purpose and goals regarding how a computer-based system can close the gap. To accomplish this goal, establish a selection committee.

2. Have the committee identify desired software products that will meet clients' needs. After reviewing systems, the committee should determine appropriate software and hardware.

3. Software integration involves comprehensive plans on how a system will be implemented. This implies that committee members have become very knowl-

---

BOX 6-1
CACG Implementation Problems

Inadequate planning
Use of "ad hoc" or "no planning" approaches
Inadequate linkage between computer use and organizational needs
Inadequate needs assessment prior to computer use
Adoption of systems overly influenced by funding or administrators
Piecemeal rather than systematic adoption of systems
Limited staff participation in decision making about CACG

Poor integration of CACG systems within career services
Lack of a suitable context for clients to process their use of information
   resources
Lack of counselor intervention for clients who need assistance
Lack of evaluation data for demonstrating accountability and for improv-
   ing CACG integration
Scheduling problems
Inconsistent support from CACG developers

Inadequate staff training
Imbalance between training expenditures and hardware/software ex-
   penditures
Inadequate training with respect to
   hands-on experience with systems
   a conceptual basis for comparing and selecting systems
   integrating CACG with various service delivery models
Unrealistic expectations about the performance of computer applications
Unrealistic expectations about the time needed for implementation
Confusion regarding the role of the counselor and the role of the computer

Staff anxiety and resistance concerning CACG
Concern over changes in the workplace
Negative staff attitude as a result of implementation problems

NOTE: Staff anxiety and resistance are negatively influenced by planning,
   integration, and training problems described above.

SOURCE: From *Effective Computer-Assisted Career Guidance: Occasional Paper Number 2,*
by James P. Sampson, 1994. Center for the Study of Technology in Counseling and Career
Development, Florida State University. Reprinted by permission.

---

edgeable about the chosen system. Plans include how to mesh the system with the
overall guidance program and to specify roles of staff members, operational procedures, and evaluation systems.

4. The next step involves comprehensive staff training. The effectiveness of a
computer-assisted guidance program is highly related to a working knowledge of
the system.

5. The trial use determines how well the staff has done its homework and how students react to using the system. The system begins operation after successful trial evaluations.

6. The system becomes operational.

7. Evaluation of service delivery is seen as an ongoing process. Evaluation feedback suggests that there should be continual refinement. Fast-paced development of hardware and software probably means that computer-assisted programs may change every year.

The seven-step implementation program was developed by Sampson (1994) of Florida State University, Center for the Study of Technology in Counseling and Career Development. Anyone seeking information about computer-assisted career guidance programs should contact this center.

Summary

1. The rationale for computerized career counseling stems from the need for up-to-date information and the unique capabilities of the computer to satisfy this need. A number of computerized counseling systems with different combinations of computer hardware and software and different sets of objectives have been developed.

2. Recent research indicates a positive reaction to computer-assisted guidance systems by users. Moreover, the results suggest that the systems evaluated are worthwhile for counseling intervention and help individuals meet career exploration needs.

3. The most common types of computer-assisted career guidance systems are information systems and guidance systems.

4. Career Information Delivery Systems (CIDS) were developed with the assistance of NOICC and the SOICCs. One of the major purposes was to give states the opportunity to develop state and local data.

5. The DISCOVER program for colleges and adults is an example of a system that includes on-line assessment programs, job descriptions, and educational information, all of which are easily accessible.

6. The Internet has tremendous potential for the career counselor. Currently, information on the Internet includes economic, labor market, job search, and career development resources.

7. A seven-step implementation model should be followed when implementing a computer-based program.

Supplementary Learning Exercises

1. Visit a school, college, or agency that has a computer-based career information system. Request to preview the system, and identify the major components in a written report.

2. Outline and discuss the advantages of having a computer-assisted career guidance system in one or more of the following: a high school, a community college, a four-year college, or a community agency providing career counseling to adults.

3. Form two groups and debate the issues relating to the following statement: Computer-assisted career guidance systems will replace the career counselor.

4. Develop a local visit file (individuals in selected occupations who agree to visits by students) that could be included as a component in a computer-assisted career guidance system. Describe the advantages of a visit file.

5. Interview a career counselor who has substantial experience in using computer-assisted career guidance systems. Write a report on the systems used and summarize the counselor's evaluation of the systems.

6. Describe the advantages of having a statewide occupational information data bank of job openings and labor forecasts. How could you incorporate this information in career counseling programs in high schools, community colleges, four-year colleges or universities, and community programs for adults?

7. Decide what is meant by an interactive computer-assisted career guidance system. Illustrate your description with your own version of an example script.

8. What do you consider to be the major components of a computer-assisted program for adults? Defend your choices.

9. Compare the DISCOVER subsystems with the SIGI-PLUS subsystems. What are the major differences? What would you adopt for a community college? Give your reasons.

10. Explain your conception of the future role of computer-assisted career guidance systems in educational settings and community programs.

CHAPTER SEVEN

Using Standardized Assessment in Career Counseling

The development of standardized tests and assessment inventories has been closely associated with the vocational counseling movement.[1] As early as 1883, the U.S. Civil Service Commission used competitive examinations for job placement (Kavruck, 1956). Multiple aptitude-test batteries developed during the mid-1940s have been widely used in educational and vocational counseling (Anastasi, 1988). Scholastic aptitude tests used as admission criteria for educational institutions were implemented through the Educational Testing Service (ETS) established in 1947 and the American College Testing Program (ACT) established in 1959.

The use of aptitude tests in career counseling—specifically using assessment instruments to predict success in an occupation or in an educational/training program—has generated considerable controversy. The results of two widely quoted studies challenged the value of tests as predictors of future success; that is, in predicting how one will perform on a job or in a training program. A longitudinal study by Thorndike and Hagen (1959) followed the career patterns of 10,000 men who had taken tests during World War II to determine whether these test results were valid predictors of their job success. The study suggested that tests given 12 years earlier did not accurately predict occupational success. A study by Ghiselli (1966) suggested that predicting success in occupational training programs on the basis of test results is only moderately reliable. These widely quoted studies and other issues—including the use of tests for special populations (ethnic groups and women)—have brought confusion concerning the proper uses of assessment instruments in career counseling programs.

Currently, more emphasis has been placed on skills identification through

---

[1]The terms *vocational* and *occupational counseling* are now incorporated in the more widely used term *career counseling*.

informal techniques (Holland, 1992; Bolles, 1993; Zunker, 1990). The growing popularity of informal methods of identifying skills strongly suggests that some assessment of individual aptitudes, skills, and other individual characteristics is of vital importance in the career decision process, despite the controversy surrounding standardized aptitude tests and job success predictions. Healy (1990) has also suggested encouraging clients to develop self-assessment skills. These skills would help them focus on their choices rather than on those suggested by a standardized measure. What seems to be the major issue is how assessment results can be used most effectively in career counseling programs. A good approach considers assessment results as only one facet of individuality to be evaluated in the career decision process.

More specifically, career decision making is seen as a continuous counseling process within which all aspects of individuality receive consideration. Skills, aptitudes, interests, values, achievements, personality characteristics, and maturity are among the more important aspects that might be evaluated by assessment measures. Thus, assessment results constitute counseling information that can provide the individual with an awareness of increased options and alternatives and encourage greater individual exploration in the career decision process.

Many of the career theorists discussed in Chapters 2 and 3 suggest that all relevant information be included in the career decision process to encourage greater individual participation and consideration of a wider range of career options. Furthermore, the more knowledge we have of individual characteristics, the greater assurance we have of a balance of considerations in career decision making. Career counseling programs that are designed to incorporate all relevant information should lessen the chances that career decision making could be dominated by any one factor.

In this chapter, we focus on the use of standardized assessment results in career counseling. We consider assessment results as information that is used with other materials to stimulate and enhance career exploration. The discussion of assessment results includes aptitude and achievement tests and interest, personality, values, career maturity inventories, and card sorts. Brief examples of applications of assessment results are included to help clarify the use of specific tests or inventories. These examples provide only brief descriptions of anonymous individuals and do not describe other materials and program considerations involved with a specific test or inventory.[2] With the exception of achievement tests (major publishers listed only), representative examples of tests and inventories are provided.[3]

Aptitude Tests

Aptitude tests primarily measure specific skills and proficiencies or the ability to acquire a certain proficiency (Cronbach, 1990). More specifically, aptitude test scores provide an index of measured skills that is intended to predict how well an

[2]The brief descriptions may appear to oversimplify the career counseling process and ignore other data and materials.

[3]The use of assessment results of culturally diverse groups and individuals with disabilities is covered in Chapters 18 and 19. The issues of gender bias and gender fairness in career interest measurement are discussed in Chapter 15.

individual may perform on a job or in an educational or training program. In addition, they indicate an individual's cognitive strengths and weaknesses; that is, differential abilities that provide an index to specific skills. For example, a measure of scholastic aptitude tells us the probability of success in educational programs. A clerical aptitude test score provides an index of ability to perform clerical duties. In the former example, we are informed of combinations of aptitudes that predict scholastic success, whereas in the latter, we are provided with more specific measures of skills needed to perform well on a specific job.

Aptitude tests may be purchased as batteries measuring a number of aptitudes and skills or as single tests measuring specific aptitudes. Combinations of battery scores provide prediction indexes for certain educational or training criteria, as well as performance criteria on certain occupations that require combinations of skills. An example of an aptitude battery is the *General Aptitude Test Battery (GATB)* published by the U.S. Department of Labor (1970b). This test was originally developed by the U.S. Employment Service for state employment counselors. The *GATB* measures the following nine aptitudes: intelligence, verbal, numerical, spatial, form perception, clerical perception, motor coordination, finger dexterity, and manual dexterity.

Other aptitude tests published as single-test booklets measure a wide range of specific skills including dexterity, mechanical comprehension, occupational attitude, clerical aptitude, design judgment, art aptitude, and measures of musical talent.

Although aptitude tests primarily provide a basis for predicting success in an occupation or in training programs, they may also be used as counseling tools for career exploration. In this approach, measured individual traits provide a good frame of reference for evaluating potential careers. The following sample cases illustrate the use of aptitude test batteries.

> Jorge, a college freshman, reports to the Career Resource Center that he is interested in architecture. While his father owns an architectural firm, Jorge is not sure of his own aptitude for architectural work. The career counselor explains that a number of skills are needed for this particular profession and suggests that Jorge should attempt to identify those skills from resources in the career library. After identifying several required skills, Jorge's past academic record and work experiences are evaluated to determine if he has used any of these skills in the past. Eventually, it is decided that two skills, space relations and form perception, would be best evaluated through standardized aptitude tests. Measurement of these particular skills was considered the most important information to be included in the career decision-making process.
>
> Susan is a senior in high school and does not plan to attend college. She is interested in obtaining work after graduation from high school. Her academic record indicates she is an average student with no particular strengths evidenced by academic grades. Her interests have not crystallized to the point at which she would be able to specify a particular occupational interest. Several assessment inventories were administered including a complete battery of aptitude tests. These scores were used to discover areas of specific strengths and weaknesses for inclusion in Susan's career exploration program. Identification of specific aptitudes was seen as a stimulus for discovering potential career considerations.

Ron is returning to the work force after a serious head injury received in a car accident. During several months of recovery, his previous job in construction work was terminated. He is now interested in "looking for other kinds of work." An aptitude battery was administered to determine possible deficits resulting from the head injury. As the counselor suspected, the test scores indicated poor finger and manual dexterity. Jobs requiring fine visual-motor coordination had to be eliminated from consideration in career exploration.

In Jorge's case, the aptitude test was used to verify or to check the feasibility of a particular career choice. That is, Jorge had decided on a career and wanted to determine whether he had the aptitude requirements of that career. In Susan's case, aptitude scores provided stimulus for the discussion of measured aptitudes along with other materials used in career counseling. Susan was provided with specific focus in career exploration. In the final example, Ron's deficiencies were found and considerable time in career exploration was saved.

Following are representative examples of multiple aptitude test batteries available on the market today.

The Differential Aptitude Test (DAT)
G. K. Bennet, H. G. Seashore, and A. G. Wesman
The Psychological Corporation
555 Academic Court
San Antonio, Texas 78204-2498

This test consists of eight subtests: verbal reasoning, numerical ability, abstract reasoning, space relations, mechanical reasoning, clerical speed and accuracy, spelling, and language usage. The entire battery takes over three hours to administer. This battery was designed primarily for use with high school and college students. When verbal and numerical scores are combined, a scholastic aptitude score is created. Other subtests are used for vocational and educational planning.

The General Aptitude Test Battery (GATB)
United States Employment Service
Washington, DC 20210

This battery is composed of 8 paper-and-pencil tests and 4 apparatus tests. Nine abilities are measured by the 12 tests: intelligence, verbal aptitude, numerical aptitude, spatial aptitude, form perception, clerical perception, motor coordination, finger dexterity, and manual dexterity. This test is administered to senior high school students and adults. Testing time is two and a half hours. Test results may be used for vocational and educational counseling and placement.

Flanagan Aptitude Classification Tests (FACT)
J. C. Flanagan
SRA-McGraw-Hill
220 East Daniel Dale
De Soto, TX 75115
1-800-843-8855

This test consists of 16 subtests: inspection, coding, memory, precision, assembly, scales, coordination, judgment/comprehension, arithmetic, patterns, components, tables, mechanics, expression, reasoning, and ingenuity. Each test measures behaviors considered critical to job performance. Selected groups of tests may be administered. The entire battery takes several hours. This test is designed primarily for use with high school students and adults.

Armed Services Vocational Aptitude Battery (ASVAB)
U.S. Department of Defense
Washington, DC 20402

The *ASVAB* form 19 consists of 9 tests: coding speed, word knowledge, arithmetic reasoning, tool knowledge, space relations, mechanical comprehension, shop information, automotive information, and electronics information. These tests combine to yield three academic scales: academic ability (word knowledge, paragraph comprehension, and arithmetic reasoning), verbal (word knowledge, paragraph comprehension, and general science), and mathematical (math knowledge and arithmetic reasoning). Four occupational scales are also checked: mechanical and crafts (arithmetic reasoning, mechanical comprehension, and auto, shop, and electronics information); business and clerical (word knowledge, paragraph comprehension, mathematics knowledge, and coding speed); electronics and electrical (arithmetic reasoning, mathematical knowledge, electronics information, and general science); and health, social, and technical (word knowledge and paragraph meaning, arithmetic reasoning, and mechanical comprehension).

Achievement Tests

Achievement tests are designed primarily to assess present levels of developed abilities. Current functioning and basic academic skills such as arithmetic, reading, and language usage are relevant to planning for educational or training programs. Academic proficiency has long been a key factor in career planning for individuals considering higher education. However, basic academic competencies are also major determinants in qualifying for certain occupations. For example, identified academic competencies and deficiencies are major considerations for placement or training of school dropouts. Achievement test results provide important information to be included in programs for adults who are entering, returning to, or recycling through the work force. Changing technology and economic conditions will force many workers to enter programs to upgrade their skills or to train for completely different positions. Assessment of present levels of abilities will be needed to determine the possible scope of career exploration for these individuals.

For our use in career counseling programs, we will consider achievement tests in three categories: (1) general survey battery; (2) single-subject tests; and (3) diagnostic batteries. The general survey battery measures knowledge of most subjects taught in school and is standardized on the same population. The single-subject test, as the name implies, measures knowledge of only one subject/content area. Diagnostic batteries measure knowledge of specific proficiencies such as reading, spelling, and arithmetic achievement.

The use of achievement tests in career counseling is illustrated in the three cases that follow. In the first example, a general survey battery is used to assist a student in determining a college major and minor. In the second example, the achievement test results are used for the same purpose, but single-subject achievement tests are used instead of a general survey battery. In the final example, a diagnostic battery is used to assist a woman who is returning to the work force after several years of being a homemaker.

> Ana is interested in determining her most proficient subject matter area for the purpose of choosing a major and/or minor in a liberal arts college. At this point in her life, she is not interested in career selection (deferring this to later) but is more interested in educational planning. The counselor chooses to administer a general survey battery, which provides meaningful comparisons of all subjects tested since the battery was standardized on the same population group. A single profile will provide Ana with an overview of comparative ability on all subjects tested.
>
> Juan is a senior in high school who is considering college, but he cannot decide between biology and chemistry as a major. All other factors being equal as far as career opportunities are concerned, the decision is made to determine which is Juan's strongest subject area. The counselor chooses to administer the single-subject tests in biology and chemistry, as these tests are relatively more thorough and precise as compared to the general survey battery and the diagnostic battery. Thus, single-subject achievement tests provide a more thorough evaluation of specific subject abilities for Juan's consideration.
>
> Betty quit school when she was in the sixth grade. After several years of marriage, she was deserted by her husband and is seeking employment. Other test data reveal that she is of at least average intelligence. A part of the evaluation for this woman includes a diagnostic battery for the specific purpose of determining basic arithmetic skills and reading and spelling levels. The counselor is especially interested in determining academic deficiencies for educational planning; that is, consideration should be given to upgrading basic skills for eventual training for a high school equivalency. This information is seen as essential for both educational and career planning.

Because of the wide range of achievement tests on the market today, individual tests will not be listed here. Instead, following are representative major publishers of achievement tests.

CTB-MacMillan-McGraw-Hill
Publishers Test Service
20 Ryan Ranch Rd.
Monterey, CA 93940

Educational Testing Service
Princeton, NJ 08540

Houghton Mifflin Company
222 Berkeley Street
Boston, MA 02116
1-800-225-3362

The Psychological Corporation
555 Academic Court
San Antonio, Texas 78204-2498

SRA-McGraw-Hill
220 East Daniel Dale
De Soto, TX 75115
1-800-843-8855

Interest Inventories

In recent years, a considerable body of literature has concerned itself with gender bias and unfairness in career interest measurement. A number of the most relevant articles have been compiled by Diamond (1975) under the sponsorship of the National Institute of Education (NIE). The NIE publishes guidelines that identify gender bias as "any factor that might influence a person to limit—or might cause others to limit—his or her consideration of a career solely on the basis of gender" (Diamond, 1975, p. xxiii).

According to Diamond (1975), the guidelines have led to some progress in reducing gender bias in interest inventories by calling for fairness in the construction of item pools ("Items such as statements, questions, and names of occupations used in the inventory should be designed so as not to limit the consideration of a career solely on the basis of gender"), fairness in the presentation of technical information ("Technical information should include evidence that the inventory provides career options for both males and females"), and fairness in interpretive procedures ("Interpretive procedures should provide methods of equal treatment of results for both sexes" [p.xxiii]). Generally, the guidelines are aimed at encouraging both sexes to consider all career and educational opportunities and at eliminating sex-role stereotyping by those using interest inventory results in the career counseling process.

Interest inventories have long been associated with career counseling. Two of the most widely used are the *Strong Interest Inventory (SII)*, originally developed by E. K. Strong (1983), and the Kuder interest inventories, developed by G. F. Kuder (1963). More recently, Holland's (1992) approach to interest identification (as discussed in Chapter 2) has received considerable attention. For example, a number of interest inventories including the *SII*, the American College Testing Program Interest Inventory, and the *Self-Directed Search* (Holland, 1987a) are constructed to correspond with Holland's personality types and corresponding work environments. In most inventories, interests are primarily designated by responses to compiled lists of occupations and lists of activities associated with occupations. The rationale is that individuals having similar interest patterns to those found in an occupational group would probably find satisfaction in that particular group.

Two methods commonly used for reporting results are direct comparison (likes and dislikes) with specific occupations and comparisons with themes or clusters of occupations. Interest inventories that provide direct comparisons with specific occupations usually include a numerical index for comparative purposes. For example, the *Kuder Occupational Interest Survey* (Kuder, 1966) provides a coefficient of correlation as an index for comparing an individual's response with an occupational group—that is, higher correlations indicate similar interest patterns to certain occupational groups (Kuder, 1963). The *SII* provides a standard score for this purpose. In addition, a number of inventories provide profiles that indicate whether interests are similar or dissimilar to those of occupational criterion groups. For example, an individual may give interest responses very similar to those of accountants and very dissimilar to those of social workers.

Clusters of occupations are presented in a variety of schemes. Some clusters are based on the *DOT* models of people, data, and things (see Appendix A, on p. 529). The *Kuder General Interest Survey* (Kuder, 1964) yields ten interest scales as follows: outdoor, mechanical, computational, scientific, persuasive, artistic, literary, musical, social service, and clerical. The *SII* yields six general occupational theme scales taken from Holland's (1992) six modal personal styles and matching work environments. The cluster systems index a group of occupations rather than a single occupation, although the individual can derive specific occupations from the clusters.

For the nonreader, picture interest inventories are used to determine occupational interests. These inventories depict occupational environments, individuals at work, and a variety of job-related activities. Individual response is recorded by circling numbers or pictures or by pointing to pictures. Picture interest inventories also provide a basis for discussion about career exploration.

Following are some representative examples of interest inventories.

Kuder Occupational Interest Survey
Publisher Test Service
CTB-MacMillan-McGraw-Hill
20 Ryan Ranch Road
Monterey, CA 93940

This survey is computer-scored and consists of 77 occupational scales and 29 college-major scales for men, and 57 occupational scales and 27 college-major scales for women. Recommended uses of the inventory include selection, placement, and career exploration. The survey is untimed, usually taking 30 to 40 minutes. Norms are based on samples of data from college seniors.

Ohio Vocational Interest Survey (OVIS)
The Psychological Corporation
555 Academic Court
San Antonio, TX 78204-2498

This survey is used by students in grades 8 through 12 and takes between 60 and 90 minutes to complete. The score results yield 24 general interest scales that are related to people, data, and things. This survey primarily measures general interest areas.

Self-Directed Search (SDS)
Psychological Assessment Resources
P.O. Box 998
Odessa, FL 33556

This interest inventory is based on Holland's (1992) theory of career development. It is self-administered and self-scored, as well as self-interpreted, and takes approximately 30 to 40 minutes to complete. The scores are organized to reveal an occupational code or a summary code of three letters representing the personality types and environmental models from Holland's typology: realistic, investigative, artistic, social, enterprising, and conventional. This inventory is used with high school and college students and with adults.

Strong Interest Inventory
Stanford University Press
Stanford, CA 94305

This inventory combines the male and female versions of the *Strong Vocational Interest Blank* into one survey. The interpretation of scores is based on Holland's typology. The interpretation format includes six general occupational themes, 23 basic interest scales, and 124 occupational scales. Administrative indexes include an academic-orientation index and an introversion-extroversion index. Time to complete: 30 to 40 minutes. Both male and female occupational scale scores are available.

Brainard Occupational Preference Inventory
P. O. Brainard and R. F. Brainard
The Psychological Corporation
555 Academic Court
San Antonio, TX 78204-2498

This inventory is designed for use in grades 8 through 12 and requires approximately 30 minutes to complete. Scores are expressed in percentiles for males and females and are used as guidelines for career exploration. Scores yield individual preference for six broad fields: commercial, mechanical, professional, aesthetic, scientific, agricultural (males only), and personal service (females only).

Career Assessment Inventory (CAI)
C. B. Johansson
National Computer Systems
P.O. Box 1416
Minneapolis, MN 55440

This is a computer-scored inventory that can be administered in approximately 45 minutes. It is designed for eighth-grade students through adults. Three types of scales reported are general occupational theme scales, basic interest scales, and occupational scales. This inventory is primarily used with noncollege-bound individuals.

Geist Picture Interest Inventory
Harold Geist, Ph.D.
Western Psychological Services
12031 Wilshire Blvd.
Los Angeles, CA 90025

This inventory is for nonreaders. Examinees are required to circle one of three pictures depicting a work or leisure activity. Separate editions are available for males and females. The male edition assesses 11 general interest areas: persuasive, clerical, mechanical, musical, scientific, outdoor, literary, computational, artistic, social service, and dramatic. The female edition assesses these same 11 general interest areas and one other—personal service. Norms for various occupational groups are also provided.

Wide Range Interest and Opinion Test
Guidance Associates of Delaware, Inc.
1526 Gilpin Avenue
Wilmington, DE 19806

This test consists of 150 sets of three pictures from which the individual is asked to indicate likes and dislikes. The pictures depict activities ranging from unskilled labor to the highest levels of technical, managerial, and professional training. The test evaluates educational and vocational interests of a wide range of individuals, including the educationally disadvantaged and the developmentally disabled.

The Campbell Interest and Skill Survey (CISS)
NCS Assessments
P.O. Box 1416
Minneapolis, MN 55440

This instrument is part of a new integrated battery of psychological surveys that currently includes the *CISS*, an attitude-satisfaction survey, and a measure of leadership characteristics. Two other instruments, a team development survey and a community survey, are being developed and will complete this integrated battery. The *CISS*, developed for individuals 15 years and older with a sixth-grade reading level, has 200 interest and 120 skill items on a 6-point response scale. The results yield parallel interest and skill scores: orientation scales (influencing, organizing, helping, creating, analyzing, producing, and adventuring); basic scales (29 basic scales, such as leadership, supervision, counseling, and international activities); occupational scales (58 scales, such as financial planner, translator/interpreter, and landscape architect). Special scales measure academic comfort and extroversion.

Personality Inventories

Major career theorists have emphasized personality development as a major factor to be considered in career development. For example, Roe (1956) postulated that early personality development associated with family interactions influences vocational direction. Super (1990) devoted considerable attention to self-concept development. Tiedeman and O'Hara (1963) considered total cognitive development in decision making. Holland's (1992) system of career selection was directly related to personality types and styles. The case for the use of personality inventories in career counseling programs seems well established. However, there is a lack of evidence that personality inventories are being widely utilized in career counseling programs.

The development of the *Sixteen Personality Factor Questionnaire (16 PF)* by Cattell, Eber, and Tatsuoka (1970) led the way for integrating personality inventories into career counseling programs. Vocational personality patterns and occupational fitness are considered major components of this questionnaire. The 16 factors measured by the *16 PF* are "source" traits or factors, which are derived from distinct combinations of an individual's personality traits (Cattell, Eber, & Tatsuoka, 1970). These traits are compared with occupational profiles and provide vocational observations and occupational fitness projections. *Vocational observations* include information concerning the individual's potential for leadership and interpersonal skills and potential benefits from academic training. *Occupational fitness projections* rank how the individual compares with specific occupational profiles as being extremely high to extremely low. Specific source traits are recorded for each occupational profile available (currently there are 24), providing a comparison of characteristic traits common to individuals employed in certain occupations. The *16 PF* is singled out because a major portion of the development of the inventory was devoted to vocational personality patterns and occupational fitness projections.

Throughout this text, references are made to the importance of satisfying individual needs associated with work, family, and leisure. As we assist individuals in career exploration, we must consider the individuality of each person we counsel. Within this frame of reference, individual personality patterns greatly assist in the task of identifying and clarifying each individual's needs. As needs change over the life span, our goal is to help individuals clarify their needs for effective planning and goal achievement. Personality inventories provide valuable information for identifying needs and providing a stimulus for career exploration.

The following examples demonstrate the use of personality inventories in career counseling programs.

> Ahmed reports that he is quite frustrated in his present working environment and is considering changing jobs. His unhappiness has caused family problems and social problems in general. His performance ratings by his superiors were high until the last two years, when they dropped to average. Assessment results indicate that he is interested in his current job as accountant. A personality inventory indicated a strong need for achievement. Group discussions that followed brought about a consensus that Ahmed was still interested in the field of accounting, but in his current position, he was not able to meet his needs to achieve. Earlier these needs were apparently met from positive reinforcement received from high ratings by his superiors. At this point in his life, he is searching for something more than "just doing a good job of bookkeeping." Recognizing his source of frustration, he decided to stay in accounting but moved to another division in the firm.
>
> Shayna had definitely decided that she was interested in an occupation that would provide her with an opportunity to help people. A personality inventory indicated that she was very reserved and nonassertive, and deferred to others. She agreed with the results of the personality inventory and further agreed that these characteristics would make it difficult for her to accomplish her occupational goal. Shayna became convinced that she would have to modify these personality characteristics through a variety of programs, including self-discovery groups and assertiveness training.

In these cases, personality inventory results provided the impetus and stimulation for action to meet individual career needs. In the first example, Ahmed recognized as the major source of his frustrations a motivational drive that he had repressed for years. Fortunately, he was able to meet his needs to achieve in another division of the firm in which he was employed. In the second example, Shayna chose to keep her career goal but increased her chances of success in that career with further training. These examples provide only two illustrations of the use of personality inventories in career counseling but clearly establish their potential usefulness. Personality inventories provide important information that can be incorporated into group or individual counseling programs to assist individuals with career-related problems.

Following are representative examples of personality inventories.

California Test of Personality
CTB-MacMillan-McGraw-Hill
20 Ryan Ranch Rd.
Monterey, CA 93940

Five levels of the test are available: primary, elementary, intermediate, secondary, and adult. The test assesses personal and social adjustment. Subscale scores are provided for the two major categories. The test is used primarily in career counseling to assess measures of personal worth and of family and school relations.

Edwards Personal Preference Schedule (EPPS)
The Psychological Corporation
555 Academic Court
San Antonio, TX 78204-2498

This inventory is designed to measure the following 15 personality variables related to needs: achievement, dominance, endurance, order, intraception, nurturance, affiliation, heterosexuality, exhibition, autonomy, aggression, change, succorance, abasement, and deference. In addition, a consistency score indicates the reliability of the responses. These scores provide an index for determining dominant individual needs to be considered in career exploration. The inventory is untimed and is hand- or machine-scored. Norms are based on data taken from college students' responses.

Guilford-Zimmerman Temperament Survey
Sheridan Psychological Services
P.O. Box 6101
Orange, CA 92667

This survey measures the following ten traits: general activity, restraint, ascendance, sociability, emotional stability, objectivity, friendliness, thoughtfulness, personal relations, and masculinity. Norms were derived primarily from college samples. Single-trait scores and total profiles may be used to determine personality traits to be considered in career decision making.

Minnesota Counseling Inventory
The Psychological Corporation
555 Academic Court
San Antonio, TX 78204-2498

This inventory was designed to measure adjustment of boys and girls in grades 9 through 12. Scores yield criterion-related scales as follows: family relationship, social relationship, emotional stability, conformity, adjustment to reality, mood, and leadership. Scales are normed separately for boys and girls. These scores provide indexes to important relationships and personal characteristics to be considered in career counseling.

Sixteen Personality Factor (16 PF)
Institute for Personality and Ability Testing
1602 Coronado Drive
Champaign, IL 61820

This instrument measures 16 personality factors of individuals 16 years or older. A major part of this questionnaire has been devoted to identifying personality patterns related to occupational fitness projections. These projections provide a comparison of the individual's profile with samples of occupational profiles. The instrument is hand-scored or computer-scored. Four forms have an average adult vocabulary; two forms are available for low-literacy groups.

Temperament and Values Inventory
Charles B. Johansson
Interpretive Scoring Systems
A Division of National Computer Systems, Inc.
P.O. Box 1416
Minneapolis, MN 55440

This inventory has two parts: (1) temperament dimensions of personality related to career choice, and (2) values related to work rewards. The inventory has an eighth-grade reading level and is not recommended for use below the ninth grade. The inventory is untimed and computer-scored. Scores help determine congruence or incongruence with an individual's career aspirations.

Myers-Briggs Type Indicator
Consulting Psychologists Press, Inc.
3803 East Bayshore Road
Palo Alto, CA 94303

This inventory measures individual preferences by personality types: extroversion or introversion; sensing or intuition; thinking or feeling; and judging or perceiving. Scores are determined according to the four categories. The publisher's manual provides descriptions of the 16 possible types (combinations). Occupations that are attractive to each type are presented in the appendixes. This inventory provides direct references to occupational considerations based on one's personality type.

Values Inventories

In the last two decades, much has been written about beliefs and values. Some argue that we have experienced significant changes in our value systems over the last 20 years. There is the ongoing debate about differences in values between the so-called establishment and the younger generation. Much of the concern has centered on lifestyle and the work role. Questioning the social worth of one's work has motivated many to reformulate their life goals. As career counselors, we must be concerned with individual beliefs and values in the career decision-making process. An important function is to act as agents who provide methods for clarifying values. In this frame of reference, we are concerned not only with work values but also with values per se as we help others find congruence with the inseparables—work and life.

For counseling purposes, we classify values inventories into two types: (1) inventories that primarily measure work values, and (2) inventories that measure values associated with broader aspects of lifestyle. Work value inventories, as the name implies, are designed to measure values associated with job success and satisfaction (achievement, prestige, security, and creativity). Values found to be high priorities for the individual provide another dimension of information that may be used in career exploration. In our second category, values are considered in much broader terms but can be related to needs and satisfactions associated with life and work. Thus, both types of inventories provide information that can be especially helpful for clarifying individual needs associated with work, home, family, and leisure.

Two examples of the use of a value measure follow.

> Ngo, a middle-aged, married man with five children, was employed for five years as a salesman in a local furniture store. He is currently seeking a change in employment, and sought out a state agency for assistance. As part of the assessment program, he took the *Survey of Personal Values* (Gordon, 1967). The results of the inventory clearly indicated that Ngo was very goal-oriented; that is, he preferred to have definite goals and plan precisely for the future. However, he felt that he had no real control over his life, particularly since in his past job as a salesman his commissions had fluctuated greatly from month to month. He expressed frustration and despair. The major focus of the group discussions that followed centered on identifying those variables through which individuals can exert control over their lives. Ngo was encouraged to recognize his past experiences as assets for his future in the job market. Exploring potential careers by identifying skills from previous work experiences gave him the confidence he lacked in the past. More important, Ngo learned of several jobs for which he was qualified that gave him the opportunity to set goals and plan for the future.

> Rosa was considered an outstanding student in high school and was very active as a member of the student council. She expressed a deep concern to the career counselor about her inability to identify a working environment in which she felt she could find satisfaction. There were no particular role models, organizations, or occupations that seemed to have the potential to satisfy her needs. In the *Work Values Inventory (WVI)* (Super, 1970) administered to her, she rated intellectual stimulus, creativity, and job placement very high. These values were incorporated into further discussions that provided her with a starting point from which she was able to launch a career exploration. Potential occupations were partially evaluated to determine how they could satisfy her work values identified by the *WVI*.

In the first example, a values inventory identified Ngo's major difficulty in career planning as stemming from a need to identify sources of discontentment with his past job. Once the unsatisfied value was revealed—a desire to have control over his life—Ngo was encouraged to identify past job skills that were applicable to new jobs over which he could have more control. In the second example, the identified work values served as a stimulus in launching a study of careers from the perspective of finding a career that could meet Rosa's needs. Once one is able to consider careers from an individual viewpoint, more realistic decisions usually follow.

Following are representative examples of work values inventories.

Work Environment Preference Schedule
The Psychological Corporation
555 Academic Court
San Antonio, TX 78204-2498

This inventory measures an individual's adaptability to a bureaucratic organization. It is untimed and self-administered. A total score reflects the individual's commitment to the sets of attitudes, values, and behaviors found in bureaucratic organizations. Separate norms by sex are available for high school, college, and Army ROTC students.

Work Values Inventory (WVI)
Houghton Mifflin Company
222 Berkeley Street
Boston, MA 02116
1-800-225-3362

This inventory measures sources of satisfaction individuals seek from their work environment. Scores yield measures of altruism, aesthetics, creativity, intellectual stimulation, independence, prestige, management, economic returns, security, surroundings, supervisory relations, value of relationship with associates, way of life, and variety. Norms are provided by grade and sex for students in grades 7 through 12. The scores provide dimensions of work values that can be combined with other considerations in career counseling.

Following are representative examples of broader values inventories.

Study of Values
Houghton Mifflin Company
222 Berkeley Street
Boston, MA 02116
1-800-225-3362

This is a self-administered inventory that measures individual values in six categories: theoretical, economic, esthetic, social, political, and religious. Norms are provided by sex for high school, college, and various occupational groups. The measured strength of values (indicated as high, average, or low) provides points of reference for individual and group counseling programs.

Survey of Interpersonal Values
SRA-McGraw-Hill
220 East Daniel Dale
De Soto, TX 75115
1-800-843-8855

This inventory measures values considered important in relationships with other people: support, conformity, recognition, independence, benevolence, and leadership. These measures assist in evaluating the individual's personal, social, marital, and occupational adjustment. Norms are available for high school and college students and adults.

> *Survey of Personal Values*
> SRA-McGraw-Hill
> 220 East Daniel Dale
> De Soto, TX 75115
> 1-800-843-8855

This inventory measures values that influence how individuals cope with daily problems. Scores yield measures of practical-mindedness, achievement, variety, decisiveness, orderliness, and goal orientation. The inventory is self-administered. National percentile norms are available for college students, and regional norms are available for high school students.

> *The Values Scale*
> Consulting Psychologists Press, Inc.
> 3803 East Bayshore Road
> Palo Alto, CA 94303

This scale measures 21 values: ability utilization, achievement, advancement, aesthetics, altruism, authority, autonomy, creativity, economic rewards, lifestyle, personal development, physical activity, prestige, risk, social interaction, social relations, variety, working conditions, cultural identity, physical prowess, and economic security. The measures are designed to help individuals understand values in relation to life roles and evaluate the importance of the work role with other life roles. Scores are interpreted by using percentile equivalents. Norms are available for high school and university students and adults.

> *Ohio Work Values Inventory (OWVI)*
> Publishers Test Service
> 20 Ryan Ranch Road
> Monterey, CA 93940

This inventory consists of 77 items yielding scores on 11 work values: altruism, object orientation, security, control, self-realization, independence, money, task satisfaction, solitude, ideas/data orientation, and prestige. It is designed for use with students in grades 4 through 12.

> *The Campbell Organizational Survey*
> NCS Assessments
> P.O. Box 1416
> Minneapolis, MN 55440

This instrument provides a measure of an overall index for the individual's satisfaction with the working environment. It is part of an integrated battery that includes several other surveys, such as the *Campbell Interest and Skill Survey*. Some of the scales include measures of the following: the work itself, working conditions, level of stress, co-workers, supervision, and job security.

Career Maturity Inventories

Career maturity inventories—also referred to as career development inventories—measure vocational development in terms of specified dimensions from which one is judged to be vocationally mature. The dimensions of career maturity are derived from career development concepts. That is, vocational maturity, like career choice, is a continuous development process that can be segmented into a series of stages and tasks (Super, 1957; Crites, 1973, pp. 5–7). Super put the process of career choice on a continuum, with "exploration" and "decline" as endpoints (as discussed in Chapter 2). Career maturity is considered the degree of vocational development measurable within this continuum. Super measured career maturity within several dimensions: orientation toward work (attitudinal dimension), planning (competency dimension), consistency of vocational preferences (consistency dimension), and wisdom of vocational preferences (realistic dimension). These dimensions identify progressive steps of vocational development and determine the degree of development relative to normative age levels.

Thus, career maturity inventories are primarily measures of individual career development. For example, attitudinal dimensions reveal individual problems associated with career choice. Competence dimensions provide measures of an individual's knowledge of occupations and planning skills. Career maturity inventories provide a focus for individual or group programs. They also evaluate the effectiveness of career education programs and curricula and help identify other career guidance program needs.

Following is a list of representative career maturity inventories.

Career Development Inventory
D. E. Super, A. S. Thompson, R. H. Lindenman,
J. P. Jordaan, and R. A. Myers
Consulting Psychologists Press, Inc.
3853 East Bayshore Road
Palo Alto, CA 94303

This inventory is a diagnostic tool for the development of individual or group counseling procedures; it can also be used to evaluate career development programs. Scores yield measures of planning orientation, readiness for exploration, information, and decision making. The reading level is sixth grade, and the inventory is applicable to both sexes. Both cognitive and attitudinal scales are provided.

Career Maturity Inventory (CMI)
Psychological Assessment Resources
P.O. Box 998
Odessa, Florida 33556

The 1995 edition of the CMI yields three scores: Attitude Scale, Competence Test, and overall Career Maturity. The test can be both hand-scored and machine-scored.

The CMI is designed to be used with students from grade 6 through 12 and with adults.

Cognitive Vocational Maturity Test (CVMT)
B. W. Westbrook
Center for Occupational Education
North Carolina State University
Raleigh, NC 27607

This test is primarily a cognitive measure of an individual's knowledge of occupational information. Scores yield measures of knowledge of fields of work available, job selection procedures, work conditions, educational requirements, specific requirements for a wide range of occupations, and actual duties performed in a variety of occupations. This inventory provides important information about career choice abilities and can be used as a diagnostic tool for curricula and guidance needs.

New Mexico Career Education Test
C. C. Healy and S. P. Klein
Monitor Book Co., Inc.
195 S. Beverly Drive
Beverly Hills, CA 90212

This test primarily assesses specific learner objectives of career education programs for grades 9 through 12. Six criterion-referenced tests yield measures of specific learner outcomes for attitude toward work, career planning, career-oriented activities, knowledge of occupations, job application procedures, and career development. Norms for the test are based completely on samples of students from the public schools in New Mexico.

Career Beliefs Inventory
Consulting Psychologists Press, Inc.
3803 East Bayshore Road
Palo Alto, CA 94303

This inventory is used as a counseling tool to help clients identify career beliefs that may inhibit their ability to make career decisions that are in their best interest. The results are computed for 25 scales under the following five headings: My Current Career Situation, What Seems Necessary for My Happiness, Factors that Influence My Decisions, Changes I Am Willing to Make, and Effort I Am Willing to Initiate. Norms are available for junior high school students as well as for separate norms for male and female employed adults. Scores can be interpreted in percentile ranks for each scale.

Adult Career Concerns Inventory
Consulting Psychologists Press, Inc.
3803 East Bayshore Road
Palo Alto, CA 94303

There are three major purposes listed for this inventory: career counseling and planning, needs analysis, and a measure of relationships between adult capability and previous, concurrent socioeconomic and psychological characteristics. Scores are related to career development tasks at various life stages as follows: exploration, establishment, maintenance, disengagement, retirement planning, and retirement living. Norms are available by age, starting at 25 to 45 and up, by combined sexes, and by age groups and sex.

The Salience Inventory
Consulting Psychologists Press, Inc.
3803 East Bayshore Road
Palo Alto, CA 94303

This instrument, a research edition in developmental stage, is designed to measure five major life roles: student, worker, homemaker, leisurite, and citizen. Use of inventory results provides counselors with an evaluation of an individual's readiness for career decisions and exposure to work and occupations.

Card Sorts

The occupational card sort was originally developed by Tyler (1961), who stressed that career decisions are significantly influenced by how clients arrange and organize alternatives in the decision-making process. Tyler saw card sorts as a means of encouraging clients to consider and discuss alternatives. Furthermore, clients can gain a perspective of a variety of factors when projecting their individuality into a career decision. Thus, card sorts are often interpreted as a symbolic picture of a client's thought process and, more specifically, about perceptions of careers and work per se.

Some of the advantages of using card sorts for career development counseling are: (1) card sorts may be used with or without other assessment data; (2) administrative costs are relatively inexpensive; (3) administrative procedures are straightforward and user-friendly; and (4) clients are often stimulated to openly express and evaluate their career preferences when discussing results.

Here are three representative examples.

Career Values: Card Sort Planning Kit
Career Research and Testing, Inc.
2005 Hamilton Avenue
San Jose, CA 95126
408-559-4945

Each of 41 cards contains one described value. The user is instructed to sort 41 cards into one of five categories: "Always Valued," "Often Valued," "Sometimes Valued," "Seldom Valued," and "Never Valued." The user then prioritizes the cards within each category. In the next step, users are instructed to list each category with selected values on a career values worksheet. Starting with the "Always Valued" list, users are to describe how each value applies to possible career choices.

Values-Driven Work
Career Action Center
445 Sherman Avenue
Palo Alto, CA 94306
415-324-1710

This instrument allows users to examine values in four different areas: (1) intrinsic values, (2) work environment values, (3) work content values, and (4) work relationships values. Each of 70 cards lists one value that the user sorts into four categories, according to the importance of that value in a working situation. Users list their top ten values on a worksheet that contains suggested exercises designed to clarify values, focus on organizational values, and methods of exploring work group values.

SkillScan
SkillScan Professional Pack
P.O. Box 587
Orinda, CA 94563

There are 64 cards used in this instrument, and each describes one of seven types of skills: (1) communication, (2) humanitarian, (3) leadership/management, (4) mental analytical, (5) mental creative, (6) creative expression, and (7) physical. Each user ranks skills according to self-assessment of abilities and records them on a skills profile sheet. The manual contains a number of exercises designed to assist users in becoming aware of specific skills in terms of the seven types of categories of skills and how they may be applied to a variety of work tasks.

Computer-Assisted Career Guidance (CACG) Assessment

In the last three decades, the use of CACG assessment has steadily increased. One of the primary reasons for the growth of computer-based assessment is that results are immediately available to clients. Computer-based assessment programs also interpret results to clients in terms of occupational fit with lists of career options. However, some concerns about the validity of instruments in computer-based assessment has been expressed by independent researchers (Sampson & Pyle, 1983; Sampson, 1994) and by professional organizations such as the American Psychological Association (1985, 1986). In this section, we will review some of the advantages and disadvantages of six computer-based assessment processes.

The six different assessment processes associated with CACG (Sampson, 1994) are as follows.

1. *Responding to an on-line instrument.* This process increases validity of instrument but also increases time clients must spend on-line.
2. *Inputting scores from an instrument completed off-line.* The obvious advantage is that clients spend less time on-line. The distinct disadvantage is

that clients may not be fully aware of how assessment results relate to occupations.

3. *User-controlled on-line self-assessment.* Clients using this system may judge variables *they* consider most important. However, considerable on-line use is a disadvantage.

4. *A system-controlled on-line self-assessment.* Simplifying assessment by reducing options is considered an advantage for some clients. The disadvantage is a significant reduction in the client's control of the system.

5. *Prestructured off-line self-assessment.* More students will have access to the system but may be overwhelmed with the comprehensive nature of some guidebooks used with this program.

6. *User-controlled on-line sequence of self-assessment, clarification, and reassessment.* This system hopefully improves the client's acceptance of using self-assessment, especially with clarification material available. However, more on-line time is needed for this process.

Other problems associated with CACG assessment include various forms of instrument validity, scoring, search, and interpretative functions. Be aware that validity of CACG assessment systems should meet the same set of standards used for other psychometric measures. For instance, the validity of scoring standardized instruments includes weighting items into scales and ensuring error-free scoring. However, errors in these two processes are difficult to identify in computer-based assessment. Thus, career service providers may not be aware of potential errors and subsequent misleading results.

Finally, interpretative statements generated by computer-based testing systems should be carefully evaluated in terms of their validity. One must ask for some evidence of proof that interpretative statements have been carefully evaluated and are indeed valid results that clients can fully understand and apply to their search process.

As computer-based assessment continues to grow, career service providers must insist that system developers and independent researchers meet the testing standards that have been clearly defined by the American Psychological Association. Evidence of valid testing standards should be clearly delineated in promotional materials, as well as in professional manuals.

Summary

1. Standardized tests and assessment inventories have been closely associated with career counseling. Skills, aptitudes, interests, values, achievements, personality characteristics, and vocational maturity are among the assessment objectives of career counseling.

2. The use of standardized assessment procedures in career counseling provides the counselee with increased options and alternatives, subsequently encouraging greater individual involvement in the career decision process. In career

counseling programs, assessment scores are used with other materials to stimulate and enhance career exploration.

3. Aptitude tests primarily measure specific skills and proficiencies or the ability to acquire a certain proficiency. Measured aptitudes provide a good frame of reference for evaluating potential careers.

4. Achievement tests primarily assess present levels of developed abilities. The basic academic skills such as arithmetic, reading, and language usage are relevant information to be included in planning for educational or training programs.

5. Interest inventories are relevant counseling tools because individuals having interest patterns similar to those of people in certain occupations will probably find satisfaction in that occupation. Interest inventories can effectively stimulate career exploration.

6. Personality development is a major factor in career development because the individuality of each counselee must be considered. Personality patterns are integral in identifying and clarifying the needs of each individual.

7. Assessment and clarification of beliefs and values are important components of career counseling. Two types of values inventories are (a) inventories that primarily measure work values and (b) inventories that measure dimensions of values associated with broader aspects of lifestyles.

8. Career maturity inventories measure the dimensions from which one is judged to be vocationally mature. Super identified dimensions of career maturity as orientation toward work, planning, consistency of vocational preferences, and wisdom of vocational preferences. Career maturity inventories have two basic purposes: (a) to measure an individual's career development and (b) to evaluate the effectiveness of career education programs.

9. Card sorts are designed to assist clients in organizing alternatives in the career decision process. Card sorts are user-friendly and encourage clients to discuss potential career choices.

10. Computer-assisted career guidance assessment has steadily increased. Validity of instruments and the proper reporting of meeting usual testing standards has been a chief concern of researchers and professional organizations.

Supplementary Learning Exercises

1. Visit a state rehabilitation office to determine the assessment programs used for rehabilitation programs. Summarize the purpose of assessment in this context.
2. Administer and interpret one or more of the tests and inventories discussed in this chapter. Summarize the results and discuss strategies for using the results in career counseling.
3. Interview a personnel director of an industrial company and discuss the company's assessment program for placement counseling. Identify the rationale for each assessment instrument used.
4. Review APA's *Standard for Educational and Psychological Tests*. Present your review to the class.

5. Interview a high school or a college counselor concerning his or her assessment programs for career counseling. Identify the counseling strategies underlying the use of assessment instruments.
6. Request permission from a university counseling center to take (or self-administer and interpret) their battery of tests and inventories used in career counseling. Summarize the results.
7. Review the evaluations of an aptitude test; an achievement test; and one interest, values, personality, and career maturity inventory in the *Mental Measurements Yearbook.*
8. Write an essay defending this statement: Assessment results can be effectively used in career counseling programs.
9. Choose one or more of the following situations and develop an assessment battery that can be incorporated in career exploration programs.
   a. a middle school in a socioeconomically deprived neighborhood
   b. a senior high school from which 70% of the graduates enter college
   c. a community college in a large city
   d. a small four-year college
   e. a large university
   f. a community agency providing career counseling for adults
   g. a rehabilitation agency
   h. a private practice in career counseling
10. Using the following reference, describe a model for using assessment results for career development counseling.

   Zunker, Vernon G. (1994). *Using assessment results for career development* (4th ed.). Pacific Grove, CA: Brooks/Cole.

CHAPTER EIGHT

The Career Resource Center

In the last decade, the growth of career resource centers in educational institutions has been phenomenal. One of the many reasons for this growth is that career resource materials have been elevated to a position of central importance as a result of renewed attention given to career guidance. For instance, comprehensive guidance programs in schools K–12 require written career plans for each student (see Chapter 10). Institutions of higher education have also focused more attention on career-related programs that require centrally located centers. The fact is, the development of career centers has paralleled the development of a variety of career counseling and career education programs (Herr & Cramer 1996).

Career resource centers are also in place at many state agencies, in communities, and in workplaces. One-stop career centers can be found in shopping centers, libraries, and other centrally located public places (Mariani, 1995-96). In essence, educational institutions, communities, libraries, workplaces, and other easily accessible areas have found an increasing demand for centrally located career information. These centrally located facilities are often referred to as Career Centers, Career Information Centers, or Career Resource Centers (CRC). The term *CRC* will be used in this chapter.

This chapter covers (1) the purpose and use of a CRC, (2) the rationale for developing a CRC, (3) organizational procedure, (4) functions of an advisory committee, (5) developing objectives, (6) location and posture, (7) resource components, and (8) innovations in the dissemination of career information.

The Purpose and Use of a CRC

CRCs have been developed as a major component of career guidance programs. The management of programs and the use of occupational information material are major responsibilities of the career counselor. The counselor's understanding of how to use occupational information is highly related to the effectiveness of the CRC. Counselors must also be well acquainted with the content of the various sources of career information. Program development for individual and group use of the center must be carefully planned.

Presentation of materials will vary according to the differing needs of groups and individuals. For example, a senior high school freshman class may be given an overview demonstration of the various resources in the center, whereas a group of high school juniors are presented with specific resources needed for a class project. Or a group of college students may be given the assignment of researching the various careers in their declared majors.

Individual use of career information is highly personalized, and the counselor must recognize that different learning styles among counselees call for flexibility in the use of career information resources. Moreover, Sharf (1984) pointed out that information-seeking behavior will vary from counselor to counselor. As counselors help individuals sort and assimilate information, they must also provide direction by generating questions concerning specific information that can be obtained from available resources. Just as career decision making is an individualized process, so too is the use and assimilation of career information.

In sum, the CRC is used by individuals who are in various phases of career decision making; some are seeking information to narrow down choices, whereas others are searching for answers in the beginning phases of decision making. It is also a place where instructors can meet with groups of students or entire classes for a variety of career guidance objectives. Finally, the entire professional staff is encouraged to use the center as a resource for ongoing projects.

Rationale

Several advantages of a CRC are worthy of consideration. First, a centralized location provides the opportunity to systematically organize all career materials into more efficient and workable units. The centralized facility also provides the opportunity to monitor materials on hand and simplifies the task of maintaining and selecting additional materials.

Second, students and faculty are attracted to centrally displayed materials that are easily accessed. Thus, a wider use of materials is usually assured, and in addition, attention is directed to programs offered by the CRC. In essence, the CRC brings into focus the career-related programs and the career resources offered by an institution.

A third consideration is the methods of promoting coordination and acceptance of career-related programs among faculty, staff, administration, students, and the community. A well-organized and well-operated CRC will encourage a variety of members of an institution to participate in development, programming, and evaluation of CRC materials and facilities. A commitment from a cross section of individuals will greatly enhance the career guidance efforts an educational institution offers.

A final consideration is programming innovations for the use of career materials and outreach activities, which are usually generated within the CRC or sponsored by the CRC. A well-planned facility can become the focal point in planning new programs and innovative activities for career guidance and career education. In essence, the CRC should facilitate a wide variety of program development opportunities among staff and faculty.

Organizational Procedures

The organizational procedures used for founding a CRC will have a significant impact on its acceptance by faculty, students, and community leaders. One should begin with a well-prepared philosophical approach for the purpose of establishing a CRC. The mission of the CRC may follow the elements suggested by Heppner and Johnston (1994), modified as follows.

1. Determine, prioritize, and promote the scope of services provided by the CRC, and relate these to the mission of both the CRC and the educational institution.
2. Design the CRC to reflect what is current and successful practice in settings where the mission is primarily to offer information and service.
3. Build the CRC on solid and psychological bases.
4. Design interventions carefully to match the clientele's developmental needs.
5. Develop a sophisticated diagnostic system for providing services.
6. Provide for continual training of staff.
7. Plan to build a strong network with other professionals on campus and in other educational institutions.
8. Provide for the increasing multicultural diversity of the student population.
9. Provide for research in terms of evaluating success of programs, basic research of practices, and review of relevant research that may be used to guide current practices.

A more practical approach is to follow the suggestions that are applicable to your situation, as outlined below.

1. Survey existing career guidance services.
2. Carefully choose an advisory committee.
3. Develop specific objectives for the above suggestions.
4. Create a budget and determine space needed.
5. Locate and request space and furniture.
6. Collect all existing career-related materials.
7. Develop methods of filing career-related materials.

8. Determine resources needed in the CRC (implementing computer-assisted career guidance programs are suggested in Chapter 6).
9. Develop a plan for operational procedures.
10. Create a plan for periodic evaluations.

Establishing an Advisory Committee

Special attention should be given to creating an advisory committee. Establishing an advisory group is a valuable and effective way to ensure early involvement from a cross section of individuals within the institution and community. This procedure is considered an effective strategy for promoting acceptance and support from faculty and community leaders, a strategy recently used to establish comprehensive guidance programs (reported in Chapter 10). The membership of this committee may consist of student users, teachers, administrators, counselors, and community leaders. Representatives of local businesses and industrial complexes should also be part of the advisory group.

At all educational levels where any advisory committee is formed, it is good procedure to include representatives from both the formal academic programs and vocational/technical training segments. At the postsecondary level, alumni are a valuable resource.

In general, the advisory committee establishes guidelines for developing the CRC, initiates early planning programs, sets policy, and eventually acts as a governing body for the appointed director. Some functions of the advisory committee could include the following.

1. Establish contacts with local businesses, industrial complexes, manufacturing firms, and labor unions.
2. Advise on the establishment of an adequate budget.
3. Assist in promoting the CRC in schools, in the community, and with parent groups.
4. Encourage faculty and counselors to become familiar with industries and businesses in the community.
5. Assist in identifying sources of funding.

Developing Objectives

Establishing objectives for a CRC provides a framework for the selection and utilization of materials to meet the institution's career guidance needs. Staffing requirements may also be determined by the objectives. Developing objectives will depend to a large extent on local needs and available resources. Therefore, consideration should be given to developing a needs assessment to document specific material and program needs, as well as needs for available resources such as innovative career-related programs and materials being used in academic departments and by individual instructors. An effective needs assessment can help clarify the CRC's goals and objectives and identify available career materials as well as ongoing career-related programs. Criteria that should be included in the assessment are (1) the existing resources; (2) how current the materials are, and how much they are being used; (3) the career guidance services currently available; (4) any support services for career guidance; (5) the personnel providing career guidance services; (6) the scope and sequence of career education programs; (7) the career-related materials used in career education programs; (8) available community resources; and (9) other related career guidance programs.

Although educational institutions and governmental agencies may develop similar objectives, they may differ significantly in organizational structure and programming needs. Therefore, consideration of the following objectives—developed for a CRC by Dittenhafer and Lewis (1973)—must take into account the specific programs, functions, and related activities that are necessary to meet the needs identified by an assessment.

1. To collect, evaluate, and disseminate accurate and relevant career information;
2. To provide assistance to the center's clientele in locating, evaluating, and using career information;
3. To help students integrate self-knowledge with relevant career information by providing counseling services;
4. To assist the faculty in integrating information into the instructional activities to support students' career development;
5. To assist parents in becoming active, concerned, and understanding participants in the career development of their children; and
6. To utilize community resources in fostering a better understanding of the relationship of education to work. (p. 1)

In summary, objectives can be developed after the institution's needs have been assessed and evaluated. Objectives should be developed with the help of a cross section of professional personnel and user groups. The objectives should communicate the CRC's purpose, programs, user groups, and materials collected. A well-developed, clearly stated set of objectives will set the pattern for staffing, space, equipment, and materials needed, as well as establish lines of communication with students, instructors, administrators, alumni, and the community.

Location and Posture

Once the CRC's objectives have been determined, its space requirements are more easily identified. In most instances, the CRC will be viewed as a multipurpose center from which a number of career-related programs and activities will evolve. The CRC may be a focal place for all career-related programs, providing a setting in which all interested parties may browse through materials. Thus, it will become a central meeting place for students, instructors, counselors, and administrators. In essence, the CRC becomes the hub of activities from which a variety of programs may be launched and to which a variety of programs may be directed. In view of the potential activities, the considerations of space and location are of major importance. Ideally, elaborate plans for constructing a new facility or for extensive remodeling would be recommended. However, in view of the increasing demand for reduced expenditures in education and in state agencies, one may have to settle for something less than ideal.

The location of the CRC should be in a high-traffic area of the campus. The importance of exposure and accessibility for students and faculty should be among the primary considerations in determining location. Existing classrooms are considered good prospective locations, and in some cases only minor modifications are necessary. In many secondary schools, existing counseling centers can be modified or adjacent classrooms can be converted to accommodate a CRC. Locating the CRC within or adjacent to the counseling center enables the most effective use of existing staff and administration. In addition, students are usually accustomed to going to counseling centers for assistance, and the CRC programs can be easily incorporated into other services offered within the center.

The CRC may also be placed within the library facility or within existing learning resource centers. In both cases, local conditions would determine the feasibility of such placement. Major considerations include the possibility of using existing equipment, materials, and space and their accessibility to both students and staff.

The CRC should not take on an institutional look but instead should communicate just the opposite atmosphere. The rationale is that the physical arrangements should be student-oriented and appear rather casual and relaxed. Students should feel welcome to browse through the attractively displayed materials.

Various media components should also be considered in the floor plans. Places for viewing television and microfilm and listening to audio components such as cassettes will be needed. Placement of computer terminals also requires careful planning. Most of the media components may be used for individual study as well as for group programs.

The Career Center at Florida State University is a good example of an effective floor plan. A sketch of the Career Center is shown in Figure 8-1. Students must be immediately impressed with the informality of design and help resources available. The organization of the layout suggests a specific place for most references and programs. For instance, a student can visualize not only where help is available for choosing a major but how that major is linked to occupations and subsequent employment opportunities. In the meantime, the resources available include videotapes, audiotapes, occupational files, reference books, and a computer-assisted career guidance laboratory. More information about programs can be obtained from the following address.

Dr. Janet Lenz
Florida State University
The Career Center
Tallahassee, FL 32306-1035
Phone: 904-644-6431
Fax: 904-644-3273

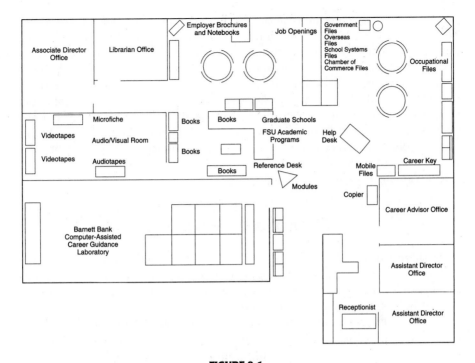

FIGURE 8-1

The Florida State University Career Center.

SOURCE: Florida State University, The Career Center, 1996. Reprinted by permission.

Resource Components

This section describes resource components that may be selected for a CRC. The component categories were chosen arbitrarily and should not necessarily be considered as a format for a filing system. The categories are logical divisions of currently available career-related materials and recently developed career counseling programs, however, and at least suggest ways to organize materials and program units to meet local needs.

All the resource components discussed are designed to provide information for career counseling programs and career education instructional units. Most provide specific information for educational and vocational planning, and a few provide techniques and strategies for developing skills needed for career planning. A list of applicable publications is provided for each component. Each list is representative but not exhaustive.

Access to the CRC's resources is a primary consideration. Instructions on how to use various resources may be given through individual or group orientation sessions or modules. An effective entry system can provide the user with a review of the resources available and the most direct means of making use of these resources.

A number of specific information-resource components should be considered, including (1) occupational descriptions, (2) occupational outlook projections, (3) postsecondary education and training information, (4) military information, (5) apprenticeship and internship information, (6) information for special populations (for example, minorities and individuals with disabilities), (7) a resource-persons file, and (8) financial aid information. (All these resource components are included in the computer-assisted career guidance systems discussed in Chapter 6.) In addition, to help students assimilate all this information, components that promote effective career planning should be considered as well. And finally, a wide variety of audiovisual materials are available to augment information and career planning resources.

Occupational Descriptions

Occupational descriptions are one of the CRC's major information components, and they can be found in a wide variety of attractively designed materials. Some publications describe occupations in a straightforward and nontechnical narrative form, whereas others like the *Dictionary of Occupational Titles (DOT)* provide very technical descriptions. Occupational information that can generally be retrieved includes (1) salary, (2) work activities, (3) working conditions, (4) physical demands of the occupation, (5) employment locations, (6) employment outlook, and (7) sources of additional information. The following list provides examples of the range of materials available.

Dictionary of Occupational Titles
Superintendent of Documents
U.S. Government Printing Office
Washington, DC 20402

Encyclopedia of Careers and Vocational Guidance
Doubleday and Company, Inc.
501 Franklin Avenue
Garden City, NY 11530

American Salaries and Wage Survey
Gale Research, Inc.
835 Penobscot Bldg.
Detroit, MI 48226-4094

Guide for Occupational Exploration
American Guidance Services, Inc.
Publishers' Bldg.
Circle Pines, MN 55014-1796
Phone: 1-800-328-2560
Fax: 612-786-9077

VGM Professional Careers Series
NTC Publishing Group
4255 West Touhy Avenue
Lincolnwood, IL 60646-1975

Vocational Biographies, Inc.
P.O. Box 31
Sauk Centre, MN 56378-0031
Phone: 1-800-255-0752
Fax: 320-352-5546

Occupational Briefs on CD-ROM
Psychological Assessment Resources, Inc.
P.O. Box 998
Odessa, FL 33556
Phone: 1-800-331-8378
Fax: 1-800-727-9329

Occupational-Outlook Projections

The competitive job market has increased the concern not only for job outlook information but also for technical and industrial developments. As a result, many individuals are at least partially basing their career decisions on projections of future job needs. This component has become increasingly popular. In addition to the following sources listed, the CRC staff should investigate local, state, and regional sources of labor forecasts. State employment agencies and other state and federal agencies are active in developing job forecast information and provide excellent resources for this component.

Occupational Outlook Handbook
Superintendent of Documents
U.S. Government Printing Office
Washington, DC 20402
(See locations of U.S. Government bookstores with their address, phone, and fax numbers in appendix A.)

Occupational Outlook for College Graduates
Superintendent of Documents
U.S. Government Printing Office
Washington, DC 20402

Modern Vocational Trends Reference Handbook
Juvenal L. Angel
Monarch Press
Division of Simon and Schuster, Inc.
12th Floor, 1320 Avenue of the Americas
New York, NY 10020

Bureau of Labor Statistics
Publication Sales Center
P.O. Box 2145
Chicago, IL 60690

U.S. Industrial Outlook
U.S. Dept. of Commerce
International Trade Commission
Washington, DC 20402

Jobs 1996
The New Career Center
1515 23rd Street
P.O. Box 339
Boulder, CO 80306

Postsecondary Education and Training

This component provides information about education and training program opportunities and the entry requirements of specific occupations. For ease of access, this component may be subdivided into three categories: (1) two- and four-year colleges, (2) technical school programs, and (3) continuing education opportunities.

College program information may be organized into one component for secondary students who are selecting a two- or four-year institution, or one for currently enrolled and graduating students seeking transfer and graduate school information. The college information desired usually includes (1) geographical locations, (2) tuition, (3) financial aid, (4) type of institution, (5) accreditation, (6) special programs, (7) college calendars, (8) campus life, (9) cultural activities, (10) residence policies, (11) social organizations, (12) religious services, (13) academic characteristics of the student body, (14) median freshman entrance test scores, (15) freshmen attrition, (16) faculty, (17) campus activities, and (18) athletic programs. In addition to the catalogs most institutions publish, a number of independent publications provide general information about most accredited institutions in the United States. Representative examples are listed later on in this section.

Vocational, trade, and technical school information should include a listing of postsecondary programs and private and public schools that offer specific entry-level trade and technical training. In particular, a listing of local, regional, and statewide programs would be most appropriate. This file may be augmented with national publications to provide general information about the trade and technical programs, and with a compilation of brochures that are usually disseminated free of charge by individual schools.

In most areas of the country, a number of outreach continuing education programs provide entry-level and advanced occupational training. A file of information about local continuing education programs can make the CRC more flexible in meeting a wide range of needs. Periodic announcements to interested individuals through available community media will increase the use of this information. Nationally published resources provide examples of the types of programs in continuing education. A few of these are listed as follows.

COLLEGE INFORMATION PUBLICATIONS

American Universities and Colleges
Otis A. Singletary and Jane P. Newman, Eds.
American Council on Education
1 Dupont Circle
Washington, DC 20036

The College Blue Book
Macmillan Information Corporation
866 Third Avenue
New York, NY 10022

American Junior Colleges
Edmund J. Gleazer, Ed.
American Council on Education
1 Dupont Circle
Washington, DC 20036

Vocational Biographies, Inc.
P.O. Box 31
Sauk Centre, MN 56378-0031
Phone: 1-800-255-0752
Fax: 320-352-5546

Peterson's Graduate and Professional Programs
Peterson's Guide to 2–4 Year Colleges
Peterson's Four-Year Colleges
(Three separate publications)
Peterson's Guides
202 Carnegie Center
P.O. Box 2123
Princeton, NJ 08543-2123

Chronicle 4-year College Data Book
Chronicle 2-year College Data Book
(Two separate publications)
Chronicle Guidance Publications, Inc.
66 Aurora Street
P.O. Box 1190
Moravia, NY 13118-1190

VOCATIONAL, TRADE, AND TECHNICAL SCHOOL PUBLICATIONS

Lovejoy's Career and Vocational School Guide—A Handbook
of Job-Training Opportunities
Clarence E. Lovejoy
Simon and Schuster, Inc.
1230 Avenue of the Americas
New York, NY 10020

Vocational Biographies, Inc.
P.O. Box 31
Sauk Centre, MN 56378-0031
Phone: 1-800-255-0752
Fax: 320-352-5546

Chronicle Vocational School Manual
Chronicle Guidance Publications, Inc.
66 Aurora Street
P.O. Box 1190
Moravia, NY 13118-1190

CONTINUING EDUCATION PUBLICATIONS

Guide to Continuing Education in America
College Entrance Examination Board
Quadrangle Books, Inc.
330 Madison Avenue
New York, NY 10017

So You Want to Go Back to School—Facing the Realities of Reentry
Elinor Lenz and Mar Hansen Shaevitz
McGraw-Hill Book Company
1221 Avenue of the Americas
New York, NY 10036

Vocational Biographies, Inc.
P.O. Box 31
Sauk Centre, MN 56378-0031
Phone: 1-800-255-0752
Fax: 320-352-5546

The Career Training Sourcebook
Sarah D. Gilbert
McGraw-Hill
1221 Avenue of the Americas
New York, NY 10036

Military Information

Another component provides information about military careers. Students generally find this component of interest because all branches of the military provide information covering special training programs. This component may provide job descriptions found in the military and related civilian jobs. The local addresses of the recruiting centers should be included. The U.S. military provides the following publications on career-related subjects:

Military Careers
U.S. Dept. of Defense
Washington, DC 20402

The U.S. Army Career and Education Guide
(Available in three editions: Student Edition; Audio/Visual Edition; and Counselor Edition)
Army Careers
U.S. Army Recruiting Command

Hampton, VA 23369
1-800-USA-ARMY

Navy Career Guide
Chief of Naval Personnel
Dept. of the Navy
Washington, DC 20370
1-800-327-NAVY

Apprenticeship and Internship Information

There is a recognized need for students to gain firsthand experience with occupations they are considering. Moreover, on-the-job training is still a very viable part of our occupational education system, and for many occupations, apprenticeship training is required. The current work-experience programs found in many educational institutions have brought a renewed interest in apprenticeship and experiential training programs. The CRC staff will want to investigate state agencies and local business and industry to compile a localized list of these programs. The following publications are examples of this type of resource.

Ferguson's Guide to Apprenticeship Programs
The New Career Center
1515 23rd Street
P.O. Box 339-GD
Boulder, CO 80306

Vocational Biographies, Inc.
P.O. Box 31
Sauk Centre, MN 56378-0031
Phone: 1-800-255-0752
Fax: 612-352-5546

Information for Special Populations

In recent years, a considerable amount of material has been published to facilitate employment of minorities, individuals with disabilities, and women. Sources of material for minorities and individuals with disabilities include the U.S. Department of Labor and other federal, state, and local agencies. The target populations reached through this component are provided with a means to increase their career options. Publications generally focus on issues faced by racial and ethnic minorities and individuals with disabilities in job placement situations. However, a substantial segment of the material discusses available training, education programs, and special financial aid programs to assist these groups.

Information about opportunities for women should contrast traditional and nontraditional jobs open to women and cover state, local, and private agencies and organizations especially designed to help women. Information for special populations may be obtained from the following sources.

INDIVIDUALS WITH DISABILITIES

Write to state and national rehabilitation agencies for up-to-date information about training programs for individuals with disabilities.

Postsecondary Education Programs for Individuals with Disabilities
Anne R. Thompson
ERIC Clearinghouse on Counseling and Student Services
ED377670
ERIC/CASS, School of Education
University of North Carolina
Greensboro, NC 27412
Phone: 1-800-414-9769
Fax: 910-334-4116

Vocational/Career Counseling and Career Education for Special Populations
National Center for Research in Vocational Education
ED354342
(Address to ERIC/CASS, as above)

MINORITIES

Write or fax the following for information on minority issues.

Quality Education for Minorities Network
Phone: 202-659-9525
Fax: 202-659-5408

National Association of Foreign Student Affairs
202-462-4811

National Black Graduate Student Association
Phone: 909-607-1244
Fax: 909-621-8390

Black Issues in Higher Education
Phone: 703-385-2981
Fax: 703-385-2981

American Council on Education
Publication Department
Department 36
Washington, DC 20055-0036
202-939-9835

WOMEN

Vocational Biographies, Inc.
P.O. Box 31
Sauk Centre, MN 56378-0031
Phone: 1-800-255-0752
Fax: 612-352-5546

AACD/NCDA Order Service Dept.
5999 Stevenson Avenue
Alexandria, VA 22304

Chronicle Guidance Publications, Inc.
P.O. Box 1190
Moravia, NY 13118-1190

Resource-Persons File

This component lists individuals from various types of occupations who volunteer to serve as resource persons. Using this resource, personal visits arranged by the CRC allow the student to make on-site investigations of a particular occupation. The name, address, telephone number, occupational field, and appointment instructions are recorded for each resource person in the file. Recorded interviews of resource persons can provide another means of personalizing occupational information. Local industrial and business directories and employment surveys of former students can serve as a valuable resource for developing a resource-persons file. At the higher education level, college alumni associations may be of great assistance in locating volunteers for the file.

Financial Aid Information

This component should include the usual types of financial aid such as loans, grants, and scholarships from federal, state, private, and local sources. Emphasis is most often placed on both local and statewide sources. A selective list of financial aid officers may also prove to be helpful. The following publications offer information on financial aid.

The Financial Aid Planner (Video)
CFKR Career Materials, Inc.
11860 Kemper Road, Unit 7
Auburn, CA 95603
1-800-525-5626

Chronicle Financial Aid Guide
Chronicle Guidance Publications, Inc.
66 Aurora Street
P.O. Box 1190
Moravia, NY 13118-1190

Vocational Biographies, Inc.
P.O. Box 31
Sauk Centre, MN 56378-0031
Phone: 1-800-255-0752
Fax: 320-352-5546

Career Planning Resources

To assist students in the most efficient use of career information resources, components that promote effective career planning skills should be considered for inclusion in the CRC. These components may be designed for independent use but will probably be more effective if used in conjunction with ongoing career counseling. Career planning resource components may include (1) career decision making, (2) vocational assessment, (3) job search skills, and (4) job simulation.

CAREER DECISION MAKING

The purpose of this component is to provide resources for teaching career decision-making techniques and self-help materials. The materials collected for this component may be used in seminars for a variety of group sessions, including seminars for older adults. A wide range of material is also available for individual study of career decision-making techniques. The following publications represent a small sample of a wide range of available materials on this topic.

> *Improved Career Decision Making in a Changing World*
> J. Ettinger (Ed.)
> Garrett Park Press
> P.O. Box 190
> Garrett Park, MD 20896

> *Choosing a Major*
> Curricular-Career Information Service
> The Career Center
> Florida State University
> Tallahassee, FL 32306-1035

> *Guided Career Exploration*
> Donald E. Super and JoAnn Bowlsbey
> The Psychological Corporation
> 555 Academic Court
> San Antonio, TX 78204-2498

> *Yes? No? Maybe? Decision Making Skills* (Video)
> Sunburst Communications
> Box 40
> Pleasantville, NY 10570-2838
> 1-800-431-1934

CAREER ASSESSMENT

A variety of tests and inventories are available for this component, including standardized cognitive measures of intelligence, achievement, aptitudes, and career maturity as well as noncognitive inventories (some of which are self-administered) of interests and other personal characteristics. Although most of these measures should be used in conjunction with a counseling program, self-administered personal assessment devices can be designed to promote self-awareness for career decision purposes. Representative examples of tests and inventories are listed in Chapter 7.

JOB SEARCH SKILLS

This component primarily provides self-help materials that assist individuals in developing interviewing skills, writing a résumé, and locating sources of job openings. There are numerous outstanding publications covering these topics, and the following list is representative of the materials available.

Job Choices Magazine
NACE
62 Highland Avenue
Bethlehem, PA 18017

Knock 'em Dead
(With great answers to tough interview questions)
Bob Adams, Inc.
840 Summer Street
Boston, MA 02127

Researching Your Way to a Good Job
The New Complete Job Search
(Two books from the following publisher)
John Wiley & Sons, Inc.
605 Third Avenue
New York, NY 10158
1-800-255-5945

The Résumé Experience
Resume Remedy
(Two videos from the following publisher)
JIST Works, Inc.
720 North Park Avenue
Indianapolis, IN 46202-3431

JOB SIMULATION COMPONENT

Career counselors have long recognized the value of experiential-learning activities in helping individuals make realistic career decisions. Job simulation exercises provide real-life experiences. The resources listed provide learning experiences that simulate working-world reality. Individuals are provided with learning experiences in exploring career fields and life and leisure activities, and they are given feedback on decisions made in the process.

Who Do You Think You Are? (CD-ROM)
The New Career Center
1515 23rd Street
P.O. Box 339-GD
Boulder, CO 80306

Life Career Game
Sage Publications, Inc.
2455 Teller Rd.
Thousand Oaks, CA 91320

Job Experience Kits
SRA-McGraw-Hill
220 East Daniel Dale
De Soto, TX 75115
1-800-843-8855

Audiovisual Materials

Many types of audiovisual materials (including filmstrips, cassettes, microfiche, films, and videotapes) are available to augment CRC information and career planning resources. Career-related information communicated via audiovisual media can often provide a refreshing break from traditional resource materials. Locally prepared audiovisual materials may be developed in addition to commercially prepared media aids. The following reference includes 650 career videos (see Appendix B).

650 Career Videos: Ratings Reviews and Descriptions
Rich Feller
Clearinghouse on Video Usage
Colorado State University
School of Education
222 Education Building
Fort Collins, CO 80523-1588
FAX: 970-491-1317

Innovations in Dissemination of Career Information

The increasing attention focused on labor forecasts and occupational data has created a genuine concern among career guidance professionals that career information be made more flexible, accessible, and attractive. Career resource materials in their traditional form can be restructured and creatively combined with nontraditional sources of material for innovative dissemination. Currently, a number of CRCs throughout the country have developed innovative means of disseminating and calling attention to their available resources. Career monographs, newsletters, posters, and other media are used to enhance access to information. These publications usually contain the employment outlook for various careers, the nature of the work, and the job status of recent graduates.

Using Past Job-Order Requests

Career planning and placement centers use past job-order requests as a means of locating prospective employers for individuals seeking placement. This material is collected by compiling the job-order requests received during the previous year in a notebook according to the date they were processed. Students are directed to scan this file for locating prospective employers who have hired individuals with qualifications similar to their own. For example, by identifying several companies that have recently hired tax accountants, the accounting major is provided with a list of prospective employers. In addition, the job-order file provides information on (1) careers available in the community, (2) actual requirements of a particular occupation, (3) realistic job descriptions, and (4) organizations that were hiring at the time the job order was processed.

Audiotapes of Major Fields of Study

Career counseling centers are developing audiotapes that describe major fields of study offered by an institution. The taped interviews usually include the department chairperson outlining areas of specialization available to students in each major field. The tapes may be structured in a variety of formats but usually contain the following information: (1) occupational forecasts for graduates in each major, (2) the occupations and graduate programs selected by previous graduates, (3) aspects of personal satisfaction experienced by others in each major field of study, and (4) special considerations for each department such as student/faculty ratio, strength of the department, research opportunities available, and other special considerations.

Videotape File

The use of videotaped presentations of individuals representing certain career fields is another innovative delivery system currently being used in some centers. These tapes may be in the form of an interview, lecture, question-and-answer format, or a combination of all three. They are often taped during career awareness week when presentations are being made to student groups. In this way, the center builds a videotape library of individuals discussing their field of work. Through these videotapes, students are able to obtain firsthand accounts of job descriptions and current requirements of particular jobs in a given career field. The videotapes appear to be an attractive method of communicating current job requirements.

The Internet

In Chapter 6, we reviewed several career resource files available on the Internet. From all indications, more career-related resources and interactive programs will be developed. The great advantage of these materials is that they are easily accessible and up to date. The increasing demand for resources the Internet can offer suggests that the CRC should provide space and equipment of equal importance for access to information on what is currently available and instructions on how to access different programs and information.

Career Resource Centers in Industrial Organizations

This chapter has been devoted primarily to the discussion of CRCs in educational institutions and in state agencies; however, industrial organizations are also interested in supporting CRCs for their employees (Moir, 1981). The purpose is to assist employees in their career development through a variety of resource components similar to those found in educational institutions. A good example of a CRC in an industry is the one established in 1976 by the University of California's Lawrence Livermore National Laboratory (LLNL) in Livermore. The LLNL is an organization devoted to applied research consisting of several thousand employees, including scientists, engineers, technicians, administrators, and clerical personnel. The CRC was established to provide information to interested employees about educational opportunities, career development, reference material for on-site training courses, and resources for training managers and supervisors (Moir, 1981).

The resource components in the LLNL CRC consist of the following: (1) educational information (catalogs of all colleges within 100 miles and other educational programs); (2) career planning (occupational references, methods for job seeking, career guides, and career planning theory); (3) world of work (resources for job opportunities and training requirements); (4) personal growth (books and cassettes containing such topics as adult development, alcoholism, employee development, assertiveness training, retirement, stress and time management, and women's issues); (5) management/supervision (resources for improving leadership effectiveness, interviewing, and managerial behavior); (6) computerized career information system; (7) periodicals (professional journals and newsletters); (8) self-study (resources for personal improvement, including in-house programs on employee development, and several courses of study, including English grammar); and (9) off-site training (resources on seminars and conventions).

The LLNL CRC has been used for educational information (25% of inquiries), management supervision (15%), job finding skills (10%), off-site training (5%), and self-study (5%) (Moir, 1981). In the first five years of its existence, the LLNL CRC received the endorsement of management and was used by a wide range of employees, including senior scientists as well as individuals in entry-level positions. Moir (1981) suggested that the career development of employees is a good rationale for maintaining interest and creativity in industrial organizations. CRCs also provide supervisors and managers with a referral source in support of career path and developmental programs as discussed in Chapter 14.

The reported innovations for using career information are only representative examples of methods in use today. We have merely scratched the surface of methodology for making the working world a relevant and meaningful part of our educational programs. It is only a matter of time before teachers and counselors build a vast volume of techniques and programs that will improve the understanding of the relatively unknown working world. The examples of innovations discussed verify that the study of occupational data can be interesting and certainly informative!

Summary

1. In the past decade, centrally located facilities for collecting and displaying career-related materials have been developed in educational institutions at all levels. The centrally located centers have often been referred to as Career Resource Centers (CRCs).

2. A CRC provides the opportunity to systematically organize all career materials into more efficient and workable units.

3. Organizational procedures include the establishment of an advisory committee consisting of a cross section of faculty members and the local business community.

4. Objectives and operational procedures for the CRC will, to a large extent, depend on local needs and available resources.

5. The ideal location for a CRC is in high-traffic areas of the campus. Existing classrooms and counseling centers may be modified to accommodate a CRC. Ideally the CRC consists of space for individual study, group meetings, browsing, displays, audiovisual equipment, and computer programs.

6. A number of specific information resource components considered for the CRC include (a) occupational descriptions, (b) occupational outlook projections, (c) postsecondary educational and training information, (d) military information, (e) apprenticeship and internship information, (f) information for special populations, (g) a resource-persons file, and (h) financial aid information.

7. Resource components that promote effective career planning skills include (a) career decision making, (b) vocational assessment, (c) job search skills, and (d) job simulation.

8. Innovative programs for dissemination of career information include career monographs that provide information to college students on employment outlook, nature of work, and job status of recent graduates, by major fields of study. Past job-order requests in placement centers are used in career counseling programs to provide information on careers available in the community, actual requirements of a particular occupation, realistic job descriptions, and organizations that were hiring at the time the job order was processed. University placement centers are also collecting audiotapes that describe major fields of study offered at the university. Videotape files of individuals representing certain career fields are another innovative delivery system being used in career planning and placement offices. Industrial organizations are interested in supporting CRCs for employee use.

Supplementary Learning Exercises

1. Visit a CRC and report on the following:
   a. resource-component classification system used
   b. square footage and floor plan
   c. programs serviced by the CRC

    d. resource materials used

    e. filing system

    f. organizational structure

2. Design and rationalize a floor plan for a CRC for one or more of the following:

    a. middle school

    b. senior high school

    c. community two-year college

    d. four-year college

    e. community center offering career counseling to adults

3. Select and name the resource components that you consider are most needed by a community college and a four-year college. Rank the components in order and defend your choices.

4. Select and name the resource components that you believe are essential for a middle school, high school, and community agency providing career counseling to adults. Defend your choices.

5. Assume that you were selected as a career counselor in a local high school and were asked to establish a CRC. Develop the goals, objectives, organizational structure, and rationale.

6. Describe the strategies you would use for improving the use of a CRC for career education programs in a middle school.

7. Visit a high school principal and a member of the local business community and discuss their ideas and suggestions for establishing a CRC in the local high school. Report your discussions, including a summary of how the community and high school could cooperate in the development of a CRC.

8. Develop a needs-assessment inventory for a community college CRC. Begin by defining the purpose of the inventory.

9. Inventory career-related materials that are available to the public in a small community. Begin by visiting the community library. Develop a plan to most effectively utilize these materials for community-sponsored career counseling programs.

10. Defend the following statement: A CRC is an essential facility for current career counseling programs.

PART TWO

Career Guidance Programs in Educational Institutions

Implications of Developmental Patterns and Research for Career Guidance in Schools

Human development is not an isolated, detached, or unrelated series of events in life; rather, it is a blend of diverse elements including psychosocial and economic variables. These interacting elements formulate life stages and cover the entire life span. Understanding human development is one of the essential ingredients leading to a greater comprehension and interpretation of career development stages and tasks.

Selected models of human development and related research are discussed in this chapter. The discussion focuses on issues that may be used to develop career guidance programs for elementary school children and adolescents in junior and senior high schools.

The vast number and variety of human development studies include many research models and theoretical orientations from several academic disciplines, including developmental psychology. Understandably, there are differences of opinion about how to interpret this accumulated wealth of information and how to apply it to programs and practices in career guidance. However, the interrelationships between human and career development are becoming more clear as investigators carry out more complete and sophisticated experiments and apply their results to more comprehensive sets of principles. Of course, more research is still needed to provide definitive evidence of relationships between career and human developmental models, but meanwhile human developmental models and selected research provide career counselors with a greater understanding of their task of building goals and developing career guidance programs.

This chapter is divided into three sections that explore the developmental patterns of and selected research on elementary school children, junior high school students, and senior high school students. At the end of each section, implications for career guidance programs are presented.

195

Studies of Early Childhood Development

Early childhood, especially the first three years, has been previously designated as the most formative years in human development (White, 1959). Before the 1970s, child development specialists seemed convinced that the first three years greatly determined a person's future motives, drives, and behavior. More recently, this viewpoint has gradually shifted to a more adaptive view of human development over the life span. Moreover, each stage of development has its own set of unique tasks to be accomplished for a smooth transition.

In studying human development over the life span, Biehler and Hudson (1986) reviewed several longitudinal studies:

1. Early personality tendencies may be diverted by the experiences one has during subsequent stages of development.
2. Predictions of adult adjustment based on child behavior were often found to be inaccurate. Individuals have a profound adaptive capacity at various stages of development.
3. Even the negative impact of infant deprivation does not have a permanent negative effect for all children.

These results suggest that *all* stages of human development are important. Infancy may be better viewed as a very important and sensitive period in an individual's development, rather than one necessarily having a permanent impact on later behavior. Moreover, the impressive adaptive capacity found in human development longitudinal studies illustrates the importance of developmental tasks at different stages of the life span.

Stages of Development and Developmental Tasks for Elementary School Children

Stage theorists have concentrated on developmental patterns that take the form of accomplishments, events, and psychological, physiological, and sociological changes in human development. During the transition process from one stage to another, developmental tasks provide a description of requirements or actions that are necessary to pass successfully through a stage of development. This perspective suggests a foundation for building effective career guidance programs. Only selected theories and research are summarized here; more in-depth coverage of these subjects can be found in developmental psychology textbooks.

Boxes 9-1 through 9-3 summarize the continuity of development by stages, ages, grades in school, and the developmental tasks assigned to stages. Erikson's (1963) developmental stages have been selected as a good example of the stage theorists' approach; Piaget's (1929) research has been selected to illustrate cognitive development; and Havighurst's (1972) well-known work is a good example of

BOX 9-1
Havighurst's Developmental Stages

Developmental tasks of infancy and early childhood
1. Learning to walk
2. Learning to take solid foods
3. Learning to talk
4. Learning to control the elimination of body wastes
5. Learning sex differences and sexual modesty
6. Forming concepts and learning language to describe social and physical reality
7. Preparing to read
8. Learning to distinguish right and wrong, and the beginning of conscience development

Developmental tasks of middle childhood (ages 6 to 12 years)
1. Learning physical skills necessary for ordinary games
2. Building wholesome attitudes toward oneself as a growing organism
3. Learning to get along with peers
4. Learning an appropriate masculine or feminine social role
5. Developing fundamental skills in reading, writing, and calculating
6. Developing concepts necessary for everyday living
7. Developing morality, a conscience, and a scale of values
8. Achieving personal independence
9. Developing attitudes toward social groups and institutions

Developmental tasks of adolescence (ages 12 to 18 years)
1. Achieving new and more mature relations with peers of both sexes
2. Achieving a masculine or feminine role in society
3. Accepting one's physique and using the body effectively
4. Achieving emotional independence from parents and other adults
5. Preparing for marriage and family life
6. Preparing for an economic career
7. Acquiring a set of values and an ethical system as a guide to behavior—developing an ideology
8. Desiring and achieving socially responsible behavior

Developmental tasks of early adulthood (ages 19 to 30 years)
1. Selecting a mate
2. Learning to live with a marriage partner
3. Starting a family
4. Rearing a family
5. Managing a home
6. Getting started in an occupation
7. Taking on civic responsibility
8. Finding a congenial social group

(continued)

BOX 9-1   *(continued)*

Developmental tasks of middle age (ages 30 to 60 years)
1. Assisting teenage children to become responsible and happy adults
2. Achieving adult social and civic responsibility
3. Reaching and maintaining satisfactory performance in one's occupational career
4. Developing adult leisure-time activities
5. Relating to one's spouse as a person
6. Accepting and adjusting to the physiological changes of middle age
7. Adjusting to aging parents

Developmental tasks of later maturity (ages over 60 years)
1. Adjusting to decreasing physical strength and health
2. Death of a spouse
3. Adjusting to retirement and reduced income
4. Establishing an explicit affiliation with one's age group
5. Adopting and adapting social roles in a flexible way
6. Establishing satisfactory physical living arrangements

SOURCE: From *Developmental Tasks and Education,* 3rd ed., by R. J. Havighurst. Copyright © 1972 by Longman Publishing Group. Reprinted by permission of Addison-Wesley Educational Publishers, Inc.

BOX 9-2
Piaget's Stages of Cognitive Development

Sensorimotor stage (0 to 2 years)
Individuals develop schemes through senses and motor actions.

Preoperational stage (2 to 5 years)
During this stage, individuals develop symbolic images but have little ability to perceptualize viewpoints other than their own.

Concrete operational stage (6 to 12 years)
This is the beginning phase of understanding differences by means of stimuli. Children solve problems only by generalizing from concrete experiences.

Formal operational stage (adolescence)
At this stage, the ability to utilize hypothetical/deductive thinking provides many solutions to a problem rather than a single answer. Individuals are able to deal with abstractions and engage in mental manipulations.

SOURCE: Adapted from Piaget, 1929.

BOX 9-3
Stages of Psychosocial Development

Trust versus mistrust (0 to 1 years)
Order in the environment and consistency in the quality of care lead to trust. Inconsistency and unpredictable care lead to mistrust.

Autonomy versus doubt (1 to 3 years)
Opportunities to explore or try out skills provide a sense of autonomy. Excessive rejection and lack of support lead to doubt.

Initiative versus guilt (3 to 5 years)
Freedom to express self through activities and language creates a sense of initiative, whereas some restrictions create a sense of guilt.

Industry versus inferiority (6 to 11 years)
Freedom to make things and to organize them leads to a sense of being industrious. Persistent failure to produce or to perform valued activities leads to a sense of inferiority.

Identity versus role confusion (11 to 18 years)
Through a multitude of experiences in different environments, the individual seeks continuity and sameness of self in search of an identity. Confusion may lead to a negative identity, perhaps a socially unacceptable one.

Intimacy versus isolation (young adulthood)
Commitment in terms of reaching out to others for a lasting relationship leads to intimacy. Isolation and a lack of close personal relationships is a result of competitive and combative behavior.

Generativity versus stagnation (middle age)
During this stage one concentrates on guiding and preparing the next generation. Focusing primarily on self creates a sense of stagnation.

Integrity versus despair (old age)
A sense of integrity is developed from acceptance of one's life and satisfaction with past achievements and accomplishments. Despair comes from the perception that life has been unsatisfying and misdirected.

SOURCE: Adapted from Erikson, 1963.

---

developmental tasks over the life span. Other developmental stages and tasks will be discussed when relevant.

According to Havighurst, the developmental tasks expected of students before leaving the sixth grade reveal a set of physical and academic skills, social role development, and personalized values. Practically all of these tasks can be related to Super's (1990) concept of career development tasks (see Chapter 2). For example, during the growth stage (ages 0 to 14), according to Super's scheme of developmental stages and tasks, individuals go through numerous experiential learning activities while developing greater self-awareness. Directed experiences in the elementary school that promote physical and academic growth, interpersonal relationships with members of the same and the opposite sex, and self-concept development are important components of career development. Students who fail to achieve the developmental tasks in both Havighurst's and Super's steps may require special attention and direction.

Erikson suggested that the stage of development from ages 6 to 11 emphasizes industriousness; that is, children learn that productivity brings recognition and reward. In Erikson's view, children develop a sense of industriousness through their accomplishments, but they may be intimidated by the requirements of success and develop a sense of inferiority. Expressing success through academic achievement, for example, is a major contributor to establishing industriousness in terms of work-role and self-concept development. A sense of inferiority at this stage of development calls for intervention strategies of an individualized nature.

Learning through Concrete Experiences and Observations

Piaget (1929), noted for his work in cognitive development, has provided a description of how humans think and what the characteristics are of their thinking at different stages of development. In early development, children cultivate "schemes" through their senses and motor activities. During the years from ages 2 through 5, children begin to develop conceptual levels but do not yet have the ability to think logically or abstractly. By the time children reach elementary school age, they have developed the ability to apply logic to thinking and can understand simple concepts. Through concrete experiences, children learn to make consistent generalizations. For example, children learn to classify persons or objects in more than one category (the Little League coach can also be a police officer).

Encouraging and directing concrete experiences to promote increasingly abstract conceptual operations during this stage of development is a vital part of educational and career guidance programming in elementary schools. An example of an exercise illustrating this process would be asking students to identify one type of skill necessary for good schoolwork and then asking them to identify a job that requires a specific school subject.

Observation is also a contributing element to early cognitive development. Krumboltz's learning theory of career choice and counseling, discussed in Chapter 2, emphasizes the importance of observation learning attributed to reactions to consequences, observable results of actions, and reactions to others (Mitchell & Krumboltz, 1996). Children are particularly prone to adopting the behavior models they observe (Fagot & Leinbach, 1989). According to Bandura (1977, 1986), there are five stages of observable learning: (1) paying attention, (2) remembering what is observed, (3) reproducing actions, (4) becoming motivated (to reproduce what is observed), and (5) perfecting an imitation according to what was observed. Within this frame of reference, parents, teachers, teachers' aides, and classmates are potential models that elementary school children will imitate. Of course, models may come from other sources, such as television, movies, and books. The potential benefits of observational learning for career development of elementary school children are of major importance. Directed observable learning experiences involving work roles are an important component of early career guidance programs.

Self-Concept Development

In Chapter 2, brief mention was made of Super's self-concept theory and its pervasive nature (Super et al., 1963). In a later publication, Super (1990) clarified his position on the nature and scope of self-concept in career development. Individuals, in Super's view, have constellations of self-concepts, or "self-concept systems," that denote sets or constellations of traits. In an elementary school setting, for example, an individual may have a different view of self as a student and as a member of a peer group. An individual may see himself or herself as gregarious while also being a weak student or not very intelligent. Elementary students are formulating sets of self-concepts as they focus on class requirements; interrelationships with peers, teachers, and important adults; and the social structure in which they live and function.

In her theory of circumscription and compromise, discussed in Chapter 2, Gottfredson focuses on the development of self-images and occupational aspirations in four stages. In the first stage, Orientation to Size and Power (ages 3 to 5), children recognize adult occupational roles and exhibit same-sex preferences for adult activities, including employment. During stage two, Orientation to Sex Roles (ages 6 to 8), children focus on what is appropriate for one's sex; they now recognize that adult activities are sex-typed. As a result, children tend to dismiss occupations that are considered appropriate for the other sex. In stage three, Orientation to Social Valuation (ages 9 to 13), children rule out low-status occupations as preferences. As Gottfredson (1996) puts it, "they reject occupational alternatives that seem inconsistent with those new elements of self" (p. 193).

Self-concept development is not a static phenomenon but an ongoing process, which changes sometimes gradually and sometimes abruptly as people and situations change. In elementary school, children experience for the first time many aspects of existence in an adult world, such as competition and expectations of productive performance. In play, they interact with peers and also assume roles in supervised and unsupervised situations. Self-esteem for some will be enhanced through academic achievement, whereas others will experience both positive and negative feedback in peer-socialization activities. Enhanced self-esteem encourages development of personal ideas and opinions of a positive nature; accurate self-concepts contribute to career maturity.

Play as a Factor in Career Development

Examining the period of childhood before age 11, Ginzberg and associates (1951) theorized that various occupational roles are assumed in play, resulting in initial value judgments of the world of work. Engaging in such activities is intrinsically rewarding for children, but their expressed occupational choices are made with little regard for reality. However, by the middle of the elementary school years, work orientation displaces play orientation. Similarly, Elkind (1981) and Gibson, Mitchell, and Basile (1993) suggested that children in the upper elementary grades have developed a more realistic view of the adult world—that is, a sense of independence and self-reliance.

Self-attributes become more prominent among children in upper elementary grades, causing them to intensify their focus on personal likes and dislikes.

Physical Development of Elementary School Children

Physical growth and maturation during the elementary school years play a major role in psychosocial development. Of particular significance is the noticeable difference in growth rate between boys and girls. At age 6 years, girls are on the average slightly shorter than boys, but by age 10, they are as tall or taller. The average age of puberty for girls is 12.5; for boys, 14 (Tanner, 1972). Many U.S. girls reach puberty before they finish the sixth grade.

Differences in growth and physiological changes between girls and boys in elementary school greatly influence social relationships and emerging self-perceptions. Learning appropriate masculine or feminine roles, according to Havighurst (1972) and Gottfredson (1996), among others, precludes greater equality between sexes, especially in occupational behavior. Of particular importance are perceptions of appropriate behavior patterns—that is, patterns regarded as acceptable for a given sex. Sex-role stereotyping is fostered through observation and imitation of male and female models. Other influences come through textbooks, other books, and popular television programs that describe and depict differences in roles for boys and girls. (See Chapters 15 and 16 for more detailed discussion.)

Influence of Cultural and Socioeconomic Diversity on Childhood Development

Our society is both economically and ethnically diverse; African American, Asian American, Hispanic American, and Native American children may have different developmental experiences than do children of the now dominant society of white European background (Sigelman & Shaffer, 1995). Differences within these groups vary considerably, primarily as a result of such factors as length of time in the United States, language usage, socioeconomic status, and level of acculturation (integration into mainstream society). Children of different cultures have been judged by the dominant society's standards for many years, but researchers have become more oriented to adopting a contextual perspective of human development (see Chapter 18 for more information on this subject).

Socioeconomic status (SES)—which is based on income, education, occupational status, and location of home—defines one's position in society (Brislin, 1993).

But, according to Garbarino (1992), about one out of five children in the United States lives in poverty. Many of these are members of ethnic groups such as African Americans, Hispanic Americans, and Native Americans. Lower-SES parents are likely to have expectations for their children that are different from those of middle- and upper-SES parents. Parenting styles may differ significantly. Lower-SES parents expect their children to be like themselves; they emphasize conformity and obedience, and they expect their children will eventually work for a boss in a blue-collar job. Middle- and upper-class parents also expect their children to be like themselves; thus they stress being independent, self-assertive, and creative and working for economic security, perhaps eventually owning their own business (Brislin, 1993).

These examples of different expectations and subsequent parenting styles influence children's development and career aspirations. Children from different cultures have special needs, which will be discussed in more detail in Chapter 18. In the meantime, we should learn to appreciate cultural diversity, be prepared to assist individuals in their career development, and in fact become advocates for the special needs of all children. The adaptive capacity found in human development, as discussed earlier, suggests that relevant strategies can also assist children from different socioeconomic and cultural backgrounds.

The National Occupational Information Coordinating Committee (NOICC, 1992) outlines three areas of career development for students in elementary school as follows:

1. Self-knowledge
   a. Knowledge of the importance of self-concept
   b. Skills to interact with others
   c. Awareness of the importance of growth and change
2. Educational and occupational exploration
   a. Awareness of the benefits of educational achievement
   b. Awareness of the relationship between work and learning
   c. Skills to understand and use career information
   d. Awareness of the importance of personal responsibility and good work habits
   e. Awareness of how work relates to the needs and functions of society
3. Career planning
   a. Understanding of how to make decisions
   b. Awareness of the interrelationship of life roles
   c. Awareness of different occupations and changing male/female roles
   d. Awareness of the career planning process

Implications for Career Guidance at the Elementary-School Level

The preceding recommended three areas of career development for students in elementary school, combined with other research reported in this section, suggest many ideas that can be applied to career guidance programs in elementary schools.

Following is a representative list; related career guidance techniques will be reported in Chapter 10.

1. Self-concepts begin to form in early childhood. Because of the influence of self-concept formation on career development, there is strong evidence of the importance of directed experiences in enhancing self-concept in the elementary school.
2. An important aspect of career development is to build an understanding of strengths and limitations. Learning to identify and express strengths and limitations is a good way to build a foundation for self-understanding.
3. Elementary school children imitate role models in the home and school. Both parents and teachers can provide children with positive role models through precept and example.
4. Children learn to associate work roles by sexual stereotyping at an early age. Exposure to career information that discourages sex-role stereotyping will broaden the range of occupations considered available by children.
5. Community resources provide a rich source of career information, role models, and exposure to a wide range of careers. Students from families whose parents did not attend high school have a special need for community opportunities.
6. Self-awareness counseling is a major goal of the growth stage in elementary schools. Methods used to enhance self-awareness encourage development of the ability to process and interpret information about self and others and about differences among people.
7. Learning to assume responsibility for decisions and actions has major implications for future career decisions. Some beginning steps include skills development that enables children to analyze situations, to identify people who can help them, and to seek assistance when needed.
8. Understanding the relationship between education and work is a key concept for enhancing career development. Skills learned in school and during out-of-school activities should be linked to work-related activities.
9. The idea that all work is important builds an understanding of why parents and others work. Reflection on the reasons for working fosters an awareness that any productive worker should be respected.
10. Learning about occupations and about people who are actually involved in occupations builds an awareness of differences among people and occupations.

Stages of Development and Developmental Tasks for Junior and Senior High School Students

Adolescence has been described as a period of turmoil resulting in a transition from childhood. Continuity of development is, for some, sporadic and chaotic. The key characteristic of this stage of development, according to Erikson, is the search for identity as one subordinates childhood identifications and reaches for a different identity in a more complex set of conditions and circumstances. The major danger of this period is role confusion; thus, this stage is often designated "Identity versus Confusion."

In Erikson's (1963) view, this is a critical period of development. As he put it, "These new identifications are no longer characterized by the playfulness of childhood and the experimental zest of youth: with dire urgency they force the young individual into choices and decisions which will, with increasing immediacy, lead to commitments for life" (p. 155).

According to Erikson, the choice of career and commitment to a career has a significant impact on identity. Because of the current difficulty surrounding occupational choice in terms of rapidly changing job markets and impersonal organizations, Erikson suggested that many careers pose a threat to personal identity; subsequently, some individuals avoid a firm career choice. Many adolescents delay commitment or place a psychological moratorium on the decision until further options are explored. Excerpts from an interview with Ted illustrate this point.

Ted: My parents want me here so that I can choose a career. They don't like it that I haven't picked one.

Counselor: As I said, we should be able to help you, Ted, but first, tell me more about jobs or careers you have considered.

Ted: I thought about a few, like photography, but I really don't know what I want.

Counselor: Tell me more about your thoughts on photography.

Ted: A photographer like Mr. Brown is not what I want to be. I guess I'd like to work for a magazine.

Counselor: You mentioned Mr. Brown. What don't you like about his job?

Ted: I don't want to take pictures of weddings and things like that. To tell the truth, I don't really know much about what a photographer or any other worker does. I just wish my parents would leave me alone until I have more time. I'm going to community college next fall and I want to decide while I'm there.

A young person unable to avoid role confusion may adopt what is referred to as a "negative identity," assuming forms of behavior that are in direct conflict with family and society. Those who soon develop a more appropriate sense of direction may find this experience positive, but for others, the negative identity is maintained throughout adulthood. Identity diffusion, according to Erikson, often results in lack of commitment to a set of values and, subsequently, to occupations.

Likewise, Super (1990) and Crites and Savickas (1996) suggested strong relationships between identity and career commitment as variables of career maturity. Career maturity implies a stabilized identity that provides individuals with a framework for making career choices, a crystallized formation of self-perceptions, and developed skills. Career maturity is a continuous developmental process and presents specific identifiable characteristics and traits essential to career development. Characteristic of career maturity are the traits of decisiveness and independence, knowledge of occupational information, and skills in planning and decision making. (Chapter 7 reviews career maturity inventories that provide specific information about other dimensions of career maturity.)

Finally, defining appropriate sexual roles and achieving relationships with peers are crucial developmental tasks for adolescents (Havighurst, 1972). Success in accomplishing these tasks is essential to social adjustment at this stage of life. Socially responsible behavior implies that the first steps have been taken in achieving emotional independence from parents and other adults. According to Havighurst, social relationship patterns learned during adolescence greatly affect an individual's adjustment to the rules and life roles, including the work role, of the dominant society.

Cognitive Development during Junior and Senior High School

Following Piaget's (Piaget & Inhelder, 1969) cognitive developmental stages, as shown in Box 9-2, the transition from concrete operational thinking to formal thought is a gradual process beginning at approximately 12 years of age. During early adolescence, patterns of problem solving and planning are quite unsystematic. Near the end of high school, however, the adolescent has the ability to deal with abstractions, form hypotheses in problem solving, and sort out problems through mental manipulations. Linking observations and emotional responses with a recently developed systematic thinking process, the adolescent reacts to events and experiences with a newly found power of thought. In formal thought, the adolescent can direct emotional responses to abstract ideals as well as to people. Introspective thinking leads to analysis of self in situations, including projection of the self into the adult world of work (Piaget & Inhelder, 1969; Elkind, 1968; Keating, 1980; Gillies, 1989).

The cognitive development of formal thought introduces sets of ambiguities. On one hand, the adolescent is developing a systematized thinking process to solve problems appropriately. On the other hand, there is unrestrained theorizing, extreme self-analysis, and more-than-usual concern about the reactions of others. By virtue of concern for others, the peer group influence is particularly strong during adolescence. Self-analysis can lead to what Miller-Tiedeman and Tiedeman (1990) refer to as "I-power" as a means of self-development. Increased self-awareness is an essential part of the adolescent's development, particularly in clarifying self-status and individualized belief systems in the career decision-making process.

In the development of formalized thinking, adolescents do not simply respond to stimuli but also interpret what they observe (Bandura, 1977, 1986). In this connection, they will perceive stimuli in the environment as having positive and negative associations. An example of a negative association is a junior high student who believes that lawyers "rip you off because they are all crooks." In this sense, perceptions and values associated with occupations are developed through generalizations formed by experience and observations. In terms of persons who have the greatest influence or impact on adolescent values, Brown, Mounts, Lamborn, and Steinberg (1993) found that parents have the greatest influence on the long-range plans of adolescents, but peers are more likely to influence immediate identity or status. Occupational stereotypes as perceived in career decision making may be generalized from interactions with both parents and peers as well as gained through other stimuli, such as films and books.

Physiological Development of Adolescents in Junior and Senior High School

A dramatic physiological change, sexual maturity, takes place for most boys and girls during junior and senior high school. Accompanying or preceding sexual maturity are dramatic bodily changes, such as increased muscle tissue and body stature, which permit the adolescent to perform adult physical tasks for the first time. Of particular importance to the adolescent is physical appearance. In junior high school, concern for appearance reaches its peak as girls compare themselves to movie and television stars, females appearing in commercials, and professional models. Boys use the standards of strength and facial and bodily hair for judging early maturity (Biehler & Hudson, 1986). Feeling comfortable within the dominant peer group is highly related to being judged as "grown-up" or mature.

Reflecting on sexual maturity, Cal related the following incident:

> I wanted to do everything I could to be grown up, but I was just a little twerp. I even tried to imitate how men walked. I guess I was 12 or 13 when I lit my first cigarette. Even though I coughed until I almost choked, I kept on smoking that cigarette! Yes sir, I wanted to be one of those "cool cats" with all the know-how.
>
> But the worst of it was P.E. I didn't want to undress in front of anybody. I made up all kinds of excuses until the locker room was clear, and then I went home and showered.
>
> You know, it was important then to be accepted by my friends. I guess I ended up being liked by most of them. Now when I look back, it seems we were all trying to fool each other.

Quiang, an early-maturing junior high school student, reflected on her experiences:

> All of a sudden it seemed I had outgrown everyone—especially the boys. Some of the girls seemed as physically mature as I was, but they usually acted uneasy around me, and I certainly felt awkward around them. It was during this time that I made friends with some older girls. As far as the boys were concerned, there were mixed feelings. The older boys didn't accept me because I was "too young," while the younger ones were too little for me. I just felt out of place for a few years until everybody caught up.

After reviewing several longitudinal research projects to determine immediate effects of early and late maturity, Livson and Peskin (1980) reached the following conclusions:

1. Early-maturing males were most likely to be viewed more favorably by adults, thus leading to a greater sense of confidence and poise.

2. Late-maturing males exhibited attention-seeking behavior to compensate for feelings of inferiority.
3. Early-maturing girls were psychologically and socially out of sync with their peers.
4. Late-maturing girls who went through less abrupt physical changes were viewed as more petite and feminine and enjoyed popularity and leadership privileges.

The effects of early and late sexual maturity provide a frame of reference for counseling intervention. There is evidence that early maturity for males holds certain benefits in terms of appropriateness among male peer groups and adults. Late-maturing girls also enjoy acceptance and popularity (Livson & Peskin, 1980).

Simmons and Blyth (1987) confirm early and late maturity differences and their related benefits and costs, and they report some additional special effects:

Early-maturing boys had more dates and dated more often than did late-maturing boys. Furthermore, they were more positive about physical development and athletic abilities.

Early-maturing girls had poorer grades in school and had more discipline problems. Also, they were more negative about their physical development.

Sexual maturity may be one basis for differentiating career guidance activities. Late-maturing males and early-maturing girls may experience a greater need for counseling intervention than do their peers. It seems justifiable to suggest that junior high school students benefit from guidance programs that inform them of the extent, type, and variation of physiological changes in early adolescence and that specifically address anxieties related to bodily changes (Thomas, 1973; Richards & Larson, 1993).

The National Occupational Information Coordinating Committee (NOICC, 1992) outlines three areas of career development for students in middle/junior high school as follows.

1. Self-knowledge
   a. Knowledge of the influence of a positive self-concept
   b. Skills to interact with others
   c. Knowledge of the importance of growth and change
2. Educational and occupational exploration
   a. Knowledge of the benefits of educational achievement to career opportunities
   b. Knowledge of the relationship between work and learning
   c. Skills to locate, understand, and use career information
   d. Knowledge of skills necessary to seek and obtain jobs
   e. Understanding of how work relates to the needs and functions of the economy and society
3. Career planning
   a. Skills to make decisions
   b. Knowledge of the interrelationship of life roles
   c. Knowledge of different occupations and changing male/female roles
   d. Understanding of the process of career planning

Implications for Career Guidance in Junior High School

The foregoing recommended three areas of career development for students in middle or junior high school, combined with research, yield numerous implications for career guidance programs in junior high school.

1. In many respects, junior high school is an educational transition from structured classroom settings to more specialized educational programs. Learning to relate acquired skills to educational/occupational goals promotes exploratory reflection and activities.

2. There appears to be a strong need to increase junior high school students' ability to realistically appraise their own abilities, achievements, and interests. Minority students and students from homes where parents' education level is low need special assistance in understanding their strengths and limitations.

3. Students in junior high school have difficulty in identifying and evaluating their interests in relation to total life experiences.

4. A limited knowledge of occupations makes it difficult for junior high school students to relate in- and out-of-school activities to future jobs. Exposure to jobs and career fields should be expanded to provide a basis for linking various activities to work.

5. The naiveté and limited knowledge of the factors necessary in evaluating future work roles suggest the desirability of introducing informational resources and teaching the necessary skills for their use. Learning about career options, for example, increases awareness of exploration opportunities.

6. Physiological development and sexual maturity during junior high school involve individual changes in self-perceptions and social interactions. Opportunities to explore, evaluate, and reflect on values seem to be very desirable activities for promoting a better understanding of self during this stage.

7. Junior high school students will greatly benefit from hands-on experience with skill activities associated with occupations. Basic and concrete experiences provide a means of learning skills utilized in work.

8. Because junior high school students should begin to assume responsibility for their own behavior, they would greatly benefit from improved knowledge of planning, decision-making, and problem-solving skills.

9. Increased awareness of sexual differences among junior high school students suggests that emphasis be placed on learning how sex-role stereotyping, bias, and discrimination limit occupational and educational choices.

10. Students in junior high school who continue the process of awareness initiated in elementary school will recognize the changing nature of career commitment. The skills and knowledge learned to evaluate initial career choices will be used to evaluate others over the life span.

Need for Career Guidance in High Schools

The results of a recent Gallup survey sponsored by the National Career Development Association and reported by Hoyt and Lester (1995) strongly suggest that high schools should give more attention to career development, help all students plan careers, help all students develop job skills, help all students find jobs, and help work-bound students develop work skills. More specifically, the respondents suggested the changes reported in Table 9-1.

It is interesting to observe that responses from both women and men did not differ very much in terms of recommended changes. In fact, none of the responses between men and women were significantly different. The results also indicate that slightly more than one-third of both women and men answered "not enough attention" was given to prepare students for college, whereas over 64% of both men and women answered that there was not enough attention given to placing high school dropouts and graduates into jobs. Also, over 55% of both men and women felt that more help was needed in developing job skills and job interviewing techniques.

Adults were asked whether they believed that the high schools in their community were sufficiently preparing students in seven areas related to the recent emphasis on school-to-work skills. Specifically, the adults were asked whether high schools pay enough attention to helping students (1) choose careers, (2) develop job skills, (3) learn how to identify local job openings, (4) obtain work after high school, (5) learn to use occupational information, (6) develop job finding skills, and (7) prepare for college. The findings indicate that more than half of the adults surveyed said high schools were not doing enough to help students in all areas surveyed except in preparing them for college (37%).

Some of the questions asked of the respondents were very similar in nature, but the first data reported focused on the idea of career emphasis in secondary education reform, whereas the other reported results reflected the public's perception of the high schools' emphasis on school-to-work skills. However, we can conclude from the data that there are specific needs that are not being met in high school career guidance programs.

TABLE 9-1

Percent of Suggested Changes among Women and Men Choosing "Not Enough Attention"

Suggested change	% Women	% Men
Place high school dropouts and graduates into jobs	64.1	64.1
Help students choose their careers	50.8	51.0
Help students who do not go to college develop skills so they can get jobs after graduation	56.8	62.6
Help students develop skills in identifying jobs that are open in their communities	54.5	53.0
Help students learn how to use occupational information about salary and working conditions	54.7	58.8
Help students develop the skills they need to get jobs such as job interviewing techniques	59.4	55.2
Prepare students for college	37.8	36.0

Note. $N = 1,046$.

SOURCE: Reprinted from *Learning to Work: The NCDA Gallup Survey,* by K. B. Hoyt and J. N. Lester, p. 63. Copyright 1995 by the National Career Development Association. Reprinted with permission of NCDA.

Recently, comprehensive school guidance programs (Gysbers & Henderson, 1988) are being developed and considered for adoption by a number of school systems. Also "school-to-work" is a new approach to learning for all students, sponsored jointly by the U.S. Department of Education and Department of Labor. Yet another program is "planning for life," sponsored by the U.S. Army Recruiting Command with the support of the National Consortium of State Career Guidance Supervisors and the Center on Education and Training for Employment at the Ohio State University. These programs are mentioned here to show the growing demand for efficient career guidance programs in schools, including the high schools. These programs will be discussed in more detail in Chapter 10.

The National Occupational Information Coordinating Committee (NOICC, 1992) outlines three areas of career development for students in high school as follows:

1. Self-knowledge
   a. Understanding the influence of a positive self-concept
   b. Skills to interact positively with others
   c. Understanding the impact of growth and development
2. Educational and occupational exploration
   a. Understanding the relationship between educational achievement and career planning
   b. Understanding the need for positive attitudes toward work and learning
   c. Skills to locate, evaluate, and interpret career information
   d. Skills to prepare to seek, obtain, maintain, and change jobs
   e. Understanding how societal needs and functions influence the nature and structure of work
3. Career planning
   a. Skills to make decisions
   b. Understanding the interrelationship of life roles
   c. Understanding the continuous changes in male/female roles
   d. Skills in career planning

Implications for Career Guidance Programs in Senior High Schools

The preceding recommendations from NOICC (1992), combined with related research reported in this section, provide an abundance of implications for career guidance programs in senior high school.

1. Career guidance at the senior high school level must provide programs designed to meet the needs of students at various stages of career development. Establishing the career development needs of entry-level high school students and a means of monitoring their progress are relevant goals.

2. According to Super (1990), the exploratory age is characterized by a tentative phase in which choices are narrowed but not finalized. Therefore, it is important for individuals to analyze their own characteristics in terms of career decisions.

3. Senior high school students should benefit from information, activities, and modules that call for matching occupations with physical characteristics and skills. Programs designed to assist senior high school students entering the labor market for the first time are of particular importance.

4. Senior high school students should understand the relationship of career choices and educational requirements. Educational awareness implies a working knowledge of educational opportunities available at specific institutions.

5. Teaching decision-making and planning skills involves guiding students through a series of steps as they formulate career goals. Refined self-knowledge—including interests, abilities, values, and occupational knowledge—is prerequisite to effective career decision making and planning.

6. Work-experience counseling provides individuals with insight into the work setting and prepares them to identify effective models. Work values, work environments, work habits, and other issues associated with work are of particular value to the novice.

7. Many senior high school students also need assistance in choosing an institution of higher learning. Knowledge of how to evaluate the advantages and disadvantages of these institutions is essential.

8. Community visits and interviews with individuals in different occupations are relevant activities for helping senior high school students relate their own personal characteristics to occupational requirements. Relating school subjects to jobs and describing sources of job information are pertinent goals for career development.

9. Students should be guided in creating a set of specific preferences and plans to implement after graduation.

10. Services to help prepare for the job search are offered through placement officers. Related activities may include résumé preparation, interview-skills training, preparation for employment tests, job testing, and listing of employment opportunities.

Summary

1. Research suggests that *all* stages of human development are important. Infancy should be viewed as an extremely important and sensitive period in human development, but one not necessarily having a permanent impact on later behavior.

2. Directed experiences in elementary school promote physical and academic growth, interpersonal relationships with members of both sexes, and self-concept development—all important components of career development. Students who fail to accomplish developmental tasks may require special attention and direction.

3. Erikson suggested that the stage of development between ages 6 and 11 emphasizes industriousness; that is, children learn that productivity brings recognition and reward.

4. Piaget described early cognitive development in children as cultivating "schemes" through motor activities and their senses. During the ages of 2 to 5, children begin developing conceptual skills but have not yet developed the abilities to think logically or abstractly.

5. Children are particularly prone to adopting the behavior of models they observe. Parents, teachers, teacher's aides, and classmates are potential models that elementary school children will imitate. Other models may come from television, movies, and books.

6. In elementary school, children experience many aspects of existence in an adult world for the first time, such as competition with others and expectations of productive performance. Differences in growth and psychological changes between girls and boys greatly influence social relationships and emerging self-perceptions. Sex-role stereotyping is quite evident in elementary school.

7. Implications of career guidance for elementary schoolchildren include the importance of self-concept development, building an understanding of strengths and limitations, providing appropriate role models, visiting community resources for career information and role models, developing self-awareness, learning to assume responsibility for decisions and actions, understanding the relationship between education and work, learning that all work is important, and learning about work environments and the people involved in occupations.

8. Adolescence has been described as a period of turmoil resulting in a transition from childhood. According to Erikson, adolescents search intensely for identity as they subordinate childhood identifications. The major danger is role confusion; thus, this stage is designated as "Identity versus Confusion." The choice of career and commitment to a career have a significant impact on identity.

9. According to Piaget, the transition from concrete operational thinking to formal thought is a gradual process beginning at approximately 12 years of age. During early adolescence, patterns of problem solving or planning are quite unsystematic, but near the end of high school the adolescent has the ability to deal with distractions and sort out problems through mental manipulations.

10. Parents have the greatest influence on long-range plans of high school students, although peers are more likely to influence current identity and status.

11. A dramatic physiological change, sexual maturity, takes place for the majority of boys and girls during junior and senior high school.

12. According to Havighurst, defining appropriate sexual roles and achieving relationships with peers are among the major developmental tasks of adolescents.

13. The effects of early and late sexual maturity provide a frame of reference for counseling intervention. The evidence suggests that early maturity for males has certain benefits in terms of appropriateness among male peer groups and adults. Late-maturing girls also enjoy acceptance and popularity. Late-maturing males and early-maturing females may experience a greater need for counseling intervention than do their peers.

14. Implications for career guidance in junior high school includes the importance of learning to relate acquired skills to educational/occupational goals. These students have a strong need to appraise their own abilities, achievements, and interests accurately. They should be given the opportunity to identify relationships between interests and total life experiences. Exposure to jobs and career fields should be expanded to provide a basis for linking various activities to work. Learning about career options increases awareness of exploration opportunities. Basic and concrete experiences provide a means of learning the skills utilized in work. Skills in planning, decision making, and problem solving are important for junior

high school students. Finally, these students should understand that sex-role stereotyping, bias, and discrimination limit occupational choices.

15. A recent Gallup survey suggests high schools should give more attention to career development by helping all students develop job skills, all students plan careers, all students find jobs, and work-bound students develop work skills.

16. Recent career development programs for high schools include a comprehensive school guidance program, school-to-work programs, and planning for life programs.

17. Implications for career guidance programs in senior high school are numerous, and they indicate that programs should be designed to meet the needs of students at various stages of career development. Programs designed to assist senior high school students entering the labor market for the first time are of particular importance. Senior high school students should understand the relationships between career choices and educational requirements. Learning decision-making and planning skills is essential. Learning more about work and what is required at work can help senior high school students identify effective role models. Many senior high students need assistance in choosing an institution of higher education.

Supplementary Learning Exercises

1. Defend the following statement with examples to prove your point: Individuals have a profound adaptive capacity at various stages of development.
2. Construct at least two activities/strategies in which concrete experiences promote abstract conceptual operations.
3. Construct at least two activities/strategies of observational learning that would promote career development of elementary school-age children.
4. Survey a sample of elementary, junior, and senior high school students to determine their perception of appropriate career roles for their sex.
5. Develop a list of behavioral characteristics of an adolescent experiencing role confusion. Develop counseling strategies designed to overcome identified characteristics.
6. Identify standardized assessment instruments that measure self-concept development. Explain how you would use the results in career counseling.
7. Identify and interview a late- and an early-maturing adolescent. Present your findings to the class.
8. Describe your development from childhood. Identify significant transitions and their influences on your career.
9. Identify at least ten reasons such a significant number of senior high school students express a need for career guidance. Discuss these issues in class.
10. Using one or more of the implications for career guidance for the elementary, junior, and senior high school levels, identify specific career guidance needs and develop activities/strategies to meet them.

CHAPTER TEN

Career Guidance in Schools

This chapter covers samples of selected strategies for career guidance in elementary, junior, and senior high school. A comprehensive school guidance program (K–12) is discussed in the first part of this chapter, followed by a discussion of planning for life strategies that are a part of the comprehensive school guidance program. Next, school-to-work programs and related programs of integrating academic and vocational education and tech-prep strategies are examined. The competencies and indicators developed by the National Occupational Information Coordinating Committee (NOICC) for elementary, junior/middle, and high school students are reviewed in the next section, along with strategies for most competencies. Other programs reviewed are the competencies for AMERICA 2000, and apprenticeship and the future of the work force. A discussion of placement in the secondary school completes this section. Finally, examples of career education collaboration and infusion are presented.

Comprehensive School Guidance Programs

Gysbers and Henderson (1988) have developed detailed plans for developing, designing, implementing, and evaluating a comprehensive school guidance program. In an earlier conceptual treatise on comprehensive guidance programs, Gysbers and Moore (1987) pointed out that a comprehensive guidance model is not an ancillary guidance service; rather, it is one in which all staff members are involved, including administrators, members of the community, and parents. Furthermore, they are involved in a common objective whose goal is the total integrated development of individual students. According to Gysbers and Henderson (1988), guidance programs should be viewed as developmental and comprehensive in that regularly scheduled activities are planned, conducted, and evaluated and comprehensive guidance programs feature a team approach. In essence, it is a full commitment to surveying current guidance programs within a district; establishing students' needs; establishing plans, activities, and staff to meet those needs; and recognizing that a comprehensive guidance program is an equal partner with other educational programs.

Human growth and development forms the foundation on which comprehensive guidance programs are built, especially within the domain of lifetime career development. The focus is the interrelationship of all aspects of life. For instance, the family role is not treated separately from other life roles. The life career developmental domains are characterized as follows: (1) self-knowledge and interpersonal skills (self-understanding and recognizing the uniqueness of others); (2) life roles, settings, and events (roles such as learner, citizen, and worker; settings such as community, home, and work environment; events such as beginning the work role, marriage, and retirement); (3) life career planning (decision making and planning); and (4) basic studies and occupational preparation (knowledge and skills found in various subjects typically offered in school curricula).

Counselor involvement and commitment in this approach is extensive. Counselors are involved in teaching, team teaching, and supporting teachers. A major innovation in this program is the development of student competencies and the methods used to evaluate them. For example, at the perceptual level, the acquisition of knowledge and skills related to selected aspects of community and self are evaluated as environmental orientation and self-orientation. The conceptual level emphasizes directional tendencies (movement toward socially desirable goals) and adaptive and adjustive behavior. The generalization level is the level of functioning students exhibit throughout the mastery of specific tasks. Each of these competencies is broken down into specific goals with identified competencies; student outcomes are specified by grade level and activity objectives.

Monitoring is accomplished using an individualized advisory system; each advisor has 15 to 20 students. The allocation of the counselor's time during the school day is suggested in percentages for participation in curriculum, individual planning, responsive services (recurring topics such as academic failure, peer problems, and family situations), and system support (consulting with parents, staff development, and compensatory programs).

The comprehensive school guidance program is a means of systematically implementing a program concept for guidance activities in kindergarten through grade 12. The value of this model is its comprehensive nature and the involvement of school professionals, selected members of the community, and parents. The program's flexibility allows for local development of needs. Another major advantage is the evaluation of student outcomes, professional effectiveness, and program design. The program's foundation centers around a life career development theme. The recognition of the importance of the interrelatedness of all life roles is a profound message to the career counseling profession.

Planning for Life Strategies

A program called Planning for Life is sponsored by the U.S. Army Recruiting Command with the support of the National Consortium of State Career Guidance Supervisors and the Center on Education and Training for Employment at the Ohio State University. This comprehensive guidance program provides a framework for improving the effectiveness of elementary, secondary and postsecondary programs; counselor education; and supervision and administration of career guidance programs. The special objectives of the National Consortium of State Career Guidance Supervisors is quoted as follows.

1. Provide a vehicle to enable states to join together in supporting mutual priorities, ongoing programs, and career development and pre-vocational services.
2. Promote the development and improvement of career guidance at all levels of education.
3. Involve business, industry and government in creating and evaluating quality career guidance programs.
4. Serve as a clearinghouse through which states can seek assistance from public and private sources for program improvement and expansion.
5. Offer technical assistance to states in developing their annual and long-term plans related to career guidance and counseling. (National Consortium of State Career Guidance Supervisors, 1996, p. iv)

The Planning for Life Program complements comprehensive guidance programs discussed in the preceding section in this chapter. First, the program places career planning within the framework of the total school guidance program; career planning for all students is a part of the comprehensive guidance plan. More specifically, elements of the Planning for Life Program are identified by the "seven C's."

1. *Clarity* of purpose is the sharing of the purposes of the program with school, family, business, and community.
2. *Commitment* suggests that an investment of resources from all parts of the community is essential.
3. *Comprehensiveness* ensures that the program addresses all participants in the community with all career and educational opportunities.
4. *Collaboration* refers to the degree to which schools, family, business, and community share program ownership.
5. *Coherence* is the term used to make certain that there is a documented plan for all students, and to see that specific assistance and program assessment is provided.
6. *Coordination* is the degree to which the program is interdisciplinary and career planning is developmental.
7. *Competency* is proof of student attainment.

Each year, outstanding programs are given a national award. The Omaha, Nebraska, public school system was one of two 1994 national award winners. An overview of their program is outlined in the accompanying box.

Omaha Public Schools Comprehensive Guidance and Counseling Program
Grade Levels Kindergarten through Twelve: Rural, Urban, Suburban

Overview

The Omaha Public Schools Comprehensive Guidance and Counseling Program provides a curriculum-based approach to address the career domain of student development.

Clarity of Purpose—The career curriculum includes an agreed-upon written statement of purpose, philosophy, goals, and outcomes. All materials were developed by program committee members who include counselors, teachers, administrators, community agencies, and industry.

Commitment—Teachers, community agency representatives, the business community, and counselors deliver the career program to all students. Personnel specializing in career planning are assigned to provide support and coordination for career planning in grades kindergarten through twelve. Advanced education planning specialist counselors are available in each high school.

Comprehensiveness—The career planning guidance curriculum is delivered to all students beginning in kindergarten. All students graduate with a career portfolio. Assessments are utilized throughout the program. At least two advanced career education evening programs for parents and students are provided each year in all district high schools.

Collaboration—Career planning program partnerships include: Urban League, University of Nebraska-Omaha, Metro Community College, Chamber of Commerce, Explorers, Nebraska Educational Planning Center, Gifted Education Instruction, vocational education and community relations agencies. The program has received over $100,000 in foundation grants each year for the past two years.

All goals and materials are designed and developed by committees representing various school departments, industry representatives and educational agencies. Advisory committees include parents/guardians, community and industry representatives, and counselors who monitor, evaluate, assess, and improve the career planning program. Parents have access to the student portfolio for comment and review.

Coherence—All students begin to develop career/educational plans in seventh grade. Students annually update their portfolios each year through grade twelve. They use the portfolio to prepare a resume and develop their career/education plan for after high school. All students graduate with a career planning portfolio.

Coordination—A written career planning curriculum is delivered to all students in grades K through 12. Specified outcomes and activities are developmentally sequenced for each grade level. Activities are delivered in conjunction with the academic curriculum. Career counselors formulate written plans that include activities, resources, and evaluation.

Competency—All students complete a career planning portfolio that includes goals, outcomes, and academic progress. Each component of the program is evaluated.

Commercial Materials Utilized:
- IDEAS Interest, Determination, Exploration & Assessment System (IDEAS)
- Self-Directed Search (SDS)
- The Harrington-O'Shea Career Decision Making (CDM)
- Myers-Briggs Type Indicator (MBTI)
- True Colors
- Guidance Information System

Noncommercial/Local Materials Utilized:
- *Look to the Future* Curriculum Guide for elementary school
- Growing through Developmental Guidance K–6
- Growing through Transitions: Career and Educational Planning Grades 7–12
- Growing through Counseling Curriculum Guide
- Educational/Career Planning Portfolio
- Parent Information Envelopes
- Career Educational Planning Brochures

Program Features—The Omaha career program is an integral component in a total, comprehensive, competency-based guidance program. The inclusion of career planning in a total program emphasizes the importance of career development in the student's total development. The K–12 career guidance curriculum provides comprehensive, extensive activities to provide students with a developmentally appropriate classroom-based approach to career development and career planning.

For more information contact:
Stan Maliszewski, Guidance Supervisor
Omaha Public Schools
3215 Cuming Street
Omaha NE 68131
402-557-2704

SOURCE: From *Planning for Life: 1995 Compendium of Recognized Career Planning Programs.* National Consortium of State Career Guidance Supervisors, Center for Education and Training for Employment, 1900 Kenny Road, Columbus, OH 43210.

One outstanding feature of the Omaha public schools plan is collaboration. The schools obviously have the support of the community, which is an important part of any comprehensive guidance program. The comprehensive nature of this program is also impressive. Parental involvement in career education programs offers tremendous opportunities for supporting the school's efforts in career guidance. As is the case with most comprehensive career guidance programs, all students graduate with a career plan. Follow-up data on implementing these plans would provide yet another measure of overall effectiveness.

Finally, planning for life suggests that career and life are both ongoing processes that require individual and community commitment. Because of the very nature of our society, individuals must periodically reevaluate their circumstances to achieve a more productive life and career. The connections and links between lifestyle and career are clearly interwoven; we can hardly separate one from the other in program development. Thus, life planning programs suggest an important lesson: planning for the future involves the interrelationship of both lifestyle and career.

School-to-Work Programs

The U.S. Department of Education and the U.S. Department of Labor have jointly sponsored a work-based program known as school-to-work. It is considered a new approach to learning for all students in which students apply what they learn to real life and to real work situations. In 1994, the School-to-Work Opportunities Act was signed into law, offering the possibility for all sectors of a community to work together in making education a more meaningful experience. Every school-to-work system must contain the following three core elements (U.S. Department of Education, 1996).

1. *School-based learning:* classroom instruction based on high academic and business-defined occupational skill standards.
2. *Work-based learning:* career exploration, work experience, structured training, and mentoring at job sites.
3. *Connecting activities:* courses that integrate classroom and on-the-job instruction; matching students with participating employers, training mentors, and building other bridges between school and work.

The major educational focus of this act is to assist students in making the transition from school to work. A work-based learning approach is designed to develop skills in critical thinking, problem solving, communications, and interpersonal relations. These skills are considered vital for all work roles.

Another major objective is to have students learn about job possibilities by shadowing existing workers and discussing work life and the workplace with someone while on a job. Experiencing multiple workplaces is stressed.

To apply academics to real tasks on a specific job, workplace mentors collaborate with classroom teachers. This rationale suggests that students will become more motivated in all academic programs when they are able to experience the connections and links between their schoolwork and what is required on a job.

Quality school-to-work programs must be expertly coordinated between the work site and the classroom. Thus, teachers must also be convinced of the program's benefits. Teachers, supervisors, and students must cooperatively plan academic content and skill development to ensure an appropriate learning experience.

Finally, it must be pointed out that school-to-work programs are not just another program for noncollege-bound students. On the contrary, this program allows students to participate in advanced academic courses while developing workplace skills. This national program recognizes that we are now a part of a technological society that requires technical skills for practically all careers, including professional ones.

Integrating Academic and Vocational Education

Vocational educators have developed a vocational reform strategy that provides a system in which students achieve both academic and occupational competencies. The major goal is to improve the educational and employment opportunities of students who face new technologies and business-management systems that require high-level worker skills. Grubb, Davis, Lum, Plihal, and Mograine (1991) described the following models for integrating academic and vocational education.

1. Incorporate more academic content in vocational courses (vocational teachers modify vocational courses to include more academic content).
2. Combine vocational and academic teachers to enhance academic competencies in vocational programs (a cooperative effort involves more academic content in vocational courses).
3. Make academic courses more vocationally relevant (academic teachers modify courses or adopt new courses to include more vocational content).
4. Modify both vocational and academic courses (change content of both vocational and academic courses).
5. Use the senior project as a form of integration (teachers collaborate in developing new courses around student projects).
6. Implement the Academy model (use team teaching of math, English, science, and vocational subjects for two or three years and then require other subjects in regular high school).
7. Develop occupational high schools and magnet schools (occupational schools have been more successful in integrating vocational and academic education than the magnet schools).
8. Implement occupational clusters, "career paths," and occupational majors (students are encouraged to think about occupations early in high school).

The interest in integrating academic and vocational education has evolved primarily from a need to encourage vocational education students to take more rigorous academic courses. A strong academic background is essential for continuing education, which is a growing trend among vocational schools (Cetron & Gayle, 1991). The models described by Grubb and colleagues (1991) underscore the interest in making significant changes in vocational education.

Tech-Prep Programs

Tech-prep is a national strategy designed to ensure that students exit high school or a community/technology college with marketable skills for job placement, have academic credentials to pursue higher education, or have both of these options. In this context, *tech-prep* means integrated academics and technical training for secondary, postsecondary, and apprenticeship students, plus curriculum development to meet the skills requirements of advanced technology jobs. Also included is an innovative, up-to-date career counseling program about high-demand occupations, a comprehensive assessment program for students in middle/junior high school, and individualized high school graduation plans.

To accomplish the goals of tech-prep programs, school systems and cooperating colleges and universities have formed consortiums with industry. Through such organizations, education and industry can coordinate work-site-based training. Additionally, follow-up assessment of graduates is enhanced.

Encouraging vocational education students to take more advanced academic courses is the major goal of tech-prep models. Typically, schools devise a variety of two-year technical curricula that include such subjects as applied mathematics, applied biology/chemistry, and principles of technology. There is often a working relationship with cooperating colleges that have agreed, by prior arrangement, to accept these courses for college credit or as entrance requirements.

Operationally, students concentrate on basic concepts their first year and learn more about applications of the concepts during the second year. In principles of technology, for example, first-year students examine principles of force, work, energy, and power; in the second year, they apply these concepts in optical systems, radiation, and transducers. Many colleges that accept the principles of technology course usually count it as a laboratory-science requirement (Cetron & Gayle, 1991). The National Career Development Training Institute plans to incorporate the counselor's role in tech-prep programs in its training programs. We should hear a great deal more about these programs in the near future.

NOICC Competencies and Indicators

The National Occupational Information Coordinating Committee (NOICC) has been very thorough in its development of competencies and indicators for schools K–12. These competencies are divided into subgroups that make them more relevant and useful. The specificity of each competency provides guidelines for planning and developing strategies for each subgroup by school level. Please be aware that the strategies for competencies reported here are not from the NOICC but are suggestions from a wide source of materials and individuals during the career education era. The strategies suggested should be considered examples that will enhance some of the competencies and indicators and as examples of activities and formats that school counselors can use in the career guidance program.

Elementary School Student: Competencies and Indicators

SELF-KNOWLEDGE

Competency I: Knowledge of the importance of self-concept
- Describe positive characteristics about self as seen by self and others.
- Identify how behaviors affect school and family situations.
- Describe how behavior influences the feelings and actions of others.
- Demonstrate a positive attitude about self.
- Identify personal interests, abilities, strengths, and weaknesses.
- Describe ways to meet personal needs through work.

Competency II: Skills needed to interact with others
- Identify how people are unique.
- Demonstrate effective skills for interacting with others.
- Demonstrate skills in resolving conflicts with peers and adults.
- Demonstrate group membership skills.
- Identify sources and effects of peer pressure.
- Demonstrate appropriate behaviors when peer pressures are contrary to one's beliefs.
- Demonstrate awareness of different cultures, lifestyles, attitudes, and abilities.

Strategies
1. In a group discussion, ask students to use open-ended sentences, such as:
   I'm happy when _____ .
   I'm sad when _____ .
   I'm afraid when _____ .
2. Have students compile a list or draw pictures of people they talked to during the week. In groups, discuss types of relationships they have with them.
3. Ask students to describe a friend and then themselves. Discuss and describe individual differences.
4. Play "Who Am I?" with one student playing a role and others trying to guess the role.
5. Have students select magazine pictures of events, places, and people that interest them. Share interests.
6. Ask students to summarize ways in which individuals may be described. Then, ask students to select descriptions of themselves.

(continued)

Strategies   (*continued*)

7. Ask students to answer the following questions in writing or orally: What do I do well? What goals do I have? What do I do poorly? Who am I like? What makes me different from others?

8. Have students make lists of "Things I like" and "Things I don't like." Compile the lists and discuss the variety of interests.

9. Form a "Who Am I?" group and meet once a week, during which each person is to describe a personal characteristic of an individual who performs a specific job. Compile list for future discussions.

10. Ask students to list several interests and to describe how they became interested in an activity.

EDUCATIONAL AND OCCUPATIONAL EXPLORATION

Competency III: Awareness of the importance of growth and change
- Identify personal feelings.
- Identify ways to express feelings.
- Describe causes of stress.
- Identify and select appropriate behaviors to deal with specific emotional situations.
- Demonstrate healthy ways of dealing with conflicts, stress, and emotions in self and others.
- Demonstrate knowledge of good health habits.

Competency IV: Awareness of the benefits of educational achievement
- Describe how academic skills can be used in the home and community.
- Identify personal strengths and weaknesses in subject areas.
- Identify academic skills needed in several occupational groups.
- Describe relationships among ability, effort, and achievement.
- Implement a plan of action for improving academic skills.
- Describe school tasks that are similar to skills essential for job success.
- Describe how the amount of education needed for different occupational levels varies.

Competency V: Awareness of the relationship between work and learning
- Identify different types of work, both paid and unpaid.
- Describe the importance of preparing for occupations.
- Demonstrate effective study and information-seeking habits.
- Demonstrate an understanding of the importance of practice, effort, and learning.
- Describe how current learning relates to work.
- Describe how one's role as a student is like that of an adult worker.

Competency VI: Skills needed to understand and use career information
- Describe work of family members, school personnel, and community workers.
- Identify occupations according to data, people, and things.

- Identify work activities of interest to the student.
- Describe the relationship of beliefs, attitudes, interests, and abilities to occupations.
- Describe jobs that are present in the local community.
- Identify the working conditions of occupations (for example, inside/outside, hazardous).
- Describe ways in which self-employment differs from working for others.
- Describe how parents, relatives, adult friends, and neighbors can provide career information.

Competency VII: Awareness of the importance of personal responsibility and good work habits

- Describe the importance of personal qualities (for example, dependability, promptness, getting along with others) to getting and keeping jobs.
- Demonstrate positive ways of performing working activities.
- Describe the importance of cooperation among workers to accomplish a task.
- Demonstrate the ability to work with people who are different from oneself (for example, race, age, gender).

Competency VIII: Awareness of how work relates to the needs and functions of society

- Describe how work can satisfy personal needs.
- Describe the products and services of local employers.
- Describe ways in which work can help overcome social and economic problems.

Strategies

1. Arrange a display of workers' hats that represent jobs in the community. Have each student select a hat that indicates a job he or she would like to do someday and explain why the job is appealing.
2. Assign students to develop a list of skills for their favorite jobs and describe how these skills are learned.
3. Ask each student to pretend that a friend wants a certain job, and ask each to describe the kinds of skills the friend would need.
4. Have students make a list of activities their parents do at home and have them identify the ones that require math, reading, and writing.
5. Have students make a list of school subjects and identify jobs in which the skills learned in the subjects are used.
6. Referring to a list of occupations, have students describe what kind of person may like a particular occupation.
7. Have students make a list of occupations involved in producing a loaf of bread.
8. Ask students to find a picture from a magazine or newspaper that depicts a female and a male in a nontraditional job.

(continued)

Strategies   *(continued)*
9. Have students interview their parents about their work roles and discuss these roles with the group.
10. Ask each student to adopt the identity of a worker and list work roles. Discuss how work has a personal meaning for every individual.

CAREER PLANNING

Competency IX: Understanding how to make decisions
- Describe how choices are made.
- Describe what can be learned from making mistakes.
- Identify and assess problems that interfere with attaining goals.
- Identify strategies used in solving problems.
- Identify alternatives in decision-making situations.
- Describe how personal beliefs and attitudes affect decision making.
- Describe how decisions affect self and others.

Competency X: Awareness of the interrelationship of life roles
- Describe the various roles an individual may have (for example, friend, student, worker, family member).
- Describe work-related activities in the home, community, and school.
- Describe how family members depend on one another, work together, and share responsibilities.
- Describe how work roles complement family roles.

Competency XI: Awareness of different occupations and changing male/ female roles
- Describe how work is important to all people.
- Describe the changing life roles of men and women in work and family.
- Describe how contributions of individuals both inside and outside the home are important.

Competency XII: Awareness of the career planning process
- Describe the importance of planning.
- Describe skills needed in a variety of occupational groups.
- Develop an individual career plan for the elementary school level.

Strategies
1. Ask students to make a list of jobs/occupations they would use to describe their neighbors and/or acquaintances. Share with others.
2. Have students identify the kinds of people who work in a selected list of occupations. Emphasize likenesses and differences.
3. In a self-discovery group, discuss how people have different interests and enjoy different/similar activities.

4. Have students describe how workers in different activities are affected by weather.
5. Ask students to collect newspaper and magazine photos of different people and describe likenesses and differences.
6. Have students identify workers that visit their home. Identify differences of work and occupations.
7. Assign students to write a short paragraph answering the question "If you could be anyone in the world, whom would you be?" Follow with a discussion.
8. Divide the class into groups of boys and girls and ask each group to make a list of jobs girls can and cannot do. Compare lists and discuss how women are capable of performing most jobs.
9. Have students describe in writing and/or orally "someone I would like to work with." Make a list of positive characteristics that each student describes.
10. Discuss how people work together and demonstrate with an example of three people building a doghouse together. What would each person do?

Middle/Junior High School Student: Competencies and Indicators

SELF-KNOWLEDGE

Competency I: Knowledge of the influence of a positive self-concept
- Describe personal likes and dislikes.
- Describe individual skills required to fulfill different life roles.
- Describe how one's behavior influences the feelings and actions of others.
- Identify environmental influences on attitudes, behaviors, and aptitudes.

Competency II: Skills needed to interact with others
- Demonstrate respect for the feelings and beliefs of others.
- Demonstrate an appreciation for the similarities and differences among people.
- Demonstrate tolerance and flexibility in interpersonal and group situations.
- Demonstrate skills in responding to criticism.
- Demonstrate effective group membership skills.
- Demonstrate effective social skills.
- Demonstrate understanding of different cultures, lifestyles, attitudes, and abilities.

Competency III: Knowledge of the importance of growth and change
- Identify feelings associated with significant experiences.
- Identify internal and external sources of stress.
- Demonstrate ways of responding to others when under stress.

- Describe changes that occur in the physical, psychological, social, and emotional development of an individual.
- Describe physiological and psychological factors as they relate to career development.
- Describe the importance of career, family, and leisure activities to mental, emotional, physical, and economic well-being.

Strategies
1. Introduce the concepts of self-image, self-worth, and self-esteem. Assign small groups to discuss the relationship of these concepts to educational and occupational planning. Compile a list from these groups.
2. Ask students to complete a standardized or original personality inventory. Using Holland's (1992) classification system, have students relate personality characteristics to work environments.
3. Have students list courses in which they have excelled and those in which they have not. Ask students to relate skills learned to their personality characteristics and traits and interests.
4. Assign students to construct a life line in which they designate places lived in and visited, experiences in school and with peer groups, and major events. Have them project the life line into the future by identifying goals.
5. Have students discuss how different traits are more important for some goals than for others. Compile a list of jobs and corresponding traits.

EDUCATIONAL AND OCCUPATIONAL EXPLORATION

Competency IV: Knowledge of the benefits of educational achievement to career opportunities
- Describe the importance of academic and occupational skills in the work world.
- Identify how the skills taught in school subjects are used in various occupations.
- Describe individual strengths and weaknesses in school subjects.
- Describe a plan of action for increasing basic educational skills.
- Describe the skills needed to adjust to changing occupational requirements.
- Describe how continued learning enhances the ability to achieve goals.
- Describe how skills relate to the selection of high school courses of study.
- Describe how aptitudes and abilities relate to broad occupational groups.

Competency V: Understanding the relationship between work and learning
- Demonstrate effective learning habits and skills.
- Demonstrate an understanding of the importance of personal skills and attitudes to job success.
- Describe the relationship of personal attitudes, beliefs, abilities, and skills to occupations.

Competency VI: Skills needed to locate, understand, and use career information
- Identify various ways that occupations can be classified.
- Identify a number of occupational groups for exploration.
- Demonstrate skills in using school and community resources to learn about occupational groups.
- Identify sources to obtain information about occupational groups, including self-employment.
- Identify skills that are transferable from one occupation to another.
- Identify sources of employment in the community.

Competency VII: Knowledge of skills necessary to seek and obtain jobs
- Demonstrate personal qualities (for example, dependability, punctuality, getting along with others) that are needed to get and keep jobs.
- Describe terms and concepts used in describing employment opportunities and conditions.
- Demonstrate skills needed to complete a job application.
- Demonstrate skills and attitudes essential for a job interview.

Competency VIII: Understanding how work relates to the needs and functions of the economy and society
- Describe the importance of work to society.
- Describe the relationship between work and economic and societal needs.
- Describe the economic contributions workers make to society.
- Describe the effects that societal, economic, and technological change have on occupations.

Strategies

1. Ask students to write a description of the type of person they think they are, their preferences for activities (work and leisure), their strengths and weaknesses, and their desires for a career someday. Discuss.
2. Have students list several occupations that are related to their own interests and abilities. Discuss.
3. Lead a class discussion by identifying relationships of interest and abilities to various occupations. Each student should explore one occupation in depth, including reading a biography, writing a letter to someone, or conducting interviews. The student should research training requirements, working conditions, and personal attributes necessary for the job.
4. Ask each student to visit a place in the community where he or she can observe someone involved in a career of interest. Have students demonstrate their observations, such as type of work, working conditions, or tools of the trade.
5. Have the students make a list of the school subjects that are necessary to the success of persons whose careers are being investigated. Discuss.

(continued)

Strategies *(continued)*

6. Ask students to research preparation requirements for several selected occupations. Have them identify one similarity and one difference in preparation requirements for each of the occupations listed. Discuss.

7. Assign students to write short narratives explaining why certain jobs have endured and others have disappeared. Discuss.

8. Have students classify ten occupations by abilities needed, such as physical, mental, mechanical, creative, social, and other. Have students select three occupations that match their abilities and interests.

9. Have students do a mini-internship program where they shadow a worker. Discuss and share with other students.

10. Have students write a story about the many jobs involved in producing a hamburger. Discuss.

CAREER PLANNING

Competency IX: Skills needed to make decisions
- Describe personal beliefs and attitudes
- Describe how career development is a continuous process with a series of choices.
- Identify possible outcomes of decisions.
- Describe school courses related to personal, educational, and occupational interests.
- Describe how the expectations of others affect career planning.
- Identify ways in which decisions about education and work relate to other major life decisions.
- Identify advantages and disadvantages of various secondary and postsecondary programs for the attainment of career goals.
- Identify the requirements for secondary and postsecondary programs.

Competency X: Knowledge of the interrelationship of life roles
- Identify how different work and family patterns require varying kinds and amounts of energy, participation, motivation, and talent.
- Identify how work roles at home satisfy needs of the family.
- Identify personal goals that may be satisfied through a combination of work, community, social, and family roles.
- Identify personal leisure choices in relation to lifestyle and the attainment of future goals.
- Describe advantages and disadvantages of various life-role options.
- Describe the interrelationships between family, occupational, and leisure decisions.

Competency XI: Knowledge of different occupations and changing male/female roles
- Describe advantages and problems of entering nontraditional occupations.
- Describe the advantages of taking courses related to personal interest, even if they are most often taken by members of the opposite gender.

- Describe stereotypes, biases, and discriminatory behaviors that may limit opportunities for women and men in certain occupations.

Competency XII: Understanding the process of career planning
- Demonstrate knowledge of exploratory processes and programs.
- Identify school courses that meet tentative career goals.
- Demonstrate knowledge of academic and vocational programs offered at the high school level.
- Describe skills needed in a variety of occupations, including self-employment.
- Identify strategies for managing personal resources (for example, talents, time, money) to achieve tentative career goals.
- Develop an individual career plan, updating information from the elementary-level plan and including tentative decisions to be implemented in high school.

Strategies
1. Present steps in a decision-making model and discuss the importance of each step. Ask students to identify a problem and solve it by applying steps in the model.
2. Organize students into groups and have them construct a list of resources and resource people who could help solve a particular problem.
3. In a group discussion, compare a horoscope from a daily newspaper with other ways of solving problems and making decisions.
4. Assign students to select three occupations and then to choose one using a decision model. Share and discuss in groups.
5. Have students prepare an educational plan for high school. Share and discuss in groups.

High School Student: Competencies and Indicators

SELF-KNOWLEDGE

Competency I: Understanding the influence of a positive self-concept
- Identify and appreciate personal interests, abilities, and skills.
- Demonstrate the ability to use peer feedback.
- Demonstrate an understanding of how individual characteristics relate to achieving personal, social, educational, and career goals.
- Demonstrate an understanding of environmental influences on one's behavior.
- Demonstrate an understanding of the relationship between personal behavior and self-concept.

Competency II: Skills needed to interact positively with others
- Demonstrate effective interpersonal skills.
- Demonstrate interpersonal skills required for working with and for others.
- Describe appropriate employer and employee interactions in various situations.
- Demonstrate how to express feelings, reactions, and ideas in an appropriate manner.

Competency III: Understanding the impact of growth and development
- Describe how developmental changes affect physical and mental health.
- Describe the effect of emotional and physical health on career decisions.
- Describe healthy ways of dealing with stress.
- Demonstrate behaviors that maintain physical and mental health.

Strategies
1. Have students list five roles they currently fill. Discuss in small groups and identify future roles, such as spouse, parent, and citizen. Discuss.
2. Discuss or show films on sex-role stereotyping. Have students identify how sex-role stereotyping prohibits many individuals from becoming involved in certain events, including work roles.
3. Assign students to select newspaper and magazine pictures and articles that illustrate societal perceptions of appropriate behavior and dress. Discuss.
4. Have students discuss physical differences among their peers. Emphasize how differences may affect individuals.
5. Discuss the value of cooperative efforts in the work environment. Have students develop a project in which cooperation is essential. Discuss.
6. Have students observe workers performing specific tasks and make notes of skills and time required to complete tasks. Discuss.
7. Have students discuss employer expectations as compared to their own. Develop a consensus about how both are justified and can be attained.
8. Have students role-play a supervisor reacting to an employee's work performance. Discuss reactions of supervisors in a variety of situations.
9. Have students research the various causes of tardiness and absenteeism among workers. Discuss.
10. Ask students to interview at least three workers and three supervisors of workers on the subject of good work habits. Discuss.

EDUCATIONAL AND OCCUPATIONAL EXPLORATION

Competency IV: Understanding the relationship between educational achievement and career planning
- Demonstrate how to apply academic and vocational skills to achieve personal goals.
- Describe the relationship of academic and vocational skills to personal interests.
- Describe how skills developed in academic and vocational programs relate to career goals.
- Describe how education relates to the selection of college majors, further training, and/or entry into the job market.

- Demonstrate transferable skills that can apply to a variety of occupations and changing occupational requirements.
- Describe how learning skills are required in the workplace.

Competency V: Understanding the need for positive attitudes toward work and learning

- Identify the positive contributions workers make to society.
- Demonstrate knowledge of the social significance of various occupations.
- Demonstrate a positive attitude toward work.
- Demonstrate learning habits and skills that can be used in various educational situations.
- Demonstrate positive work attitudes and behaviors.

Competency VI: Skills needed to locate, evaluate, and interpret career information

- Describe the educational requirements of various occupations.
- Demonstrate use of a range of resources (for example, handbooks, career materials, labor market information, and computerized career information delivery systems).
- Demonstrate knowledge of various classification systems that categorize occupations and industries (for example, *Dictionary of Occupational Titles*).
- Describe the concept of career ladders.
- Describe the advantages and disadvantages of self-employment as a career option.
- Identify individuals in selected occupations as possible information resources, role models, or mentors.
- Describe the influence of change in supply and demand for workers in different occupations.
- Identify how employment trends relate to education and training.
- Describe the impact of factors such as population, climate, and geographic location on occupational opportunities.

Competency VII: Skills needed to prepare to seek, obtain, maintain, and change jobs

- Demonstrate skills to locate, interpret, and use information about job openings and opportunities.
- Demonstrate academic or vocational skills required for a full- or part-time job.
- Demonstrate skills and behaviors necessary for a successful job interview.
- Demonstrate skills in preparing a résumé and completing job applications.
- Identify specific job openings.
- Demonstrate employability skills necessary to obtain and maintain jobs.
- Demonstrate skills to assess occupational opportunities (for example, working conditions, benefits, and opportunities for change).
- Describe placement services available to make the transition from high school to civilian employment, the armed services, or postsecondary education/training.
- Demonstrate an understanding that job opportunities often require relocation.
- Demonstrate skills necessary to function as a consumer and manage financial resources.

Competency VIII: Understanding how societal needs and functions influence the nature and structure of work

- Describe the effect of work on lifestyles.
- Describe how society's needs and functions affect the supply of goods and services.
- Describe how occupational and industrial trends relate to training and employment.
- Demonstrate an understanding of the global economy and how it affects each individual.

Strategies

1. *To identify geographical factors that can affect choice of a career* (Geary, 1972). Obtain newspapers from urban and rural areas. Compare employment opportunities and contrast differences.
2. *To identify high school courses required for entry into trade schools, colleges, or jobs* (Walz, 1972). Discuss elements of required courses and develop brochures that list jobs and corresponding high school courses required.
3. *To understand how human values are significant in career decision making* (Bottoms, Evans, Hoyt, & Willers, 1972). Develop a list of values that may influence selection of a career. Each student selects two values of importance and locates a career that would be congruent with values. Discuss.
4. *To understand the principles and techniques of life planning* (Brown, 1980). In small groups, in eight 1-hour meetings, six components are presented and discussed: "Why People Behave the Way They Do," "Winners and Losers," "Your Fantasy Life," "Your Real Life," "Setting Goals," and "Short- and Long-term Planning."
5. *To prepare for entrance into college* (Hansen, 1970). A college-bound club discusses in weekly meetings such topics as how to read a college catalog, how to visit a college campus, and college study.
6. Discuss the value of leisure activities. Have students report on the benefits involved in five leisure activities of their choice. Discuss.
7. Have students develop a list of leisure activities they enjoy and estimate the amount of time necessary to participate in each. Form groups to decide which occupations would most likely provide the necessary time and which ones would not.
8. Ask students to debate the pros and cons of selected leisure activities.
9. Assign students to develop a list of leisure activities they enjoy now and project which of these can be enjoyed over the life span. Have students collect and discuss brochures from travel agencies and parks.
10. Have students discuss the concept of lifestyle in terms of work commitment, leisure activities, family involvement, and responsibilities and share their projections of future life roles and lifestyle.

CAREER PLANNING

Competency IX: Skills needed to make decisions

- Demonstrate responsibility for making tentative educational and occupational choices.
- Identify alternatives in given decision-making situations.
- Describe personal strengths and weaknesses in relationship to postsecondary education/training requirements.
- Identify appropriate choices during high school that will lead to marketable skills for entry-level employment or advanced training.
- Identify and complete required steps toward transition from high school to entry into postsecondary education/training programs or work.
- Identify steps to apply for and secure financial assistance for postsecondary education and training.

Competency X: Understanding the interrelationship of life roles

- Demonstrate knowledge of life stages.
- Describe factors that determine lifestyles (for example, socioeconomic status, culture, values, occupational choices, work habits).
- Describe ways in which occupational choices may affect lifestyle.
- Describe the contribution of work to a balanced and productive life.
- Describe ways in which work, family, and leisure roles are interrelated.
- Describe different career patterns and their potential effect on family patterns and lifestyle.
- Describe the importance of leisure activities.
- Demonstrate ways that occupational skills and knowledge can be acquired through leisure.

Competency XI: Understanding the continuous changes in male/female roles

- Identify factors that have influenced the changing career patterns of women and men.
- Identify evidence of gender stereotyping and bias in educational programs and occupational settings.
- Demonstrate attitudes, behaviors, and skills that contribute to eliminating gender bias and stereotyping.
- Identify courses appropriate to tentative occupational choices.
- Describe the advantages and problems of nontraditional occupations.

Competency XII: Skills needed in career planning

- Describe career plans that reflect the importance of lifelong learning.
- Demonstrate knowledge of postsecondary vocational and academic programs.
- Demonstrate knowledge that changes may require retraining and upgrading of employees' skills.
- Describe school and community resources to explore educational and occupational choices.
- Describe the costs and benefits of self-employment.
- Demonstrate occupational skills developed through volunteer experiences, part-time employment, or cooperative education programs.

- Demonstrate skills necessary to compare education and job opportunities.
- Develop an individual career plan, updating information from earlier plans and including tentative decisions to be implemented after high school.

Strategies
1. Ask students to review several job search manuals. Discuss the steps suggested in the manuals and develop strategies for taking these steps.
2. Assign students to visit a state employment agency and describe its functions. Discuss.
3. Have students research newspaper want-ads and select several of interest. Discuss and identify appropriate occupational information resources.
4. Have students demonstrate the steps involved in identifying an appropriate job, filling out an application, and writing a résumé. Discuss.
5. Have students participate in a mock interview. Critique and discuss appropriate dress and grooming.
6. Help students develop planning skills (Hansen, 1970). A one-year course, taught as an elective, covers six major areas of study: (a) relating one's characteristics to occupations; (b) exploring manual and mechanical occupations; (c) exploring professional, technical, and managerial occupations; (d) relating the economic system to occupations and people; (e) exploring roles, clerical, and service occupations; and (f) evaluating and planning ahead.
7. Help students evaluate careers in terms of standards of living and lifestyle (Steidl, 1972; Sorapuru, Theodore, & Young, 1972a). Students project themselves 10 to 15 years in the future and identify the kind of lifestyle they would like to have. Each student selects four careers and conducts research to determine if the projected lifestyle can be met through these careers.
8. Provide good job search procedures (Sorapuru, Theodore, & Young, 1972b). Students who have had part-time jobs explain how they got them. Groups investigate local organizations that help people find jobs. Students investigate telephone directories, school placement center files, and state employment agencies for leads to jobs. Students write résumés and "walk through" steps for applying and interviewing.
9. Help students understand the stressors of work responsibility (Bottoms et al., 1972). Students identify individuals who recently attained a position of prominence and compare changes in lifestyle (work, leisure, and family).
10. Involve parents in career planning and decision making in high school (Amatea & Cross, 1980). Students and parents attend six 2-hour sessions per week and discuss the following at school and at home: self-management and goal setting, elements in career planning and decision making, comparing self with occupational data, information gathering skills, and training paths.

Understanding Sex-Role Stereotyping

All children need to be prepared for self-sufficiency in the future. One of the major challenges is to assist both boys and girls in overcoming the problems associated with sex-role stereotyping. Counseling-component modules for the classroom present one method of accomplishing this objective. The following case study uses a counseling module for junior high school.

> Jane, Sari, Bart, and John are in a junior high school self-discovery counseling group. The counselor asks each member to study an advertisement that uses a man and a woman on television and also to locate one in a magazine. Each will record the product being advertised and describe the individual in the ad.
>
> Sari and John recorded the information for two ads, which were discussed in the next group session. Sari's notes included the following: "This woman was beautiful on television, in a long flowing dress with gorgeous hair blowing in the wind. She was advertising a soap to be used for the face and hands for keeping them soft and pretty."
>
> John's notes were taken on a magazine ad: "This ad was on a full page in a magazine. It showed a man advertising cigarettes who had a tatoo on his hand. He looked like a cowboy with a weather-beaten face."
>
> The counselor asked the group to discuss the characteristics of each character in the two ads. The adjectives used to describe each character were recorded. On the woman in the ad, the list included beautiful, graceful, clean, dainty, and sexy. The list for the man included macho, handsome, outdoorsman, self-assured, and rugged.
>
> The counselor asked the group to discuss the appropriate roles in life for men and women implied by these advertisements. The apparent differences in roles were then extended to typical sex-role stereotypes such as women are to be pampered, dependent, and pretty, whereas men are strong, free to do as they please, and independent. The group discussed how these ads and other types of sex-role stereotyping have influenced their own perceptions of lifestyles for men and women and subsequently the careers they find appropriate for men and women. The counselor summarized the influence of sex-role stereotyping found in advertising and elsewhere in society. Finally, the changing role of women in general and specifically in the work force was emphasized.

Role models may also be used as a counseling component that can effectively emphasize the occupational potential of girls. Examples of women who have enjoyed successful careers provide girls with concrete evidence that women do have opportunities to develop careers in a working world thought to be dominated by men. Numerous techniques are applicable to such a component. One method is to have students interview working women and write a summary of their work-related experience. Biographies of women may also be reviewed and discussed (*Vocational Biographies*, 1985). These examples should emphasize how women can overcome sex-role stereotyping and find equal opportunity in the job market. They also illustrate that women can effectively assume leadership roles in the world of work. Finally, role models provide support for girls seriously considering a career-oriented lifestyle and may also provide some potential mentors.

Locating a mentor from whom one can directly learn the skills of a given career is usually highly productive. Therefore, career education and career counseling programs that instruct girls on the values of mentor relationships are very useful. A mentor is usually an older person who is admired and respected and has tremendous influence on the young. Levinson (1980) suggested that women who aspire to professional careers have fewer opportunities to find a mentor than do males, primarily because there are fewer female mentors available. There is some evidence that cross-gender mentoring can be of value, but because men have a tendency to not take career women seriously, there is the danger of increasing the chances of sex-role stereotyping.

Career Videos

Before leaving this section, it should be noted that there are some excellent career videos available for educational purposes. Feller (1994) has collected a list of 650 career videos, 161 of which have been reviewed and rated by career development specialists. The titles of the 161 rated videos are listed in Appendix B. More information and a complete list of videos may be obtained from:

Dr. Rich Feller
Colorado State University
School of Education
222 Education Building
Fort Collins, CO 80523-1588
Office: 970-491-6897
Fax: 970-491-1317
E-mail: feller@condor.cahs.colostate.edu

Strategies for Implementing Career Development Guidelines

Splete and Stewart (1990) reviewed the career development abstracts included in the ERIC database between 1980 and 1990. On completing their review, they made the following recommendations for how competencies could be achieved at various levels.

Elementary school level
- More parents and community persons should be involved in presenting career information.
- Increased attention should be given to self-knowledge activities, especially as they relate to the development of a positive self-concept.
- Use of media (computer programs, videos, films) should be increased.

Middle/junior high school level
- Place more emphasis on self-knowledge competencies.
- Get business persons involved with students to help them with educational and occupational exploration and career planning.

- Increase attention to the benefits of educational achievement as the amount of education for different occupations varies.
- Emphasize skills necessary to seek and obtain jobs.

High school level
- Emphasize activities related to awareness of interrelationship of life roles.
- Increased emphasis on understanding the relationship of work to the economy and how work influences lifestyles.
- Find opportunities for students to improve skills to interact with others, a needed workplace characteristic. (Splete & Stewart, 1990, pp. 1–36)

The strength of the NOICC competency-based program models is that they describe goals and objectives in terms of specific tasks. These competencies also lend themselves quite readily to task statements and activities devised to develop the skills necessary to complete each task. And perhaps even most important, criteria for successful task performance can be specifically defined.

NOICC established the National Career Development Training Institute (CDTI) in 1992. The CDTI's major responsibility has been to design career development training programs for states to use in training the personnel who help students and adults acquire career planning skills and make career decisions. The focus has been on in-service training for professional counselors and other advisors and on preservice training through counselor education programs at universities and other institutions. The CDTI also designs and develops training models and reviews the certification and credentials required of career development personnel. Competencies for staff who deliver career guidance and counseling programs have been defined by the National Career Development Association (NCDA) and are included in Appendix A.

Government-Sponsored Programs: Planning for the Future

In the late 1980s, the Department of Labor formed the Secretary's Commission on Achieving Necessary Skills (SCANS) to determine the level of skills required to enter employment. Specifically, SCANS was to define the skills needed for employment; propose acceptable levels of proficiency; suggest effective ways to assess proficiency; and develop a dissemination strategy for the nation's schools, businesses, and homes.

After lengthy interviews with workers in a wide range of jobs and after discussions and meetings with business owners, public employers, unions, workers, and supervisors in shops, plants, and stores, the prevailing message was that good jobs increasingly depend on people who can put knowledge to work. The commission concluded that young people in general leave school without the knowledge or foundation required to find and hold jobs. In labeling job performance as *workplace know-how,* SCANS suggested that know-how has two elements: competencies and a foundation. The five identified competencies are found in Box 10-1, and the three-part foundation of skills and personal qualities is reported in Box 10-2.

Box 10-1

Five Competencies for AMERICA 2000

Resources

Identifies, organizes, plans, and allocates resources

A. *Time*—selects goal-relevant activities, ranks them, allocates time, and prepares and follows schedules

B. *Money*—uses or prepares budgets, makes forecasts, keeps records, and makes adjustments to meet objectives

C. *Material and facilities*—acquires, stores, allocates, and uses materials or space efficiently

D. *Human resources*—assesses skills and distributes work accordingly, evaluates performance, and provides feedback

Interpersonal

Works with others

A. *Participates as member of a team*—contributes to group effort

B. *Teaches others new skills*

C. *Serves clients/customers*—works to satisfy customers' expectations

D. *Exercises leadership*—Communicates ideas to justify position, persuades and convinces others, responsibly challenges existing procedures and policies

E. *Negotiates*—works toward agreements involving exchange of resources, resolves divergent interests

F. *Works with diversity*—works well with men and women from diverse backgrounds

Information

Acquires and uses information

A. *Acquires and evaluates information*

B. *Organizes and maintains information*

C. *Interprets and communicates information*

D. *Uses computers to process information*

Systems

Understands complex interrelationships

A. *Understands systems*—knows how social, organizational, and technological systems work and operates effectively with them

B. *Monitors and corrects performance*—distinguishes trends, predicts impacts on system operations, diagnoses systems' performance, and corrects malfunctions

C. *Improves or designs systems*—suggests modifications to existing systems and develops new or alternative systems to improve performance

Technology

Works with a variety of technologies

A. *Selects technology*—chooses procedures, tools, or equipment including computers and related technologies
B. *Applies technology to task*—understands overall intent and proper procedures for setup and operation of equipment
C. *Maintains and troubleshoots equipment*—prevents, identifies, or solves problems with equipment, including computers and other technologies

SOURCE: U.S. Department of Labor. (1991). *What Work Requires of Schools: A SCANS Report for AMERICA 2000.* Washington, DC: U.S. Government Printing Office.

BOX 10-2
A Three-Part Foundation for AMERICA 2000

Basic Skills

Reads, writes, performs arithmetic and mathematical operations, listens, and speaks

A. *Reading*—locates, understands, and interprets written information in prose and in documents such as manuals, graphs, and schedules
B. *Writing*—communicates thoughts, ideas, information, and messages in writing; and creates documents such as letters, directions, manuals, reports, graphs, and flow charts.
C. *Arithmetic/mathematics*—performs basic computations and approaches practical problems by choosing appropriately from a variety of mathematical techniques
D. *Listening*—receives, attends to, interprets, and responds to verbal messages and other cues
E. *Speaking*—organizes ideas and communicates orally

Thinking Skills

Thinks creatively, makes decisions, solves problems, visualizes, knows how to learn, and reasons

A. *Creative thinking*—generates new ideas
B. *Decision making*—specifies goals and constraints, generates alternatives, considers risks, and evaluates and chooses best alternative
C. *Problem solving*—recognizes problems and devises and implements plan of action

(continued)

BOX 10-2   *(continued)*

D. *Seeing things in the mind's eye*—organizes, and processes symbols, pictures, graphs, objects, and other information

E. *Knowing how to learn*—uses efficient learning techniques to acquire and apply new knowledge and skills

F. *Reasoning*—discovers a rule or principle underlying the relationship between two or more objects and applies it when solving a problem

Personal Qualities

Displays responsibility, self-esteem, sociability, self-management, and integrity and honesty

A. *Responsibility*—exerts a high level of effort and perseveres toward goal attainment

B. *Self-esteem*—believes in own self-worth and maintains a positive view of self

C. *Sociability*—Demonstrates understanding, friendliness, adaptability, empathy, and politeness in group settings

D. *Self-management*—assesses self accurately, sets personal goals, monitors progress, and exhibits self-control

E. *Integrity/honesty*—chooses ethical courses of action

SOURCE: U.S. Department of Labor. (1991). *What Work Requires of Schools: A SCANS Report for AMERICA 2000.* Washington, DC: U.S. Government Printing Office.

The five competencies are applicable to nearly all jobs and reflect the attributes the employer seeks in tomorrow's employee. A large portion of these competencies involve human resources and interpersonal skills, mixed with technological skills and knowledge. The elements of the three-part foundation emphasize basic skills but also place extreme importance on thinking skills and personal qualities. In this respect, the basic skills take on a new meaning in the workplace; now, not only is an employee expected to read well, but, even more important, he or she must also understand and interpret information. Furthermore, tomorrow's workers must be prepared to communicate with others, work in teams, and describe complex systems and procedures. What we must communicate to future workers is that proficiency in each competency requires proficiency in the foundation. The report ends with the pronouncement that what "America 2000" will need from our schools is progress in teaching skills (the competencies and academic foundations needed by students in the year 2000).

Apprenticeship and the Future of the Work Force

In recognition of the changing needs of the work force, especially the need for technical skills, the U.S. Department of Labor has established a committee on apprenticeship. Like other work-based learning, training under the supervision of a master worker is a desirable learning experience. Building technical skills and observing how technical tasks relate to theoretical knowledge and interpretation is a major advantage of apprenticeship.

The Federal Committee on Apprenticeship suggests training strategies with the following eight essential components.

- Apprenticeship is sponsored by employers and others who can actually hire and train individuals in the workplace, and it combines hands-on training on the job with related theoretical instruction.
- Workplace and industry needs dictate key details of apprenticeship programs—training content, length of training, and actual employment settings.
- Apprenticeship has a specific legal status and is regulated by federal and state laws and regulations.
- Apprenticeship leads to formal, official credentials—a Certificate of Completion and journeyperson status.
- Apprenticeship generally requires a significant investment of time and money on the part of employers or other sponsors.
- Apprenticeship provides wages to apprentices during training according to predefined wage scales.
- Apprentices learn by working directly under master workers in their occupations.
- Apprenticeship involves both written agreements and implicit expectations. Written agreements specify the roles and responsibilities of each party; implicit expectations include the right of program sponsors to employ the apprentice, recouping their sizable investment in training, and the right of apprentices to obtain such employment. (Grossman & Drier, 1988, pp. 28–63)

Apprenticeships are independent of vocational-technical education programs, tech-prep programs, and cooperative education. This distinction is made because only apprenticeship produces fully trained journeypersons with the skills needed to perform effectively in the workplace. The concept of apprenticeships is important in meeting the ever- and fast-changing technical needs of the workplace.

Placement as Part of Career Planning

This section covers the role of placement officers in secondary schools and also the role of the state employment agency.

The integration of career planning and placement services in many educational institutions has slowly evolved over the last three decades. A current suggestion is to eliminate the word *placement* as a part of the name of the center where career services are offered (Carter, 1995). This name change is the result of changing missions in educational institutions. For instance, more emphasis in many career centers has focused on preplacement services, such as general information about educational programs, outreach programs, cooperative education and internships, part-time jobs, and computerized career guidance and information systems.

Placement should remain as a primary service offered by educational institutions; but in institutions where career planning and placement services have been combined into career centers, the focus of services includes a wide variety of programs that have received equal and in many cases more attention than placement has. Thus, a more appropriate name for locations that provide career-related services, including placement, is the more generic reference to career services as *career centers.*

The Role of Placement in Senior High School

A major component of the placement part of career planning involves job listings from local, state, regional, national, and international sources. The numerous federal and state programs that provide job placement for high school graduates and dropouts are valuable referral sources for secondary schools. A cooperative venture between the school, the business community, and federal and state agencies is essential in developing local sources of job listings. One of the most effective approaches is through a community advisory committee (Gysbers & Henderson, 1988). Local service clubs, chambers of commerce, federal and state agencies, and professional and personnel organizations are excellent resources for developing a local career advisory committee. As demand for hands-on experience increases, local career opportunities will be essential to the success of these programs. A viable listing of local part-time and full-time jobs will also enhance the popularity of the career planning and placement office.

Programs that enhance the transition from school to work should also be offered in senior high schools. In this respect, placement should be viewed as a vital function and a continuation of career guidance programs (Herr & Cramer, 1992). Some suggested program topics include how to: prepare for an interview, write a résumé, locate job information, apply for a job, know if you are qualified for a job, and find the right job.

Finally, computer-assisted career guidance programs (discussed in Chapter 6) provide vital, up-to-date information on the current job market. The ability to generate local job information on available computer programs is extremely helpful to the job seeker. In fact, the fast-changing job market may very well require that computer capabilities keep up to date.

Placement services can also provide the vital link between academics and the working world. Career planning and placement services offered early in secondary programs should provide the student with knowledge of career skills to be developed in secondary education. Such programs should be established not to discourage future formal academic training but to provide relevance and added motivation for learning per se. Career planning and placement in this sense should be an ongoing program for students in various levels of secondary education, with the placement function playing a vital role in student services.

Placement by State Employment Agencies

State employment agencies consist of a network of local offices in cities and rural areas across the nation. This network is based on federal and state partnerships with the U.S. Employment Service, providing broad national guidelines for operational procedures in state and local employment offices. One of the principal sources of job information has been compiled into what is referred to as a *job bank*. The job bank is a listing of all job orders compiled daily within each state. Microfiche copies are distributed daily to authorized users and all state employment offices. Those offices with computer terminals have direct access to the job bank. This up-to-the minute job information is available to all job seekers, who are required to fill out an application and be interviewed before they are given access to the job bank.

The functions of state employment agencies, which have very active placement programs, are to help the unemployed find work and to provide employers with qualified applicants for job orders. Many state agencies divide their services into two categories: (1) placement for job seekers and (2) services to employers. For job seekers, state agencies offer the following services.

1. Job listings in professional, clerical, skilled, technical, sales, managerial, semiskilled, service, and labor occupations
2. Personal interviews with professional interviewers
3. Assistance with improving qualifications
4. Referral to training
5. Testing
6. Counseling
7. Service to veterans
8. Unemployment benefits (for those who qualify while they are looking for work)

Services offered to employers are as follows.

1. Screening for qualified applicants
2. Professional interviews
3. On-site recruitment and application taking
4. Computerized job listing in most areas of the state
5. Aptitude and proficiency testing
6. Labor market information on technical assistance
7. Technical assistance with job descriptions, master orders, and turnover studies
8. Unemployment insurance tax information

Job placement is the focus of state employment agencies, but career counseling is available when requested. State employment agencies also administer assessment instruments that are typically used in career counseling, such as aptitude and achievement tests. Individuals are regularly referred to state employment agencies by other state agencies. For example, rehabilitation agencies refer clients who have had extensive career counseling and are in need of job listings. The placement function is enhanced by computerized job banks and lists of qualified job applicants that provide a readily accessible matching system. Employment opportunities are quickly available to job seekers who need immediate placement.

Career Education

A new concept of education that emerged in the 1970s specifically addressed career development, attitudes, and values in addition to traditional learning (Hoyt, 1972). This comprehensive career education concept focused on relationships between traditional educational programs and the world of work. The major purpose of career education was to prepare each individual for living and working in our society.

Thus, career education was considered integral to the educational process, from kindergarten through adulthood. The integration of career education programs into existing educational curricula had been considered the most feasible method of accomplishing these objectives and goals. Career education programs were not simply additional courses to be added to traditional curricula but were actually infused into existing curricula.

This chapter reviewed a number of existing career-related programs; their foundations were solidly built from career education concepts. And because career education strategies can be most useful in current programming, some are included here.

Career Education Collaboration and Infusion

In the career education framework, *collaboration* is the cooperative effort of educators, the family, the work force of the community, and governmental agencies that implement career education programs. Increased cooperation between school and community enhances and increases opportunities for work experience programs and on-site visits, as well as promotes the mutual advantages of job placement arrangements. Furthermore, family members and individuals from the business community are very valuable as career role models who can participate in classroom activities. Community representatives are also a valuable resource to school personnel; the importance of community cooperative effort and involvement in the development and operation of career education programs cannot be overstated.

Career education is not considered simply an extra course in the curriculum but an instructional strategy that relates established subject matter to career development concepts. The idea of integrating career development concepts into existing curricula is referred to as *career education infusion*. Career education infusion requires that teachers expand their current educational objectives to include career-related activities and subjects. For example, teaching decision-making skills can be infused with traditional academic courses. Planning a term project in a history class involves certain decisions, such as specifying the goals of the project, determining the possible approaches to the project and selecting the best one, and actually following through. Decision-making and planning skills are applicable to many—if not all—subjects and should be consciously taught as skills to be developed and refined. The proponents of career education infusion contend that formal attention should be given to career-related skills and tasks. Examples of infusion models for elementary, junior/middle, and high schools are presented in the following pages.

ELEMENTARY SCHOOL

Career counselors may find that the purposes of career education infusion need careful delineation to teaching and administrative staffs. Assisting elementary school teachers to conceptualize the role of career education infusion is a fundamental task for the career counselor. Career counselors advocate career education concepts by emphasizing that learning modules infused in formalized instruction foster greater self-awareness, knowledge of occupational roles, and an understanding of the purpose of work in our society. Examples of career education infusion modules are an effective means of illustrating the important role teachers play in career guidance programs.

The following career education infusion module is designed to improve career awareness. This module provides rationale, objectives, description, place of activity, personnel required, cost, time, resources, and evaluation measures.

Subject: Math, reading, language
Concept: Career awareness

Answering a Job Advertisement

Rationale
Students should have an understanding of the jobs described in want ads in order to develop an awareness of various occupations. Students should also learn about the requirements of various occupations and draw conclusions of whether they would like to work in the environment described by a want ad and during follow-up.

Objective
Students will describe in writing how different occupations are described in terms of salary, hours of work, training, and educational requirements.

Description
1. Discuss the various ways people find out about openings in the job market.
2. Present a page from the local newspaper with want ads listed.
3. Have students select three careers in which they are interested and research the requirements, salary, training, and education necessary for the job being advertised.
4. Have the students write a description of the job that appeals to them the most and explain their choices.
5. Have students share their findings with classmates in a 3–5 minute report.

Where activity occurs: classroom
Personnel required: teacher
Cost: cost of newspaper

Time: discussion, one-quarter period; research and select careers, one and one-quarter periods; share with classmates, one-quarter period

Resources: newspaper

Evaluation measures: oral and written report[1]

JUNIOR HIGH SCHOOL

Many goals of career education in elementary school are relevant for junior high school students. However, there is a shift of emphasis from general knowledge of work roles to more specific learning activities. Learning to differentiate individual characteristics and to identify broad occupational areas of interest are goals to foster. Awareness of self in relation to personal interests, values, abilities, and personal characteristics is an important objective during this developmental period.

Planning and decision-making skills are emphasized in junior high school. The following career infusion module for a geography class is designed to include planning, decision making, and awareness of career opportunities in geography.

Subject: Social studies, geography

Concept: Planning and decision making

   Career awareness

Chamber of Commerce Exercise

Rationale

Students should be exposed to different ways in which different groups make decisions, in order to improve their own decision making.

Objectives

1. Students will be able to describe their part in the project to accord with teacher observation.
2. Students will list all the Republics of South America and at least one feature from the tourist bulletin for each.
3. Students will identify at least two ways in which their project activity corresponds to duties in two specific occupations.

Description

During a unit on South America, divide the class into six groups. Each group will be a Chamber of Commerce for a Republic of South America. Each group can plan a tourist bulletin with articles and drawings.

1. Students will tell how their group decided who would research information, write articles, draw pictures, etc.
2. Students will describe their responsibilities in preparing the tourist bulletin and tell how they think those responsibilities were like some they might have on a job.
3. Students will answer the question, "Can you see how assuming responsibility for something in this project might help you assume responsibilities in an adult occupation?"

[1]*SOURCE: Project Cadre: A Cadre Approach to Career Education Infusion,* by C. C. Healy and O. H. Quinn, 1977. Unpublished manuscript. Reprinted by permission.

Personnel required: teacher
Cost: none
Time: 3 or 4 periods estimated
Resources: maps and information on South America
Impact on regular offering/curriculum goals: complement regular unit on South America; help students remember important information about the area
Evaluation measures: paper/pencil test[2]

HIGH SCHOOL

The career preparation stage in high school requires intensive self-awareness exploration. An important goal is to help students crystallize self-concepts; career education infusion modules are designed to help students become more aware of their aptitudes, interests, values, and lifestyle preferences. The development of planning skills for future educational and vocational choices also involves a multitude of learning activities and guidance programs. Decision-making skills and knowledge of occupations and job placement are key factors to emphasize in career education infusion. The following career education infusion module for a high school English class should help students become more aware of the importance of decision making.

Subject: English
Concept: Planning and decision making
        Self-awareness
           Decision Making Exemplified in Literature

Rationale
Students should become more aware of the importance of decision making.

Objectives

1. Students will arrange in order the steps in the systematic decision-making model discussed in class.
2. Students will analyze either a personal decision or a decision made by a literary character by listing the steps taken in making the decision; students will write in one page how that decision followed the steps in the model, or if it didn't how it could.

Description
Read and hold a class discussion on Robert Frost's poem, "The Road Not Taken," having students express their thoughts about the importance of decision making and talk about experiences that led them to make an important decision or to change their minds after making one. Bring out the following points in the discussion:

1. It is important that the student make a decision systematically and participate in its formulation.
2. Before making a decision, one must examine the consequences of the decision, both pro and con.

[2]*SOURCE: Project Cadre: A Cadre Approach to Career Education Infusion,* by C. C. Healy and O. H. Quinn, 1977. Unpublished manuscript. Reprinted by permission.

3. To do this, one must try to get accurate information about each decision.

4. Decision making can be thought of as a series of steps: (a) set the goal; (b) figure out alternative ways of reaching the goal; (c) get accurate information to determine which alternative is best; (d) decide on an alternative and carry it out; (e) figure out if the choice was correct and why; and (f) if you did not reach the goal, try another alternative or start the process over again.

Personnel required: teacher

Cost: none

Time: one period

Resources: Robert Frost's poem, "The Road Not Taken"[3]

Summary

1. Comprehensive school guidance programs are a means of systematically implementing a program concept for guidance activities in grades K–12. The value of this model is its comprehensive nature and involvement of school professionals, selected members of the community, and parents.

2. The Planning for Life Program complements comprehensive guidance programs. "Planning for life" suggests that career and life are ongoing processes that require individual and community commitment.

3. A work-based program, known as school-to-work, assists students in making the transition from school to work. The rationale of this program suggests that students will become more motivated in all academic programs when they are able to experience the connections between schoolwork and what is required on a job.

4. Models for integrating vocational and academic education are designed to encourage vocational education students to take more rigorous academic courses.

5. Tech-prep programs have stressed the need to integrate academics and technical training. Students who opt for tech-prep would also qualify for higher education.

6. The NOICC competency-based program models lend themselves readily to task statements and activities. The CDTI conducts training programs to facilitate the proper use of competencies and indicators.

7. Other government-sponsored programs address changes in vocational education in order to place a greater emphasis on technology. Work-based programs are being stressed.

8. Secondary placement offers a variety of programs to assist high school students in transition to work and entering college.

9. Career education infusion is a strategy requiring that teachers expand their current educational objectives to include instruction on career-related activities and subjects in addition to traditional academic subjects.

10. Career education collaboration is a cooperative effort among educators, family, the total community, the work force, and government agencies.

[3]*SOURCE: Project Cadre: A Cadre Approach to Career Education Infusion,* by C. C. Healy and O. H. Quinn, 1977. Unpublished manuscript. Reprinted by permission.

Supplementary Learning Exercises

1. Interview a representative from the business community for suggestions on how to establish collaborative efforts to meet school-to-work objectives. Summarize your recommendations.
2. Interview a school counselor to determine the role and scope of his or her career guidance program. Evaluate your findings and offer suggestions.
3. Develop objectives and strategies for introducing life planning concepts in the elementary school.
4. What strategies would you use to convince a junior high class that life and career planning are important goals?
5. Develop a format that could be used to annually evaluate the career planning progress of high school students.
6. Interview at least two parents of school-age children who are willing to participate as career models in career education programs. Develop a format for presenting the career to a class or an assembly.
7. Develop course objectives and goals for a minicourse on decision making for junior and senior high school students.
8. Visit a local industry to determine the kinds of on-site job experiences available. Write a description of at least five possible on-site jobs.
9. Develop at least five counseling strategies for junior high school students to promote opportunities for reflecting on self-in-situation.
10. Develop at least five counseling strategies for senior high school students designed to help them choose a training program or a college.
11. Visit a senior high school placement office. Report your findings to the class.

CHAPTER ELEVEN

Career Guidance in Institutions of Higher Learning

This chapter begins with a discussion of characteristics of college students and how college affects students' career choice and development. This chapter also explores the *National Occupational Information Coordinating Committee* recommendations for college career guidance programs. Examples of career guidance programs in institutions of higher learning include representative models of innovative career counseling programs, such as a curriculum module model, a metroplex model, a decision-making approach, and work-experience models. Finally, the chapter covers the role and function of college placement services.

Some Characteristics of College Students

Marcia (1967, 1980, 1991) described college students in terms of four identity statuses: the "foreclosed student," the "identity-diffused student," the "moratorium student," and the "achieved-identity student." These statuses were determined by the students' capacity for intimacy, moral awareness, respect for individual rights, and reliance on a universal principle of justice. The statuses also represent styles of coping with identity developmental tasks. For example, foreclosed students are closed off from self-exploration and limit their contacts and challenges. Identity-diffused students have few commitments to the future and are less mature than achieved-identity and moratorium students. Moratorium students (described by Erikson as "delaying commitments") are able to effectively use the college experience in coming to terms with their quest for identity. Achieved-identity students have successfully resolved ego identity, as evidenced by firmer commitments to future goals.

The diverse levels of development among college students, as revealed by Marcia's work, are not unexpected but do point out a wide range of career guidance needs. Mauer and Gysbers (1990) also determined the career concerns of college students (entering freshmen) from a study of 3600 undergraduates, and they grouped these concerns in the following categories.

1. *Anxiety:* undecided about a career and confused about the process of career exploration
2. *Confidence:* uncertain about an occupation
3. *Self-assessment:* Major strengths and weaknesses are unknown
4. *Occupational information:* lacks knowledge of work and what workers do

The needs expressed in this survey suggest strategies that would greatly assist entering freshmen.

Recent evidence overwhelmingly supports career guidance programs in institutions of higher learning. More than 945,000 high school students responded to an American College Testing Program questionnaire during the 1994–1995 academic year, and 41% indicated that they needed help with educational and occupational plans (American College Testing Program, 1996b). Accomplishing the tasks required of the transition from Super's (1990) exploration stage to his establishment stage is not easy, as Healy (1982) observed. Almost half of all college students change majors, and even more change career goals while in college.

Before concluding this section, it should be mentioned that returning adult students are a growing population in institutions of higher learning. Hirschhorn (1988) reported that students over age 25 make up 45% of campus enrollments. This group of students has special needs that must be addressed by postsecondary career centers. Splete (1996) has been one of the leaders in developing adult career counseling centers and has successfully built a model for such programs during the last 12 years at Oakland University. One of the goals of this center is to provide no-cost career exploration and planning opportunities to adults in the community. Splete (1996) has also supported research efforts in promoting effective career guidance practices for adults.

How College Affects Students' Career Choice and Development

Over a 20-year-period, Pascarel and Terenzi (1991) conducted a comprehensive study of research findings on how college affects students. The following conclusions were selected and paraphrased from the chapter on career choice and development.

1. Students frequently change their career plans.
2. Significant occupational status differences between high school and college graduates are sustained over the life span.
3. Individuals with a bachelor's degree are more likely to obtain high-status managerial, technical, and professional jobs.

4. College graduates are less likely to be unemployed than are high school graduates.
5. College graduates are less likely to suffer the effects of prolonged periods of unemployment.
6. Employers see college graduates as possessing requisite skills and values that make them more desirable for employment and advancement.
7. College graduates enjoy significantly higher levels of career mobility and advancement.
8. College experiences tend to produce conflicting influences on satisfaction with one's work. College tends to develop a capacity for critical judgment and evaluation that in turn provides sensitivity to shortcomings of jobs.
9. Maturity of career thinking and planning can be modestly improved through various career development courses.
10. Socialization in college increases student occupational aspirations.
11. College may enhance occupational success by facilitating development of traits that describe a psychologically mature person, such as symbolization (reflective intelligence), allocentrism (empathy and altruism), integration (ability to combine a variety of views), and stability and autonomy.
12. In terms of reducing unemployment, a college education was more important for non-whites than for whites.

The results of this study suggest that the benefits of a college education are quite significant in the world of work. This conclusion comes as no surprise but does give credence to recommendations counselors have made for years about the influence of higher education on lifestyle and future opportunities for career development. Not only does the college experience provide for career mobility and advancement, but it also increases occupational aspirations. In essence, the benefits of higher education improve the quality of life and the capacity to make appropriate judgments over the life span.

NOICC Goals for a College Career Guidance Program

We include the NOICC's 1992 competencies and indicators for adults to underscore the necessity of preparing students for the work world and integrating life roles into a future lifestyle. These competencies and indicators present a significant challenge to institutions of higher learning and point out the importance of and need for an effective career guidance program. Not only is the importance of educational and occupational exploration suggested by these competencies and indicators, but also the importance of work as it affects values and lifestyle. The far-reaching influences on college students suggested by these guidelines are quite apparent. To accomplish these goals will require a comprehensive program and commitment on the part of the college or university.

Adult: Competencies and Indicators

SELF-KNOWLEDGE

Competency I: Skills needed to maintain a positive self concept
- Demonstrate a positive self-concept.
- Identify skills, abilities, interests, experiences, values, and personality traits and their influence on career decisions.
- Identify achievements related to work, learning, and leisure and their influence on self-perception.
- Demonstrate a realistic understanding of self.

Competency II: Skills needed to maintain effective behaviors
- Demonstrate appropriate interpersonal skills in expressing feelings and ideas.
- Identify symptoms of stress.
- Demonstrate skills to overcome self-defeating behaviors.
- Demonstrate skills in identifying support and networking arrangements (including role models).
- Demonstrate skills to manage financial resources.

Competency III: Understanding developmental changes and transitions
- Describe how personal motivations and aspirations may change over time.
- Describe physical changes that occur with age and adapt work performance to accommodate these.
- Identify external events (for example, job loss, job transfer) that require life changes.

EDUCATIONAL AND OCCUPATIONAL EXPLORATION

Competency IV: Skills needed to enter and participate in education and training
- Describe short- and long-range plans to achieve career goals through appropriate educational paths.
- Identify information that describes educational opportunities (for example, job training programs, employer-sponsored training, graduate and professional study).
- Describe community resources to support education and training (for example, child care, public transportation, public health services, mental health services, welfare benefits).
- Identify strategies to overcome personal barriers to education and training.

Competency V: Skills needed to participate in work and lifelong learning
- Demonstrate confidence in the ability to achieve learning activities (for example, studying, taking tests).
- Describe how educational achievements and life experiences relate to occupational opportunities.
- Describe organizational resources to support education and training (for example, remedial classes, counseling, tuition support).

Competency VI: Skills needed to locate, evaluate, and interpret information
- Identify and use current career information resources (e.g., computerized career-information systems, print and media materials, mentors).
- Describe information related to self-assessment, career planning, occupations, prospective employers, organizational structures, and employer expectations.
- Describe the uses and limitations of occupational outlook information.
- Identify the diverse job opportunities available to an individual with a given set of occupational skills.
- Identify opportunities available through self-employment.
- Identify factors that contribute to misinformation about occupations.
- Describe information about specific employers and hiring practices.

Competency VII: Skills needed to prepare to seek, obtain, maintain, and change jobs
- Identify specific employment situations that match desired career objectives.
- Demonstrate skills to identify job openings.
- Demonstrate skills to establish a job search network through colleagues, friends, and family.
- Demonstrate skills in preparing a résumé and completing job applications.
- Demonstrate skills and attitudes essential to prepare for and participate in a successful job interview.
- Demonstrate effective work attitudes and behaviors.
- Describe changes (e.g., personal growth, technological developments, changes in demand for products or services) that influence the knowledge, skills, and attitudes required for job success.
- Demonstrate strategies to support occupational change (e.g., on-the-job training, career ladders, mentors, performance ratings, networking, continuing education).
- Describe career planning and placement services available through organizations (e.g., educational institutions, business/industry, labor, and community agencies).
- Identify skills that are transferable from one job to another.

Competency VIII: Understanding how the needs and functions of society influence the nature and structure of work
- Describe the importance of work as it affects values and lifestyle.
- Describe how society's needs and functions affect occupational supply and demand.
- Describe occupational, industrial, and technological trends as they relate to training programs and employment opportunities.
- Demonstrate an understanding of the global economy and how it affects the individual.

CAREER PLANNING

Competency IX: Skills needed to make decisions
- Describe personal criteria for making decisions about education, training, and career goals.

- Demonstrate skills to assess occupational opportunities in terms of advancement, management styles, work environment, benefits, and other conditions of employment.
- Describe the effects of education, work, and family decisions on individual career decisions.
- Identify personal and environmental conditions that affect decision making.
- Demonstrate effective career decision-making skills.
- Describe potential consequences of decisions.

Competency X: Understanding the impact of work on individual and family life
- Describe how family and leisure functions affect occupational roles and decisions.
- Determine effects of individual and family developmental stages on one's career.
- Describe how work, family, and leisure activities interrelate.
- Describe strategies for negotiating work, family, and leisure demands with family members (e.g., assertiveness and time management skills).

Competency XI: Understanding the continuing changes in male/female roles
- Describe recent changes in gender norms and attitudes.
- Describe trends in the gender composition of the labor force and assess implications for one's own career plans.
- Identify disadvantages of stereotyping occupations.
- Demonstrate behaviors, attitudes, and skills that work to eliminate stereotyping in education, family, and occupational environments.

Competency XII: Skills needed to make career transitions
- Identify transition activities (e.g., reassessment of current position, occupational changes) as a normal aspect of career development.
- Describe strategies to use during transitions (e.g., networks, stress management).
- Describe skills needed for self-employment (e.g., developing a business plan, determining marketing strategies, developing sources of capital).
- Describe the skills and knowledge needed for preretirement planning.
- Develop an individual career plan, updating information from earlier plans and including short- and long-range career decisions.

Implications for Career Guidance Programs in Institutions of Higher Learning

Several career guidance strategies in the senior high school apply to career guidance at postsecondary institutions. For example, career guidance must meet the needs of students at various stages of career development. Understanding the relationships between career choice and educational requirements is essential. College students must learn to relate their personal characteristics to occupational requirements. Career planning and decision-making skills are essential. College students need assistance in choosing graduate schools.

In general, college students should be assisted in systematically analyzing college and noncollege experiences and in incorporating this information into career-related decisions. In addition, career guidance services should help students select major fields of study and relate these to career fields. Career life planning that focuses on factors that influence career choices over the life span is a valuable concept to incorporate in career guidance programs. Placement offices should provide a wide range of services, including projected job markets and overall employment statistics, job search strategies, interview skills training, and job fairs.

Career guidance activities in institutions of higher learning must provide assistance in helping each student understand that career development is a lifelong process based on a sequential series of educational and occupational choices. Each student should be given the opportunity to identify and use a wide variety of resources to maximize his or her career development potential.

Examples of Career Guidance Programs in Institutions of Higher Learning

There are numerous career counseling programs in institutions of higher learning. Some institutions offer credit for 1- or 3-hour courses that are built around some aspect of career guidance. Others offer seminars or workshops that typically do not include credit hours. In some institutions, instructors assign projects that include career exploration, typically done in a career counseling center. Individual and group counseling is available at most institutions, and most institutions have a placement office or an employment services office available to students. One can expect to find computerized career guidance systems at most institutions of higher learning. Finally, some institutions offer career-related services to the community.

In the next section, examples of strategies designed to meet the needs of some students are presented. The first is a curricular career information service module that covers a wide range of needs and contains modules for special populations groups. The second is a career counseling program at a large metropolitan university that must serve not only its large student enrollment but also its alumni. The third example is a decision-making approach built for group counseling.

Curricular Career Information Service (CCIS): A Module Model

A very innovative program for delivery of educational and vocational information was initiated at Florida State University in 1975. The program emphasizes an instructional approach to career planning services. The CCIS is self-help-oriented, utilizes instructional models, and is multimedia-based. The program delivery system is accomplished through paraprofessionals. The CCIS is an outreach program used in residence halls and the university student center. In addition, the modules have been used as the nucleus of a three-credit course in career planning offered by two academic departments at Florida State University. The instructional modules were conceptualized to meet specific counseling goals and are structured around behavioral objectives. Modules I through V are shown in Table 11-1; modules VI through XII are presented in Table A-1 of Appendix A.

After a brief interview, a typical student is directed to the first module, which begins with a 10-minute slide presentation outlining the goals and purposes of the CCIS. The second module provides an overview of variables considered desirable in career planning using slides and selected materials. The third module requires self-assessment, primarily accomplished through self-administration and self-interpretation of the SDS (*Self-Directed Search*) interest inventory (Holland, 1987b). The fourth module consists of a slide presentation of career information resources. The fifth module assists the student in locating careers related to academic majors. Other modules include employment outlooks, leisure planning, career planning for African Americans, career decision making for adult women and students with disabilities, and career interest exploration through work and occupational skills.

The instructional approach to career planning used in the CCIS has potential application for all career counseling programs. There is greater opportunity for accountability in the evaluation of career counseling effectiveness when behavioral objectives are specified as they are in these modules. Major and minor components of the instructional unit can be effectively evaluated through a systematic review process. Effectiveness of materials and of instruction techniques can be measured in relation to specific objectives. Thus, the system provides the opportunity for continuous modification and upgrading of each instructional component. As career-related materials and programs change rapidly in the future, the opportunity to systematically evaluate and subsequently upgrade them will be a major asset.

Additional modules can be developed as needs are identified. As new program needs are identified, such as career assistance for minority groups, an instructional module can be built using materials already at hand and examples of existing modules. Thus, instructional modules are very flexible. Once the system of instructional modules has been established, the building of additional modules can be based on a review of needs identified by the professional staff. Inherent in this process is also the identification of additional career materials.

Instructional modules provide the opportunity for more effective choice of entry into career counseling for individuals seeking career decision assistance. The diversity of the learning activities provided through a series of career planning modules allows the individual a greater variety of options and a more effective means of choosing a point of entry. The development of modules for specific groups (such as adults, females, minority groups) represents a multifaceted approach to career counseling that eliminates the necessity of prescribing the same program for everyone. A diversity of programs also provides an attractive means of creating interest in career exploration activities. Career counseling programs that provide the opportunity to identify goals and desired outcomes have much greater appeal and assist the individual in identifying expectations of career planning experiences. (See Appendix A for additional modules.)

TABLE 11-1
Curricular Career Information Services (CCIS) Modules

Module Title	Objectives	Activities
I. Everything You've Always Wanted to Know About CCIS	1. To introduce you to the CCIS. 2. To help you select activities that will assist you in solving your career problem.	a. Examine a Career Center brochure located on the yellow rack near the Career Center entrance to learn more about CCIS services and programs. b. Ask a Career Advisor to explain CCIS and the career advising process to you. c. Attend a Career Center tour. d. Browse the remaining module sheets on the yellow rack to learn more about some of the common concerns addressed through the career advising process.
II. What's Involved in Making a Career Decision?	1. To dispel common misconceptions about career planning; 2. To help you identify areas that are important to consider development; and 3. To help you establish some guidelines for the process of career decision making.	a. Review the "What's Involved in Career Choice" sheet to gain a greater awareness of the career decision-making process. b. Review "A Guide to Good Decision Making" sheet to explore more effective ways to make career decisions. c. Review the "Career Choice Resources in CCIS" and/or books catalogued IA in The Career Center Library. d. Review materials in the Module II folder in the Mobile File (File 1). e. Attend a "Choosing a Major/Career" workshop in CCIS. f. With the assistance of a Career Advisor, complete the "Guide to Good Decision Making Exercise." g. Register for Unit I and II of the Introduction to Career Development Class—SDS 3340. A course syllabus is available for your review in the Module XVI section of the Mobile File (File 1).
III. Looking at You	1. To help you examine some of your interests, values, and skills. 2. To help you identify some occupations or fields of study for further exploration.	**INTERESTS** a. Complete the Self-Directed Search (SDS). b. Complete the "Career Areas" topic in the Explore section of the CHOICES computer program. c. Complete the Interest Inventory in the "Learning About Yourself" module of the DISCOVER computer program. d. Complete the "Self-Assessment" section of SIGI PLUS. **VALUES** a. Interact with the SIGI PLUS computer program. b. Complete the Values Card Sort. c. Complete the Values inventory in the "Learning About Yourself" module of the DISCOVER program. **SKILLS** a. Complete the aptitudes section in the CHOICES Guidebook. b. Interact with the Micro Skills computer program.

TABLE 11-1 *(continued)*

Module	*Title*	*Objectives*	*Activities*
			c. Complete the Motivated Skills Card Sort. d. Complete the Abilities Assessment in the "Learning About Yourself" module of the DISCOVER computer program. e. Use the Skills section of SIGI PLUS.
IV.	Information: Where to Find It and How to Use It	1. To help you locate all Career Center information related to your educational and career planning needs.	a. Perform a search using Career Key for the topic of interest to you. b. Review the diagram on the back of this sheet to locate various multimedia resources available in The Career Center Library.
V.	Matching Majors and Jobs	1. To help you learn how specific job titles relate to college majors or fields of study.	a. Review printed materials in the Module V "Matching Majors and Careers" folders in the Mobile File (File 1), specifically the "Match-Major" sheets. b. Read sections in these books or others found in Area IIC of The Career Center Library. IIC AA C7 The College Board Guide to 140 Popular College Majors IIC AA M3 What Can I Do with a Major in . . .? IIC AA N3 College Knowledge and Jobs IIC AA P4 College Majors & Careers IIC AA O2 The Occupational Thesaurus (Vols. 1 & 2) IIA 025 Occupational Outlook Handbook c. Perform a search on Career Key under the topic *Occupations by Major* to get a list of relevant CCIS resources. Ask a Career Advisor for assistance. d. Use the *College Majors Card Sort* to find majors and occupational opportunities. e. Review employment information in the *Undergraduate Academic Program Guide* for FSU majors. f. Use the SDS code assigned to a particular FSU major to search for occupations in the *SDS Occupations Finder* or the *Dictionary of Holland Occupational Codes* (IA G6). g. Examine materials on FSU academic programs in File 3. h. Review selected Employer Directories that list organizations by major, career, or geographical areas. i. Consult with Career Center staff members in Placement Services and Career Experience Opportunities (CEO). j. With assistance from a Career Advisor, explore opportunities on Career Key for informational interviews, extern experiences, and networking assistance with participating professionals and FSU alumni.

SOURCE: From *Curricular Career Information Service,* by R. C. Reardon, 1996. Unpublished manuscript, Florida State University. Reprinted by permission.

Library System for the CCIS

The CCIS Library has divided its material into two types: career planning information and occupational information. The career planning information is classified according to the Dewey Decimal Classification (DDC). The *Dictionary of Occupational Titles (DOT)* is used to classify all materials related to occupations (Reardon & Domkowski, 1977).

As material reaches the library, it is classified and assigned a DDC or *DOT* number. A cutter number is also assigned to each piece of material to distinguish it from materials with the same DDC or *DOT* number. Because the CCIS uses a large number of materials that have *DOT* numbers printed on them, the classification process is greatly simplified. All material is classified by alphabetical order into one of three catalogs: (1) *DOT* index, (2) *DOT* subject, or (3) DDC subject.

Students are provided with step-by-step instructions in the use of the CCIS Library. For occupational information, the student uses Card Catalog 1 (*DOT* Index) and locates the *DOT* number. The number is used to locate the filed information and may also be used in Catalog 2 (*DOT* Subject Catalog) for information in books and tapes. For curriculum and career planning information, a student is referred to Catalog 3 (DDC Listing), in which information is filed alphabetically according to subject matter.

The CCIS adopted this system for flexibility of use and for ease of cross-referencing. Many students are interested only in information and want easy access to materials filed by occupations. Cross-referencing is considered very important because each brief, book, chapter, or pamphlet describing a certain occupation is contained in the subject catalog and is available to the student for his or her career search. Students thus have easy access to information from a variety of sources.

The CCIS is an inexpensive system for career information delivery. The use of paraprofessionals is recommended for on-line supervision and various outreach locations. A relatively small staff commitment is needed for module development and evaluation. The instructional modules developed for the CCIS have a flexible design and can be converted to computer-based career information systems. The most recent use of the CCIS was described by Peterson, Sampson, and Reardon (1991) and by Reardon (1996b).

Career Counseling at a Large University:
A Metroplex Model

A large university located in a metropolitan area may have the added responsibility of satisfying heavy alumni demand for career guidance. Not only is the career center faced with a large volume of currently enrolled students choosing from a diversity of academic programs, but it must also respond to a wide variety of alumni requests for career guidance. Alumni contemplating career changes with subsequent reentry into the work force represent a unique dimension of career counseling encountered by a university located in a metropolitan area. The following examples of unique client needs exemplify the complexity of programs needed

in such a career center: (1) individuals (young adults through middle age) anticipating a change of career direction; (2) individuals seeking relocation within their
career field; (3) individuals desiring mobility within their career field through
further educational training; (4) individuals seeking information about specific,
current job market trends; (5) individuals seeking college reentry planning; and
(6) individuals seeking second careers after early retirement from a primary career.
In addition, many adults residing in the metropolitan area will seek assistance for
career education planning prior to university enrollment. Thus, a career center
metroplex model must be able to provide a wide range of services not only for
currently enrolled students but also for alumni and others in the community seeking assistance or career redirection.

The UCLA Placement and Career Planning Center is a good example of a
metroplex model. Located in its own building, the center offers career planning
and placement services to students and alumni from all University of California
campuses. Along with several in-house programs, this center also offers outreach
programs on a number of subjects. For example, in conjunction with the Alumni
Association and various academic departments, the center offers specific career
panels on a broad spectrum of career fields such as mental health, allied health,
banking and investments, motion pictures, advertising, and marketing and sales.
The programs are videotaped and available on request.

From the results of a national survey, Hoyt and Lester (1995) found that there
is a growing need for career centers to offer their services to the general public.
This finding was underscored by the results of a national survey conducted by the
New York Times, reporting that large numbers of U.S. workers have lost their jobs
through downsizing of industrial corporations and now need career planning assistance (Uchitelle & Kleinfield, 1996). (Both surveys are discussed in more detail
in Chapters 12 and 13.) Therefore, in the context of a university metroplex model,
the variety of program needs for students, alumni, and the general public is almost
unlimited. In fact, universities and colleges in most all communities can offer a
valuable and needed service to community members.

Samples of career-related programs generally offered in heavily populated
areas include direct job referral services, seminars on job search strategies, assistance with résumé preparation, interview skills training, job clubs (individuals engaging in similar job searches), life/work relationships, seminars on career decision
making and problem solving, career information resources (including computer-
based career information resources, both local and Internet), graduate school selection, and retraining for a different or related career. One way to determine the
need for specific career-related programs is through a survey of alumni and community members.

A Decision-Making Approach

How to make a career decision is a subject with roots that go back to the origin
of occupational guidance. Deciding was perceived as a relatively simple task in
early vocational guidance approaches. The trait-and-factor approach measured an

individual's aptitudes, interests, and achievements and matched this profile with the traits necessary for certain occupations. As more sophisticated career counseling approaches evolved, the process of deciding was seen in a broader perspective. Moving away from authoritative procedures, the counselor would often leave the client stranded along the road of career exploration with the statement, "We can't decide for you—you must make up your own mind." The client's alternatives in many instances were not as "cut and dried" as the nondirective counselor implied. However, it was not until the 1960s that career decision-making strategies made a significant impact on the counseling scene.

Decision making is now viewed as a learned skill that should be part of everyone's educational program. The acquisition of decision-making skills is a vital objective of career counseling. Decision making is distinguished from problem solving in that decision making involves examination of a variety of variables to arrive at satisfying solutions, whereas in problem solving there are no clear-cut right or wrong solutions.

Decision making is complex in that individuals must apply their own values, interests, aptitudes, and other unique qualities to each decision. Thus, decision making is a learned skill that should lead to more satisfying solutions according to personally held values. Decision making is a relatively easily learned skill that becomes complex when applied to individual lives. Individuals faced with the same decision often take different paths; varying personal values, knowledge, and strategies of action lead to different outcomes.

Krumboltz and Sorenson (1974) designed a decision-making system for high school students. Its application is extended not only to ongoing decisions but also to those each individual will face in a lifetime. There are eight steps in the decision-making process that can be taught either to groups or to individuals. Group discussion appears to have several advantages, because it presents opportunities for reinforcement from peers. Therefore the eight steps are described in the context of group counseling. Following this description, the model for decision making and specific objectives and tasks appropriate for each step are outlined.

The first step requires that the individual state the reason or problem that motivated him or her to seek career counseling. When individuals describe their own problems, individual goals can more easily be formulated within a group. Therefore, step 1 is to *formulate individual goals* for each member of the group. Goals should be described in behavioral terms for more effective evaluation of each individual's progress.

The second step is to *commit time.* The counselor should point out the necessary time commitment required of each member to meet his or her individual goals. It is imperative that the counselor be realistic concerning the amount of committed time and receive a firm commitment from each member. Time commitments will be necessary for specific meetings and individual research. Some resistance to time commitment can be expected, but the counselor must remain firm in receiving a pledge from each individual to make the necessary time available.

The third step is to *generate activities.* The purpose of this step is to narrow the alternatives in the career search. Students will be required to complete individual projects (such as taking interest inventories, reviewing filmstrips and films, and studying occupational literature) on their own. Individual conferences may be necessary to reinforce this part of decision making.

The fourth step is to *collect information.* The students now return to the group meeting and share the activities that they have completed during the previous step. Peer group interaction will tend to reinforce students in further career exploration. The counselor should be prepared to suggest specific kinds of resources for each individual student. Group discussion should include the nature of career clusters, job market information, opportunities for advancement, worker associates, preparation time for certain occupations, pay scales, and other information of this type for each career being considered. The information collection phase could also include job-site visitation in the community. When it is not possible to visit a job site, job-experience kits (Mitchell & Krumboltz, 1996), which contain exercises simulating actual work experiences, are recommended.

The fifth step entails *sharing information* and *estimating consequences.* This step should assist the student in predicting success, based on information collected. The counselor could provide local expectancy tables for predicting success in specific colleges.

The sixth step is entitled *reevaluate* and is usually accomplished through group discussion. The students share the possibilities of success in specific kinds of occupations that they have explored through the previous steps. The objective of this session is to provide the stimulus for firming up a decision on a career or for changing direction and going back to previous steps in the decision-making process. Individual conferences may be necessary, particularly for those students returning to previous steps.

The seventh step is to *decide tentatively.* Here the objective is to have students narrow their choices and eliminate least-desirable possibilities that have been considered up to this point. The elimination process may require that students team up and explore possibilities together or, for certain individuals, explore the remaining jobs under consideration. The students should be encouraged to recall the skills they have learned up to this point when considering alternatives.

The last step in the career decision-making process is referred to as *recycle.* Each group member is encouraged to view career decision making as an ongoing process that can be used in various situations other than the immediate one in which the group is involved. Ideally, the group should recognize that although decision making should be systematic and will lead most individuals to satisfying solutions, it is also a process that is repeated over and over again as one recycles information, crystallizes career expectations, and learns more about personal values related to the world of work. Zunker, Ash, Evans, Kight, Sunbury, and Walker (1979) developed objectives and tasks for the Krumboltz and Sorenson model of decision making to be covered in five counseling sessions, which are outlined in Box 11-1.

Work- and Experienced-Based Programs

There appears to be a growing trend in all levels of education to provide students the opportunity of work experience as a vital part of their educational program. Although student teaching and a variety of intern and extern experiences are not

BOX 11-1
Objectives and Tasks of Krumboltz and Sorenson's Model of Decision Making

Session I: Formulate individual goals and commit time
A. Objectives:
1. Each student will formulate at least one career goal.
2. Each student will commit herself or himself to six hours of group time and four to six hours of individual research.
B. Tasks:
1. Members will introduce themselves to the group.
2. Through brainstorming, some rules and regulations for group time will be established.
3. The counselor will define behavioral goals and introduce the goal development process.
4. The group will divide into pairs and help each member decide on an individual goal.
5. Goals will be shared with the group, and the counselor will provide reinforcement as discussion progresses.
6. The counselor will discuss the time commitment necessary for group participation.
7. Group accomplishments of Session I will be summarized.

Session II: Generate activities
A. Objectives:
1. To familiarize students with career information system and assessment instruments that may be used.
2. To explain the purpose of assessment instruments and the occupational information system.
B. Tasks:
1. Group members will be reintroduced to goals established at the last meeting.
2. The purpose and objectives of Session II will be explained.
3. The interest inventory will be administered and interpreted.
4. Through discussion of the interest inventory (with counselor input), each student will select two or more occupations that he or she wishes to explore.
5. Through visual aids or demonstration, available career information materials and the system to be used will be introduced.

Session III: Collect Information
A. Objectives:
1. To introduce career information resources, their purpose, and their use.

    2. To introduce important components of occupational information for career exploration.

B. Tasks:

    1. Individual career exploration and choices will be reviewed.

    2. The format of published occupational information resources will be clarified. Job-site visitation resources will be identified.

    3. The purpose and use of alternatives for previewing occupations, such as a job-experience kit, will be discussed.

    4. The counselor will present a sample module of the format for previewing an occupation.

    5. Each group member will present his or her individual goals and objectives for the career information search.

    6. Through group interaction, each member will commit himself or herself to completing job previews in the following two weeks.

    7. Accomplishments and commitments will be reviewed, and the time for the next meeting will be set.

Session IV: Share information and estimate consequences

A. Objectives:

    1. Each group member will share compiled information on a chosen career with the group.

    2. Each group member will select a tentative career field for further exploration.

B. Tasks:

    1. The meeting format will be set, and careers to be discussed will be selected.

    2. Through oral presentation, each group member will share compiled information on occupations reviewed with the group.

    3. Each group member will state tentative conclusions, reasons for conclusions, and ideas for further exploration.

    4. The counselor will summarize conclusions for each member and introduce data that will help students estimate their chances of success in an occupation and/or career.

    5. The counselor will assist each group member with estimating his or her chances of success in a chosen occupation, or suggest the need to recycle within the decision-making process.

    6. The session will conclude after the next session's format is decided on.

Session V: Reevaluate, decide tentatively, or recycle

A. Objectives:

    1. To share the possibilities of success in specific kinds of occupations.

    2. To provide the stimulus for firming up a decision for further exploration on a career, or changing direction and going back to previous steps in the decision-making process.

novel ideas in institutions of higher learning, some innovations should be of interest to the career counselor. One such innovation is the extern experience.

The extern model provides the student with an opportunity to observe ongoing activities in his or her major field of study and to interact with individuals on the job. Generally, during senior year, students submit a proposal of their career goals on graduation with a statement of how the extern experience would help them meet these goals. Career planning and placement centers or other administrative entities have agreements with host agencies to offer such experiences. Selected students will spend a specified time with a host agency during midsemester break or during an interim semester.

Intern models, on the other hand, provide students with the opportunity to spend more time in a workplace and are more work-experience-oriented than are extern models. Students actually do the work they are being trained to do. For example, junior-level students planning to become accountants may be chosen by an accounting firm to intern in one of its offices. Actual accounting work will be done under the supervision of a selected employee. The time spent in this experience is usually negotiated so as not to interfere with the student's progress toward a degree.

The practice of providing college students with actual work experience related to their college major should proliferate over the next decade. The length of the experience should also increase; students will find a longer time more beneficial than current extern programs allow. As colleges attempt to help students make more realistic career choices, more experience-based models will certainly emerge.

College Placement

The traditional placement service in our educational institutions has evolved into the career planning center. As suggested in the previous chapter, the use of the word *placement* in the name, such as the "Career Planning and Placement Center," has in the minds of some professionals become obsolete (Carter, 1995). The major argument centers around the students' perception of such a center: this is where you interview for a job. Thus, students overlook the fact that placement is only *one* of the services offered. The philosophical stance is that placement is subsumed in a center that offers a wide variety of career services that are of at least equal status with placement; therefore, the name of the center should reflect this change. What has been suggested are more generic names, such as Career Planning Center, Career Service Center, or simply Career Center. Regardless of the name, such centers should be student-service-oriented and should indeed offer a wide variety of services to all students—and in some cases, also to alumni or individuals in the community. In this context, placement continues to be an important part of services offered.

Partially to emphasize a changing philosophical position, national, regional, and local placement organizations have also undergone name changes. The national organization formerly called the College Placement Council is now the National Association of Colleges and Employers (NACE), a name change that reflects the broad-based approach of career service centers. Employers are now an important part of national, regional, and local organizations, and their participation in planning and sharing in all organizational matters has distinctly improved services to students. For instance, college representatives and employers have found a tremendous arena for exchanging information, such as salary surveys, job market information, internship programs, and workshops.

Don't be surprised to continue seeing the term *placement* used in the name of centers and programs being offered, at least until students and faculty become more familiar with the current changes that are taking place. In the meantime, many of the following programs may be found at typical career planning and placement offices.

1. Full-time employment listings
2. Temporary-work files
3. Full-time vacation jobs
4. Job-search strategy meetings
5. Résumé-preparation workshops
6. Interview practice sessions
7. Career interest testing.
8. Career exploration workshops
9. Individual and group counseling in career searching
10. Special programs such as minority recruiting opportunities for employers
11. Follow-up studies of previous graduates

Many colleges and universities have installed automated placement services. For a fee of $30 to $50, students can send résumés to regional, national, and international employment networks. Also, students can phone in 24 hours a day to hear about full-time vacancy listings; to schedule interviews; and to receive information on part-time jobs, summer job vacancies, and internships (Herr & Cramer, 1996).

As the demand for services from the placement office increased, the more fortunate centers were given adequate facilities. As mentioned before, the University of California at Los Angeles has designed and built a modern facility for its placement and career planning functions. A floor plan for this building is shown in Figure 11–1. The commitment at UCLA to career planning and placement exemplifies the changing placement role and the emerging services of a university placement office.

The conference room next to the Career Resource Library provides the space needed for orientations to acquaint students with the services and use of the center. A separate educational career services unit provides room for storage and study space for individuals searching for graduate and professional school information. Audiovisual equipment is available for teaching interview techniques and other job search strategies. A secretarial pool provides clerical assistance for the entire office.

At Richland College, a Dallas County Community College, the career planning and placement office is referred to as the Center for Choice (CFC). The CFC includes career counseling, a comprehensive career information area, financial aid information, a comprehensive test center, a veterans' service center, an alcoholic-education specialist center, and a job placement program. The CFC is housed in a

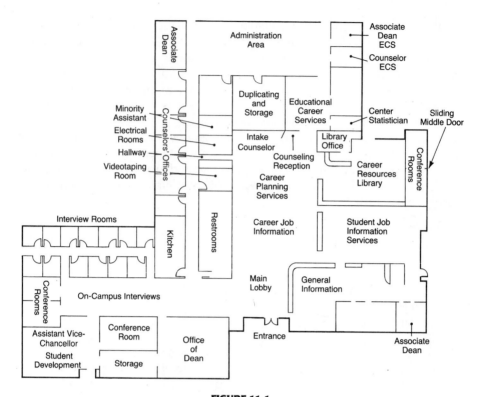

FIGURE 11-1

The UCLA placement and career planning center

SOURCE: The University of California, Los Angeles, 1980. Reprinted by permission.

building adjacent to the counseling center. The floor plan for the CFC is shown in Figure 11-2.

The CFC is informal in nature and is staffed by peer counselors (called student service aides) and professional personnel. The easily identifiable areas of the CFC are separated and delineated by 4-foot-high partitions. The resulting atmosphere is informal. This physical setting provides students with the opportunity to easily establish relationships with the center personnel or browse through the career information resources. The CFC offers numerous programs, including a 1-hour credit course in human development as well as noncredit classes such as assertiveness training and life-planning seminars. An advisory committee, including faculty representatives, has been established to evaluate and plan for future programs for the CFC.

Interview Skills Training

The importance of training programs designed to improve interview skills is underscored by the fact that employers' decisions are often heavily based on their impressions of the interviewee. Also, many college students are, at best, only mod-

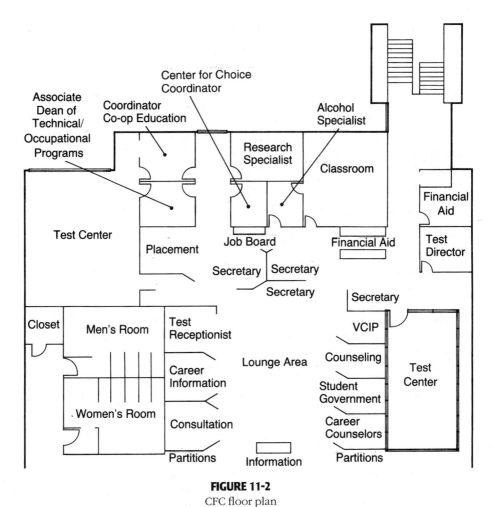

FIGURE 11-2

CFC floor plan

SOURCE: Center for Choice, Richland College, Dallas County Community College District, Dallas, Texas, 1980. Reprinted by permission.

erately experienced with interview procedures. Instruction has primarily been through role playing, videotape feedback, and mock interviews with personnel directors.

The use of videotape has become a popular method of preparing individuals for an interview. A number of commercial videos produced in the last decade have been compiled by Feller (1994). He includes ratings, reviews, and descriptions of 650 videos, some of which assist individuals in preparing for an interview (see Appendix B for more information).

Some videotapes that discuss interview preparation illustrate poor interview techniques and then follow with suggested changes and demonstrations of interviewee skills. Others demonstrate techniques, including establishing good eye contact; assuming the appropriate posture, voice level, and projection; closing the interview; following up; negotiating; and making a decision.

Videotapes can be used for individual training or in a workshop format, and they are also effective for group viewing—with or without discussion. For large groups, individuals can be divided into dyads or triads for practice interviewing. This procedure provides individuals with role-playing opportunities that can be videotaped for immediate feedback.

Snodgrass and Wheeler (1983) suggest that simulated interviews for videotaping could be derived from questions frequently asked during job interviews. One of the advantages of using videotape is that segments of the interview can be replayed and analyzed to afford greater flexibility of training.

Résumé Writing

As jobs become more competitive, personnel managers rely more heavily on résumés to select individuals for further evaluation. The résumé is the first criterion of the selection process, and its importance cannot be overstressed. The primary purpose of a résumé is to obtain an interview for the desired position. An effective résumé is one that "sells" the candidate's qualifications to the employer and thus provides the candidate the opportunity for an interview. Most effective resumes relate the candidate's skills, experiences, education, and other achievements to the requirements of the job. Résumés are essential for individuals seeking professional, technical, administrative, or managerial jobs and are often needed for clerical and sales positions. Preparation of a good résumé is an essential part of the job search sequence. The following outline may be used as a guide in preparing a résumé.

I. Personal data
   A. Name, address, and telephone number.
   B. Other personal data are optional, such as date of birth, marital status, citizenship, dependents, height, and weight.
II. Job or career objectives
   A. Prepare a concise statement of job objective and the type of position desired.
III. Educational history (If the previous work experiences are more closely related to the job objective, list them before educational history.)
   A. In reverse chronological order, list the institutions attended for formal education.
   B. High school can be omitted if a higher degree has been awarded.
   C. List dates of graduation and degrees or certificates received or expected.
   D. List major and minor courses related to job objectives.
   E. List scholarships and honors.
IV. Employment history
   A. In reverse chronological order list employment experiences including:
      1. Date of employment
      2. Name and address of employer and nature of firm or business

   3. Position held
   4. Specific job duties
   5. Scope of responsibility
   6. Accomplishments
V. Military experience
   A. List branch and length of service, major duties, assignments, rank, and type of discharge.
VI. Achievements related to job and career objectives (optional)
   A. List other assets, experiences, and skills significant to job objective. For example, knowledge of foreign language, volunteer activities, and special skills.
VII. References
   A. It is often not necessary to list references on the résumé. One may state that references are available on request.
   B. If references are listed, the name, position, and address of at least three persons is usually sufficient.

Here are some additional suggestions.

1. Because of affirmative action laws, many employers prefer that optional personal information (with the exception of citizenship) be deleted from the personal data section (I).
2. The job objective section (II) is designed to bind the parts of the résumé together into a common theme or direction and should be carefully stated.
3. The educational history section (III) should relate academic skills and achievements to the requirements of the job objective. Specific, relevant courses and experiences as well as degrees or specializations of formal education should be recorded.
4. The employment history (IV) should relate previously acquired working skills and accomplishments to the requirements and duties of the job objective. Voluntary as well as paid experiences should be included.
5. The military experience section (V) should relate skills and accomplishments acquired during military duty to the requirements and duties of the job objective.
6. The achievements (VI) listed should relate to the job objective, delineating any relevant special skills or accomplishments that were not recorded previously.

Examples of résumés are an important teaching instrument. The career counselor will want to accumulate copies of résumés from former students who have applied for different types of positions. A good model will make the job of writing a résumé much easier for the novice. There are many formats, and a number of publications on the market today provide examples of them. Such publications should be included in the counseling center's bibliography on job search strategy.

The following outline may be used as a guide in preparing a functional résumé.

I. List of achievements
   A. Begin with most impressive, relevant achievement.
   B. Disregard chronological sequence.
   C. List your achievements in the order in which you wish to highlight your background.
II. List work experience
   A. Offer an agenda of employers and job titles.
   B. Provide information about your past work experience.
III. List educational background
   A. List schools, colleges, and technical schools with dates of attendance.
IV. References
   A. It is often not necessary to list references on the résumé.
   B. One may state that references are available on request.

The functional résumé is designed to emphasize an individual's qualifications for a specific job. This type of résumé is often used by individuals who have had extensive work experience, particularly if they are applying for a job in the same area in which they have had experience or for a job that is related to their experience. The functional résumé stresses selected skill areas that are marketable, and it allows the applicant to emphasize professional growth.

International Job Market

As more businesses expand their operations globally, placement offices will be required to provide information for individuals interested in the international job market. More multinational corporations, small businesses, and entrepreneurs are expanding internationally. Krannich and Krannich (1990) suggested that the 1990s will be a highly competitive decade for international opportunities for college graduates. They will need the right "mix" of skills and the correct information to know how to find jobs in the international market. Because of the rapid and sometimes chaotic changes in political entities and the international economy, placement offices are faced with a formidable challenge.

Krannich and Krannich (1990) have compiled a list of the major trends in the 1990s that will affect the way individuals approach the international job market:

1. International jobs will be available, but students must learn how to find them. Different approaches are needed, such as making a contact in a foreign country or being willing to take other jobs available in the country of choice.
2. The competition for international jobs will more than likely increase as more individuals pursue them.
3. Most international jobs will require highly specialized, technical skills.
4. Students must prepare early in their academic training for the international job market. Language training, business courses, and technical skills that

are marketable in the country of choice are recommended. Internships in foreign countries are also desirable.

5. Corporations based in this country will have few entry-level jobs available. Most will have hired local talent for these jobs.

6. Some ways to break into the international job market are through a volunteer organization working in the country of choice or through educational institutions and the travel industry.

7. Fewer traditional jobs will be available. Engineering, architecture, construction, and public administration will be in demand.

8. Networking skills will be required to locate and develop job information.

9. International career patterns will have a life of their own, as individuals move frequently from job to job and from country to country.

10. International jobs could be dangerous, especially in countries with increased political instability and terrorism.

Some of these suggestions for obtaining jobs in the international arena are similar to other job search strategies. Networking and obtaining internships are good examples. Nevertheless, decentralized and fragmented information makes it difficult to ascertain the overall structure of the international job market. It almost appears to be a closed system to outsiders. Therefore, it is extremely important to begin gathering information and networking early in the college experience, perhaps as early as the freshman or sophomore year. Perhaps the international job market will gain more structure in the near future, particularly when organizations have more experience in this market.

Computer-Assisted Career Guidance Programs

As discussed in Chapter 6, computer-assisted career guidance programs provide up-to-date information on the job market. Many of the systems contain local information about jobs. Computer-assisted programs also have components that provide information to students and notify them of other vital information that can be used in the job search. Employers can register job vacancies, salary, interview schedules, and so forth.

Computer-assisted programs also provide a quick method of matching qualified students and requests for job orders from prospective employers. For instance, an employee asks the placement office by phone or through fax printouts for junior-level accounting majors who have at least a 3.0 grade point average and have plans to graduate in two semesters. Through prearranged agreements with students, the placement office can fax a list of students who meet the requirements. Speed may be of the essence in the competitive job market, and placement offices that are able to quickly provide information to students as well as to prospective employers may have an important advantage. Second, computer-assisted programs place current information at the fingertips of the placement office. The example presented is only one method of assisting students and employers through computer-assisted career guidance programs, but it points out the potential of these programs.

The Follow-Up

Follow-up information provides a valuable resource for multiple utilization by the college placement office. However, this section covers only the use of follow-up data as an aid in assisting college students in career planning. The overall employment status of graduates paints a realistic picture of the variety of jobs available to graduates from a particular institution. In addition, information on the current employment status of graduates according to majors can be most useful to the prospective graduate. Thus, follow-up is a very important resource that indicates employment trends and employment potential according to specific educational goals offered at the university level.

Follow-up is an important function of the Career Planning and Placement Office, especially in light of the competitiveness of the job market. The information obtained from a follow-up is valuable in helping students plan their education and careers. Even though the labor market may make abrupt changes, the follow-up has many implications for the job search strategy: (1) this information should aid the student in thinking in terms of the type of organization in which he or she is likely to find employment if holding a particular degree; (2) a realistic salary is usually listed according to field of study; (3) the employment potential is better understood by field of study; and (4) the job satisfaction of working in a particular field is known. In essence, follow-up information should aid the individual in clarifying values and subsequently establishing goals; it also provides practical information concerning initial career search activities and probable geographical location of prospective jobs.

The UCLA Placement and Career Planning Center conducts an annual follow-up of the most recent graduating class, usually during the first week of September. The survey reports data in seven areas: (1) plans after graduation, (2) job commitment, (3) type of organization, (4) field of employment, (5) job satisfaction, (6) helpfulness of degree in employment, and (7) salary (*Job Market for UCLA 1987 Graduates,* 1988).

Using this data, the placement office can compile information about jobs that graduates currently hold, including the graduates' field of study and employer, the nature of the job (part- or full-time), job satisfaction, salaries, plans for the future, and the satisfaction with the university's academic program.

Summary

1. Studies of the characteristics of college students suggest a diversity of needs for career guidance programs. Research has consistently shown that almost one-half or more of college students desire help with educational and vocational planning.

2. College affects students' career choices and development by providing career mobility and advancement and by increasing career aspirations. The benefits of higher education can also lead to a fulfilling lifestyle and the capacity to make appropriate judgments over the life span.

3. The NOICC has provided competencies and indicators for self-knowledge, educational and occupational exploration, and career planning for adults. These guidelines can be used to develop career guidance programs at institutions of higher learning.

4. Implications for career guidance includes a wide variety of programs to maximize each student's career development potential.

5. The CCIS developed at Florida State University utilizes an instructional approach to career planning. The model is self-help-oriented, uses instructional models, and is multimedia-based. A number of modules have been developed to perform a career search sequence; several other modules have been developed for special groups such as minorities and blind students. The diversity of learning activities provided through a series of career planning modules allows the individual a greater variety of options and a more effective means of choosing a point of entry.

6. Career counseling centers located in metropolitan areas have heavy alumni demands for educational and career planning. The UCLA Placement and Career Planning Center is a good example of a metroplex model. This center is divided into several units to meet demands of currently enrolled students in undergraduate and graduate programs, as well as alumni and others in the community requesting educational and career planning assistance.

7. Decision making is a learned skill that is vital to educational programs. As distinguished from problem solving, decision making is a means of discovering a satisfying solution through the evaluation of options and alternatives; whereas in problem solving, there are no clear-cut right or wrong solutions. Krumboltz and Sorenson designed a decision-making system involving the following steps: (a) formulate individual goals, (b) commit time, (c) generate activities, (d) collect information, (e) estimate consequences, (f) reevaluate, (g) decide tentatively, and (h) recycle.

8. The typical college placement office has drastically changed its image in the last 20 years. The intensification of the job search has led college placement centers to assume a wider scope of responsibilities. The placement office is no longer just an employment agency; it offers a variety of seminars and programs that assist students in planning for careers as well as in searching for jobs.

9. Typical programs being offered in career planning and placement centers in two- and four-year colleges include career search strategies, interview skills training, and instructions on writing résumés.

10. The demand for work- and experienced-based programs for college students is increasing. Extern models provide the opportunity to observe ongoing activities in a major field of study. Intern models are more work-oriented and cover a longer time.

11. The international job market is expected to grow. Students will need to plan early in their college career to meet job requirements in the international marketplace.

12. Computer-assisted career guidance programs provide the placement office with a wide range of options to react quickly to employers' requests and student needs.

13. Follow-up studies serve as important resources for placement offices when they include (a) types of job opportunities available by geographical areas, (b) general employment patterns and fields of employment of graduates with specific majors and degrees, (c) employment potential within specific industries, and (d) current salary schedules. Follow-up information is being incorporated into career planning programs.

Supplementary Learning Exercises

1. Using the CCIS model, develop a module to introduce high school students to career information resources.
2. Develop a philosophical statement that includes the placement office as a vital part of the career guidance efforts in postsecondary schools.
3. Develop a strategy that would justify adult career guidance centers as an extension of college career guidance programs.
4. Write to several large universities located in a metropolitan area and request descriptions of their career counseling programs. Compare the programs for commonalities and innovative components.
5. Visit an industry to determine potential extern experiences available for college students. Compile the available experiences with recommendations for college majors that could benefit through an extern experience.
6. Survey a community to determine the number and kinds of agencies that are actively involved in career planning and placement activities. Develop plans to involve all agencies in a cooperative career planning and placement effort.
7. Develop plans and strategies that would focus on career planning and placement of school dropouts. Include in your plans the strategies you would use for encouraging the dropout to continue in an educational or training program.
8. Defend the following statement: Career planning and placement programs are essential in secondary schools and in two- and four-year institutions of higher learning.
9. Compare the decision-making model discussed in this chapter with another. What are the strengths and weaknesses of each?
10. Interview a personnel director in a local firm who is responsible for interviewing prospective employees. Summarize your conclusions of what are considered to be the most important variables in hiring a new employee.

PART THREE

Career Guidance Programs for Adults in Transition

CHAPTER TWELVE

Some Perspectives of Work

Work is at the heart of our concerns as professionals and individuals fortunate enough to live in a free society. Work can involve the most simple step-by-step procedures or be physically and mentally demanding, complex, interesting, boring, creative, or menial; or it can involve all of the descriptions listed and many more. Throughout our history, work has fascinated researchers who have attempted to delineate the complexities of the labor itself and the problems of individuals who do it. Today, work has prevailed as a most viable subject within the scientific community and has occupied the thoughts of scholars from a variety of disciplines who dared venture into the complex arena associated with work. Work in America has a fascinating, extensive history.

This chapter covers the vast changes in the work force and the workplace. First, it discusses how work has changed, what has happened to work in America, and rethinking the idea of work. Next are occupational projections and how to focus on clients' needs. Several other perspectives of work are discussed, including occupational insecurity, coping with joblessness, the new entrepreneurial climate, work values, work commitment and work ethic, the personal agency person, stress at work, career burnout, healthful work, demand for quality of work, and aging workers.

Case Example:
How Work Has Changed—The Secretary

Joan took a secretarial job a few years ago that primarily required that she take shorthand, type, and make appointments. During most of her tenure of 15 years, the job requirements remained the same. But when the technology revolution arrived, the entire atmosphere of her office changed drastically. Joan was retrained to learn new skills, shorthand was no longer a requirement, typing was done on a computer, and appointments were made quite differently. The following description of how a secretarial position has changed is a good example of new skills required in the workplace.

> A person who filled a secretarial position 15 years ago may have been expected to type, take shorthand or dictation, manage files, make appointments, take telephone messages, and arrange for meetings, travel, or other appointments. Today, a secretary may be expected to perform all these tasks and, in addition, to make use of one or more software programs, usually including word processing, a spread sheet, and list processing. The secretary may be expected to maintain an interactive calendar, posting the calendar to a network of linked associates. The secretary may be required to use electronic mail to communicate with clients at remote locations, to post and retrieve information from electronic bulletin boards, and to keep abreast of software changes to upgrade the office system. In many offices, the secretary is also expected to be familiar with the basic operating principles of high-speed copiers, laser printers, and fax machines, at least in order to serve as the first line of defense when the system fails. (Newman & Newman, 1995, p. 576)

This example should serve as a point of reference for the work changes discussed in this chapter. It was chosen as an example of change because it is straightforward and easily understood. However, the complexity of changes in the many areas of the workplace are somewhat difficult to comprehend, especially for clients who have not experienced industrial organizations. Career counselors should find that visiting local industrial plants may prove to be time well spent.

What Has Happened to Work in the United States?

As discussed in the opening paragraphs, there have been major changes in the U.S. work force during the last 15 years. The U.S. Department of Labor estimates that 36 million jobs were eliminated in the United States between 1979 and 1993; a recent *New York Times* poll puts the number up to 43 million through 1995. Although many of these jobs would have been eliminated by the development of new products and new procedures, the latest casualties are white-collar jobs that have been the victims of severe downsizing. A large percentage of total jobs lost were the result of contracting work with other companies. This type of job loss is referred to as "out-sourcing" (Uchitelle & Kleinfield, 1996).

An astonishing development is the fact that far more jobs have been added to the workplace that have been lost! However, many of the newly created jobs offer fewer benefits and less pay, and many are part-time jobs. Individuals who are unable to find full-time work usually settle for temporary part-time work. Thus, the country's largest employer is Manpower, Incorporated, which "rents out" 767,000 substitute workers each year (Uchitelle & Kleinfield, 1996).

The news is not great for those who manage to find full-time work or become self-employed. Many take huge cuts in salary and benefits; for example, an executive who made $150,000 is lucky to make $50,000, and a manager who made

$50,000 may now have a job that pays $25,000 (Uchitelle & Kleinfield, 1996). For literally millions of people in this country, the American dream of upward and onward is fading.

Chief executive officers who eliminate vast numbers of workers use the rationale that they must have leaner organizations to compete in the new global economy. Some of the hardest-hit organizations in the 1990s were AT&T, 123,000 jobs; Delta Airlines, 18,800 jobs; and Eastman Kodak, 16,800 jobs. Advancing technology has also taken some tasks away from human beings and given them to machines. For example, General Motors Corporation had 500,000 employees in the 1970s but now can make the same number of cars with 315,000 workers (Uchitelle & Kleinfield, 1996). Many workplaces are in transition; the old certainties about work no longer apply. A summary of what has happened to two workers in the special report on downsizing by the *New York Times* and written by Uchitelle and Kleinfield (1996) are good examples.

A loan officer, age 51, who made $1000 weekly was told that he no longer had a job when he returned from a family vacation. The news was devastating, but the worst of it was yet to come. He pumped gas, was a guinea pig in a drug test, drove a car for a salesman, and, at the time the story was written, was currently employed as a tour guide at $1000 per month. His wife divorced him, and his children shunned him, ashamed of a father who had lost his job.

This example may not be completely typical of all workers who lose their jobs, but it does point out the potential problems encountered by those whose jobs have been terminated by downsizing.

Next is the story of a woman who lost three jobs because of downsizing. More specifically, this is an example of a woman, still in her forties, whose pay dropped each time she experienced downsizing. Her first job was in a meatpacking plant at $8.50 per hour, her second job was in a bank mailroom at $7.25 per hour, and her third job was at $4.75 per hour loading newspapers. She is currently employed at $4.25 per hour cleaning office buildings in Baltimore. She has not had a raise for three years. She has a high school diploma and studied one year at a community college.

This is an example of the difficulty workers face at the lower end of the economic ladder. In addition to the personal/social problems faced by these individuals, they need assistance to find resources for training programs to upgrade their skills.

Later in this chapter, we will see that occupational projections reveal that manufacturing will have 1.3 million fewer workers in 2005 that it did in 1994. However, there will be 16.2 million new wage and salary jobs during the period from 1994 to 2005. These jobs will be concentrated in health, education, business service, and eating and drinking establishments ("Charting the projections," 1995).

Rethinking the Idea of Work

Skills associated with organizational work grow more complex, as advances in technology are usually followed by changes in the workplace. Job descriptions have had difficulty in keeping abreast with the ever-changing needs of organizations that are both operating and competing globally. *Job restructuring* is the desired term used to describe these changing perceptions of work and the skills that organizations currently consider necessary for efficient operation.

To add to the confusion, organizations are reorganizing and abandoning fundamental assumptions that underlie previous operating procedures. The fact is they are making significant changes in operational procedures as well as in job requirements in order to prepare for 21st-century capitalism (Reich, 1991). Some have labeled this process of change "reengineering the corporation" (Hammer & Champy, 1993). More about this subject will be discussed in the next two chapters.

Many attempts have been made to explain the ongoing changes in a variety of media, but the career counselor may have little information to pass on to the counselee about what is actually happening in the real world of organizational work. A part of this problem is that the change process in job requirements is in its early stages. Second, the constant reconfiguration of the job market has been exacerbated by work force reductions through downsizing and subsequent retraining programs. Finally, as corporations reengineer or restructure their work forces—a move to compete for the global market—the emerging strategies to meet their goals will, in effect, provide them with a more discernible definition of job requirements in the future. However, there very well may be a constant evolution of new and different products in our current and future organizations that subsequently will require new and different skills from their employees (Drucker, 1992).

In sum, the transformation of industries into smaller working units with vastly different operating procedures has created particular needs for individuals with certain types of skills. Meister (1994) identified six core workplace competencies employers require, as paraphrased below.

1. *Learning skills:* Organizations must adjust to new demands and improve their systems and processes in order to survive. Learning skills rank high in importance as organizations introduce changes. Employees must learn from a variety of sources, including co-workers, customers, suppliers, and educational institutions. The goal is for continuous improvement and to transform these skills into how an employee thinks and behaves.

2. *Basic reading, writing, computation, and cognitive reasoning skills:* Basic skills are a minimum requirement, but they are not narrowly defined as an ability to read, write, and perform mathematical computations. Employees must be able to apply information they read, for example, into action on a job.

3. *Interpersonal skills:* Good job performance in the past meant repeating tasks associated with each job. In current organizations, teams have become the vehicles of performance; thus individual performance is linked to well-developed interpersonal skills. The following skills are considered important: how to work in groups successfully and resolve conflicts, how to gain cooperation with peers, and how to network within the organization.

4. *Creative thinking and problem-solving skills:* The worker of today should be able to relate every phase of the production process, from obtaining raw materials to improving processes and procedures. Problem-solving skills should include being able to analyze situations, ask questions, seek clarification of what is not understood, and think creatively to generate options. The overall goal is for em-

ployees to develop skills that enable them to handle situations effectively without direction.

5. *Leadership (and visioning) skills:* In the new emerging organizations, employees are encouraged to be active agents of change; not passive recipients of instructions. The employee today needs to develop abilities to envision improvement in work areas or establish a new direction and—perhaps most important—elicit the active commitment of others to accomplish his or her visions.

6. *Self-development (and self-management) skills:* These skills require that employees take charge of their careers and manage their own development. Employees must become aware of the changes in the workplace and be sure they have the requisite skills, knowledge, and competencies for their current assignment and potential future ones. The management of one's career is considered to be a learned competence and a necessary and important condition in the emerging corporation structure.

Reich (1991) also delineated worker skills that will be necessary for the effective operation of current and future organizations. He framed these skills in what he refers to as the "new web of enterprise" (p. 87). Such organizations are referred to as high-value enterprises that resemble a spider's web. New connections from multiple locations on the globe will be spun continuously. Teams of workers will generate concepts of new products, how to produce them, and how they will be marketed. During the give and take of debate among team members, mutual learning will occur through shared insights, experiences, and solutions. Workers will learn from each other, learn about each other, and learn how to help one another perform better. Each point on the web will be unique and will represent its own combination of skills.

Within this frame of reference, three different but related skills will be needed by each team member. First are *problem-solving skills.* Problem solvers continuously search new combinations and applications that might solve all kinds of emerging problems. They must have intimate knowledge of, say, semiconductor chips and what can be expected of them if they are reassembled or redesigned for a new product.

The second skill is referred to as *problem identification* or, as team members, *problem identifiers.* This skill requires an intimate knowledge of a customer's business and how a new and different product can give this customer the competitive edge. Instead of using the art of persuasion to sell a product, the operational procedure here is identifying new problems and possibilities to which a product may be applicable.

The third skill requires that the worker play the role of *strategic broker.* This high-value position requires knowledge of specific technologies and markets to the point of foreseeing the potential for new products. This individual must coordinate the role of the *problem solver* and *problem identifier* and raise necessary funds to launch projects. These people are characterized as being continuously engaged in managing ideas.

What we see here is a recognition that survival in the 21st century will, in large part, depend on a well-trained work force. Newly acquired skills in problem solving and team building are designed to make improvements in job production, but work environments must also be redefined. The major goal appears to be the development of work environments that may be ever-changing, where workers conceptually understand their work and look for methods to improve it. The ideal organizational work environment promotes a culture of lifelong learning and a working atmosphere that encourages all employees to *want* to learn (Meister, 1994).

Finally we must remember that not all organizations have been restructured or reengineered. Some organizations, particularly government ones, have retained a bureaucratic structure. Some clients may find congruence within these structures rather than in the emerging ones, although Reich (1991) points out that these older, structured organizations are decreasing in number.

Occupational Projections

The 1995 fall issue of the *Occupational Outlook Quarterly* ("Charting the projections," 1995) has charted, through the year 2005, occupational projections developed by the Bureau of Labor Statistics. Following are some of the highlights of these projections.

Highlights of the Projections

The bureau's projections contain considerable detail about the structure of the economy, the demographic makeup of the labor force, and changes in employment in more than 500 occupations and 260 industries. The following trends are of special significance.

Labor force
- The number of Hispanics, Asians, and others in the labor force will continue to increase much faster than white non-Hispanics, but white non-Hispanics will still account for the vast majority of workers in 2005.
- The rate at which women enter the labor force will continue to be much faster than the rate for men, and women's share of the labor force will increase to 48%.
- The number of blacks in the labor force will grow slightly faster than the labor force as a whole.

Gross domestic product
- Exports will grow very rapidly, but employment will grow little in most industries producing goods for export because of rising productivity.

Industry employment
- Industry employment growth will be very concentrated. The services and retail trade industry divisions will account for 16.2 million new wage and salary jobs, about 96% of the total. Most of the growth will be in just four areas: health, education, business services, and eating and drinking places.

On the other hand, manufacturing will have 1.3 million fewer workers in 2005 than it did in 1994.

Occupational employment

- Because of the close relationship between industries and occupations, most health occupations, which are concentrated in the rapidly growing health services industry, will grow faster than average.
- Employment will grow in occupations requiring all levels of education and training. The contradictory beliefs that all growing occupations require little education or all require high levels of training are both incorrect. However, jobs requiring greater education and training clearly dominate those occupations that are growing fastest and also have the highest pay rates.

The following figures from the Bureau of Labor Statistics present some interesting data. For example, Figure 12-1 depicts thousands of jobs that will be lost from 1994 to 2005. Bookkeepers, accountants, and bank tellers may very well be displaced by greater use of home computers and from direct deposits of paychecks by employers. Ironically, jobs for computer operators will also decline as industry restructures its work force.

Figure 12-2 shows that the fastest growing industry is home health care services. In fact, the ten fastest growing industries are in the service division. Eight of these ten are related to health care or computer technology, as shown in Figure 12-3. Occupational groups that require the most education have above-average growth, as seen in Figure 12-4. Finally, Figure 12-5 indicates that workers over 45 will account for a larger share of the labor force by the year 2005, though not larger than the total "under 45" group.

In the preceding paragraphs, we have discussed organizational changes that will greatly affect the work force and workplace. However, services and retail trade will account for most job growth from 1994 to 2005, as shown in Figure 12-6. Although some changes are expected in the service industries, most of the projections for drastic changes in the work force discussed earlier have been suggested for industrial complexes. Service occupations will also make use of changing

Thousands of jobs, 1994–2005

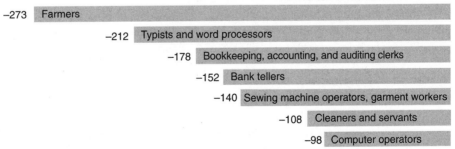

FIGURE 12-1

Occupational declines stem from industry declines and technological change

SOURCE: U.S. Department of Labor, Bureau of Labor Statistics

Percent change, 1994–2005

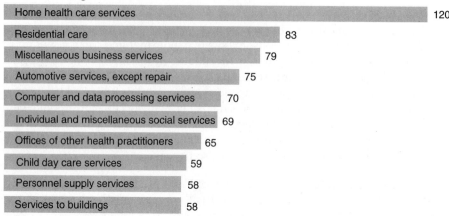

FIGURE 12-2

All of the ten fastest growing industries are in the services division
SOURCE: U.S. Department of Labor, Bureau of Labor Statistics

Percent change, 1994–2005

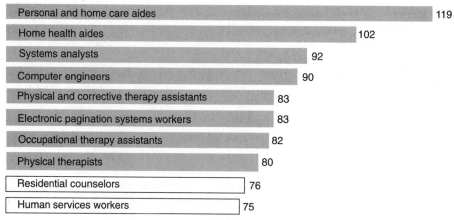

FIGURE 12-3

Eight of ten fastest growing occupations are related to health care or computer technology
SOURCE: U.S. Department of Labor, Bureau of labor Statistics

technology, but many of the skills needed to effectively perform in these occupations will remain relatively the same. The point here is that although career counselors must be prepared to discuss the projected changes in skills needed for future occupations, they also must be prepared to point out occupational descriptions that are projected to have the greatest potential for job growth.

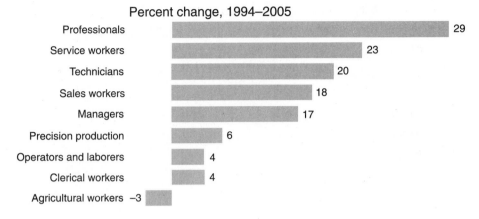

FIGURE 12-4
Occupational groups requiring the most education have above average growth
SOURCE: U.S. Department of Labor, Bureau of Labor Statistics

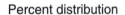

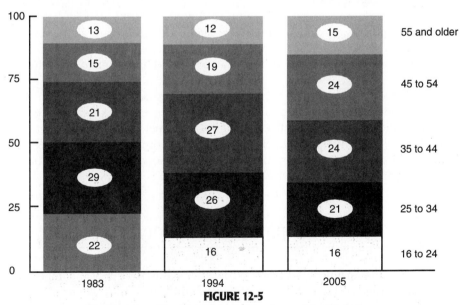

FIGURE 12-5
Workers over 45 account for a larger share of the labor force
SOURCE: U.S. Department of Labor, Bureau of Labor Statistics

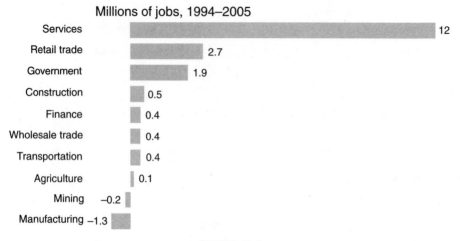

FIGURE 12-6
Services and retail trade account for most job growth
SOURCE: U.S. Department of Labor, Bureau of Labor Statistics

Focusing on the Client's Needs

Most clients will be looking at future work from a different perspective than in the recent past. Those not aware of changing work environments must be educated to view future work realistically. For example, some may want to follow the career path of their parents, who spent their entire career with one organization, periodically moving up the career ladder, and enjoying health benefits and other rewards of long-term service. These workplaces may be more difficult to find in the future (Reich, 1991; Meister, 1994).

The career counselor who focuses on the client's needs provides each with the opportunity to express his or her individuality, desired life roles, and lifestyle and occupational plans. The pathways to finding the person-environment fit may contain roadblocks that justify intervention strategies of more in-depth career information, including descriptions of work changes and workplaces in the future. Obviously, not all clients will need this information.

Occupational Insecurity

The massive downsizing of jobs, discussed earlier, has led to a new and unnerving workplace. Many workers who were considered middle class—following the typical American dream of job, home, and family—find themselves worrying about survival rather than a new car or an addition to the house or a second home. Dreams have faded with the cruel reality that one could be cast among the jobless at any time in today's workplace climate. Typical of this group is to worry about what was once taken for granted. The loss of home, retirement pensions, and health benefits are troubling thoughts that occupy the minds of the insecure. When they witness the plight of their fellow jobless workers, they are quick to recognize a loss of dignity that is often severe and pervasive.

A *New York Times* telephone poll conducted in December 1995 (Uchitelle & Kleinfeld, 1996) surveyed 1265 adults throughout the United States and found that many intact workers were struggling to adjust to downsizing. The majority polled stated they would work more hours, take fewer vacations, or accept lesser benefits to keep their job. These workers, almost desperately looking for job security, are willing to work harder and longer to maintain their occupational status.

The loss of control over one's future work role can lead to poor mental health (Roskies & Louis-Guerin, 1990) and subsequent devastating consequences to other life roles, such as family member and citizen. It also can take individual tolls, such as loss of self-esteem, which often leads to depression. Career counselors must recognize the potential conflicts that could result from occupational insecurity.

Coping with Joblessness

Closely related with occupational insecurity is the impact of unemployment. According to the 1992 U.S. Bureau of Census report, the unemployment rates by race, age, and sex in 1991 were as follows:

	Male %	Female %
White		
35–44	5.0	4.3
45–54	4.4	3.9
African American		
35–44	9.6	7.6
45–54	8.6	6.2
Hispanic		
35–44	8.6	7.6
45–54	7.9	8.1

According to these figures, African Americans and Hispanics have a greater unemployment rate than do whites; an advocacy role for ethnic minorities should be a priority for career counselors.

It is important to realize that men and women seem to experience the same degree of distress following loss of a job (Leana & Feldman, 1991). And according to Defrank and Ivancevich (1986), middle-aged men are more vulnerable to negative effects of job loss. The degree of negative effects of unemployment has been associated with both physical and psychological consequences such as withdrawal, decline of self-respect, loss of identity and affiliation, and disruptive behavioral reactions (Herr, 1989; Newman & Newman, 1995).

Among other counseling techniques, a supportive role while monitoring a new job search may be quite helpful. The consequences of repeated job search failures can be devastating, and the career counselor may find that a long-term commitment to unemployed individuals may be necessary.

The New Entrepreneurial Climate

The opportunity to own your own business may increase in the new business climate that exists in today's economy. Changes in operational procedures for organizations have created more opportunities for small businesses to offer their services and skills. One advantage of owning your own business is that you can operate out of your home and, in most cases, live where you are most comfortable.

The entrepreneur should be multifunctional; one may be required to develop marketing strategies, plan for finances, act as a salesperson, and maintain an office. The entrepreneur must be willing to spend long hours in launching a new business and must be willing to take chances and be innovative. It has often been said that the first steps are the hardest ones, and this is certainly true for the entrepreneur. However, the challenge of owning your own business has been very satisfying for many who have entered this arena.

The Fall 1994 issue of the *Occupational Outlook Quarterly* gives the following encouragement to future entrepreneurs (Mariani, 1994).

The Entrepreneurs Among Us

People who want a career working for themselves can develop their own businesses. The opportunities do exist. According to the Bureau of Labor Statistics, over 10 million members of the U.S. labor force (16 years and older) worked for themselves in their own unincorporated businesses in 1992. Another 3.5 million people head their own incorporated enterprises and can be considered self-employed even though, technically, they are salaried employees of their corporations.

Service occupations and executive, administrative, and managerial occupations had large numbers of self-employed workers in 1992, and self-employment is expected to increase much faster than average within these occupational groups through 2005. Marketing and sales occupations accounted for much self-employment, even though the number of self-employed workers in these occupations will grow much more slowly than average from 1992–2005. Two other large groups—professional specialty occupations and precision production, craft, and repair occupations—include many detailed occupations with a high share of self-employed workers. (p. 7)

Work Values

Cultural values can sometimes be difficult to separate from work values. As Rosenberg (1957) noted several decades ago, occupational choice is made on the basis of values, which are the principles that guide individuals in making decisions and developing behavioral patterns. Values are influential in determining individual goals and lifestyles and influencing work motivation, behavior, and satisfaction.

Attitudes toward work are also reflected in changing cultural values. Spindler (1955), who studied changing values in American mainstream culture after World War II, found significant changes from traditional values to what he called "emergent values." For example, the traditional value of future-time orientation or working toward future goals was contrasted with the emergent value of hedonistic, present-time orientation, which reflected a new focus on living for the present because the future is unknown. Following this logic, all work is perceived as temporary, with little value placed on longevity of the job, job identity, or the value of work itself.

Pine and Innis (1987) suggested that individual work values are influenced by a number of factors, including ethnicity, subcultures, historical cohorts, socioeconomic status, significant others, society, and economic conditions. Work values are influenced by changing conditions in our society, as illustrated by Schnall's (1981) study of longitudinal value shifts. Schnall found that basic belief systems in our society had shifted in stages over a half-century: (1) during the period from the 1930s through the 1950s, more attention was paid to the welfare of others than self; (2) during the 1960s, the focus changed to self-indulgence and instant gratification with little regard for others; (3) during the 1970s, distrust for others was manifested in a strong movement toward self-reliance; and (4) during the 1980s, there was a shift back to concern for others with the growing need for individuals to experience self-fulfillment (Pine & Innis, 1987). Schnall's study clearly suggests that we have returned to some of the dominant values of the 1950s.

In a related study of value changes of college students, Astin (1984) suggested that students in the 1980s had value orientations similar to students in the 1950s: they wanted security, jobs that were indicators of success, and a home in the suburbs. However, Wall (1984) indicated that value orientations of college students in the 1950s and 1980s differed significantly because the possibility of moving up the career ladder, a foregone conclusion in the 1950s, was uncertain in the economically unstable 1980s.

The uncertain economic forecast changed the process of choosing careers from idealism to pragmatism—"where do I have the best chance of being employed?" and "how can I best market myself for that occupation?" Economic realities influence not only career choice but also how individuals work at jobs they otherwise may not have chosen. Self-fulfillment, which Schnall mentioned as a prevalent goal in the 1980s and yet not fully attainable in the uncertain economic conditions, may cause some people to withhold a firm emotional involvement in their work (Yankelovich, 1979).

The implications of observing work values in the context of changing cultural values and economic patterns in our society are profound. For example, career counseling should focus more on available opportunities than on individual psychology. This shift in emphasis implies that career counseling must become more realistic to be most effective. Finally, individual perceptions of work and commitment to work are inextricably connected with economic and societal forces. How these factors influence individual value systems must always be considered when evaluating work values (Pine & Innis, 1987).

A Synthesis of Opinion about Work Commitment and Work Ethics

Growing evidence suggests that causes of job satisfaction and dissatisfaction are indeed complex issues. Just as intricate are the issues surrounding work commitment and work ethics. Some researchers have proposed that a common bond connecting these issues is rooted in our society. O'Toole (1981), among others, has postulated that low productivity is a cultural problem rather than a result of national economic policy. Yankelovich (1981a) suggested that our work ethic is an inextricable part of social issues. Both positions have common themes related to our national social development.

According to O'Toole (1981), there is overwhelming evidence that culture is a fundamental determinant of our economic performance. He cited the economic superiority of Germany and Japan as examples of cultures that encourage efficiency and productivity. He suggested that the Japanese especially have adopted managerial policies compatible with their culture. The answer is not simply to adopt another country's philosophy and orientation toward work but to develop policies that are compatible with our own culture. Furthermore, the major problem in the U.S. workplace today is that most of our current managerial and organizational policies and practices were developed in the 1940s and 1950s. These policies were compatible with the culture at the time, but in the last 30 years there have been dramatic social shifts. The rules for work commitment have been altered, and Americans simply are unwilling to do work under outdated mandates. The new work values are congruent with changes in the broader culture.

Yankelovich (1981b), in search of answers for self-fulfillment in work, has suggested that we are in need of an ethic of commitment. He, like O'Toole, also addressed the changes of values in our culture, attacking in particular the self-psychology practices promoting the idea that sacredness lies within self. According to Yankelovich, the impact of the "duty-to-self" ethic has led to development of selfishness and hedonistic values. These self-indulgent values have subverted self-fulfillment. Yankelovich suggested that what is now needed is a new ethic that promotes a more cooperative attitude among workers and places less emphasis on competitiveness for personal gain.

Yankelovich contended that an ethic of commitment would emerge slowly over the next several decades. Changes in self-concept and attitude are key ingredients for self-fulfillment under the ethic of commitment. The first step is to discard the goals of the duty-to-self ethic and to concentrate on sharing, showing more concern for others, being cooperative, and striving to develop closer and deeper personal relationships. Relationships with others are to be simple, direct, and unencumbered by pursuit of status or financial rewards. Ultimately, more satisfying personal achievements will come from *sacred expressive values*. Sacred values include increased concern and dedication to improving community and country. Expressive values are personal, but they do not originate from me-first attitudes; they are broader in concept and allow for greater self-involvement and a closer connection to others.

Following the logic of Yankelovich (1981b), the shift in attitudes and values associated with the ethic of commitment will change workers' perspectives of their jobs and work environment. The primary motivation to work will not be based on moving up the career ladder at all costs. Commitment to work will be a sharing of producing, creating, and mutually expressive accomplishments. The work environment is to be one in which direct, honest, and straightforward communications are exchanged. The organization is to adopt leadership policies that are conducive to openness of communication between workers and supervisors and involve a caring interest in each worker. Work will continue to be an important commitment but will not be all-absorbing. Sufficient time to enjoy leisure and develop family relationships will be emphasized. Self-fulfillment is achieved when "one understands that the self must be fulfilled within the shared meanings of psychoculture" (p. 242).

Samuelson (1995) suggests that, as Americans, we expect such institutions as "big business" and "big government" to guarantee us secure jobs, rising living standards, clean environments, safe cities, and satisfying work, among other entitlements. As Samuelson puts it, "we feel entitled" (p. 4). Moreover, entitlement's fatal flaw is utopianism—that is, the false impression that we are working our way toward a perfect society. The problem is that we expect the perfect society to be handed to us; we also expect to assume little personal responsibility. This attitude is pervasive in all our life roles, according to Samuelson, including our work role. As individuals, we should expect to do more for ourselves and expect less from our government. In essence, we are to assume more responsibility for our own actions now and into the 21st century.

The Personal Agency Person

Throughout this chapter, references have been made to the worker of the future. Key descriptions have been used or implied, such as "self-developing person," "one who uses personal agency," or "one who can adapt to change." There have been references to the fact that the worker of the future must develop new and different attitudes about work per se and about career development.

The idea of *positive uncertainty,* a term originated and recently discussed by Gelatt (1996), suggests that the future worker will shed obsolete beliefs and narrow views of the past in order to develop a future sense. Thus, limited thinking will change to prospective visions of what the future may offer. In essence, the uncertainty of the future should not inhibit but instead should challenge the worker to meet changes that will surely come.

The personal agency person has an evolving profile that lends itself to some descriptors at this time. First, we consider some basic assumptions. The true personal agency person may not exist. The profile of the personal agency person will change and evolve along with changing work environments and requirements. The degree to which a person matches the descriptions of the personal agency person does not guarantee success and satisfaction in the workplace, now or in the future. What we have are some descriptions of what is considered to be the future archetypal organization person (Kleinfield, 1996).

The Personal Agency Person Profile

Examples of basic shifts in thinking
Does not feel entitled
Assumes responsibility for the future
Assumes a lifelong learning responsibility
Dismisses obsolete beliefs about work
Does not take any job for granted
Assumes that personal involvement is key to success
Depends on own initiative
Views the future with vision and imagination
Has little fear of change
Can deal with uncertainty
Believes creativity is a basic requirement
Believes good interpersonal relations is an employee's responsibility
Is completely receptive to new ideas
Assumes that there are few guarantees for the future
Assumes that the organization does not owe anyone a career

Mode of action
Is very functional in basic skills
Creates effective changes in work assignments
Cooperates with teams of workers and supervisor
Develops methods to improve effectiveness of job assignment
Exhibits high levels of resourcefulness and imagination
Takes advantage of opportunities to develop skills and learn more about job assignment
Develops overview and knowledge of total work environment and company purpose and policies
Creatively demonstrates how product or products can be improved
Assumes total responsibility for career development

Many characteristics of the personal agency person are not new qualities in an employee an organization seeks, but, more important, the basic shifts in attitude and beliefs are key requirements of the future worker. The personal agency person accepts the future for what it is. It is through individual effort, personal initiative, and self-development that one's career develops, with no future assurances from the organization. The mindset of the personal agency person is similar to that of a freelance performer who must "sell" himself or herself each day. Finally, the personal agency person believes that planning for unknown changes in the future is each person's total responsibility.

Stress at Work:
Its Implications and How to Deal with It

One factor inherent in modern working life is stress, induced by work and the work environment. Stress in this context has been defined as a psychophysical response to various stimuli. Work-related stressor sources have been studied by a number of researchers (Kasl, 1978; Ivancevich & Matteson, 1980; Shostak, 1980; Levi, 1984). Sources of stress compiled by these researchers dramatize the complexity and variety of potentially stressful conditions most workers face:

1. Conditions of work (unpleasant work environment, necessity to work fast, excessive and inconvenient hours)
2. Work itself (perception of job as uninteresting, repetitive, overloaded, and demanding)
3. Shift work (rotating shifts affecting bodily functions and role behaviors)
4. Supervision (unclear job demands, close supervision with no autonomy, scant feedback from supervisors)
5. Wage and promotion (inadequate income)
6. Role ambiguity (lack of clarity about one's job and scope of responsibilities)
7. Career development stressors (little job security, impending obsolescence, dissatisfaction over career aspirations and current level of attainment)
8. Group stressors (insufficient group cohesiveness, poor group identity in the organization)
9. Organizational climate (impersonally structured organizational policies)
10. Organizational structure (too bureaucratic or too autocratic)

Job-Related Stress Is a Global Phenomenon

Job-related stress afflicts British miners, French nurses, and Australian government workers as well as U.S. executives. Blue-collar workers also experience job stress, perhaps because they have less control over their jobs and lives than do higher paid white-collar workers. An international survey conducted by the United Nation's International Labor Organization found that women suffer as much or more job-related stress than men do ("Job stress at work," 1993).

One reason suggested for the increase in job stress is that many workers are involved in a sort of electronic assembly line, which allows supervisors to evaluate them constantly during the workday. Perhaps more important are job demands that do not match a worker's current abilities, needs, or expectations. That is, there is a poor fit between workers and their work environments and subsequent requirements. Job-related stress has many roots and causes, but among the important ones are organizational management and work environment.

Magnuson (1990) suggested the following indicators of job-related stress:

- Low self-esteem
- Low motivation to work
- Poor concentration on work tasks
- Poor work relationships with peers and supervisors
- Poor communications with others on the job site
- Feelings of inadequacy and resentment
- Depression
- Excessive tardiness and absenteeism

The effects of stress are pervasive; work performance and interpersonal relationships are often affected. Stress has been linked to numerous physical problems, including cardiovascular diseases. Stress exists at all levels of the work force, extending from executives to blue-collar workers (Shostak, 1980). As organizations grow in complexity, potential stressor sources will multiply.

Career Burnout

In the early 1970s, the term *burnout* emerged in career counseling articles and in the popular media. Freudenberger (1974) is generally given credit for first using the term to describe certain kinds of career behavior (Herr & Cramer, 1996). Later, Freudenberger and Richelson (1980) defined *burnout* as the depletion of an individual's physical and mental resources caused by excessive attempts to meet self-imposed, unrealistic goals. A number of symptoms have been associated with burnout, including depression, fatigue, irritability, sleeplessness, and uncontrollable anger. Important to our discussion is the fact that Freudenberger identified the work environment and work situation as precipitating factors that lead to symptoms of burnout.

A more precise explanation of burnout was discussed by Cherniss (1980), who concentrated on workers in the "helping" professions. Conceptually, Cherniss perceived burnout within the helping professions in three stages: (1) workers experience stress due to demands of job, (2) workers experience strain due to emotional responses of anxiety and tension, and (3) workers attempt to cope defensively by changing their attitude toward commitment to their job. For example, they may treat clients in a manner that reflects an attitude of little concern for them. He observed that when helping professionals experience burnout, devotion to helping others is no longer a strong commitment. Cherniss suggested that in response to work-related stress and strain, workers in helping professions will actually disengage from their work. Other writers, such as Maslach, have come to similar conclusions concerning mental health workers (Maslach, 1976, 1981; Maslach & Jackson, 1981; Pines & Maslach, 1979).

Burnout has been used to describe a number of work-related behaviors. For example, Cordes and Dougherty (1993) describe burnout as a stress syndrome, characterized by emotional exhaustion, depersonalization, and diminished personal accomplishment. Burnout has been associated primarily with individuals in the helping professions such as teaching, social work, and health care. Similarly, the terms *burnout* and *stagnation* are used interchangeably to describe individuals who have lost enthusiasm for work (Edelwich & Brodsky, 1980). Another comparable term is *plateauing,* which is used to describe individuals who have reached their highest level in an organization (Drucker, 1992). In essence, burnout has not been delineated clearly and has received only preliminary and small-scale validation (Herr & Cramer, 1996). Therefore, the correlates of burnout described next should be considered to be preliminary observations in lieu of further research and delineation of the term.

There appears to be general agreement among investigators that burnout is not a single event but a process of gradual change in behavior, eventually reaching intense reactions and leading to crisis if left unresolved. Burnout has been associated with work overload, repetitive work tasks, boredom, ambiguity, lack of advancement opportunities, and time pressures (Forney, Wallace-Schultzman, & Wiggens, 1982). Schwab (1981) contended that burnout is highly related to role conflict. Farber and Heifetz (1981) and Emener and Rubin (1980) suggested that excessive work with very disturbed people is highly correlated with burnout. Other researchers suggested that off-the-job stress should also be evaluated when counseling individuals who exhibit symptoms of burnout (Pardine et al., 1981).

There appears to be a high degree of relationship between work-associated stress and burnout. Perhaps one strategy to use in dealing with individuals who exhibit symptoms of burnout is to evaluate work-related stressor sources, as outlined earlier. Support groups designed to foster self-acceptance and coping skills through the use of relaxation techniques and biofeedback are also recommended (Argeropoulos, 1981), and leisure therapy has been proposed by Garte and Rosenblum (1978). The variety of strategies suggests that burnout is a viable counseling consideration for individuals throughout the life span.

Pines and Aronson (1988) suggested a four-step plan for dealing with career burnout: (1) recognize the symptoms of burnout, (2) activate a plan for solving the causes of burnout, (3) distinguish between what can be changed and what cannot be changed, and (4) develop new coping skills and refine old ones. The first step is intended to promote awareness of stressors that cause individuals to believe they are helpless. Some, for example, may feel that burnout is "life's course" and little can be done to change that course. Others try to ignore existing problems. Even though awareness may increase anxiety, it is a necessary first step in solving career burnout problems. When individuals become aware of problems, they are usually willing to take action. For example, a worker who receives poor feedback on job performance from a supervisor may elect to either confront the supervisor or transfer to another work environment.

In many work environments, it is difficult to assess the causes of burnout; but to make progress toward change, the individual must carefully evaluate the underlying causes. Pines and Aronson (1988) pointed out that some bureaucracies cannot change their unresponsiveness to individuals; the system simply does not provide for it. For example, the work of a rehabilitation counselor is demanding and has many frustrating aspects. Even when success is attained, the counselor may only receive an increased client load as a reward. In this case, the counselor views the organizational changes to make the job more fulfilling as overwhelming. However, the counselor at least recognizes that the source of the problem is in the system rather than in himself or herself. In this scenario, the fourth step, developing coping skills, might include teaching the rehabilitation counselors to reinforce each other's work. This method promotes appreciation and respect for peers.

Other coping skills involve a careful evaluation of individual needs to solve a specific problem. Individuals may accomplish this through self-introspection or through professional help.

In conclusion, Pines and Aronson (1988) suggested that career counselors can help clients who may be experiencing burnout by (1) clarifying symptoms of burnout, (2) helping them develop the ability to distinguish sources of stress that they can control and those that are inherent in the work itself, and (3) developing tools for coping with stress by teaching how to focus on positive work aspects and develop positive attitudes.

Healthful Work

In the last decade, a number of publications have addressed the sources of job-related stress, whereas others have suggested methods of dealing with it. The relationship between job stress and disease has also been exposed as an ongoing problem that has been ignored in many workplaces. Recently, however, the connection between work and health has focused attention on designing more healthful workplaces. The physical, psychological, and psychosocial consequences of work are significantly related to job design (Karasek & Theorell, 1990). For example, bad job design fosters social isolation, little feeling of the social value of work, unrestrained job competition, sex-role conflicts, little or no freedom or independence, long periods of intense time pressures, and little autonomy for workers.

Jobs designed for the future and considered healthful work—that is, beyond the material rewards of work—are described by Karasek & Theorell (1990) as follows.

1. More jobs are to be designed to make maximum use of every worker's skill and provide opportunities to improve and increase skills.
2. More work freedom exists when workers are able to select their work routines and peer affiliates. Some work may be done in the home.
3. Workers are given equal status in making decisions as far as work demands are concerned. Jobs may require routine tasks, but they also provide new learning challenges.
4. Social contacts are encouraged to promote new learning and prevent work isolation. Advanced technologies are made available to encourage new learning.

5. Democratic procedures are prevalent in the workplace. Grievance procedures protect workers from arbitrary authority.
6. Workers receive feedback from customers, and in fact, customers and workers are encouraged to work together to customize products.
7. All workers are to share in family responsibilities and tasks, especially in two-earner homes. Time is set aside for family activities. (pp. 316–317)

In sum, healthful work reduces the sources of job stress prevalent in current work environments primarily by giving the worker more freedom and autonomy. Social interactions are encouraged to reduce threats associated with job competition. New learning is encouraged by making new technologies accessible to workers. Finally, more freedom of choice concerning work roles and greater autonomy in the workplace are recommended as key ingredients for designing jobs for the future.

Will There Be a Demand for Increased Quality of Work?

As we become more involved with global economics and multinational work forces, the quality of our products will become increasingly important. A quality product has been defined as one that is without defects or mistakes and is delivered on time. There have been significant signs that an international standard for certain products may be in the making. The International Organization for Standardization (ISO) in Switzerland may provide the framework from which quality is assured ("ISO 9000," 1992). The ISO 9000 standard series explains fundamental quality concepts and guides organizations in tailoring and designing production systems to ensure quality. Other countries, including the United States (National Institute of Standards and Technology), also have organizations for standards.

Does this movement mean that there will be global supervision of products, and will these products only be exported and imported if they are registered under some system of standards? That question has yet to be answered, but changes in the workplace may follow adoptions of some system of standardization. Some U.S. chemicals and associated products are registered under the ISO 9000. Currently, few changes affect workers and management, but there has been some concern that this kind of standardization approach could evolve into a rating system affecting job security.

Workers' welfare and mental health will continue to be our concern as counselors, and we will always be faced with ongoing changes that make our job a challenge. No doubt situations will continue to occur that create the need to develop new intervention strategies to assist individuals in making career decisions and adjusting to fast-paced changes in the workplace. The ISO 9000 approach to standardization may be a method of creating satisfaction among workers or a situation of change that creates more job-related stress. Within the next 10 to 20 years, we should have some answers.

Aging Workers

A question often considered in the hiring process is, Are aging workers more motivated to do good work than younger workers are? Research has shown that age per se is not a good predictor of how well a person will perform in either a blue-collar or a white-collar job. However, older workers may be as competent as younger ones and typically have a more positive attitude toward their work. Furthermore, they seem to be more satisfied in their job, more involved in their work, and less interested in finding a different job (Warr, 1992).

One explanation for these findings is that older workers have found jobs that satisfy them, and they have accepted the downside of a job realizing that it may be difficult to find a new one. The point here is that older workers, in their fifties and sixties, can make good employees.

Summary

1. Changes in work requirements and skills have evolved with the technological revolution. Up to 43 million jobs were lost to downsizing by 1995.

2. Organizations are reorganizing and abandoning fundamental assumptions that underlay previous operating procedures. Some skills individuals will need to compete are in the areas of reading, writing, computation, cognitive reasoning, interpersonal relations, creative thinking and problem solving, leadership, self-development, and self-management. In the "new web of enterprise," team members will function with problem solvers, problem identifiers, and strategic planners.

3. Occupational projections include jobs that will be lost from 1994 to 2005, and the fastest growing industry is identified as home health care services. Occupations that require the most education have above-average growth. Workers over age 45 will account for a larger share of the labor force.

4. Occupational insecurity can lead to mental health problems. All life roles can be affected.

5. Clients need assistance in coping with joblessness. Men and women can experience the same degree of stress.

6. The opportunities for entrepreneurs may be expanded by changes in organizational procedures.

7. Work values are influenced by a number of factors, including changing cultural values and economic patterns in our society. Career counselors should focus more on opportunities and choices that individuals perceive as available to them; career counseling must be realistic to be most effective. Individual perceptions of work and commitment to work are inextricably connected with economic and social forces.

8. Work commitment and work ethics could be cultural issues and may be related to our national social development. A new self-development ethic may be

emerging that will change workers' perspectives of their jobs and the work environment.

9. The personal agency person is a self-developing person who uses personal agency to succeed and can adapt to change. The personal agency person accepts the future for what it is and shifts other attitudes to meet the uncertainty of the future.

10. Stress, defined as a psychophysical response to various stimuli, is inherent in modern working life. The effects of stress are pervasive: work performance and interpersonal relationships are often affected. Stress affects all levels of workers, from executives to blue-collar workers.

11. The term *burnout* is used to describe a number of work-related behaviors. Burnout is a gradual process of behavioral change. Burnout is associated with stress caused by work overload, boredom, repetitious work tasks, time pressures, and other work-related stressor sources.

12. Healthful work reduces the sources of job stress by giving workers more freedom of choice for work roles and autonomy.

13. The International Organization for Standardization (ISO) may provide the framework used in organizations to ensure quality of work. The effects of change in the workplace may create opportunities for greater work-related satisfaction or change that creates job-related stress.

14. Older workers, in their fifties and sixties, may be as competent as younger workers and typically have a more positive attitude.

Supplementary Learning Exercises

1. Describe your own work ethic and how it developed. Compare your description with a classmate's.
2. Develop a counseling component that is designed to help individuals overcome job stress.
3. Defend or criticize the following statement in writing or in a debate: Work ethics change because society changes.
4. How did teamwork displace assembly-line work that required one task to be repeated? Give an example.
5. What is the difference between the problem solver and the problem identifier? Which one has the most difficult task?
6. Explain the concept of a "new web of enterprise." How does it operate?
7. Give several reasons the home health care services is the fastest growing industry. Identify some specific jobs in this industry.
8. Develop counseling strategies for individuals who feel insecure in their occupation.
9. How would you assist an individual who has lost his or her job? Describe your procedures and their purpose.
10. Using the following source, write an essay on the changes in the organization that will be experienced by the year 2005.

    Hammer, M., & Champy, J. (1993). *Reengineering the corporation: A manifesto for business revolution*. New York: HarperCollins.

CHAPTER THIRTEEN

Career Counseling for Adults in Career Transition

This chapter concentrates on the growing need for programs and strategies to assist adults in career transition. Traditionally, career counseling programs have focused on strategies for initial career choices, giving only limited help to adults who change careers. However, in the last decade, greater attention has been focused on the development of counseling programs for individuals who choose to make a career change and for those who are forced into it. In the 1970s, Arbeiter, Aslanian, Schmerbeck, and Brickell (1978) found that 40 million U.S. adults were in some phase of career transition. Many were victims of an economic slowdown, which triggered the downsizing of organizations as discussed in the preceding chapter. More recently, the changing workplace has become somewhat dismal, with the decline of manufacturing, downscaling of jobs, and high unemployment (McDaniels, 1990). However, Waterman (1992) argued that change is to be expected, especially in an environment where advanced technology makes some jobs obsolete while creating new ones. Change is a way of life and can provide exciting new challenges. An individual's response to change should be the counseling focus for those who work with adults in career transition. The NOICC (1992) emphasized this point when developing the national guidelines for career guidance programs, in particular the competencies for adults making career transitions. Two other important facts should also be understood: society's needs and functions affect occupational supply and demand, and a global economy can directly affect the career development of many individuals.

Because individuals in any generation differ from each other and from one generation to the next, counseling programs cannot be expected to meet everyone's needs. However, components of existing programs may be effectively combined and used in counseling a broad spectrum of adults. As we learn more about various aspects of the life span, stages of development, vocational maturity, motivation, and specific tasks related to life and work, better guidelines for developing programs will become available. Meanwhile, the development of counseling components that meet specific needs should provide for flexibility in program structure. Specific components can then be combined to meet the general needs of a particular population. In addition, interchangeable techniques and alternative procedures are needed to provide flexible strategies. Finally, specific counseling objectives need to be developed as guidelines for accomplishing various parts of specific counseling programs. These factors have been considered in developing the counseling program discussed in the second section of this chapter.

This chapter begins with the plight of an individual who has changed jobs several times. Next are examples of results from a national survey of working America. This is followed by a discussion of issues facing adults in career transition and then by a multidimensional model of career and individual development. The section "Major Themes in Human Development" is followed by implications of adult career development. Next, basic coping skills are presented for managing transitions, followed by counseling components for adults in career transition. Finally, occupational projections for 1994 to 2005 are discussed.

Case Example: Ben Is Changing Jobs Again

When Ben finished high school, he was referred to as a vocational educational student. Much of his course work was in woodworking and auto repair. Ben had always liked working with his hands, and he became a skilled cabinetmaker. He was first hired by a local builder, but he left this job after only a few months. His work history included a number of jobs in construction; he had also worked for several manufacturing firms and had lived in several states. When Ben reached the age of 41, he, along with several other employees, was dismissed from his current job. He and his fellow workers were told that the company was downsizing its work force.

When he returned to his home town, he informed his friends that he was tired of "drifting" from one job to another and was ready to settle down. However, the world of work was in the process of making rapid changes, as many industries were downsizing and restructuring job requirements. Even for Ben, who had developed several skills in different working environments, jobs were hard to find.

Ben was not aware of any local counseling assistance and turned to his friends for advice. They could offer little assistance, as most were either unemployed themselves or were greatly concerned about keeping their jobs. For the first time in his life, Ben seriously worried about future employment. He began to consider strategies to find a job. He started by jotting down what he knew of the current changing conditions in the workplace.

> Many workers are being retrained because of new technology. Maybe I could be one of them.
> New skills are needed in the workplace.

More corporations are having their products manufactured in foreign countries. I
   don't want to move again!
They are referring to workers as labor pools that are contracted for certain jobs.
A lot of workers are being replaced by robots.
Job guarantee seems to be a thing of the past.

Ben began to explore the possibility of starting his own business. He had
discovered that a number of firms were contracting for product assembly, rather
than hiring a labor force to produce them. Ben recalled his work experiences,
especially in the garment industry, where it was not unusual for goods to be partially assembled in several countries around the globe. His thoughts turned to
products that could be manufactured locally. He realized that he could not compete with cheap labor in foreign countries that could handle certain products like
garments or straw hats. He remembered hearing that some straw hats were woven
in India, had the hat bands inserted in Thailand, and were shaped for shipping in
the Philippines.

After several days of researching the needs of local firms, Ben found no leads.
About the time when Ben was ready to give up the idea of becoming an entrepreneur, he made a startling discovery. When shopping, he found that a large department chain contracted for the production of some of their furniture and wooden
cabinets. Ben knew he could build cabinets as good as and even better than the
ones he saw. But there were many other factors to consider, including costs of raw
products, building rentals, costs of production, and financial assistance. But Ben
had learned that giving up easily was not very rewarding.

This was a success story of how one individual used his past experiences and
skills to become an owner of his own business. He had received little assistance with
his career plans as a high school student and even less later when he was unemployed.
This is typical of many adults in career transition today (Hoyt & Lester, 1995).

National Survey of Working America

The National Career Development Association (NCDA) sponsored a national survey of working America conducted by the Gallup Organization from September
27, 1993, through October 27, 1993. A national sample of adults ($N = 1046$) were
surveyed by telephone. Of this group, 713 were working either full or part time.
Some of the key findings (percentages were rounded to whole numbers) are in
abridged form as follows:

1. When asked about sources of help and counseling they would use, the responses were:
       40% would turn to friends or family.
       37% would go to a career counselor.
       17% would go to present employer.
       10% would return to community.
       8% would not know where to go for help.

The results also indicate that 68% of all adults sampled had *not* visited a professional school or college counselor. In contrast, 50% of the 18 to 25 years olds *had* visited a professional school or college counselor.

2. When asked about career information sources they had used in the past, the responses were:

> 47% had used newspapers, magazines, and television.
>
> 10% used college, university information centers, public libraries, public job services, or job training centers.
>
> 7% used computerized career information systems (CIDS).
>
> 33% used no job information sources.

When asked what they would do if they were given the opportunity to start over in search of a career, more than 70% of all adults surveyed stated they would try to get more information about career options. When asked how much special job training their employers had provided, approximately two-thirds indicated their employers had provided them with some type of training (Hoyt & Lester, 1995).

Returning to the story of Ben's plight to find a work role, we discover that his problems were similar to many adults in the national survey. For example, he turned to friends for advice about job opportunities. He was not aware of job information sources. Like 70% of the adults surveyed, Ben wanted more information about career options when he started a new career search. The next section covers some of these issues.

Issues Facing Adults in Career Transition

The first issue is a practical one: the unavailability of career counseling programs for adults. Adults are generally unaware of available jobs and lack directions in making satisfactory career changes. Furthermore, many adults have not developed career exploration skills, such as decision making, and do not know about resources that give job descriptions, requirements, and so forth (Brown & Minor, 1989). In essence, many adults are generally confused about future directions and where to find assistance (Hoyt & Lester, 1995).

However, counseling should do more than just supply exploration skills. The important components of career counseling not addressed in original career decisions (such as values, needs, goals, and developed skills) are major targets of career counseling for adults who have lost their jobs due to downsizing or have voluntarily made a job change. The issue here involves helping individuals reassess the contributing factors that led to the desire for a career change and to provide relevant career information to those who have lost their jobs. The complex nature of arriving at a career decision underscores the need for career counseling programs that meet individual needs at all age levels and in a variety of settings.

Downsizing is an important issue facing adults in the workplace. This term is used to describe the removal of significant numbers of managers, professionals, and blue-collar workers from organizations. The corporate message in the 1990s is to "think small." For example, General Electric reduced their work force by 100,000 over 11 years by 1992, and during that time their net income increased from $1.5 billion to $4.7 billion (Naisbitt, 1994).

There are many reasons for the continuing retrenchment of organizations, such as strong overseas competition, declining manufacturing, declining energy and commodity prices, free trade policies, and deregulation. The globalization of U.S. companies, making them multinational enterprises, has also contributed to the weakening of the U.S. job market (Barnet & Cavanagh, 1994).

Reich (1991) presents the following example of how products are produced and marketed internationally: "Precision ice hockey equipment was designed in Sweden, financed in Canada, and assembled in Cleveland and Denmark for distribution in North America and Europe, respectively, out of alloys whose molecular structure was researched and patented in Delaware and fabricated in Japan" (p. 112). This example illustrates the mode of operation of multinational corporations, underscoring the fact that many organizations will lose their national identity.

These events have triggered a rethinking of bureaucratic assumptions about long-term employment commitments. As Kanter (1989) put it, "Climbing the career ladder is being replaced by hopping from job to job" (p. 299). The lack of certainty and clear direction for the future work role has generated many personal dilemmas. Adults who find themselves in career transition as a result of downsizing need career intervention strategies that focus on establishing a career direction in the ever-changing workplace.

Along with evolving organizational structure changes will come a work force that is more diverse in terms of culture and gender. By the year 2000, white males will no longer dominate the work force as the number of women, minorities, and immigrants significantly increase (U.S. Department of Labor, 1992–1993). These new demographics offer challenges to supervisors and fellow workers as well as to the career development specialist. A greater sensitivity to such diverse populations in the workplace will become increasingly important. Evolving organizational settings will reflect the new demographics, and effective team members will have to be able to function well with all groups of people. Career counselors must be able to offer professional leadership to help individuals develop these skills. (In this section, we will focus on cultural diversity; for more information on women, see Chapter 15.)

Organizations will also become more globally oriented, which translates into a greater potential for working with people from many cultures (Kanter, 1989). A multicultural work force may include natives of Mexico, Japan, Germany, and France, for example, and U.S. team members will have to understand the basic differences in cultural perceptions of work, in processing information, and in responding to tasks and fellow workers (Wigglesworth, 1992). Here are some examples of differences between cultures, as compiled by Harris and Moran (1991).

Nonverbal signals—the "A-OK" gesture
- In America, it means everything is fine.
- In Germany and Brazil, it is interpreted as obscene.

- The Japanese interpret it as money.
- To the French, it means "zilch" or zero.

Eye contact

- In America, poor eye contact translates into a "shifty" character.
- In Japan, children are taught to look at the tie knot or Adam's apple.
- In Latin America, prolonged eye contact can be considered disrespectful.
- Arabs look at each other squarely in the eye.
- The widening of the eyes in China is a danger signal and may indicate suppressed anger.

These few examples are indicative of the vast array of differences among cultures and underscore the increasing need to become more culturally aware. Other differences include time factors, body language, physical distance, and what gives rise to conflict (Wigglesworth, 1992). The acquisition of skills to be an effective worker in a diverse work force is long overdue and should be a high-priority focus for career counselors. For more information on multicultural groups, see Chapter 18. In the next paragraphs, we will discuss the relationships between workers and companies, among workers, and between workers and supervisors.

A survey done in 1993 by the *New York Times,* as reported in Chapter 12, found some interesting reactions from individuals who were now in career transition. In what was labeled a National Economic Insecurity Survey, numerous tables were compiled from adults about the current job market and economic climate. The following are selected examples.

When asked whether companies are more or less loyal to their employees than they were ten years ago, 75% of all adults surveyed answered "less loyal." When asked whether workers are more or less loyal to their employers, 64% of all adults surveyed responded "less loyal." When asked whether most working people today cooperate more with one another at the place where they work or whether they compete more with each other, 70% of all adults surveyed answered "compete more." When asked whether they think the mood at many workplaces is more angry or more friendly, 53% of all adults surveyed answered "more angry."

These results, providing some perceptions of the current workplace, give a rather dismal picture of its climate. That companies are less loyal to their workers and workers are less loyal to their employers than they were ten years ago may mean that some workers may have difficulty establishing any degree of trust with their employers. Many other negative reactions from employees and employers are possible within such an atmosphere.

The relationships among workers do not look any better from the results of the survey. Workers see their peers as being more competitive and more angry than in the past. These perceptions, whatever their cause, significantly add to insecurity in the workplace and to the potential of increased stress among workers and between workers and supervisors. The adult in career transition may indeed face a hostile work environment.

Finally, we must deal with the variety of expectations individuals have concerning their career choice. Many have enthusiastically entered a career with the expectation of a continuous, challenging, intrinsically rewarding work environment, only to experience something quite different. For these individuals, the realities of working somehow have been misinterpreted. Many see this as a broken promise of what they were led to expect from their careers and react as if in a crisis, ultimately seeking changes in their lifestyles. The conflicts between career and expectations are characteristically intense, leading many toward a search for a second career. Their message is quite clear—help us find fulfillment from life and work.

Career and Individual Development

As we consider a more integrated approach to career development, career issues and individual issues must be dealt with jointly. Kram (1985) proposed a developmental model of career issues, displayed in Table 13-1, that reflects (1) *concerns about self,* including comparisons with peers and career role; (2) *concerns about career,* including work involvement and commitment; and (3) *concerns about family,* including family role and work-family conflict. These issues are examples of adult concerns that can serve as reference points for counseling intervention, as this model presents multidimensional tasks at successive career stages.

In the early career stage, concerns of self include questions about one's competence at work and one's effectiveness as a spouse or parent. There is striving for identity, and key questions about occupational skills and aspirations are addressed. In this stage, the individual questions his or her commitment to an organization and the possible advancement pathways. The family role in the early career stage includes a concern for establishing an appropriate lifestyle and for

TABLE 13-1
Characteristic Developmental Tasks at Successive Career Stages

	Early career	*Middle career*	*Late career*
Concerns about self	*Competence:* Can I be effective in the managerial/ professional role? Can I be effective in the role of spouse and/or parent? *Identity:* Who am I as a manager/professional? What are my skills and aspirations?	*Competence:* How do I compare with my peers, with my subordinates, and with my own standards and expectations? *Identity:* Who am I now that I am no longer a novice? What does it mean to be a "senior" adult?	*Competence:* Can I be effective in a more consultative and less central role, still having influence as the time to leave the organization gets closer? *Identity:* What will I leave behind of value that will symbolize my contributions during my career? Who am I apart from a manager/ professional and how will it feel to be without that role?

(continued)

TABLE 13-1 *(continued)*

	Early career	*Middle career*	*Late career*
Concerns about career	*Commitment:* How involved and committed to the organization do I want to become? Or do I want to seriously explore other options?	*Commitment:* Do I still want to invest as heavily in my career as I did in previous years? What can I commit myself to if the goal of advancement no longer exists?	*Commitment:* What can I commit myself to outside of my career that will provide meaning and a sense of involvement? How can I let go of my involvement in my work role after so many years?
	Advancement: Do I want to advance? Can I advance without compromising important values?	*Advancement:* Will I have the opportunity to advance? How can I feel productive if I am going to advance no further?	*Advancement:* Given that my next move is likely to be out of the organization, how do I feel about my final level of advancement? Am I satisfied with what I have achieved?
	Relationships: How can I establish effective relationships with peers and supervisors? As I advance, how can I prove my competence and worth to others?	*Relationships:* How can I work effectively with peers with whom I am in direct competition? How can I work effectively with subordinates who may surpass me?	*Relationships:* How can I maintain positive relationships with my boss, peers, and subordinates as I get ready to disengage from this setting? Can I continue to mentor and sponsor as my career comes to an end? What will happen to significant work relationships when I leave?
Concerns about family	*Family role definition:* How can I establish a satisfying personal life? What kind of lifestyle do I want to establish?	*Family role definition:* What is my role in the family now that my children are grown?	*Family role definition:* What will my role in the family be when I am no longer involved in a career? How will my significant relationships with spouse and/or children change?
	Work/family conflict: How can I effectively balance work and family commitments? How can I spend time with my family without jeopardizing my career advancement?	*Work/family conflict:* How can I make up for the time away from my family when I was launching my career as a novice?	*Work/family conflict:* Will family and leisure activities suffice, or will I want to begin a new career?

SOURCE: From *Mentoring at Work: Developmental Relationships in Organizational Life*, by K. E. Kram. Copyright 1988 by University Press of America. Reprinted by permission of the publisher and the author.

balancing work with family commitments. Middle career and late career stages contain similar questions that foster the idea of considering all life roles in developmental tasks at successive career stages.

Our level of awareness must increasingly be directed to the multidimensional nature of human and career development. We should not attempt to isolate one from the other in our development of counseling activities for all age groups, including the adult in career transition. As we converge our counseling processes to include all life roles and life's problems, we have a greater assurance that our effectiveness as counselors will be enhanced and—more important—will provide avenues for identifying clients' core problems. In the next section, major themes of human development provide further clues to adult development and subsequent issues facing adults in career transition.

Major Themes in Human Development

Many academic disciplines have contributed to the understanding of human development; it is certainly multidimensional as well as comprehensive in nature and scope. In this tradition, we must recognize the prolific amount of research involved in delineating human development over the life span.

Adult life stage models were not used in this chapter because some observers have suggested either that they have little relevance to practice (Courtenay, 1994) or that research concerning adult career development has reached only tentative conclusions (Herr & Cramer, 1996). We can, however, propose some implications of adult career development from the following general themes of human development, adapted from Sigelman and Shaffer (1995).

1. *We are whole persons throughout the life span.* There is an intermeshing of physical, cognitive, personal, and social development throughout the life span. There is also a distinctive and coherent quality to each individual's development.

2. *Development proceeds in multiple directions.* There are significant changes in development over the life span, but they are viewed in terms of gains and losses, not by the old notion of progression that consisted of growth and improvement up to adulthood, stability into middle age, and decline in old age. Within this framework of development, for every gain there is a loss. For example, the amount of time spent on becoming an expert in a field means a loss of opportunity to develop other areas of specialization.

3. *There is both continuity and discontinuity in development.* The point here is that predicting the character of an adult from knowledge of the child is very risky. Continuity can continue from early childhood, but discontinuity can be fostered by events in one's environment, such as child abuse, inferior schools, or parental neglect.

4. *There is much plasticity in human development.* People can be adaptable throughout their life span. Potentially harmful early experiences need not have a permanent effect on one's development.

5. *Nature and nurture truly interact in development.* There are multiple causal forces in human development; both nature and nurture interact in the change process. One or the other may be more influential in certain aspects of human development, but there are usually ongoing influences from both.

6. *We are all individuals, becoming even more diverse with age.* We do share common experiences with others, but we are indeed individuals and we accumulate our own unique history of life experiences.

7. *We develop in a cultural and historical context.* We must recognize that human development takes place in different cultures, social classes, and racial and ethnic groups. Cultural variations in development should include contextual influences.

8. *We are active in our own development.* We create our own environment and influence those around us; but at the same time all participants are influenced in a reciprocal way.

9. *Development is best viewed as a lifelong process.* The linkages between early and late development are important connections to study. But it is also valuable to view behavior during each phase of life, because development is a process. Understanding where we have started from and where we are heading leads to an understanding of the processes involved.

10. *Development is best viewed from multiple perspectives.* Many disciplines have contributed to the understanding of human development. In this tradition, we must recognize that a multiple of theories are often integrated when explaining human development.

Implications of Human Development as Related to Adult Career Development

The intermeshing of physical, cognitive, personal, and social development that gives each period of the life span a distinctive quality should make us more aware of considering the overwhelming possibilities of an individual adult's development. Perhaps we have been guilty of attempting to oversimplify development into categories that appeared to be more manageable.

The concept of multiple directions of development, with its gains and losses, challenges the older view of development as consisting of continuous growth and improvement into adulthood, stability, and decline. We must recognize that we give up something in almost every step we take toward specialization. One suspects that many adults do not view choices in this manner.

As humans, we have a remarkable capacity to change in response to experience. This translates into providing opportunities for growth even though an individual's past record may be dismal.

The match between a person and his or her environment as a contributing factor of human development has overtones of several career development constructs (discussed in Chapters 2 and 3). When there is goodness of fit, positive things begin to happen.

The cultural and historical context in which one develops has enormous implications for counseling adults. This multicultural developmental position recognizes the centrality and primary importance of culture as an internalized subjective process that must be included in counseling programs developed for different ethnic groups.

There has been a greater recognition of individual agency in career development. We do indeed have an active role in our own development. Focusing adults' attention to this position will hopefully lead to more positive assertive action.

Finally, viewing development as a lifelong process reinforces the current importance placed on retraining and lifelong learning.

As we continue to view development from multiple perspectives, we are humbled by the comprehensive nature of human development itself. Hopefully, the ongoing research efforts will provide more solid guidelines in the future. In the meantime, we can use what we have as tentative support for program development, as the comprehensive nature of this subject will continue to provide more questions that need to be answered.

Basic Coping Skills for Managing Transitions

Brammer and Abrego (1981) have developed a model for basic coping skills that assist adults in managing transitions (see Box 13-1). The first set of coping skills relates to perceiving and responding to transitions, such as developing self-control and a style for responding to change. The second set of skills relates to assessing, developing, and utilizing external support systems. By developing a personal support system network, the individual can use friends and professionals in crisis situations. The third set is related to assessing, developing, and utilizing an internal support system, such as assessing positive and negative attitudes and personal strengths and activating these strengths when needed. The fourth set involves reducing emotional and physiological distress through relaxation exercises and the verbal expression of feelings associated with distress. The fifth set, which involves planning and implementing change, promotes planning various courses of action and formulating strategies for implementing them.

One example of applying these skills might be a man who is given the news that his job is to be terminated because of economic conditions. He can use self-control skills to perceive the current situation realistically. By recognizing he has time to make future plans before the termination turns into a financial crisis, he can call on friends for emotional support and for suggestions on how to conduct a job search. He can rely on skills used to develop inner strength to help him evaluate the current job market and make plans for the future.

Brammer and Abrego (1981) suggested that people often feel powerless to respond to change. Coping skills help adults in transition react more rationally when responding to changing conditions over the life span. Coping skills are often best taught in seminars or in small groups.

Box 13-1
Basic Coping Skills for Managing Transitions

1 *Skills in perceiving and responding to transitions*

  1.1 The person mobilizes a personal style of responding to change. He or she

    1.11 Accepts the proposition that problematic situations constitute a normal part of life and that it is possible to cope with most of these situations effectively (perceived control over one's life).

    1.12 Recognizes the importance of describing problematic situations accurately (problem definition).

    1.13 Recognizes the values and limitations of feelings as cues to evaluate a transition (feelings description).

    1.14 Inhibits the tendency either to act impulsively or to do nothing when confronted with a problematic situation (self-control).

  1.2 The person identifies his or her current copying style (style of responding to change).

2 *Skills for assessing, developing, and utilizing external support systems*

  2.1 The person can assess an external support system. He or she can

    2.11 Identify his or her emotional needs during times of transition.

    2.12 Identify people in his or her life who provide for personal needs.

    2.13 Describe a personal support network in terms of physical and emotional proximity.

  2.2 The person can develop a personal network based on data from 2.1 or he or she can

    2.21 Seek sources (groups, organizations, locales) of potential support persons.

    2.22 Apply social skills to cultivate persons to meet identified needs.

  2.3 The person can utilize an established support network. He or she can

    2.31 Develop strategies for spending time with persons considered most helpful.

    2.32 Apply skills for utilizing persons in his or her network when a transition is anticipated or arrives.

3 *Skills for assessing, developing, and utilizing internal support systems*

  3.1 The person can assess the nature and strength of positive and negative self-regarding attitudes. He or she can

    3.11 Identify personal strengths.

    3.12 Identify negative self-descriptive statements, as well as the assumptions and contextual cues that arouse such statements.

  3.2 The person can develop positive self-regard attitudes. He or she can

    3.21 Affirm personal strengths.

    3.22 Convert negative self-descriptions into positive descriptive statements when the data and criteria so warrant.

(continued)

Box 13-1   *(continued)*

3.3 The person can utilize his or her internal support system in a transition. He or she can

3.31 Construe life transitions as personal growth opportunities.

3.32 Identify tendencies to attribute personal deficiencies as causative factors in distressful transitions.

4 *Skills for reducing emotional and physiological distress*

He or she can

4.1 Practice self-relaxation responses.

4.2 Apply strategies to control over-stimulation/under-stimulation.

4.3 Express verbally feelings associated with his or her experience of transition.

5 *Skills for planning and implementing change*

5.1 The person can analyze discrepancies between existing and desired conditions.

5.2 The person exercises positive planning for new options. To the best of his or her abilities, the person can

5.21 Thoroughly canvass a wide range of alternative courses of action.

5.22 Survey the full range of objectives to be fulfilled and the values implied by the choice.

5.23 Carefully weigh whatever he or she knows about the cost and risk of negative consequences that could flow from each alternative.

5.24 Search intensely for information relevant to further evaluation of the alternatives.

5.25 Utilize feedback to reassess his or her preferred course of action.

5.26 Reexamine the positive and negative consequences of all known alternatives.

5.27 Make detailed provisions for implementing or executing the chosen course of action including contingency plans.

5.3 The person successfully implements his or her plans. He or she can

5.31 Identify stressful situations related to implementing goals.

5.32 Identify negative self-statements that interfere with implementing plans.

5.33 Utilize self-relaxation routines while anticipating the stressful implementation of plans.

5.34 Utilize self-rewards in goal attainment.

5.35 Identify additional skills needed to implement goals (for example, anxiety management, training in assertiveness, overcoming shyness).

SOURCE: From "Intervention Strategies for Coping with Transitions," by L. M. Brammer and P. J. Abrego, 1981. *The Counseling Psychologist, 9,* p. 27. Reprinted by permission.

Occupational Projections, 1994–2005

The 1995 fall issue of the *Occupational Outlook Quarterly* contains some very interesting forecasts of occupational projections to the year 2005 that have implications for adults in career transition. Although Figure 13-1 reflects conditions in 1994, these trends are expected to continue in the future. For example, according to Figure 13-1, the lowest-earning jobs will be those that require the least amount of education. Above-average earnings will be received by individuals who have an associate or higher degree. Below-average earnings will be paid to individuals who have only on-the-job training experience.

Figure 13-2 informs us that professionals and service workers account for over half of the projected job growth. The projected employment growth within the services is presented in Figure 13-3. Professions within the service industry—such as social work, nursing, and many other health professions—will also experience significant growth.

It is significant to observe that eight of the ten industries with the most rapid job declines are in manufacturing, as seen in Figure 13-4. The highest loss is in footwear. According to Barnet and Cavanaugh (1994), Nike, the largest maker of sport shoes in the world ($2 billion a year) has almost all of their shoes manufactured and assembled in Asia. Nike shoes made in Indonesia at a cost of $5.60 are sewed primarily by girls who earned about 82¢ a day in 1991.

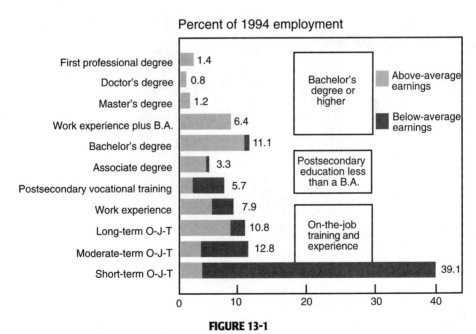

FIGURE 13-1
Low-earnings jobs are concentrated in occupations requiring the least
amount of education and training
SOURCE: U.S. Department of Labor, Bureau of Labor Statistics

Millions of jobs, 1994–2005

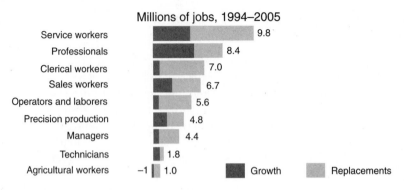

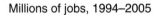

Service workers	9.8
Professionals	8.4
Clerical workers	7.0
Sales workers	6.7
Operators and laborers	5.6
Precision production	4.8
Managers	4.4
Technicians	1.8
Agricultural workers	−1 1.0

Growth   Replacements

FIGURE 13-2

More job openings stem from replacements than from growth

SOURCE: U.S. Department of Labor, Bureau of Labor Statistics

Millions of jobs, 1994–2005

Total 12.0

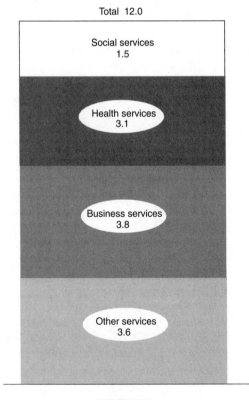

Social services
1.5

Health services
3.1

Business services
3.8

Other services
3.6

FIGURE 13-3

Where projected employment growth within services is concentrated

SOURCE: U.S. Department of Labor, Bureau of Labor Statistics

Percent change, 1994–2005

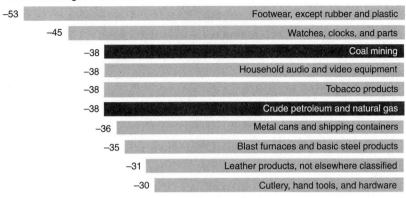

FIGURE 13-4

Eight of the ten industries with the most rapid job declines are in manufacturing

SOURCE: U.S. Department of Labor, Bureau of Labor Statistics

Percent of labor force

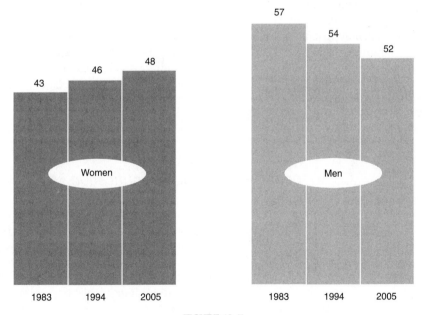

FIGURE 13-5

Women's share of the labor force edges up

SOURCE: U.S. Department of Labor, Bureau of Labor Statistics

In Figure 13-5, projections indicate that women's share of the labor force will increase steadily from 1994 to 2005, to 48%. Their rate of entry into the labor force will continue to be much faster than men's.

The major implication of these projections for adults in career transition is that jobs requiring greater education and training will dominate as the occupations that grow the fastest and will have the highest pay rates. This appears to be in agreement with the projection that job changes will require retraining of the work force. Finally, women will continue to need assistance in career exploration procedures that are free of sex-role stereotyping.

Career Counseling Components
for Adults in Career Transition

Career counseling programs for adults in career transition have many elements in common with programs designed for initial career choice. However, there are enough different and distinct factors involved in career transition to merit the development of specific programs for adults considering career change. Of major consideration are the individual adult experiences associated with work, leisure, family, and individualized lifestyle. Life's experiences provide both the counselor and the individual with a rich source of information from which to launch a career exploration. Identifying developed skills, interests, work experiences, and reformulated goals are examples of program strategies for the adult in career transition.

A counseling program for adults in career transition is outlined in Table 13-2. This program consists of seven components referred to as *strategies*. Each component has suggested technique options and specific tasks. The technique options suggested do not rule out other methods of accomplishing the specific tasks. In many instances, reference will be made to other chapters in this text and other publications for program considerations. Following are brief explanations of each component.

Component I—Experience Identification

Valuable assets often overlooked in career counseling are work and life experiences. One of the main purposes of this component is to carefully evaluate past experiences in relation to potential use in career selection. Typically, the adult overlooks the value of developed skills or only casually considers them in career exploration. This component emphasizes providing the structure from which counselor and counselee can effectively evaluate an individual's background of experiences and relate them to interests, work requirements, and other variables associated with occupations.

The technique options suggested for Component I provide the counselor with alternatives to meet individual needs. In most instances, combinations of suggested options may be used. For example, after an individual writes an autobiography, the counselor can follow with an interview or work experience analysis or both. In other instances, it may be feasible to use only one of the options. This decision may often be based on time availability and the educational level of the counselee.

TABLE 13-2
Counseling Program for Adults in Career Transition

Strategy component	Technique option	Specific tasks
I. Experience identification	1. Interview 2. Autobiography 3. Background information format and guide 4. Work- and leisure-experience analysis	1. Identify and evaluate previous work experience 2. Identify and evaluate life experiences 3. Identify desired work tasks and leisure experiences 4. Assess familial relationships 5. Identify reasons for job change 6. Identify career satisfaction variables 7. Identify factors that contributed to job changes 8. Identify reasons for current interest in career change
II. Interest identification	1. Interest inventories	1. Identify and evaluate occupational interests 2. Identify specific interest patterns 3. Relate interest to past experience 4. Compare interest with identified skills 5. Relate interest to potential occupational requirements 6. Relate interests to avocational needs
III. Skills identification	1. Self-analysis of developed skills 2. Self-estimates of developed skills 3. Standardized measures of developed skills	1. Identify and evaluate developed skills from previous work tasks 2. Identify and evaluate developed skills from leisure learning experiences 3. Identify and evaluate developed skills from formal learning experiences 4. Identify and evaluate developed functional, technical, and adaptive skills
IV. Value and needs clarification	1. Value and needs assessment through standardized inventories 2. Values clarification exercises	1. Clarify values in relation to life and work 2. Determine level and order of needs in relation to life and work 3. Identify satisfaction and dissatisfaction variables associated with work

(continued)

TABLE 13-2
Counseling Program for Adults in Career Transition   *(continued)*

Strategy component	Technique option	Specific tasks
		4. Identify satisfaction and dissatisfaction
		5. Identify expectations of future work and lifestyle
		6. Identify desirable work environments, organizations, and peer affiliates
		7. Realistically assess potential future achievements
		8. Assess potential movement within current work environment
		9. Identify work roles and leisure roles and how they interrelate with lifestyle
		10. Relate values to factors that contribute to obsolescence
		11. Identify personal factors associated with career decision
V. Education/ training planning	1. Published materials	1. Identify sources of educational/training information
	2. Locally compiled information resources	2. Identify continuing education programs
	3. Microfiche system	3. Identify admission requirements to educational/training programs
	4. Computerized system	4. Investigate potential credit for past work experience and previously completed training programs
		5. Evaluate accessibility and feasibility of educational/training programs
		6. Identify and assess financial assistance and other personal assistance programs
		7. Relate identified skills to educational/training programs for further development

TABLE 13-2   *(continued)*

Strategy component	Technique option	Specific tasks
VI. Occupational planning	1. Published printed materials 2. Microfiche system 3. Computer information systems 4. Visit files	1. Identify sources of occupational information 2. Identify and assess occupational opportunities 3. Relate identified skills and work experience to specific occupational requirements 4. Evaluate occupations from a need-fulfilling potential 5. Relate identified goals to occupational choice 6. Relate family needs to occupational benefits 7. Identify educational/training needs for specific occupations
VII. Toward a life learning plan	1. Decision-making exercises 2. Life-planning exercises	1. Learn decision-making techniques 2. Clarify short-term and long-term goals 3. Identify original and reformulated career goals 4. Contrast differences between original and reformulated goals 5. Identify alternative goals 6. Clarify goals in relation to family expectations 7. Develop a flexibility plan for life learning 8. Develop life-planning skills 9. Identify lifestyle preferences

The first of the technique options is the interview. The primary purpose of the interview is to assist the counselee in evaluating work and leisure experiences, training, and education in relation to potential occupational choices. The focus of the interview should include (1) specific work experiences, (2) specific educational/training experiences, (3) specific leisure experiences and preferences, (4) specific likes and dislikes of former jobs, and (5) special recognitions. In general, the interview should provide the basis from which the next step in the counseling program is determined. (See Chapter 20.)

The format for the autobiography can be either structured or unstructured. In the latter approach, the individual is instructed to write an autobiography without being given any specific guidelines. In the structured approach, the individual may be instructed to follow an outline or answer specific questions or both. The structured approach has obvious advantages for our purposes in that we are attempting to identify and evaluate specific information.

An autobiographical sketch can be used to identify developed skills (Radin, 1983). First, the individual is instructed to describe a significant accomplishment, such as starring in a dramatic production, being a leader in a scout group, or teaching photography. Descriptions of the accomplishment are analyzed to determine the use of functional, adaptive, and technical skills. Each autobiographical sentence is analyzed and later compiled and related to Holland's six modal personal styles. The following sentence is taken from a description of teaching photography and is analyzed for functional, adaptive, and technical skills.

"I started each class by demonstrating the proper use of a number of different cameras."

Functional	Adaptive	Technical
teaching	leadership	knowledge of cameras
communication	articulate	
	orderly	

Skills that are easily identifiable are those that are explicitly stated, whereas other skills are only implied, such as those needed to accomplish the task. In this case, teaching, communication, and camera knowledge are fairly explicit, while being articulate, orderly, and showing leadership are only implied.

The next option, background information, requires that the individual fill out a specified form. The information requested includes demographic data, marital status and family size, a list of jobs held and duties, education and training completed, armed services experiences, honors and awards, leisure preferences, hobbies, and other related information. A variety of approaches may be used to identify satisfaction and dissatisfaction variables associated with work and other experiences. One technique is to ask the individual to rank-order or to list likes and dislikes of each past job held. Another option is to provide spaces for free-response reactions to work and other experiences.

Following the example of Bolles (1993), a work and leisure experience analysis form was designed (Figures 13-6 and 13-7), on which the individual lists specific work (Part I) and leisure experiences (Part II). In addition, the individual indicates likes and dislikes of the experiences listed. The objective is to identify tasks and experiences that may be considered in future career choices.

Part I

Work experience	General duties	Specific tasks O over number if liked X over number if not liked
Bank Teller	Customer accounts Transactions	① Record + deposit receipts ② Payout Withdrawals X Cash Checks X Record transactions X Exchange Money

FIGURE 13-6
Work experience analysis form

Part II

Leisure experience		Specific tasks O over number if liked X over number if not liked
PTA Secretary		① Record Minutes X Call roll ③ Read minutes

FIGURE 13-7
Leisure experience analysis form

A review of the tasks for Component I suggests that the major objective is to identify specific desired work tasks, leisure experiences, family concerns associated with work, lifestyle, and potential reasons for job change. Using this information, the counselor and counselee should be able to identify a partial list of career satisfaction variables. The tentative conclusions and outcomes of this component will usually provide information for Component III, Skills Identification, but will also be integrated into other components of the program.

Component II—Interest Identification

Career counseling and interest identification have had a close association in their respective developments. Measured interests have been used primarily in predicting job satisfaction in career counseling programs. In our efforts to assist the adult in career transition, we must also be concerned with interests and their relationship to potential occupational choices. Conceptually, it is thought that interest identification can broaden and stimulate adults' exploratory career options. Adults should be in a relatively good position to identify individual interests, primarily from past experiences. However, some are able to identify uninteresting tasks and jobs but are unable to identify positive interests. For these individuals, interest identification is essential.

The suggested technique option for this component consists of the use of interest inventories. Careful consideration should be given to the selection of the inventory; it should assess the counselee's educational level, expectations of the future, reading level, and educational and training potentials, among other factors. A number of inventories are also available for nonreaders. A list of inventories is provided in Chapter 7.

The task for Component II is to identify interest clusters or patterns as well as specific interest indicators. A major task is to relate identified interests to occupational variables and education/training opportunities in the following components to ensure that all components are well integrated.

Component III—Skills Identification

In recently developed career counseling programs, skills identification has received special attention (Bolles, 1993; Holland, 1992). The focus is on identifying skills developed from previous experiences in work, hobbies, social activities, community volunteer work, and other leisure experiences. (See examples of skills in Figures 13-8 and 13-9.) The rationale for this objective is that people, in general,

Skills used in tasks

a. Functional
1. Clerical
2. Communication
3. Editing
4. Organizational

b. Adaptive
1. Articulate
2. Leadership
3. Diplomatic
4. Courteous

c. Technical
1. Accounting
2. Knowledge of foreign money exchange

FIGURE 13-8
Skills identification form

Classification:
Conventional
1. Clerical
2. Bookkeeping
3. Teller

Rate yourself as:

Good   Average   Poor
            ✓
✓
✓

FIGURE 13-9
Lifestyle identification form

fail to recognize developed skills and also do not know how to relate them to occupational requirements.

Skills-identification techniques have been used by Bolles (1993), Holland (1992), and Burton and Wedemeyer (1991). Bolles suggested that functional/transferable skills can best be identified by using a "quick job-hunting map." Holland provided a method to identify developed skills through self-estimates of ability. These methods concentrate on self-estimates of developed skills. Traditional standardized measures of skills and aptitudes may also be used.

The first technique option, self-analysis of developed skills, can be accomplished through the use of the work and leisure experience analysis forms used in Component I. For example, the compiled specific tasks on this form provide sources for identifying developed skills. Following are some examples of this process.

Three steps are necessary to identify skills from the work and leisure analysis form: (1) list specific work tasks; (2) identify functional, adaptive, and technical skills for each work task; and (3) relate each functional, adaptive, and technical skill to one or more of Holland's six modal personal styles. For those skills that are difficult to identify with Holland's six modal personal styles, *The Occupations Finder* (Holland, 1987c) will be most helpful.

The second technique option, self-estimates of developed skills, can be accomplished by having the individual rate each functional, adaptive, and technical skill as good, average, or poor as illustrated in the above example. These rankings provide self-estimates of skills within Holland's (1992) modal personal styles and corresponding work environments model.

A more traditional method of evaluating skills is through standardized testing, which is our third technique option. A variety of aptitude tests on the market today provide methods of evaluating skills based on normative data. A number of aptitude tests have been identified in Chapter 7.

The importance of specific skills identification is to encourage the counselee to consider skills developed from a variety of experiences as important factors in career exploration. By requiring that the individual identify skills in terms of adaptive, functional, and technical groups, a more precise relationship to occupational requirements is understood, thus promoting a more realistic evaluation for future goals. This component stresses the identification of skills from the individual's total lifestyle experiences.

Component IV—Lifestyle Identification

The emphasis thus far has been on considering the "whole person" when counseling adults. This component correspondingly includes the adult's total lifestyle. Component IV focuses on the individual adult's values and needs. More specifically, these individualized values and needs are considered in relation to work, leisure, peer affiliates, and family. Each value and need must be considered in relation to the others. For example, work values are only one part of the value system that must be considered in career counseling programs for adults. Individuals who are unable to clarify or satisfy their goals and needs concerning family may express dissatisfaction with work-associated tasks when in reality the source of difficulty is unrelated to the work environment itself. Hence, the need for the lifestyle identification approach used in this component is established.

The first of the technique options is the assessment of values and needs through standardized inventories. A number of inventories on the market today can be used for this purpose. Most inventories provide complete instructions for interpretation and counseling use. (See Chapter 7 for available inventories.)

Values clarification exercises are suggested as a second technique option. Values clarification may be accomplished in groups as well as in individual counseling programs. It is most important to select strategies that emphasize skills that assist individuals in identifying and developing their value systems. See the *Life Values Inventory* (Crace & Brown, 1996) for suggestions of value clarification strategies.

The lifestyle component is indeed a broad, rather all-encompassing concept of career counseling. In this context, we consider the individual's entire system of values and needs associated with lifestyle. Individually developed values and needs may be thought of as an integrated system that determines satisfaction with life. We may dichotomize value systems for clarification, but eventually we must address the entire system of values. Our goal is to communicate to the adult in career transition that life is indeed multifaceted and that satisfactory solutions cannot be oversimplified. We must consider what we are, where we have been, and that our future is relatively unpredictable. A change in career may reflect a desire to change lifestyle.

Component V—Education and Training

Education/training information was ranked as a high-priority interest among adults in career transition (Burton & Wedemeyer, 1991). The major purpose of Component V is to assist adults in identifying sources of educational/training information and making the most effective use of it. As community colleges and four-year institutions offer a greater variety of continuing education programs, the working adult will be in a much better position to upgrade and improve occupational skills. Exposure to educational/training opportunities should enhance the career decision-making process.

There are four technique options for this component. As with most components, and particularly with this component, the use of all or combinations of the options is recommended. The first option suggests the use of published materials. As illustrated in Chapter 8, there are a variety of publications from which education/training program information may be obtained. One of the most important sources for working adults is locally compiled information resources, suggested as the second technique option. Educational/training programs within reasonable commuting distances provide opportunities for training while maintaining occupational and family obligations.

Microfiche systems, the third technique option, provide another resource for educational/training information delivery. First, an advantage of a microfiche system is that it requires a relatively small storage area. Second, updating the system can be accomplished easily and regularly to ensure accurate information delivery. Third, accessing and refiling is very quick and systematic. Of major importance to the working adult is the accessibility of information provided by microfiche systems.

The fourth technique option for this component is the computerized career information system. A number of interactive and information-oriented computer-assisted guidance programs are available today (as discussed in Chapter 6). Generally, two types of educational/training information files are available by computer: files containing programs for all states, and files containing program information on a regional basis within states. The latter has the advantage of providing current localized programs.

The specific tasks for this component encourage a systematic approach to using educational/training information. Exposure to educational training opportunities will no doubt encourage many adults to consider methods of upgrading their skills for higher level job opportunities. Second, many adults will be encouraged to consider educational/training programs to keep from becoming obsolescent. Possible educational credit from past work experiences should also provide the incentive to enter continuing educational/training programs. Finally, we must encourage the fullest development of identified skills through educational/training opportunities delivered in this component.

Component VI—Occupational Planning

Occupational planning and the previously discussed educational/training component have many commonalities. Both focus on providing information to assist the adult in making the most effective use of occupational information. In fact, these two components are so closely related that they are often accessed at the same time (because occupational planning must take into account educational/training requirements). Therefore, many of the published materials combine educational/training requirements with occupational information.

Three of the technique options for this component suggest the use of published materials, microfiche, and computer-assisted programs. Representative samples of published materials that provide occupational information are provided in Chapter 8. Microfiche systems, discussed for the educational/training component, provide occupational information, as do computer-assisted programs. Most computer-assisted programs contain national occupational information files, but many provide occupational information on a local or regional basis within states. Many state and federal agencies provide labor forecasts and occupational information that should be incorporated into this component.

The fourth technique option, visit files, can be an important segment for delivering relevant occupational information. This file provides the names of individuals or organizations who agree to visits and interviews by people interested in obtaining firsthand information about certain occupations. This file is usually compiled locally through personal contacts, and in some cases may be available through purchased programs. Many computer-assisted programs that provide localized and regional data contain visit files.

The tasks for this component suggest that occupational information is more than just information about a job. Indeed, occupational information should enable individuals to evaluate the variables that will influence their lifestyles. For example, personal goal satisfaction, family/financial needs, and use of identified skills are just some of the variables to consider when accessing occupational information. Of major importance are the potential need-fulfilling opportunities available in each occupation under consideration.

In 1987, the National Career Development Association (NCDA) commissioned the Gallup Organization to survey a sample of adults about their career planning processes and workplace. One major finding suggested that six out of ten adults would request more information if they were to begin another career search. Another one out of two adults did not know how to interpret and use career information (Brown & Minor, 1989). These findings suggest that a greater effort should be made to introduce adults to career decision-making techniques, with thorough instruction in how to interpret occupational information.

Component VII—Toward a Life Learning Plan

This component assists in the development of a life learning plan. The introduction of decision-making techniques and life-planning exercises provides two methods of developing effective planning. The rationale for life learning is based on a continuing need to develop planning strategies to (1) meet technological changes, (2) stay abreast of the information explosion, (3) upgrade skills, and (4) reduce the chances of become obsolete. In addition, and perhaps more important, changing individual needs and reformulated goals also create a demand for effective planning. The techniques and skills developed in this component enhance decision-making techniques for meeting both occupational changes and changing individual needs associated with work, leisure, and lifestyle. Furthermore, these skills not only provide methods for formulating current plans but also provide strategies for continued life learning–planning in the future.

The first technique option, decision-making exercises, helps individuals effectively decide on options related to their future. As adults are faced with more options for continuing education/training and career choices, learning how to decide becomes a most relevant skill. In addition to the decision-making strategies discussed in Chapter 11, see *Career Decision Making* (Walsh & Osipow, 1988).

The second technique option promotes life-planning strategies. The specific task of establishing alternative plans for the future should be emphasized in this component. Skills identification and personal lifestyle preferences are integrated to provide the basis for alternative plans to meet future goals. Clarifying differences between original goals and reformulated goals is one way to show how changes in an individual's priorities change lifestyle patterns. Effective life-planning strategies help individuals in developing options and making effective decisions (as discussed in Chapter 4).

The tasks for this component may suggest to the adult in career transition that the career counseling program has ended. On the contrary, a life learning plan should be viewed as cyclic; individual changes and external conditions may require the individual to recycle through one or more of the counseling components. A life learning plan should be viewed as continuous, with intermittent pauses. The important message is that the skills learned through these components will provide effective methods of finding and using resource information, clarifying individual needs, making decisions, and planning for the future.

Summary

1. Ben, a fictitious worker who had been the victim of downsizing, used past experiences and skills to become an owner of a business.

2. The results of a national survey of U.S. workers indicated that adults usually turn to friends for career advice. Among the findings was that many adults need sources of career information and career exploration skill training.

3. Current issues related to career problems among adults are (a) lack of available career counseling programs, (b) the downsizing of organizations, (c) the globalization of U.S. companies, (d) the multicultural work force, and (e) a potentially hostile workplace.

4. Career and individual development is a multidimensional model that includes concerns about self, family, and career.

5. Major themes in human development suggest that there are multiple directions of development, humans have a remarkable capacity to change in response to experiences, a match between person and environment is an important factor, the importance of culture as an internalized subjective process must be included in counseling programs, individual agency in development is important, development is a lifelong process, and human development is a comprehensive process.

6. Basic coping skills are identified by sets of skills to assist in managing transitions.

7. Occupational projections indicate that service workers will account for over half the projected job growth by the year 2005. Women's share of the labor force will also increase.

8. Career counseling programs for adults in career transition have many elements in common with programs designed for initial career choice. However, there are enough different and distinct factors to merit the development of specific programs for adults considering career change. Counseling components that meet specific needs of adults include (a) experience identification, (b) interest identification, (c) skills identification, (d) values and needs clarification, (e) educational/training planning, (f) occupational planning, and (g) a life learning plan.

Supplementary Learning Exercises

1. Develop a list of the ten most dominant needs in your life at the present time. Share these with a colleague and project how these needs may change over a life span. Identify major sources of satisfaction and dissatisfaction and how these factors may cause you to become an unfulfilled individual.

2. What are your suggestions for counseling programs that would meaningfully interpret the realities of working? Obtain your suggestions by interviewing workers and by observing working climates.

3. Develop an outline for writing a work autobiography. Using the outline, write your own work autobiography.

4. Using the experience-identification component strategy, develop a counseling program to accomplish two or more of the specific tasks.

5. Compile a list of your own skills developed through previous work, leisure, and learning experiences. Relate these skills to specific kinds of occupations. Why is skills identification important for adults in career transition?

6. Develop a set of counseling strategies to clarify values and needs associated with expectations of future work and lifestyle. Why is it important to clarify values and needs for the adult in career transition?

7. Review several community college and four-year college catalogs' financial aid information. Compile this information and specify how you would use it in counseling adults in career transition.

8. Identify and list your personal goals and relate these to your career choice. Why is it important for adults to identify personal goals for career exploration?

9. Take any four major themes of human development and develop a list of implications for adults in career transition.

10. Debate the accuracy of occupational projections. Use references to support your position.

CHAPTER FOURTEEN

Career Development of Adults in Organizations

Career counseling programs have grown over the last decade to include a variety of new and different components. However, providing the individual with information about organizations has not been a major counseling effort. The center of attention has been on other occupational choice variables. Yet, experienced career counselors are well aware that career choices are often directed at organizations as well as at specific career fields. In addition, individuals tend to identify with organizations as well as with their occupations.

Despite the need for information about organizations, career guidance professionals have documented vast amounts of materials and programs aimed at helping students evaluate occupations, whereas little attention has been given to helping students evaluate organizations. Moreover, a review of the literature of industrial and management psychology suggests that a number of characteristics of organizations are important to consider in the career decision process (Hall, 1990). Thus the relevant question for the career counselor is, "How can we make the assumption that individuals are making realistic and effective organizational choices?" Underlying this question is the obvious need for programs, procedures, and materials that build a better understanding of the organizations in which we work. The scope of the issues is indeed complex, but such efforts are greatly needed by the career counseling profession. Along with the growing list of career counseling concerns, organizations must also receive our attention.

In the 1990s, referred to as an age of transition, we are experiencing significant changes in organizational structure and, as we observed in the previous chapter, numerous operational changes in the work environment. Advances in technology, accompanied by competition from foreign markets, has led to downsizing and restructuring of the organization. Work itself will be different; many new jobs are being created and others will become obsolete. The counseling issues that evolve from vast changes must receive our attention.

This chapter introduces factors to consider in evaluating an organization and discusses how they can be incorporated into the career counseling process. This information may be used to assist individuals who are choosing an organization and those who are contemplating a career change. Many researchers, including Drucker (1992) and Kanter (1989), predict that the organization of the future will undergo vast changes. Most authorities seem to agree that major changes have begun to occur in management style and structure of the work environment. Middle management has been drastically reduced, and all workers are expected to learn new skills and develop positive attitudes for work in new and changing projects. The implications of these two changes greatly affect the career development of individuals who work in organizations. More specifically, some organizations will not offer predictable career paths and job security as in the past, and most will require continual retraining to develop skills to meet ever-changing demands. Career development in organizations may indeed require greater initiative, interpersonal skills, and the ability to adapt to changing and different work environments.

This chapter begins with a discussion of changing organizations and new concepts in career development. This discussion is followed by a review of changing organizational patterns, including reengineering the corporation and boundaryless organizations. Third, the evolution of career development in organizations is covered. The fourth part covers a variety of counseling programs in organizations. Finally, suggestions are presented for evaluating organizations.

Changing Organizations and New Concepts in Career Development

In the 1970s and 1980s, career development in organizations was related to upward mobility with predictable promotions and job descriptions. An employee aspired to reach the top of the pyramid in an orderly progression of steps. However, numerous forecasts predict the replacement of the pyramidal organizational structure with a "flat" model, in which workers move laterally and use their skills in different projects. In this environment, workers are expected to learn new skills and adapt to the requirements of working with a team. Workers rotate to different projects and are required to initiate objectives that meet goals through innovation and learning. Management coordinates projects and participates directly in achieving these objectives. There appears to be a partnership between workers and managers and between workers and workers. Greater cooperation—sharing skills and mentoring—is encouraged. In sum, structural changes are already under way, accompanied by closer relationships between employees and employers and the reshaping of careers.

Tomasko (1987) suggested that organizations' structure will have the following components: (1) a lean headquarters (limited staff); (2) networks, not conglomerates (workers can be rotated); (3) vertical disintegration and decentralization (no superstructures); (4) staff services that can be sold to others (once an efficient staff has been assembled they can be marketed to other users); (5) expert systems rather than experts (development of computer-based expert systems); and (6) greater human resource planning (switch from personnel administration).

The old models of organizational structure are compared with the new evolving models in Table 14-1. Included among the changes for workers are broader roles and more demanding skill requirements. In the previous models, there were

TABLE 14-1
Changing Organizational Patterns in U.S. Industry

Old Model *Mass production,* *1950s and 1960s*	*New Model* *Flexible decentralization,* *1980s and beyond*
Overall strategy	
• Low cost through vertical integration, mass production, scale economies, long production runs. • Centralized corporate planning; rigid managerial hierarchies. • International sales primarily through exporting and direct investment.	• Low cost with no sacrifice of quality, coupled with substantial flexibility, greater reliance on purchased components and services. • Decentralization of decision making; flatter hierarchies. • Multimode international operations, including nonequity strategic alliances.
Product design and development	
• Internal and hierarchical; in the extreme, a linear pipeline from central corporate research laboratory to development to manufacturing engineering. • Breakthrough innovation the ideal goal.	• Decentralized, with carefully managed division of responsibility among R&D and engineering groups; simultaneous product and process development where possible; greater reliance on suppliers and contract engineering firms. • Incremental innovative and continuous improvement valued.
Production	
• Fixed or hard automation. • Cost control focuses on direct labor. • Outside purchase based on arm's-length, price-based competition; many suppliers. • Off-line or end-of-line quality control. • Fragmentation of individual tasks, each specified in detail; many job classifications. • Shopfloor authority vested in first-line supervisors; sharp separation between labor and management.	• Flexible automation. • With direct costs low, reduction of indirect cost become critical. • Outside purchasing based on price, quality, delivery, technology; fewer suppliers. • Real-time, on-line quality control. • Selective use of work groups; multiskilling, job rotation; few job classifications. • Delegation of shopfloor responsibility and authority to individuals and groups; blurring of boundaries between labor and management encouraged.

(continued)

TABLE 14-1
Changing Organizational Patterns in U.S. Industry   *(continued)*

Old Model *Mass production,* *1950s and 1960s*	New Model *Flexible decentralization,* *1980s and beyond*
Hiring and human relations practices	
• Work force mostly full-time, semiskilled. • Minimal qualifications acceptable. • Layoff and turnover a primary source of flexibility; workers, in the extreme, viewed as a variable cost.	• Smaller core of full-time employees, supplemented with contingent (part-time, temporary, and contract) workers, who can be easily brought in or let go, as a major source of flexibility. • Careful screening of prospective employees for basic and social skills, and trainability. • Core work force viewed as an investment; management attention to quality-of-working life as a means of reducing turnover.
Job ladders	
• Internal labor market; advancement through the ranks via seniority and informal on-the-job training.	• Limited internal labor market; entry or advancement may depend on credentials earned outside the workplace.
Training	
• Minimal for production workers, except for informal on-the-job training. • Specialized training for craft and technical workers.	• Short training sessions as needed for core work force, sometimes motivational, sometimes intended to improve quality control practices or smooth the way for new technology. • Broader skills sought for all workers.

SOURCE: Office of Technology Assessment, U.S. Congress, 1990. *Worker Training: Competing in the New International Economy.* Washington, DC, Government Printing Office.

numerous job classifications that were narrowly focused. Currently, the term *multi-skilling* is used to reflect the notion that many skills are to be learned in a lifelong learning program that may involve formal training as well as on-the-job training and job rotation. As discussed in the previous chapter, organizational training programs cover a variety of skills, including the basic skills of reading, writing, and computation; interpersonal skills; problem-solving skills; and leadership skills.

There is a smaller core of full-time employees that are supplemented with part-time temporary workers or contract workers. The work environment is highly automated, and workers who have learned several skills are used selectively. When necessary, short training programs for the core workers are used to improve quality practices.

The overall strategy of the evolving organizational model is to lower costs of operations and at the same time improve product quality. Organizations have increased the purchase of quality components and services. For example, if some component can be produced better and cheaper elsewhere, the organization will contract for this component with another organization, which may be located in a foreign country.

The fact is, we currently have many multinational organizations that have some or all of their products produced in foreign countries such as Mexico, India, Thailand, South Korea, and many others. In the global web of organizations described in the previous chapter, products become international composites. Reich (1991) clearly illustrates this point.

> When an American buys a Pontiac Le Mans from General Motors, for example, he or she engages unwittingly in an international transaction. Of the $20,000 paid to GM, about $6,000 goes to South Korea for routine labor and assembly operations, $3,500 to Japan for advanced components (engines, transaxles, and electronics), $1,500 to West Germany for styling and design engineering, $800 to Taiwan, Singapore, and Japan for small components, $500 to Britain for advertising and marketing services, and about $100 to Ireland and Barbados for data processing. The rest—less than $8,000—goes to strategists in Detroit, lawyers and bankers in New York, lobbyists in Washington, insurance and health-care workers all over the country, and General Motors shareholders—most of whom live in the United States, but an increasing number of whom are foreign nationals. (p. 113)

Organizations have also decentralized to speed up the process of taking action on relevant issues, such as making transactions with different entities in the manufacture of a Pontiac Le Mans. The emphasis in the evolving models is on simultaneous product and process development to get new products on line. There is a greater reliance on suppliers and contract firms, which has drastically changed working environments in organizations and the skills required of workers.

The implications for career development in restructured organizations are quite significant. Kanter (1989) has suggested that organizations will no longer provide highly structured guidelines for careers; the individual must be more assertive in developing his or her destiny. Self-reliance and the ability to adapt to new and different work circumstances are key factors in career development. The new workplace will require greater flexibility from employees and the ability to do several jobs; that is, in some cases, to be more of a generalist than a specialist. Competency in new skills—and, more important, the ability to anticipate future skills—will make individuals more marketable and secure. Although technical competence is extremely important, people skills and the ability to create synergy within a team will also have high priority.

Reengineering the Corporation

The standard pyramidal organizational structure has been replaced recently by what was earlier referred to as "flat models." New organizational structures are currently being developed from evolving operational changes in order to effectively meet the demands of doing business in a world that is also experiencing rapid and significant changes. There seems to be agreement that the massive bureaucracies of yesterday's organization were not structured to keep up with the fast pace of competitiveness U.S. corporations are facing today.

In bureaucratic organizations, labor was fragmented into specialized work. In reengineered corporations, work is more integrated and has shifted to teams of employees. Instead of one worker performing one particular task, it is now teams of workers as generalists who complete the total process—assembling an automobile, for example.

The following illustration is an example of what influenced leaders to rethink standard organizational procedures. One company discovered that it took seven days to process an order; several steps in the process passed through layers of bureaucracy. It was quickly discovered that the person who took the order could "walk" it through this process in just a few hours, thus delivering the product to the customer in one day instead of seven. In developing organizations today, it is the renewed interest in serving the customer that has caused changes in standard practices.

According to Hammer and Champy (1993), the following "three C's" are the driving force behind the changing organizations: *customers, competition,* and *change.* Today's customers expect products to meet their individual needs and are no longer satisfied with what the seller may have mass-produced to be only "good enough." High-quality goods are what today's more sophisticated consumer wants. *Price, selection,* and *service* are three key words used to describe customer satisfaction.

Reengineering is about "starting over" in organizational design. It is basically a search for new models of work and new approaches to process structure (Hammer & Champy, 1993). The old models of bureaucratic organizations must be rejected along with the assumptions of the past. Focusing on labor, reengineering casts out hierarchical controls and divisions of labor. Focusing on process structures, such as research and development of new products and accounting, reengineering stresses creative use of information technology. Following are two examples that illustrate process structures.

A large U.S. camera manufacturing company discovered that its major rival in Japan had produced a 35mm single-use camera for which they had no competitive offering. Traditionally, the product design process would take 70 weeks to produce a rival camera. Because this time lapse would give its competitor a huge advantage, the corporation decided to reengineer its product-development process. In the old model of development, some groups waited for earlier steps to be completed before their work began (referred to as "fragmented work").

In another design process, parts were designed simultaneously and then integrated. The major problem with this process was that all subsystems did not mesh, and the newly designed product could be significantly delayed. In this division of labor, the groups were not adequately communicating with each other.

To solve the problem, the organization developed a computer-integrated product design database. The database collects each engineer's work and combines it daily for an overall design review by the contributing engineers. Each group or individual can resolve problems immediately, instead of facing weeks or months of delay. The organization was successful in getting out its rival camera in 38 weeks.

Another example of reengineering is in the procurement process. In a large automobile manufacturing plant, the receiving clerk accepted deliveries of products without prior knowledge of an order for them. He had to assume they had been ordered, and he would let the accounts payable office handle any errors. Evidently, there were a large number of them, for the accounts payable department had 500 employees.

The organization reengineered the procurement process that included the accounts payable function. Eventually, the procurement process produced three documents: the purchase order, the receiving document, and the invoice. Now the receiving clerk matches the three and is empowered to order payment. The organization currently has 125 people working in the vendor payment process (Hammer & Champy, 1993).

These two examples introduce changes that organizations are undertaking to successfully compete in the global marketplace. Even more changes are expected in the future. How many individuals will lose their jobs is unknown at this time. A better understanding of current organizational changes should assist counselors in developing a clearer perspective of this revolutionary process, which is expected to continue.

The Boundaryless Organization

To break the chains of organizational structure Ashkenas, Ulrich, Jick, and Kerr (1995) have proposed yet another restructuring philosophy—a boundaryless organization. These corporate leaders have suggested methods of breaking through slow-moving bureaucracies in order to mobilize multiple constituencies for change. Identifying priorities for change includes methods for breaking through four boundaries that block success: *vertical, horizontal, external,* and *geographic.* The questionnaire on the next two pages was developed to determine how far each organization has progressed in breaking through the four boundaries, and the statements on the questionnaire also describe the behavior in boundaryless organizations. The 16 statements define general philosophical operational procedures in each boundary, and each boundary is evaluated in terms of speed, flexibility, integration, and innovation.

The *vertical boundary* in boundaryless organizations has less to do with who has authority and rank and more to do with processing ideas and innovations. Notice that most decisions are made "on the spot" at the workplace, and members operate more informally than in the lockstep methods of bureaucratic organizations.

Horizontal boundaries refer to boundaries between functions found within organizations. For example, engineering, marketing, and accounting were functions that maximized their own goals, sometimes to the exclusion of organizational goals. In contrast to previous organizational structures, resources and innovative ideas would move quickly across functions for more effective product lines. In the new scheme, products would reach markets much more quickly.

The removal of *external boundaries* will hopefully lead to more effective communication with customers, suppliers, and other firms. Suppliers and customers are seen as strategic helpers to improve or develop new products.

Global boundaries have been disappearing quickly as the need grows for globally integrated products and services. Shared experiences across country lines

Questionnaire #1

Stepping Up to the Line: How Boundaryless Is Your Organization?

Instructions: The following 16 statements describe the behavior of boundaryless organizations. Assess the extent to which each statement characterizes your current organization, circling a number from 1 (not true at all) to 5 (very true).

	Speed	Flexibility	Integration	Innovation	Total Score
Vertical boundary	Most decisions are made on the spot by those closest to the work, and they are acted on in hours rather than weeks. 1 2 3 4 5	Managers at all levels routinely take on front-line responsibilities as well as broad strategic assignments. 1 2 3 4 5	Key problems are tack-led by multilevel teams whose members operate with little regard to for-mal rank in the organization. 1 2 3 4 5	New ideas are screened and decided on without fancy overheads and multiple rounds of approvals. 1 2 3 4 5	
Horizontal boundary	New products or services are getting to market at an increasingly fast pace. 1 2 3 4 5	Resources quickly, fre-quently, and effortlessly shift between centers of expertise and operating units. 1 2 3 4 5	Routine work gets done through end-to-end process teams; other work is handled by proj-ect teams drawn from shared centers of experience. 1 2 3 4 5	Ad hoc teams represent-ing various stakeholders spontaneously form to explore new ideas. 1 2 3 4 5	

(continued)

Questionnaire #1   *(continued)*

	Speed	Flexibility	Integration	Innovation	Total Score
External boundary	Customer requests, complaints, and needs are anticipated and responded to in real time. 1 2 3 4 5	Strategic resources and key managers are often "on loan" to customers and suppliers. 1 2 3 4 5	Supplier and customer reps are key players in teams tackling strategic initiatives. 1 2 3 4 5	Suppliers and customers are regular and prolific contributors of new product and process ideas. 1 2 3 4 5	
Geographic boundary	Best practices are disseminated and leveraged quickly across country operations. 1 2 3 4 5	Business leaders rotate regularly between country operations. 1 2 3 4 5	There are standard product platforms, common practices, and shared centers of experience across countries. 1 2 3 4 5	New product ideas are evaluated for viability beyond the country where they emerged. 1 2 3 4 5	
TOTAL SCORE					

SOURCE: From *The Boundaryless Organization: Breaking the Chains of Organizational Structure,* by R. Ashkenas, D. Ulrich, T. Jick, and S. Kerr, pp. 28–29. Copyright 1995 by Jossey-Bass, Inc., Publishers. Reprinted by permission.

and respect for local differences as sources of innovation have erased many of the roadblocks.

In sum, the boundaryless organization provides for significant changes in work procedures and work environments. Supervisors and managers become coaches rather than authority figures to whom workers must pledge their loyalty. The worker is given empowerment to make decisions and offer innovations directly to key people in the vertical structure. This empowerment was unheard of in the old organizational structure.

The process of advancement can come faster in the boundaryless organization, as more workers will have the opportunity to be innovative—by suggesting new product lines or new and different procedures in handling products, for example. There appears to be more freedom of expression and more opportunities to establish relationships with other personnel, customers, and suppliers.

There are several methods a career counselor can use to inform clients about the new organizational climate and the new skills required to function in this ever-changing workplace. The career counselor can provide a good reference, supply a videotape, organize a visit, have workers or managers from nearby organizations give presentations, or introduce these topics in individual and group counseling. The wise career counselor may use a combination of two or more of these suggestions to accomplish this task effectively.

However, as Meister (1994) points out, "The skills and training required of both frontline workers and managers has changed significantly in the past two decades, and *will continue to change in the next*" [italics added for emphasis] (p. vii). What we clearly have are emerging rules, regulations, and procedures that have not been clearly defined in the new, forming organizational structures. We *do know* that lower-level employees are required to take much more responsibility and cooperate more closely. They must somehow learn to better understand how their jobs relate to the organizational mission. Employees will not repeat the same task over and over but will perform varied roles, so they must develop a broader set of skills.

Currently, there are 30 known corporate universities that provide training for their employees, presented in the following list. Career counselors should find this information helpful but should remember that this list may grow in the very near future; thus clients should be directed to inquire about training programs for any organization they consider joining.

Amdahl University
Amdahl Corporation
1250 East Arques Avenue
Sunnyvale, California 94088

American Express Quality University[SM]
American Express Travel Related
   Services Division
20022 North 31st Avenue
Phoenix, Arizona 85027

Apple University
Apple Computer, Inc.
20525 Mariani Avenue
Cupertino, California 95014

Arthur Andersen Center for Professional Development
Arthur Andersen & Co. SC
1405 North Fifth Avenue
St. Charles, Illinois 60174-1264

Banc One College
Banc One Corporation
100 Broad Street
Columbus, Ohio 43215

Bristol-Myers Squibb Pharmaceutical College
Bristol-Myers Squibb Company
P.O. Box 4000
Princeton, New Jersey 08543

CMDS Team University
Computer Management and
    Development Services
P.O. Box 1184
Harrisonburg, Virginia 22801

Corning Education and Training Center
Corning Incorporated
Corning, New York 14831

Dana Customer Training Center
Dana Corporation
8000 Yankee Road
Ottawa Lake, Michigan 49267

Disney University
The Walt Disney Company
P.O. Box 10,000
Lake Buena Vista, Florida 32830-1000

Federal Express Leadership Institute
Federal Express Corporation
3035 Directors Row
Memphis, Tennessee 38131

Fidelity Investments Retail Training Services
Fidelity Investments
82 Devonshire Street
Boston, Massachusetts 02109

First of America Bank Corporation Quality Service University
First of America Bank Corporation
108 East Michigan Avenue
Kalamazoo, Michigan 49007

Ford Heavy Truck University
Ford Motor Company
100 Renaissance Center
Detroit, Michigan 48243

General Electric Management Development Institute
General Electric
Old Albany Post Road
Ossining, New York 10562

Hamburger University
McDonald's Corporation
Ronald Lane
Oak Brook, Illinois 60521

Hart Schaffner & Marx University
Hartmarx Corporation
101 North Wacker Drive
Chicago, Illinois 60606

Iams University
The Iams Company
7250 Poe Avenue
Dayton, Ohio 45414

Skill Dynamics, an IBM Company
IBM
500 Columbus Avenue
Thornwood, New York 10594

Intel University
Intel Corporation
2565 Walsh Avenue
Santa Clara, California 95051

KPMG Peat Marwick Quality Institute
KPMG Peat Marwick
Three Chestnut Ridge Road
Montvale, New Jersey 07645-0435

MBNA Customer College (MBNA America)
MBNA America Bank N.A.
400 Christiana Road
Newark, Delaware 19713

Motorola University
Motorola Inc.
1303 East Algonquin Road
Schaumburg, Illinois 60196

Saturn Training Center
Saturn Corporation
100 Saturn Parkway
Spring Hill, Tennessee 37174

Southern Company College
The Southern Company
64 Perimeter Center East
Atlanta, Georgia 30346

**Sprint University of
  Excellence**SM
Sprint Corporation
2330 Shawnee Mission Parkway
Westwood, Kansas 66205

Sun U
Sun Microsystems
2550 Garcia Avenue
Mountain View, California 94043

Target Stores University
Target Stores (Division of Dayton-
  Hudson Stores)
33 South 6th Street
Minneapolis, Minnesota 55402

Walton Institute
Wal-Mart Stores, Inc.
702 Southwest 8th Street
Bentonville, Arkansas 72716-8074

Xerox Document University
Xerox Corporation
P.O. Box 2000
Leesburg, Virginia 22075

SOURCE: From *Corporate Quality Universities,* by J. C. Meister, pp. 228–231. Copyright 1994 by
Richard D. Irwin, Inc., Publisher. Reprinted by permission.

Evolution of Career
Development in Organizations

Just as each developmental stage of career and human development is accompanied by a set of tasks necessary for completing the transition from one stage to another (see Chapters 2 and 3), stages of career development in organizations consist of tasks and transitions. Stages of development in organizations may be referred to as "employee socialization"; new employees are transformed from outsiders to participating, effective corporate members.

Feldman (1988) proposed a three-stage employee socialization process: *getting in* (the individual presents a realistic picture of self to the organization), *breaking in* (the individual is accepted by peer affiliates and supervisor), and *settling in* (the individual resolves conflicts between work life and home life and within the work environment). Kram (1988) suggested the following four stages, based on individuals' personal needs.

Stage	*Needs*
Establishment	Support and direction
Advancement	Coaching, exposure, and role models
Maintenance	Making a contribution, sharing with others, serving as a mentor
Withdrawal	Letting go of work identity

These models form a frame of reference from which steps in career development can be observed. As individuals progress through stages, they learn new skills, are exposed to previously unknown jobs, become more self-aware, and find more opportunity for self-expression. Within this process, there is an ongoing search for job satisfaction, future career goals, and a direction for lifestyle preferences. Each developmental stage has unique and overlapping needs.

The stages in career development in organizations have been identified as entry, early, mid-career, and late career (Hall, 1990). Some researchers have focused on tasks needed to accomplish each stage in terms of individuals' socioemotional and psychological needs. Although these stages were developed during the old model of organizational structure, they have relevance for individuals who are entering the evolving organizations of today. For example, individuals have expectations of organizations in terms of identifying with the new work force, workplace, and assignment. During the early career stage, workers become oriented to the organization and begin to acquire new skills. In mid-career, individuals are finding that they must balance life roles and find stabilization in their work role. In late career, the individual maintains status in the organization but is also preparing to "let go" of responsibilities.

Entry Stage

Organizations and the counseling profession have given little attention to how and why people choose organizations. Although individual career choice variables have occupied the attention of many researchers in the counseling profession, organizations have been more interested in selection variables to meet personnel needs. Yet both groups have researched the importance of matching individual traits to appropriate work environments. Meanwhile, the individual has little in the way of direction for organizational choice and less in the way of meaningful literature to review.

Work environments researched by Holland (1992) and Dawis (1996), among others, provide individuals with direction in matching their personal styles with occupational environments. Although the attraction of different occupational environments is indeed helpful in career decision making, the task of finding the appropriate work environment has not been fully delineated by organizations or career information materials.

We can only speculate that organizational choice is greatly influenced by an individual's expectations of what the organization is about and what it has to offer. Kotter (1984) compiled the following list of such expectations.

1. A sense of meaning or purpose in the job
2. Personal development opportunities
3. Amount of interesting work
4. The challenge in work
5. Empowered responsibility in the job
6. Recognition and approval for good work
7. The status and prestige in the job
8. The friendliness of people; the congeniality of the work group
9. Salary
10. The amount of structure in the environment
11. The amount of security in the job
12. Advancement opportunities
13. The amount and frequency of feedback and evaluation (p. 501)

These examples of expectations are primarily what make an organization attractive to an individual. The individual's effort in determining the likelihood of a match between an organizational climate and self is a very relevant factor in the selection process. However, final selection is usually based not only on organizational attractiveness but also on the individual's effort to join the organization (Kotter, 1984). Clearly, the career counseling profession needs to place more emphasis on guiding individuals in how to choose an organization. Some suggestions are given later in this chapter.

Early Career Stage

Early career experiences provide individuals with opportunities to establish themselves in organizations. For the beginning worker, it is an exciting time of entering the work force. For those who have been in the work force for some time, the content of their experiences may differ from those of the novice, but the developmental process will be very similar.

During early career, individuals demonstrate their ability to function effectively in organizations. The novice will be naive about the complexities of the work environment and will expend considerable effort in learning how to function within the organizational milieu. Employees who have worked in other organizations will concentrate more on learning the structure of the organization. Some individuals in both groups will move through early career in a few months, whereas others will take considerably longer; some may never become fully established.

The major tasks of early career, compiled by Campbell and Heffernan (1983), are as follows:

1. Become oriented to the organization.
   a. Learn and adhere to regulations and policies.
   b. Learn and display good work habits and attitudes.
   c. Develop harmonious relationships with others in the work environment.
   d. Integrate personal values with organizational values.
2. Learn position responsibilities and demonstrate satisfactory performance.
   a. Acquire new skills as tasks or position change.
   b. Take part in on-the-job training as appropriate.
3. Explore career plans in terms of personal goals and advancement opportunities.
   a. Evaluate current choice of occupation.
   b. Evaluate advancement opportunities.
   c. Develop a plan for advancement or position change.
   d. Consider alternatives in other occupations.
4. Implement plan for advancement or position change.

Although the pathway to a successful early career has pitfalls and stumbling blocks, there is a relatively well-defined direction. For example, building harmonious relationships in the work environment, becoming oriented to organizational rules and regulations, and demonstrating satisfactory performance are common concrete tasks of early career. The individual's personal reaction to advancement opportunities and acceptance of the values associated with organizational goals and peer affiliates are less tangible. Objective indexes (salary, merit pay, regulations, policies, and so on) and subjective indexes (meeting expectations, goal attainment, match between personal needs and organizational needs) are evaluative criteria the individual can use to determine future direction in the organization or change to another work environment.

In the following counseling session, Shanika, who has been with an organization for ten months, reflected a need to withdraw and find another work environment.

Counselor: Yes, we do have some information about the organization you asked about. But first I would like to know about the one you are leaving.

Shanika: As you know, it's a well-known organization, and I was excited about the opportunity of working there. But I don't seem to fit in.

Counselor: Could you be more specific?

Shanika: Well, the job assignment was not what I expected. The recruiter told me I would have a lot of responsibilities and interact with people at high levels, but in actuality there was little of either.

Counselor: So it really wasn't the kind of job you expected?

Shanika: No, I was put off in a side office and no one seemed to pay much attention to me. I did have a few assignments that seemed more like busywork than anything else.

Counselor: Could this have been a part of the training program?

Shanika: Well, partly, but my supervisor hardly ever came around, and when he did, he seemed preoccupied.

In this case, reality shock and unused potential, as described by Hall (1990), were frustrating experiences for Shanika. She had high expectations from what she was told about the job and hoped to be challenged, but she experienced far less. There also appeared to be a communication gap between Shanika and her supervisor.

Wanous (1980) suggested that reality shock and lack of appraisal and appropriate feedback while in early career are major causes of withdrawal from an organization. In such cases, the career counselor must focus on the individual's perception of these two conditions and his or her level of sophistication in appraising them. Some individuals in early career will have unrealistically high expectations, whereas others may indeed find their jobs to be less than challenging and experience poor feedback from their supervisors.

Work environments in organizations also provide a variety of learning experiences that are relevant to career development. For example, exposure to unknown jobs could begin career direction for some members of an organization. In other cases, the individual's work experiences provide a meaningful sense of direction in career development. Developing harmonious relationships, for example, means learning effective communication skills, interpersonal relationships, and general modes of behavior that are easily transferable to other work environments.

Mid-Career

Mid-career has been identified as the middle phase of an individual's work life, with its own set of tasks and social-emotional needs (Hall, 1986). In terms of Super's vocational developmental stages, mid-career may be thought of as the beginning of the maintenance stage, which is characterized by a continual adjustment process to improve working position and situation. In Tiedeman's model of implementation and adjustment, mid-career is characterized by greater self-understanding and identification within the total system of a career field. Feldman (1988) labeled the mid-career experience as "settling in," characterized by resolution of conflicts and conflicting demands within the organization and in personal life. Mid-career is not necessarily age-related; individuals who make career changes may experience several mid-career stages.

The transitional process from early to mid-career has residual effects, as individuals establish themselves in an organization. In early career, the major course of change is the socialization process, but in mid-career, changes are from diversified sources, such as new and different technology, product demand, and changes in the labor market. Developing a perspective of positive growth orientation in organizations and encouraging individuals to adapt to changes is a healthy attitude to promote. Also, finding a meaningful area of contribution is part of the process of establishing an organizational identity. Individuals must distinguish between real barriers (no growth, slow growth, and organizational decline) and perceived barriers (role confusion, poor career identity, nebulous perceptions of career success and direction) that affect their ability to reach personal goals.

The following dialogue demonstrates some sources of organizational and individual plateaus.

Counselor: Tell me how you arrived at the decision to change jobs.
Ying: Well, you know I've been with the company for twelve years, but I don't have the same enthusiasm for the job. I just can't put my finger on it.
Counselor: Is the company doing well financially?
Ying: That's a part of it; no promotion to speak of now.
Counselor: Is this a company policy?
Ying: No. John, a friend of mine, got one the other day. He's a lucky guy. He seems to always be in the right place at the right time.
Counselor: Did you say that John was in your division?
Ying: Yeah, he's always got something going. I don't understand how he does it. He went to this training program and six weeks later there he goes—up the ladder!
Counselor: Tell me more about the training program.
Ying: The company sponsored it. I could have gone, but I don't believe I like that kind of extra work. Besides, it would have interfered with the city golf tournament.

It appears from this conversation that Ying is not willing to be more assertive in his career development. The source of his plateau appears to be primarily a lack of a strong desire to advance. Perhaps Ying felt that he only needed to put in time for the next advancement. In mid-career, individuals may have difficulty balancing commitment to outside activities with intense competitiveness for promotions.

Mercedes, also in mid-career, tells how she discovered a career path in an organization:

Mercedes: I kept looking in the want ads for a career in management after I finished college. I don't know how many times I was turned down. Finally, I took an entry-level job in this company just to tide me over. As I kept looking at the want ads, I also started meeting more people in the company. I began to realize that this wasn't such a bad place after all. But what really did it for me was when I met Linda. When she told what she was doing in the company, I knew I wanted to know more about it. Well, you know the rest of the story. I found out about several jobs I never knew existed and I landed one I like very much. I guess I'll stick around.

In Mercedes' case, she was exposed to occupations and career opportunities she had never known before. An entry-level job provided the means to discover unknown opportunities, and after a successful socialization period, she discovered a career path that appealed to her.

In a more preconceived manner, Al began his career in a high-tech organization with the goal of reaching the management level.

Al: I started out as a computer salesman. After a few years, the company offered me a retail store management job in the eastern part of the state. My wife didn't want to move. That was a tough decision; the kids didn't want to leave either. We spent eight years there, but made the best of it. Meanwhile, I took advantage of every career development opportunity through a variety of training programs. I got good feedback from my supervisor, which really helped. During that process, I became familiar with many aspects of the company. It finally paid off when I was made regional manager a few years ago. It worked out well. I live near a lake now and in a delightful part of the state.

Counselor: What are your future plans?

Al: I like what I'm doing, but I have become more interested in civic organizations and church work.

Counselor: Do you have as strong a commitment to the organization as you once had?

Al: Yes and no. It's different than before. My wife is happy that I devote more time to other things, but I still get excited about the future. I enjoy working with these young kids. They have good management skills, and I enjoy helping them.

As shown in this interview, mid-career is a time when individuals develop an increased awareness of the long-term dimensions of a career and shift their focus from the work world to personal roles. Attention is focused not only on career maintenance but also on life issues, such as parenting, joining civic organizations, and caring for aging parents. Priorities between work roles and personal roles fluctuate according to circumstances. A healthy attitude to promote is a balance of roles, as career and life changes become increasingly connected.

Mid-career is also a time when individuals become more aware of life stages in terms of time spans and begin to view career in terms of implementing future opportunities, as shown in Super's (1977) model of vocational maturity in mid-career. Super's concept of vocational maturity defines life stages and tasks as inter-related in career development. His earlier studies of vocational maturity followed the vocational development of secondary students through adulthood (discussed in Chapter 2). More recently, he has been concerned with establishing the criteria of vocational maturity for older adults in mid-career. The developmental tasks associated with mid-career developed by Super (1977) are provided in Box 14-1.

Super's model for adults has five basic dimensions of developmental tasks, similar to those in his adolescent model. The first dimension, *planfulness* or *time perspective,* focuses on the awareness of life stages and tasks. The second dimension, *exploration,* considers the tasks of exploring both goals and jobs for an eventual established position. *Information,* the third dimension, focuses on tasks dealing with the proper use of occupational sources, options, and outcome probabilities. The fourth dimension, *decision making,* considers skills, principles, and practices in decision making. The final dimension, *reality orientation,* considers the vocationally mature adult as having acquired self-knowledge, consistency, and stabilization in occupational preferences, choices, and work experiences.

The model provides a basis for determining which of the developmental tasks the adult has accomplished. It is useful for counseling because the identified dimensions and substages provide a frame of reference from which counseling procedures can be built. The vocational maturity in the mid-career model should also provide the basis for informative research projects in the future.

Late Career

In late career, the major focus of an individual's life is on activities outside the organization. The individual builds outside interests and begins a gradual detachment from the organization. Activities within the organization may also shift from a power role to a minor role. Super refers to this stage as decline characterized by preretirement considerations. Within the organization, the individual is preparing to "let go" of responsibilities and pass them on to others. One of the major adjustments during late career is learning to accept a reduced work role and changing focus away from a highly involved work identity.

Emotional support in late career comes primarily from peers and particularly from old acquaintances. Moving away from the stress and turmoil associated with younger workers who are striving to move upward, late-career employees identify with peers and rekindle closer attachments to spouses. Having resolved many of the uncertainties of mid-career, they tend to focus on broader issues, such as the organization as a whole and the future of their profession or work (Kram, 1985).

BOX 14-1
A Theoretical Model of Vocational Maturity in Mid-Career

I. Planfulness or time perspective
   A. Past: Exploration
      1. Crystallizing
      2. Specifying
      3. Implementing
   B. Present and immediate future: Establishment
      4. Stabilizing
      5. Consolidation
      6. Advancement
   C. Intermediate future: Maintenance
      7. Holding one's own
      8. Keeping up with developments
      9. Breaking new ground
   D. Distant future: Decline
      10. Tapering off
      11. Preparing for retirement
      12. Retiring
II. Exploration
   E. Querying
      1. Self
         a. In time perspective
         b. In space (organizational geography)
      2. Situation
         a. In time perspective
         b. In space (organizational geography)
   F. Resources (attitudes toward)
      3. Awareness of
      4. Valuation of
   G. Participation (use of resources)
      5. In-house resources (sponsored)
      6. Community resources (sought out)
III. Information
   H. Life stages
      1. Time spans
      2. Characteristics
      3. Developmental tasks
   I. Coping behaviors: Repertoire
      4. Options in coping with vocational development tasks
      5. Appropriateness of options for self-in-situation
   J. Occupational outlets for self-in-situation

(continued)

Box 14-1 *(continued)*

    K. Job outlets for self-in-situation

    L. Implementation: Means of access to opportunities

    M. Outcome probabilities

IV. Decision making

    N. Principles

        1. Knowledge of

        2. Valuation of (utility)

    O. Practice

        3. Use of in past

        4. Use of at present

V. Reality orientation

    P. Self-knowledge

        1. Agreement of self-estimated and measured traits

        2. Agreement of self-estimated and other estimated traits

    Q. Realism

        3. Agreement of self- and employer-evaluated proficiency

        4. Agreement of self- and employer-evaluated prospects

    R. Consistency of occupational preferences

        5. Current

        6. Over time

    S. Crystallization

        7. Clarity of vocational self-concept

        8. Certainty of career goals

    T. Work experience

        9. Floundering versus stabilizing in mid-career

      10. Stabilizing or maintaining versus decline in mid-career

SOURCE: From "Vocational Maturity in Mid-Career," by D. E. Super. In *Vocational Guidance Quarterly,* June 1977, *25*(4), p. 297. Copyright 1977 by American Personnel and Guidance Association. Reprinted by permission.

Implications for Career Guidance Programs

The stages of career development in organizations provide guidelines for career guidance needs and program development. The case for the need to assist individuals in organizational choice and the processes involved in organizational choice has not been clearly delineated by the counseling profession or by organizations. However, the need for counselors to encourage careful evaluations of organizations on the basis of individual needs and realistic expectations has been clearly established. Learning to evaluate and to choose an organization and to establish realistic expectations is an important component of counseling.

The stages of entry in early career are highlighted by the socialization processes that take place in each organization. The individual evaluates self-in-situation by observing the many facets of environmental working conditions, supervisor-worker relations, opportunities for advancement, and congruence with peer affiliates. During the socialization process, the individual needs support in developing a sense of direction in the worker social milieu, where he or she is also being observed and evaluated. Helping individuals assess the complexities associated with organizational life and establish an identity with a new organization are major counseling goals of this stage. For those who decide to withdraw and try again in a different organization, the decision process must include a careful analysis of the reasons for the desired change.

Learning to deal with competition is one of the major social-emotional needs of middle career, when individuals may need to reevaluate their career direction in organizations. As an individual integrates skills and becomes aware of organizational career paths, help in establishing a set of new goals is a relevant counseling objective. The hazards associated with obsolescence and "career plateaus" suggest that counseling programs encourage continuing education and training.

In late career, the individual is preparing to "phase out" or "let go" of major work responsibilities. Super (1990) used the term *decline* to indicate that a minor work role is imminent. Many people may be reluctant to accept the fact that their work life is almost over. For others, this stage has been eagerly anticipated as a time of freedom from work and obligations. Counseling strategies that help all workers prepare for this phasing out should include preretirement and retirement programs. More specifically, career programs should be designed to help individuals assess future needs, as discussed in Chapter 13.

Counseling in Organizations

The career counselor's role in organizations has not been fully determined or evaluated. However, Osipow (1983) has suggested that career counselors can fulfill definite needs in organizations. Some of his suggestions include programs to help individuals: (1) identify hazards in work, (2) identify work styles that match work sites, (3) deal with work-related stress, (4) deal with problems associated with dual-career roles, (5) deal with the effects of transferring to another job, (6) deal with interpersonal problems on the job, (7) deal with job loss, (8) deal with family problems, (9) deal with health care issues, and (10) prepare for retirement. The competencies necessary to meet the counseling needs of individuals in organizations suggest specialized training programs for career counselors.

Hall (1990) has suggested that organizations in general are not fully prepared to manage an individual's career development in terms of resources and information materials. He suggested that individuals should be persuaded to assume responsibility for their own career development and to develop career competencies as opposed to job skills. The key word used by Hall to describe career competencies is *adaptability;* that is, learning to manage changes personally and tolerate the ambiguities of uncertainty. Organizations, on the other hand, should provide a supportive environment for career development by making it possible for individuals to use in-house human-management systems to explore various work roles and to experience various work sites in organizations.

Finally, Hall (1996) warns that a career with an organization may not offer a series of upward moves with steadily increasing incomes, power, status, and security. A sense of affiliation with one organization over a lifetime may be a relic of the past. However, if one redefines a career as a series of lifelong learning and experiences, the idea of career will never die. Thus, the new career contract with an organization may include the *personal agency person* approach, as described in Chapter 12, which requires that individuals adapt quickly, learn continuously, and take responsibility for their own career development.

Employee Assistance Programs

Over the last ten years, organizations have been making greater use of employee assistance programs (EAPs). Recognizing the variety of counseling needs of their employees, especially on such problems as alcoholism and alcohol abuse, organizations are providing at least minimal services. The reasons for the growing popularity of EAPs have been identified by McGowan (1984): (1) increased public sophistication about the interaction of psychological stress, work, and health; (2) limited availability of low-cost community mental health and family services; (3) increased concern about worker productivity and morale; (4) increased labor and management recognition of the value of maintaining a stable work force; and (5) repeated research findings that indicate that 15% to 20% of the working population have personal problems that may interfere with job performance.

Although the functions of EAPs may vary significantly in different organizations, they usually perform one or more of the following functions: (1) identification of employees with problems or potential problems, (2) intake and assessment counseling, (3) case coordination, (4) monitoring, information, and referral to other agencies, and (5) follow-up (Myers, 1984).

Some EAPs are part of the organization's personnel and human resources offices and are used primarily as a referral service. Organizations also contract with EAP consortiums for services. There is a wide range of program service arrangements, and many have specified numbers of visits for counseling assistance. For example, some organizations pay for intake and diagnosis and the employee pays the charges for treatment services. Other organizations may pay for five or six counseling sessions. EAPs are found in every type of organization and are staffed by social workers, psychologists, personnel administrators, educational counselors, alcohol counselors, and occupational program consultants (McGowan, 1984).

In a study of personal problems presented by employees to EAPs, Myers (1984) found the following problems to be most prevalent: (1) alcoholism and alcohol abuse, (2) compulsive gambling, (3) drug abuse, (4) employee theft, (5) family and marital problems, (6) personal finances, (7) legal problems, and (8) mental health problems and stress.

Career counselors should be aware of services available to employees and the specific services offered through EAPs. The evidence suggests that such programs will move increasingly toward comprehensive services while developing new types of programs to meet the special needs of a variety of groups. For example, childcare planning, health care planning for elderly relatives, preretirement counseling, and single-parent groups may be future EAP services.

The Emergence of Outplacement Counseling

The relatively new term *outplacement counseling* is used to define counseling services offered to employees terminated from industrial and governmental organizations and educational institutions. Outplacement counseling grew out of a need to help terminated employees assess individual strengths, evaluate career options, and learn effective job search strategies. The costs of outplacement counseling are absorbed by the terminating employer. There is little reference in the literature to outplacement counseling prior to the mid-1970s. This counseling service is expected to grow rapidly in the next decade.

Knowdell, McDaniels, and Walz (1983) have studied the contributing factors that led to the emergence of outplacement counseling:

1. *Technical change:* The increased use of computers and other technological changes have made many traditional employees obsolete. Robot systems are expected to replace many assembly-line positions in the near future.

2. *Corporate reorganization:* Rapidly growing corporations will have periodic reorganizations and power struggles. Many corporate executives will be terminated.

3. *Economic downturns:* Some organizations will find it necessary to periodically reduce staff because of changing economic conditions.

4. *Takeovers, mergers, and divestitures:* During the 1970s and 1980s, many corporations were merged, and as a result, executive officers were displaced.

5. *Stagnation and burnout:* Organizations have discovered that many executives have become ineffective because of various factors, including burnout, divorce, and identity crisis. These managers have difficulty focusing their energies on a job that they have had for a significant time.

6. *Obsolescence and overspecialization:* Many career specialists have difficulty finding use for their highly specialized skills when they are displaced from some organizations. For example, the space industry drew many workers into engineering positions that were highly specialized. As the aerospace industry declined, many of these individuals were displaced.

7. *Promotion to a level of incompetence:* It has been the practice to promote technically competent workers to managerial positions, but many have not had the necessary managerial skills and competencies. The result has been that many of these individuals are ineffective managers and need to be displaced.

8. *Changing value systems in society:* The stigma of being terminated by an organization is not as great as it once was. Tomasko (1987) suggests that downsizing organizations will result in more terminations of staff and executives.

Organizations have discovered that outplacement counseling provides them with many benefits. For example, most organizations wish to keep a good public and community image, and they have resorted to outplacement counseling to help preserve this image. Also, organizations want to minimize lawsuits and grievance procedures (Drucker, 1992).

COUNSELING STRATEGIES FOR OUTPLACEMENT COUNSELING

Outplacement counseling is designed primarily to assist adults in career transition; therefore, most of the counseling components discussed in this chapter are relevant strategies for outplacement counseling. For example, the terminated employee will be encouraged to identify experiences and skills that are marketable in other organizations. Interest identification and value clarification are major counseling efforts. Decision-making exercises are relevant learning experiences for employees.

Among the special needs of displaced employees are strategies designed to help them deal with their anger and frustration. One useful strategy is helping displaced employees accept their anger as a normal reaction. Providing opportunities to express anger and frustration, individually or in groups, is considered helpful for adults in career transition. Résumé writing and development of interview skills are other needs to be addressed by the career counselor in outplacement counseling (Knowdell, McDaniels, & Walz, 1983).

Retirement Counseling

Throughout this book, career development has been presented as a continuous process over the life span. It is influenced by many variables; some are externally generated (for example, economic crisis and job loss) and others are internally generated (for example, perceptions of retirement), but all are integrated into the continuous career development process. Nevertheless, retirement counseling may often be overlooked as part of the career development process and as a career counseling objective. As we prepare to meet the needs of individuals in the 21st century, the evidence suggests that retirement counseling will be a major component of the career development process. For example, Sheppard and Rix (1977) pointed out that 31 million Americans will be 65 or older by the year 2000 and 52 million will be that age by the year 2030, clearly indicating that over the next decades, there will be significantly more retirees.

To meet this increasing need, organizations have developed preretirement programs (Morrow, 1985) that offer assistance in projecting pensions and other future benefits when the individual reaches retirement age. This type of preretirement program has often been referred to as a "probable inflation" model from which the individual can project his or her financial status at retirement. Other topics often addressed in organizational preretirement programs are optional retirement plans (such as partial retirement, which allows the individual to work part time), time management, financial planning, leisure alternatives, and marital and social relationships (Feldman, 1988).

Some organizations also offer planning services to individuals near retirement age. There are two types: limited and comprehensive. Limited retirement programs typically provide guidance in pension planning, Social Security and Medicare information, health insurance options, and information on retirement benefits at various ages of retirement. Areas included in comprehensive programs commonly include those covered in the limited programs plus the following: maintaining good health, marital/emotional aspects of retirement, leisure activities, relocation advantages and disadvantages, legal concerns (wills, estate planning, inheritance laws), family relations, employment possibilities, and lifestyle change.

Evaluating the Organization

This chapter has presented several suggestions on how we might help others evaluate an organization. These suggestions were offered in different contexts. You will recall that the purpose of this chapter is to build a frame of reference on organizational structure, leadership styles, motivation studies, and other factors that would help us evaluate an organization. We will, therefore, develop a number of key questions to help us in our evaluation. The questions that follow are, in most cases, very general and will be difficult to answer. They are only representative samples and are not inclusive of all that should be learned about organizations during the career search.

Our first question is, Can we evaluate an organization effectively enough to justify including organization evaluations as another step in the career exploration process? This and many of the questions we may pose concerning organizations are similar to those we attempt to answer about occupations. Admittedly, the evaluation of organizations will be difficult and time-consuming, but this is an important challenge; similar problems were faced by the early pioneers in vocational counseling in their quest for occupational information.

At this point, we have little research that might give us guidelines on how to effectively choose an organization (Hall, 1990). Therefore, our attempt here to develop a format and guidelines for evaluating an organization will have to be considered exploratory and tentative. The question of whether we can effectively evaluate individuals who will work in organizations is academic—for, after all, they must do it.

Let us begin by reviewing the major components of this chapter in order to generate questions that may be used as an evaluation format. (The sequence of the major components addressed in an evaluation format need not be the same as that presented in the chapter.) One of our major concerns was organizational structure. This immediately led to a consideration of the authority relationships in the organization. Thus, we will first ask questions concerning the form of structure, policies, and formal control systems, as these appear to be relevant to our observations. We will primarily want to consider how the structure of the organization influences the individual's role. Questions to be answered include the following.

- What is the pattern of the formal organizational structure?
- Where and by whom are organizational decisions made?

- What are the requirements for promotion in the organizational structure?
- What kinds of "movement" are available in the organizational structure?
- How would you characterize the organizational structure?
- Are the social systems compatible with my lifestyle?
- Will the entry point in the organization provide opportunities to meet goals and needs?

Our next major component for consideration is that of leadership style found in the organization. As you will recall, leadership style is a very important determinant of the role of subordinates. Another important point to remember is that some organizations take a contingency approach and determine a leadership style for each situational difference within the organization. In these organizations, there may be combinations of differing approaches to leadership. Questions in this part of the evaluation include the following.

- Do the leaders appear to be task-oriented or people-oriented?
- What is the organization's philosophy or procedure for developing leaders?
- Do the leaders appear to be autocratic or democratic?
- What interaction, if any, takes place between leader and subordinate in the decision-making process?
- How are the goals and needs of the individual considered by the leaders?
- To what degree do leaders involve subordinates in sharing organizational goals?

Our third and final major component is our concern for work motivation in the organization. The evaluation of this component, like others, should be very individualized. Identifying individually developed goals and needs may be considered a prerequisite to evaluating this aspect of the organization. Of major consideration are opportunities for satisfying needs for affiliation, achievement, power, status, recognition, actualization, and so on. In Chapter 2, we discussed Tiedeman and O'Hara's (1963) paradigm of decision making within which goals can be categorized as crystallized, reaffirmed, and integrated. Tiedeman postulated that an individual modifies goals or realigns them to find consistency in the working environment. Thus, the organizational work environment does provide a frame of reference within which certain individual considerations can be made. It is important to find congruency with as many organizational variables as possible to ensure a satisfactory work environment. Even though we may modify personally held goals, we should not be expected to change them completely. Finding a satisfactory work environment, like making an occupational choice, is an individual matter; both choices may be painstakingly difficult to make but are essential in satisfying individually developed goals and needs. Key questions about motivation include the following.

- Will the working environment provide a means of satisfying immediate goals?
- What are the job satisfactions that can be realized in the organizational work environment? Do these opportunities satisfy my goals and needs?
- Will the social interaction satisfy my needs for affiliation?
- Will there be a fulfillment of need for recognition and status with this organization?

- Will my need for achievement be met now and in the future?
- Are there adequate reinforcers provided by the organization and in what form?
- Can I find consistency between the organizational goals and my own values, beliefs, and attitudes?
- Do all persons have equal opportunities for achieving their individual goals?

Now that the questions have been generated, we must turn our attention to how they may be answered. Our first approach is to investigate published materials that may provide us with pertinent information. Because there have been such rapid changes in the last decade, we should attempt to obtain the most recent publication describing a corporation. One way to do this is to request information by using the list of corporate universities reported earlier in this chapter.

We should also consult the local library or career center for published information. However, publications can only partially help us evaluate an organization from the frame of reference we have established. They are generally designed to provide only a broad exposure to corporations and organizations, reporting some operational aspects, management procedures, and institutional structures. Information found on computerized programs may have the same limitations, but, more than likely, they are frequently updated. We should not expect to fulfill our quest for evaluating organizations by using only published materials.

The suggested alternatives are visitation and interview. Career counseling programs have long suggested on-site job visits as valuable experiences during career exploration. From our frame of reference, assessment of occupational climate and other organizational variables are of equal importance. On-site visits may also present the opportunity to interview a variety of individuals within the organization.

When visitations are not practical, the interview becomes our primary method of evaluating an organization. In this context, the interview becomes a "mutual interview" in which the individual not only provides information but also receives information from organizational representatives. Both this method of evaluating an organization and the on-site visit method have obvious limitations. Organizational representatives are hired to project a "good image" of their organizations and may present a biased appraisal of organizational climate. On-site visits may often do the same. Nevertheless, the individual with a good understanding of organizational structure, leadership styles, and organizational behavior will be in a much better position to evaluate an occupation within an organization during the career decision-making process. In the meantime, research is needed to develop more effective methods of evaluating organizational climate.

Summary

1. Organizations are changing from pyramidal structures to "flat models." Workers move laterally and use different skills in different projects.

2. Organizations no longer provide structured guidelines for careers; individuals must be more assertive in developing their destiny.

3. The term *multiskilling* is used to reflect the notion that many skills are to be learned in a lifelong learning program.

4. The role of manager is also going through transformation; a manager is now considered a coach or mentor.

5. In reengineered corporations, work is more integrated and has shifted from individuals to teams of employees.

6. Customers, competition, and change are driving forces behind organizational change of structure.

7. In the boundaryless organization, the following boundaries must be penetrated: vertical, horizontal, external, and geographic.

8. Models of career development stages in organizations offer a frame of reference for observing the steps in career development. Each developmental stage has similar yet unique needs.

9. The major tasks of early career include becoming oriented to the organization, learning position responsibilities and demonstrating satisfactory performance, and implementing plans for advancement or position change.

10. Mid-career is a "settling-in" process characterized by resolutions of conflicts and conflicting demands within the organization and in personal life.

11. In late career, the individual turns his or her attention to activities outside the organization. One of the major adjustments is learning to accept a reduced work role and work identity.

12. Although the relationship between age and job performance is not clear, the type of work seems to be the most important variable.

13. The changing organization will bring about new concepts in career development. The individual must be more assertive in developing his or her destiny. Learning new skills and adapting to new and different work environments are key factors to success.

14. Organizations are using EAPs to meet the personal counseling needs of their employees. The primary functions of EAPs are identifying employees with problems or potential problems, intake and assessment counseling, and referring employees to other agencies for counseling.

15. Outplacement counseling is offered to employees terminated from industrial and governmental organizations and educational institutions. Outplacement counseling evolved from the need to assist terminated employees in assessing individual strengths, evaluating career options, and learning effective job-search strategies.

16. Retirement counseling is also being offered by organizations. Some organizations provide comprehensive programs, including information concerning leisure activities, legal concerns, and lifestyle change.

17. Procedures for evaluating an organization have not been fully developed. Important considerations include authority relationships in the organizations, leadership style found in the organization, and potential opportunities for satisfying individual needs. Publications, visitations, and interviews provide some means for evaluating organizations.

Supplementary Learning Exercises

1. Using the references listed in this chapter and others, develop strategies for evaluating an organization from published material. Explain how these evaluations could be incorporated into career counseling programs.
2. Develop a counseling component that gives an orientation to the realities of working in an organization.
3. Compare a bureaucratic organization structure with a boundaryless structure. Describe the differences in the workplace.
4. What kind of leader would you prefer in an organization? Describe the leader's characteristics and basic assumptions about the role of subordinates. List the reasons you consider leadership an important element to be considered in career counseling programs.
5. Interview an individual who has a leadership position in an organization. Focus your questions on relationships with subordinates. Develop a set of questions that could be used by your counselees to assess leader-subordinate relationships.
6. Interview an individual who has worked in an organization for several years to determine how that individual would evaluate an organization, based on past experience. Compare this evaluation with the questions listed in this chapter for evaluating an organization. What are your conclusions?
7. Develop at least five counseling strategies to meet the needs of individuals in early career. Discuss.
8. Compare the career development of an individual who works for an organization with someone who owns his or her own business. Discuss similarities and differences.
9. Develop a counseling component for individuals who are planning to retire.
10. Project what you consider to be an organization of the future. Focus on the roles of the worker, management, and the work force.

PART FOUR

Career Guidance Programs for Special Populations

CHAPTER FIFTEEN

Special Issues in Career Counseling for Women

A few short years ago, career counseling programs for women consisted of an exploration of the traditionally held working roles. The choices were narrowed to such occupations as clerk, teacher, or nurse. One of the first questions asked was, "How will this job fit into your husband's occupational goal?" The message to women was quite clear: you have but a few jobs to choose from, and your career is secondary to your husband's or other family obligations. Currently, career counselors find that women are rearranging their career priorities—planning for a life-long career in a wide range of occupations has become the highest priority. A career first and marriage maybe or later is the new order of preference for many.

In this post–women's movement era, women continue to look beyond the traditional feminine working roles. The women who embark on this career course will find that a variety of barriers still remain. First, the bias associated with sex-role stereotypes in the working world still exists (McBride, 1990; Wentling, 1992; Wood, 1994). Second, the woman who gives her career development equal status with her husband's will find acceptance of her role personally challenging, with little support from many men and women (Betz & Fitzgerald, 1987). There may also be resistance by male and female counselors in accepting women's changing career priorities (Harway, 1980; Unger & Crawford, 1992). In essence, there continues to be resistance in our society—albeit somewhat less since the women's movement—to the role of women in the working world from men and women at all levels of the work force, from managers and professionals to blue-collar workers. A number of professional counselors and organized groups have recommended the development of counseling programs to assist women who are strongly committed to pursuing a full-time career. However, for many other women who are unable to perceive themselves as career-oriented but who wish to break away from traditional feminine roles, the need for counseling programs may be even greater. For these women, the consideration of a lifelong career is entirely new and conflicts with the concepts developed in early socialization; that is, women were primarily "socialized" to see themselves as homemakers while men pursued careers (Smith, Smith, Stroup, & Ballard, 1982; Betz, 1994a). The rapidly changing values regarding traditional sex roles in the United States suggest that a number of additional factors influence the type and magnitude of critical career decisions women are currently making. For example, the decline of motherhood as a full-time occupation is becoming increasingly prevalent in our society ("Chipping Away," 1991; "Charting the Projections," 1995); consequently, women feel freer to consider full-time careers outside the home. In addition, families' current financial needs have made it necessary for both husband and wife to work. Also, jobs traditionally allocated to men are now available to women (U.S. Department of Labor, 1992-1993). Finally, research has shown that we have not adequately addressed the role of women in our work force or the special needs of women who work (Gianakos & Subick, 1986; Siltanen, 1994).

In this chapter, we discuss women's special career counseling needs and describe several career counseling components. The chapter is divided into six sections: the first part reviews women's career development patterns; the second part identifies and discusses special career counseling needs; career counseling and career counseling programs for girls and women are discussed in the third part; the fourth part describes some career counseling components that meet the special needs identified in part two; counseling bias is discussed in the fifth part; and finally issues of gender bias and gender fairness in interest assessment are reviewed.

The term *gender role* will be used from here on instead of the more familiar *sex role*. Although many researchers have used these terms synonymously, Money (1982) pointed out that an individual's sex role is a component of his or her gender role; the sex roles are physiological components of sex-determining role sets for men and women. The more inclusive term, *gender role,* is composed of nonphysiological components of sex, including behaviors, expectations, and roles defined by society as masculine, feminine, or androgynous (Unger, 1979).

Career Development Theories and Women

Women's career development has received only cursory attention by career development theorists (Osipow, 1983). The need for career development theories free of gender-role stereotyping has been suggested by Betz and Fitzgerald (1987). Super (1990) is one of the major career development theorists (discussed in Chapter 2) who addressed women's career development patterns, which he classified into seven categories: stable homemaking, conventional, stable working, double track, interrupted, unstable, and multiple trial. Still significant today is Super's double-track career pattern, which establishes homemaking as a second career. Conflicts between homemaking and career remain a concern that must be addressed in career counseling programs (Wilcox-Matthew & Minor, 1989).

Ginzberg (1966) considered three lifestyle dimensions for women that may be used in career counseling approaches: (1) *traditional* (homemaker-oriented), (2) *transitional* (more emphasis on home than on job), and (3) *innovative* (giving equal emphasis to job and home). These dimensions seem to represent realistic lifestyles found among today's working women, with the addition of a *career-oriented* dimension—one in which the highest priority is given to the development of a career. It is difficult for many women to move toward the innovative dimension, primarily because of psychological barriers; some women may be reluctant to become more career-oriented for fear of losing the stereotypical female identity so readily accepted by our society. For many, the loss of this identity is indeed threatening and deters a serious focus on career development.

According to Betz and Fitzgerald (1987), occupational choices for women are greatly influenced by home and family responsibilities. They suggest that social class, plus attitudes generated by marriage, financial resources, educational level, and general cultural values of past and immediate families, are major determinants influencing occupational choice. Furthermore, women's occupational choices are not made independently of other variables in our society. Women do indeed have special needs that must be addressed in career counseling programs.

Zytowski (1969) denoted the vocational development patterns of women as (1) mild vocational, (2) moderate vocational, and (3) unusual vocational. These patterns closely follow the lifestyle dimensions developed by Ginzberg in that each category is progressively more occupationally oriented. According to Zytowski, the modal life role for women in our society is that of homemaker. Through vocational participation, a woman may change her modal lifestyle. Patterns of vocational participation for women are determined by age at entry, the length of time the woman works, and the type of work undertaken. Further determinants of vocational patterns for women are individual motivation, ability, and environmental circumstances, such as financial needs (Wolfson, 1972). Of significance to our considerations is that women do differ and have special needs to be included in career development programs.

Sanguiliano (1978) emphasized the theme of different and special needs of women. Although she agreed that women do follow a serial life pattern, there are unique times of hibernation, renewal, postponement, and actualization. She contended that life-stage theorists such as Erikson (1950), Havighurst (1953), Kohlberg (1973), and Levinson (1980) reveal significant shortcomings in describing the development of women. Stage theorists do not account for the unexpected, critical events and the myriad of unusual influences that shape feminine life patterns. Sanguiliano suggested that a woman's life cycle does not follow a rigid progression of developmental tasks but is similar to a sine curve representing the impact of unique experiences and critical events.

According to Sanguiliano, the formulation of self-identity is one of the fundamental differences between men's and women's developmental patterns. Women's self-identification is significantly delayed because of the conflicting expectations ascribed to feminine identity. Men learn their masculinity early and are better prepared to adapt to changes; but women do not have comparable, clearly defined boundaries and images of appropriate gender-linked roles. Men are reinforced in their efforts to attain clearly defined masculine roles; women depend on loosely defined feminine roles and have few support systems.

Sanguiliano's principal argument is that women's individual life patterns require special consideration. Attention should focus on unique paths women take to break away from gender-role stereotyping. Individual progress toward self-identity is germane to Sanguiliano's approach to determining counseling components for women.

Spencer (1982) supported Sanguiliano's denial that women's development follows the rigid progression suggested by life-stage theorists. She contended that feminine developmental tasks are unlike masculine tasks and that women follow unique patterns of development. Using Levinson's life-cycle sequence and transitional periods of men discussed in Chapter 16, Spencer compared women's development to the men's model: early transitions (ages 17–28), age-30 transitions (ages 28–39), midlife transitions (ages 39–45), and late-adult transitions (ages 65–?).

The early transitional period, the time when one reappraises existing structures, begins the search for personal identity (Erikson, 1950; Levinson, Darrow, Klein, Levinson, & McKee, 1978). Spencer contended that separating from the parental home is more difficult for the young woman than for the young man; women receive less encouragement and experience less social pressure to become independent. Furthermore, women do not have adequate support systems to encourage self-expression in a society that presents conflicting messages. In essence, women have a more difficult time developing self-identity.

During the age-30 transitions, marital conflicts are prevalent in women who look for new directions. For example, women who want to spend time in career development often find difficulty forming egalitarian marital relationships. The frustrations women face in dual family/career commitment are often misunderstood. On one hand, women are socialized to think of themselves only as homemakers; but on the other hand, they have a strong need to express themselves in a career. Women have to struggle to realize that greater freedom and satisfaction are options.

Midlife transitions are periods of reappraising the past and of continuing the search for meaning in life. This period is marked by an increased awareness that some long-held beliefs may not be valid. For women, successful appraisal of life accomplishments is usually reflected in what others (husband and children) have done (Troll, Israel, & Israel, 1977). Therefore, when their children leave home, women have difficulty creating a new identity and a new life purpose.

The late-adult transition is a continued reappraisal of self in society. According to Spencer, the primary task of this period is to gain a sense of integrity in one's life. Spencer (1982) concluded that women rarely achieve the developmental goal of ego autonomy—"They are doomed from the start" (p. 87).

Spencer and Sanguiliano suggested that women have different developmental patterns than men: (1) women experience intense role confusion early in their development; (2) women are more inhibited in their self-expression; (3) women tend to delay their career aspirations in lieu of family responsibilities; and (4) women's developmental patterns are more individualized. These unique and individualized developmental patterns may present significant problems in career decision making. Career counselors should carefully consider self-concept development and value assessment in career decision-making programs for women.

Chusmir (1983) identified characteristics and background traits of women in nontraditional vocations (construction trades, skilled crafts, technical fields, science, law, engineering, and medicine). He suggested that women who choose nontraditional occupations have personality characteristics usually attributed to men. For example, they tend to be more autonomous, active, dominant, individualistic, intellectual, and psychologically male-identified than do women who choose traditional careers (social work, nursing, teaching, and office work). Motivational characteristics of women who choose nontraditional occupations are also similar to those attributed to men: achievement orientation, status seeking, and strong need for self-regard and recognition. Examples of background traits of women in nontraditional occupations are better education, better mental health, fewer or no children, eldest or only child, postponed marriages, fathers who were younger and in management roles, well-educated fathers, and enrollment in women's studies courses.

Chusmir suggested that personality and motivational traits of women who choose nontraditional occupations are formed by the time they are teenagers. Clearly, the research focuses on the importance of feminine early developmental patterns. Intervention strategies designed to expand occupational choice for girls should be introduced during elementary school years.

In each of the career developmental patterns of women briefly reviewed, emphasis was placed on the woman's role as homemaker, and the special needs of women interested in developing careers were stressed. Women who give at least equal emphasis to job and home were considered "innovative" (Ginzberg, 1966) or "unusual" (Zytowski, 1969) because they differed in lifestyle from the "typical" homemaker. However, these terms are very misleading today, as there are increasing numbers of women in the work force and more are expected in the future (U.S. Department of Labor, 1992-1993). Even more important are the considerations we should give to women as individuals, free of gender-role stereotyping, in an expanding job market.

The general developmental patterns of women suggest that a woman's life cycle does not follow life-stage models developed from the study of men. Compared with men, self-identity is slower to develop, primarily as a result of gender-role stereotyping. Our society accords a secondary priority to career choice as well as to career development for women. Women's difficulty with career decision making is closely associated with role confusion and the lack of role models and support systems.

More recently, career development theorists have given some attention to women's career development. For example, some gender issues are addressed in the individual developmental constructs in the theory of work adjustment and person-environment-correspondence counseling (Dawis, 1996) discussed in Chapter 2. Although gender is not considered as a defining variable in the theory, it becomes important when it influences work skills and work needs that have not been identified. The point here is that women have not been given the opportunity equivalent to men to develop a full range of work skills required in the world of work. Therefore, what reinforces women in a number of work environments is unknown. However, this theory considers gender as an important "background" variable that may account for personality structure, style, and adjustment style of workers. Therefore, when more gender variables are identified in the world of work, more emphasis can be given to gender as a defining variable.

Gottfredson (1996) makes an interesting observation about gender concerning group differences, for instance, how gender, ethnic, and social groups and how group membership per se might shape career aspirations (see Chapter 2). Gottfredson asserts that group-based identities influence and shape one's preference for place and fit in the social order. Moreover, the theory of circumscription and compromise "assumes that most young people orient to their own gender and social class when contemplating careers" (p. 202). Gottfredson stresses that orientation to sex roles in early childhood (ages 6 to 8) results in a concern for individuals to do what is considered appropriate for one's sex, particularly in vocational aspirations.

In the theory of sociological perspectives on work and career development discussed in Chapter 2, Hotchkiss and Borow (1996) suggest that long-standing social inequities constrain females' work-related achievements. Although there is some evidence of decline in gender segregation of occupations (Roos & Jones, 1993), there is much more to be done in the way of reducing gender barriers to the work world.

In an outstanding article, Fitzgerald and Betz (1994) suggest that women's career development is affected by discrimination and sexual harassment, cultural constraints as occupational gender stereotypes, and gender-role socialization, in addition to the "motherhood mandate." One point well taken is that women's abilities are not being fully utilized both in education and in occupations; thus, many women are functioning in jobs for which they are overqualified. Fitzgerald and Betz suggest that each career development theory should determine its applicability to particular groups, such as gender and ethnic groups. Second, information should be given about the utility of a theory for groups or how people's characteristics affect the predictive validity of a theory. Third, each theory should be scrutinized as to its conceptualization of structural and cultural factors and how they relate to important theory variables. Using structural and cultural factors as a measure of a theory's effectiveness will provide new perspectives for career theories, particularly for greater insights into women's career development.

Identifying Women's Special Needs

Our society has seen a significant number of women go to work in nontraditional jobs during times of emergency. For example, during World War II, women assumed many jobs that were then considered reserved for men. The concept of the working role of women during this time was well exemplified in the then-popular song, "Rosie the Riveter," as most people saw the situation of women in nontraditional jobs as somewhat humorous and temporary. The trend today is toward equalization of job opportunities, particularly those jobs that were predominantly held by men. That the number of women working in skilled occupations (as defined in the Bureau of Census Classifications) has significantly increased underscores that attitudes toward working women are changing.

The emerging trend toward equalization suggests a number of special needs for women. One need is for information resources about nontraditional occupations for women. To make a wider range of choices available to women, several federal agencies have sponsored programs to inform them of nontraditional jobs. These programs will be expanded into public schools; two- and four-year colleges; and relevant federal, state, and local community agencies.

One program, Women in Nontraditional Careers (WINC) (Alexander, 1985), is designed to help women consider nontraditional occupations. This model consists of three major components: (1) training of school staff to alert them to the need for broadly based career planning and how occupational choice affects lifetime earnings, (2) classroom instruction that provides students with information about the labor market and other topics that is free of gender bias, and (3) the establishment of nontraditional job exploration in the community. In addition, the program activities include women working with other women who are employed in nontraditional occupations.

Federal Law Requirements

Women need to be made aware of the federal laws under Title VII of the Civil Rights Act of 1964 and Title IX of the Educational Amendments of 1972. These laws prohibit discrimination on the basis of gender in employment, payment received for work, and educational opportunities, and they assist women in attaining equal opportunity in these three important areas. Title VII applies to all employers with 15 or more employees, employment agencies, and labor organizations. Discrimination is prohibited against employees on the basis of race, color, religion, gender, or national origin. Policy on discrimination applies to hiring, upgrading, promotion, salaries, fringe benefits, training, and all other terms and conditions of employment. Title IX refers to all educational agencies and institutions receiving federal assistance. This law prohibits discrimination against students and employees on the basis of gender, including the admission and recruitment of students, the denial or differential provision of any aid, benefit, or service in an academic, extracurricular, research, occupational, or other educational program or activity, as well as in any term, condition, or privilege of employment (including hiring, upgrading, promotion, salaries, fringe benefits, and training).

Career Information

Through affirmative action and other programs, women are more frequently considered for leadership positions previously reserved for men. However, the number of women in doctoral training programs and in certain scientific fields has remained relatively out of proportion (Betz & Fitzgerald, 1987). Clearly, women are in need of career information that encourages them to consider a wide variety of careers—especially those previously pursued only by men. Women who have the interest and ability to pursue assertive, managerial careers need direction and encouragement, as do women who are interested in skilled labor and technical occupations.

Dual Roles

Economic conditions have greatly contributed to an increase in the number of married women who are employed full time. For many families, it has been essential that both parents work to fulfill financial responsibilities. Today's husband and wife consider their work efforts a joint venture. The family stereotype of homemaking mother and breadwinning father is no longer typical. In greater numbers, women are assuming a dual role of homemaker and worker. Managing both roles has caused conflicts for many women, particularly in meeting their own individual needs (Hansen, 1990). Although the dual role of working women has found greater acceptance, personal contradictions that need clarification persist in the working woman's life (Nadelson & Nadelson, 1982). Today's women need to more fully value an independent lifestyle and clarify their self-concepts. More specifically, counseling should help women identify their abilities and skills and provide them with the same opportunities given to men in making use of their talents in our society.

An Integrative Life Planning (ILP) model by Hansen (1996) incorporates career development, life transitions, gender-role socialization, and social change. This model is designed to expand career options for both men and women because fragmented approaches to development and life roles place limits on decisions clients will make in their lifetime. A more integrative approach to career development recognizes that an individual's total development includes a broad spectrum of domains. The impact of decisions on lifestyle, including relationships, is a major part of a more comprehensive view of development.

As women make a greater commitment to education and training, their willingness to accept full responsibility for household tasks, including childrearing, is decreasing (Benin & Agostinelli, 1988). The increasing pressure for an equitable division of household responsibilities focuses on what men actually do in the home. Coleman (1988) found that men spend over 50% of their time in play with their children, whereas women spend only 10% of their time in this way. However, some evidence suggests that women are frequently reluctant to delegate household tasks to men (Bernardo, Shehan, & Leslie, 1987). See Chapter 17 for more information on dual-career families.

Child Care

Although this topic is considered relevant for both parents, research has shown that mothers shoulder the greater burden with regard to child care issues (Lott, 1994). The enormity of child care problems is evidenced by the fact that the percentage of married women with children under the age of 6 has increased from 12% in 1950 to 57% in 1992 (National Commission on Children, 1993). Child care providers include caretakers in the home, day care centers, adult members of the household, older siblings, and no provider at all—some children are left to look after themselves. More recently, some organizations have provided on-site day care centers (Gilbert, 1993; see Chapter 17 for more information on child care sites).

Many work, family, and personal difficulties for women evolve from child care problems. Examples of work-related problems are arriving late for work, leaving early from work, scheduling problems, missing work, and having difficulty concentrating on work tasks. Family-related problems primarily focus on family conflicts over child care arrangements. Personal problems usually involve stress and the conflict that results between the need to achieve in a work situation and the need to be a responsible parent. Some women may decide not to take a promotion because the new position may interfere with child care. Others may decide not to return to work after childbirth because child care problems cannot be resolved to their satisfaction. The problems of child care are exacerbated for workers who have less money to budget for it (Fernandez, 1986).

Working Environment

The working environment is relatively unknown to women who have considered themselves primarily homemakers. Because a significant number of women will work outside the home (U.S. Department of Labor, 1992-1993), programs that inform women about what typically can be expected in work settings are needed more than ever. Employee expectations, effective communication with peers and supervisors, promotional policies, and authority relationships are examples of items requiring clarification.

Needs of Displaced Homemakers

This group is usually identified as comprising women over the age of 35 who have been out of the labor force for an extended period of time. They are ineligible for unemployment insurance and do not qualify for various government aid programs, such as Aid to Families with Dependent Children (AFDC). Many of these women may have to turn to public support for assistance (Lott, 1994). Because of their previous lifestyle, many displaced homemakers lack job search skills and are completely unprepared for entry into an occupation.

Needs of Divorced Women

Similarly, divorced women are often unprepared for self-sufficiency and often have children who depend on them. Not only are many forced to seek employment, but they also have the sole responsibility for rearing their children. This new lifestyle requires balancing the responsibilities of parenthood and home management with the responsibilities of work. In addition to the recommendations for the displaced homemaker, other possible counseling components may cover day care centers, transportation information, and quick, efficient methods of food preparation. These women must learn to set priorities to effectively meet both home and employment responsibilities.

Internal Restrictions

Of major importance are the internal restrictions women experience when considering full-time careers or nontraditional roles. To project oneself into an occupational environment dominated by men may indeed be a difficult task for many women who grew up under the influence of traditional gender stereotyping of occupations. Women who have considered only traditional jobs such as teacher, nurse, or clerical worker find the contemplation of many other careers foreign to them. On one hand, early socialization has instilled identification with certain society-sanctioned gender roles; on the other hand, women are being told to break away from the traditional gender role. Indeed, many find this dichotomy too great to bear. In general, some women lack confidence and self-esteem, which tends to limit their career choices. There is also evidence that gender-role orientation adversely affects achievement motivation (Frenza, 1982; Eccles, 1987; Wood, 1994).

Need for Leadership Roles

Other inhibiting barriers prevent women from reaching their full potential in the world of work. Epstein (1980) suggested that our cultural heritage does not encourage women to excel in business-related occupations. In our culture, the model for a business manager is typically masculine (Lindsey, 1990). Through social conditioning, men are perceived as leaders and better able to carry out demanding tasks. Women who have taken on leadership roles are often regarded merely as tokens, and their abilities and skills are questioned, even by their colleagues. Women are often made to feel like outsiders in organizations and are ostracized by the existing formal and informal structures. Wood (1994) contends that women need more experience (access to formal and informal structure) and exposure to feminine leadership role models to encourage a greater degree of motivation to attain leadership positions.

The Glass Ceiling

The so-called glass ceiling is an invisible barrier that consists of subtle attitudes and prejudices that have blocked women and minorities from ascending the corporate ladder. For example, one method used to block women and minorities from top-level corporate jobs is to insist that senior executives have 25 years' experience.

Another method used to exclude women is to groom them for either lower-level positions or for those positions not on track for senior-level positions. Garland (1991) reported that white males most often prefer mentoring other white males. *Nations Business* magazine ("Chipping Away," 1991) pointed out that although women and minorities account for 50% of the nation's work force, only 5% hold senior-level management positions. According to this same source, women are chipping away at the glass ceiling and will have more success in industries where the customer base is women. Through affirmative action policies, the government is also attempting to break the glass ceiling (U.S. Department of Labor, Bureau of Labor Statistics, 1991).

The Trials and Tribulations of Women Who Want to Climb to the Top

Wentling (1992) suggested that the following actions are necessary for women to attain senior-level management positions:

1. *Educational credentials:* Obtain at least an MBA or equivalent.
2. *Hard work:* Be ready and willing to work at least 54 hours per week at the office and take work home.
3. *Mentors:* Find and network with the most qualified mentor.
4. *Interpersonal/people skills:* Female executives have several common characteristics, including the ability to manage people.
5. *Demonstrate competency on the job:* Expect to be more thoroughly evaluated and screened than men.
6. *Willingness to take risks:* Be innovative and initiate projects.

Women and Entrepreneurship

In 1992, women owned 5.4 million businesses, and in 1990, they employed 11 million people. Also, women own 30% of *small businesses,* and it is predicted that their share will increase to 40–50% by the year 2000 (Aburdene & Naisbitt, 1993). In spite of substantial gains in business ownership and the increases projected for the future, women entrepreneurs face barriers not usually encountered by men. As suggested by Gould and Parzen (1990), (1) women lack socialization to entrepreneurship in the home and society; (2) women have been excluded from business networks; (3) women lack capital and information on how to obtain it; (4) women suffer from discriminatory attitudes of lenders; (5) women are often ostracized in the business community because of gender stereotypes, which in turn influences expectations of women as entrepreneurs.

Clearly, women need more assistance in learning about pathways and barriers to owning their own business. However, a very encouraging fact is that so many women have successfully ventured into the world of entrepreneurship. Federal support programs include the Women's Business Ownership Program, the Women's

Network for Entrepreneurial Training (a national training program), and the Women's Business Ownership Act of 1988, which offers incentive loans.

Sexual Harassment

The issue of sexual harassment has been well documented in the workplace for several years. For example, in 1980 the Working Women's Institute concluded that sexual harassment was the single most widespread occupational hazard women face in the work force (Lott, 1994). The attention given to sexual harassment was dramatically increased by (1) the 1991 Senate hearings involving Supreme Court nominee Clarence Thomas and his accuser, Anita Hill; and (2) the U.S. Navy Tailhook scandal involving the mistreatment of women by U.S. Navy personnel.

What constitutes sexual harassment has been the central issue of a number of recent court cases. The "reasonable woman" standard was applied as the appropriate legal criterion for determining whether sexual harassment had occurred: if a reasonable woman would consider behavior offensive even though a man would not, the court would rule that sexual harassment had occurred (Fitzgerald & Ormerod, 1991).

Other factors used to determine when a behavior is considered offensive are: (1) if the behavior was judged extreme, (2) if the victim was responsible for what happened, (3) if the perpetrator was a direct supervisor of the victim, and (4) if there was significant frequency of occurrence (Kail & Cavanaugh, 1996).

In a *Newsweek* poll in October 1992 (Lott, 1994), 21% of women respondents claimed they had been harassed, and 42% said they knew someone who had. Some descriptions of harassment are sexual remarks, suggestive looks, deliberate touching, pressure for dates, letters and calls, pressure for sexual favors, and actual or attempted rape.

Beginning over a decade ago, many large organizations developed policies, procedures, and programs to define sexual harassment, to decide what to do about it, and to determine how to prevent it. In June 1992, 81% of Fortune 500 companies offered their employees sensitivity training programs designed to make them more aware of acts that constitute sexual harassment (Lott, 1994).

Lesbian Women

There appears to be a growing trend for more open discussion about the effects of sexual orientation on career development. Kronenberger (1991) reported that more lesbian women and gay men are coming out of the closet and discussing issues they face, especially in the workplace. In fact, gay men and lesbian women are creating support networks, educating co-workers, and pushing for reforms for benefits and freedom to move up the career ladder. However, there are many homosexuals who don't identify with being gay and find it easier to assimilate into a heterosexual workplace. There is evidence to suggest that more companies are supporting gay associations and networks, including Xerox, AT&T, Lockheed,

RAND Corporation, Hewlett Packard, Sun Microsystems, U.S. West Communications, and Levi Strauss. Many of these organizations have looked on gay men and lesbian women as another diverse group in the work force and are dealing with this group just as they do multiethnic groups; they have added a sexual-orientation component to diversity training programs.

However, the negative bias against homosexuals can be very intense (Goleman, 1990). For example, anti-gay legislation was introduced in two states in the fall of 1992 and passed in one of them. On the other hand, it appears that gay men and lesbian women will no longer be excluded from the armed services (Barry & Glick, 1992). The issues surrounding homosexuality in general and its effect on career development and bias in the workplace are far from being settled.

In the meantime, there is some evidence that lesbian women are more satisfied with their career choices than are gay men and heterosexual men and women (Hetherington & Orzek, 1989). Nevertheless, research is so meager that most conclusions about adaptability in the workplace, self-efficacy, career choice, and career development are only tentative at best. (Further discussion on this subject can be found in Chapter 16.)

Implications for Career Counseling

Thus far, we have identified or implied several career counseling needs for women. More specifically, these needs include (1) job search skills, (2) occupational information, (3) self-concept clarification, (4) strategies and role models for managing dual roles—homemaker and worker, (5) assertiveness training, (6) information on a variety of working environments, (7) lifestyle clarification, and (8) development toward a value of independence. These needs suggest specially designed programs for women in terms of program content, techniques, and subject matter. For example, many job search skills are universal for all job seekers, but women have a special need to develop strategies for negating employer discrimination. Other examples of specific programming needs include providing a more complete understanding of job search techniques, teaching women to use occupational information, encouraging women to evaluate a wide range of careers, and alerting them to the stereotyping of female workers. Programs designed to assist women with managing dual roles, child care, and lifestyle skills may be accomplished in a variety of counseling settings, including groups of women or with their spouses.

Components for Counseling Women

In the next section of this chapter, four counseling components that partially meet these needs are presented. These components can also be combined with the counseling components of the previous chapter to provide more options for meeting women's special needs. For example, occupational information on nontraditional jobs can be obtained through the occupational information component of the previous chapter and combined with suggested technique options and specific tasks developed here (as shown in Table 15-1). The suggested technique options do not exhaust all possible methods of accomplishing the specific tasks. Following is a brief explanation of each component.

Component I—Job Search Skills

A specially designed job search skills component is recommended to help women deal with potentially discriminatory practices. The primary purpose of this component is to prepare women to apply for nontraditional jobs, although the skills learned may be applied to any job search. The point is that women need special assistance with preparing applications for jobs that are primarily reserved for men. Displaced homemakers especially need this component because most have little experience in applying for a job. To be effective, women must not only learn the general skills needed for interviewing and résumé writing, they must also be prepared to deal with discriminatory practices associated with gender-role stereotyping. For example, in typical gender-role stereotyping, the woman is considered best suited as a homemaker and mother. When women work, it is assumed to be a necessity, as the man is perceived to be the primary breadwinner. Thus, men are typified as leaders who make decisions; women are seen as passive, cooperative, and unable to rise to leadership positions in the world of work. In essence, traditional gender-role stereotyping implies that women are generally inferior in marital roles and work roles (Reschke & Knierim, 1987).

The technique options suggested to accomplish this component are workshops, group or individual counseling, and resource exploration. As with other components, combinations of the technique options are recommended. Examples of materials that may be used to develop this component are found in Chapter 11. Three representative resources that may be used to build resource exploration and other parts of the program are *Exercises for the Résumé Workshop: A Program for Women, Résumé Preparation Manual—A Step-by-Step Guide for Women*, and *Launching Your Career* (all available from Catalyst, 220 Park Avenue South, New York, NY 10003: Fax 212-477-4252).

Component II—Working Climate

The purpose of this component is to prepare women for typical gender-role stereotyping found in many working environments. Unfortunately, gender-role stereotyping has been prevalent in many sectors of our society. For example, advertising portrays women as being very dependent and almost helpless (Comstock, with Paik, 1991; Wood, 1994). There is also evidence of stereotyping in textbooks and in teachers' interactions with students (Basow, 1992). One of the most serious problems facing working women is the large gap in earning power between men and women. Fundamental to this problem are sex-based wage discrimination and occupational sex segregation (Lott, 1994). It appears that women continue to select

TABLE 15-1
Components for Counseling Women

Strategy component	Technique options	Specific tasks
I. Job search skills	1. Workshop 2. Group and/or individual counseling 3. Resource exploration	1. Evaluate and clarify purpose of the interview. 2. Require that each counselee demonstrate interview skills. 3. Evaluate and clarify purpose of résumé. 4. Require that each counselee demonstrate résumé preparation skills. 5. Clarify potential discriminatory employment practices. 6. Clarify federal laws that prohibit discrimination on the basis of gender in employment, pay, and education. 7. Clarify possible strategies for combating employer discrimination.
II. Working climate	1. Workshop 2. Group and/or individual counseling 3. Role-clarification exercises	1. Identify typical stereotyping of female workers by peer affiliates. 2. Clarify competitive nature of working environment. 3. Identify and clarify interpersonal skills associated with peer affiliates. 4. Identify and clarify interpersonal skills associated with supervisors. 5. Increase understanding of work setting.
III. Lifestyle skills	1. Workshop 2. Group and/or individual counseling 3. Role-clarification exercises	1. Clarify goals and specific needs associated with potential career. 2. Identify methods of jointly meeting family and personal needs. 3. Identify and require that each counselee demonstrate an understanding of the dynamics associated with dual careers. 4. Identify and require that each counselee demonstrate assertiveness skills. 5. Identify and clarify the implications of early socialization and needs for establishing a value of independence. 6. Clarify the concept of implementing one's self-concept into a career.
IV. Support and follow-up	1. Group and/or individual counseling support 2. Follow-up visits	1. Identify and clarify problems associated with working environment. 2. Identify and clarify problems associated with family. 3. Identify and clarify problems associated with personal goals.

occupations from a more restricted range of options and continue to see fewer suitable occupations (Poole & Clooney, 1985; Fitzgerald & Betz, 1994). Women need special assistance to cope with typical stereotyping of women workers.

Basow (1992) presents the current picture of the barriers women face to reach the top-ranked jobs as rather discouraging.

> Women confront a "glass ceiling" when trying to reach top-ranked jobs. In 1990, fewer than three percent of the 6502 top jobs at Fortune 500 companies were held by women, although this is up from one percent a decade before. At the current rate of increase, gender equity will be reached in the executive suite in the year 2466. (p. 264)

A combination of role plays, discussion groups, and effective use of audio-visual material is recommended for accomplishing the specific tasks of this component. A speaker who is willing to share experiences can also be effective. "How to listen" exercises and clarification of differences among assertiveness, nonassertiveness, and aggressive behavior are important segments of this component. Other learning outcomes include (1) effective methods of communicating in a working environment, (2) identifying and understanding authority lines in typical organizations, (3) effective group decision-making techniques, (4) factors contributing to good worker-supervisor relationships, (5) understanding the role of the informal group in a typical organization, and (6) effective methods of establishing rapport with peer affiliates.

Following are some representative resource materials that may be used for this component.

Corporate Quality Universities: Lesson in Building a World-Class Force
Jeanne C. Meister
American Society for Training and Development
1640 King Street
Box 1443
Alexandria, VA 22313-2043

Gendered Lives: Communication, Gender, and Culture
Julia T. Wood
Wadsworth Publishing Company
Belmont, CA 94002

Women and Corporations—Breaking In
Women and Corporations—Moving Up
(two videotapes)
National Innovative Media Co.
Route #2 Box 301B
Calhoun, KY 42327
1-800-962-6662

Women in Business (videotape)
Cambridge Educational
P.O. Box 2153
Charleston, WV 25328-2153
1-800-468-4227

Component III—Lifestyle Skills

To learn that every person is unique and should be considered as an individual who has certain aptitudes, interests, and aspirations is the primary purpose of this component. Women especially have more control over their lives than ever before. We have not yet reached the ultimate androgynous society, but we have taken giant steps away from gender-role stereotypes. The time has come for all women to consider their individual needs in determining their lifestyle. What should be communicated is that every woman is an individual who has certain strengths and weaknesses and, like everyone else, is unique. The challenge is to clarify the uniqueness (self-image, skills, and aspirations) and to project those characteristics into work, family, and life planning.

In this component, special attention is directed toward goal setting from an individualized frame of reference. Identifying and clarifying individual strengths and weaknesses through self-concept exercises is recommended. Assertiveness training with emphasis on interpersonal work relationships is another technique for accomplishing the tasks of this component. Individual personality development could be explored through discussion of background experiences, including those involving family, peers, school, and other life events.

Special consideration should be given to the task of identifying and clarifying dual-career family problems (Pleck, 1985). Rapoport and Rapoport (1978) identified five areas of stress common to couples who are both pursuing full-time careers and have at least one child: (1) *overload dilemmas* (the management of household and child-rearing activities), (2) *personal norm dilemmas* (conflicts arising from what parents consider proper lifestyle and what other individuals consider proper), (3) *dilemmas of identity* (intrinsic conflicts associated with life roles), (4) *social network dilemmas* (conflicts associated with relatives, friends, and other associates), and (5) *role cycle dilemmas* (conflicts associated with family life cycles such as birth of a child, child leaving home, and other domestic issues that produce stress on career development). Suggested solutions include shared responsibility exercises, time-management techniques, and effective planning between parents who have discussed and established individual and family priorities.

The following representative materials may be used for this component.

The Three-Career Couple: Mastering the Art of Juggling Work, Home, and Family
Peterson's Guides
202 Carnegie Center
P.O. Box 2123
Princeton, NJ 08543-2123

Planning for Work
Catalyst
220 Park Avenue South
New York, NY 10003
Fax: 212-477-4252

Sex, Career and Family
Sage Publications, Inc.

2455 Teller Rd.
Thousand Oaks, CA 91320

American Lifestyles
Vocational Biographies, Inc.
Sauk Centre, MN 56378
Phone: 1-800-255-0752
Fax: 320-352-5546

The Best Jobs in America for Parents
Ballantine Books
201 E. 50th St.
New York, NY 10022
Phone: 1-800-733-3000
Fax: 212-872-8026

Working Parents: Balancing Kids and Careers
(videotape)
The Learning Seed
330 Telser Road
Lake Zurich, IL 60047

Component IV—Support and Follow-Up

A follow-up component provides support through either group participation or individual visits. The primary purpose of this component is to reinforce those skills learned from other components. The need for this component is underscored by research that suggests that women have difficulty finding acceptance of their ability to contribute significantly in a working environment. In fact, more than likely they will experience rejection and isolation, which often leads to withdrawal and the subsequent assumption of a more passive position (Wilcox-Matthew & Minor, 1989). In addition, women who are actively expressing their needs through a career may also receive negative reactions from spouse, family members, relatives, and friends (Sigelman & Shaffer, 1995). Research indicates that the chances are high that a woman may experience difficulty in attaining fulfillment in a career because many of her associates will strongly suggest that she change her position. Because of the potential negative feedback from associates, friends, relatives, and spouse, reinforcement is considered an essential component in counseling women.

The specific task suggests that problems that may be encountered ought to be identified and clarified. In the process of clarification, a recycling through one or more of the components may prove valuable. For example, more effective methods of home management may be needed, or a reformulation of goals may be required. The follow-up component provides support as well as problem identification associated with work, family, and personal goals. Exercises that promote problem identification and provide subsequent alternative solutions are recommended.

Counselor Bias

During the 1970s, there was an explosion of research concerning counselor bias—more specifically, that is, gender bias that frequently occurs in career counseling by both male and female counselors. The problem centered around the charge that counselors of both sexes may dissuade women from choosing a traditionally masculine role. Betz and Fitzgerald (1987) conducted an excellent review of the literature from the 1970s through the mid-1980s and concluded that the methodology and other factors make the results less than definite. The authors suggest that some sex-role bias among counselors did exist during this time, but the research results do not necessarily substantiate this conclusion.

Although all research findings do not point to gender discrimination among counselors, there appears to be sufficient evidence that counselors need to give more consideration to an androgynous model (counseling free of gender roles) in their career counseling approaches. More specifically, all career options in educational programs should be made available as a viable part of career exploration for all individuals, regardless of their gender. Counselors should be challenged to evaluate their personal views of the world of work and to understand that others may have legitimately different views.

The federal law requirements in Titles VII and IX, identified earlier in this chapter, should be carefully reviewed by career counselors for their counseling implications. A major implication is that women must be informed about the equal opportunities provided by these acts. More explicitly, women are not to be dissuaded by counselors from considering any career for which they are qualified. In addition, women should be encouraged to feel free to pursue jobs that may traditionally be reserved for men only. Finally, women should be encouraged to seek admission to educational or training programs for which they qualify. Clearly, counselors should be supportive of women and foster equal opportunities in employment, wages, and educational/training programs.

Gender Bias and Gender Fairness of Interest Assessment

Since the mid 1970s, a considerable body of literature has been published on issues of gender bias and unfairness of career interest measurement. A major issue has been the limited career options available for women forecast by the results of interest measures. In the meantime, the American Psychological Association (APA) has addressed sex bias in its publication of ethical principles (APA, 1990). This prestigious national association focused on "individual and role differences" in mental health practices, more specifically in this context, "role differences" associated with gender. Much earlier, in the 1970s, the National Institute of Education (NIE) voiced its concern of sex bias found in interest inventories; this group argued that occupational options are limited primarily on the basis of gender (Diamond,

1975). Thus, the concern for sex bias has been pervasive in the mental health professions and continues to be the focus for career service providers when using interest inventory results.

As the debate of sex bias in interest inventories continues to evolve, the issues have remained basically the same. First, do men and women have different interests? Fouad and Spreda (1995), Harmon and Meara (1994), and Hansen, Collins, Swanson, and Fouad (1993) all agree that men and women *still differ* in the way they endorse interest inventory items. For instance, women are influenced to endorse items according to their socialization—that is, by what is considered appropriately feminine, such as nurturance, caring, warmth, and expression of emotion—the results of which may serve to reinforce traditional occupations for women (Betz, 1994a). Thus, interest inventory results may not reflect actual differences between men and women for occupational groups or for specific occupations (Fouad & Spreda, 1995). Therefore, specific items on interest inventories require careful scrutiny to determine whether they appropriately represent interests of both genders.

Second, are interest inventories constructed with the assumption that work is dichotomized into man's work and woman's work; or in the language of measurement, is there content bias? For instance, items that encourage role stereotyping, such as "salesman" or "policeman," should be omitted (Hackett & Lonborg, 1994). As Betz (1992a) points out, the main problem of sex restrictiveness in interest inventory results is that different score patterns for men and women encourage gender-stereotypic occupations.

Other psychometric qualities, such as the internal structure of inventories, may be another source of bias. For example, how raw scores are converted to norms used in profile interpretation may contribute to bias (Hackett & Lonborg, 1994). In recent years, publishers have restructured and revised their inventories to lessen this problem. However, although improvements have been made in the psychometric quality of tests, this does not automatically translate into using the results of instruments in a fair manner.

A related issue is whether to use raw, same-sex, or sex-balanced inventory scores. According to Holland, Fritsche, and Powell (1994), the role of interest inventories is to provide a reflection of the current interests men and women have; and when standardized scores are used, the interests become modified and reality becomes obscured. Spokane and Holland (1995) obviously endorse raw scores as a most effective method of interpreting the results of interest inventories. Fouad and Spreda (1995) and Prediger and Swaney (1995) argue that whereas raw scores may reflect reality, they may also endorse occupational segregation for women or sex-restrictive options. It appears that the argument boils down to the suggestion that raw scores should be used because they accurately reflect vocational aspirations of men and women that may differ because of their life history, whereas Fouad and Spreda (1995) and Betz (1992a) suggest that other methods be used to increase a wider range of options for women.

Yet another issue involves the norm reference groups used for interpreting completed interest inventories. More explicitly, the prevailing question is whether sex bias in interest inventories can be most effectively overcome through the use of separate norms (reference group by gender, often referred to as same-sex norms) or combined-gender norms (reference groups combining males and females).

Same-sex norms have the advantage of having one's score compared to patterns of interest of others who have similar gender-related socialization experiences. For instance, a woman can view her scores in reference to both male and female samples. Also, same-sex norms provide more options for exploration of interests (Hansen, 1990). Separate sex norms for men and women have been developed for the *Strong Interest Inventory* (SII) and the *Kuder Occupational Interest Survey*. Apparently, both inventories plan to expand the number of feminine occupational scales as more data become available about women in different occupational roles.

Finally, the argument about whether to use gender-based norms or raw scores may simply be negotiated by the *purpose* of the assessment. For instance, if the purpose of assessment is to increase an individual's options by including those typically underrepresented by his or her gender, then one would use gender norms and explain the purpose of their use to the client. Conversely, if the purpose of assessment is to measure congruence with respect to individuals in an occupation or a major field of study, then one could use raw scores. In this respect, both men and women are provided with a broader range of options, and thus gender bias is not viewed as exclusively a matter of women's interests.

According to Prediger and Swaney (1995), one way of reducing sex bias in interest inventories is by using sex-balanced scales found in the UNIACT, an interest inventory published by the American College Testing Company. This instrument was designed to measure basic interests common to occupations while "minimizing the effects of sex-role connotations" (Prediger & Swaney, 1995, p. 432). The construction of this inventory included the introduction of items that were considered typical of male and female role socialization; items that produced an appreciable difference in response by gender were eliminated. The rationale is that sex-balanced items will elicit similar responses from men and women, thereby eliminating different sets of scales. Prediger and Swaney argued that different sets of occupational scales for men and women perpetuate sex-role stereotyping because such tests inherently suggest that some work is typically male-oriented and other work is typically female-oriented.

What we have here are difficult decisions for the career counselor regarding which inventory is most appropriate for specific clients. Perhaps a compromise is the best solution. Betz (1993) suggests that the counselor use both a same-sex norm inventory and a sex-balanced inventory. The basis for this recommendation is that both sets of norms will likely provide more options for career exploration (Zunker & Norris, 1998). (See the five-step process for using assessment results for career development in Chapter 21.)

Summary

1. Women are reassessing their career priorities and are looking beyond the traditional feminine working roles. However, even though they are being given greater opportunities to expand their career choices, barriers to the changing role of women in the working world still exist.

2. Super was one of the major career development theorists who addressed career development patterns of women. Ginzberg denoted three lifestyle dimensions—traditional, transitional, and innovative—in career counseling approaches for women. Zytowski labeled vocational developmental patterns of women as *mild vocational, moderate vocational,* and *unusual vocational.* Sanguiliano suggested that a woman's life cycle does not follow a rigid progression of developmental tasks and that attention should focus on unique paths women take to break away from gender-role stereotyping. Spencer supported Sanguiliano's denial that women's development follows the rigid progression suggested by life-stage theorists. She contended that feminine developmental tasks are unlike masculine tasks and that women follow a unique pattern of development. Chusmir suggested that personality and motivational traits of women who choose nontraditional occupations are formed by the time they are teenagers.

3. The emerging trend toward equalization suggests specially designed career counseling programs for women. Special career counseling needs for women are job search skills, occupational information, self-concept clarification, managing dual roles, assertiveness training, information on a variety of working environments, lifestyle clarification, and development toward a value of independence.

4. The family stereotype of a homemaking mother and a breadwinning father is no longer typical. In greater numbers, women are assuming a dual role of homemaker and worker. Managing both roles has created conflicts for women, especially in meeting their own individual needs.

5. Career counseling approaches should be androgynous; that is, free of gender-role stereotyping. Counseling strategy components include job search skills, working climate, lifestyle skills, and support and follow-up.

6. Developmental components for girls prepare them for career-related events that are highly probable during their life spans. Counseling components can assist girls in overcoming gender-role stereotyping, and may include identifying successful career women as role models and mentors.

7. Issues of gender bias and gender fairness of interest assessment are indeed complex and involve numerous technical problems such as test item development and norm references, as well as issues concerning societal changes. Guidelines developed for assessment of gender bias and gender fairness in career interest inventories primarily encourage both males and females to consider all career and educational opportunities.

Supplementary Learning Exercises

1. Support or disagree with Spencer's contention that feminine developmental tasks are unlike masculine tasks. Back up your arguments through interviews with at least two females.
2. Interview a woman who has had a successful career. Identify her reactions to the gender-role stereotyping of women and to the barriers that still exist for the woman in the working world. If she is married, ask her how she has managed the dual career of homemaker and career woman.

3. Write to the Women's Bureau (Employment Standards Administration, U.S. Department of Labor, Washington, DC 20402) and request materials developed to promote equalization for women in the work force. Indicate how several examples of materials may be used in career counseling programs for women.

4. Divide the class into three groups and identify and clarify dual-career family problems. One group considers problems associated with the husband, another group considers problems associated with the wife, and the third group considers problems associated with other family members. Build counseling components for solving the identified problems.

5. Visit a women's center and obtain descriptions of career-related counseling programs. Summarize your findings and point out the potential use of the women's center as a referral source.

6. Develop a list jointly or independently of the early socialization processes that promote gender-role stereotyping. Explain how this information can be used in career counseling programs for women.

7. Develop a scenario to be used for emphasizing gender-role stereotyping in a work setting. Present it to the class for critiquing.

8. Develop a list of questions that women are typically asked in a job interview. Provide guidelines for answering these questions.

9. Interview at least two women who are currently holding nontraditional jobs. Summarize the problems they have faced and their recommendations to other women.

10. Using the counseling components developed for women in this chapter, develop strategies for one or more components designed to accomplish the specific tasks.

CHAPTER SIXTEEN

Special Issues in Career Counseling for Men

The previous chapter examined the recent changes in working roles for women. It stands to reason that when there are role changes for one sex, pressure develops toward changes for the other. Since the beginning of the feminist movement, men have reexamined their roles, beliefs, and values regarding their relationships with women. Basow (1992) and Wood (1994), among others, suggest that men do not have an easy time adjusting to the egalitarian movement toward equal rights for women in the workplace and in other areas in our society.

To change their perspective of what is an appropriate masculine role, men will have to modify their belief that they are supposed to dominate women. Moreover, the change in lifestyle for men will be difficult because they are the products of a socialization process that mandates that men should be aggressive and competitive, acting as protectors and providers. It is no surprise, then, that men are confused when faced with a new set of values suggesting that the traditional masculine role should be significantly modified.

In this chapter, we examine the socialization process that has shaped men's lives and influenced their perspective on an appropriate masculine role. We attempt to understand why men have adopted stereotyped behavioral roles that are not conducive to equality and cooperation in the working environment. We attempt to analyze why men behave so aggressively in their attempts to gain career achievement and success. All the answers to these questions are related to career counseling procedures designed to help men meet the demands of their career and their life roles in a changing society.

This chapter begins with a discussion of the influence of parents, school, and media on gender-role development. Next, the special needs of men are identified and discussed. In the final part, four counseling components are presented and analyzed.

Influences on Gender-Role Development

This section examines three sets of influences on gender-role development: parents, the schools, and the media.

Parental Influence

The purpose of this section is to determine whether parents treat boys and girls differently and the effects, if any, that parents' reactions to children have on gender-role stereotyping. An introduction to research studies that attempt to answer these questions is a good starting point for understanding the socialization process children experience from interaction with important adults in their environment. Insights into potential reasons that individuals behave the way they do is relevant information for career counselors.

According to Basow (1992), the preference for male children over female children is a worldwide phenomenon. In some cultures, female infants are swiftly disposed of following birth (French, 1992). Thus it should not be surprising that many pregnant women place a higher value on giving birth to a boy than to a girl. These parental attitudes are relayed to children in terms of gender stereotypes that affect children's development. For example, Lindsey (1990) supports the concept of differential parental attitudes toward infants, finding that parents regard boys as sturdier than girls and tend to play more roughly with baby boys. Evidence supports the contention that parents expect sons to be more active and aggressive and daughters to be passive and nonassertive (Basow, 1992).

Solomon (1982) contends that the growing boy is surrounded by a multiplicity of social influences, including parental attitudes, that facilitate his internalization of the masculine role. For example, parents tend to choose different types of toys for boys than for girls (Wood, 1994). Although this method of gender typing has decreased in recent years, there is evidence that parental choice of toys continues to be based on perceived appropriate gender roles (Lytton & Romney, 1991).

Differential parental expectations of boys and girls may, to some extent, influence career choices and other roles children envision for themselves. Parents as models and children's tendencies to identify with same-sex parents are powerful gender stereotypes that lead children to prescribe to certain roles they have observed. Boys are vigorously socialized into gender by their fathers; fathers and men in general appear to enforce appropriate roles on children more intensely than women do (Chodorow, 1989; Wood, 1994). For example, fathers tend to attribute independence and aggressiveness to boys and passivity and dependence to girls. Boys look to their fathers as role models that define manhood for them; they emulate fathers' examples to become masculine.

According to cognitive development theory, once gender identity is developed, much behavior is organized around it (Lindsey, 1990). Parents who have been gender-role socialized provide models for their children, who actively seek identification with the same-sex parent. As boys learn gender concepts, there is an increasing agreement with adult stereotypes (Leahy & Shirk, 1984). Thus, home tasks that parents consider appropriate for boys and girls reinforces learned gender-role concepts. Rosenwasser (1982) suggested that although there are changes in mothers' perceptions of appropriate tasks for girls and boys, tasks still tend to be gender typed.

School Influence

The process of formal education further reinforces expectations learned in the home. Elementary school is often described as being very feminine in that the vast majority of teachers are women, thus providing feminine models for children (Rosenwasser, 1982; Tracy, 1990). Moreover, evidence suggests that teachers in elementary school treat boys and girls differently. After reviewing research on this subject, Doyle (1983) found that boys were encouraged to be more aggressive than girls, whereas girls were more likely to be noticed for dependent, clinging behaviors. Boys are portrayed as being resourceful, brave, and creative, whereas girls are portrayed as passive, helpless, and dull (Scott, 1981).

According to Etaugh and Liss (1992), there is a significant influence from our educational system on the development of gender-stereotyped work roles. "Feminine-appropriate" courses are language, home economics, and typing; boys are encouraged to take math and science courses. Sadker and Sadker (1986) argued that teachers respond differently to boys and girls in all grade levels, K–12, partly because teacher-education training books are gender biased.

Wood (1994) also suggests that schools reinforce gender-role stereotypes in their curriculum by making women's achievements invisible. For instance, men's accomplishments are highlighted in curricular materials, whereas women's roles are often excluded. Thus, more attention given to males emphasizes that males are more important than females and that they are more able than females to lead and exert influence. Following this logic, men are to be the chief executive officers, whereas women are more suited for supportive roles.

The appropriate future work role is made clear by educators and counselors, who further socialize boys and girls to conform to the established norms society has fostered. Teachers and counselors who endorse traditional gender-role behavior directly influence the choice of career options, and the message is clear to the boy that much more is expected of him in the way of career achievement.

Media Influence

TELEVISION

By 1991, most U.S. households (98.3%) owned a television, and approximately two-thirds of households owned one or more sets. In addition, 60.2% had installed cable television (Television Bureau of Advertising, 1991, cited in Wood, 1994). Although many children and adolescents watch television on the average of

2 to 3½ hours a day, some watch up to 7 hours (Nielsen Media Research, 1989). What is relevant to our concerns here is that masculine and feminine roles children observe on television programs may affect their perception of reality and of what is appropriate for adults to do in the real world (Signorielli & Lears, 1992). As Wood (1994) points out, media are the "gatekeepers of information and images" (p. 231). Furthermore, the media greatly influence how we perceive gender roles.

Several researchers have charged that television programs continue to reiterate the gender stereotyping of women as dependent and passive, as needing to look good in order to please men, and as greatly involved in relationships or housework (Davis, 1990; Pareles, 1990; Woodman, 1991). Conversely, children's television shows typically portray men as aggressive, dominant, and involved in masculine accomplishments. Men are also seen in high-status positions, whereas women are expected to be younger, very physically attractive, and less outspoken than males. In sum, children see more males in significant roles, whereas females are usually relegated to minor roles with little responsibility concerning the outcome of a story (Wood, 1994).

Television commercials may also contribute to children's perceptions of appropriate gender-role stereotypes (Jones, 1991). Products advertised by men represent a broad variety of uses and depict men in more dominant roles or as tough and rugged, as in the "Marlboro man." On the other hand, women have been used to advertise products used in kitchens or bathrooms.

BOOKS

There appears to be substantial evidence that boys and girls are highly stereotyped in children's books as well (Nelson, 1990). S. St. Peter (1979) reviewed 206 children's books and grouped them into the following three categories: books published before the women's movement, books published since the women's movement, and books selected from nonstereotyped lists (*Little Miss Muffett Fights Back*) of books about girls. Her results revealed that boys were the central character twice as often as girls in the first two categories of children's books. Furthermore, boys were pictured more often—a 3:2 ratio—on the covers of the books reviewed. The titles of books in the first two categories used boys more often than girls by more than 2:1. Interestingly, she found that, with the exception of books from nonstereotyped lists, the proportion of boys to girls on the covers of children's books has increased since the women's movement. An examination of the character roles portrayed in children's books indicated that girls were more expressive than boys, whereas boys were more likely to be portrayed as fulfilling goals.

In a more recent study of children's books, Purcell and Stewart (1990) concluded that significant differences still appear in how male and female roles are presented. Males continue to be presented as clever, brave, adventurous, and as primary breadwinners, while females continue to be presented as passive, victimized, and goal-constricted. Basow (1992) argues that because males have greater visibility in children's readers and are given more active roles than females are—especially in occupations—stereotyped gender roles are reinforced.

Identifying Men's Special Needs

The emerging trend toward androgyny will create a need for counseling programs to help men reevaluate their roles, beliefs, and values in all areas of their lifestyle, including their relationships with women in the home and workplace. Rabinowitz and Cochran (1994) and Lott (1994), among others, pointed out that the idea of androgyny has freed both men and women to consider alternative lifestyle behaviors and gives both the opportunity to acknowledge their masculine and feminine qualities. Career counselors are to be especially concerned with social changes that affect career development and interpersonal relationships in the home and at work.

Fear of Femininity

Researchers seem to agree that men's fear of being perceived as feminine has been indoctrinated through gender-role socialization (O'Neil, 1982, 1990; Solomon, 1982). Gender-role socialization has created a masculine/feminine polarity, as found by a prominent research group (Levinson et al., 1978) and more recently by Levinson (1996). O'Neil (1982) summarized the roles associated with masculine/feminine polarity as follows.

Masculinity is associated with:
1. Power, exercising control over others; (and being recognized as) a person of strong will, a leader who "gets things done";
2. Strength, bodily prowess, toughness, and stamina to undertake long, grueling work and endure severe bodily stress without quitting;
3. Logical and analytical thought, intellectual competence, understanding of how things work;
4. Achievement, ambition, success at work, getting ahead, earning one's fortune for the sake of self and family.

Femininity is associated with:
1. Weak, frail, submissive, and unassertive behavior; victimized by others who have more power and are ready to use it exploitatively; limited bodily resources to sustain a persistent effort toward valued goals;
2. Emotions, intuition; likelihood of making decisions on the basis of feelings rather than careful analysis;
3. Building a nest, taking care of needs of husband and children;
4. Homosexuality. (pp. 21–22)

According to the Levinson research team (Levinson et al., 1978; Levinson, 1996), the integration of masculine/feminine polarity is usually achieved during midlife, because younger men tend to identify strongly with the stereotypic masculine characteristics and are reinforced by cultural conditions. The Levinson studies suggest that evolving tasks in early adulthood make it difficult for men to deviate from learned masculine roles.

Other investigators have concentrated on problems associated with fear of femininity (O'Neil, 1982, 1990; Cochran, 1994). O'Neil (1982) suggested that the fear of femininity among men contributes to their obsession with achievement and success and is associated with (1) restrictive self-disclosure (fear their thoughts and actions will be associated with femininity), (2) health problems arising from conflicts, and (3) stress and strain.

Skovholt (1990), who researched gender differences in self-disclosure, concluded that men tend to avoid emotional intimacy with one another. Furthermore, he suggested that women were more willing than men to disclose to intimates. Another of these conclusions suggests that fear of femininity is one of the major factors that contributes to men's avoidance of emotional intimacy. Clearly, the fear of femininity is an appropriate topic in helping men understand the effects of their gender-role socialization.

Placing Achievement and Success in Perspective

According to Russo, Kelly, and Deacon (1991), men are conditioned to perceive career success and achievement as primary measurements of manhood and masculinity. These researchers suggested that a man's work represents his status in society and is the primary base for measuring success over the life span. Basow (1992) pointed out that men are conditioned to be overly competitive, ambitious, and status-seeking because these are the qualities associated with a successful man. Furthermore, a man's obsessive work behavior stimulates him to seek power and control and to become overly aggressive (Tannen, 1990). Men who exhibit obsessive patterns of work behavior clearly need counseling assistance to help them place achievement and success in perspective.

Learning to Relax

Highly valued masculine traits (such as competitiveness, independence, and self-reliance) make it difficult for men to learn to relax (Solomon, 1982). Masculinity is associated with work that consumes energy and imposes stress. Being passive is considered feminine and drives men to constant activity. Solomon (1982) suggested that men's leisure activities are not always conducive to relaxation. For example, a "friendly" game of tennis or golf often turns into a highly competitive activity that is not compatible with relaxation.

Learning to relax during leisure time appears to be an important need for men who are overly ambitious and competitive. Kail and Cavanaugh (1996) suggested that when there is a balance between work and leisure, leisure is a definite source of need satisfaction. Herr and Cramer (1996) contended that choice and control of leisure is important to self-esteem and holistic health. Career counselors can provide a valuable service by helping individuals determine practical, satisfying, and relaxing sources of leisure. Leisure counseling, as suggested by Leclair (1982) and McDaniels (1990), is a productive activity for professional counselors. Leisure counseling activities include (1) value clarification of work and leisure, (2) interest and attitude clarification, (3) identification of leisure opportunities, and (4) application of decision-making skills.

Restrictive Emotionality

As a result of research in the 1970s by Skovholt (1978) and more recently (Skovholt, 1990), he has determined that emotional expression and self-disclosure are serious problems for men. Lindsey (1990), while concentrating on the social perspective of gender-role development, contended that expression of grief, pain, or weakness is perceived to be unmanly. The fear of being perceived as unmanly makes many men resist being open, honest, and expressive, for such expressions are considered an open admission of vulnerability and loss of control so important to the masculine role (Rabinowitz & Cochran, 1994). O'Neil (1982) believed that restrictive emotionality is one of the leading causes of poor interpersonal relationships between men, between men and women, and between men and children. These authors suggested that men and women have developed two different styles and levels of communication: men deemphasize interpersonal relationships in communication, whereas women tend to be more expressive and more concerned with interpersonal processes. Different levels and styles of communication can lead to misunderstandings and conflicts in many social situations, including interactions in the home and the workplace.

Dealing with Competition

Some men have been socialized to be highly competitive; winning is perceived as important to maintaining the masculine role (Smith & Inder, 1993). In other words, men validate their masculinity through competition at work. Intense competition among men in the workplace may result in some men being very reluctant to be honest with their peers and having difficulties in developing interpersonal relationships. That is, intense competition among men may be highly related to stressful work environments and work anxiety (O'Neil, 1982; Lowman, 1993).

As discussed in Chapter 12, work environments in the United States have changed dramatically. Workers at all levels are worrying about survival as more organizations downsize their work force. Men as well as women feel stress from occupational insecurity in the workplace climate. Many are competing by working longer hours and for less pay to maintain job status (Roskies & Louis-Guerin, 1990). Future organizations may require more cooperation among workers, and workers will be required to deal with a wider variety of assignments and other workers (Hammer & Champy, 1993). In such work environments, openness and honesty with peer affiliates are important qualities to foster.

Learning to Recognize Self-Destructive Behavior

Closely related to issues of dealing with competition are behaviors that lead to health care problems. One pattern of work overcommitment is the widely studied Type A behavioral pattern. Friedman and Rosenman (1974), and more recently Strube (1991), conceptualized a model of how men behave in the workplace and designated the two masculine styles of functioning as Type A and Type B. Type A persons have an accelerated overall lifestyle, with involvement in multiple functions. They are overcommitted to their vocation or profession, have an intense drive for achievement, and develop feelings of guilt when relaxing. Other characteristics include excessive drive, impatience, competitiveness, restlessness; abrupt speech; nervous gestures; and rapid walking, eating, and moving. Type B persons are the opposite. They are characterized as serene, having the ability to relax, and lacking a sense of time urgency.

According to Thompson, Grisanti, and Pleck (1987), there is a higher elevation of Type A behavior in males compared with females. However, Greenglass (1991) found that professional women were predominantly Type A. Type A behavior has been linked to cardiovascular problems; workers who experience stress may have a higher rate of heart disease than non–Type A workers (Baker, Dearborn, Hastings, & Hamberger, 1988; Houston & Kelly, 1987). More recently, a five-year study at the Duke University Medical Center found that mental stress may hold the key to future heart problems. The major conclusion is that reducing abnormal responses to mental stress can lead to a reduction of cardiac problems (Jiang et al., 1996).

In the workplace, Type A individuals have an intense sense of time urgency and attempt to participate in most tasks, job assignments, and events that are ongoing in the workplace. Type A individuals give the impression that they can meet all challenges and successfully cope with any challenge, especially at work. Goldfried and Friedman (1982) suggest a program of cognitive restructuring as an effective intervention to modify Type A behavior. In cognitive restructuring, individuals learn to recognize behaviors that are self-destructive by acknowledging unrealistic and irrational beliefs that have reinforced their Type A behavior patterns. Counseling sessions, designed to promote cognitive restructuring, help them identify anxiety-arousing situations so they can take steps to modify their behavior (Doyle, 1992). Relaxation training, developed by Wolpe (1958), is another method of helping Type A individuals deal with anxieties.

Changing Male Roles in Dual-Career Homes

In a provocative study of dual-career couples, Wilcox-Matthew and Minor (1989) pointed out some concerns, benefits, and counseling implications. Because men have been socialized to play the role of "king of the hill," they may have difficulty sharing family roles and feeling comfortable in a nurturing role. One of the major issues is the management of household tasks. Counselors need to encourage men to share household duties, particularly in dual-career homes. The concept of shared responsibility is a step toward accepting new learning patterns that may require shifting roles for both husbands and wives in dual-career homes. (The next chapter has a more in-depth discussion about men in dual-career marriages.)

Needs of Househusbands

In the 40-year span from 1940 to 1980, the percentage of employed mothers with children under age 18 rose from 8.6% to 56.6% (Hoffman, 1983). Another dramatic social change is the fact that, in 1950, 12% of married women with children under age 6 worked outside the home, and in 1991 that figure reached 57% (Chadwick & Heaton, 1992).

These figures underscore the possibility of more involvement among men in primary and shared household/child care activities. A significant question involves how men react to the role of househusband. In the scanty literature that exists, there is evidence of resentment among fathers involved in paternal caretaking (Lamb, Frodi, Hwang, & Frodi, 1982). Russell (1982) reported that fathers involved in shared care giving were bored with their role, desired adult interaction, and were pressured by male peers. On the other hand, Russell (1982), Radin (1983), and Sagi (1982) found that shared caregiving fathers experienced an enhanced father-child relationship.

Perhaps men need to be made aware of the benefits of primary and shared responsibility for household/child care activities. In a study of 16 fathers who had assumed 50% or more of the responsibility of child care and household tasks, Rosenwasser and Patterson (1984) found that all but one indicated that they would recommend their lifestyle to other men. The results of this study provide some encouragement for men who assume the role of househusband.

When we learn more about the problems men face with child care and household tasks, appropriate guidelines for counseling consideration may emerge. In the meantime, counseling considerations for househusbands may include methods for dealing with ridiculing peers, boredom, household management, role conflict, and balancing household tasks with career.

Needs of Divorced Men

In the preceding chapter, the needs of divorced women were identified and discussed. Divorced men have similar needs. In particular, men who have dependent children will find that balancing the responsibilities of parenthood and managing a home with the responsibilities of work is a definite need. Halle (1982) studied 26 men whose wives filed for divorce and identified the following problems these men experienced: depression, self-blame, suicidal ideation, rage, jealousy, stress of new demands, vulnerability, being judged less of a man, and needing help with child-rearing. As with divorced women, men must learn to cultivate composure to effectively meet both home and employment responsibilities.

Men in Nontraditional Careers

Nontraditional occupations, as identified by Chusmir (1990), are those that have less than 30% of the same-sex workers. For example, four careers that are female-dominated (57% women) are social work, nursing, elementary school teaching, and office work. Although there is greater acceptance of men in nontraditional careers, there continues to be prejudice, ridicule, and negative perceptions of the men who choose them. It appears that gender typing of careers is still prevalent in our society and those who deviate experience the scorn of those whose thinking is dominated by gender-role stereotyping.

The career counselor should make it clear that all careers are to be considered in the decision-making process. Both negative and positive aspects of choosing an atypical career should be discussed. The negative aspects have been mentioned; the positive ones include faster opportunities for promotion, upward mobility, and increased compensation (Chusmir, 1990).

Gay Men

As discussed in the preceding chapter, more gays are making their sexual orientation known. Two major objectives are to find acceptance in the workplace and remove barriers that discriminate and inhibit their career development. Gay men appeared to have less certainty about their career choice and less job satisfaction with their career than do gay women and heterosexual men and women (Hetherington, Hillerbrand, & Etringer, 1989). Furthermore, these researchers suggested that gay men are sensitive to negative stereotyping (such as assuming certain occupations are mainly for them), employment discrimination, and limited role models.

Hudson (1992) suggested that counselors should prepare for counseling gays by building an extensive body of resources including specific information on those organizations and companies that support gay employees and a list of gay professionals who would provide support and information. Eldridge (1987) provides the following recommendations for counselors: (1) keep in mind the subtle, insidious nature of heterosexual bias and use this knowledge as a reminder for reflection; (2) use gender-free language; (3) become familiar with models of gay identity formation; (4) identify a consultant who can provide helpful information or feedback on working with gay clients; and (5) become familiar with local support networks for gays.

Implications for Career Counseling of Men

The preceding sections identified some effects of gender-role conflicts in men. These conflicts are important considerations in counseling men on career development, maintenance, and lifestyle orientation. Of particular value are programs that foster the idea that both men and women are gender-role socialized. Generally speaking, men are more resistant to self-disclosure than women are, suggesting a greater need for men to understand socialization processes. The importance of learning about leisure and relaxation techniques suggests programs designed to assist men in identifying and planning for appropriate leisure activities. The problem many men have with putting work achievement in proper perspective and learning to deal with competition suggests programs that delineate differences between aggressiveness and assertiveness. Finally, the concept of dual-career roles needs clarification.

Components for Counseling Men

The four counseling components that follow (outlined in Table 16-1) address general as well as specific career issues that arise from gender-role conflicts in men. Within each component there are specific tasks that can be selected as counseling objectives to meet specific needs or interests of groups or individuals. Likewise, each counseling component may be selected for its special appeal to specific individuals or groups; the components need not be offered in any particular sequence. The technique options do not exhaust all possible methods of accomplishing the specific task.

Component I—Expressiveness Training

The two goals of this component are to help individuals identify situations in which it is appropriate to express their emotions and learn that it is acceptable to freely express emotions in those situations. Dosser (1982) reported that men have a more difficult time experiencing their emotional feelings than do women. Specifically, they have more difficulty expressing emotions of happiness, sorrow, tenderness, delight, sadness, and elation. Jourard (1964), who initiated studies of self-disclosure, suggested that men reveal less information about themselves than women do. Research has shown that there is a high correlation between self-disclosure/self-awareness and interpersonal functioning (Dosser, 1982). In general, men devalue what they perceive as feminine traits of gentleness, expressiveness, and responsiveness (Solomon, 1982; O'Neil, 1982). In the work environment, men tend to be much more guarded than women are against revealing weaknesses to fellow workers and may resist certain cooperative tasks that could expose their vulnerability (Lindsey, 1990). Inexpressiveness can become highly dysfunctional in many relationships, including those with peer affiliates in the working environment, children, spouse, and friends.

The workshop described for this component should incorporate all or most of the other technique options. For example, inexpressive behavior can be succinctly illustrated through videotaped presentations or other video media. Role clarification exercises can be used to demonstrate the impact of inexpressive behavior on

TABLE 16-1
Components for Counseling Men

Strategy component	Technique options	Specific tasks
I. Expressiveness training	1. Workshop 2. Group and/or individual counseling 3. Role clarification exercises 4. Videotaped feedback 5. Homework assignments	1. Clarify how men's behavior has been shaped through socialization. 2. Identify and clarify inexpressive behavior. 3. Require that each counselee demonstrate an inexpressive behavior. 4. Clarify the advantages of expressive behavior and disadvantages of inexpressive behavior. 5. Clarify the advantages of a less rigid masculine role. 6. Clarify potential problems of inexpressive behavior in the working environment. 7. Clarify potential problems of inexpressive behavior in the home, with colleagues, and with friends. 8. Identify and discuss factors that prohibit expressive behavior. 9. Clarify strategies for becoming more expressive. 10. Demonstrate consequences of inexpressive and expressive behaviors in the work environment. 11. Clarify the differences between self-control and inexpressive behavior. 12. Role-play/rehearse expressive behavior.
II. Assertiveness training	1. Workshop 2. Group and/or individual counseling 3. Role clarification exercises 4. Videotaped feedback 5. Homework assignments	1. Clarify the differences between assertive, aggressive, and unassertive behavior. 2. Develop a philosophy of assertiveness (i.e., one's assertive bill of rights). 3. Identify behavioral expressions that are assertive. 4. Identify behavioral expressions that are aggressive. 5. Identify positive assertive responses to interpersonal situations with friends, fellow employees, and strangers. 6. Identify positive responses that are assertive. 7. Identify the differences between aggressive and passive behaviors. 8. Clarify factors of socialization that inhibit assertiveness. 9. Identify and clarify the concept of self-disclosure.

(continued)

TABLE 16-1
Components for Counseling Men   *(continued)*

Strategy component	Technique options	Specific tasks
III. Dual-career roles	1. Workshop 2. Group and/or individual counseling 3. Role clarification exercises 4. Videotaped presentations 5. Homework assignments	1. Clarify the concept of dual careers. 2. Clarify reasons women have the same rights as men in developing a career. 3. Clarify reasons men have the same rights as women in nurturing their families. 4. Clarify how socialization has determined gender roles in our society. 5. Clarify the concept of an egalitarian marriage. 6. Identify and discuss methods of sharing household management and tasks. 7. Clarify how husband and wife can look on their dual career and work roles as a joint venture. 8. Clarify the role of a "liberated" husband in a dual-career marriage. 9. Identify and clarify fears about possible loss of status or self-esteem among men when adjusting to changing roles in dual-career families. 10. Identify and clarify changing styles of interaction between spouses who both support dual-career concepts. 11. Identify changing attitudes in relation to work and responsibilities in dual-career families. 12. Clarify the family-nurturing role for men in dual-career marriages.
IV. Support groups	1. Group and/or individual counseling 2. Role clarification exercises 3. Videotaped presentations 4. Homework assignments	1. Identify the concept of androgyny. 2. Identify and clarify problems associated with the modification of masculine roles. 3. Identify and clarify problems associated with reactions to the women's movement. 4. Increase understanding of the masculine socialization process. 5. Increase understanding of the feminine socialization process. 6. Identify stereotyped work roles for men and women. 7. Identify and clarify problems men will encounter when they adopt a more androgynous role. 8. Identify and clarify problems associated with maintaining modified behaviors of expressiveness, sharing in dual-career homes, and assertiveness. 9. Identify and clarify the purpose of men's consciousness-raising groups.

interpersonal relationships. Videotaped feedback is a good procedure to help individuals perceive how others may see them. Homework assignments can be quite varied and inclusive and may include an assignment of recording one's behavior for a week and reporting back to a group, or keeping records of the behavior of others. Individual goals and strategies should be identified, and group counseling may be used to provide the counselee with feedback from his peers regarding his progress toward accomplishing established goals. Peer-group interaction is also a valuable means of support for individual and group efforts.

The specific tasks for this component can be sequenced to meet the needs of individuals or groups. The tasks of identifying and clarifying inexpressive behaviors are especially important for men, because they have been socialized to regard their inexpressiveness as an appropriate masculine trait. Indeed, these tasks may be used at various times to provide the framework from which men can learn to identify the differences between inexpressiveness and expressive behavior and to judge their progress toward becoming more expressive.

Other tasks to be emphasized by the career counselor are those that direct attention to behaviors that interfere with establishing appropriate interpersonal relationships with fellow workers, family, and friends; expressiveness is an important characteristic for establishment of relationships at work, in the home, and during leisure time.

Component II—Assertiveness Training

Assertiveness training has become immensely popular during the last 20 years, providing a basis for research in the scientific community and training programs for the general public. Programs for women have included assertiveness training to help them achieve individual goals for improving interpersonal relationships. Recognition of the need for special programs for men has led to a reexamination of several existing programs for women—including assertiveness training. There is evidence from research that men also benefit from programs designed to help them become more assertive (Dosser, 1982; Goldberg, 1983). Wolpe's (1973) discussion of assertive behavior suggested that men generally need to be more assertive when expressing affection, admiration, and praise. Wolpe also suggested that differences between hostile/aggressive behaviors and assertive behaviors need to be delineated. Wolpe pointed out that some individuals might experience embarrassment when expressing affection, admiration, and praise. Goldberg (1983) suggested that men need to learn how to become less competitive and aggressive when interacting with colleagues and spouses.

The specific tasks of this component are primarily designed to assist men in clarifying the differences between aggression and assertiveness. The technique options provide several strategies to help them recognize the benefits of appropriately expressing their emotions, thoughts, and beliefs in a direct and honest manner. Assertiveness training can provide behavioral guidelines for men to use in modifying their aggression when interacting with peer affiliates on the job and with their families at home. Examples of appropriate verbal and nonverbal behaviors help men target specific situations in the process of modifying their behaviors. Dosser (1982) suggested that it is advantageous to concentrate on the expression of positive feelings in assertiveness training. Rich and Schroeder (1976) compiled a list of suggested techniques and procedures for assertiveness training, including developing a philosophy of assertiveness, role playing, role reversal, response practice, constructive criticism, modeling, relaxation, exaggerated role taking, postural and vocal analysis training, and homework assignments. Most of these suggested procedures can be accomplished with the technique options recommended for this component.

Component III—Dual-Career Roles

In Chapter 15, we learned that an increasing number of women are planning lifelong careers in a wide range of occupations. In their life plans, women are a giving career development a higher priority or at least equal status to other priorities, such as marriage and family. Dual-career families are becoming less of a novelty in the 1990s, but the increased prevalence of this lifestyle has not been accompanied by changes in the values, beliefs, or behavior of many of the men or women in these marriages. Men may have difficulty making the transition from traditional attitudes of man-at-work/woman-at-home to that of negotiating dual-career and family roles. These entrenched attitudes and perceptions of appropriate masculine roles will die slowly because of the long-standing socialization process that has stereotyped gender-role models. The process of change requires the recognition of deeply rooted patterns of masculine role behavior and attitudes toward women in general. However, there is recent evidence that when men are challenged to modify their behavior in dual-career families, they change their attitudes and actions (Wilcox-Matthew & Minor, 1989). The recent shift of roles in dual-career families gives this counseling component credibility for helping husbands make adjustments in their attitudes toward their wives' career aspirations, demonstrating advantages of fathers' being able to participate in their children's lives more directly, and encouraging men to assume a greater role in household management responsibilities.

The specific tasks in this component are designed to clarify the concept of dual-career families and to introduce changes in male role models. Special attention should be given to identifying and clarifying dual-career family problems as discussed in Component III—Lifestyle Skills for Women in Chapter 15. Other suggested solutions contained in this component for women, such as shared responsibility and role-coping exercises, can also be used in this component for men.

Component IV—Support Groups

Other counseling considerations may evolve as men begin to reexamine their roles as males. During the process of reexamination, some men may experience a sense of loss of status and self-esteem when confronted with the prospect of egalitarianism. At the beginning of the transition process, husbands may make pseudo attempts at conforming to newly established goals of sharing, but they may continue to consider their wives as being primarily responsible for fulfilling household and family needs. A combination of role playing and discussion groups is recommended for encouraging men to share these responsibilities. Other special issues that may be addressed include the following: (1) men may place more importance on their careers because they have considered themselves the primary breadwinners, (2) men may react negatively toward women who are successful and strong, (3) men may experience difficulty in changing and modifying the nature of adult relationships, and (4) men may have difficulty adopting a different male role in work and recreation (Stein, 1982). These issues clearly indicate the need for career counselors to provide support groups for men to express their needs in career-related issues and lifestyle concerns. Stein (1982) suggested that support groups for men provide an effective environment for addressing gender-role and career-related issues.

The technique options and specific tasks for this component provide the opportunity for men to freely express their emotions. Men should be encouraged to recognize and express emotions and behaviors that are usually associated with the feminine role, such as gentleness, sadness, caretaking, and nurturing. Conversely, they should also be encouraged to express typical masculine role traits of assertiveness, dominance, and competitiveness when appropriate. Both activities provide a rich source of learning how men react and relate to each other when assuming feminine and masculine role models. These experiences should be designed to help men establish caring and empathic interpersonal relationships in the work environment. In essence, men should be encouraged to modify traditional, stereotyped patterns of behavior in order to build personal relationships that do not require that they resort to rigid, masculine role models.

A men's support group also provides the opportunity to introduce specific topics of interest, such as difficulties in parenting, excessive need to achieve, expressing emotions, sharing household tasks, and competitiveness in the work place. The group can be divided into dyads and triads to discuss specific topics of interest.

The general goal of a men's support group is to change rigid, gender-role masculine behavior in order to build better relationships with women and other men. The peer interaction in men's groups should lead to greater flexibility in all interpersonal relationships.

Summary

1. Recently, men have begun reexamining their roles, beliefs, and values regarding their relationships with women. Boys exhibit gender-role appropriate behavior at a very early age. The learned framework of societal expectations intensifies in early childhood through social learning from parents, the schools, and the media.

2. Parents expect sons to be more active and aggressive and daughters to be passive and nonassertive. Parents' treatment and expectations of children in early childhood foster developmental patterns that may determine future role behavior.

3. The process of formal education further reinforces expectations of gender-role behavior learned in the home. Our educational system fosters the development of gender-typed work roles.

4. Television programs and commercials, children's books, and comic strips foster the development of gender-typed roles.

5. Special career counseling needs of men include fear of femininity, placing achievement and success in perspective, learning to relax, restrictive emotionality, dealing with competition, learning to recognize self-destructive behaviors, changing roles in dual-career homes, support for househusbands and divorced men, difficulties in nontraditional careers, and workplace acceptance of gay men.

6. Career counseling approaches should be free of gender-role typing. Counseling strategy components include expressiveness training, assertiveness training, dual-career families, and support groups.

Supplementary Learning Exercises

1. Develop a counseling component to help individuals identify typical masculine aggressive responses.
2. Review several history textbooks and identify descriptions of strong, masculine characters.
3. Develop a script that demonstrates the "Sturdy Oak" gender role.
4. Develop a list of masculine roles that interfere with cooperative efforts in the work environment.
5. Interview a husband and wife of a dual-career family to determine the extent of sharing of household planning and duties.
6. Using the dimension of the masculine role descriptions, develop a list of behaviors that are detrimental to career fulfillment.
7. While observing several television programs, develop a list of characters that represents the dimensions of the role appropriate behavior.
8. List your experiences in school that influenced gender-role appropriate behavior.
9. Develop a counseling component that is designed to help men modify their masculine role behavior in the work environment.
10. Develop counseling strategies that could be used to help men deal with competition.

CHAPTER SEVENTEEN

Special Issues in Family Systems Featuring Issues for Dual Careers

The family's influence on career development has been a significantly relevant issue for a number of career development theorists. Roe (1956), and more recently Roe and Lunneborg (1990), directed considerable attention to the developmental period of early childhood in their study of parent-child relations. Super (1990) projected the homemaker role as a major life role in the life-span, life-space approach to career. Gottfredson's (1996) treatise on sex-role orientation emphasizes the role of family influence. Mitchell and Krumboltz (1996) suggest that environmental conditions and events are factors that influence career paths. In sociological perspectives on work and career development, family effects on career development are considered a major variable: "The focus is on how family structure (intact, not intact) and maternal work roles influence development of work-related attitudes and choices of youth" (Hotchkiss & Borow, 1996, p. 284).

Many other factors of parental actions and behaviors—such as parents' expectations for their children's success, and parents' perceptions of their children's competence, interests, skills, and activities (Eccles, 1993)—are potential causal factors of career development. These examples, among others, suggest that more emphasis should be given to the study of familial variables to determine the degree to which these variables affect career development. As we move closer to the 21st century, we are encountering a different world in which traditional family systems have been altered, transformed, and reconstituted. Furthermore, determining the degree to which such variables as single parents, dual-worker parents, divorce, and remarriage shape career development is a challenge for professionals from several academic disciplines. These changes in family systems suggest that career development may also be changing its course. To fully delineate career development, the career counseling profession will likely require a closer alliance with other academic disciplines that view the work role as a pervasive variable in the lives of current and future generations.

In recent years, it has been essential that both parents work to fulfill financial responsibilities, and it should be recognized that many women *choose* to work and pursue a career. In greater numbers, women are assuming a dual role of homemaker and worker. Families in which both parents work are referred to as either dual-career or dual-earner households. Both types share some common goals and common issues. The term *dual career* is usually reserved for families in which both spouses hold professional, managerial, or technical jobs. Most of our discussion will be devoted to dual-career families.

As more women have changed roles, men also have changed by assuming a larger share of the homemaker role. But sharing responsibilities, particularly in the home, has caused role conflicts. This chapter will discuss some aspects of family dynamics in a changing world and the challenges that face couples in dual-career roles. More specifically, the first part of the chapter discusses the family as a system and some aspects of family relationships. In the second part of the chapter, issues facing dual-career families, some of which relate to dual-earner families, are covered. Finally, implications for career counseling are presented.

The Family as a System

In this chapter, the family is conceptualized as a social system. Any system, whether a corporation, a city government, or a family, comprises interdependent elements that have interrelated functions and share some common goals. In this perspective, we view individuals in families as interconnected elements, each of whom contributes to the functioning of the whole. Thus, we cannot wholly understand the system by focusing on the component parts, as each is affected by every other part; it is the relationships of those parts that results in a larger coherent entity. Families are viewed as composites of many factors, such as genetic heritage from parents, that are passed on to their children; members share common experiences and develop common perspectives of the future. The family system is embedded in larger social systems.

The nuclear family, most common in the United States, consists of husband/ father, wife/mother, and at least one child. The extended family, the most common form around the world, is one in which parents and their children live with other kin. The sequences of changes in families are referred to as *family life cycles*. In this respect, the family itself is also a developing organism of roles and relationships that occur over the family life cycle (Sigelman & Shaffer, 1995; Kail & Cavanaugh, 1996).

Rowland (1991) points out that an increasing number of people do not experience the traditional family life cycle; social changes have altered the makeup of the typical family in a changing world. Sigelman and Shaffer (1995) suggest that the following trends of change in family systems alter the quality of family experience.

1. *Increased number of single adults.* Although more adults are staying single, over 90% of today's young adults are expected to marry eventually.

2. *Postponement of marriage.* More adults are delaying marriage. The average age at first marriage for men is 26 and for women, 24.

3. *Decreased childbearing.* The average number of children in U.S. families is two. Adults are waiting longer to have children, and increasing numbers of young women are choosing to remain childless.

4. *Increased female participation in the labor force.* About 12% of married women with children under age 6 worked in 1950; the figure changed in the early 1990s to 57%.

5. *Increased divorce.* Up to 60% of newlyweds are expected to divorce.

6. *Increased numbers of single-parent families.* Projections indicate that about half of the children born in the 1980s will spend some time in a single-parent family. Fathers as single parents are increasing faster than are mothers as heads of single homes.

7. *Increased numbers of children living in poverty.* The increasing number of single-parent families has led to the increase in numbers of impoverished children.

8. *Increased remarriage.* About 75% of divorced individuals are remarrying. About 25% of U.S. children will spend some time in a *reconstituted family,* usually consisting of a parent, a stepparent, and children from another marriage.

9. *Increased years without children.* Adults are spending more of their later years without children in their homes for the following reasons: some who divorce do not remarry, people are living longer, and couples bear children in a shorter time span.

10. *More multigeneration families.* Because people tend to live longer, more children establish relationships with grandparents, and some with great-grandparents. Parent/child relationships last longer, some for 50 years or more.

These trends of change in family systems pose some interesting questions concerning career development. For example, will perceptions of life roles including the work role be altered? What impact will family transitions have on career development? Gilbert (1993) found that some aspects of men's behaviors in the home appear crucial to children's developing self-concepts. Moreover, fathers in dual-career families are likely to model less stereotypic behaviors, thus providing children with a more positive role of being involved in parenting. Also, observing women as economically independent and having more choices and opportunities influences children's perceptions of what women can do and become (Gilbert, 1993). The point is that although these trends may not have negative effects on images that children form about career and life roles, we need to remain aware of potential causal factors that contribute to and influence career development in these rapidly changing times.

Family Relationships

Mothers have traditionally been the primary caregivers for children. But recent research indicates that mother-child relationships cannot be fully understood without the addition of the father's influence (Sigelman & Shaffer, 1995). Both parents indirectly affect their children through their own interactions—the way in which they influence each other. For example, mothers who experience a supporting relationship with their husbands tend to respond to children in a more sensitive manner (Cox, Owen, Henderson, & Margand, 1992). Fathers, on the other hand, are likely to become more involved with their children when their wives suggest that they have an important role in their children's lives (Palkovitz, 1984). Thus, in the family system, mothers, father, and children all affect one another in the socialization process.

The previous discussion of changing family systems suggests that U.S. children are being reared in a diversity of environments, for example, in single-parent families, reconstituted families, and multigeneration families. There are many other variables within family structures that account for more diversity, such as poverty or the number of children within a family system. Therefore, it is difficult to predict or develop a profile of a successful marriage for these diverse groups. However, longevity of marriage appears to have at least some relationship to marital satisfaction. Berry and Williams (1987) found that marital satisfaction is highest at the beginning, drops in satisfaction when children leave home, and rises in later life. Figure 17-1 illustrates the level of overall marital satisfaction from start of marriage to retirement from work.

Lauer and Lauer (1986, p. 385) interviewed women and men who were married at least 15 years and compiled their reasons for staying married. The first seven

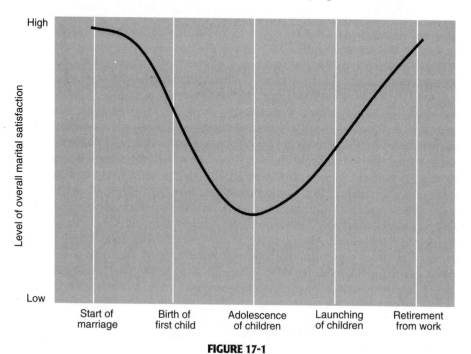

FIGURE 17-1

Level of overall marital satisfaction

SOURCE: From *Human Development,* by R. V. Kail and J. C. Cavanaugh. Copyright 1996 by Brooks/Cole Publishing Company, a division of International Thomson Publishing Inc.

responses were the same for both men and women, and they are listed here in order of frequency: (1) My spouse is my best friend; (2) I like my spouse as a person; (3) Marriage is a long-term commitment; (4) Marriage is sacred; (5) We agree on aims and goals; (6) My spouse has grown more interesting; and (7) I want the relationship to succeed.

In dual-career marriages, Newman and Newman (1995) report that the degree of marital satisfaction is related to agreement between husband's and wife's attitudes and aspirations. The way conflicts are expressed and negotiated and the manner in which resources are shared appear to be strong binding forces. Not surprisingly, couples that have more traditional sex-role attitudes tend to experience greater stress in a dual-career marriage. This conclusion supports Gilbert's (1993) findings on dual-career families. For instance, husbands who witnessed their father in actual involvement in family work were more comfortable in assuming family roles. In the next section, dual-career families will be discussed, but first is a case example of a dual-career couple in conflict.

Case Example: A Dual-Career Couple in Conflict

A conversation between a hair stylist and her customer went something like this:

Customer: I just don't know how Jose and I can keep our sanity. He is gone most of the time, and now I have to leave for a few weeks. I hope the children will be okay.

Stylist: Both of you sure travel a lot. I know Jose flies to New Orleans every week and now you are going overseas. When do you do fun things?

Customer: Fun things!! What's that?? All we ever do is argue about who is supposed to do what at the house and with the children.

Stylist: You know, Maria, you have been telling me the same story every week. And I think you are depressed over the whole situation. I do hope you and Jose can work something out.

The customer, a married women named Maria, has two children, ages 9 and 5. The family lives in a fashionable home in an exclusive neighborhood. Almost everyone but the stylist views Maria and Jose's relationship as dynamic and exciting because of their prestigious career positions. Although their marriage situation is unusual in a number of ways, Maria was expressing typical problems associated with dual-career marriages.

Maria was reared on the West Coast with two siblings. Both parents were professionals. Her mother was a medical doctor specializing in internal medicine, and her father was an electrical engineer who had built his own consulting firm. Maria recalls that even though her parents were very busy with their careers they made time for their children. They had a maid who also served as their nanny when they were small, but both parents shared in household tasks and driving Maria and her playmates to fun places.

Maria is now an internationally known architect employed by a prestigious international firm based in Phoenix. She is very pleased with her current position.

Her husband Jose is a college professor currently employed at a university in a southern state more than 1000 miles from their home. Jose flies to his job every week, leaving on Monday and returning on Friday. He now has tenure and does not want to give up his current position.

Jose and Maria moved to Phoenix when a position opened in an architectural firm. Jose decided that if someone had to travel on a regular basis, it should be him. When Jose is asked about this decision, he usually replies, "It's best for the kids to have their mother with them." However, Maria is not particularly pleased with this response, as it indicates that Jose doesn't recognize her achievements and the fact that she had been selected after a highly competitive search by the firm. By his response, Jose seems to ignore the fact that she receives more than three times his pay and that they had agreed that most of her earnings would be set aside for the children's education. Maria doesn't expect Jose to tell every casual acquaintance about all these details, but she does expect more of an appreciation for a mutual decision that had been thoroughly discussed and agreed on.

Jose, on the other hand, feels that Maria overlooks his traveling time and the hardships associated with it. Maria seems to view his position as just another professor's job that is relatively unimportant.

The conversation in the salon continued:

Stylist: I don't believe your husband gives you credit for all you have done.
Maria: Well, sometimes he does, but it seems harder for him to express those kinds of feelings.
Stylist: Why can't he do that? Why doesn't he just say it?
Maria: Hmm . . . that's something I have to think about.

On the way home, Maria was worried. She was now having difficulty with her oldest son, who is losing interest in all school subjects. At home, he has refused to obey her on a number of occasions. When she discussed this situation with her mother by phone, she got the usual response: "Maybe you should give more attention to your children."

Jose grew up in a midwestern state with three siblings. Jose's father was a corporate lawyer and had built a reputable practice. His mother was a homemaker who had no intentions of working outside the home. Jose recalls the scrumptious meals his mother would prepare and that she always seemed to be there when he needed her. Jose's relationship with his father was one of respect, but there was never much affection expressed between the two, and his father was often too busy to spend time with him and his siblings. Jose describes his family system as a traditional one.

Jose and Maria met in graduate school. After a courtship of two years, they became engaged and were married soon after graduation. They lived in the Northwest and on the Atlantic coast. They moved to Jose's New Orleans teaching location when a position opened. Each move was made to improve Jose's career. Maria had taken jobs in nearby cities in each location, and her growing reputation as an outstanding architect finally gave her the opportunity to take "the job of a lifetime," and so the family moved to Phoenix.

It was Friday, and Jose was on his way home for the weekend. He had invited one of his male colleagues, Bob, to join him. They had planned for time to prepare a research project.

Bob: Jose, this is a nice flight, but doesn't it get tiresome to do this every week?
Jose: I'm used to it by now, but I have to admit that there are times I would much prefer to stay at home. Actually, it's not the flight as much as it is the nights away from home that bother me.
Bob: Well, I hated to see you move. I still don't know why you had to do it.
Jose: Maria just had to have this job, and I guess I had to cave in just this once. But I hope you understand that I get my way most of the time. Anyway, let's start talking over our plans for this research project. You know, Bob, I think this project could get us an international reputation.

The first year in Phoenix was a relatively happy one, as Maria tried her best to take most of the responsibility of managing the household. It was during the second year that Jose began to argue about household tasks and spending time with the children on weekends, and he often refused to attend business-related events with Maria's firm. The small arguments seemed to get bigger, and Jose was often irritable. Both Jose and Maria felt they had reached a crucial stage in their marriage.

The next section addresses issues facing dual-career families. As you read this section, identify issues and potential sources of problems Maria and Jose are experiencing in their marriage. Following this discussion is a summary of Maria and Jose's case.

Issues Facing Dual-Career Families

The following issues are representative of current problems found among dual-career families, some of which apply to dual-earner families as well. This relatively new family structure was made popular in the early 1970s by Rapoport and Rapoport's (1978) studies involving graduates of British universities. Following their work, many studies involving dual-career families contained serious methodological limitations, such as focusing on women only and using only academics as samples (Herr & Cramer, 1996). Nevertheless, the following issues emerged as potential career counseling concerns and should be viewed from the perspective that many more may come forth in future research.

Expectations and Intentions about Work and Family

In a study of university students, Gilbert (1993) found that young women and men reared in dual-career families were highly committed to a role-sharing marriage. In other words, children raised in dual-career families were more likely to develop positive views of integrating occupation and family work. This is in contrast to the usual situation in traditional family structures, where the husband assumes the primary employment role and home roles are assumed by the wife.

These findings suggest that the kind and type of role sharing observed in the home by both women and men greatly influence their expectations of roles in marriage. Silberstein (1992) argues that a lack of agreement between expectations of roles in marriage has the potential to create interpersonal tension. The point is that role overload typically occurs between spouses when family roles are not clearly defined. For example, if the husband's occupational role is assumed to be primary, or if a wife views the husband's employment as a less important career, there is a greater potential for minimal sharing of household work.

Role Conflict

Role conflict is generally thought of as a system of competing demands of different roles; in the case of the dual-career family, the conflict is between family roles and work roles. Society has generally viewed the woman as the primary homemaker. The division of labor between spouses usually results in negotiating family roles, which are more complex when the family responsibilities include child care. When a husband does little sharing of household tasks, his wife may experience role overload. Role conflict results when husbands or both husbands and wives believe that men should continue to fulfill the traditional role of family breadwinner.

There is evidence to suggest that role conflict and role overload are decreasing somewhat in dual-career families; men seem to be increasing their willingness to share in household tasks and child care (Dancer & Gilbert, 1993). There is also some evidence to support the position that, in heterosexual marriages, African American and Hispanic American men tend to spend more time doing household tasks than do European American men (Shelton & John, 1993). Although women have been somewhat relieved of household tasks over the past two decades, they continue to do the most work and assume the most responsibility for household tasks (Kail & Cavanaugh, 1996).

Klinger (1988) developed a model designed to delegate household tasks based on interests, aptitudes, and time available. This flexible model provides for changes in tasks and in who performs them as the situation or as economic factors change. It also addresses the fact that some tasks may be viewed as more desirable than others, so that the most-preferred and least-preferred tasks should be rotated between the spouses. The last part of the model provides for a "recycling" that ensures an equitable division of labor.

Part I Formulate list of household tasks.

Part II Agree on the frequency of the tasks (daily, biweekly, weekly, monthly, annually).

Part III Agree on the person(s) responsible for accomplishing the task (considering each person's available time, interest, abilities). Highly desirable or highly undesirable tasks are rotated.

Part IV Review of the tasks to determine the following:
  a. Did the person(s) designated perform the task?
  b. Was the task viewed as satisfactorily completed?
  c. If "no" responses to questions a or b, what were the obstacles to completing the task?
  d. What additional resources (time, dollars, people, or other factors) are needed to complete the task successfully?
Part V Recycle: Add or delete tasks, change person(s) responsible for completing task if changes are necessary to maintain the perception of both persons that the division of labor is equitable.

The model can also be adapted to include child care. When the couple begins using the model, both partners should go through all the stages on a weekly basis. As they become familiar with the model, and if they are generally satisfied, then they can cycle through less frequently. The main determinant in how frequently the process is reviewed should be the level of dissatisfaction: the greater the level of dissatisfaction, the greater the need for the couple to recycle through the process.

Child Care

When both parents work, the care of children becomes a critical issue. Because over half of the mothers in the United States do work outside the home, child care has been an increasing concern. According to the National Commission on Children (1993, cited in Newman & Newman, 1995), there has been a steady increase in the use of day care since 1965. Forms of day care used include sitters, day care homes, and relatives.

Organizations have also recognized the need to provide for child care and may offer one or more of the following alternatives.

  Emergency care: The company provides temporary care when employees' regular arrangements fail.
  Discounts: The organization arranges for a discount from national day care chains or pays a small portion of the fees.
  Vouchers: Some organizations pay subsidies or offer special assistance to some low-paid employees.
  Referral services: Organizations may offer employees a list of approved day care centers.
  On-site day care: Day care centers are located on site.
  Flexible benefits: Money paid to day care centers is deducted from each employee's salary, thus, it is not considered taxable income.

One of parents' major concerns is the potential negative effects on children who are placed in day care centers. Research indicates that day care infants are no different from infants who were reared in their homes on measures of cognitive, linguistic, and social development (Clark-Stewart, 1993). In fact, most studies suggest that children benefited from their day care experiences (Sigelman & Shaffer, 1995).

Geographic Moves

A very pivotal point in dual-career families is a geographical relocation to enhance the husband's or the wife's career. First of all, a move could represent a sacrifice on the part of one spouse. According to Silberstein (1992), it is usually the husband who receives the major benefits from geographical moves. However, more couples are deciding to move to favor the wife's career. In some situations, a decision is made to commute in order to maintain the current residence.

Competition

Competition usually emerges when one spouse develops feelings of insecurity or frustration associated with his or her career (Silberstein, 1992). Feelings of competition may not be expressed directly but instead may result in debates over a variety of family or career concerns. For example, the tendency to address the issue of competition indirectly may lead to arguments over such issues as work schedules, vacation schedules, and child care commitments. The view that competition is largely inappropriate may cause dual-career partners to deny or avoid the issue.

Other Personal Factors

The need to dominate is a personality factor that influences how partners combine occupational and family roles. Typical of a dominating partner is to expect the other partner to take a secondary role in career aspirations and subsequent effort, thought, and time relegated to a career. For example, a dominating male may view his spouse as primarily responsible for raising children and the spouse's income as providing extra money. Or a deferring female may see her spouse as being the major breadwinner who must work full time, while she works part time and assumes the role of rearing children (Gilbert, 1993).

The attitudes, values, and subsequent views about women as professionals and about who should assume responsibility for which major roles in dual-career marriage may determine to a great extent the degree of the partners' "fit" in dual-career home environments. For instance, do both spouses have a favorable attitude toward a role-sharing marriage? Do both agree to work full time and share financial responsibilities? In essence, how interested and committed are both partners to an egalitarian marriage?

The stages of career development of both partners are also important considerations. For example, one partner may have reached the point where career has become rather secondary in life's priorities and, as a result, may not give support to the other partner's career advancement. Second, personal factors may make one partner resist accepting nontraditional roles in order to provide time for the other partner's career efforts. In this case, one partner debunks the other partner's career aspirations and offers little in the way of role sharing for the other partner's career growth and productivity.

Relationship Factors

One very important aspect of dual-career relationships is the decision-making process within the family—more specifically, who is empowered to make decisions. This factor seems to boil down to the question of equity in the decision process. For dual-career families, it is particularly important to reach mutual agreement on both major and minor decisions. Otherwise, one partner may feel unjustly treated.

The sharing of decision making and subsequent agreement of common life goals can serve as a foundation of support for family roles. Likewise, the sharing of perceptions of women's and men's roles in dual-career marriages is considered significantly relevant to how partners combine occupational and family roles (Gilbert, 1993).

Family-Oriented Work Policies

The work situation itself may provide obstacles that become relevant issues in a dual-career marriage. Fortunately, many organizations are offering parents flexible work policies. The following is a summary of the information compiled by Gilbert (1993).

1. Telephone access is an organization's policy that permits parents to make personal calls to their children or receive them.
2. Parental leave is also provided by many organizations. This type of leave is different from maternity leave in that it is primarily for care of children who are seriously ill.
3. Flextime is a policy that permits parents to choose arrival and departure times within a set range.
4. Flexible work arrangements permits arranging part-time work, job sharing, flexplace work (part of the day at home and part at the office), or telecommuting (work from home or satellite office).

Implications for Career Counseling

Clearly, one of the major problems of dual-career marriages is gender equity. The subtleties of male dominance that are often present in dual-career marriages lead couples to deal indirectly with their anxieties. Instead of attacking the underlying reasons for their frustrations, couples may resort to arguments over role assignments, child care, or other surface problems. In many instances, women may very well be searching for equity, while men may fear giving up power. The gap between expectations and reality for both spouses could be a productive intervention strategy, particularly if it is designed to clarify disparate expectations between spouses (Silberstein, 1992).

The major decision points in any marriage are crucial, but in dual-career marriages specific decision points can be identified. When or whether to have children can be particularly perplexing for spouses in dual-career marriages. It is usually during early career when women can more easily have children, which makes this decision a complex one. One method of resolving this issue is through negotiated compromises. Each spouse must share not only in this decision but also in actions and responsibilities that follow the decision.

Another major decision point that may provoke anxiety and stress in dual-career marriages is the necessity of moving to another location to foster one spouse's career. Again, who has the major role in being breadwinner? Decisions of this type highlight underlying questions that may have been avoided in the past. Counselors should be prepared to develop strategies that would prompt a reexamination of individual and collective priorities for both partners. The issues and individual feelings about work and family are indeed complex, and many couples may not be fully aware of personal issues involved in a geographic move to benefit one spouse's career. The counselor's task is to illuminate these issues for clarification.

So far we have dismissed concrete issues such as management of household tasks and sharing of duties as if they have little relevance to the welfare of dual-career marriages. But it appears more appropriate to address the possibility of underlying and unresolved issues before the more concrete ones can be effectively dealt with. The idea of role sharing, planning for children, making time for leisure, and offering support to one's spouse are examples of viable topics for the career counselor.

Finally, it is important to recognize that some couples may need to be referred to a marriage counselor to enhance marital satisfaction. Marital relationships may best be addressed in couples therapy.

Case Example Continued

The case of Jose and Maria illustrates some of the stress associated with dual-career marriages. Both have highly advanced career positions that are quite demanding. Their high income level permits them to hire domestic help, but the responsibilities of managing a household and rearing children cannot be completely relegated to others outside the family system. The task of managing a two-career household has caused some of the following problems for Maria and Jose.

Gap between Marital Expectations and Reality

For Maria and Jose, the gap between expectations and reality has led to some of their frustrations. Perhaps Maria, who was reared in a dual-career home, had not fully realized that family responsibilities cannot be fully delegated the way she had envisioned from her childhood experiences. It may have appeared easy for her mother, but in reality her mother was in a much better position than Maria is to control the demands of her workload and to keep a firm hand on household and family-related tasks.

Jose was not reared in a dual-career home; in fact, he was the product of a typical traditional system in which family roles were sex-role stereotyped. For the first years of marriage, Jose was happy; his expectations of married life, the roles of husband and wife, were mostly being met. Even though Maria was working full time, most attention was directed to his work-role advancement through geographical moves. And even though he had agreed to the fourth move for Maria's benefit, he expected the traditional role of husband and wife to continue, though perhaps with some modifications. When Maria had to ask for more of his support for household and child care activities, as well as support for her work, he felt betrayed.

Role Overload

For her part, Maria was an aggressive worker. She had multiple abilities and creative talents that needed to be expressed. Her work was now a challenge to her previously unused creativity, and it required that she devote most of her energy and cognitive skills to several ongoing projects. She would often arrive at home feeling fulfilled but also drained of energy. She also felt guilty when she was unable to devote more time to her children.

Competition and Empowerment Issues

Jose also experienced high levels of frustration associated with his career and his home life. The reality was that Jose was away from home and from his children on a regular basis. He also blamed commuting to work for his lack of productivity (research projects) in his academic discipline. Jose could very well have developed a fear of losing empowerment in his home. These two assumptions on Jose's part were troublesome ones. Being away from home four days a week can be stressful for all family members. However, Jose had not let any distractions interfere with his academic productivity in the past.

Jose's high anxiety level was a product of fear associated with losing control over family matters. He had developed a strong need to be empowered to make decisions, and, more important, he expected most family decisions to agree with his perceived role as head of the family. When his family position was threatened, Jose fought back by competing with his spouse for career recognition.

The problems identified in this dual-career relationship are complex but are typical of dual-career marriages. A closer look at the identified problems suggests that there was no significant indication of dysfunctional work, unsatisfactory work environments, or unstable peer and supervisory relationships. In fact, both spouses were well satisfied with their career positions. There were indications that some role sharing had been successful, and the family had functioned relatively well for several years. Their financial future was very promising.

The identified problems also reveal a gender equity battle between a highly successful wife and a successful husband. Some of the identified problems are typical of equity disagreements. For instance, their expectations of marriage were quite different.

Jose foresaw a more traditional marriage, with the husband assuming the primary work role, the wife working only for extra income, and the wife assuming the primary responsibility for house and child care. Maria had quite a different view of marriage—an egalitarian one of sharing and appreciating each other's independence. When these two different perspectives begin to collide, stress, anxiety, and frustration were predictable outcomes.

The reactions of partners in conflict may vary considerably, but in this case—other than both being identified as having conflicting expectations of marriage—Maria's other problem was role overload. On the other hand, Jose's multiple problems are clearly a part of expectations of marriage and his views of gender roles.

The recommendations for intervention strategies in this case could include couples counseling designed to illuminate conflicting expectations of marriage and resulting conflicts. The major goal would be to address marriage roles of sharing and gender equity. The needs and problems of the children also need to be addressed.

In conjunction with couples counseling, the career counselor can provide: (1) role-sharing strategies; (2) leisure time commitments, including family leisure time; (3) restatement of career goals, which center on agreement of plans for the future; (4) career development of children as a sharing venture; and (5) reformulation of life-span goals.

A number of outstanding counseling models are available for dual-career marriages, among them are the integrative strategies by Stoltz-Loike (1992). This integrative approach is based on the following assumptions.

1. A family has a variety of responsibilities that must be performed to function properly. How they are performed depends on the couple's skills, talents, and preferences.
2. Couples must communicate attitudes toward responsibilities. Conflicts need to be discussed and resolved.
3. Dual-career couples can effectively serve as models to help other couples balance career and family roles.
4. Communication, negotiation, and problem solving are to be viewed as ongoing processes over the life span.
5. Interventions are to be tailored to meet a variety of presenting problems among dual-career couples.
6. A spouse must balance his or her own family and work responsibilities with those of the other spouse.
7. Solutions to issues must be contextual to include each spouse's life, workplace, and community setting.

The major goal of this approach is to achieve balance of family and career equity. Helping couples recognize that role conflicts can occur at any time over the life span is another major goal. Because of overlapping roles and responsibilities, basic relationship skills of communication, negotiation, conflict resolution, and life-span success are stressed.

Summary

1. The families' influence on career development has been a significantly relevant issue for a number of career development theorists.

2. The family is conceptualized as social system. The nuclear family is the most common in the United States. The extended family is the common form around the world.

3. Current trends in family systems include: increased number of single adults, postponement of marriage, decreased childbearing, increased female participation in the labor force, increased divorce, increased number of single-parent families, increased numbers of children living in poverty, increased remarriage, increased years without children, and more multigeneration families.

4. The example presented of a dual-career couple in conflict is typical of issues involving struggles for gender equity of household and child care tasks and of work recognition.

5. Issues facing dual-career couples are expectations of work and family, role conflict, child care, geographic moves, competition, relationship factors, family-oriented work policies, and a number of personal factors.

6. Implications of career counseling include illuminating underlying issues of gender equity, couple communication, sharing exercises, family and career status, and conflict resolution.

Supplementary Learning Exercises

1. Does the nuclear family or the extended family have more influence on a child's career development? Defend your answer.
2. What strategies would you suggest for a single parent who is concerned about a child's career development?
3. Defend the following statement: Mother-child relationships cannot be fully understood without the addition of the father's influence.
4. Which two trends in changing family systems do you consider to be the greatest threat to the traditional U.S. family system? Defend your choice.
5. What are major differences between dual-career and dual-earner families? Of the two, which would have the greater difficulty with role conflicts?
6. Explain how expectations of marriage influence behaviors in dual-career marriages. Give at least five examples.

7. Give three examples of how parents in a traditional marriage influence their children's perceptions of dual-career marriages.
8. How can agreement on life-span goals affect a dual-career marriage? Give at least three examples.
9. Explain how you could assist a dual-career couple negotiate a geographic move that will benefit the wife's career.
10. Interview one couple in a dual-career and one in a dual-earner marriage. Explain the similarities and differences.

CHAPTER EIGHTEEN

Career Counseling for Multicultural Groups

The challenge of counseling various ethnic groups has received renewed impetus with recent changes in educational and employment opportunities. Legislation requiring that ethnic groups have equal access to training and employment has generated career counseling programs that aid the "culturally different." Career counselors are intent on developing career counseling objectives and strategies that will assist individuals of various ethnic groups overcome a multitude of barriers including prejudice, language differences, cultural isolation, and culture-related differences. Because this group is composed of persons from a wide variety of ethnic backgrounds, counselors are being challenged to become culturally aware, evaluate their personal views, and understand that other people's perspectives may be as legitimate as their own (Sue & Sue, 1990).

The need to develop career guidance strategies for multicultural groups will increase in the next century. An article ("Minority Numbers," 1993), based on a report from the Population Reference Bureau of the U.S. Census Bureau, suggested that by the middle of the next century, the United States will no longer be a predominately Anglo society. The more appropriate reference will be "a global society," in which half of all Americans will be from four ethnic groups: Asian Americans, African Americans, Hispanic Americans, and Native Americans. As more multicultural groups gain access to opportunities for education and higher-status jobs, the career guidance profession should be prepared to assist them. These projected demographics of diversity will present a significant challenge to all the helping professions.

This chapter begins with an introduction of the meaning of culture as it relates to career counseling. Culturally related work values are also discussed. Next, a multicultural counseling and therapy theory is introduced, with a summary of its propositions and corollaries. The next part of the chapter describes and discusses the needs of African Americans, Asian Americans, Hispanic Americans, and Native Americans. Suggested developmental strategies are given for each group. Finally, the remainder of the chapter presents some counseling strategies for multicultural groups and a list of assessment instruments.

What Is Culture?

Cultural diversity is an important topic for all counselors, and especially for the career counselor. In many respects, we have not addressed the issue of culture in the counseling profession. For example, researchers have given little attention to appropriate intervention strategies and assessment instruments for specific ethnic groups (Betz & Fitzgerald, 1995), which are among the many issues and questions to be resolved. Because of the variety of ethnic groups found in the United States today, we may find the answer to these issues and questions to be very evasive and quite complex. In the meantime, the career counselor must give high priority to cultural variables that influence career development.

Returning to the question of identifying culture, perhaps each one of us could offer an explanation of what culture means. We would be able to illustrate our definition with examples of cultural aspects, variables, customs, and perceptions of different individuals from a variety of "cultures." We could describe activities associated with a culture, we could refer to heritage and tradition of cultures, we could describe rules and norms associated with cultures, we could describe behavioral approaches associated with cultures, and we could describe the origin of cultures. These are examples of different meanings associated with the definition of *culture* and the different interpretations we use to identify people of different cultures. Thus, culture is a complex concept that can refer to many aspects of life and living.

Matsumoto (1996) defines *culture* "as the set of attitudes, values, beliefs, and behaviors shared by a group of people, but different for each individual, communicated from one generation to the next" (p. 16). This definition, although leaving a lot to be said about culture, provides a good fit for the career counselor's use of the word. For example, the use of sharing implies the degree to which an individual holds the same value, attitude, belief, norm, or behavior of a particular group. Furthermore, the emphasis is on cognitive processes of psychological sharing of a particular attribute among members of a culture. The lesson to be learned is that even within cultures, each individual should be treated as such and not from a stereotypical viewpoint one may have about a particular culture. We must be alert to cultural diversity among members of a particular ethnic group; the Asian American population, for instance, is not homogeneous.

It is true that culture is a learned behavior. Therefore, two people from the same race may share some values, attitudes, and so on but may also have very different cultural makeups. How much has been *acculturated* from racial heritage through socialization varies even within the dominant cultural group of a country (Triandis, 1992, cited in Matsumoto, 1996). Therefore, we must not make assumptions from cultural stereotypes; as we have heard so often in counseling, we enter into counseling relationships with *individuals*.

Cultural Differences in Work-Related Activities

Many clients have different work values, including people from different cultural backgrounds. Value orientations to work can be serious sources of conflict and misunderstanding in the workplace. One of the most provocative studies of work-related values was done by Hofstede (1984). His study included 50 different countries in 20 different languages and 7 different occupational levels (Matsumoto, 1996). His aim was to determine dimensions of cultural differences of work-related values. His findings are paraphrased as follows.

1. Power distance.   This dimension attempts to answer the basic hierarchical relationship between immediate boss and subordinate. In some countries, such as the Philippines, Mexico, Venezuela, and India, individuals tended to maintain strong status differences. In countries such as New Zealand, Denmark, Israel, and Austria, status and power differentials were minimized. In the United States, there was some degree of minimizing power differences.

2. Uncertainty avoidance.   This term is used to describe how different cultures and societies deal with anxiety and stress. Countries that had low uncertainty avoidance indexes on a questionnaire designed for this study differed significantly from countries that had high scores. Examples of connotations from those with low scores were that workers had lower job stress, less resistance to change, greater readiness to live by the day, and stronger ambition for advancement. Examples of high uncertainty avoidance scores were fear of failure, less risk taking, higher job stress, more worry about the future, and higher anxiety.

3. Individualism/collectivism.   This dimension attempted to answer the question about which cultures foster individual tendencies as opposed to group or collectivist tendencies. In this study, the United States, Great Britain, Australia, and Canada had the highest scores for individualism. Peru, Colombia, and Venezuela were most collectivistic. People in high individualistic countries were characterized as placing more importance on employees' personal lifestyle, were emotionally independent from the company, found small companies attractive, and placed more importance on freedom and challenge in jobs. People in countries with low individualism were emotionally dependent on companies, frowned on individual initiative, considered group decisions better than individual ones, and aspired to conformity and orderliness in managerial positions.

4. Masculinity.   This dimension is thought to be an indicator of which cultures would maintain and foster differences between sexes in the workplace. However, most employees who answered the questionnaire were men, so the conclusions drawn here are to be considered tentative. People in countries that had high scores on this variable were characterized as believing in independent decision making, having stronger achievement motivation, and aspiring for recognition. People in countries that had low scores on this variable were characterized as believing in group decisions, seeing security as more important, preferring shorter working hours, and having lower job stress.

These results appear to suggest conclusive evidence that culture does have an important role in work-related values. Moreover, we can conclude that employees' perceptions of work roles—as well as of other life roles—are influenced by culture-related values. Differences between cultures help us understand employee attitudes, values, behaviors, and interpersonal dynamics. Nevertheless, we must remember that differences between countries, as outlined in this study, need not necessarily correspond with similar differences on the individual level. The cultural differences found in this study suggest that we may use them as general guidelines to understand how cultural dimensions influence work-related values, to see that they can lead to conflicts in the workplace, to be aware that cultural differences are legitimate, and to challenge us to recognize that individual differences exist within cultures (Matsumoto, 1996).

Multicultural Counseling and Therapy Theory

Recognizing that a theory for multicultural counseling and therapy was long overdue, Sue, Ivey, and Pedersen (1996) have proposed a multicultural counseling and therapy theory (MCT). These authors have suggested that contemporary theories of counseling and psychotherapy do not adequately deal with the complexity of culturally diverse populations. Specifically, current theories do not describe, explain, or predict current cultural diversity. But even more important, the shortcomings in current contemporary theories and practices will not adequately prepare the mental health profession to meet the needs of an increasingly more diverse population that will become a numerical majority within several decades.

Following is a summary of other underlying assumptions that prompted the development of MCT.

1. Individualism should not dominate the mental health field (consider self-in-situation and people-in-context discussed in Chapter 3).
2. Learning occurs within a cultural context.
3. Cultural identity is changing.
4. Culture should be defined inclusively and broadly.
5. Counselors must possess an understanding of the culture and sociopolitical context of a client's behavior in order to develop appropriate intervention strategies and use appropriate assessment instruments.
6. To develop multicultural competence, the counselor must increase his or her own self-awareness.
7. Multicultural training will be necessary to increase the skills and perspectives needed in the future.

The MCT has six propositions, each with several corollaries, as shown in Box 18-1. The comprehensive nature of this metatheory should promote a large body

Box 18-1
Propositions and Corollaries Underlying MCT Theory

Proposition 1

MCT is a metatheory of counseling and psychotherapy.

Corollary 1A

MCT theory assumes that all theories of counseling and therapy are culture-centered, the values, assumptions, and philosophical bases of which must be made explicit.

Corollary 1B

Each theory of counseling and psychotherapy was developed in a particular cultural context. To the extent that each theory is appropriate to a particular cultural context, it is likely to be biased against contrasting cultural contexts.

Corollary 1C

Different worldviews lead to different constructions of client concerns.

Corollary 1D

MCT theory combines elements of psychodynamic, behavioral, humanistic, biogenic, and other perspectives to the extent that the person's culturally learned assumptions share these salient features.

Corollary 1E

MCT theory seeks to work with and learn from clients through the process of co-construction, thus minimizing potential problems of oppression.

Corollary 1F

MCT theory is ultimately concerned with freeing individuals, families, groups, and organizations to generate new ways of thinking, feeling, and acting—living with intentionality—both within their own cultural framework and with understanding and respect for other worldviews.

Corollary 1G

MCT theory qualifies as a theory by predicting that failure results from the overemphasis of either cultural differences or cultural similarities and that success results from a combined perspective.

Proposition 2

Both counselor and client identities are formed and embedded in multiple levels of experiences (individual, group, and universal) and contexts (individual, family, and cultural milieu). The totality and interrelationships of experiences and contexts must be the focus of treatment.

Corollary 2A

MCT theory acknowledges that all individuals possess individual, group, and universal levels of identity that are fluid and vary in salience.

(continued)

Box 18-1   *(continued)*

Corollary 2B
The importance of the person-environment interaction is basic to MCT theory. A person's identity is formed and continually influenced by her or his context.

Corollary 2C
The Complexity of cultural identity presumes that each client will be able to identify shared features of co-membership with each counselor no matter how different they may appear from each other.

Corollary 2D
The complexity of cultural identity presumes that each client will be able to identify cultural assumptions unique to the client or the counselor, no matter how similar they may appear to each other.

Corollary 2E
Culture is a complex construct that one can define in multiple ways.

Corollary 2F
Counselors and psychotherapists bring their own cultural background to the session; the worldviews associated with their cultural groupings deeply affect the way they conduct therapy.

Corollary 2G
The salient cultural feature (individual, group, or universal) will change for the client during the interview, and a skilled counselor will be able to accurately track that changing salience from one cultural referent to another.

Corollary 2H
Cultural identity is a constantly evolving perspective for both client and counselor, as each is shaped by different experiences over time.

Proposition 3
Development of cultural identity is a major determinant of counselor and client attitudes toward the self, others of the same group, others of a different group, and the dominant group. These attitudes are strongly influenced not only by cultural variables but also by the dynamics of a dominant-subordinate relationship among culturally different groups.

Corollary 3A
Developing a cultural identity represents a cognitive/emotional/behavioral progression and expansion through identifiable and measurable levels of consciousness, or stages.

Corollary 3B
Each client (individual, family, group, organization) has multiple cultural identities, which most likely will not progress or expand at the same rate.

Corollary 3C
Treating the individual, family, or group in isolation may ultimately defeat interconnectedness.

Corollary 3D
Issues of dominance and power have been insufficiently considered in helping theories.

Corollary 3E
MCT counselors or therapists constantly seek to expand awareness of cultural identity issues for both themselves and their clients.

Corollary 3F
Culturally learned assumptions are the primary features of each person's identity or concept of self as a learned perspective.

Corollary 3G
Because power differences influence each group's view of itself and others, MCT theory recognizes the importance of these differences among culturally defined groups.

Corollary 3H
Misunderstanding will likely occur when a client's behavior is interpreted or assessed outside of its cultural context and without regard to shared positive expectations of common cultural ground between therapist and client.

Corollary 3I
Cultural identities are complex but not chaotic; culturally learned patterns provide orderly and systematic narratives in a dialogical perspective where each part is related to the whole of the client's identity.

Corollary 3J
Two people from culturally different backgrounds may disagree without one necessarily being right and the other wrong.

Corollary 3K
Because culture influences both the process and the content of thinking in counseling and therapy, linear thinking may be appropriate for understanding some clients, whereas nonlinear thinking may be appropriate for others.

Corollary 3L
Individual differences and cultural differences are not the same.

Corollary 3M
MCT theory recognizes the dangers of unintentional as well as intentional racism.

(continued)

Box 18-1 *(continued)*

Proposition 4

The effectiveness of MCT theory is most likely enhanced when the counselor uses modalities and defines goals consistent with the life experiences/cultural values of the client.

Corollary 4A

MCT theory recognizes at least two valid conceptual frameworks for culturally sensitive helping: the universal and the culture-specific.

Corollary 4B

One can generate new theories and strategies by starting from a cultural frame of reference.

Corollary 4C

Because counseling and psychotherapy are language-based phenomena and worldviews exist in language, it is vital that awareness of the power of a dominant language (whether that of a therapeutic theory or that of a culture) over a client or client system be fully recognized.

Corollary 4D

To the extent that the client is culturally different from or similar to the counselor in status, affiliation, or ethnographic or demographic variables, the counseling process will be blocked or facilitated.

Corollary 4E

In matching a client with a counselor, considerations of cultural similarity must come second to client preferences, which may be for a culturally different counselor.

Corollary 4F

Counselors who are culturally different from their clients can learn multicultural skills to become effective with those clients.

Corollary 4G

Each intervention may be appropriate for one client in one cultural context and inappropriate for another client in another cultural context.

Corollary 4H

MCT theory recognizes that sympathy—how the counselor would feel if he or she were in a particular situation—is less appropriate than empathy, which focuses on how the client actually in that particular situation feels.

Proposition 5

MCT theory stresses the importance of multiple helping roles developed by many culturally different groups and societies. Besides the one-on-one encounter aimed at remediation in the individual, these roles often involve larger social units, systems intervention, and prevention.

Corollary 5A

Community resources, which include the extended family, people in the neighborhood, spiritual advisors, and government officials, can enrich therapy.

Corollary 5B

In multicultural counseling, formal methods in formal settings are supplemented by informal methods and/or settings.

Corollary 5C

Though the Western meaning of *counseling* developed from a Euro-American academic setting in the 20th century, counseling has been available historically whenever individuals helped other individuals with personal problems.

Corollary 5D

Because counseling and counselors have frequently been stereotyped as protecting the system and the status quo against the minority, individual counseling has sometimes suffered a stigma in multicultural settings.

Corollary 5E

Because contemporary ethical guidelines are based on a culturally narrow perspective of counseling, the multicultural counselor might need to violate or reframe particular ethical guidelines in order to counsel in an ethically appropriate manner.

Corollary 5F

Because problems usually develop in a cultural context, the definition of counseling as one-on-one problem solving may be superficial. Problems may be defined as residing in the family, group, or community.

Corollary 5G

Although a one-directional description of counseling might emphasize outcome measures of pleasure, happiness, or other good feelings, a two-directional description of counseling in an asymmetrical balance perspective might stress the importance of meaning that incorporates both pain and pleasure, happiness and sadness, and good and bad.

Corollary 5H

A multicultural perspective in counseling contributes to accurate assessment and diagnosis in every therapeutic setting, not just for minority populations.

Proposition 6

The liberation of consciousness is a basic goal of MCT theory. MCT theory emphasizes the importance of expanding personal, family, group, and organizational consciousness of the place of self-in-relation, family-in-relation, and organization-in-relation. This results in therapy that is not

(continued)

Box 18-1 *(continued)*

only ultimately contextual in orientation, but also draws on traditional methods of healing from many cultures.

Corollary 6A

The process of *conscientizacao*, or critical consciousness, is a constant dimension of the helping process.

Corollary 6B

There is a strong psychoeducational component to MCT theory. The role of the counselor or therapist often includes teaching the client about the underlying cultural dimensions of present concerns.

Corollary 6C

MCT therapists or counselors draw on both Western and non-European systems of helping.

SOURCE: Adapted from *A Theory of Multicultural Counseling and Therapy* by D. W. Sue, A. E. Ivey, & P. B. Pedersen, pp. 13–29. Copyright 1996 by Brooks/Cole Publishing Company, a division of International Thomson Publishing Inc.

---

of research well into the 21st century. In fact, Sue, Ivey, and Pedersen (1996) have developed suggestions for various research approaches for their theory. They have suggested that past research has focused on social biases of Eurocentric society and subsequently have not addressed the study of positive attributes and characteristics of racial and ethnic minority groups.

The MCT theory has many implications for the future of counseling, but its main focus is on changing conventional counseling. As we learn from research that this theory will certainly promote, we will be in a better position to consider counseling strategies to meet the needs of culturally diverse groups. Here are some of the suggested changes at this point (Sue, Ivey, & Pedersen, 1996).

1. *Balance the focus of counseling.* We are to move away from the traditional focus on the individual; more attention should be given to family and cultural issues. Thus, a balance is needed between self-oriented help and self-in-relation help.

2. *Expand the repertoire of helping responses.* Some of the helping responses that counselors now use—and, in fact, their approach to helping responses—may be inappropriate for culturally different clients. For example, passive attending and listening skills may confuse some clients from different cultures.

3. *Identify indigenous helping roles.* Dealing with human problems is quite different from one culture to another. Counselors should be trained to understand different culturally based roles and that traditional healers found in a culture are viewed with high credibility.

4. *Develop alternatives to the conventional counseling role.* New and different counseling roles may require that counselors practice outside of their office, such as in the community or in an organization. Counselors are to become more externally focused—that is, advocate changes in the community, enhance job opportunities, and intervene on behalf of the client. In sum, counselors are to become

advisors, advocates, facilitators of indigenous support systems, consultants, and change agents.

Other Cultures' Opinions about Preparing for Work

In 1989, the National Career Development Association (NCDA) commissioned the Gallup Organization to survey the opinions of three cultural groups (African Americans, Hispanics, and Asian Pacific Islanders) about their own career planning processes and workplaces. African Americans strongly expressed a need for career planning and access to appropriate occupational information. They also expressed problems of discrimination in the workplace. The Asian Pacific Islander group reported that their skills were not fully used on the job. They also experienced more job-related stress than did other cultural groups surveyed. Hispanics indicated that pay was the greatest incentive to motivate them to do more on a job (Brown, Minor, & Jepsen, 1991).

Although these findings are helpful in determining career guidance programs for other cultural groups, the limitations of the study should be carefully scrutinized. For example, a telephone survey was used, thus limiting the subgroups studied to those who have telephones; the sample size was relatively small, and Native Americans were excluded. As a result of these limitations, the results should be used with caution. However, the need for career planning and access to appropriate occupational information found in this study is not surprising and was also expressed as a need in a similar research project reported in 1989 (Brown & Minor, 1989).

African Americans

The largest racial minority group in this country is African Americans. Most African Americans live in urban areas and have assumed a moderate position in our society. For the most part, they have been wage earners as opposed to being self-employed. In essence, they have been blue-collar workers rather than managers or proprietors. African American men have achieved greater career mobility than African American women have. Although some of both sexes have managed to achieve upward mobility to professional occupations, the overall success of upward movement of African Americans is minimal. Those who have attained middle-class status are also in the position to take advantage of educational opportunities and career mobility. Others, particularly those classified as underclass—primarily from three-generation families on welfare—are without job skills and lack motivation to change their status (Smith, 1983; Axelson, 1993).

According to Jackson (1975), African Americans have a unique psychological development. He has devised four developmental stages that depict the psychological development:

1. *Passive acceptance:* In this stage, African Americans imitate whites as a way of coping with them.

2. *Active resistance:* In this stage, African Americans reject white cultural patterns and become active in militant groups.
3. *Redirection:* In this stage, African Americans give less attention to the cultural mores of whites and focus on their own identity.
4. *Internalization:* In this stage, cultural and self-identity are achieved.

In all stages of a developmental approach, counselors must be aware of their counselees' current stage and the tasks associated with transitions and moving from one stage to another. In this model, for example, an individual in stage 2 may have difficulty relating to a white counselor.

African Americans in School

Many African Americans are made to feel as outsiders in public schools, according to Vontress (1979) and more recently McBay (1992). Even after several decades of integration, they are treated differently from whites. More important, they continue to receive inferior educational opportunities compared to whites. What is implied here is that African Americans have reached or soon should reach the point of not being considered so unlike whites; thus, special expertise to counsel or teach them may not be warranted. In the meantime, they remain socially isolated in church, school, and work.

Achievement and motivation among African Americans in college have been found to be equally high for both men and women. This finding suggests that African American women have high expectations for work and a sense of responsibility to contribute to family income. However, they tend to choose the more traditional feminine professional occupations at about the same rate as white women do (Woody, 1992). The message to the counselor is twofold: encourage and enhance the high level of achievement motivation of African American women; and encourage more to consider nontraditional, professional occupations.

The National Science Foundation (1989) gathered statistics on the number of African Americans enrolled in graduate courses in doctorate-granting institutions as a percentage of total graduate enrollment: 1.7% in both computer sciences and life sciences, 1.3% in physical sciences, and 1.4% in mathematical sciences. The number of doctoral degrees awarded to African Americans from 1975 to 1989 in physical sciences, life sciences, and engineering ranged from a low of 101 in 1980 to a high of 133 in 1978 (Vetter, 1989). Malcolm (1990) suggested that we must encourage more African Americans to major in mathematics and the sciences by engaging children in these subjects early in their educational experience and by encouraging parents to influence their children in this direction. In essence, we must encourage African Americans to choose majors in a wider variety of career fields.

African American Workers

Taylor (1990) suggested that the major reasons for fewer job prospects for African Americans are related to industrial decentralization and shifts from manufacturing to service industries. These events have significantly reduced job prospects for unskilled and semiskilled workers and have had devastating effects on the poorly educated. However, Johnson (1990) reported that underemployed and underpaid African Americans have developed coping strategies to maintain self-worth and self-esteem through personal and familial achievements.

Woody (1992) researched work patterns of African American women and found that many lack requisite skills to compete for technical work and will fail to qualify for higher-level jobs. She argued that African American women have severe job limitations, and many are restricted to low-end jobs because of discrimination. She suggested that there is a "women's work subculture" that may be alleviated only through an improved national employment policy.

Suggested Developmental Strategies for African Americans

Selected developmental strategies to help African Americans include assisting self-concept development, developing more internally directed behavior, becoming more aware of job opportunities, clarifying motivational aspirations, and dealing with ambivalence toward whites.

1. *Developing self-concept:* Many African Americans can benefit from being made keenly aware of how feelings of personal inadequacies affect their perception of current and future work roles.
2. *Learning to be more internally directed:* Programs designed to help African Americans take control of their career direction and break away from old patterns of life will help them toward self-improvement.
3. *Learning about job opportunities:* Career information that delineates trends in the labor force and explains equal opportunity laws will alert African Americans to job opportunities. Careful attention should be directed toward the effective use of materials and the steps involved in a job search.
4. *Clarifying motivational aspirations:* This module should include causes of low expectations and fear of failure and methods of improving motivation.
5. *Learning to cope with the white society:* This component should include interrelationships in work environments and the development of sense of identity.

Asian Americans

Asian Americans represent a culturally diverse group that includes Cambodians, Chinese, Filipinos, Indians, Japanese, Pakistanis, Thai, and Vietnamese (Sue & Abe, 1988). Many Asian American groups place a high value on education. Sue and Okazaki (1990) suggested that Asian Americans perceive education as a means of upward mobility and are highly motivated to remove barriers that may limit them. However, Leong and Serafica (1995) argued that Asian Americans are often victimized by discriminatory employment practices. Asian women are given especially low status and are exploited in the working world (Chu, 1981; Kumata & Murata, 1980). Hsia (1981) argued that Asian Americans are hindered in the job market because of poor communication skills, which accounts for their tendency to choose jobs such as engineering, computer science, and economics.

In evaluating counseling processes as a source of conflict for Chinese Americans, Sue and Sue (1990) made several pertinent observations: (1) Chinese American students inhibit emotional expression and do not actively participate in the counseling process, (2) Chinese Americans are discouraged from revealing emotional problems by their cultural conditioning, and (3) Chinese American students react more favorably to well-structured counseling models. Sue's conclusions emphasize the importance of understanding cultural influences when counseling Chinese Americans.

Fernandez (1988) argued that Southeast Asian students should be counseled using behavioral approaches. She considered it inappropriate to use counseling techniques that require clients to verbalize excessively. Evanoski and Tse (1989) have successfully used bilingual materials and role models in workshops directed toward parents of Chinese and Korean children that exposed them to methods of accessing a variety of occupations. The basic assumption was that these parents have a tremendous influence on their children.

The following special needs and problems associated with Asian Americans in counseling are summarized from suggestions by Kaneshige (1979), D. W. Sue (1992), and Ivey (1986).

1. Asian Americans are very sensitive about verbalizing psychological problems, especially in group encounters.
2. Asian Americans tend to be inexpressive when asked to discuss personal achievements and limitations.
3. Asian Americans tend to misinterpret the role of counseling in general and the benefits that may be derived from it.
4. Asian Americans may be perceived as very passive and nonassertive with authority figures, but in reality they are reacting to cultural inhibitions that discourage them from being perceived as aggressive.
5. Asian Americans may strongly resist suggestions to modify behavior that is unassuming and nonassertive.

In recent years, Vietnamese have presented particular problems to career counselors who have assisted them in relocating in this country. The needs and problems of this adult cultural group are good examples for illustrating limitations of employment for first-generation Asian Americans. In addition to the need to learn English, other problems and difficulties are (1) recognizing the importance of transferable skills, (2) considering past work history as relevant, (3) understanding the concept of career ladders, (4) locating information about unemployment, and (5) recognizing the importance of résumé preparation and interview skills training.

As a group, Asian Americans have the lowest rate of unemployment (Smith, 1983). In general, Asian Americans are very industrious workers, seem to value education, and have taken advantage of higher education to enhance their career development. They are also known to do well in business administration, engineering, and sciences. However, the stereotype of the Asian American as being good in sciences but lacking in verbal skills may limit their access to careers that require communication skills.

Finally, among traditional Asian cultures, offering what is considered to be desirable help includes giving advice and suggestions but avoiding confrontation and direct interpretation of motives and actions. When discussing personal issues, it is more appropriate to be indirect, and the counselor should do most of the initial verbalization with a rather formal interactive approach (D. W. Sue, 1994).

Suggested Developmental Strategies for Asian Americans

Although the following strategies meet the specific needs of Asian Americans, they can probably be generalized to other groups discussed in this chapter. In fact, many of the counseling strategies, models, and components discussed in other chapters are relevant for all groups discussed in this chapter, so that the strategies suggested here should not be considered exhaustive of all pertinent counseling strategies.

Components of counseling for Asian Americans include the following.

1. *Learning self-assertion skills:* This component should be designed to help Asian Americans overcome the stereotype of being passive and noncommunicative.
2. *Learning to understand organization systems and bureaucracies:* This component should be especially useful for first-generation Asian Americans.
3. *Improving communication skills:* Many Asian Americans may be hampered in their career development and career options because of poor communication skills.
4. *Improving interpersonal skills:* Learning how to establish satisfying and productive relationships with others should help Asian Americans meet social-emotional needs.
5. *Learning to understand work environments:* Forming relationships with supervisors and peers should help Asian Americans adjust to work roles and work environments.
6. *Using parents as role models:* Asian American parents tend to encourage their children in career pursuits. Parents who are aware of potential job opportunities are in a very strong position to advise their children.

Hispanic Americans

Hispanic Americans compose the second largest minority group in the country. The largest subgroup of Hispanics are Mexican Americans, followed by Cubans and Puerto Ricans. The states with the largest Hispanic populations are California, Texas, New York, and Florida. Most Hispanics live in metropolitan areas (Smith, 1983; Axelson, 1993).

Although Ponterotto (1987) reported that Hispanics underutilize counseling services in both mental health and academic settings, there is good evidence that they could benefit from these services, especially when intervention strategies meet special needs. Rodriguez and Blocher (1988) found that interventions with academically and economically disadvantaged Puerto Rican women produced positive results by raising their level of career maturity and developing beliefs that they can control their own destiny.

Social factors such as social-class membership, environment of the home and school, and the community in which the individual resides significantly influence career perspectives and attitudes toward work (Osipow, 1983; Pietrofesa & Splete, 1975). Arbona (1995) supported this conclusion by debunking the idea that cultural traits have restricted Hispanics in career choices. Instead, socioeconomic status and lack of opportunity have restricted Hispanics from access to higher education and subsequently to their occupational aspirations. However, Hispanics are not a homogeneous group; there are important differences between subgroups and between Hispanics from different socioeconomic backgrounds (Arbona, 1995). Career counselors should attempt to assess levels of acculturation before developing intervention strategies. Ponterotto (1987) recommended obtaining the following information as a measure of acculturation: socioeconomic status, place of birth, language preference, generation level, preferred ethnic identity, and ethnic group social contacts.

It is not a good idea, however, to overgeneralize about the Hispanic students in our schools today; many are acculturated and fit well into the mainstream of society. One can expect, for example, to find diverse value systems among Hispanics. There are, however, those Hispanics who cling to their traditional heritage and consequently may have difficulty in adjusting to an Anglo-dominant school and culture. Caught between conflicting cultures, the adolescent Hispanic seeks out the support of peers who are experiencing similar conflicts. As a result, there is usually less interaction with other groups of students and, typically, school becomes a low priority.

The Mexican American family, in particular, has been characterized as a closely knit group that greatly influences the values of its members. For example, Axelson (1993) suggested that Spanish-speaking children are generally taught to value and respect family, church, and school as well as masculinity and honor. Families are primarily patriarchal (as far as the center of authority is concerned) with a distinct division of duties; that is, the father is the breadwinner, and the mother is the homemaker. Spanish is the primary language spoken in the home and in the barrio.

Fouad (1995) recommends several career intervention strategies for Hispanics. Researchers are encouraged to assess these recommendations and to aim their research efforts toward examining the career behavior of Hispanics. The following career counseling recommendations have been paraphrased from Fouad (1995, pp. 186–187).

1. Career counseling must consider the cultural context of all clients, including Hispanics. Some Hispanics have retained traditional value systems, whereas others may not be traditional. When we are not certain about the client's

cultural background, we need to be creative, or as Leong (1993) has labeled it, to have "creative uncertainty." Using this approach, we are to guide our counseling efforts toward the client's willingness to inform us of how culture has influenced his or her life.

2. Flexibility is essential in the career counseling process, especially when we incorporate familial and environmental factors in decision making.

3. Assessment instruments should be chosen with care as to what is appropriate for Hispanic cultures.

4. Use immediate intervention to retain Hispanic students in school. Career information should include reasons for taking math and science courses.

5. Develop strategies to include self-efficacy as a key to future career success.

6. Focus on Hispanic females. Provide them with a wide variety of career information, including information on nontraditional careers.

Suggested Developmental Strategies for Hispanic Americans

The vast differences in origins and diversity of Hispanics make it difficult to generalize counseling needs and subsequent career counseling strategies. The suggested developmental strategies for other groups are particularly relevant for first-generation Hispanic Americans. For example, learning about effective communication skills, work environments and organizations, the use of career information, job search strategies, and interpersonal relationships are viable components of counseling. Other suggestions include the following.

1. *Learning goal-setting and problem-solving skills:* The major goal of this component is to help Hispanics set goals and priorities, analyze situations, and apply realistic and productive techniques in planning.

2. *Developing working-parent skills:* The purpose of this component is to help Hispanics develop more awareness of the need to effectively balance parenting responsibilities with work responsibilities.

3. *Improving financial management of resources:* The goal of this component is to help Hispanics effectively utilize anticipated monetary resources from employment. The focus should be on principles of budgeting.

Native Americans

The American Indian and Alaska Native population in the United States is estimated at 1.9 million (U.S. Bureau of the Census, 1990). More than 1.5 million American Indians, also referred to as Native Americans, live in the United States. Approximately half of them live on Native American lands and some 275 reservations. Of those Native Americans who live outside the reservations, the largest concentrations are in Los Angeles, San Francisco, and Chicago, but Minneapolis, Denver, Tulsa, Phoenix, and Milwaukee also contain significant numbers. The states with the highest numbers of Native Americans are Oklahoma, California,

Arizona, New Mexico, Alaska, Washington, North Carolina, Texas, New York, and Michigan.

According to the Bureau of Indian Affairs (1993), there are 318 recognized tribes, not including 200 Alaska Native tribes. Each tribe may have a different language, religious beliefs, and social characteristics that are common to that tribe. However, almost two-thirds of Native Americans live in urban areas; they are there for training, college, or employment. Many keep close contact with their family and friends who live on the reservations (Johnson, Swartz, & Martin, 1995).

On the reservations, many are involved in farming, ranching, fishing, and lumber production. Off the reservations, Native Americans work in factories, on farms, and as skilled craftsworkers. Some tribes are engaged in various enterprises, such as motel management; others offer bingo and lottery games to the general public (Axelson, 1993).

Career Development of Native Americans

An important variable in the career development of Native Americans is the degree to which they adhere to cultural customs, language, and traditions (Johnson, Swartz, & Martin, 1995). The degree of cultural heritage is described on a continuum by Ryan and Ryan (1982, cited in LaFromboise, Trimble, & Mohatt, 1990), as follows.

1. *Traditional:* Speak only Native language and observe traditions.
2. *Transitional:* Speak both Native language and English and may question traditions of the past.
3. *Marginal:* Speak of themselves as Indian but identify with roles in dominant society.
4. *Assimilated:* Have generally embraced the dominant society.
5. *Bicultural:* Are accepted by dominant society but also identify with tribal traditions and culture.

As with other ethnic groups, we should not stereotype Native Americans but instead focus on the degree to which each client adheres to cultural customs, language, and traditions. Significant differences between individuals within cultural groups must be addressed in the career counseling process. But we should also remember that old traditions should be respected, and some may be used to foster career development; the use of role models and experientially related activities are recommended (Johnson, Swartz, & Martin, 1995).

Counseling Native Americans

Martin (1995) has developed the following initial intervention strategies for Native Americans that include cultural and contextual variables.

1. The first step is to obtain information about the Native American client. For instance, the counselor should have information about the client's tribe and reservation community and should visit the reservation, if possible. Relevant informa-

tion includes tribal history, customs, and family systems. As in all career counseling strategies, the counselor should have up-to-date educational and career information and as much information about workplace affiliates as possible.

2. Establishing communication with the client is the major focus of the second step. It is recommended that the counselor use what is referred to as cultural/environmental/contextual focusing; this "includes not only knowledge of and respect for the values of other cultures, but comfort with and knowledge of one's own values and ethnicity" (Betz & Fitzgerald, 1995, p. 263). Perspectives of presenting problems are better understood by both counselor and client within this context.

3. The counselor should be alert to the fact that extended families play an important role in the decision-making process. A major goal is to gain the family's support and provide them with specific methods that will assist in the career development process.

4. Obtain an evaluation of the client's English ability, preferably from an educational institution that offers courses in English for Native Americans.

5. Use strategies to increase the client's knowledge of the world of work. Recommended are structured reading-discussion techniques using current occupational resources. Video resources may also be used, and group guidance can be an effective technique with Native Americans.

6. For a Native American to obtain firsthand knowledge of an occupation, job shadowing (spending time in the workplace with an individual engaged in a particular occupation), interviewing individuals on job sites, or enrolling in an on-the-job training program are recommended.

Most of the counseling strategies discussed in this chapter are often referred to as specially focused interventions (Betz and Fitzgerald, 1995). The name certainly applies to ethnic groups who have special needs that counselors must become increasingly aware of, especially for Native Americans. Bowman (1995) argues that it is impossible for career counselors to be aware of all variables within a culture; let us acknowledge that fact, but the proper attitude is to be open to continued learning about cultural diversity.

Another variable to be considered in counseling approaches is that tribes do differ in value orientations and individuals differ within tribes. Thus, as in all minority groups, general recommendations for counseling have to be modified to meet individual needs. Thomason (1991) pointed out that a major consideration is the degree of acculturation in the dominant society. Furthermore, he suggested that the client's set of beliefs as to how changes occur is an important consideration for developing intervention strategies for Native Americans.

However, Herring (1990) argued that there are many career myths about Native Americans; he believes that we simply do not have the necessary research results to draw many conclusions about their career development. Like other minority groups, Native Americans have not been exposed to a wide range of careers and have limited opportunities to attend college because of high unemployment rates. He suggested that Native Americans be introduced to more nontraditional occupations and be provided with career information using Native American role models to expand their career considerations.

Native Americans have a strong desire to retain the symbolic aspects of their heritage, much of which is different from the dominant culture. The challenge for counselors is to assist them in preserving the positive aspects of their heritage while encouraging them to modify some behaviors. For example, the ability to enjoy the present should be combined with planning skills, and the ability to share with others should be combined with assertive behavior. The value orientation of Native Americans is a sensitive issue for career counselors.

Native American resistance to counseling in general is exemplified by the group's underuse of existing mental health services. According to Manson (1982), Native Americans are the most neglected group in the mental health field. Miller (1982) suggested that more Native Americans would take advantage of counseling relationships if appropriate counseling strategies were used. Trimble and LaFromboise (1985) summarized Miller's strategies as follows.

1. Personal ethnic identity in itself is hardly sufficient for understanding the influence of culture on the client.
2. The client's history contains a number of strengths that can promote and facilitate the counseling process.
3. The counselor should be aware of his or her own biases about cultural pluralism—they might interfere with the counseling relationship.
4. The counselor should encourage the client to become more active in the process of identifying and learning the various elements associated with positive growth and development.
5. Most important are empathy, caring, and a sense of the importance of the human potential. (p. 131)

Developmental Strategies for Native Americans

The following strategies are designed to help Native Americans maintain their cultural heritage and at the same time introduce concepts of career development of the dominant society.

1. *Using parents and relatives as counseling facilitators:* The rationale for this approach is embedded in the strong family ties of Native Americans.
2. *Using Native American role models:* They should assist in helping to break down resistance to counseling objectives. Native Americans should react more favorably to other Native Americans.
3. *Emphasizing individual potential in the context of future goals:* Identity conflicts make it difficult for Native Americans to project themselves into other environments, including work environments.

Counseling Strategies for Multicultural Groups

The preceding personal and environmental characteristics serve as barriers to the career development of those whose culture differs from the dominant one, and they establish the need for specific counseling strategies that help overcome these barriers. Feck (1971) noted that essential counseling strategies for the multicultural groups generally include frequent rewards and reinforcements of positive behaviors. It is important in the planning process to relate ongoing activities with long-term goals. Operationally, the counselor presents short-term plans and gradually introduces plans for the future. Exposure to success models, particularly from the individual's ethnic community and cultural background, is highly recommended as a means for developing positive self-concepts.

Sue and Sue (1990) suggested that current mental health practices cannot be applied universally to culturally different populations without recognition of those differences. They implied that counselors who are unaware of different world views (psychological orientation, manners of thinking, ways of behaving and interpreting events) are essentially ineffective; counselors must learn to accept the worldviews of others. The following characteristics are necessary to be a culturally effective counselor (Sue, 1978).

1. An ability to recognize which values and assumptions the counselor holds regarding the desirability or undesirability of human behavior;
2. Awareness of the generic characteristics of counseling that cut across many schools of counseling theory;
3. Understanding of the sociopolitical forces (oppression and racism) that have served to influence the identity and perspective of the culturally different;
4. An ability to share the world view of his or her clients without negating its legitimacy; and
5. True eclecticism in his or her counseling. (p. 451)

Sue implied that counselors can use their entire repertoire of counseling skills as long as they are accepting of different views and are cognizant of the experiences and lifestyle of the culturally different. He emphasized that counselors must be alert to the influences of different views and environmental factors. Finally, counselors must be cautious not to impose their values on others.

Sue (1981) also developed a minority identity model that describes the psychosocial development of minority group members. Stages of development and transitions between stages are expressed in terms of the minority members' attitude toward self, others of the same minority, others of a different minority, and the dominant society or groups.

Stage 1: Conformity—The individual is self-deprecating and prefers to be identified with dominant cultural values.

Stage 2: Dissonance—The individual develops conflicts about the dominant system and is in a state of cultural confusion.

Stage 3: Resistance and immersion—The individual is more self-appreciating and rejects the dominant society.

Stage 4: Introspection—The individual carefully evaluates his or her attitude toward self and the dominant society.

Stage 5: Synergetic articulation and awareness—The individual accepts his or her cultural identity and develops selective appreciations of the dominant culture.

In addition to providing guidelines for career guidance activities, this model also provides counselors with a greater understanding of the stress and adjustment problems of minorities and the role of environment and culture in minority identity development.

Axelson (1993) suggested basic points of awareness for improving counseling in a multicultural society, including cultural-total awareness, self-awareness, client awareness, and counseling procedure awareness. These basic points of awareness lead to focusing on the client's needs. Needs are most appropriately conceptualized from a broad base of human experiences to more discrete distinctions. The broad base of human experiences includes common human experiences, specific cultural experiences, individual experiences, and the unique individual. This approach to counseling in a multicultural society consists of the following four steps.

1. Recognize the fact that all human beings possess the like capacity for thought, feeling, and behavior.
2. Be knowledgeable in several cultures; study differences and similarities among people of different groups and their special needs and problems.
3. Gain an understanding of how the individual relates to important objects of motivation, what his or her personal constructs are, and how they form his or her worldview.
4. Blend steps 1, 2, and 3 into an integrated picture of the distinctive person as experienced during the counseling process. (p. 18)

The counseling procedures outlined by Sue and Sue (1990) and by Axelson (1993) suggest an awareness of the fact that when we counsel in a multicultural society, we are likely to have clients who have a distinctively different cultural background and thus different worldviews. An important step is to recognize other worldviews and discover what those views might be in order to eventually arrive at a point where the uniqueness of the individual dictates the counseling intervention strategies. In the next section, relational counseling focuses on realistic self-appraisals.

Relational Counseling

The major goal of relational counseling is to assist individuals in developing realistic self-images by focusing on positive aspects of self and relating these images to existing opportunities. Axelson (1993) suggested that individuals with self-doubts have difficulty projecting into a work environment with any degree of expectation for success. On the surface, such individuals may appear lazy or lacking ambition or motivation, but in reality, they are reacting to pessimistic expectations. Counseling can help these individuals alter their poor self-perceptions by emphasizing individual strengths and resources, highlighting resources in the community, and providing a positive approach to what can be accomplished within the boundaries of existing conditions, including labor trends and economic realities.

The focus of relational counseling is on *realistic* opportunities and conditions. Economic conditions, for example, should help shape the individual's perception of what can realistically be achieved in the working world. Specific techniques of relational counseling follow.

1. Identify and reinforce self-perceived qualities and accomplishments. Identify areas of desired improvement with accompanying short-term goals.
2. Point out that negative feelings are related to low expectations and may be a negative factor throughout a lifetime.
3. Practice positive visual imagery, such as imagining oneself in a successful job interview.
4. Validate self through identification with others, using role models from everyday life rather than celebrities. Emphasize characteristics such as honesty, forthrightness, and persistence.
5. Learn self-assertion skills, which increase self-respect.
6. Understand and use services and resources. Many minority group members are not aware of or question the credibility of these resources.
7. Disseminate knowledge and information through career guidance and education. Career guidance with a life-centered focus in the social context of "individual, family, culture, national, and international" (Axelson, 1993, p. 256) should be available at all levels.

Relational counseling focuses on developing realistic self-appraisals, developing personal strengths, and expanding perceptions of occupational choices. Removing self-doubts that interfere with personal expectations is a major goal, accomplished through the identification and strengthening of personal abilities. The individuals' perception of life must be evaluated from environmental experiences, and negative factors are balanced by positive ones. Emphasizing positive experiences is an important method to reduce negative perceptions in mind-sets. Finally, social factors that influence values and attitudes, economic factors that impact an individual's career opportunities, political factors that impact special interests, and chance factors of events that are beyond one's control are to be emphasized in career development counseling.

A Sample Counseling Component for Multicultural Groups

In considering the special problems and needs of ethnic groups, countless options for program objectives come to mind. Therefore, the following counseling component should not be considered a comprehensive counseling program that resolves all needs and special problems of ethnic groups; rather, it is just one example of a counseling component that accomplishes only one of many possible objectives. This component illustrates how a counselor can assist members of various ethnic groups to take charge of their lives.

Rotter's (1966) concept of *locus of control* suggests that there are internal and external personality types. The locus of control for internal people is contingent on their behavior and their own characteristics; external people consider rewards and outcomes as independent of their actions and behavior. Putting it another way, internal people feel they can control their lives through their actions and behavior, whereas external people feel they have little control over their lives. Powell and Vega (1972) suggested that internal people generally have a good self-concept, are more independent and self-reliant, and show more initiative and effort in controlling their environment than do external people. Rotter postulated that a person's locus of control is highly related to the events in life and subsequent positive and negative reinforcements received. The following individual counseling sessions illustrate techniques to assist the culturally different individual in establishing greater feelings of control of life.

Rosalita, a 17-year-old Mexican American girl and a junior in high school, was referred to the counseling office when she indicated she planned to drop out of school to get a job. During the course of the interview, Rosalita indicated that she really felt powerless to change the direction of her life. She expressed despair when thinking in terms of her family situation because most of her older brothers and sisters had taken menial jobs and lived in the "barrio." Her feeling was that this was a matter of fate and there was little she could do about it. After looking over Rosalita's academic record, the counselor discovered that her grades were average and above. There were also indications from previous test data that Rosalita had the aptitude to continue with academic training beyond the high school level.

Counselor: Well, let's state it in more specific terms. How high do you think you could raise your grade?
Rosalita: I might be able to raise it to a B on my next paper.
Counselor: Okay, let's set that as a goal.

The day following Rosalita's meeting with her English teacher, she returned to the counselor's office very enthusiastic about the conference. She stated that the teacher was very cordial and had offered constructive criticism and encouragement. The counselor quickly made the point that this is one example of how individuals can control the outcomes of their lives if they are willing to take initiative to effect change.

The importance of this approach in counseling disadvantaged individuals is that it can provide them with concrete evidence that some control over their lives can be effected through their own actions. By arranging learning situations that prove individuals can gain control through appropriate action, specific behavior and subsequent outcomes are reinforced. As the individual recognizes alternatives to past unsuccessful behaviors, more internally oriented behavior can evolve.

Prevocational Training
Program for Multicultural Groups

A prevocational training program for adults of ethnic groups was launched at Southwest Texas State University. The program was designed to provide prevocational training to adults residing in small towns and rural areas within a 50-mile radius of the university. The major purpose of the program was to assist these adults to prepare for employment. The classes were held four hours each day, five days a week, for six weeks. The class size ranged from 10 to 15 students.

The major components of the prevocational training program were adapted from two manuals, *Prevocational Training Manual* and *Career Orientation Manual*, developed by the Texas Rehabilitation Commission (1980, 1985) and used for similar training programs within the state. The instruction involves lecture, group discussion, role playing, individual instruction, homework assignments, visitation, and audiovisual presentations. Table 18-1 delineates several of the components.

Orientation Component

The instructor is required to make advance preparations before each group of students enters the program. Most class members are individually interviewed and cumulative files are reviewed. This phase of the program is crucial in that the ground

TABLE 18-1
Prevocational Training Program

Components	Class periods	Activities
Orientation	2	Sharing individual family history; setting goals and objectives; reinforcement of individual and group involvement
Exploring	5	Group discussion of self-image, self-worth, self-esteem, and locus of control; administer attitude scale; group discussions on self-assessments; role-playing using stereotyped models; discussion groups relating self-concept to work
Communication skill and relationships	3	Role-playing various situations using assertiveness training; role-playing using listening skills with group discussion; reinforcement of appropriate behavior; client involvement in self-exploration of values toward others and work
Goal setting and problem solving	4	Discussion of time-management principles; self-exploration of goals; reinforcement of appropriate behavior; advising on individual goals and problems
Working parents' skills	1	Problem solving using daily chore schedule
Occupational information	5	Administer interest inventory; group discussion of results; field trip to university Career Development Resource Center; individual and group career exploration
Job interview skills	5	Role-playing an interview; filling out job application forms; advising on individual basis
Expectations in the world of work	4	Group discussion of employer expectations, employee expectations, and peer group affiliation
Consumer information	1	Discussion of budgeting principles; presentation of sample budget; review of wise use of credit and filling out a sample credit application form

rules for class have to be firmly established. The important objective here is to empha-size class attendance and participation in class projects. Students are encouraged to view the classes as if they were working at a job and were expected to be on time; that is, they are expected to attend regularly and to put forth a maximum effort.

Exploring Component

The exploring component is considered of major importance primarily because it is designed to improve the student's self-image. Many participants will have had very few positive experiences in their lives, particularly in work-related activities. This component is structured to promote a more positive attitude regarding future work expectations. Group discussion is the major delivery system for accomplish-ing the learning and action objectives outlined for each student (Texas Rehabilita-tion Commission, 1980).

1. Every person is unique and worthwhile and has important contributions to make to others.
2. How you feel about yourself determines to a large extent how you act and what you do.
3. Identify at least five things about yourself that you like and that will be helpful to you on a job.
4. Identify some things in yourself that you don't particularly like and would like to change.
5. Learn to use what you know about yourself to your best advantage. To do this, choose activities and goals in which the strengths you have are important and can be used well. Accept some of your weaknesses and choose activities in which those weaknesses are not very important. Decide to change some of your weaknesses. (p. 15)

Other components provide students with the opportunity to identify their strengths and weaknesses as related to successful employment. Throughout the entire program, students are encouraged to focus on effective behavior patterns necessary in maintaining employment and a productive lifestyle. The program focuses on future expectations. Many students may express that they feel power-less to change the direction of their lives and, in fact, feel that they have very little control over their own lives. In an attempt to change these perceptions, modules were structured to emphasize that students should (1) accept more responsibility for their behavior, (2) become less dependent on others, (3) be more willing to cor-rect their weaknesses, (4) be willing to experiment with new behaviors, (5) improve decision-making skills, (6) become more realistic in their aspirations, and (7) show more initiative and effort in controlling their environment.

The evaluation of the prevocational training program was accomplished through comparisons of pretest and posttest scores on an attitude scale developed by the TRC from the *Career Maturity Inventory* (Crites & Savickas, 1995), *The Locus of Control* (Rotter, 1966), and a follow-up of the graduates. The results of the pretest and posttest scores suggest that there was a significant change in the graduates' attitude toward making a career choice and entering the world of work. There was significant improvement in orientation toward work, independence in career decision-making tasks, and involvement in the career decision process. A follow-up of the graduates of the program revealed that 78% were either attending other training programs or were actively seeking employment.

Group Counseling Procedures: Communication Skills

The communication skills component has been selected to illustrate the group counseling procedures and techniques used in this program. In this component, each counselee should be able to demonstrate (1) effective listening skills and the ability to express thoughts clearly and precisely, (2) effective methods of communicating in working situations, and (3) effective methods of communicating as a working parent. The following scenario demonstrates the techniques used to accomplish the first two objectives.

There are six participants: Sam, a 34-year-old African American male; Yolanda, a 27-year-old Mexican American female; Carla, a 24-year-old Mexican American female; Jane, a 30-year-old white female; Rod, a 32-year-old African American male; and Georgia, a 32-year-old African American female.

SESSION 1

Objective: Each group member will be able to demonstrate effective listening skills.

Counselor: Carla, I would like you and Georgia to move to the center of the room. Now, Carla, you tell Georgia about two people you know, including their ages, how you met them, where they work, and anything else you can think of that would be of interest about the individuals. Georgia, I would like you to listen carefully to Carla's description of those individuals and try to remember as much as you can. The rest of the group is to observe both Carla and Georgia.

The counselor gave the group members a handout outlining listening skills to sharpen their observations. After Carla had described two individuals, the following exchange took place.

Sam: Hey, Georgia, why can't you look people in the eye when they are talking to you? That turns me off!

Yolanda: I agree! I don't like talking to people who don't pay attention.

Rod: Well, maybe she was listening—you know—but it was hard to tell.

Counselor: Carla, tell us how you felt.

Carla: I thought she was listening, but I wasn't sure. But anyway, I didn't think she was interested.

Georgia: I thought I was listening too! But maybe I didn't get that message across.

The counselor then asked the group to review what had been said. The following points were made and listed on the chalkboard: (1) Georgia did not maintain eye contact; (2) she tended to lean away from Carla; and (3) she seemed uninterested. The counselor had two other group members repeat the same procedure, which was followed by a more positive reaction from the group members.

Counselor: Now, let's think of some other listening skills that are important. Jane, can you give us another skill that you think is important?
Jane: Well, some people interrupt you too much. They just can't shut up.
Georgia: They just jump in and talk before thinking—like they don't understand you or have no feeling for you.
Sam: You can say that again—they judge before you can say much.
Counselor: That's good. Now, let's list some listening skills on the board.

SESSION 2

Objective: Each group member will be able to demonstrate effective methods of listening and communicating in a working environment. This scenario includes the same group members.

Counselor: Let's all pretend we are working in a factory where car radios are made. Our supervisor tells Yolanda that we are going to have to work all day next Saturday, which happens to be Thanksgiving weekend. Yolanda goes to Sam and tells him that the supervisor said we have to work next Saturday because the plant boss wants to show more profit. How would you respond, Sam?
Sam: Man, I'd say they're off their rocker. I'd probably plan to call in sick because I'm going to see that football game on TV. More profit, what are they thinking about?
Carla: We got our rights—they ought to remember that!
Yolanda: Hey, and what about our families? Just to make more money isn't worth it!
Counselor: Now, let's go back to the conversation between Jane and Yolanda. Remember the reason for working on Saturday was to make more profit. Did anyone think to check out this statement with the supervisor? Let's pretend that Yolanda checked out the story with the supervisor before she talked to Sam and found that the real reason for working on Saturday was that the major contractor with the factory had put in a special order. Now, Sam, how would you react?
Sam: [After a brief pause] Well, I wouldn't like working on a Saturday, but this reason makes it easier.
Rod: Those guys (major contractors) give us the bread—you know—we don't want to lose them.

The counselor then made the point that communication and listening skills were important factors for motivation and maintenance in the working environment.

Counselor:	All of you experienced a change of mind when the reason for working was properly communicated. Perhaps the supervisor did not make it clear to Yolanda, or maybe Yolanda wasn't listening.
Georgia:	Man, when you get things mixed up you sure can cause unnecessary trouble.
Jane:	I guess you have to listen to get it straight.
Sam:	Yeah, and you better talk straight too!

The counselor followed this exercise by having group members pretend they were a supervisor delivering a message to the group concerning change of policies, announcement of new regulations, and other relevant topics. The group members were required to repeat the most important parts of the announcement. Each member was provided with reinforcement of his or her listening and communicating skills by the group and the counselor.

Career Assessment

Publishers of certain standardized tests that predict future performance are now required to make public their studies on validity, release test questions and correct answers to students who have taken a test, and provide information concerning the meaning of test scores and how the results will be reported. These issues point out the growing concern for the use of standardized tests in general and focus greater attention on the issues surrounding the use of standardized tests with various ethnic groups.

The solutions to these issues and others will no doubt occupy the research efforts of numerous individuals in the counseling profession in the future. More important, research is needed for the use of assessment instruments with specific ethnic groups, for example, relevant norms, and statistical evidence of their use within ethnic groups. Also, publishers of currently used assessment instruments for career guidance will hopefully devote more research to the utility of tests and inventories for culturally diverse groups. In the meantime, counselors have the option of using tests and inventories designed for certain racial and ethnic groups; representative examples of these instruments are provided in the following section.

U.S. Employment Service (USES) Tests for Different Cultural Groups

Since the mid-1930s, USES and the training administration of the U.S. Department of Labor have been involved in test development and research. Since the mid-1960s, the major emphasis has been toward developing tests for different cultural groups. One of their major goals was to develop a nonreaders' edition of the *General Aptitude Test Battery (GATB)*. In the early 1970s, research priorities were directed toward developing specific aptitude tests and pretesting orientation techniques for other cultural groups (Division of Testing Staff, USES, 1978).

After ten years of research, USES produced several aptitude tests and related publications designed to expand occupational and educational training programs for the undereducated. Research efforts attempted to assure test fairness; that is, the aim was to provide illiterate, bilingual, or undereducated individuals with an equal opportunity to demonstrate their abilities. Of these tests, the *Nonverbal Aptitude Test Battery (NATB)* is a measure of aptitudes of individuals unable to take the *GATB* because of an inability to read. This test measures the same aptitudes as the *GATB* (intelligence, verbal, numerical, spatial, form perception, clerical perception, motor coordination, finger dexterity, and manual dexterity).

Another test developed by USES, the *Specific Aptitude Test Batteries,* measures an individual's potential to acquire skills needed in specific occupations. Separate norms for minority groups have been developed for more effective use of these tests.

A *Basic Occupational Literacy Test (BOLT)* is a measure of achievement for reading and arithmetic. The four parts of this test (reading vocabulary, reading comprehension, arithmetic computation, and arithmetic reasoning) are easily related to general educational development requirements of jobs. The four levels of the test measure achievement for grades 1 through 11.

A Spanish edition of the *GATB, Bateria de Examenes de Aptitud General (BEAG),* has also been published. This edition may be used for all Spanish-speaking individuals.

USES has developed several publications designed to orient people from other cultures to test-taking techniques, among them: *Doing Your Best on Aptitude Tests* (Spanish and English), *Group Pretesting Orientation on the Purpose of Testing* (Spanish and English), *Doing Your Best on Reading and Arithmetic Tests,* and *Pretesting Orientation Exercises.*

Although the USES tests were developed primarily for public employment-service systems, they are available for release to some agencies. Counselors may develop cooperative arrangements with state employment systems for the purpose of referring clients for testing. Tests are also released to agencies for use in counseling and research. The following are examples of other tests and inventories that may be used to assist people of different cultures in career exploration.

The Adult Basic Learning Examination (ABLE)
The Psychological Corporation
555 Academic Court
San Antonio, TX 78204-2498

ABLE was designed to measure the general educational level of adults who have not completed high school. Three levels of the test measure achievement in vocabulary, reading, spelling, and arithmetic. Norms are available for job-corps trainees and adults enrolled in basic education courses.

Escala de Inteligencia Wechsler para Niños
The Psychological Corporation
555 Academic Court
San Antonio, TX 78204-2498

A Spanish-American translation of the *Wechsler Intelligence Scale for Children,* developed in Puerto Rico, yields three IQ scores—verbal, performance, and full-scale. Norms are available for several Puerto Rican groups.

Tests of General Ability
SRA–McGraw-Hill
220 East Daniel Dale
De Soto, TX 75115

These tests are appropriate for students from culturally deprived backgrounds as a measure of general intelligence and basic learning ability. All items are pictorial, and the examiner's manual has been translated into Spanish. One part of the test measures the individual's ability to recognize relationships and understand meanings and basic concepts. The second part of the test measures reasoning ability.

Chicago Nonverbal Examination
The Psychological Corporation
555 Academic Court
San Antonio, TX 78204-2498

This is an intelligence test designed specifically for individuals with reading difficulties or those who have been reared in a foreign language environment. The test is administered with either verbal directions or pantomime directions. Standardization sample includes 70% white and 30% foreign-born students.

Test de Aptitud Diferencial
The Psychological Corporation
555 Academic Court
San Antonio, TX 78204-2498

This is an authorized translation of the *Differential Aptitude Test* for use with Latin Americans. Its coverage includes verbal reasoning, numerical ability, abstract reasoning, space relations, mechanical reasoning, clerical speed and accuracy, and language usage.

California Occupational Preference Survey
Educational and Industrial Testing Service
P.O. Box 7234
San Diego, CA 92107

This test has been translated into Spanish and is primarily designed to assist individuals in defining broad areas of interest.

Geist Picture Interest Inventory for Men, Spanish Edition
Western Psychological Services
12031 Wilshire Boulevard
Los Angeles, CA 90025

An interest inventory for Spanish-speaking and bilingual males. The interest areas are depicted by occupational activities. The general interest areas assessed are persuasive, clerical, mechanical, musical, scientific, outdoors, literary, computational, artistic, social service, and dramatic.

Summary

1. Culture is a very complex concept that can refer to many aspects of life and living. Culture is a learned behavior. Two people from the same race may share some values, attitudes, and so on but may also be very different in their cultural makeups. Counselors should be alert to value orientation to work among different cultural groups.

2. A multicultural counseling and therapy theory (MCT) was developed by Sue, Ivey, and Pedersen, who felt that current theories did not describe, explain, or predict current cultural diversity. Several propositions and corollaries have been developed for research.

3. The largest racial minority group in this country is African Americans. Culturally different African Americans tend to remain social isolates in church, school, and employment.

4. Many Asian Americans place a high value on education. Asian Americans tend to inhibit emotional expression, and so many do not actively participate in counseling programs. In general, Asian Americans are reluctant to admit personal problems because of their cultural conditioning. Asian Americans tend to misinterpret the role of counseling and its potential benefits.

5. The second largest minority group in this country is Hispanic Americans. General cultural characteristics of Hispanic Americans appear to distinguish them as the least "Americanized" of the ethnic groups. The Hispanic family is typically a closely knit group that greatly influences the value systems of its members.

6. Native Americans are culturally conditioned to view life from a different perspective than that of the dominant culture. Native Americans are generally not motivated to achieve status through the accumulation of wealth. The lifestyle of most Native Americans is extremely democratic, and their culture promotes egalitarianism.

7. Effective counselors have knowledge of and are sensitive to different cultural orientations when establishing rapport in counseling relationships. To be effective with populations of different cultures, counselors must be aware of different worldviews (the psychological orientation of thinking, behavior, and interpretation of events). Counselors must be cautious not to impose their values on others.

8. An effective model of minority development provides guidelines for career guidance activities designed to meet the needs of members of other cultures in terms of their adjustment to the dominant culture. The model should also provide counselors with a greater understanding of adjustment problems of minority groups.

9. Relational counseling focuses on developing realistic self-appraisals, personal strengths, and perceptions of occupational choices. The individual's perception of life must be evaluated from environmental experiences, and negative factors are to be balanced by positive ones.

10. Prevocational training programs for adults include components designed to develop and improve self-image, communication skills, goal-setting and problem-

solving techniques, working parent skills, job interview skills, and expectations of the world of work.

11. Interpretation and use of assessment inventories for multicultural groups remains a controversial issue. One of the major arguments is that most standardized assessment instruments are discriminatory, primarily because they have been developed from data based on white male middle-class values, beliefs, attitudes, and experiences. Recent controversies concerning the use of standardized tests have focused on the use of standardized tests with people from other cultures.

12. The descriptive characteristics relative to different cultures cannot be generalized to all members of any group. However, homogeneity is greater within groups than among them.

Supplementary Learning Exercises

1. Define your cultural background and that of a classmate. Compare differences and similarities.
2. How would you explain the differences between individualism and collectivism? What socialization variables influenced the differences between them?
3. Do you believe the multicultural counseling and therapy theory (MCT) is necessary? Support your conclusion.
4. Justify Corollary 2B of the MCT from Box 18-1. Present referenced positions for your support.
5. Review the suggested developmental strategies for each ethnic group. Which group do you feel would best be served by all of them? Justify your answer.
6. Describe how you would help someone from another culture overcome distrust and suspicion of counselors and authority figures.
7. Develop counseling strategies for two or more of the components of the prevocational training program for adults described in this chapter.
8. Write a review of two or more of the tests or inventories listed in the "Career Assessment" section of this chapter.
9. In the following reference, read Chapter 2, "The Culture of the Counselor," and summarize the major points made about the ethics, training, and professional dimensions of the professional counselor.

   Axelson, John A. (1993). *Counseling and development in a multicultural society* (2nd ed.). Pacific Grove, CA: Brooks/Cole.

10. In the following reference, read pages 567–584 on the subject of other approaches to testing minority group members. Summarize your findings.

    Kaplan, Robert M., & Saccuzzo, Dennis P. (1993). *Psychological testing: Principles, applications, and issues* (3rd ed.). Pacific Grove, CA: Brooks/Cole.

CHAPTER NINETEEN

Career Counseling for Individuals with Disabilities

Rehabilitation services and special education programs on career counseling for persons with disabilities have recently received considerable attention. Innovative career-related educational programs and counseling strategies have been developed to assist individuals with disabilities in making the best possible life/work adjustment. The major emphasis in these programs is to maximize each individual's potential for employment. Career counseling programs for individuals with disabilities have elements in common with traditional career counseling programs. However, the diversity of needs requires specially designed assessment instruments, career counseling techniques, materials, and career-related educational training programs.

The terms used to describe people with disabilities have been changed to negate stereotypes and false ideas. The major objection was the labeling of individuals with demeaning names. For example, a spastic does not describe a person but refers to a muscle with sudden involuntary spasms. It is much more acceptable to think of a disability as a condition that interferes with an individual's ability to do something independent such as walk, see, hear, or learn. Thus, it is preferable to say "people with disabilities" rather than "the disabled"; "Joe is a wheelchair user," not "confined to a wheelchair"; "has a hearing impairment" rather than "is deaf-mute"; and "persons with mental retardation" rather than "the mentally retarded." The focus should be on the unique identity of a person as opposed to a label that implies that everyone with that particular label is alike and has a separate status. A person's identity should be an individual matter that focuses on a unique condition, and the words we use should convey this message.

The first section of this chapter focuses on the Americans with Disabilities Act (ADA). The second section describes special problems and needs of individuals with disabilities. Implications for career guidance and the role of state rehabilitation agencies are then discussed. An actual counseling case of an individual with a disability who sought services from a state rehabilitation agency is described in the next section. A career education program for students with disabilities is covered in the next section, followed by a description of a group counseling program for individuals with disabilities who have been hospitalized. Finally, assessment instruments for individuals with disabilities are discussed.

The Americans with Disabilities Act

The Americans with Disabilities Act (ADA), signed into law on July 26, 1990, is a comprehensive law. For example, Title III regulations require public accommodations (including private entities that own, operate, or lease to places of public accommodation), commercial facilities, and private entities to make reasonable modifications of policies, practices, and procedures that deny equal access to individuals with disabilities. Box 19-1 provides an overview of requirements in public accommodations.

The ADA identifies individuals with disabilities as follows.

- An individual with a disability is a person who has a physical or mental impairment that substantially limits one or more "major life activities," or has a record of such an impairment, or is regarded as having such an impairment.
- Examples of physical or mental impairments include, but are not limited to, such contagious and noncontagious diseases and conditions as orthopedic, visual, speech, and hearing impairments; cerebral palsy, epilepsy, muscular dystrophy, multiple sclerosis, cancer, heart disease, diabetes, mental retardation, emotional illness, specific learning disabilities, HIV disease (whether symptomatic or asymptomatic), tuberculosis, drug addiction, and alcoholism. Homosexuality and bisexuality are not physical or mental impairments under the ADA.
- "Major life activities" include functions such as caring for oneself, performing manual tasks, walking, seeing, hearing, speaking, breathing, learning, and working.
- Individuals who currently engage in the illegal use of drugs are not protected by the ADA when an action is taken on the basis of their current illegal use of drugs. (U.S. Department of Justice, 1991, pp. 3–4)

Of interest to the career counselor are the ADA's requirements concerning employment of individuals with disabilities and transportation accessibility. Box 19-2 includes a fact sheet prepared by the U.S. Department of Justice on employment and transportation requirements and the dates on which these requirements are effective.

One of the major issues covered in this act is employment discrimination. The ADA prohibits discrimination in all employment practices including job application, hiring, firing, advancement, compensation, training, and other terms and

Box 19-1
Americans with Disabilities Act
Requirements in Public Accommodations Fact Sheet

General
- Public accommodations such as restaurants, hotels, theaters, doctors' offices, pharmacies, retail stores, museums, libraries, parks, private schools, and day-care centers may not discriminate on the basis of disability. Private clubs and religious organizations are exempt.
- Reasonable changes in policies, practices, and procedures must be made to avoid discrimination.

Auxiliary aids
- Auxiliary aids and services must be provided to individuals with vision or hearing impairments or other individuals with disabilities, unless an undue burden would result.

Physical barriers
- Physical barriers in existing facilities must be removed, if removal is readily achievable. If not, alternative methods of providing the services must be offered, if they are readily achievable.
- All new construction in public accommodations, as well as in "commercial facilities" such as office buildings, must be accessible. Elevators are generally not required in buildings under three stories or with fewer than 3,000 square feet per floor, unless the building is a shopping center, mall, or a professional office of a health care provider.
- Alterations must be accessible. When alterations to primary function areas are made, an accessible path of travel to the altered area (and the bathrooms, telephones, and drinking fountains serving that area) must be provided to the extent that the added accessibility costs are not disproportionate to the overall cost of the alterations. Elevators are required as described above.

SOURCE: U.S. Department of Justice, Civil Rights Division, 1991. *Americans with Disabilities Act Handbook,* Coordination and Review Section.

conditions of employment. Also included are advertising for employment, fringe benefits, and tenure. However, employers are free to select the most qualified applicant available and to make decisions based on reasons unrelated to a disability. For example, two individuals may apply for a typist job and one is able to accurately type more words per minute. Thus, the employer can hire the better typist even though that particular person does not have a disability and the other does. The key to such decisions appears to center around job performance needs, and in this case, typing speed is needed for successful performance of the job.

Box 19-2
Americans with Disabilities Act Requirements Fact Sheet

Employment
- Employers may not discriminate against an individual with a disability in hiring or promotion if the person is otherwise qualified for the job.
- Employers can ask about one's ability to perform a job, but cannot inquire if someone has a disability or subject a person to tests that tend to screen out people with disabilities.
- Employers will need to provide "reasonable accommodation" to individuals with disabilities. This includes steps such as job restructuring and modification of equipment.
- Employers do not need to provide accommodations that impose an "undue hardship" on business operations.

Who needs to comply:
- All employers with 25 or more employees must comply, effective July 26, 1992.
- All employers with 15–24 employees must comply, effective July 26, 1994.

Transportation
- New public transit buses ordered after August 26, 1990, must be accessible to individuals with disabilities.
- Transit authorities must provide comparable paratransit or other special transportation services to individuals with disabilities who cannot use fixed route bus services, unless an undue burden would result.
- Existing rail systems must have one accessible car per train by July 26, 1995.
- New rail cars ordered after August 26, 1990, must be accessible.
- New bus and train stations must be accessible.
- Key stations in rapid, light, and commuter rail systems must be made accessible by July 26, 1993, with extensions up to 20 years for commuter rail (30 years for rapid and light rail).
- All existing Amtrak stations must be accessible by July 26, 2010.

SOURCE: U.S. Department of Justice, Civil Rights Division, 1991. *Americans with Disabilities Act Handbook,* Coordination and Review Section.

Other subjects covered in the ADA that may be of interest to the career counselor are job descriptions, job application forms, job application process, interviews, testing and medical examinations, hiring decisions, benefits, working conditions, raises and promotions, and reasonable accommodations. More information about the ADA can be obtained at the following address:

Office on the Americans with Disabilities Act
Civil Rights Division
U.S. Department of Justice
P.O. Box 66118
Washington, DC 20035-6118

Special Problems and Needs
of Individuals with Disabilities

The problems and needs associated with disability are inclusive and pervasive. Career counselors address adjustment problems associated with disability as well as career choice and career development factors. The severity of functional limitations and the individual's adjustment to his or her limitations are the most important factors to consider in career counseling. The special problems and needs of disabled individuals discussed in this section should be considered as representative examples from a diverse population.

Adjustment

Individuals whose disabilities result from physical trauma may have difficulty adjusting to and accepting disability, which may interfere with motivation to seek retraining and employment. Cook (1981) postulated that individuals may experience shock, depression, and denial before accepting and adjusting to a disability. Psychological denial of a disability is discussed frequently in rehabilitation literature. Failure to accept its limitations can impede counseling assistance; the individual will not be open to retraining or to experiences provided by rehabilitation agencies or educational institutions.

Wright (1983) contended that individuals with physical disabilities are given an inferior status position in our society. The frustrations produced from a physical disability can be accompanied by shame and feelings of inferiority. The acceptance of one's physical condition is often linked with one's total self-esteem. Careful consideration is to be given to the sources of poor self-concept, ways of reacting to physical disability, and ways of adjusting to it.

Attitudinal Barriers

Individuals who are labeled *handicapped* or *disabled* face attitudinal barriers to employment. Employers are reluctant to hire individuals with disabilities because of erroneous assumptions: more sick leave will be required, insurance rates will be affected, safety on the job will be endangered, and plant modifications will be mandatory. People with mental retardation are especially considered to need constant supervision and are perceived as incapable of learning. In general, employers have stereotyped views of individuals with disabilities, resulting in discrimination (Daniels, 1981).

Wright (1980) suggested that one of the most successful methods of improving employers' hiring attitudes is through placement of individuals with disabilities who turn out to be successful workers. An advocacy role through personal contact with potential employers is also an effective method for building positive attitudes. The importance of the advocacy role in career counseling is underscored by Neff (1985), who contended that individuals with disabilities face an impressive array of negative social attitudes, prejudice, and other social barriers.

Generalizations Formed as a Result of Being Labeled Disabled or Handicapped

Being identified as disabled or handicapped may limit access to the job market. For example, the label *amputee* may conjure up an image of someone who has lost a leg because of amputation and is severely restricted. Another individual who has had successful open heart surgery may be perceived as sickly and weak. Such generalizations inhibit opportunities for employment, especially for individuals who have minor functional limitations because of an amputation or illness. The career counselor should emphasize that each individual is to be judged on his or her own merits; a disability is only one individual characteristic to be considered in the employment process.

Lack of Models and Norm Groups

The current lack of visibility of individuals with physical disabilities working successfully in a broad spectrum of career fields may reinforce low self-esteem and negative attitudes about labor market potential. Standardized tests and inventories are not always normed for those with physical disabilities, resulting in conflicting or misleading assumptions concerning employment potential.

Kriegel (1982) addressed problems of societal acceptance of individuals with disabilities. He suggested that they are often perceived as second-class citizens, and he contended that society ignores the reality of having a disability: "The terms of our visibility have been created not by us but by those who see what they want to see rather than what is there" (p. 55). Kriegel also appealed to individuals with disabilities to learn to accept their disability and to make the most of their assets. Those who have accomplished these goals are good role models.

Onset of Disability

The age at which a disability occurs is a relevant factor to be considered in career counseling. Stone and Gregg (1981) suggested that the effects of a childhood disability can result in parental or community overprotection. In early onset of a disability, an individual's exposure to occupations is limited and career development is usually delayed. The type of disability is also a factor for consideration; adolescents with hearing impairments are more limited in career development than are hearing adolescents.

Early onset of disability may greatly influence career choice. For example, juvenile diabetes may later result in heart disease or visual impairment that could limit an individual's ability to function in occupations requiring keen vision or physical exertion (Stone & Gregg, 1981). Finally, Smith and Chemers (1981) suggested that individuals may be deficient in assertiveness and in independence if they have experienced early onset of a disability.

Onset of disability in adulthood often requires that career counselors introduce the process of career redevelopment. By assessing the realities of their functional limitations, individuals may be required to change career direction. In sum, later onset of disability (1) may have disturbing effects on personal adjustment, (2) may be related to lower levels of educational or vocational aspirations (Thurer, 1980), and (3) may be related to indecisiveness in career choice, especially with individuals whose medical conditions will be improved or stabilized in the future (Roessler & Rubin, 1982).

Social/Interpersonal Skills

Persons with disabilities have special needs, including a restrictive view of career opportunities. Misconceptions about disabilities have limited intervention strategies that would usually be considered in career development theories (Curnow, 1989), such as social skills training. Fine and Asch (1988) suggested that social and psychological problems for persons with disabilities should receive greater or at least equal attention as the disability itself.

Individuals with disabilities tend to limit their social lives to interactions with other persons with disabilities. Curnow suggested that they are reluctant to develop friendships outside the disabled community. Positive reinforcement received from peer groups is especially important. Strategies to assist these individuals to develop more inclusive interpersonal relationships is an important counseling component.

Self-Concept

Disabling conditions have the potential to create a poor self-concept (Humes, Szymanski, & Hohenshil, 1989). Individuals with disabilities tend to report lower self-esteem. A life associated with constant rejection and being labeled as different can potentially create a poor self-image. "Who am I?" may indeed be a difficult question to answer positively. Our goal in this context is to assist individuals in accurately assessing strengths and weaknesses in order to help them modify their self-perceptions. Programs that include components to help develop positive self-images are of critical importance in meeting the needs of these individuals.

Skills for Independent Living

Individuals with disabilities need special help in developing skills for independent living. For some, the greatest problem is learning to accept limitations that may restrict their ability to become fully independent. For others, increasing their desire to be independent may be the counseling challenge. In essence, some individuals may be unrealistic about their ability to be fully independent, whereas others may lack the motivation to become independent, preferring to maintain their dependence on others.

The following special problems and needs were compiled from *Barriers and Bridges* (California Advisory Council on Vocational Education, 1977).

1. Architectural barriers place limits on the mobility of people with orthopedic disabilities. Inaccessible transportation, training, and workplaces will eventually be overcome by legislation, but progress is slow.
2. Employers' bias and reluctance to hire people with disabilities limit placement opportunities.
3. There is a lack of trained personnel in vocational education to deal effectively with special problems of people with disabilities.
4. The general public's lack of knowledge concerning the needs and problems of people with disabilities creates barriers to employment.
5. Families of persons with disabilities, who are often the main source of physical and psychological support, often fail to understand the problems and needs of the person with a physical disability. Without professional training, family members may find it difficult to determine whether to foster acceptance of limitations or motivation for independence.

Implications for Career Guidance

The problems associated with the career development of individuals with disabilities exemplifies the need for career counselors to adopt advocacy roles. In addition to directly assisting the client with physical disabilities, career counselors should support community education and training programs to foster acceptance in the work world. Programs that assist educators, families, and employees in working with individuals with disabilities can be invaluable in reducing the physical and psychological barriers that currently exist. People with disabilities face negative attitudes, prejudice, discrimination, and other social barriers. As a consequence, counseling programs should provide more positive roles and role models. Developing positive self-images and interpersonal relationship skills are important counseling components. Finally, the role of an advocate implies considerable dedication to removing social barriers and to providing supportive counseling.

Rehabilitation Programs

This section focuses on programs for individuals with disabilities sponsored by state rehabilitation agencies and on rehabilitation centers sponsored by the private sector.

State Rehabilitation Agencies

State rehabilitation agencies provide career counseling and other services to individuals who meet two eligibility requirements: (1) the person must have a disability that results in a substantial handicap to employment, and (2) vocational rehabilitation services must reasonably be expected to benefit the person in terms of employability (Texas Rehabilitation Commission, 1984). The disabling conditions among populations served by state agencies are extensive and inclusive. Rehabilitation services have been extended to individuals with mental illness, orthopedic problems, mental retardation, visual and hearing problems, circulatory problems, amputation of limbs, and other disabling conditions such as alcoholism, cancer, epilepsy, kidney disease, multiple sclerosis, muscular dystrophy, and cerebral palsy (Porter, 1981).

To meet the needs of such a diverse group of individuals, state rehabilitation agencies have developed numerous and varied programs designed to assist individuals reentering the work force or maintaining their chosen occupation. Parker and Hansen (1981) have compiled a list of services provided by state rehabilitation agencies: (1) counseling and guidance; (2) medical and psychological evaluation; (3) physical and mental restoration services; (4) prevocational evaluation and retraining; (5) vocational and other training services; (6) expense allowances; (7) transportation; (8) interpretive services for the deaf; (9) reader, orientation, and mobility services for the blind; (10) prostheses and other technical aids and devices; (11) work adjustment and placement counseling, (12) job placement services; (13) occupational license, tools, equipment, and so forth; and (14) other goods and services to benefit the client in achieving employability.

Privately Supported Rehabilitation Agencies

Among the most widely known, privately sponsored, nonprofit rehabilitation agencies are Goodwill Industries, Salvation Army, Jewish Vocational Services, St. Vincent De Paul Society, National Society for Crippled Children and Adults, United Cerebral Palsy Association, Volunteers of America, and Deseret Industries. Although a diversity of programs are sponsored by these organizations and other national, state, and local private rehabilitation agencies, Goodwill Industries of America serves as a good example of a national network of programs for individuals with disabilities. Goodwill Industries of America is generally recognized as the world's leading privately sponsored agency for training individuals and with facilities for individuals with disabilities.

Local Goodwill Industries are autonomous, having their own board of directors, and are affiliated with the national organization, Goodwill Industries of America of Bethesda, Maryland. Goodwill Industries conducts a wide range of activities, including classroom instruction, sheltered workshops, encounter sessions, therapy (physical, occupational, or speech), counseling, and placement. Many local Goodwill Industries collect donated clothing, furniture, household goods and appliances, books, art objects, radios, and televisions for repairing, refurbishing, and rebuilding by individuals with disabilities. These items are sold in a network of bargain retail outlets. Another method Goodwill Industries uses to provide jobs is to subcontract with private industries and with state and federal government agencies for assembling and manufacturing of goods, janitorial, grounds maintenance, and other services.

Goodwill Industries also provide educational skills training programs. For example, Goodwill Industry of San Antonio provides the following services: psychological testing, vocational evaluation, personal and social adjustment, work adjustment, prevocational training, special academic instruction, therapeutic recreation, skills training, and job placement. The individualized services offered by this agency are funded from service fees charged to referring agencies, such as the Texas Rehabilitation Commission, the Commission for the Blind, local independent school districts, the City of San Antonio Manpower Consortium, the Veteran's Administration, and private insurance firms.

Most age groups can be served by privately supported, nonprofit rehabilitation agencies. Services include provisions for assistive devices such as artificial limbs, braces, wheelchairs, glasses, and hearing aids. Assistance is also given to help individuals develop independent living skills through programs in which individuals share supervised apartments. The Salvation Army and Volunteers of America have emphasized programs for homeless individuals with alcohol or psychological problems.

Career counselors need to be aware of the goals, objectives, and services of private rehabilitation agencies in their community or local area. Programs that help prepare individuals with disabilities for employment (such as work-adjustment seminars, prevocational classes, personal counseling, medical management, and mobility training) are valuable referral resources for career counselors. Sheltered workshops, supported by a number of private rehabilitation agencies, provide a workplace for individuals who are unable to meet work requirements in the competitive job market. Career counseling for disabled individuals is greatly enhanced through a wide variety of programs offered by rehabilitation programs supported by the private sector.

Counseling Program: A Case Study

The following is an actual case of an individual who received rehabilitation services from a state agency. Names, dates, and other information have been changed to protect client confidentiality. This example illustrates rehabilitation services provided by a state agency in a small town of about 25,000 people. The following steps in the rehabilitation process are covered in this case: (1) initial contact, (2) diagnostic workup, (3) evaluation and certification, (4) vocational assessment, (5) service planning, (6) placement, and (7) postemployment services.

Initial Contact

The purposes of the initial contact are to establish a counseling relationship, provide the client with information about the state agency, and obtain information from the client to determine eligibility for rehabilitation services. In this case, Sam, the rehabilitation counselor, interviewed the client to obtain personal/social information, educational background, past work experiences, physical limitations, and financial needs. Excerpts from the case file are used to illustrate examples of information recorded from the initial contact.

Dora was a self-referred high school graduate and had never received rehabilitation services. She was 40 years old, divorced for approximately three years, and had two children. Her older child was married and living nearby, but the younger had chosen to live with her. Dora had married at age 18 and had lived in several cities and states with her salesman husband. Sam noted in his report that her mood was very flat and that she seemed remorseful and lethargic. She became extremely emotional when she referred to her marriage, stating, "I resent that my husband left me because of my arthritis."

Dora reported that she had suffered serious problems with arthritis for the past ten years, requiring five surgical procedures on her hands. During the interview, she demonstrated lack of finger flexibility and restricted hand mobility. She was taking two prescribed medications.

Dora's only source of income was $600 monthly child support, and she had no savings. She was unable to insure her five-year-old automobile, and her current rent and utility bills totaled $310. Dora's work experience was very limited; she had worked as a teacher's aide for approximately nine months but was unemployed at the present time.

Sam decided that Dora was a good candidate for rehabilitation services and had her fill out an official request form. She was then scheduled for a medical and psychological evaluation. Sam had to verify reported physical problems, and he wanted a full report on potential psychological disturbances associated with the emotional instability he had observed. Sam also requested reports of previous medical diagnosis and treatment.

Diagnostic Workup

The orthopedist's report indicated that Dora had a severe case of rheumatoid arthritis. After carefully studying the medical report, Sam arrived at the following functional limitations and vocational handicaps.

1. Can stand for short periods of time only	1. Orthopedic report from Dr. Bone
2. Unable to lift anything over 10 lbs. on a repetitive basis	2. Orthopedic report from Dr. Bone
3. Unable to push or pull	3. Client's statement
4. Cannot bend for prolonged periods	4. Client's statement
5. Has limited finger dexterity	5. Orthopedic report from Dr. Bone

The psychological report discussed results of intelligence, achievement, personality, and several aptitude tests. Sam summarized Dora's assets from the psychological evaluations as follows:

1. Normal intelligence
2. Good clerical skills
3. Ability to learn and retain new information
4. Good reading skills
5. Good oral expressive skills
6. Average academic achievement for her educational level
7. Potential for college-level training

In addition, Sam summarized Dora's limitations:

1. Diagnosed as depressive reaction
2. Poor self-concept
3. Lacks confidence
4. Subject to mood swings
5. Limited work history
6. Poor manual dexterity
7. Easily fatigued

Evaluation and Certification

After reviewing medical and psychological reports, Sam approved Dora's request for rehabilitative services. The results of her disability as well as the degree of her handicap were evaluated. In this case, her physical disability was considered severe enough to merit services. Psychological problems associated with the depressive reaction would also be considered in planning services for her. In developing a rehabilitation plan, Sam was required to address all services that would help Dora reach her rehabilitation goal. Dora was notified of her acceptance, and an appointment was set for the following day.

In preparation for the next counseling appointment, Sam carefully reviewed the material that had accumulated in Dora's file. He paid particular attention to medical problems resulting in functional limitations. The psychological report clearly indicated that Dora would need supportive counseling. However, he decided that his first goal was to establish a vocational objective.

Vocational Assessment

In the counseling sessions that followed, limitations and assets were thoroughly discussed. Although Dora had strongly considered teaching as a vocational objective, she agreed that an interest inventory would help verify her interests and introduce other career considerations. Dora was given a computer-scored inventory, and a date was set for the next counseling session.

The vocational assessment phase of the rehabilitation process continued with an interpretation and discussion of interest inventory results and the test data contained in the psychological report. Dora decided that she would like to explore a career in either elementary school teaching or social work. With these two careers in mind, Sam directed her to references describing these occupations in detail. Dora spent considerable time reviewing job descriptions and requirements. At Sam's suggestion, she made on-site visits to a school and a social welfare agency. Shortly after these visits, Dora decided that she would prefer a career as an elementary education teacher.

Service Planning

Sam developed a comprehensive vocational plan for Dora. This plan, known as the Individualized Written Rehabilitation Program (IWRP), contains the following aspects of action.

1. The rehabilitation goal and immediate rehabilitation objectives
2. Vocational rehabilitation services
3. The projected date of initiating services and the anticipated duration of services
4. Objective criteria, evaluation procedures, and schedules for determining whether the rehabilitation goal and intermediate objectives are being achieved
5. Explanation of availability of a client assistance program. (Roessler & Rubin, 1982, p. 132)

Sam postulated that Dora would need assistance with medical and emotional problems during the course of her college training. He also recognized that he would have to assist Dora in obtaining grants and other benefits that might be available to her. Excerpts from Sam's service plan suggestions follow: (1) enrollment in a local college with financial assistance for tuition, fees, and transportation; (2) other financial assistance through grants and Social Security benefits; (3) physical treatment to be continued as necessary; and (4) regular counseling sessions necessary to address reported psychological problems. Sam decided to provide supportive counseling and, if necessary, refer Dora to a college counseling center or local mental health unit.

Thomas and Butler (1981) suggested that rehabilitation clients often need extensive personal counseling designed to assist them in accepting their disability, adjusting to reactions of others to their disability, reintegrating their self-concepts, and adjusting to changes in relationships with family and others in their lives. Career counselors are to evaluate different counseling theories and techniques in meeting the needs of different types of clients. In essence, individuals with disabilities may require extensive personal adjustment counseling.

During the course of the next four years, Dora made remarkable academic progress in spite of recurring physical and psychological problems. She had three operations on her hands to improve flexibility, and the regular supportive counseling provided by Sam helped her overcome the depressive reaction. Financial assistance provided by the state and other agencies helped Dora maintain subsistence. During her final year in college, Sam directed Dora to attend seminars on résumé preparation and job interview skills.

Placement

In a conference with Sam, Dora decided that she wanted to remain in the area. Sam evaluated the local job market for teachers and found it to be keenly competitive for elementary school teachers. However, he decided that he could improve Dora's chances of obtaining a position by assisting her in job interview preparation. Sam also helped Dora develop a list of alternate school systems to which she could apply.

Postemployment Services

Sam plans to follow Dora's work for at least 60 postemployment days. He will focus on her adjustment to the new job and adaptations she must make in her daily schedule. Finally, Dora will be notified that if services are needed in the future, he can reopen her case.

This case illustrates the comprehensive nature of rehabilitation counseling for individuals with disabilities. The services offered involved considerable client contact and coordination of functions provided through training programs, financial assistance resources, and medical treatment. Although state rehabilitation programs follow a general pattern, there are variations in services given. Nevertheless, it is clear that rehabilitation counselors must possess numerous skills and considerable knowledge to foster client career development.

Career Education
for Students with Disabilities

Brolin and Gysbers (1989) have developed the Life-Centered Career Education Curriculum (LCCE) for individuals with disabilities. This program has been widely adopted in school systems in several states and in some foreign countries. This curriculum focuses on 22 major competencies that students need to succeed in daily living, personal/social, and occupational areas after leaving school. For daily living, competencies include buying and preparing food, managing finances, and caring for personal needs. For personal/social skills, competencies include achieving self-awareness, achieving independence, and making adequate decisions. Finally, for occupational preparation, competencies include selecting and planning occupational choices and obtaining a specific occupational skill. This model is competency based and specifies counselor time for carrying out guidance activities in each component.

Counselors are provided with a trainer/implementation manual, activity books, and an inventory to assess competency levels. The suggested competencies for this model are infused into the kindergarten through grade 12 curriculum. Some school systems have used this model to facilitate and improve community awareness of students' needs and increase parent participation in learning activities. It has also been used for staff in-service training to make them aware of the structure and purpose of the model.

Brolin and Gysbers (1989) suggested that career awareness, career exploration, and preparation are major benefits of this model. The career awareness phase is very important during the elementary years. Programs that focus on helping students with disabilities should emphasize developing self-worth, socially desirable behaviors, communication skills, positive attitudes toward work, and desirable work habits.

The career exploration phase includes guidance activities that explore abilities, needs, and interests. The use of work samples, simulated job tasks, and community jobs are important hands-on experiences. In addition, this phase includes experiences with the work roles of homemaker, family member, volunteer, and individuals engaged in productive avocational/leisure activities.

The preparation phase includes guidance activities that help clarify personal/social and occupational competencies. Interests, aptitudes, and skills are further clarified. Lifestyle and career choices are more clearly delineated. This phase emphasizes that many students with disabilities require more than the usual amount of time to prepare for an occupation.

One issue that needs to be addressed in the 1990s is the place of proficiency tests required for graduation in many states. Should all students with disabilities be required to take and make acceptable scores on these tests? Perhaps more important, what kind of criteria should be used for students with disabilities to determine high school graduation? Finally, can the stereotypes and negative attitudes toward individuals with disabilities be erased from many professionals, including some members of the counseling profession? No doubt, some students with disabilities need individual attention, but counselors need to view these students' needs in perspective rather than in a stereotypic manner. As with other special populations, students with disabilities should receive career counseling first by identifying their individual needs and second by building programs to meet them (Brolin & Gysbers, 1989).

A Module for Specific Needs of People with Disabilities

Counseling considerations for people with disabilities was developed by Ettinger and associates (1991), focusing on special needs, making the school-to-work transition, and the impact of federal legislation on future programming. The authors suggested four major areas that should be included in the career development plans of persons with disabilities.

1. Career information, such as an understanding of the roles, responsibilities, and the realities of the workplace.
2. Learning strategies to enable individuals to master the information they need to know.
3. Prevocational skills, such as responsibility, initiative, punctuality, care of materials, and task completion.
4. Social skills, with an emphasis on job interviewing, accepting and providing criticism, and relating to authority figures. (Ettinger, 1991, pp. 9–3)

In making the school-to-work transition, persons with disabilities often need assistance in establishing and clarifying goals. This transition also involves a change in environment, which is sometimes difficult for people with disabilities. The counselor's role here is to assist the individual change roles from student to employee. This task could involve group discussions of self-concept, developing communication and interpersonal skills, and learning the expectations in the work world.

Ettinger (1991) points out that career counselors in schools are essential advocates for assisting students in making the transition from school to work. This transition period refers to the first year of employment after high school, postsecondary education, or training. Transition services are defined in the Individuals with Disabilities Education Act of 1990 (IDEA) (U.S. Department of Education, 1990) as

> a coordinated set of activities for a student, designed within an outcome-oriented process, which promotes movement from school to postschool activities, including postsecondary education, vocational training, integrated employment (including supported employment), continuing and adult education, adult services, independent living, or community participation. The coordinated set of activities shall be based upon the individual student's needs, taking into account the student's preferences and interests, and shall include instruction, community experiences, the development of employment and other postschool adult living objectives, and when appropriate, acquisition of daily living skills and functional vocational evaluation. [Sec. 602 (a) (19)]

School-to-work transition has been an extremely popular topic for workshops and seminars since the early 1990s. The National School-to-Work Learning and Information Center opened in Washington, D.C. in August 1995. This office serves as a training center and an information resource facility. (See Chapter 10 for more information on school-to-work programs.)

A Group Counseling Program for Individuals with Disabilities

The following counseling program illustrates a group counseling procedure for individuals with disabilities. The descriptions include excerpts that illustrate relevant counseling techniques. The counseling activity sequence consisted of four highly structured meetings, shown in Table 19-1. The counselees were hospitalized male patients who were accepted as clients for a vocational rehabilitation project.

John had been injured in a car accident and was almost totally paralyzed. The other counselees had been injured in industrial accidents. Rex's right leg was amputated below the knee. Roberto had lost three fingers. Harold's injury prevented him from bending his left leg.

Several days before the first counseling meeting, each counselee completed a vocational counseling inventory. The inventory was to be used as a counseling tool for each of the group meetings.

SESSION I: PERSONAL/SOCIAL ADJUSTMENT COUNSELING

The counselor began the first session by introducing himself and having each member introduce himself. The counselor briefed the counselees on the purpose of the counseling session.

Counselor: We're going to have four meetings to talk about some problems that you may experience when you return to the work force. Today we're going to cover some personal problems that you might experience in readjusting to a work role and general factors that influence the performance of workers who have similar problems.

The next excerpt illustrates the use of the previously completed vocational counseling inventory and the importance of group interaction. The counselor selected items to stimulate discussion. For example, the item, "Now that I have a disability, life is going to be difficult," generated considerable discussion.

Harold: I've thought about this a lot since I've been in the hospital, and things are really going to be different when I get out.

TABLE 19-1
Vocational Rehabilitation-Counseling Activity Sequence

Title	Activity
Personal/social adjustment counseling	Briefing on the purpose of counseling session; discussion of problems of workers with disabilities, personal/social adjustment problems, and factors influencing work performance
Peer group affiliation	Counseling session on the importance of good peer relations, factors influencing peer group affiliation, the give-and-take of working with others, and the influence of the working environment on job satisfaction
Worker-supervisor affiliation	Counseling session on the factors determining good relations with a supervisor, the role of the supervisor, and the influence of good worker-supervisor relations on work proficiency and job satisfaction
Job attitude	Counseling session on factors determining vocational success, factors influencing attitudinal development, and the influence of job attitude on work proficiency and job satisfaction

Roberto: Well, I've been here for almost eight months, and I've learned to accept the fact that I probably will be doing a different kind of work than I did before. By the way, what kind of work did you do? (*looking at Harold*)

Harold: I was a foreman on a construction job, and I had to go around the different jobs for this contractor I worked for.

Roberto: Well, you might be able to do the same kind of thing.

During this meeting, it was difficult for John to enter into the discussion, for he had been recently injured and was almost completely paralyzed. However, toward the end of the session he spoke.

John: I used to play in a band before I had this car accident, but I don't know what I am going to be able to do now. Anyway, I'm going to this Warm Springs Foundation, and I hope I will get some feeling back in my body and I will find out something.

John's response had a great impact on the entire group because his message was quite clear; here was someone who still had hope even though his injury had the potential of being much more restrictive than those of the other members of the group.

SESSION II: PEER GROUP AFFILIATION

The next excerpt illustrates how group interaction enhanced Session II. This meeting began with the counselor's question, "What kind of people did you like to work with on previous jobs?" During the course of exchanging ideas, several opinions were expressed. It became apparent to the counselor that all but one member of the group seemed to have a fairly healthy attitude toward peer workers. The counselor used several key questions and phrases to stimulate discussion: "Are most people you work with easy to talk to during breaks?" "Some people feel like an outsider on the job." "A friend of mine prefers working alone." "Are most of the people you have worked with friendly?"

Through group interaction, the point was made that good peer relations are most important for the worker with disabilities. Examples of statements from group members follow:

John: Some people are going to try to pity me because I've got a disability, while some are going to be very uncomfortable when I'm around.

Rex: To have a friend, you have to be a friend, and you can also do that as a disabled person.

Harold: Not everybody you work with is going to be friendly, but it sure helps if *you* try.

SESSION III: WORKER-SUPERVISOR AFFILIATION

The excerpts from this session illustrate how the counselor took advantage of the experiences of one group member to enhance the discussion. Harold had been employed in a supervisory position before his accident but was rather hesitant in communicating his viewpoint as a supervisor. The counselor began this session by having each member of the group discuss his relationships with a past supervisor or a boss. Each counselee stated that he had very little difficulty in worker-supervisor relationships. However, the counselor suspected that the relationships between employee and supervisor were not as appropriate as expressed by the counselees. Therefore, the counselor introduced several topics, hoping to elicit further responses from the group. An example of the exchange among group members follows:

Counselor: I've had some bosses that I would have worked harder for had they been a little more friendly. How about the rest of you?

Roberto: I remember a few guys like that, and we used to really chew them up during our bull sessions.

John: Yeah, sometimes bosses give too many orders and are not really interested in you.

Harold: (*Finally responding*) Well, when I was the boss, sometimes I had to get on people to make them work. Look at it this way, bosses have bosses, and they also have pressure to get the job done.

Rex: I never thought of it that way!

John: Yeah, I guess everybody has to answer to someone.

The discussion continued, centering on how one's perception of a supervisor influences personal reactions to the work environment.

SESSION IV: JOB ATTITUDE

The following excerpt illustrates how the counselor continued with the very productive previous counseling session and related the previous topic of discussion to the purpose of this final meeting.

Counselor: Well, last time we raked bosses over the coals, but we finally agreed that bosses and supervisors do have a pretty tough job and they are generally good guys if you act like you want to work with them and do a good job. This will be especially important as a worker with disabilities.

The counselor then asked each group member to restate what he had learned from the previous meeting.

Counselor: Each of you has illustrated how your attitudes about a supervisor influence your perception of the work environment. Now, let's direct our attention to how your attitudes will affect your return to the work force as a worker with disabilities.

Roberto: If you have a good attitude about your boss and people you work with, you will probably like your job too.

John: We have gotta think positive or we'll lose hope.

Harold: Sometimes it's going to be hard to have the right attitude—but you only hurt yourself.

This group counseling program encouraged group interaction by sharing concerns about new and different lifestyles as persons with disabilities. The program emphasized (1) personal/social adjustment problems that might be encountered by each member of the group when he or she returned to the work force, (2) retraining that may be necessary for a different occupation, (3) peer affiliation and supervisor relationships as a person with disabilities, and (4) the influence of one's attitudes on work proficiency and job satisfaction.

Assessment Instruments for Individuals with Disabilities

Micro-Tower—A Group Vocational Evaluation System

The *Micro-Tower* system of vocational evaluation was developed by ICD Rehabilitation and Research Center of New York City. The original instrument, *Tower,* is an acronym for Testing, Orientation, and Work Evaluation in Rehabilitation. *Tower* is an evaluation system consisting of 94 work samples that are individually administered. The *Micro-Tower* system is a group of 13 work samples that can be administered in a group session lasting three to five days. The *Micro-Tower* work samples are objectively scored and are considered to be performance tests. Work samples are measures of aptitude for a number of unskilled and skilled occupations grouped according to five broad areas of aptitude:[1]

Primary aptitude	*Work sample tests*
Motor	Electronic connector assembly; bottling, capping, and packing; lamp assembly
Clerical Perception	Zip coding; record checking; filing; mail sorting
Spatial	Blueprint reading; graphics illustration
Numerical	Making change; payroll computation
Verbal	Want-ads comprehension; message taking

A third- to fourth-grade reading level is required to take the *Micro-Tower* system test. Work samples can be administered to an individual who is seated but do require the use of at least one hand. The individual must understand spoken English.

A unique feature of the *Micro-Tower* system is the involvement of the clients in group discussions that explore their interests, values, lifestyles, and so on. A separate manual is provided, which has specific procedures and variations for the discussion groups. One of the major objectives of the discussion group is to improve the client's motivation for job placement. Discussion groups are also used as an entrée for the testing period in an effort to make the testing situation as nonthreatening as possible.

There are several sets of normative data available, including sets for groups who are in general rehabilitation, are Spanish-speaking, are left-handed, have

[1]*Micro-Tower: The Group Vocational and Research Center,* ICD Rehabilitation and Research Center, 1977.

physical disabilities, have psychiatric disturbances, have brain damage, have cerebral palsy, are in special education, are of a different culture, are ex-drug abusers, are ex-alcoholics, and are adult offenders. Interpretive materials for the *Micro-Tower* system are elaborate and thorough. The results are plotted on a graph from weak to strong for the skill area and specific work samples. Additional reports for the counselor include (1) behavioral observations made during testing, (2) a summary of the client's interest and perceived performance, (3) a client data sheet, (4) a summary report that includes a narrative of the test results, (5) a recommendation summary sheet that covers such areas as special training recommended, (6) referral recommendations, and (7) vocational recommendations (*Micro-Tower*, 1977).

The *Micro-Tower* system grew out of a need for a work evaluation instrument that could be administered to a group in a relatively short period. The evaluation system may also be used as a screening device to determine which clients would benefit from a more extensive evaluation of specific aptitudes. A manual is provided to convert *Micro-Tower* scores into estimates of *DOT* aptitude levels. The variety of norms available for interpretation increases the usefulness of the instrument.

Valpar Component Work Sample System

The *Valpar Component Work Sample System* (*VALPAR*) (Peterson, 1982) was developed by the Valpar Corporation of Tucson, Arizona, for disabled and nondisabled in all age groups. Its purpose is to assess vocational and functional skills through a series of 16 work samples. Each work sample measures a certain universal worker characteristic. The work samples involve hands-on tasks; some focus on general work characteristics, and others are related to specific job requirements. The following is a brief description of each of the work samples.

1. *Small tools:* Measures the ability to work with small hand tools, including screwdrivers and small wrenches.
2. *Size discrimination:* Measures visual discrimination by requiring that the individual screw correct-sized nuts onto threads mounted in a box.
3. *Numerical sorting:* Measures the ability to sort, file, and categorize by number code.
4. *Upper extremity range of motion:* Measures the range of motion of upper extremities and fatigue factors, finger dexterity, and sense of touch.
5. *Clerical comprehension and aptitude:* Measures the ability to perform certain clerical tasks and aptitude for typing.
6. *Independent problem solving:* Measures the ability to perform work that requires detailed visual comparisons of colored shapes.
7. *Multilevel sorting:* Measures the ability to sort according to number, letter, and color.
8. *Simulated assembly:* Measures the ability to do repetitive assembly tasks.
9. *Whole-body range of motion:* Measures gross motor abilities and fatigue factors.
10. *Tri-level measurement:* Measures the ability to perform precise measurements.

11. *Eye-hand-foot coordination:* Measures the ability to use eyes, hands, and feet simultaneously in a coordinated manner.
12. *Soldering and inspection:* Measures the ability to solder.
13. *Money handling:* Measures skills that are necessary in dealing with money and making change.
14. *Integrated peer performance:* Measures work behavior in interaction in small group assemblies.
15. *Electrical circuitry and print reading:* Measures the ability to understand and apply principles of electric circuits.
16. *Drafting:* Measures basic drafting skills and ability to learn drafting.

Each of the *VALPAR* work samples can either be used as a separate evaluation or be integrated with a combination of other work samples or other testing instruments. The administrator gives the directions verbally, and each work sample can be completed in one or two hours. Modifications of the work samples are available for people with visual and hearing impairments. Norm groups include institutionally retarded, culturally disadvantaged, U.S. Air Force recruits, San Diego employed workers, low-income unemployed, hearing impaired, and what is described as employer workers that were unselected.

VALPAR is well designed and easy to administer and score. The value of work sample testing is the ease of associating the results with requirements of a particular job. Counselors who need work-sample evaluations should carefully consider the content of each work sample in the *VALPAR* system. The focus of this system is on physical skills and the ability to use eyes, hands, and feet in a coordinated manner (Peterson, 1982).

Other work-sample tests include the following:

Jewish Employment Vocational Service Work Sample System—JEVS
Vocational Research Institute
Jewish Employment and Vocational Service
1700 Sansom St.
Philadelphia, PA 19103

SINGER Vocational Evaluation System
SINGER Career Systems
80 Commerce Drive
Rochester, NY 14623

Vocational Information and Evaluation Work Samples— VIEWS
Vocational Research Institute
Jewish Employment and Vocational Service
1700 Sansom St.
Philadelphia, PA 19103

Social and Prevocational Information Battery (SPIB)

The *SPIB* (Halpern, Raffeld, Irvin, & Link, 1975) was designed for use with students with educable mental retardation (EMR) in junior and senior high schools. The *SPIB* is useful for EMR program identification, individual evaluation for placement in EMR programs, and monitoring progress and outcomes of EMR programs. There are nine tests that can be used to assess students' needs for social and vocational skills. The tests measure nine domains identified by the authors as part of five long-range goals for the EMR that should be achieved in secondary schools. These five goals are (1) employability, (2) economic self-sufficiency, (3) family living, (4) personal habits, and (5) communication skills. Tests have been developed to measure the objectives of each goal. The nine tests consist of 277 mostly true-or-false items that are administered orally. The authors identify the goal of economic self-sufficiency as one of the major objectives necessary to postsecondary adaptation. The three domains set for this particular goal are (1) purchasing habits, (2) budgeting, and (3) banking. Test items were subsequently developed to measure self-sufficiency in these three domains. For example, in measuring purchasing habits, test items include measures of knowledge of sales tax, knowledge of types of stores, and effectiveness in using newspaper ads for best buys.

The *SPIB* can be compared with three reference groups. A junior high school–level conversion table permits comparisons from the derived raw scores with equivalent percentage correct scores and percentile ranks with junior high school–level students on each *SPIB* test. Likewise, a senior high school–level conversion provides comparisons with high school–level students on each *SPIB* test. The third conversion table is a combination of junior and senior high school–level normative samples.

The authors suggest a "task analysis" method of evaluating specific competencies within each domain *SPIB* measures. To accomplish this, each content area is divided into subcontent areas. For example, see how the domain of job-related behavior is divided into content and subcontent areas in Table 19-2. Each subcontent area defined provides the basis for developing instructional activities and measuring outcomes for each domain. In this way, the *SPIB* provides the foundation for establishing instructional programs for the EMR, as well as being a tool for measuring the outcomes of the instructional activities. The *SPIB* is a well-devised test battery for assessing and evaluating programs and provides the framework from which to build instructional programs for the EMR.

American Association of Mental Deficiency's (AAMD) Adaptive Behavior Scale

The *AAMD Adaptive Behavior Scale* (Nihira, Foster, Shellhaas, & Leland, 1975) is designed to replace the IQ test as a means of identifying individuals with mental retardation. It is primarily a rating scale for identifying adaptive behavior of individuals who have mental retardation and other special needs. The American Association of Mental Deficiency has endorsed this effort of using descriptions for identifying an individual's adaptive behavior, as opposed to the use of a single intelligence quotient (Nihira et al., 1975).

Of major importance in this approach is that adaptive behavior can be described from a developmental frame of reference. Thus, an individual is observed

TABLE 19-2
Content and Subcontent Areas for the Domain of Job-Related Behavior

Domain	Content areas	Subcontent areas
Job-related behavior	1. Knowledge of role and duties of a supervisor	a. Instruction b. Criticism c. Praise d. Hiring and firing e. Inspection of work f. Promotion g. Task assignment
	2. Knowledge of appropriate job-related communications	a. Job progress reports b. Relaying messages c. Reporting serious errors d. Requesting supplies e. Asking for help when needed f. Knowing whom to ask for help g. Asking for clarification
	3. Knowledge of what constitutes job completion	a. Importance of finishing a job b. Factors affecting job completion c. The effect of mistakes on job completion
	4. Recognition and knowledge of appropriate work relations with fellow employees	a. Compromising b. Cooperation c. Friendliness d. Showing appreciation e. Controlling temper f. Responsibility to others

SOURCE: From *Social and Prevocational Information Battery, Examiner's Manual,* by A. Halpern, P. Raffeld, L. D. Irvin, and R. Link, p. 3. Reprinted by permission of the publisher, CTB/McGraw-Hill, 2500 Garden Rd., Monterey, CA 93940. Copyright © 1975 by the University of Oregon. All rights reserved.

from an established standard that provides certain descriptive information as to the individual's functioning. Using this technique, a more comprehensive and informative description in terms of skills, habits, social expectations, and personal independence is provided.

The *AAMD Adaptive Behavior Scale* (Nihira et al., 1975) has two parts. Part I is a measure of 10 behavioral domains and 21 subdomains. The examiner is required to react to statements descriptive of behavior in certain identified situations. The examiner may circle a number representative of the individual being observed or may be required to check all statements that apply to the individual being observed. For example, in evaluating independence functioning, the examiner is required to rate individuals according to which statements may apply to them, such as "drops food on the table or floor" or "talks with mouth full" or "chews food with an open mouth." The behavioral domains evaluated include economic activity, language development, domestic activities, vocational activities, self-direction, responsibility, and socialization.

Part II is a measure of social expectations in 14 domains related to personality and behavioral disorders. The examiner is required to rate whether the individual occasionally or frequently is involved in a particular behavior. For example, in rating violent and destructive behavior, the examiner may be required to evaluate whether the individual occasionally or frequently "tears up magazines or books" or "rips or tears clothing." Other domains measured include antisocial and rebellious behaviors and unacceptable and eccentric behaviors.

The *AAMD Adaptive Behavior Scale* is designed to provide information that can be used to determine classroom instructional programs. A profile summary is provided for all adaptive behavioral domains measured by the rating scale. The scores are interpreted in terms of percentiles and deciles. Percentiles are arranged according to age groups. Comprehensive information received from the scale should assist teachers in planning specific programs for individuals and groups according to behavioral domains. Thus, the behavioral domains can be used to formulate objectives to be achieved. Systematic evaluation of the objectives can be provided by periodic retesting. The adaptive behavior scale is an instrument that can serve many purposes: it can be used to identify students for placement in certain programs, provide evaluation of ongoing special programs, assist in administrative decisions for students with special needs, and provide specific objectives for instructional planning.

Summary

1. The terms used to describe people with disabilities have changed to negate stereotypes and false ideas.

2. The passage of the Americans with Disabilities Act (ADA) has focused more attention on career counseling programs designed especially to meet the needs of individuals with disabilities. The ADA is a comprehensive document that covers a number of subjects significant to the rights of individuals with disabilities, including fair employment practices and access to public accommodations and transportation.

3. Special problems and needs of persons with disabilities include difficulty adjusting to and accepting physical disabilities, attitudinal barriers, being labeled "disabled," lack of role models, onset of disability, social/interpersonal skills, self-concept, skills for independence living, and architectural barriers. Educational programs that develop a better understanding of the special problems are needed by both employers and families.

4. State rehabilitation agencies provide numerous and varied programs for persons with disabilities. An actual case of an individual who received rehabilitation services from a state agency included the following steps: initial contact, diagnostic workup, evaluation and certification, vocational assessment, service planning, placement, and postemployment services.

5. Privately supported rehabilitation agencies provide educational, work, and counseling programs. Among services offered are psychological testing, vocational evaluation, personal/social adjustment counseling, work adjustment, prevocational training, special academic instruction, skills training, job placement, and sheltered workshops.

6. A career education program for students with disabilities uses a Life-Centered Career Education Curriculum. Included are a career awareness phase, a career exploration phase, and a preparation phase.

7. A group counseling program that promotes the vocational rehabilitation of individuals with disabilities included activities in (a) personal/social adjustment, (b) peer group affiliation, (c) worker-supervisor affiliation, and (d) job attitude counseling.

8. The *Micro-Tower* system of vocational evaluation consists of a group of 13 work samples and is used as a screening device to determine which individuals would benefit from more extensive evaluation of specific aptitudes.

9. The *Valpar Component Work Sample System* consists of 16 work samples used to measure certain universal worker characteristics. The focus of this system is on physical skills and the ability to use eyes, hands, and feet in a coordinated manner.

10. The *SPIB* was designed for use with students with educable mental retardation (EMR) in junior and senior high schools. Nine tests are used to assess students' needs for social and vocational skills.

11. The *AAMD Adaptive Behavior Scale* provides a means of identifying individuals with mental retardation. It is primarily a rating scale for identifying adaptive behavior of individuals with mental retardation and other special needs.

Supplementary Learning Exercises

1. Interview a rehabilitation counselor and obtain program descriptions for individuals with disabilities.
2. Make several observations of a special education class. Compile a list of common problems based on your observations. Relate these problems to job placement.
3. Develop a list of rehabilitation journals that publish articles of interest concerning career counseling programs for individuals with disabilities.
4. Visit an industry that employs individuals with disabilities. Compile a list of jobs performed and worker function activities.
5. Survey your campus to find physical barriers that restrict individuals with disabilities. Discuss how these barriers and others contribute to psychological barriers.
6. Using the *SPIB* goals and domains, develop a rationale for using assessment results of this type in career counseling programs.
7. Compile a list of audiovisual materials that can be incorporated in career counseling programs for individuals with disabilities. Review and report on at least two.
8. Develop counseling components designed to meet two or more special problems and needs.
9. Survey a community to determine programs available for individuals with disabilities. Using the survey results, develop plans for utilizing these programs in a high school and/or community college counseling program.
10. Interview a personnel director of an industry that employs individuals with disabilities to determine common problems experienced by these workers. Develop counseling components to help individuals overcome the common problems reported.

Techniques for the Career Counseling Intake Interview

CHAPTER TWENTY

Career Counseling Intake Interview and Assessment Techniques

The preceding chapters contained examples of the growing knowledge of the foundations for career guidance, different perspectives of career development, and strategies for career intervention. The wide range of content in these chapters provides background information for developing techniques that assist individuals in making career decisions. Recently, more attention has been directed toward personal problems such as faulty cognitions that can adversely affect career decision making and behavioral problems that inhibit career development. For example, Brown, Brooks, and Associates (1990) suggested that deficits in cognitive clarity require intervention other than career guidance for individuals who cannot objectively assess their own strengths and weaknesses and relate them to environmental situations. Gysbers and Moore (1987) pointed out that individuals who have been found to have irrational beliefs more than likely have distorted views of self and the career decision-making process. Spokane (1991) suggested that an increasing proportion of career counseling clients have a combination of career and personal problems. Furthermore, because career problems are often an integral part of personal problems, treatment requires intervention strategies to deal with them simultaneously. In other words, one affects the other to the point that it is less productive to separate them in treatment. Finally, Krumboltz (1983) argued that certain faulty cognitions lead to serious problems in career decision making such as, "I can do anything if I work hard enough for it," or "There is only one career for me." Career counselors should make every attempt to identify problems that would impede career development or the ability to adequately process information in career decision making. One way to accomplish this goal is through an intake interview.

The Intake Interview

The intake interview has different meanings and purposes for mental health professionals. In counseling, the interview assists clients in developing self-understanding, forming conclusions, looking at alternative actions, and so forth; it is viewed as a "helping interview." As a key tool for establishing objectives and goals, the interview is used by social workers to build a social history. Psychiatrists and clinical psychologists use the interview as a diagnostic tool to help form treatment considerations. For career counselors, the proposed purposes of the intake interview borrow from each of these functions. As a diagnostic tool, the interview should help uncover behavioral problems that can lead to work maladjustment and faulty cognitions, which may in turn interfere with the client's ability to make career decisions. In a helping role, the interview assists clients in understanding the integral relationship of all life roles. Finally, all parts of the interview (including historical and demographic data) are used to help develop goals.

This chapter focuses on accomplishing the objectives of an intake interview by providing some techniques for conducting the interview, a suggested sequence for interviewing, and a brief discussion of selected life roles with suggested topics for discussion. In addition, there is a supplement to the interview that will assist in discovering problems that interfere with career development, such as problems in living, work maladjustment, faulty cognitions, and memory and persistence. Depending on the needs of the client, the interview may take several sessions. In Chapter 21, the interview process is illustrated using case studies.

A Suggested Sequence for an Interview

The following interview sequence is designed to provide career counselors with structured guidelines for observing their clientele while in dialogue with them. Most of the topics, such as demographic information and educational history, are typically found in career counseling programs. However, the discussion of selected life roles significantly increases the options for obtaining pertinent information. For example, work history and preference for a future career are discussed as a part of the work role and in association with other life roles. Individual client needs will directly determine the major focus of the interview and the sequence to be followed. For instance, an interview may be terminated during the discussion of life roles if it is determined that the individual is unable to communicate effectively with a counselor because of major clinical depression. In another case, the interview may focus on only selected life roles. Yet, in another case, the counselor may need to evaluate memory and persistence. The flexibility suggested for using the interview provides the opportunity for meeting the needs of a wide range of clients. This is the suggested sequence provided by Brown, Brooks, and Associates (1990).

    I. Current status information
       A. General appearance
       B. Attitude and behavior

    C. Affect and mood
    D. Demographic information
    E. Work experience
    F. Medical history
    G. Educational history
    H. Family history
  II. Discovering the significance of life roles and potential conflict
    A. Worker role
      1. Work history
    B. Homemaker
      1. Spouse
      2. Parent
    C. Leisure role
    D. Citizen role
  III. Supplement to the interview: Discovering problems that interfere with career development
    A. Problems in living
    B. Behaviors that may lead to work maladjustment
    C. Faulty cognitions
    D. Memory and persistence
  IV. Developing goals and objectives [see Chapter 19]
    A. Identifying client goals
    B. Determining the feasibility of goals
    C. Establishing subgoals
    D. Assessing commitment to goals

Interviewing Techniques

The techniques for interviewing discussed in the following paragraphs are used within a counselor-client dyadic relationship. The objectives focus on techniques and strategies that foster productive dialogue and focus on potential deficits in career decision making and other career development concerns. The major purpose for the interview, in this context, is to determine client needs and the subsequent direction that intervention strategies will take. In some instances, the following techniques are illustrated by counselor-client dialogue: (1) rapport; (2) observation; (3) self-disclosure; (4) open- and close-ended questions; (5) echoing, restatement, or paraphrasing; (6) continuation; and (7) staying on track.

Techniques for Establishing Rapport

Jan, a 28-year-old woman, was considering a return to graduate school at a local university. She asked for an appointment at the career counseling center.

    On the morning Jan reported for the appointment, she was frowning noticeably and moved around the waiting room picking up one magazine and then another. She constantly looked at her watch, sighing aloud as if impatient.

Ali, the counselor assigned to Jan, observed this behavior while finishing with another client. A few minutes before the time for the appointment, Ali greeted Jan with enthusiasm.

Counselor: Jan, my name is Ali, and I'm here to help you.
Client: Yes, I'm Jan.
Counselor: This is Rita, our secretary, and she will help also, especially for appointments, just call either one of us for anything you need.
Client: (*Nodding*) Okay, thanks.
Counselor: Let me show you around. Here is our career library. There is one of my clients reading about careers. Notice another person is using the computer program to find information. To our left is a room used for taking tests, as you see two people are currently taking an interest inventory. Now here is my office.

As they entered Ali's office, he made the following comments:

Counselor: I'm pleased that we've been able to help most everyone who comes to us either directly through one or more of our programs or by referring people to proper sources.

Thus far, Ali had responded to his client's signs of tension and continued to establish rapport. However, some clients do not exhibit signs of tension or apprehension as clearly as Jan did, so it is important to communicate to each client an expression of sincerity and competence. After a short period of explanation of ethical issues and confidentiality rules, Ali asked the following question.

Counselor: How may we help you?
Jan: My parents want me to choose another job, so I promised them I'd come here. I'm really upset and mad about this whole idea!
Counselor: You do seem upset, particularly with your parents.

By responding with empathy, the counselor continued to build rapport. Also, Ali used the client's terms for expressing an emotion rather than a psychological one. Paraphrasing responses using the client's wording communicates understanding to the client (Othmer & Othmer, 1989). He also helped improve rapport by expressing an interest in the anxiety that he observed through Jan's body language and verbal expressions. Ali had learned that he must be genuine and resist using psychological jargon, or the client might withdraw. For example, the conversation may have gone as follows:

Counselor: You were apprehensive and overwrought when I met you, you must really be somewhat unstable.
Jan: Oh really! Do you honestly think you know me that well? I've heard that psychological claptrap before.

Counselors must communicate to their counselees an understanding of their emotional status and empathetically appreciate the frustrations they are experiencing. Instead of using technical language, clear behavioral descriptions are suggested (Hersen & Turner, 1985). The use of more technical terms may be appropriate in sessions that follow the establishment of rapport and trust.

Techniques for Observation

Mental health workers have a long history of using observation as a tool to provide insights into their client's behavior. Psychiatrists, psychologists, clinical social workers, and counselors have refined systematic procedures for observation. Then they use the information gained, along with other data, to determine intervention strategies.

Throughout the interview, the effective interviewer is alert to any clues that provide insights into the client's personality, mood, social functioning, and other characteristics. General appearance, behavior, affect, nutritional status, hygiene and dress, eye contact, psychomotor activity, speech, attitude, and other characteristics provide important information for the intake interview.

A career counseling intake interview may be conducted in a number of different types of settings, such as a high school, college or university, private practice, mental health center, rehabilitation and employment agency, or other agency. Physical appearance may then be judged from the perspective of what is considered appropriate to the environment and to the purpose for which the interview is conducted. Appropriate physical appearance in this context is relative, but in all instances, it can provide important information. The following examples illustrate this point.

> Angelo, a 17-year-old high school student, made an appointment with the school counselor for the stated purpose of "I want help in choosing a future job." He reported promptly for the interview. The counselor made the following notes: Angelo was neatly dressed in freshly pressed trousers, a clean shirt, and shined shoes. He was of average weight, clean-shaven, with combed, short hair. There were no unusual movements and he made eye contact throughout the interview. Angelo expressed himself well and had an impressive vocabulary. There were no indications of depression.

At first glance, one may conclude that little was revealed about Angelo other than his physical appearance was unremarkable—that is, nothing negative. However, the observer could conclude that his dress was appropriate and that he was aware of social convention and had insights into how to function adequately during the interview. His appearance gave an initial impression that he was indeed serious and highly motivated to initiate a counseling relationship.

The next example takes place in a state employment agency:

> Fred was age 33 and had had several different jobs during the last ten years. The reason he gave for coming for counseling was that he was out of work and looking for a job. The counselor made the following notes: Fred was a disheveled-looking man whose clothes were unpressed and soiled. He seemed to have very poor personal hygiene; he had not shaved for several days and had very strong body odor. Fred appeared to be anxious during the interview, as observed by his

behavior. First of all, he spoke at times with a differently pitched voice, particularly when past work experiences were discussed. He also seemed to be very guarded about his reasons for leaving certain jobs. He was quite fidgety, moving around in his chair and clenching his fists. There was a strong smell of alcohol on his breath.

From just these few notes, the client's problems with getting and keeping employment were rather clear. At least two needs were obvious: personal hygiene and substance abuse. Other information obtained from Fred in the interview reinforced these conclusions.

In these two cases, the counselor jotted down first impressions. Careful scrutiny of these impressions, along with other data, may reinforce or justify modification of them. Without spending more time with a client and looking beyond surface information, recommending appropriate programming may be questionable. The skilled counselor is willing to modify early conclusions when it is justifiable.

Other descriptions of behavior include the following.

Rapport was difficult to establish and maintain.
Appeared to be nervous.
Seemed to tire easily.
Gave up on tasks easily.
Did not appear to be well.
A speech-articulation disorder was noted.
Seldom initiated conversation.
Responded impulsively to many questions.
Talked in a loud voice.
Talked in a low voice and was hard to understand.
Was easily distracted.
Had short attention span.
Daydreamed.
Had nervous tics.
Expressed negative view of self.
Lacked interest in personal appearance.
Expressed feelings of sadness, cried readily.

Techniques for Using Self-Disclosure

At certain times during the interview, counselors may find it advantageous to convey information about themselves to their clients. This technique is known as self-disclosure and may be positive or negative in nature. Successful personal experiences, such as "I'm known as a task-oriented person and my persistence has paid off for me," convey successful positive experiences, whereas "I lacked self-confidence on my first job" conveys a negative type of experience. Both types of self-disclosure may be used effectively for establishing rapport, communicating empathy, and facilitating dialogue during the interview. Self-disclosure by counselors can also facilitate self-disclosure from clients (Cozby, 1973; Cormier & Cormier, 1991). However, counselors should be very selective when using self-disclosure and should use this technique only sparingly. The following example illustrates the effective use of self-disclosure.

Jin: My father has always wanted me to follow in his footsteps like owning your own business. But I have no interest in business and especially in retail—I just wish they would leave me alone.

Counselor: This sounds so familiar! My parents wanted me to become an architect and applied plenty of pressure before I went to college. I thought they would never get off my back.

Jin: I can't believe it. We had similar experiences—wow! Let me tell you more about my dad. . . .

By sharing common experiences, the counselor attempts to increase the client's disclosure level and foster discussion of unresolved relationship issues. The counselor's responses to Jin's problems through self-disclosure influenced, structured, and directed the discussion topic during the interview. Immediate feedback through self-disclosure about a client's personal problems usually enhances the client's willingness to discuss them in greater depth (Halpern, 1977; Thase & Page, 1977; Cormier & Cormier, 1991).

Techniques for Using Open- and Close-Ended Questions

The types of questions used during an interview are usually selected to obtain specific information or encourage clients to express themselves more fully by elaborating on certain subjects, emotions, or events. The two options discussed here are the use of open- and close-ended questions. Research on the use of these two types of questions suggested that open-ended questions facilitate emotional expression (Hopkinson, Cox, & Rutter, 1981), whereas close-ended questions have higher reliability and narrow the focus of the interview (Othmer & Othmer, 1989). Open-ended questions usually are formed with the words *tell me, explain more fully, what, how, when,* or *where.* For instance, "Tell me more about your work experiences" gives the client the opportunity to select the direction and subject of his or her response within the broad category of work experiences. Close-ended questions request more specific information; for example, "Have you served in the armed services?" Both types of questions are useful during an interview, as illustrated below.

Counselor: How far did you go in school?
Ben: I quit in the tenth grade.
Counselor: Why did you quit?
Ben: I don't know. I didn't like it.

Now the counselor turns to more open-ended questions in the interview.

Counselor: What kind of problems did you have at school?
Ben: I couldn't get along with the teachers and the principal didn't like me, so I just quit.

Counselor: Can you tell me more about your problems?
Ben: Well, I was absent a lot, and they must have known I was doing drugs and selling them, because they were always watching me. Man, I didn't do anything in school—I just quit.

In this case, the counselor quickly realized that there was more to the story about quitting school than Ben had suggested earlier. He shifted from questions used to get specific information to a free-response type, and Ben responded with pertinent information. Inconsistencies suggested by clients' statements or "mixed messages" can be clarified through the use of both open-ended and close-ended questions.

Techniques for Using Echoing, Restatement, or Paraphrasing

To focus attention on the cognitive or affective content of a client's statement, the counselor can use the techniques of echoing, restatement, or paraphrasing. One purpose of these techniques is to focus attention on the situation, object, person, or general idea of a statement. Paraphrasing or echoing the cognitive portion of a statement provides greater chances for obtaining a measure of the emotional tone associated with its content. Client affect may be expressed through nonverbal communication (gestures, facial expressions) or through descriptive words such as *sad, angry,* and *depressed* or *happy, affectionate,* and *supportive.* The degree to which affect is associated with the content of a client's statement provides counselors with important evaluative information. The following case illustrates this point.

Kanisha: My father thinks I should plan my life around a typical stereotyped role like homemaker, but—well, I've already told you that my father and I don't agree. He is just impossible!
Counselor: You obviously do not agree with your father about future life roles.
Kanisha: On some things I guess I do, but most of the time no.
Counselor: You mentioned the role of homemaker.
Kanisha: I really don't know at this time. Most of my friends are going after a career and not worrying about marriage and kids. I guess I'd like to get married someday, but I'm not sure. Honestly, it depresses me to even think about it.

In this case, the counselor wanted to find out more about Kanisha's feelings about her father and particularly her feeling about the role of homemaker. The counselor was interested in determining whether there were perceived role conflicts that might influence career development. Kanisha seemed to be struggling with the message of her father's view of the appropriate role for women and with what friends were projecting as a role model. Such conflicts may inhibit ongoing career decision making well into the future.

Techniques for Using Continuation

Continuation is one of the so-called steering techniques used to encourage clients to go on with a topic and provide reinforcement that he or she is on the right course. Techniques used include nonverbal gestures such as keeping eye contact, nodding, staying silent, and using hand movements that invite the client to continue. Typical statements include "Go on," "Tell me more," "Hmm," and "What happened after that?" (Othmer & Othmer, 1989). An example follows:

Counselor: What do you consider to be your major problem in selecting a career?
Abe: I don't know very much about different kinds of jobs.
Counselor: Go on.
Abe: What's the future look like? What are the possibilities? I'm not sure what I like, but I know what I don't like.
Counselor: Hmm. Tell me more.
Abe: How can you find out about all these things? Sometimes I feel like giving up and just taking any old job. But, then I may not be happy with it and have to start all over again. How does anyone really decide what to do?

In this case, the counselor steered Abe to elaborate on his lack of career information, interests, and decision-making procedures. Armed with such information as "What's the future look like" and "I'm not sure about what I like," the counselor is in a good position to obtain client agreement for specific career counseling goals.

Techniques for Staying on Track

Maintaining content focus is an effective technique for gainful productivity in a dyadic relationship. The counselor may have clients who are rather nonverbal, whose responses are short and abrupt, or clients who enjoy verbalizing. In both cases, keeping the conversation within the interview guidelines is one way of avoiding the possibility of wasting time with irrelevant information.

Some clients have difficulty maintaining focus on a subject for a variety of reasons, including the defense mechanism of denial, lack of motivation to persist, and conflicting thoughts that make staying on track difficult. When clients have consistent patterns of difficulty maintaining focus on the subject of discussion, referral for an in-depth analysis of the problem may be warranted. In those cases where clients deviate from the subject with unessential circumstantial information, abrupt and assertive action by the counselor may be necessary. The following case illustrates this point.

Counselor: Tell me more about your interest in working with people.
Kyung: I think I like people. My friend Julie was working in a day care center and the children there were okay. She got married and is taking a trip to the Bahamas. She and her husband like to swim and sail, they will probably go there every vacation and—
Counselor: (*Interrupts*) Kyung, let's continue talking about *your* interests.

The process of interviewing clients for career counseling is a dynamic one and requires the skillful use of the techniques discussed in this section. Assessing and generating hypotheses about clients involves the possibility of a profound number of career-related problems. In the next sections, each part of the interview is discussed.

Current Status Information

General Appearance

General appearance is a generalized observation of the client's personal grooming, posture, facial expressions, and mannerisms. Forming a visual perception of the client's general appearance provides a reference point as the interview progresses. For example, appearance may provide some important clues about personality, awareness of social conventions, and ability to function in current life roles.

Attitude and Behavior

Attitude and behavior are also obtained through observation and, more specifically, through the quality of the interaction with the counselor. One client may relate easily and be cooperative, whereas another may be suspicious and guarded, requiring that the counselor offer reassurance and frequently refer to the confidentiality of the interview. Specific examples of a client's attitude and behavior should be recorded for later review. Some descriptive examples follow: articulate, avoids eye contact, shy, elated, depressed, relaxed, aggressive, anxious, tense, overbearing, alert, oppositional, self-righteous, sullen, insubordinate.

Affect and Mood

Affect is evaluated through observation of the client's emotional tone during the interview, whereas mood is the client's current reported status. Affect is a momentary reaction to a current situation or conversation and may change as stimuli change. Mood, on the other hand, is self-reported for a specified period. Affect and mood can differ; for example, a client may appear happy (affect) when meeting the counselor but later report depression and despair (mood). Inappropriate affect refers to clients who demonstrate incongruence with the content of conversation, such as laughing inappropriately when a sad topic is discussed.

Demographic Information

Demographic information should include sex, ethnicity, age, and marital status. This information may be obtained by direct questioning or by self-report to questions on a structured form.

Work Experiences

Past work experience may also be recorded by the client or obtained through questioning. Report forms usually require listing both part- and full-time jobs. Other information commonly required on report forms includes likes and dislikes about jobs, career successes and failures, and jobs that may be considered for the future. Work roles are further discussed in the next section.

Medical and Educational History

Likewise, medical and educational history may also be obtained by direct questioning or by self-report. Both topics may have a significant effect on life roles. For example, physical and academic limitations are important factors to be considered in educational and career planning.

Family History

Family roles may be obtained by various methods, such as through career genograms. Gysbers and Moore (1987) describe these methods in detail. Another method referred to as an occupational family tree asks clients to list the occupations of grandparents, parents, aunts and uncles, and brothers and sisters. The respondent is questioned about his or her reactions to relatives' occupations in terms of pride or embarrassment. Other questions probe such subjects as family satisfaction with occupations and the benefits the family has received from specific occupations. The client is also asked to identify with any of the family members (Dickson & Parmerlee, 1980).

Direct questioning has the important advantage of observing client behaviors and emotional reactions. It is therefore suggested that even if a written self-report is used to obtain demographic data and work, medical, educational, and family history, a discussion of this information should be included in the interview.

Discovering the Significance
of Life Roles and Potential Conflicts

There is an abundance of evidence, as suggested in Chapters 2 and 3, that career counseling is not just concerned with strategies for selecting a career but is much broader in scope and content. Among others, Super (1990) has suggested an integrative approach to career counseling that focuses on the development of life roles over the life span, with emphasis on interrole congruence. The key to this concept is the effect of the development of one role on others. For instance, has the homemaker role inhibited career development or does the work role leave ample time for fulfillment of the citizen role? As Super (1980) pointed out, "Success in one facilitates success in others, and difficulties in one role are likely to lead to difficulties in another" (p. 287).

Hansen's (1996) Integrative Life Planning (ILP) model incorporates career development, life transitions, gender-role socialization, and social change. This model involves a "lifelong process of identifying our primary needs, roles, and goals and the consequent integration of these within ourselves, our work, and our family" (Hansen, 1990, p. 10).

The ILP model evolved from Hansen's (1978) *BORN FREE* project, which was designed to expand career options for both men and women. She suggested that fragmented approaches to development place limits on decisions clients will make in their lifetime. A more integrative approach recognizes that an individual's total development includes the broad spectrum of domains: social/emotional, physical, sexual, intellectual, vocational, and spiritual. Finally, in the context of our discussion, this model suggests that life roles are to be integrated in our planning and not isolated from the career decision-making process. The impact of decisions on lifestyle, including relationships, is a major part of a more comprehensive view of development.

The life roles to be evaluated in the interview include worker, homemaker, leisurite, and citizen. Included in the work role is work history and in the homemaker role, spouse and parent. Life roles increase and decrease in importance according to the individual's current status. For example, the student role is much more dominant in early life, even though career development is continuous and requires a lifetime learning involvement. The potential complexity and variety of life roles over the life span may include a multitude of possible scenarios that warrant exploration. In the following paragraphs, each role is identified and examples of topics to be covered in the interview are presented.

Worker Role

Over time, the term *work* has generated many definitions and has meant different things to the individuals who do it. Also, the objectives people have for work may be quite different and may change as they pass through stages of career development. For example, some individuals may work for the intrinsic enjoyment of it; for others, the primary objective may be a narrowly concerned way of making a living; and yet others work for social status or for self-identity. For many, a combination of objectives and other factors are of equal importance. Super (1984) suggested an inclusive perspective of the work role that covers most segments of lifestyle.

> The approach of recent years has shifted from a focus on work alone as a central life concern to an interest in the quality of life, life in which work is one central concern in a constellation of roles such as homemaking, citizenship, and leisure that interact to make for life satisfaction. The terms work motivation and job satisfaction are now perhaps not displaced by, certainly incorporated into, the terms quality of life and life satisfactions. (p. 29)

The different purposes individuals have for the work role are central to our concerns in the interview. Herr and Cramer (1996) suggested that the purposes of work can be classified as economic, social, and psychological. For example, a major economic purpose is to provide the individual with assets to satisfy current and future basic needs. In the social realm, friendships and social status are established through peer group affiliations where mutual goals are achieved. A work identity, self-efficacy, and a sense of accomplishment are examples of the psychological purposes of work.

The purposes and meanings of work are uniquely individualized. For example, a family-oriented individual who has strong needs to spend ample time with his or her children may be somewhat unhappy in a work role that limits family activities. A strong orientation for work leadership roles may inhibit an individual's needs associated with the life roles of citizen and leisurite. Although it may be difficult to satisfy the needs of all life roles, a greater balance of roles may enhance some people's quality of life. The following list of topics for discourse and samples of content for work-role interviewing represent only a few of the possibilities that can be discussed. Client needs should dictate the selection of subjects.

For a client making an initial choice of work role, the counselor should assess the following:

- Knowledge of life role concepts
- Acceptance of the idea of different life roles
- Ability to evaluate how work roles affect other life roles
- Ability to project an ideal work role
- Ability to identify purpose of the work role
- Ability to project self into work roles
- Ability to identify future work roles
- Knowledge of personal characteristics
- Level of skill development

Although many of the variables considered in the initial choice may need to be reevaluated with individuals who wish to change careers, the degree to which the individual is able to do the following should also be explored:

- Adapt to changes
- Learn new and different skills
- Function under different management styles
- Assess reasons for career changes and work commitments
- Assess his or her abilities, limitations, interests, and values to adapt to work environment changes
- Use decision-making procedures
- Identify career resources and how to use them
- Identify sources of stress
- Apply methods of modifying behavior
- Identify educational and training programs

Homemaker Role

The role of homemaker has a wide spectrum of possibilities. For example, a 35-year-old single person may not consider this role a very important one, whereas a married 35-year-old who has children may consider the role of homemaker a major role. A high school student may consider this role as something to be dealt with in the future, whereas a 50-year-old who has reared several children will place less emphasis on this role when planning a career change. The more recent phenomenon of the househusband and more emphasis on the male role as a homemaker adds to the diversity of possible interrole conflicts (see Chapters 15, 16, and 17).

The number of working mothers is expected to increase. There is a definite trend of more working mothers who have children under the age of 6; for instance, 12% were employed in 1950, whereas 57% were employed in the early 1990s (Chadwick & Heaton, 1992). Hoffreth and Phillips (1987) have suggested that 7 out of 10 mothers with infants and young children will be employed before or by the end of the 1990s. A major concern of maternal employment is its effect on children, the family, and the working women themselves. In a comprehensive review of the literature concerning the effects of maternal employment on children, Herr and Cramer (1996) concluded that in general it does no harm to children (infants, preschoolers, and adolescents). Working mothers also seem to fare well according to Ferree (1984), who conducted a national research study concerning satisfaction variables. She concluded that there were no significant differences of life satisfaction between working mothers and those who did not work outside the home. In a related study, results indicated that stress experienced by working women can be offset by spousal approval, dependable child care, and shared family responsibilities (Suchet & Barling, 1985; Scarr, Phillips, & McCartney, 1989).

The issues surrounding the homemaker role in families where both husband and wife work outside the home (dual-earner and dual-career) have major significance as a result of the expected growing number of working mothers. In dual-earner and dual-career families, both husband and wife work outside the home, but dual-career families are characterized as more career-oriented and committed to career development on a continuous basis. Both types of families share some common goals as well as sources of stress, such as role conflict, role overloads, and decreased opportunity for leisure. The following is a list of subjects for general discourse.

- Degree of commitment to the role of homemaker
- Career now and homemaker later
- The woman as a homemaker and the husband as a breadwinner
- The reason both spouses may have to work
- The homemaker-worker connection
- Family life versus career commitment
- The significance of integrated life roles

Potential conflict issues such as the following should also be assessed.

- Decreased leisure
- Share of homemaker responsibilities

- View of traditional gender-based roles
- Stress from physical and emotional demands
- Multiple role demands
- Commitment to household chores
- Commitment to sharing child care responsibilities
- Commitment to development of spouse's career
- Nonsupport of spouse's career development
- Dissimilar levels of involvement in both work and family needs
- Decision-making procedures for such family matters as when to have children
- Expectations of family roles in dual-career marriages

Leisure Role

There are a number of clichés about the relationship of work and leisure that have endured for generations. The primary message has been that a quality lifestyle is one in which there is a balance between time spent at work and time devoted to leisure activities. This message still prevails and has received renewed recognition as a means of fostering need satisfaction (Leclair, 1982). Within this frame of reference, quality of life is attained through a more holistic viewpoint of human and career development. Simply stated, individuals are to recognize that quality of life is associated with all life roles. Central to our concerns as career counselors is a balance of life roles that gives clients the freedom for self-expression to meet their needs. Moreover, when interrole conflicts are discovered, we have at our disposal a menu of suggestions designed to enhance all life roles.

The complementary role that leisure has to the work role is expressed by Kando and Summers (1971) as two-dimensional; that is, it reinforces positive associations that are also expressed in the work role (supplemental compensation) and provides activities to reduce stress associated with unpleasant work experiences (reactive compensation). Following this logic but with a somewhat different twist, Jackson (1988) suggested that individuals can receive psychological benefits from leisure, but only if they learn how to use the time spent in leisure in a purposeful manner. Remember that sources of stress found in work, such as competition, can also become sources of stress in leisure activities.

The availability of time that can be devoted to leisure for any one individual is situational. However, McDaniels (1990) advocated planning for different types of leisure as a part of a counseling model. He also suggested that counselors act in an advocacy role to promote leisure activities in schools, workplaces, homes, and communities.

In sum, the leisure role should be assessed as a prolific means of complementing other life roles. The proportion of time a person allocates to leisure should be judged from the perspective of lifestyle. For example, the ambitious accountant may consider leisure activities as a luxury that has little current relevance, whereas the individual who is working full time as a bus driver and part time on two other jobs may view leisure as something other, more fortunate people do. The *involvement* in leisure may simply be haphazard and left to chance. Although there is not a plethora of research suggesting the benefits of leisure activities, some research conclusions strongly suggest that effective participation in leisure can be therapeutic (Ragheb & Griffith, 1982) and can compensate for dissatisfaction found in work (Bloland & Edwards, 1981). Suggested subjects for discourse are:

- Benefits of leisure activities
- Purpose for planning activities
- Types of leisure, including intellectual, creative, social, and physical activities
- Resources for information on leisure activities
- How to become involved in a leisure/work model
- Perspectives of a holistic lifestyle
- Recognition of conflicts with other life roles
- The role of leisure and career development
- The advantages of balancing life roles with leisure
- Identification of needs and values associated with the leisure role
- Psychological needs satisfied through leisure activities
- The work/leisure connection
- Developmental tasks related to leisure development
- Development of a greater level of interest in leisure activities

Citizen Role

Similar to the leisure role's link to quality of life, the citizen role may serve as an additional or compensating source of satisfaction. Also, this role provides opportunities for fulfillment of individual needs in a wide variety of activities found in most communities. Local civic organizations offer an abundance of opportunities to express civic responsibility as a way of responding to community needs. Although involvement in volunteerism was on the increase for community, state, national, and international projects in the late 1980s and the early part of the 1990s, the recent downsizing of the U.S. work force has created a different atmosphere in many communities. According to Rimer (1996), who reflects on a national poll sponsored by the *New York Times,* many communities have fewer volunteers for community service. Workers who have lost their jobs are desperately searching for ways to maintain their lifestyle and no longer have the time or the inclination to volunteer for civic services. Thus, counselors need to observe the citizen role in the context of current conditions within communities.

The concept of balanced life roles implies that there are numerous opportunities to build a quality lifestyle. Individual work situations may not provide outlets to meet client needs associated with, for example, reading to blind students or being a tutor or hospital aide. Productive opportunities outside the work role are means of satisfaction that enhance interrole activities. That is, some needs that might otherwise be left to go to seed or produce stress can be satisfied through civic activities.

Among others, Bolles (1993) has suggested that skills learned and developed through participation in civic organizations and activities may be used in career decision making. These skills can be matched with work requirements in career exploration (see Chapter 13). Also, volunteer experiences, along with education and other experiences, are considered in job placement (McDaniels, 1990).

In the interview, the counselor should assess the client in terms of

- perception of the citizen's role;
- knowledge of civic organizations;
- knowledge of benefits from participating in civic activities;
- knowledge of benefits from participating in volunteerism;
- evaluation of skills learned through participation in civic activities;
- knowledge of how skills can be transferred to work roles;
- degree of participation in civic organizations;
- desire to participate in civic organizations;
- reasons for lack of participation in community activities;
- likes and dislikes of civic activities; and
- family involvement in civic activities.

Interviewing Multicultural Groups

Developing a greater sensitivity to culturally diverse clients has become increasingly important for career counselors; we must foster specific counseling techniques to accommodate the human diversity that exists in our society. The core dimension of interviewing is effective communication between clients and counselors. Also, during the course of the interview, counselors form opinions and assumptions about clients from both verbal and nonverbal communications. Because of cultural and ethnic differences between counselor and client, the counselor must be alert to a wide spectrum of ethnic and cultural characteristics that influence behavior. For example, some cultural groups may conceptualize their problems differently from those of the dominant white culture and seek solutions based on these assumptions. For instance, a client who views his problem as being ostracized because of race may be much more interested in finding immediate employment than pursuing a program for identifying a long-term career goal. Another client may be reluctant to share her personal problems with someone outside the family circle, and in fact, direct questioning can be interpreted as an infringement on privacy.

Although it is difficult to generalize techniques suggested for different cultural groups, it seems feasible to first determine the level of acculturation by socioeconomic status, language preference, place of birth, generation level, preferred ethnic identity, and ethnic group social contacts (Ponterotto, 1987). Questions must be carefully selected and presented so as not to offend the client. For example, directness may be judged as demanding, intrusive, or abrupt by some cultural groups. Furthermore, an open person may be seen by some cultures as weak, untrustworthy, and incapable of appropriate restraint (Copeland & Griggs, 1985).

Here are some other points to remember when interviewing people from other cultures.

- General appearance may be quite distinctive for some subcultures and should be accepted on that basis.
- Attitude and behavior are considered difficult to ascertain. Major belief themes of certain cultures may influence members' attitudes about themselves and others. Their perceptions of the world may be quite different from those of the counselor.
- Affect and mood are also related to cultural beliefs and to what is considered appropriate within a culture. The meaning given to gestures often differs by culture. Work experience may be quite limited because of lack of opportunity. Also, in some cultures, it is considered very immodest to speak highly of yourself and the skills you have mastered.
- Life roles, and particularly relationships, are unique to cultural socialization. In some cultures, females are considered equal to males, whereas in others they are expected to be subservient.

These examples illustrate the necessity of building an extensive body of resources for interviewing ethnic minorities. Other general recommendations include (1) use straightforward, slang-free language, (2) become familiar with cultural life-role models, (3) identify a consultant on other cultures who can provide helpful information, and (4) become familiar with support networks for different cultural groups. Finally, Chapter 18 provides suggestions and strategies for career development for some multicultural groups.

Supplement to the Interview: Discovering Problems that Interfere with Career Development

The focus of this part of the interview is on behavioral patterns of maladjustment. The identification of specific behavior domains that may contribute to conflicts in the work environment provides a practical and workable system for the career counselor to identify goals and objectives for counseling intervention. For instance, individuals whose basic behavior style has been identified as overtly hostile and aggressive may respond to programs designed to manage anger and reduce aggression.

"Problems in living" and methods of coping with these problems need to be identified. This approach does not rule out psychiatric etiology as a source of work maladjustment but focuses more on the individual's ability to cope with work demands. Perhaps more important, mental disorders may or may not affect work behavior. Neff (1985) pointed out that the ability to function on a job is related to the nature of both an individual's mental health and his or her mental illness. However, more research is needed to establish the relationship between work maladaption and mental disorders.

Some research has suggested that career competence is not grossly affected by mental illness (character and affective disorders, severe psychoneurosis, and functional psychosis) when the mental illness subsides (Huffine & Clausen, 1979). The findings of this longitudinal research project suggested that developed competencies and socialization into the work world were not necessarily affected by the mental illness of the men studied.

The fourth edition of the *Diagnostic and Statistical Manual of Mental Disorders* (DSM-IV) (American Psychiatric Association [APA], 1994) has several categories of mental, social, and behavioral disorders. Although all these disorders can appear in the workplace, references to work impairment or dysfunctions are very generalized. The following quote from the DSM-IV (APA, 1994) is a guideline for how we must individualize our interpretation of mental disorders and the subsequent behavior associated with a disorder.

> In DSM-IV, there is no assumption that each category of mental disorder is a completely discrete entity with absolute boundaries dividing it from other mental disorders or from no mental disorder. There is also no assumption that all individuals described as having the same mental disorder are alike in all important ways. The clinician using the DSM-IV should therefore consider that individuals sharing a diagnosis are likely to be heterogeneous even in regard to the defining features of the diagnosis and that boundary cases will be difficult to diagnose in any but a probabilistic fashion. (p. xxii)

Behaviors that May Lead to Work Maladjustment

One of our objectives in the assessment interview is to identify individualized behavior patterns that impair the work role. Table 20-1 presents symptoms of behavior and faulty cognitive functioning that can lead to work impairment. These symptoms were adapted from personality disorders and descriptions of depression found in DSM-IV (APA, 1994). The information can be used as guidelines for identifying similar patterns of behavior in clients being interviewed. The purpose of this table is not to classify clients according to any particular disorder but, more important, to serve as a guide to identify behavioral contingencies and faulty assumptions that may lead to work impairment. A client who may be identified as having poor social interaction skills, for instance, may also have difficulty relating to work affiliates and thus develop negative meanings associated with work.

Table 20-1 identifies disorders by behaviors, beliefs, and traits. The column "Work Impairments" suggests that some clients may have difficulty in the workplace when the behaviors, beliefs, or traits listed in the column are dominant and extreme. On the other hand, behaviors, beliefs, and traits associated with disorders may not necessarily lead to work impairment as suggested in the column "Other Work Role Observations." Using this logic, the interviewer attempts to determine the degree to which an identified behavior or trait affects the work role. For example, work involving interpersonal interactions may be difficult for some clients, but these clients have managed to become productive workers. Perhaps they could improve their potential with counseling designed to help them overcome this

TABLE 20-1
Work-Role Projections

Identification	Behaviors, beliefs, traits	Work impairment	Other work role observations
Cluster A[1] Paranoid career client	Suspicious of others, especially authority figures Avoids participation in group activities Reluctant to self-disclose Hostile and defensive Strong need to be self-sufficient	Poor interpersonal relationships with boss and peer group.	May meet demands of work role because of high ambition, especially in work environments that are highly structured and nonthreatening.
Schizoid career client	Very indecisive Vague about goals Does not desire or enjoy close relationships Prefers solitary activities Often aloof	Work involving interpersonal interactions is difficult.	May work well in an environment that provides social isolation.
Cluster B[1] Antisocial career client	Truancy, vandalism, stealing Nonconformity to social norms Very aggressive Inconsistent work behavior Poor emotional control	Difficulty in sustaining productive work.	Clients who are identified as having only several characteristics of this disorder may be able to function successfully in a work role. However, full-blown antisocial career clients have considerable interference with work roles.
Borderline career client	Poor self-concept Difficulty in establishing long-term goals Difficulty with career choice Difficulty with identifying preferred values Impulsive Unstable interpersonal relations Uncertainty about life roles	Impulsive behavior interferes with work role functioning; poor commitment to work.	The instability and impulsive nature of borderline career clients presents considerable interference with most life roles, including the work role.

[1]Not all personality disorders are included in Clusters A, B, and C.

TABLE 20-1 (continued)

Identification	Behaviors, beliefs, traits	Work impairment	Other work role observations
Narcissistic career client	Exploits others Shows little concern for others Expects favorable treatment Excessive feelings of self-importance Constantly seeks attention	Poor interpersonal relationships; may pursue unrealistic goals while exploiting co-workers.	Because of a strong need for success and power, these clients are able to meet requirements and sometimes excel in work role functioning.
Cluster C[1] Obsessive-compulsive career client	Preoccupied with trivial details Seeks perfection in work tasks to the point that task completion is constantly delayed Has strong need for inflexible routines Avoids decision making Unnecessarily devoted to organizing tasks	Poor task completion. Poor productivity. Subject to stress because of indecision.	Because of excessive conscientiousness and extreme attention to detail, these clients are able to function in work roles that require highly organized procedures.
Avoidant career client	Poor interpersonal skills Avoids occupational activities that involve interpersonal contact Is preoccupied with being criticized or being rejected Is reluctant to take personal risks	Work role is affected by poor interpersonal skills.	Work role functioning is limited to environments that are nonthreatening and only require minimum social contacts.
Depressed[2] career client	Lacks interest and pleasure in most activities Has difficulty in concentrating on tasks Behavior is typically lethargic and shows loss of energy Has difficulty sleeping or sleeps excessively Expresses negative feelings toward and about self Dejected mood Low self-evaluations	In severe cases, clients are not able to function in work role.	In mild to moderate cases of depression, some interference can be expected, but not all clients are totally inefficient.

[1]Not all personality disorders are included in Clusters A, B, and C.

[2]The depressed career client is not considered a personality disorder.

SOURCE: Adapted from *Diagnostic and Statistical Manual of Mental Disorders*, 4th ed. rev., by the American Psychiatric Association, 1994.

problem in all life roles, but their needs are not as obvious as someone who simply cannot function effectively with others. In sum, the severity of the identified needs determines the course and extent of intervention strategies.

In the DSM-IV, personality disorders are grouped into three clusters—A, B, and C—to accommodate the commonalities found among them. For example, career clients who resemble the characteristics, traits, and behaviors found in the Cluster A group may appear strange, peculiar, and bizarre. Likewise, those career clients who resemble the characteristics associated with the Cluster B group may appear highly emotional and dramatic. Those identified with Cluster C may appear anxious and fearful. The commonalities and overlap of symptoms found in personality disorders suggest to the interviewer that clients may demonstrate behaviors, beliefs, and traits of more than one personality disorder.

In an attempt to organize qualities of work behavior that lead to failure in work, Neff (1985) identified five types or patterns of work psychopathology using classifications ranging from Type I to Type V, as shown in Table 20-2. Individuals can be "typed" only when the characteristics listed predominate work behavior. Neff warns that not all clients will fit into these categories; some may have characteristics of several.

Lowman (1993) has attempted to devise a clinically useful taxonomy of psychological work-related dysfunctions, as reported in Table 20-3. One of his major premises is to illuminate the distinction between psychopathology and work dysfunctions, but at the same time he reminds mental health workers that the two types of problems can coexist. For example, psychopathology may or may not affect work performance, and the presence of worker dysfunctions may or may not have an impact on psychopathology.

The disturbances in the capacity to work are useful categories for delineating worker dysfunctions. These patterns are summarized as follows. Underachievement is an apparent discrepancy between the individual's ability and performance. Possible causes are passive-aggressive behavior, procrastination, or periodic inhibition to work. Fear of success refers to intentional underachievement because of perceived negative consequences associated with being successful. Fear of failure suggests that an individual withholds work efforts for fear of not being successful.

Other disturbances in the capacity to work such as patterns of overcommitment (see Chapters 12 and 16), work-related anxiety (see Chapter 12), personality dysfunctions and work, life role conflicts (see Chapter 17), and transient, situational stress (see Chapter 13) have been discussed in previous chapters and in other sections of this chapter. The last category in this section, perceptual inaccuracies, refers to differences between the individual worker's perception of the workplace and what actually exists.

Finally, category III, dysfunctional working conditions, refers to problems associated with the assigned job itself (such as too demanding or too difficult work), the quality or lack of supervision, and the possibility of poor interpersonal relationships. All these issues represent potential conflicts associated with working conditions.

The guidelines for identifying characteristics that could lead to work impairment or work dysfunctions associated with personality disorders, Neff's patterns

TABLE 20-2
Neff's Patterns of Work Psychopathology

Type	Characteristics
I—Individuals who lack motivation to work	• Have a negative concept of the work role. • Are indifferent to productive work. • Will work if coerced. • Meet minimum standards of work tasks. • Resist work commitment. • Require close supervision. • Lack need or desire to work.
II—Individuals who experience fear and anxiety in response to being productive	• Feel incapable of being productive. • Feel too inept to meet work demands. • Have low self-esteem. • Competition at work is extremely threatening. • Cooperative work efforts are difficult. • Lack self-confidence. • May retreat from work environment if severely threatened.
III—Individuals who are hostile and aggressive	• Underlying hostility is easily aroused. • Peer affiliation is viewed as potentially dangerous. • Are quick to quarrel with others. • Relation with supervisory personnel is precarious and threatening. • Work roles are often viewed as too demanding and restrictive. • Have very poor interpersonal relationships.
IV—Individuals who are very dependent on others	• Early socialization convinces them that the way to self-preservation is to please others. • Believe that the key to work success is pleasing authority figures. • Have a strong need for constant approval, particularly from supervisors.
V—Individuals who display a marked degree of social naivete	• Have very little knowledge of work environment and demands of work role. • Lack simple understanding of work role involvement. • Have no perception of self as a successful worker to meet even minimal standards. • Unable to project self into work role.

SOURCE: Adapted from Neff, 1985.

of work psychopathology, and Lowman's taxonomy of psychological work-related dysfunctions must be used with caution. Identified characteristics must predominate to be significant. Moreover, work behavior is considered to be a semiautonomous area of personality, and as such may not be affected by personality disorders. On the other hand, work maladaption may be linked to personality disorders. In essence, work dysfunctions are the result of a complex interaction of personal characteristics and the workplace. In sum, these guidelines present examples of potential work behavior problems and should be used as such. In the

TABLE 20-3

Toward a Clinically Useful Taxonomy of Psychological Work-Related Dysfunctions

I. Determining the relation between psychopathology and work dysfunctions
   A. Affecting work performance
   B. Not affecting work performance
   C. Affected by work performance
   D. Not affected by work performance
II. Disturbances in the capacity to work
   A. Patterns of undercommitment
      1. Underachievement
      2. Temporary production impediments
      3. Procrastination
      4. Occupational misfit
      5. Organizational misfit
      6. Fear of success
      7. Fear of failure
   B. Patterns of overcommitment
      1. Obsessive-compulsive addiction to the work role ("workaholism")
      2. Type A behavioral pattern
      3. Job and occupational burnout
   C. Work-related anxiety and depression
      1. Anxiety
         a. Performance anxiety
         b. Generalized anxiety
      2. Work-related depression
   D. Personality dysfunctions and work
      1. Problems with authority
      2. Personality disorders and work
   E. Life role conflicts
      1. Work-family conflicts
   F. Transient, situational stress
      1. Reactions to changes in the work role (e.g., new job) whose impact on the work role is time limited
   G. Other psychologically relevant work difficulties
      1. Perceptual inaccuracies
III. Dysfunctional working conditions
   A. Defective job design (role overload, ambiguity, etc.)
   B. Defective supervision
   C. Dysfunctional interpersonal relationships

SOURCE: From *Counseling and Psychotherapy of Work Dysfunctions,* by R. L. Lowman, pp. 43–44. Copyright 1993 by the American Psychological Association. Reprinted by permission.

next chapter, examples of methods of identifying potential work behavior problems are illustrated.

Faulty Cognitions

We are challenged to give more attention to cognitive processes in career counseling from the social-learning theory approaches to career development discussed in Chapter 2 (Mitchell & Krumboltz, 1996). Somewhat similar approaches to cognitive functioning are irrational beliefs (Ellis, 1962) and faulty reasoning (Beck, 1985). More specifically, the individual's perceptions of self and of people, events, experiences, and environment are seen as potential sources of mistaken and troublesome beliefs. Inaccurate information, faulty alternatives, and negative constructs derived from life experiences are sources of faulty cognitions.

Faulty cognitions inhibit systematic, logical thinking and as such can be self-defeating. For example, a client's expectations and assumptions can cause distorted perceptions and unrealistic thinking such as "There is only one career for me." Doyle (1992) presented the following examples of faulty cognition that he suggested can lead to false conclusions and negative feelings.

1. *Self-deprecating statements:* These expressions reveal poor self-worth, for example, "I'm not a good student" or "No one really likes me."

2. *Absolute or perfectionist terms:* When an individual sets up overly stringent guidelines for his or her behavior, the individual sets himself or herself up for self-criticism and a negative self-image. Conclusions that are absolute or perfectionistic often include the words *must, ought, should, unless,* or *until.* For example, "I should have been the one promoted" or "Unless I get an 'A,' I can't go home."

3. *Overgeneralization of negative experiences:* These are deductions based on too few examples of situations. Frequently, they are based on negative experiences that make clients think there are many obstacles making the future hopeless and bleak. For example, "Since I failed the first exam, I will fail the course" or "All the children in school hate me."

4. *Negative exaggerations:* These statements greatly magnify the true meaning of an event or reality. For example, "All professional athletes are greedy" or "You insulted my mother—you hate my family!"

5. *Factually inaccurate statements:* These remarks are based on inadequate or incorrect information. These erroneous data distort the client's perceptions of reality. For example, "You need an 'A' average to get into college" or "Autistic children are lazy."

6. *Ignorance of the effects of time:* These assertions ignore growth, maturation, and the effect that the passage of time can have on experience or events. For example, "He was a very poor student last year—he will surely fail this year" or "I have to go back to the lake and relive my vacation there." (p. 85).

Although faulty cognitions can lead to a multitude of personal problems, Mitchell and Krumboltz (1996) argued that the career decision-making process is most affected. Looking at it from a positive viewpoint, individuals with accurate, constructive beliefs will have fewer problems reaching their career goals. Moreover, realistic expectations foster positive emotional reactions to self and others.

In sum, this portion of the interview requires an assessment of the client's beliefs, generalities that cause a belief, other bases for a belief, and the actions that are a result of a belief (Mitchell & Krumboltz, 1987). Chapter 21 provides other criteria for evaluating faulty cognitions and also presents counseling intervention strategies designed to introduce more rational, productive ways of thinking.

Memory and Persistence

A prerequisite to more complex capabilities is the client's ability to concentrate on tasks without being distracted by other stimuli (Schwartz, 1989). In the context of career counseling, clients must be able to process information about work environments and themselves in order to make decisions in their best interests. The ability to attend selectively and to concentrate over time is a vital part of cognitive functioning necessary in the career decision-making process.

Some of the specific tasks for evaluating memory and concentration are reported in Hersen and Turner (1985), Craig (1989), and Othmer and Othmer (1989). Techniques suggested are straightforward, informal, and designed to screen clients for gross deficits in memory and concentration.

Memory is usually classified into three types: immediate (the client's ability to recall information he or she has just been told), recent (the client's ability to recall events that took place in the last several days, weeks, or months), and remote (the client's ability to recall events that happened several years in the past). Assessment for each type of memory provides important insights into each client's current cognitive-functioning capabilities. Impairment of memory may indicate the client is easily distracted, preoccupied, confused, anxious, or depressed or may have psychiatric disorders. The important point for the counselor to ascertain is the degree of severity of impairment in memory and concentration. The counselor will want to find out if the client is capable of adequately attending to the tasks of a selected career counseling program. The rule of thumb here is, when in doubt, seek assistance from other professionals. A client with significant deficits in concentration or memory should be referred for a formal inquiry (Rosenthal & Akiskal, 1985).

Memory can be evaluated during the course of the interview in an informal manner. For example, one way to check immediate recall is to spell your name or the name of the school or a city and ask the client to repeat the spelling. To check recent memory, ask the client to give directions to a well-known location or to your office. Remote memory can be evaluated during a discussion of past events (Othmer & Othmer, 1989). A more formalized method of evaluating memory is described in Hersen and Turner (1985).

Assessing immediate recall.   To assess immediate recall, the client is asked to remember three things that are presented verbally; for example, pen, blue, and the number 14. After the client successfully repeats the items, he or she is instructed to keep remembering them, because the counselor will ask for a repetition in approximately 5 minutes.

In another assessment technique, the client is instructed to listen carefully to a series of numbers; he or she will be asked to repeat them immediately after the presentation. For example, "Listen carefully and repeat these numbers after I'm finished." (Present them at the rate of one each second.) "2–7–9." After each successful answer, the number of digits is increased, 1–5–4–7, and so forth. When the client is no longer able to recall the digits in proper sequence, the process is repeated with the instructions to recall the digits in backward order, starting with two numbers and increasing the number of digits each time. Individuals with normal intelligence and without any organic impairment can usually repeat six digits forward and five in reverse (Hersen & Turner, 1985).

Assessing for recent memory.   A measure of recent memory can be accomplished by asking clients about verifiable information that has transpired within a few days. Some example questions are:

What did you eat for lunch yesterday?
Who was the presidential candidate who spoke at the municipal auditorium this week?
Tell me what you saw on TV news last night.
What national holiday did we celebrate on Wednesday?

Assessing remote memory.   Remote memory can be evaluated by asking clients to assess recollections of significant historical events. The ability to cognitively select and recall significant events in the past is a measure of remote memory. Some examples are:

Where were you born?
Where did you go to high school?
What was the Great Depression?
What was your first job outside the home?
What was Watergate?
What was Desert Storm?

Assessing concentration and task persistence.   Concentration and task persistence refer to the ability to sustain focused attention sufficiently to permit the completion of tasks commonly found in career counseling programs. For example, is the client able to sustain focused attention to permit the completion of such tasks as gathering information; generating, evaluating, and selecting alternatives; and formulating plans to implement decisions? According to Hersen and Turner (1985), deficiencies in concentration and memory can be observed through serial subtraction.

For assessment of concentration, the client is asked to subtract 3 from 100, then 3 from that number, then 3 again, and so forth. If this task is done correctly for five or six subtractions, then the client is asked to subtract 7 from 100, and so forth. The counselor will need to determine whether an inability to perform these calculations is due primarily to educational level and calculating ability or to the inability to concentrate. For example, if a client has a college degree and is unable to calculate beyond one subtraction, the counselor could probably conclude that the ability to concentrate has been adversely affected.

Summary

1. Recently, more attention has been directed to personal problems and faulty cognitions that can adversely affect career decision making.

2. Deficits in cognitive clarity require intervention other than career guidance. Because career problems are often an integral part of personal problems, intervention strategies deal with both simultaneously.

3. The intake interview is designed to identify client needs for career counseling or other career needs that could interfere with career development and life role functioning.

4. The intake interview includes gathering current status information, discovering problems that interfere with career development, discovering the significance of life roles and potential conflicts, and developing goals and objectives.

5. Techniques for interviewing include establishing rapport, observation, self-disclosure, open- and close-ended questions, echoing, continuation, and staying on track.

6. General appearance is a generalized observation of the client's personal grooming, posture, facial expressions, and mannerisms.

7. Attitude and behavior are observed through the quality of the interaction with the counselor.

8. Affect and mood are evaluated by the client's emotional tone and reported status.

9. Demographic information and work, medical, educational, and family history are obtained by self-report or through direct questioning.

10. Life roles selected for interviewing include worker, homemaker, citizen, and leisurite. Life roles are considered an integral part of each individual's development. Success in one life role enhances success in another.

11. Behavior patterns that impair the work role are identified in the intake interview as needs that determine intervention strategies.

12. Faulty cognitions inhibit systematic, logical thinking and can be self-defeating. Sources of faulty cognitions are primarily from life experiences.

13. Memory is classified as immediate, recent, and remote. Memory can be evaluated during the course of the interview through informal questioning and by more formalized procedures.

Supplementary Learning Exercises

1. Develop a list of reasons to support intake interviewing for career counseling. Give specific examples to support your reasons.
2. Present two examples of irrational beliefs that could interfere with career decision making.
3. Develop interview objectives for a specific ethnic client. Justify your rationale.
4. Discuss how work history can identify work maladjustment. Build two cases to illustrate.
5. Defend or criticize the following statement: Life roles are to be considered a significant part of career development.

6. Develop two examples to illustrate how self-disclosure can or cannot be effective in the interview.
7. Present several examples of dialogue to illustrate the effective use of open- and close-ended questions.
8. Have the benefits of leisure activities been overemphasized? Defend your arguments to classmates.
9. Develop a list of intervention strategies that could be used to encourage shared responsibilities in the home for dual-earner families.
10. Give several examples of behavior that could be identified with career client personality disorders in Table 20-1. Explain how these identified behavior patterns would or would not interfere with the work role.

CHAPTER TWENTY-ONE

Career Counseling Intake Interviews: Case Studies

In the preceding chapter, the rationale for interviewing clients for career counseling pointed out the need for developing an intake interview to determine appropriate intervention strategies. Embedded in this rationale is the recognition that some career clients may not fully benefit from career decision-making procedures for a variety of reasons, including illogical thinking, irrational beliefs, other faulty cognitions, or severe psychological problems. What is needed are methods of identifying potential problems that inhibit clients from making decisions in their best interests. For example, clients who cannot reason in a rational manner have erroneous perceptions of work roles and are unable to accurately process career information because of false beliefs; they would best be served by intervention programs to correct these problems before continuing in career decision making.

We cannot, of course, deal only with factors that inhibit career decision making. We must also deal with contingencies that contribute to work role maladjustment and potential problems associated with family, homemaker, citizen, and leisure roles. The assumption that life role development is the outcome of the long process of personal and interpersonal development gives credence to the position of focusing attention on each client's perception of the interrelationship of these roles. For example, poor interpersonal skills found as limiting factors in the work role may also impair the development of the citizen role (interpersonal relations in civic clubs) and the leisure role (activities involving others). Although life roles are discussed as separate entities, problems in one life role may affect development in another. In essence, the career counselor's ability to effectively tease out problems that inhibit positive growth must be recognized as a necessary skill for using the intake interview.

In the first section of this chapter, an intake interview closely follows the sequence for interviewing suggested in Chapter 20, starting with current status information. The second section contains a discussion of problems that interfere with career development; identification of these problems is illustrated with case studies. Part three covers life roles and potential conflicts. Finally, the development of goals and objectives is discussed.

Current Status Information

Techniques for observing clients were illustrated in Chapter 20; therefore, in this section, more emphasis will be devoted to the value of demographic information and work, medical, and educational histories.

THE CASE OF WHAT WAS LEFT UNSAID

Ida, a 36-year-old woman, was referred by a mental health agency to a state-supported agency that provided career counseling. The information sent with the referral contained demographic data, a sparse educational history, a diagnosis of clinical depression, and prescribed medication. The following notes were made by the career counselor as she interviewed Ida.

A. General appearance
- Client was appropriately dressed.
- Hair had not been recently washed.
- Wore little or no makeup.
- Wore glasses.
- Gait was normal.
- Movements were without tremor.
- Carried envelope and placed it on desk.

B. Attitude and behavior
- Introduced herself.
- Eye contact was appropriate.
- Showed no evidence of unusual behavior.

C. Affect and mood
- Said she was depressed but did not look it.
- Appeared rather lifeless.
- Stated that she was somewhat nervous about being interviewed.
- Stated she "felt good" especially when she was alone.
- Said she didn't like "being around a lot of people."
- Was vague when expressing herself.

D. Demographic information
- Said she was married four times, but could not remember the sequence of birth of four children or which marriage they were from.
- High-pitched voice used during discussion of marriages.
- Currently living with a cousin who helps care for her children.

   E. Work experiences
- Difficulty in recalling work experiences.
- Held part-time job in fast-food restaurant during senior year in high school.
- Held part- and full-time jobs in fast foods for several months after graduation.
- Waitressed in different local restaurants.
- Was a receptionist in accounting firm for about four months.
- Disliked restaurant work.
- Enjoyed work as a receptionist; claims she left because she was hospitalized.

   F. Medical history
- Stated that she was in good health until age 29 when she was hospitalized for depression. Stayed in a psychiatric hospital for five days. Has been treated as an outpatient with medication for several years but was unable to specify exactly how long.
- Felt that failure in marriage was a major cause of depression.
- Reported problems with sleeping.
- Reported no other significant illnesses.

   G. Educational history
- Finished high school with average grades.
- Did not finish a course in computer programming. Said she had a strange feeling "that she should not finish this course."

During the interview the counselor became concerned about vague references to past history. Even with further questioning, she could not get appropriate feedback:

Counselor: Ida, could you tell me more about the feeling you experienced that convinced you not to finish the computer programming course?

Ida: I don't know how to explain it—it was just like something told me not to finish.

Counselor: Something told you not to finish?

Ida: Yeah, I can't explain it.

Another example was expressions about work experiences.

Ida: I quit working with them because my uncle told me to.

Counselor: Does your uncle often give you advice?

Ida: He helps me a lot—he just seems to know what's best.

The counselor decided to end the interview and get more information about Ida's past history. Another appointment was set to continue the interview. In the meantime, a complete report was received from a mental health agency, which contained a signed release, a social history, and psychological workup. Ida had been diagnosed as a schizophrenic, undifferentiated type, and had been hospitalized on three occasions in the last five years.

When Ida was asked why she didn't mention the hospitalization, she responded with a shrug. The counselor also discovered that the uncle who was currently advising Ida had died ten years earlier.

In the case of severe psychiatric problems, there is usually evidence of marked impairment of life role functioning, particularly in the work role and homemaker role. The client's suggestion of a "sixth sense" telling her to abruptly quit an educational program and the fact that she felt controlled by someone else was enough evidence to request more in-depth information. Because the psychiatric and psychological evaluation was three years old, the counselor requested a complete update.

One of the major learning outcomes of this case is the importance of obtaining all available client information. The documented history of severe psychological problems does not always translate into suspending career counseling but may require an up-to-date evaluation of current psychological status.

Discovering Problems that Interfere with Career Development

Faulty Cognitions

Examples of faulty cognitions from Doyle (1992) in Chapter 20 offer a sound basis for assessing a faulty deductive-thinking process. Doyle's (1992) six examples are ways of thinking that reflect negative feelings about oneself. Irrational expectations of career counseling, as suggested by Nevo (1987), are examples of faulty cognitions and irrational thoughts often found in prospective clients.

1. There is only one vocation in the world that is right for me.
2. Until I find my perfect vocational choice, I will not be satisfied.
3. Someone else can discover the vocation suitable for me.
4. Intelligence tests would tell me how much I am worth.
5. I must be an expert or very successful in the field of my work.
6. I can do anything if I try hard, or I can't do anything that doesn't fit my talents.
7. My vocation should satisfy the important people in my life.
8. Entering a vocation will solve all my problems.
9. I must sense intuitively that the vocation is right for me.
10. Choosing a vocation is a one-time act.

The goal for the interviewer is to help clients identify maladaptive thinking. Using "choosing a vocation is a one-time act" as an example, the counselor asked the client to explain this expressed belief.

THE CASE OF FAULTY ASSUMPTIONS

Client: I want to find my lifetime job now and get it over with so I can go on to other things.

Counselor: What kind of job did you have in mind?

Client: I thought that's what you're supposed to help me with . . . anyway, I want a job that I can start in when I graduate.

The counselor then asked the client to describe the basis for his belief.

Counselor: Do you think you will stay with the job you choose now for the rest of your life?

Client: Well, I guess so. My father has worked as a bookkeeper as long as I can remember.

Counselor: Was he always a bookkeeper?

Client: Umm, come to think of it, he did work somewhere else.

Counselor: Do you think you might also have other job opportunities in the future?

Client: I never thought of that, but I guess I will.

The counselor was now in a position to explain the idea of career development over the life span and the importance of learning career decision-making techniques. In addition, he could help the client analyze faulty reasoning and false assumptions. The path to a more logical approach to career decision making had been established.

Doyle (1992) suggested a technique for helping this client work through faulty reasoning. The client writes out beliefs and conclusions and the assumptions on which they are based. For example:

All bankers are rich.
Once you are a banker, you drive a big car.
The only way for me to get rich is to become a banker.

The rationale for this exercise is based on the premise that faulty reasoning and faulty logic usually have underlying faulty assumptions. Having clients write out their assumptions in this manner assists them in recognizing that their beliefs may be inaccurate.

Yet another way of helping clients identify faulty cognitions is through the use of the *Career Beliefs Inventory* (*CBI*) (Krumboltz, 1991) discussed in Chapter 7. If a counselor strongly suspects that a client has developed faulty assumptions, which are measurable with the *CBI*, this instrument could prove to be a valuable counseling tool. Career counselors should be familiar with such inventories, particularly those that help clients expose false beliefs that interfere with wise decision making.

Another technique used to help clients recognize that they have some control of their destiny is illustrated in Chapter 18. This technique is based on Rotter's (1966) concept of locus of control. In sum, counselors arrange learning situations that prove clients can gain control of their lives through appropriate actions.

Behaviors that May Lead to Work Maladjustment

Observing current behavior and recording behavioral patterns from past events is a means of studying life experiences and their relationship to how clients have learned to behave. In this part of the interview, the focal point is on clients who manifest maladaptive behavior and methods to teach them appropriate ways to behave. Two case summaries are used to illustrate how behaviors may lead to work maladjustment.

THE CASE OF THE CONFUSED DECISION MAKER

Gui, a 17-year-old high school student, asked for help in choosing a career. She reported to the counselor's office with one of her older brothers. She stated, "I cannot decide what to major in at college."

Gui was neatly dressed and well groomed. Her speech was fluent and of normal rate and rhythm. She tended to speak very softly. She seemed to be somewhat anxious about making a career decision. She did not appear to be depressed. She constantly looked to her brother for approval.

In the top 10% of her class, Gui had a record of being a very capable student. She had good rapport with teachers as well as with her peer group. She strongly identified with several girls her age at the high school.

Gui had five brothers and her father was a meat inspector in a local plant. He worked hard to maintain the family. Her mother had never worked outside the home.

When the counselor asked Gui to come into his office alone, she seemed very uncomfortable and asked if her brother could attend the session with her. The counselor reassured her that they would have ample time to talk with her brother later. She reluctantly agreed to begin the interview.

From the description Gui gave of her home environment, the counselor assumed it was very traditional. Moreover, the chores assigned to the children were typically based on what the parents considered appropriate work for boys and for girls. There seemed to be strict stereotypical roles embedded in Gui's perception of traditional work roles for women. She appeared to be very passive and gave the impression that she expected someone else to make decisions for her.

When discussing future objectives, Gui seemed quite confused when the counselor suggested she consider all careers including nontraditional ones. At one time she had expressed an interest in architecture but considered it to be for men only and therefore decided against it as a possible choice.

Gui's behavior pattern reflected little confidence in her own abilities and deference to others for decision making. She appeared to be quite uneasy when she was asked to leave her brother and constantly referred to him as giving her good advice and reassuring her of what was best for her. The following dialogue demonstrates her dependency needs.

Gui: My parents will help me choose the right kind of work.
Counselor: Could you tell me more about your parents' choosing the right kind of work for you?
Gui: My mother and father usually help me with most of the things that I decide on, and if they don't, my older brothers do.

From these excerpts, it seemed clear that Gui was quite dependent on others for decision making. Gui's background and behavior patterns closely matched Neff's (1985) Type IV pattern of individuals who are very dependent on others. The counselor feared that Gui might make career decisions based on what her family considered best for her, rather than on her own interests, values, and abilities. Also, the counselor suspected that if Gui's current behavior patterns continued as is, she would suffer the consequences of a Type IV worker and develop work-related dysfunctions as outlined by Lowman (1993).

The counselor's strategy consisted of building greater rapport with Gui and establishing a basic trust, using the following guidelines.

1. Be respectful and genuine.
2. Focus on developing self-awareness by using reflective procedures.
3. Assist her in understanding how environmental circumstances influenced her behavior.
4. Help her establish alternative ways of thinking and behaving.
5. Assist her in recognizing how she can control her own destiny by illustrating the concept of locus of control; that is, how external and internal people think.
6. Help her recognize the relevance of her values and interests in a career decision-making mode.
7. Introduce career decision-making steps as discussed in Chapter 11.

To promote more realistic goals for career decision making, especially toward self-direction, the counselor chose a cognitive behavioral-intervention strategy (Ellis, 1971; Corey, 1991). The first step included techniques to help Gui separate rational beliefs from irrational ones. Second, the counselor assisted Gui in modifying her thinking, especially the thoughts associated with stereotypical gender-role development. Third, the counselor challenged Gui to develop a greater self-awareness and a more realistic philosophy of integrated life role development. To help her reduce stereotyping in career options, Gui was also scheduled to view the *BORN FREE* series (Hansen, 1978).

THE CASE OF THE ANXIOUS COMPUTER TECHNICIAN

A 28-year-old male computer technician named John sought out the services of a career counselor in private practice. His major complaint was a recent upsurge in anxiety when a new group of workers was assigned to his department. He felt threatened by them and, as he saw it, was treated as an outsider and definitely not a part of their group. He feared that he would be fired and considered resigning and finding a different job or asking for reassignment to another department.

John appeared to be anxious; he moved around in his chair and the pitch of his voice changed, particularly when talking about this new group of people. He constantly moved his arms and hands and clenched his fists. He did not appear to be depressed and stated that he felt very anxious.

John had never seriously considered marriage; he saw himself as a "loner." Furthermore, he had few friends and spoke of himself as being shy with limited social contacts.

John evaluated his educational background as average or above in academics. He had received computer training from a local community college. He was currently taking more courses. John characterized his student life in much the same way as his current situation—that is, few social activities and a feeling of isolation.

He interpreted his role as citizen as voting in most elections; he did not partic-ipate in any civic activities. He expressed a feeling of rejection by the individuals in organizations he had met. John collected musical records from the Big Band era and enjoyed listening to them when he was alone. He occasionally attended mov-ies, visited his parents, and watched TV.

When expressing work role experiences, his anxiety seemed to peak, as ob-served by increased motor activities. Earlier trends of isolating himself from contact with others continued in the current work environment; he ate by himself in the cafeteria and did not join bull sessions during breaks. He did not have a "good" friend among the peer group. He characterized his work role as quietly getting the job done.

John's symptoms of anxiety seemed to be related to a long-standing pattern of difficulty with social interactions. Low self-esteem, feelings of rejection, and avoid-ance of social activities were embedded in most of his statements. These character-istics are found in Neff's (1985) Type II work psychopathology, in Cluster A personality disorders, and in Lowman's (1993) work-related anxiety work dysfunc-tion taxonomy (see Chapter 20). However, John does not exhibit all of the Type II characteristics; likewise, he cannot be identified with any one personality disorder but has characteristics of two or more. This example could be quite typical of many career clients and supports the assumption that identified behaviors, actions, be-liefs, and thinking can be generically evaluated as contingencies that could lead to work maladjustment. In sum, John had a history of being an acceptable worker. His life roles could be enhanced with better social skills and more positive self-concepts as a worker and social being. John wanted to change jobs for the wrong reasons. The counselor suggested that he could explore other career opportunities and simultaneously participate in a counseling program designed to help him recognize sources of stress. Other intervention strategies selected were anxiety-management training, social skills and assertiveness training, and relaxation train-ing. In addition, thought-stopping techniques (Cautela & Wisock, 1977; Doyle, 1992) were used to eliminate inappropriate thinking, negative self-concepts, and worry-oriented thinking.

The counseling intervention strategies proposed for John were based on the fol-lowing premise: emotions are often the result of how we think, and a change in John's thinking process could reduce or eliminate emotional disorders and dysfunctional behaviors (Trower, Casey, & Dryden, 1988; Ellis & Grieger, 1977; Lazarus, 1989).

There are many sources of stress in the work environment, as discussed in Chapter 12, including poor communications between management and workers and between peer groups. Techniques for group-counseling procedures designed to improve communication skills are illustrated in Chapter 18.

Memory and Persistence

This part of the interview is used when there is sufficient evidence to suspect problems with immediate, recent, or remote memory. Typical examples of mem-ory loss include forgetting names, telephone numbers, directions, and so forth. In more severe cases, memory loss may interfere with social and occupational functioning. Excerpts from a case history are used to illustrate the identification of memory loss and persistence.

THE CASE OF THE FORGOTTEN WORK ADDRESS

A 52-year-old man named Jack was accompanied by his wife to see a career counselor in private practice. She stated that she wanted her husband to get a steady job with a guaranteed salary.

Jack was neatly dressed and groomed. He had short combed hair and was freshly shaven. He appeared confused and was somewhat bewildered as to why he was there and what he was to do. His speech patterns suggested he had difficulty in recalling words to complete sentences. He stated that he felt well and was looking forward to being "talked to." There had been no indications of depression. Jack had been married on two occasions. His first marriage lasted only about 18 months because, as he put it, "I was very young." He has two children from his current marriage of 20 years. He lives with his wife in a home they own. One child is currently attending college.

For over 20 years, Jack's main occupation was cafeteria manager in a small town. Approximately a year ago, he was fired from his job and was currently selling cosmetics as a door-to-door salesman. When asked why he was fired, Jack stated that they told him he was not capable of doing the work anymore. When asked what he would like to do in the future, he replied "I like to read a lot and wouldn't mind working in a bookstore."

Jack appeared to be in good health and was of medium build and weight. He stated that he did have hypertension, which was controlled by medication.

Jack had gone to the local high school and received a B.S. degree from the state university. He had above-average grades in high school and college. When asked why he had planned to change jobs, Jack responded by asking that his wife be allowed to come in and describe his current condition. Jack's wife mentioned that he had been an effective cafeteria manager until about 18 months ago, when he started having difficulty remembering chores that he'd done automatically in the past. He misplaced cash receipts, forgot to make assignments of the personnel (causing chaos in the cafeteria), and forgot the address of the cafeteria. Jack was given a second chance but was not able to improve his work efficiency. He had now taken a sales job selling cosmetics and had not been too successful. His wife also pointed out that he had difficulty coordinating his clothing; he selected conflicting color combinations and at times put his T-shirt on backward. He also stumbled frequently, and when he mowed the yard, he made criss-cross patterns, leaving part of the lawn unmowed. At night when he got up to go to the bathroom, he would return to the wrong room.

At this point, the counselor got agreement from the couple to evaluate Jack's memory. When Jack was asked to repeat the spelling of the city in which he lived, he was able to spell it only with prompting. He also failed to repeat other spellings that were presented. When asked, Jack was unable to give directions to several well-known locations within the city. The counselor then asked Jack to listen carefully to a series of numbers and repeat them immediately after presentation. He was unable to respond correctly after two trials with only three digits. He was not able to recall any digits backward.

The procedure used for assessing recent memory was as follows: When Jack was asked what he had for lunch yesterday, he responded with a typical luncheon menu, but his wife stated that this was not the food that she served him. When he was asked what he saw on the TV news the night before, he simply responded by saying "the same old thing."

The assessment of remote memory was more encouraging. Jack was able to state his birthdate, where he went to high school, and where he obtained his first job outside his home. The counselor concluded that he had poor immediate and recent recall but that his remote memory was fairly well intact.

Jack's wife verified that he had difficulty concentrating and following tasks through to completion. She gave several examples in which he had difficulty maintaining focus on a particular task, like mowing the yard or going to a local store to purchase a single item. It seemed that Jack would easily leave a task without giving much thought to the consequences of his actions.

The counselor referred Jack to a neurologist, who discovered Jack had a brain tumor. An operation followed shortly thereafter, and the tumor turned out to be benign. Several months after rehabilitation, Jack returned to the counselor's office ready to search for a new occupation. He had decided during his recovery time that he wished to follow his desire of working in a bookstore. The counselor began the assessment interview once again.

Discovering the Significance of Life Roles and Potential Conflicts

Life roles are considered significant determinants of an individual's lifestyle (Super, 1990) and as such constitute a formidable influence on career development. Intake interviews also help discover whether clients have significant role conflicts and the degree to which such conflicts inhibit career development. However, the evaluation of life roles for this interview should be based on individual needs and interests. For example, not everyone needs or wants to participate in a civic organization. What is profound, however, is to identify a need that can be fulfilled in civic activities. Life roles should be viewed as having individualized meanings and purposes and as developmentally linked to career development; conflicts in one role can hamper the development and satisfaction of other roles. The following excerpts from interviews illustrate the significance of life role evaluations.

THE CASE OF THE FIRED PLUMBER

Yuri, a 40-year-old plumber, requested career counseling to change jobs. "I don't like this plumbing work anymore," he said. He was dressed in soiled work clothes and hadn't shaved for several days. Yuri appeared to be anxious; he constantly moved in his chair, raised his arms, and clenched his fists. He was grossly over-weight and asked that he be given permission to smoke. His speech was fluent and of normal rate and rhythm.

Yuri completed high school but had no other formal training. He claimed to be an average student and never failed a grade. During on-the-job training, he learned the skills to become a licensed plumber.

Starting at the lowest level in plumbing, he had advanced to the master plumber status and had been employed as a plumber for 12 years. He was recently fired for disruptive behavior and fighting with two fellow workers.

Yuri reported no serious medical problems and had no history of psychiatric treatment. He had been a tobacco smoker for 15 years and occasionally drank alcohol.

For leisure, Yuri watched sports on TV and enjoyed renting movies for home viewing. He also enjoyed watching his son play Little League baseball and regularly practiced with him. Short family vacations consisted of visiting relatives and camping.

Yuri was not active in civic affairs, other than annually helping organize the local Little League. He claimed that he had such little time off from his work that it would be difficult for him to actively participate in civic organizations.

Evidently Yuri felt that household duties were "woman's work," and even though his wife worked full time outside the home, he did not help with such tasks as cooking, shopping, washing, or housecleaning. He did mow the yard and water the grass. Yuri complained that his wife had recently demanded his help with household chores, which resulted in several major arguments that lasted for days. It was obvious that Yuri and his wife were not on very good terms and had seri-ously considered divorce. Shortly after his wife chose to spend several days with her mother to "sort things out," Yuri was fired for fighting on the job.

The fact that Yuri had worked for the same plumbing company and with most of the same peer affiliates for 15 years indicated that he had the skills necessary to interact appropriately within the work environment. It was also clear that Yuri's relations with his wife were in turmoil. Although it was difficult for the counselor to determine at this time whether serious marital problems had existed for a long time, it was clear that Yuri's refusal to help with household chores precipitated the most recent problems. Yuri admitted that he enjoyed working as a plumber, but the stress associated with dual-earner problems had probably influenced how he felt about his current work environment.

This case is a good example of how one life role affects another. The major problem was conflict between husband and wife who both worked full time out-side the home, not wanting a job change. The counselor's plan was to have Yuri and his wife commit to counseling with emphasis on sharing responsibilities and household tasks.

The techniques suggested were based on Hansen's (1996) Integrative Life Plan-ning Model, which encourages couples to move away from dominate-subordinate relationships to being equal partners. Among other changes suggested in this model are movement from the position of "job to life roles, and from achievement only to achievement and relationships for both women and men" (Hansen, 1991, p. 84). Career decision making for a different job would be deferred for the time being. Yuri agreed to relocate with a different company as a plumber.

Work and family are not separate worlds, and the case of the fired plumber illustrates how conflict in the homemaker role influenced Yuri's behavior in the work role. Other problem areas that may contribute to conflicts include:

Shift work
Separation and travel
Relocation
Work spillover (preoccupation with work role)
Relationships with supervisors
Relationships with co-workers

THE CASE OF THE UNFULFILLED WORKER

Karen, a 42-year-old married woman, was self-referred to a career counselor in private practice because, as she put it, "I really don't know what's wrong with me. I like my job and I'm happy with my marriage and my family, but something is missing in my life." Karen was very attractive and neatly and appropriately dressed. She had a new hairdo and made an outstanding appearance. She was very fluent and her speech was of normal rate and rhythm. Although Karen had a positive attitude about her work and many other factors of her life, she still felt that she could improve her lifestyle. She expressed dismay at not being able to be more specific about what was troubling her. She seemed to be somewhat depressed but stated that she was feeling well.

Karen had been married on two different occasions. Her first marriage lasted only a short period, and as she put it, she married when she was very young and made a mistake. She'd been married the second time for over 20 years and had one child from this marriage. Her child was now attending college. Her husband was a professional engineer and had a good income.

Karen had several odd jobs while in high school and college working in fast-food places and dress shops. She was currently managing a local dress shop and had had this job for at least six years. She felt very comfortable in this work and enjoyed meeting people and doing the usual tasks that were involved in running and managing the shop. She expressed no particular desire to get another job but would be willing to if she were able to fulfill her needs better.

Karen stated that she was in excellent health and had never had significant problems with bad health. She was of medium height and weight.

Karen had received an A.A. degree at a local community college and was currently taking courses at a nearby college. She hoped to receive a degree in business management in the near future.

Karen and her husband, a dual-career couple, seemed to have worked out a very satisfactory relationship in their homemaker roles. Her husband participated in household tasks and assumed responsibilities that gave Karen more time to take care of her work and attend classes at college. She expressed no problems with her marital life and stated that her husband also seemed to be very happy.

As stated earlier, Karen felt that her work role was satisfactory. She had dreamed of managing a dress shop while she was an employee several years ago and now the opportunity had been given to her. The dress shop she currently managed had been very successful, and she had received several awards from the parent company for exceptional sales. She claimed to relate well to both employees and customers. She was taking a business management course to improve her skills in management.

Because of the strong commitment to upgrade their careers, both Karen and her husband devoted little time to leisure activities. They exercised together in the morning by jogging or walking and attended various events in the community such as theater, movies, and art exhibits. Karen stated that they took the usual vacations, had taken their son to national parks, and had visited historical places.

When asked about participation in civic activities, Karen seemed somewhat bewildered and stated that she simply wouldn't have time to participate in these activities because of her full schedule. She was not aware of activities in local civic organizations and had not considered volunteerism.

The counselor returned to Karen's statement, "Something's missing in my life." The counselor asked her to express this feeling more fully:

Karen: I don't know how to really explain it, and I feel guilty about even talking to someone about this. For gosh sakes, I have a great husband and a marvelous child and a very good job. I can't put a finger on what's wrong with me, but I seem to have a feeling that I want to do other things that I'm not doing at this time.

Counselor: Tell me more about the feeling that you want to do "other things."

Karen: Well, I have to give that some thought, but I guess what I really mean is I have a lot of interests and I haven't been able to fulfill many of them.

Counselor: Tell me more about your interests.

Karen: The first one that strikes my fancy is that I had dreams of being an artist, but when I took art classes and started painting, I quickly realized that I didn't have the talent to go on. But, I'm still interested in art and miss being around arts-and-crafts people.

Counselor: Have you ever thought of taking an art class in college?

Karen: Yes, I've had several of those, but I don't want to continue taking art classes.

As the conversation continued, the counselor felt that a values inventory might help Karen clarify needs she could not identify. The counselor recalled that values tend to remain fairly stable and endure over the life span. She felt that this might be an area that would help Karen come to some realization of what she would like to do in the future.

The counselor decided to use the Five-Step Process for Using Assessment Results developed by Zunker (1994). The steps are paraphrased as follows.

Step 1: Analyzing needs.   In this step, the counselor ascertains the client's perception of her need for information in order to foster self-knowledge. In evaluating Karen's lifestyle, she decided that work climate, family responsibilities, and leisure time had been committed, but rewarding activities in the community had been given little attention.

Counselor: Karen, you've expressed a very positive viewpoint of your work, family, and leisure activities. In fact, you had no negative thoughts concerning these life roles. It seems to be that other areas of your lifestyle may be lacking—what do you think?

Karen: You're probably right, but the only thing that you've mentioned so far has been civic activities, and as I told you, I know very little about them.

Counselor: Okay, well, I can give you more information about them, but at the same time I would like to know more about your needs and how you might fulfill them. Since we cannot identify specific needs at this time, let's agree that we want to identify some unknown need that gives you the feeling that something is "missing in your life."

Step 2: Establishing a purpose.   Following the needs analysis, the counselor and the counselee decide on the purpose of testing. Both should recognize that testing cannot be expected to meet all identified needs. In Karen's case, however, the counselor was thinking of only one or two tests to foster self-knowledge. The purpose of each test and inventory should be explained in terms that the counselee can understand. In the following dialogue, the counselor attempts to link the purpose of the test to Karen's needs.

Counselor: As you recall, we've been talking about a number of needs that you feel have not been satisfied or, as you put it, fulfilled. Would you agree that an exploration of your values would be helpful?

Karen: Yes, I do, but what kind of test do you have in mind?

Counselor: Well, I was thinking of a values inventory that would help us establish priorities of values and also introduce sets of values for dialogue.

Step 3: Determining the instrument.   The client and the counselor agree on the type of assessment instrument to be administered. The counselor relates the characteristics of the test and the kinds of information that it will provide.

Karen: Well, I think it would be great to take a values inventory, but I don't quite understand how it's going to help.

Counselor: You expressed a need to fill a gap in your life, and I think a values inventory that provides such measures as ability utilization, aesthetics, altruism, creativity, and lifestyle would be helpful.

Karen: Oh, that sounds great! Maybe they will tell me just what I need to know.

Counselor: A word of caution, Karen. These tests will help us discover some life career values, but they are not designed to tell you what to do in the future. They will provide us with some information to discuss.

Step 4: Utilizing the results.   The counselor interprets the test scores in a manner that the client can understand and relates the results to the established purpose of testing.

Counselor: Karen, here is a profile of your scores. You will notice that you have high scores in aesthetics, creativity, and social interaction. A high score in aesthetics means . . .

As the counselor went through an explanation of scores, she made certain that Karen understood that test scores from a values inventory are not necessarily more valid or accurate than her own perceptions of her problems. However, the results do provide new ideas and opportunities for specificity in the counseling dialogue. In Karen's case, this was important because she had been very vague about what she felt were her unfulfilled needs. As they discussed the results of the test, Karen agreed with the results from the standpoint that she did have a very high value in aesthetics; perhaps this was one area that was lacking in her life. It could provide other opportunities and interesting social interactions and creative endeavors.

Step 5: Making a decision.   The final step is to make a decision based on the assessment's results. Karen decided that she would set aside more time to become involved as a volunteer at the local art museum. She also felt that it would be a good idea to eventually become a docent. She would seek agreement for her plans from her husband and son. The counselor was to see Karen after she had established herself at the art museum to continue dialogue and evaluate her progress.

Developing Goals and Objectives

The unique and distinct information obtained from an intake interview is used to generate individualized goals for career intervention counseling. The information that emerges about how clients interact in their environment and function in a diversity of life roles provides a clearer understanding of needs and subsequent counseling strategies and interventions. In an informative discussion of the goals of career intervention, Spokane (1991) suggests that clients become more positive about their ability to obtain major life goals as follows: "The goal of career intervention is to enhance the mobilization of persistently constructive attitudes, emotions, and behaviors that will improve the client's career attainment" (p. 56).

As part of a strategic planning model for practitioners and human service organizations, Kurpius, Burrello, and Rozecki (1990) recommend systematic planning as a necessary element to improve effectiveness, and part of this model includes a section that addresses the formulation of goals and objectives (p. 5):

1. Specify objectives.
2. Generate strategies.
3. Implement action plans.
4. Recycle.

Brown and Brooks (1991) recommend the following sequence for goal setting.

1. Identify client goals.
2. Determine the feasibility of goals.

3. Establish subgoals.
4. Assess commitment to goals.

Using the case of the unfulfilled worker, we will apply the sequence for goal setting recommended by Brown and Brooks (1991).

Karen's identified goals were:

1. to identify sources of anxiety
2. to identify resources for a more balanced lifestyle
3. to identify values and their application to unmet needs

The feasibility of these goals was established as being realistic.

1. The client was highly motivated to explore and discuss solutions.
2. There was mutual agreement on the overall goal of lifestyle direction.
3. There was mutual agreement on subgoals such as assessing values.

Subgoals were established as follows:

1. Assess values.
2. Visit the local art museum.
3. Share plans with family.

The commitment to goals was established by a mutually agreed-on systematic plan that the counselor carefully and fully explained. Her systematic approach enhanced Karen's willingness to participate. The key ingredients were the identification of needs and mutually agreed-on goals with systematic plans for action.

Summary

1. Specially designed intervention programs are most useful for identifying clients who cannot reason in a rational manner, have erroneous perceptions of work roles, or have false beliefs.

2. Work role maladjustment behaviors are also identified and modified through intervention programs. Attention should be focused on life role development and the interrelationships of these roles.

3. The "Case of What Was Left Unsaid" points out the importance of obtaining all client background information available.

4. The "Case of Faulty Assumptions" illustrates the rationale that faulty reasoning and faulty logic are based on false assumptions.

5. The "Case of the Confused Decision Maker" illustrates how sex-role stereotyping can influence behavior and career decision making.

6. The "Case of the Anxious Computer Technician" illustrates how fear and anxiety can interfere with work behavior and other life roles. Counseling intervention strategies focused on helping the client recognize the sources of stress.

7. The "Case of the Forgotten Work Address" illustrates how memory can be evaluated with clients who demonstrate the inability to do routine work tasks.

8. The "Case of the Fired Plumber" illustrates how one life role can influence behavior in another role.

9. The "Case of the Unfulfilled Worker" is an example of how an unidentified need can be clarified through a five-step interpretation procedure using a values inventory.

Supplementary Learning Exercises

1. Using the "Case of What Was Left Unsaid," specify how the interviewer could have probed for more background information. Identify clues to the client's problems.
2. Suggest intervention strategies to deal with the following beliefs: "Psychological tests can tell me what to do in the future" and "I am destined to have only one vocation."
3. How can the concept of locus of control be effectively used to assist clients in controlling their future? Identify symptoms of behavior that would support the use of this procedure.
4. Develop a profile of behaviors that indicate stereotyped gender roles. Suggest intervention strategies.
5. What are the major symptoms of interpersonal relationship problems? Develop goals and objectives for modifying behavior.
6. Develop a supportive argument for the idea that life roles have individualized meanings.
7. Present examples of how one life role affects another. Give suggestions for identifying such problems in the interview.
8. Develop a case that illustrates how a narcissistic career client may behave in the workplace.
9. Illustrate the five steps for using assessment results with an interest inventory and an abilities test.
10. Present suggestions for detecting serious psychological problems in the interview. Illustrate with examples.

Explanation of Relationships within Data, People, and Things Hierarchies

Data. Information, knowledge, and conceptions related to data, people, or things, obtained by observation, investigation, interpretation, visualization, and/or mental creation; incapable of being touched; written data take the form of numbers, words, and symbols; other data are ideas, concepts, and oral verbalization.

0. *Synthesizing*—Integrating analyses of data to discover facts and/or develop knowledge concepts or interpretations.
1. *Coordinating*—Determining time, place, and sequence of operations or action to be taken on the basis of analysis of data; executing determinations and/or reporting on events.
2. *Analyzing*—Examining and evaluating data. Presenting alternative actions in relation to the evaluation is frequently involved.
3. *Compiling*—Gathering, collating, or classifying information about data, people, or things. Reporting and/or carrying out a prescribed action in relation to the information is frequently involved.
4. *Computing*—Performing arithmetic operations and reporting on and/or carrying out a prescribed action in relation to them. Does not include counting.
5. *Copying*—Transcribing, entering, or posting data.
6. *Comparing*—Judging the readily observable functional, structural, or compositional characteristics (whether similar to or divergent from obvious standards) of data, people, or things.

People. Human beings; also animals dealt with on an individual basis as if they were human.

0. *Mentoring*—Dealing with individuals in terms of their total personality to advise, counsel, and/or guide them with regard to problems that may be resolved by legal, scientific, clinical, spiritual, and/or other professional principles.

1. *Negotiating*—Exchanging ideas, information, and opinions with others to formulate policies and programs and/or arrive jointly at decisions, conclusions, or solutions.
2. *Instructing*—Teaching subject matter to others, or training others (including animals) through explanation, demonstration, and supervised practice; or making recommendations on the basis of technical disciplines.
3. *Supervising*—Determining or interpreting work procedures for a group of workers, assigning specific duties to them, maintaining harmonious relations among them, and promoting efficiency.
4. *Diverting*—Amusing others.
5. *Persuading*—Influencing others in favor of a product, service, or point of view.
6. *Speaking-Signaling*—Talking with and/or signaling people to convey or exchange information. Includes giving assignments and/or directions to helpers or assistants.
7. *Serving*—Attending to the needs or requests of people or animals or the expressed or implicit wishes of the people.
8. *Taking Instructions-Helping*—Attending to the work assignment instructions or orders of supervisor. (No immediate response required unless clarification of instructions or orders is needed.) Helping applies to "non-learning" helpers.

Things.   Inanimate objects as distinguished from human beings; substances or materials; machines, tools, equipment; products. A thing is tangible and has shape, form, and other physical characteristics.

0. *Setting Up*—Adjusting machines or equipment by replacing or altering tools, jigs, fixtures, and attachments to prepare them to perform their functions, change their performance, or restore their proper functioning if they break down. Workers who set up one or a number of machines for other workers or who set up and personally operate a variety of machines are included here.
1. *Precision Working*—Using body members and/or tools or work aids to work, move, guide, or place objects or materials in situations where ultimate responsibility for the attainment of standards occurs and selection of appropriate tools, objects, or materials and the adjustment of the tool to the task require exercise of considerable judgment.
2. *Operating-Controlling*—Starting, stopping, controlling, and adjusting the progress of machines or equipment designed to fabricate and/or process objects or materials. Operating machines involves setting up the machine and adjusting the machine or material as the work progresses. Controlling equipment involves observing gauges, dials, and so on, and turning valves and other devices to control such factors as temperature, pressure, flow of liquids, speed of pumps, and reactions of materials. Setup involves several variables and adjustment is more frequent than in tending.
3. *Driving-Operating*—Starting, stopping, and controlling the actions of machines or equipment for which a course must be steered, or which must be

guided, in order to fabricate, process, and/or move things or people. Involves such activities as observing gauges and dials; estimating distances and determining speed and direction of other objects; turning cranks and wheels; pushing clutches or brakes; and pushing or pulling gear lifts or levers. Includes such machines as cranes, conveyor systems, tractors, furnace charging machines, paving machines and hoisting machines. Excludes manually powered machines, such as hand trucks and dollies, and power-assisted machines, such as electric wheelbarrows and hand trucks.

4. *Manipulating*—Using body members, tools, or special devices to work, move, guide, or place objects or materials. Involves some latitude for judgment with regard to precision attained and selecting appropriate tool, object, or materials, although this is readily manifest.

5. *Tending*—Starting, stopping, and observing the functioning of machines and equipment. Involves adjusting materials or controls of the machine, such as changing guides, adjusting timers and temperature gauges, turning valves to allow flow of materials, and flipping switches in response to lights. Little judgment is involved in making these adjustments.

6. *Feeding-Offbearing*—Inserting, throwing, dumping, or placing materials in or removing them from machines or equipment which are automatic or tended or operated by other workers.

7. *Handling*—Using body members, hand tools, and/or special devices to work, move, or carry objects or materials. Involves little or no latitude for judgment with regard to attainment of standards or in selecting appropriate tool, object, or material.

Note.   Included in the concept of Feeding-Offbearing, Tending, Operating-Controlling, and Setting Up is the situation in which the worker is actually part of the setup of the machine, either as the holder and guider of the material or holder and guider of the tool (U.S. Department of Labor, 1977, pp. 1369–1371).

The *Standard Occupational Classification Manual*

For a number of years, occupational analysts have expressed a need for an occupational classification system that could combine occupational data into one system. Traditionally, occupational data have been gathered from a variety of sources and compiled under different classification systems. Combining the data has been a growing problem. In 1940, only two major classification systems, the Census Classification System and the *DOT* system, existed. The problem of combining occupational data was compounded in the 1960s when several other classification systems evolved. It was during this period that the first steps were taken toward developing a classification system that standardized occupational data collection. For over ten years, the interagency Occupational Classification Committee met; it eventually published the first edition of the *Standard Occupational Classification Manual* in 1977 (U.S. Executive Office of the President [USEOP], 1977).

Format and Structure of the SOC Manual

The *SOC Manual* format is divided into four levels of successively greater detail as follows: (1) division, (2) major group, (3) minor group, and (4) unit group. The first level of the format, *division*, is broad in scope, providing a general description of an occupational field.

There are 21 divisions of occupational groups included in the 1977 *SOC*.

Executive, Administrative, and Managerial Groups
Engineers and Architects
Natural Scientists and Mathematicians
Social Scientists, Social Workers, Religious Workers, and Lawyers
Teachers, Librarians, and Counselors
Health Diagnosing and Treating Practitioners
Nurses, Pharmacists, Dietitians, Therapists, and Physicians Assistants
Writers, Artists, Entertainers, and Athletes
Health Technologists and Technicians
Technologists and Technicians, except Health
Marketing and Sales Occupations
Clerical Occupations
Service Occupations
Agriculture and Forestry Occupations, Fishers, and Hunters
Construction and Extractive Occupations
Transportation and Material Moving Occupations
Mechanics and Repairers
Production Working Occupations
Material Handlers, Equipment Cleaners, and Laborers
Military Occupations
Miscellaneous Occupations

Each division is further subdivided into *major groups*. The following examples of two division groups followed by major groups illustrate this part of the format and structure of the *SOC* system (USEOP, 1977, pp. 35–59).

(Divisions)	
Executive, Administrative, and Managerial Occupations	Engineers and Architects
(Major Groups)	
11 Officials and Administrators; Public Administration	14 Management-Related Occupations
12–13 Officials and Administrators, other	15 Architects
	16 Engineers and Surveyors

The two-digit numbers adjacent to the major groups in the preceding example are the actual numbers assigned to those major groups in the *SOC* system. All major groups are assigned two-digit numbers; minor groups three-digit numbers; and unit groups four-digit numbers. All minor groups and unit groups begin with the first two digits of their major group. Likewise, the third digit of the unit group corresponds to the third digit of its minor group. The following example illustrates the numerical scheme used in the *SOC* system (USEOP, 1977, p. 166).

Major Group	55	Farm Operator and Manager
Minor Group	551	Farmer (Working Proprietors)
Unit Groups	5512	General Farmer
	5513	Crop, Vegetable, Fruit, and Tree Nut Farmer
	5514	Livestock, Dairy, and Poultry Farmer
	5515	Horticultural Specialty Farmer

A *minor group* of the major group 14, management-related occupations, is illustrated in the following box (USEOP, 1977, p. 49).

The following illustration is typical of minor group levels found in the *SOC*. The 705 digits are *DOT* industry designations that identify the industry in which the occupation is most commonly found. In this illustration, the industrial designation is professional and kindred. The nine-digit numbers assigned to each occupation are the fourth edition *DOT* codes.

A *unit group* is provided when it is necessary to further break down a minor group. For example, in the case of a Natural Resource Program Administrator, other occupations involving administration of related programs are listed in the unit group, as illustrated on page 490 (USEOP, 1977, p.37).

The *SOC* is designed for conversion of *DOT* data, thus making it possible to use data collected by *DOT* codes or by the broader *SOC* for analysis. The system is flexible in that unit groups can be analyzed for specific information. For example, sales supervisors are classified according to products sold, which allows for combining one unit group with another sales group for supplemental analysis according to products or other combinations. Governmental agencies will be encouraged to use *SOC* for collecting occupational data as well as for research and planning occupational, educational-training programs.

The *SOC*'s four levels of detail seem to provide the flexibility needed for the ever-changing world of work. New and unique occupations can be classified according to similar minor or unit groups within the system. The grouping of classifications is designed to allow for additional breakdown into units when necessary. To move from the currently diverse occupational classification systems, each with its own uses, to a national standard is a technically demanding process. The Office of Federal Statistical Policy and Standards, which is responsible for the continued development of *SOC*, has emphasized its flexibility and the need to adapt it to various analytical situations (USEOP, 1977, p. 9). The first use of *SOC,* and its first revision, was made for the 1980 Census of Population. The numerous revisions to the 1977 edition reflect the needs of the Census Bureau. No doubt *SOC* will be closely scrutinized in the years ahead by the many agencies that collect occupational data and are charged with the responsibility of projecting labor-market trends.

---

142 Management Analysis

This minor group includes occupations concerned with reviewing, analyzing, and improving business and organizational systems to assist management in operating with greater efficiency and effectiveness. Activities such as conducting organizational studies and evaluations, designing systems and procedures for new work processes, conducting work simplification and measurement studies, and preparing and maintaining systems and procedures manuals are performed in these occupations.

Director, records management	705	161117014
Management analyst	705	161167010
Manager, farm analysis	705	161167014
Manager, records analysis	705	161167018
Manager, reports analysis	705	161167022
Clerical methods analyst	705	161267010
Records-management analyst	705	161267022
Reports analyst	705	161267026

1133 Natural Resource Program Administrator

This unit group includes occupations involving administering programs related to preservation, management, and restoration of natural or man-made environments within the public domain.

Chief, fishery division	425	188117018
Commissioner, conservation of resources	425	188117026
Federal Aid Coordinator	425	188167054
Park superintendent	425	188167062
Wildlife agent, regional	425	379127018

Curricular Career Information Service (CCIS) Modules

The Curricular Career Information (CCIS) program for delivery of educational and vocational information emphasizes an instructional approach to career planning services. The program consists of 12 modules. The first 5 modules were discussed in Chapter 11; the remaining 7 modules are described in Table A-1.

TABLE A-1

Curricular Career Information Services (CCIS) Modules (continued from Chapter 11)

Module	Title	Objectives	Activities
VI.	Job Forecasts and Your Career Plans	1. To describe the present distribution of workers in different job areas, e.g., sex, race.	a. Read the materials in the Module VI folders in the Mobile File. "Employment Outlooks" contains information regarding forecasts nationwide, and "Florida Outlooks" contains projections for the various geographic sections of Florida.
			b. Scan such books as:
			IIA 025 Occupational Outlook Handbook
			IIA S6 Jobs! What They Are . . . Where They Are . . . What They Pay!
			IC C3 Careers Tomorrow
			IC O2 Employment Projections
			IC W6 Work in the 21st Century
			ID M5 Occupations in Florida 1982–1995
			IIA P4 "Jobs '94"
			IC W7 American Almanac of Jobs and Salaries
			c. Review occupational information materials located in the vertical files for outlook information on specific careers (File 2).
			d. Consult with staff in The Career Center for special concerns.
VII.	Your Lifestyle	1. To understand the need for balancing one's work role with nonwork roles.	a. Perform a computer search on Career Key to locate specific resources in The Career Center Library on lifestyle. Topics are listed under "Careers and Life Planning."
			b. Complete Module 8: "Planning Your Career" on the DISCOVER computer.
			c. Review the section of "The Three Boxes of Life" pertaining to "Lifelong Leisure or Playing," IIA B62.
		2. To understand one's personal characteristics in relation to leisure planning.	a. Review "The Leisure Activities Finder" for activities related to Holland Codes.
			b. Use the "Leisure Activities Card Sort" to assist you in identifying activities for leisure time.

(continued)

TABLE A-1

Curricular Career Information Services (CCIS) Modules (continued from Chapter 11) (continued)

Module	Title	Objectives	Activities
VIII.	For African American Students	1. To assist you in locating sources of career planning information of special interest to African American students.	a. Perform a search using Career Key to locate any Career Center Library materials on career planning or educational planning for special populations. b. Review materials in Module 8: "Opportunities for African Americans" located in the Mobile File (File 1). c. Read occupational files for current information on opportunities for African Americans in various fields (File 2). d. Skim through current minority student magazines in the library reception area that feature career planning articles (i.e., "The Black Collegian" and "Equal Opportunity"). e. Stop by the Sigma Chi Iota office (Room 1463) or see a CEO staff member for information regarding Sigma Chi Iota, a career development honorary society for minority students. f. Review the "Directory of Special Programs for Minority Group Members" (IG1 J6) for information on internships, occupations, scholarships, employment assistance, summer jobs, etc. g. Consult with staff in The Career Center for special concerns.
IX.	Especially for Her	1. To provide you with the opportunity for self-assessment: to examine your strengths, interests, accomplishments, experiences, and motivations.	a. Review Module III: "Looking At You," to identify self-assessment activities that may be beneficial to you. b. Discuss your situation with a Career Advisor. c. Pick up a copy of "Career Resources for Women" in The Career Center Library next to Career Key to see what resources are available. d. Perform a search using Career Key under the topic "Education and Training—Special Groups—Women" and "Career Life Planning—Lifestyle—Dual-Career Couples" to locate available resources in The Career Center Library. e. Read the material in Module 9: "Opportunities for Women" in the Mobile File (File 1).

TABLE A-1 *(continued)*

Module	Title	Objectives	Activities
			f. Read the magazines located in The Career Center relating to women and work.
			g. View "Working Parents: Balancing Kids and Careers."
			h. Complete the Nonsexist Vocational Card Sort.
X.	Career Planning for Students with Disabilities	1. To assist you in locating sources of career planning information of special interest to students with disabilities including information on the Americans with Disabilities Act.	a. Review current articles and pamphlets in the Module X folder in the Mobile File.
			b. Read sections in the following books:
			III E3 L4 A World of Options for the 90's: A Guide to International Educational Exchange, Community Service and Travel for Persons with Disabilities
			IG3 B6 Job Hunting Tips for the So-called Handicapped
			IG3 U5 *Americans with Disabilities Act Handbook*
			IG3 W4 Job Strategies for People with Disabilities
			c. Perform a computer search on Career Key under "Career & Life Planning—Special Groups" to locate any Career Center Library materials on career planning or educational planning for persons with disabilities.
			d. Read the amended version of The Americans with Disabilities Act of 1990 located in the Module X folder in the Mobile File.
			e. Consult with the Coalition for Careers Project Manager, 4th Level, University Center, room 1442, the Disabled Students Services Coordinator, 216 William Johnston Building, or the Division of Blind Services, 255 A&B William Johnston Building.
			f. Consider participation in Advocates for Disability Awareness, an FSU student organization (644-9566).
			g. Consult with Career Center staff members for special concerns.
XI.	Career Changes	1. To explore the issues involved in job and career changes.	a. Discuss your situation with a Career Advisor and evaluate options; individual counseling through the evening career clinic or using services available during normal hours are both possible.

(continued)

TABLE A-1
Curricular Career Information Services (CCIS) Modules (continued from Chapter 11) *(continued)*

Module	Title	Objectives	Activities
			b. Review the materials in the Module XI: "Career Changes" folder in the Mobile File (File 1).
			c. Perform a search using Career Key to locate the Career Center Library resources that address "Career Change" or review "Career Center Resources for Mid-Life Career Change" located on the cabinet near the Career Key computer.
		2. To identify the kind of change desired.	a. Interact with the MICRO SKILLS computer-assisted career guidance program to review skills from previous work roles, rate level of satisfaction, and relate them to future possibilities. (Provides Holland Codes, list of occupations compatible with skills, references to DOT, OOH, and GOE.)
			b. Review CCIS Module II: "What's Involved in Making a Career Decision?" for possible activities.
		3. To begin the change process.	a. For career changes, review CCIS Module III: "Looking At You," for available self-assessment activities.
			b. For lifestyle changes, review CCIS Module VII: "Your Lifestyle."
			c. For job changes, review CCIS Module XIII: "Your Job Campaign."
			d. Interact with the DISCOVER and SIGI PLUS computer-assisted career guidance programs.
XII. Get Experience!		1. To assist you in identifying resources that will help you obtain experience relevant to your area of career interest.	a. Read selected resources in the Career Center Library:
			Volunteer
			Volunteer! IVD C6
			Volunteer USA IVD C2
			Volunteer Vacations IVD M2
			Connections 1993 (A Directory of Lay Volunteer Opportunities IVD C3)
			Response-Volunteer Opportunities Directory IVD C4
			Summer/Holidays
			Summer Employment Directory IVC S8
			Directory of Overseas Summer Jobs IF2 P3
			Opportunities in Part-Time and Summer Jobs IF2 P3
			Jobs in Paradise: The Exotic Jobs Everywhere IVC M2

TABLE A-1 *(continued)*

Module	Title	Objectives	Activities
			Co-op/Internship

Co-op/Internship

The Insider's Guide to Washington Internships

The Student's Guide to International Internships

Internships in Federal Government IVB I6

Internships in State Government IVB 17

Internships Leading to Careers IVB 18

Internships in Law, Politics, and Medicine IVB 19

Internships Programs for Women IVB M8

Student Guide to Business Internships IVB P6

Internships: Advertising, Marketing, Public Relations, and Sales IVB F81

Internships: Newspaper, Magazine, and Book Publishing IVB F82

Internships: Travel and Hospitality Industries IVB F84

The Student Guide to Mass Media Internships IVB C5

b. Perform a search using Career Key under the topics in "Work Experience" to locate other Career Center resources.

c. Refer to the Job Choices series to find out about companies currently seeking candidates in the areas of Business, Health Care, and Science and Engineering.

d. Review articles in Module XII in the Mobile File (File 1).

e. Refer to "Volunteer Tallahassee Style" for contacts and information related to volunteering in Tallahassee.

f. Check the Florida State University General Bulletin for internship information in selected majors.

g. Attend a CEO orientation session and review the resources at the CEO Office, 4th floor University Center. Paid and nonpaid placements are available with employers in Florida, the Southeast, and nationwide along with information on federal and state co-ops, internships, summer jobs and volunteer experiences.

(continued)

TABLE A-1

Curricular Career Information Services (CCIS) Modules (continued from Chapter 11)   *(continued)*

Module	Title	Objectives	Activities
			h. Visit the Student Employment Services Office, 2472 University Center, for information on the college Work-Study Program and the College Career Work Experience Program. Review the job boards outside the Financial Aid Office on the 4th level of the University Center.
XIII.	Your Job Campaign	1. To help you start your job hunt.	a. View the 40 min. videotape "How to Get the Job You Want" (Audiovisual Room).
			b. Attend a "Job Hunting Workshop" offered by The Career Center or view the videotape "Job Hunting" (Audiovisual Room).
			c. Review current articles in the "Job Hunting" file located in the Module XIII section of the Mobile File (File 1).
			d. Pick up a copy of "Job Hunting Resources in CCIS," located on top of the cabinets near Career Key. Review sections in the many resource books catalogued in Section V of The Career Center Library.
			e. Pick up a copy of the *Career Objective Guide* located in Module XIII of the Mobile File (File 1).
			f. Look through the job files for current openings.
		2. To write a résumé appropriate for your job objective.	a. Pick up a copy of the *Résumé Writing Guide* from the Module XIII section of the Mobile File (File 1) and examine sample résumés available in The Career Center Library.
			b. Attend a "Résumé Writing Workshop" offered by The Career Center.
			c. Review current articles in the "Job Hunting" file located in the Module XIII section of Mobile File (File 1).
			d. Use Career Key to obtain a list of Career Center Library sources on résumé writing. Choose #5, "Job Hunting," from the main menu. Then choose #1, "Résumé Writing," from the next menu.
			e. Use the résumé section (located in "Instruction About Job-Seeking Skills") of Module 7 in the DISCOVER computer system.

TABLE A-1 *(continued)*

Module	Title	Objectives	Activities
		3. To write letters for your job campaign.	a. Pick up a copy of the *Letter Writing Guide* from Module XIII of the Mobile File (File 1).
			b. Review current articles in the "Job Hunting" file located in the Module XIII section of the Module File (File 1).
			c. Use Career Key to obtain a list of Career Center Library resources on writing letters. Choose #5, "Job Hunting," from the main menu. Then choose #3, "Letter Writing," from the next menu.
		4. To become informed about services available to you from Career Placement Services.	a. Attend a Placement Services orientation session. See the schedule on the Career Advisor desk.
			b. Visit Career Placement Services for special questions and information (Fourth Level, The University Center).
			c. Obtain a copy of the *Placement Manual*, the manual describing services available through Placement Services (Fourth Level, The University Center).
			d. Register with Placement Services for any on-campus interviews appropriate to your career objectives.
			e. Attend Seminole Future and/or the Education Expo to meet prospective employers.
		5. To prepare yourself for your job interview.	a. View the 40 min. videotape "How to Get the Job You Want" (Audiovisual Room).
			b. Pick up a copy of the Interview Preparation Guide from the Module XIII section of the Mobile File (File 1).
			c. Attend an Interview workshop offered by The Career Center.
			d. Review current articles in the "Job Hunting" file located in the Module XIII section of the Mobile File (File 1).
			e. Use Career Key to obtain a list of resources on interviewing. Choose #5, "Job Hunting," from the main menu. Then choose #2, "Interviewing," from the next menu.

(continued)

TABLE A-1

Curricular Career Information Services (CCIS) Modules (continued from Chapter 11)   (continued)

Module	Title	Objectives	Activities
XIV.	Going Abroad	1. To help you explore issues and locate opportunities for study abroad.	a. Perform a search on Career Key under the topic of "Education and Training," "Alternative Education" to get a list of relevant resources in the Career Center Library. b. Review the "Study Abroad" guide located in the mobile file in Module XIV. c. Review materials in the "Summer Study Abroad" folder in the Mobile File 1 Module XIV. d. Review materials in the "Overseas Study Programs" files located in The Career Center Library (File 7). e. Contact the Study Abroad Programs Office or the International Programs Office, on the 5th level, University Center.
		2. To help you explore issues and locate opportunities to work abroad.	a. Perform a search on Career Key under the topic of "Employment Information," "Overseas Employers" to get a list of relevant sources in The Career Center Library. b. Review the "Work Abroad" guide located in the Mobile File in Module XIV. c. Review materials in the Work Abroad folder in Module XIV, located in the Mobile File (File 1). d. Review Module XIII, "Your Job Campaign," for resources that may assist you with other components of your job search.
XV.	Going to Graduate School	1. To explore issues and activities that are important to you in pursuing graduate/ professional education.	a. Read "Part 1—Before You Apply" in "How to Get into and Finance Graduate and Professional Education" (III C2 W5). b. Review the folder labeled *Module XV:* "Graduate School" in the Mobile File (File 1). c. Look at The Career Center Library *Going to Graduate School Guide* located in the folder listed above. d. Attend a "Going to Graduate School" workshop.
		2. To identify graduate/ professional education programs in your chosen field of study.	a. Review selected resource books: (For additional information on graduate programs and advanced degrees, get a complete Career Key printout.) III C2 Pf4—Peterson's Annual Guides to Graduate Study III C2 A7—An Assessment Research—Doctorate Programs in the United States

TABLE A-1 (continued)

Module	Title	Objectives	Activities
			III C2 P4—Accounting to Zoology. A Comprehensive Look at 300 Graduate Fields of Study
			III C2 W5—How to Get into and Finance Graduate and Professional School
			IIB 10 K8—The Official Guide to MBA Programs, Admissions, and Careers
			IIB 211 B4—Barron's Guide to Law Schools
			IIB 211 P68—The Best Law Schools
			IIB 261 P7—The Best Medical Schools
			b. Use Career Key to perform a search under the topic "Occupations." (Often occupational materials contain information valuable in identifying and selecting graduate/professional programs.)
		3. To investigate selected graduate/professional education programs.	a. Review the appropriate sections of the general resource books listed on the previous page.
			b. Review the collection of graduate program materials in File 4; also see the information on FSU programs in File 3.
			c. Obtain program and university materials for your own use by writing/telephoning both the program office and the graduate admissions office of those programs you wish to consider further (this information can easily be found in the *Peterson's Guides*).
			d. Arrange for a personal interview with appropriate faculty/staff in programs you are seriously considering. If this is not possible, write or telephone.
			e. Talk to FSU faculty or students who might be familiar with the programs you are considering. Ask to see the FSU *Faculty Resource Directory* located at the Career Advisory desk.
		4. To develop an application strategy for gaining admission to your graduate/professional programs of choice.	a. Read appropriate sections of "How to Get into and Finance Graduate and Professional Education" (III C2 W5).
			b. Read articles related to graduate/professional school admissions located in Module XV: "Graduate School" of the Mobile File (File 1).
			c. Read the chapters "Applying to Graduate and Professional Schools" and "Financial Aid for Graduate and Professional Education" located in "Peterson's Graduate and Professional Programs: An Overview."

(continued)

TABLE A-1
Curricular Career Information Services (CCIS) Modules (continued from Chapter 11)   *(continued)*

Module	Title	Objectives	Activities
			d. Find out about, register for, prepare for and take the appropriate admission test(s). Visit Evaluation Services in 106 William Johnston building for information on various tests. See specific resources in The Career Center Library: Barron's Guide to the New Law School Admission Test (LSAT). (IIB 211 B3). Barron's Guide to How to Prepare for the New Medical College Admission Test (MCAT). (IIB 26 B3). e. Investigate financing options for graduate/professional education. Review financial aid resource materials located in Section IIIF. Visit the STAR Center. Write to your program(s) of choice to ask about financial aid.

XVI.	Choosing a Major	1. To identify what factors are important to you in selecting a major.
		2. To discover fields of study that you might find interesting.
		
		1. To broaden your general awareness of majors available at Florida State and elsewhere.
		2. To find detailed information about specific majors.
			a. Attend a "Choosing a Major Workshop." See the schedule at the Career Advisor desk for date, time, and location.
			b. Complete the "Major Expectations" section of the Career Center booklet "Choosing a Major or a Career." Ask a Career Advisor to get it for you.
			c. Complete appropriate self-assessment activities; review Module III: "Looking at You" and discuss your situation with a Career Advisor.
			d. Review the "F.S.U. Undergraduate Programs by Holland/SDS Categories" sheet to identify FSU programs consistent with your self-assessments.
			
			a. Acquaint yourself with the variety of college majors available at institutions around the country.
			1. Examine the "areas of study" section on the shelf in front of the library reference desk.
			  a. *Peterson's Guide to Four-Year Institutions*
			2. Review: College Majors and Careers: A Resource Guide for Effective Life Planning IIC AA P4
			  The College Board Guide to 150 Popular College Majors IIC AA C7
			  The Career Connection: A Guide to College Majors and Their Related Careers IIC AA R61

TABLE A-1 *(continued)*

Module	Title	Objectives	Activities
			3. Use the College Majors Card Sort to help identify majors that would be of interest to you.
			b. Learn more about specific majors available at FSU:
			1. See the *Florida State University General Bulletin* for a list of degree and certificate programs.
			2. Get specific information about majors that interest you in the *Undergraduate Academic Program Guide and the FSU General Bulletin.*
			3. Perform a computer search using Career Key to locate Career Center Library resources that address majors of interest to you.
			4. Review printed materials in File 3 on FSU Academic Programs.
			5. Refer to the *Faculty Resource Directory,* at the career Advisor desk, to find faculty names and phone numbers. Make an appointment with a faculty member to acquire more information about a particular major.
			c. Learn more about majors available at other colleges/universities.
			1. Use the directories on the shelf in front of the Library Reference Desk to identify institutions with programs in which you have an interest.
			2. Obtain further information about programs at other institutions.
			a. Write or call the institution and/or specific departments for catalogs and academic program information.
			b. Search out catalogs available on the FSU campus:
			1. Strozier Library, micromaterials department.
			2. Undergraduate Studies, 3rd Level, University Center, Room, 5304.
	3. To enhance your ability to make an informed decision.		a. Review sheet, "A Guide to Good Decision Making."
			b. Review Module II: "What's Involved in Making a Career Decision?"
			c. Complete the "Guide to Good Decision Making Exercise."
			d. Talk to a Career Advisor about special programs getting in the way of your "major decision."

SOURCE: From *Curricular Career Information Service,* by R. C. Reardon, 1996. Unpublished manuscript, Florida State University. Reprinted by permission.

A High School Student's Experience in a Cooperative Education Program

The following account of a student's participation in a high school cooperative education program points out the values of work experiences.[1] Experiential activities involved money management, cooperative work activities with regular work staff, coping with work-related stress, and responsibility for work tasks. This student credits the cooperative education program as the single most influential aspect of her career education.

During my high school years, I was enrolled in a cooperative education program—I was a co-op student. As many people know, a co-op program is where a high school or college student earns academic credit and sometimes wages by working in the "real world" as part of a specified vocational curriculum. For example, a student in a retail merchandise program can earn credit and money through working in a department store. A food services student can work in a restaurant, a welding student can work for a sheet metal company, and so on.

I attended a high school that contained an areawide vocational skill center. Because I planned to attend college, I enrolled in the typical college prep courses, but I was also able to combine a college prep track with a vocational course (two hours a day for two years) that led to vocational certification by the State of Michigan. Early in my high school career, I had chosen elective courses from business: typing, shorthand, general business. I did quite well in these courses, and although I had no aspirations of becoming a business tycoon, I thought that having a background in business could prove helpful in the future, so I planned to take the Stenographer/Secretarial vocational program in my junior and senior years.

Immediately after finishing my sophomore year I was told of a co-op job working in the County Treasurer's Office, which sounded more interesting than cleaning motel rooms (which I had done the previous summer). So I interviewed for, and subsequently landed, the position of clerk/"go-fer"/secretary in the Office of the County Treasurer of Chippewa County.

It was then that my real education began. As a 16-year-old, my work experience consisted of being a paper girl for two years, extensive babysitting, and cleaning motel rooms. I was now in an "adult" job, one full of responsibility and of learning a tremendous amount of information. During the two-and-a-half years I worked in that office, I learned more about the world of work than I did in any class I have ever taken—in high school, college, or graduate school.

The first major concept I learned was responsibility. I was required to be on time, day-in, day-out, even if I did not feel like going to work. However, my responsibility did not end with punctuality. I also had to *perform*, usually in pressure situations, under legal deadlines imposed by the State. I was responsible for accepting delinquent taxes and penalties and had to figure out the charges. At certain times of the year the office would become extremely hectic, but I was still expected to be accurate. After all, I was dealing with public funds.

Another area of my on-the-job education involved money management. For the first time in my life I was receiving a substantial amount of money in the form

[1]From *My Vocational Experience,* by M. K. Wiinamaki, 1988. Unpublished manuscript, Southwest Texas State University. Reprinted by permission.

of a regular paycheck. Granted, it was only minimum wage, but working 20 hours per week during the school semester and 40 hours per week during summer, even minimum wage looked good to a high school girl with few expenses. I began to buy all my own clothes, my own gas, and was responsible for all of my entertainment expenses. Looking back, I believe both my parents and I appreciated this step of "economic independence."

Another crucial concept learned through my co-op experience was decision making, particularly the idea that decisions do have consequences and should be weighed before plunging head-first into one. I learned this in a variety of ways: first, by watching the adults with whom I worked, and second, by becoming aware of the political process around me. Decisions I made during those years still affect my life today.

The most generalizable skills I learned through co-op were interpersonal skills. I worked in an office with three women; though all of us had vastly different personalities, we had to cooperate and learn to co-exist peacefully, even when we did not agree. I also dealt with the public, people who were often paying delinquent land taxes, plus penalties, and who were generally unhappy about having to do so. I learned to be tactful, diplomatic, patient, and above all, to have a sense of humor about myself and about people. Working in such a stressful environment also taught me the importance of dealing with stress in a productive manner.

Time management was another skill I learned in my co-op job. When I began working regular hours, I was forced to use free time in a more productive manner—suddenly I had less time to goof off, do homework, and participate in household chores. I gained respect for adults who dealt with their job, spouse, children, and home. Life was more complicated than it had previously seemed.

In my position in the County Treasurer's Office, I had many occasions to talk to and become acquainted with a variety of people who held various city and county positions, such as county clerk, registrar of deeds, district attorneys, judges, and county commissioners. While students my age were learning about local politics in government class, I knew the officials by name and discovered what they actually did in their respective positions.

Also significant was the fact that I had greatly increased my job experience during the time I worked as a co-op student. Many of the skills, such as typing, interpersonal skills, and problem-solving proved invaluable in subsequent positions.

While all these skills and concepts were worthwhile, I think the most valuable benefit was a very positive increase in my self-esteem. I was now capable of working in the real world, of earning a living, of sticking with something that was not always pleasant. And that is a tremendous benefit.

So what happened after I left the County Treasurer's Office? During the time I worked there, I discovered some things about myself and the kind of environment I wanted to work in, and office work as a career was not what I envisioned. I learned that I did not enjoy the rigid structure, the routine, the repetition, but I did like working with people rather than with things. I entered college as a psychology major and thoroughly enjoyed the world of concepts, ideas, theories, and speculation. Throughout my years in college, I worked as a typist, a secretary in the Admissions Office, and as a word processor. Upon receiving a B.A. in psychology and realizing that graduate school was a necessity, I moved to Texas and promptly got a job as a word processor in a large law firm in Austin. Once again I was using the skills learned first in my co-op job as a high school student. In fact, that word-processing job supported me throughout graduate school, and also confirmed my decision to work in the field of counseling. I am glad to say that I am now working as a counselor, and I think I appreciate it more due to the years I spent in various secretarial jobs.

In summary, I learned a great deal about working, life, and myself through my experiences in cooperative education, experiences that continue to influence my life. For me, being a co-op student was the single most influential aspect of any career education I received. It was valuable not because it showed me what I wanted to do with my life, but rather what I did *not* want to do—at a time when I was not forced to make irrevocable decisions on majors, careers, and locations. It provided me with the opportunity to navigate the transition from adolescence to adulthood gradually, and it is an experience I will never forget.

Section II: Career Counseling Competencies (Adopted by NCDA Board January 11, 1991)

Introduction to Career Counseling Competency Statements

These competency statements are for those professionals interested and trained in the field of career counseling. For the purpose of these statements, career counseling is defined as counseling individuals or groups of individuals about occupations, careers, life/career roles and responsibilities, career decision making, career planning, leisure planning, career pathing, educational and career placement, and other career development activities, such as employability skills, together with the issues or conflicts that individuals confront regarding their careers.

These competency statements are a revised version of the "Vocational/Career Counseling Competencies" of 1982. They were revised by counselor educators and career counseling practitioners, then reviewed and approved by the Board of Directors of the National Career Development Association (NCDA). Career development competency statements developed by other groups, such as the National Occupational Information Coordinating Committee (NOICC), the National Board for Certified Counselors (NBCC), the Council for the Advancement Standards for Student Services/Development Programs (CAS), and the Council for Accreditation of Counseling and Related Educational Programs (CACREP), were reviewed as part of this revision. The NCDA Standards Committee responsible for this review and revision included Edwin Herr, James Sampson, Larry Burlew, Linda Gast, James Benshoff, and Janet Treichel.

NCDA's "Career Counseling Competencies" are intended to represent minimum competencies for those professionals at or above the master's degree level of education. They can also serve as guidelines for any professional or paraprofessional working in a career development setting.

Purpose

Professional competency statements provide guidance for the minimum competencies necessary to perform effectively a particular occupation or job within a particular field. Professional career counselors (master's degree or higher) or persons in career development positions must demonstrate the knowledge and skills for a specialty in career counseling that the generalist counselor might not possess. Skills and knowledge are represented by designated competency areas which have been developed by professional career counselors and counselor educators. The Career Counseling Competency Statements can serve as a guide for career counseling training programs or as a checklist for persons wanting to acquire or to enhance their skills in career counseling.

Minimum Competencies

In order to work as a professional engaged in Career Counseling, the individual must demonstrate minimum competencies in ten designated areas. These ten areas are: Career Development Theory, Individual and Group Counseling Skills, Individual/Group Assessment, Information/Resources, Program Management and Implementation, Consultation, Special Populations, Supervision, Ethical/Legal Issues, and Research/Evaluation. These areas are briefly defined as follows:

> *Career Development Theory:* Theory base and knowledge considered essential for professionals engaging in career counseling and development.
>
> *Individual and Group Counseling Skills:* Individual and group counseling competencies considered essential to effective career counseling.
>
> *Individual/Group Assessment:* Individual/group assessment skills considered essential for professionals engaging in career counseling.
>
> *Information/Resources:* Information/resource base and knowledge essential for professionals engaging in career counseling.
>
> *Program Management and Implementation:* Skills necessary to develop, plan, implement, and manage comprehensive career development programs in a variety of settings.
>
> *Consultation:* Knowledge and skills considered essential in enabling individuals and organizations to impact effectively upon the career counseling and development process.
>
> *Special Populations:* Knowledge and skills considered essential in providing career counseling and development processes to special populations.
>
> *Supervision:* Knowledge and skills considered essential in critically evaluating counselor performance, maintaining and improving professional skills, and seeking assistance from others when needed in career counseling.
>
> *Ethical/Legal Issues:* Information base and knowledge essential for the ethical and legal practice of career counseling.
>
> *Research/Evaluation:* Knowledge and skills considered essential in understanding and conducting research and evaluation in career counseling and development.

Professional Preparation

The competency statements were developed to serve as guidelines for persons interested in career development occupations. They are intended for persons training at the master's level or higher with a specialty in career counseling. However, this intention does not prevent other types of career development professionals from using the competencies as guidelines for their own training. The competency statements provide counselor educators, supervisors, and other interested groups with guidelines for the minimum training required for counselors interested in the career counseling specialty. The statements might also serve as guidelines for professional counselors who seek in-service training to qualify as career counselors.

Ethical Responsibilities

Career development professionals must only perform activities for which they "possess or have access to the necessary skills and resources for giving the kind of help that is needed" (see ACA's Ethical Standards). If a professional does not have the appropriate training or resources for the type of career concern presented, an appropriate referral must be made. No person should attempt to use skills (within these competency statements) for which he/she has not been trained. For additional ethical guidelines, refer to the NCDA Ethical Standards for Career Counselors in Section V of this document.

Career Counseling Competencies and Performance Indicators
CAREER DEVELOPMENT THEORY

Theory base and knowledge considered essential for professionals engaging in career counseling and development. Demonstration of:

1. Knowledge about counseling theories and associated techniques.
2. Knowledge about theories and models of careers and career development.
3. Understanding and appreciation of differences in knowledge and value about work and productive roles associated with gender, age, ethnic and race groups, cultures, and capacities.
4. Knowledge about career counseling theoretical models, associated counseling and information techniques, and resources to learn more about them.
5. Knowledge about developmental issues individuals address throughout the life span.
6. Knowledge of role relationships which facilitate personal, family, and career development.
7. Knowledge of information, techniques, and models related to computer-assisted career guidance systems, career information delivery systems, and career counseling.
8. Knowledge of the information, techniques, and models related to career planning and placement.
9. Knowledge of career counseling theories and models that apply specifically to women or are inclusive of variables important to women's career development.

Individual and Group Counseling Skills

Individual and group counseling competencies considered essential to effective career counseling. Demonstration of:

1. Ability to establish and maintain productive personal relationships with individuals.
2. Ability to establish and maintain a productive group climate.
3. Ability to collaborate with clients in identifying personal goals.
4. Ability to identify and select techniques appropriate to client or group goals and client needs, psychological states, and developmental tasks.
5. Ability to plan, implement, and evaluate counseling techniques designed to assist clients to achieve the following:
   a. Identify and understand clients' personal characteristics related to career.
   b. Identify and understand social contextual conditions affecting clients' careers.
   c. Identify and understand familial, subcultural and cultural structures and functions as they are related to clients' careers.
   d. Identify and understand clients' career decision-making processes.
   e. Identify and understand clients' attitudes toward work and workers.
   f. Identify and understand clients' biases toward work and workers based on gender, race, and cultural stereotypes.
6. Ability to challenge and encourage clients to take action to prepare for and initiate role transitions by:
   a. Locating sources of relevant information and experience.
   b. Obtaining and interpreting information and experiences.
   c. Acquiring skills needed to make role transitions.
7. Ability to support and challenge clients to examine the balance of work, leisure, family, and community roles in their careers.

INDIVIDUAL/GROUP ASSESSMENT

Individual/group assessment skills considered essential for professionals engaging in career counseling. Demonstration of:

1. Knowledge about instruments and techniques to assess personal characteristics such as aptitude, achievement, interests, values and personality traits.
2. Knowledge about instruments and techniques to assess leisure interests, learning style, life roles, self-concept, career maturity, vocational identity, career indecision, work environment preference (e.g., work satisfaction), and other related life style/development issues.
3. Knowledge about instruments and techniques to assess conditions of the work environment (such as tasks, expectations, norms, and qualities of the physical and social settings).
4. Ability to evaluate and select instruments appropriate to the client's physical capacities, psychological states, social roles, and cultural background.

5. Knowledge about variables such as ethnicity, gender, culture, learning style, personal development, and physical/mental disability which affect the assessment process.
6. Knowledge of and ability to use computer-assisted assessment measures and techniques effectively and appropriately.
7. Ability to identify assessment (procedures) appropriate for specified situations and populations.
8. Ability to evaluate assessment procedures in terms of their validity, reliability, and relationships to race, gender, age, and ethnicity.
9. Ability to select assessment techniques appropriate for group administration and those appropriate for individual administration.
10. Ability to administer, score, and report findings from career assessment instruments.
11. Ability to interpret data from assessment instruments and present the results to clients and to others designated by clients.
12. Ability to assist the client and others designated by the client to interpret data from assessment instruments.
13. Ability to write a thorough and substantiated report of assessment results.

INFORMATION/RESOURCES

Information/resource base and knowledge essential for professionals engaging in career counseling. Demonstration of:

1. Knowledge of employment information and career planning resources for client use.
2. Knowledge of education, training, and employment trends; labor market information and resources that provide information about job tasks, functions, salaries, requirements and future outlooks related to broad occupational fields and individual occupations.
3. Knowledge of the changing roles of women and men and the implications for work, education, family, and leisure.
4. Knowledge of and the ability to use computer-based career information delivery systems (CIDS) and computer-assisted career guidance systems (CACGS) to store, retrieve, and disseminate career and occupational information.
5. Knowledge of community/professional resources to assist clients in career/life planning, including job search.

PROGRAM MANAGEMENT AND IMPLEMENTATION

Knowledge and skills necessary to develop, plan, implement, and manage comprehensive career development programs in a variety of settings. Demonstration of:

1. Knowledge of designs that can be used in the organization of career development programs.
2. Knowledge of needs assessment and evaluation techniques and practices.

3. Knowledge of organizational theories, including diagnosis, behavior, planning, organizational communication, and management useful in implementing and administering career development programs.
4. Knowledge of leadership theories, evaluation and feedback approaches, organizational change, decision-making and conflict resolution approaches.
5. Knowledge of professional standards for accreditation and program development purposes.
6. Knowledge of personal and environmental barriers affecting the implementation of career development programs.
7. Knowledge of using computers for forecasting, budgeting, planning, communicating, policy analysis, and resource allocation.
8. Knowledge of educational trends and state and federal legislation that may influence the development and implementation of career development programs.
9. Ability to implement individual and group programs in career development for specified populations.
10. Ability to train and/or inform teachers and others about the use and application of computer-based systems for career information.
11. Ability to plan, organize, and manage a comprehensive career resource center.
12. Ability to work as a lead person in developing and implementing career development programs involving collaborative arrangements with teachers and other professionals or paraprofessionals.
13. Ability to prepare budgets and time lines for career development programs.
14. Ability to identify staff competencies needed to remain current in the field of career counseling and development.
15. Ability to identify, develop, and use record-keeping methods.
16. Ability to implement a public relations effort in behalf of career development activities and services.

CONSULTATION

Knowledge and skills considered essential in relating to individuals and organizations that impact the career counseling and development process. Demonstration of:

1. Knowledge of and ability to use consultation theories, strategies, and models.
2. Ability to establish and maintain a productive consultative relationship with people in roles who can influence the client's career, such as the following: parents, teachers, employers, business and professional groups, community groups, and the general public.
3. Ability to convey career counseling goals and achievements to business and professional groups, employers, community groups, the general public, and key personnel in positions of authority, such as legislators, executives, and others.
4. Ability to provide data on the cost effectiveness of career counseling and development intervention.

SPECIAL POPULATIONS

Knowledge and skills considered essential in relating to special populations that impact career counseling and development processes. Demonstration of:

1. Knowledge of the intrapersonal dynamics of special population clients while understanding resistances and defenses that may occur naturally during the counseling process.
2. Sensitivity toward the developmental issues and needs unique to minority populations.
3. Sensitivity toward and knowledge of various disabling conditions and necessary assistance and requirements.
4. Ability to define the structure of the career counseling process to accommodate individual cultural frames of reference and ethnic and racial issues.
5. Ability to distinguish between the special needs of the culturally different, immigrants, the disabled, the elderly, persons with the AIDS virus, and minority populations.
6. Ability to find appropriate methods or resources to communicate with limited-English-proficient individuals.
7. Ability to identify alternative approaches to career planning needs for individuals with specific needs.
8. Ability to identify community resources and establish linkages to assist clients with specific needs.
9. Ability to assist other staff members, professionals, and community members in understanding the unique needs/characteristics of special populations with regard to career exploration, employment expectations, and economic/social issues.
10. Ability to advocate for the career development and employment of special populations.
11. Ability to deliver and design career development programs and materials to hard-to-reach special populations.

SUPERVISION

Knowledge and skills considered essential in critically evaluating counselor performance, maintaining and improving professional skills, and seeking assistance from others when needed. Demonstration of:

1. Knowledge of supervision models and theories.
2. Ability to provide effective supervision to career counselors at different levels of experience.
3. Ability to utilize supervision on a regular basis to maintain and improve counselor skills.
4. Ability to consult with supervisors and colleagues regarding client and counseling issues and issues related to one's own professional development as a career counselor.
5. Ability to recognize own limitations as a career counselor and to seek supervision or refer clients when appropriate.

ETHICAL/LEGAL ISSUES

Information base and knowledge essential for the ethical and legal practice of career counseling. Demonstration of:

1. Knowledge about the codes of ethical standards of ACA, NCDA, NBCC, CACREP, and other relevant professional organizations.
2. Knowledge about current ethical and legal issues that affect the practice of career counseling.
3. Knowledge about ethical issues related to career counseling with women, cultural minorities, immigrants, the disabled, the elderly, and persons with the AIDS virus.
4. Knowledge about current ethical/legal issues with regard to the use of computer-assisted career guidance.
5. Ability to apply ethical standards to career counseling and consulting situations, issues, and practices.
6. Ability to recognize situations involving interpretation of ethical standards and to consult with supervisors and colleagues to determine an appropriate and ethical course of action.
7. Knowledge of state and federal statutes relating to client confidentiality.

RESEARCH/EVALUATION

Knowledge and skills considered essential in understanding and conducting research and evaluation in career counseling and development. Demonstration of:

1. Knowledge about and ability to apply basic statistics and statistical procedures appropriate to research related to career counseling and development.
2. Knowledge about and ability to use types of research and research designs appropriate to career counseling and development research.
3. Knowledge about and ability to convey major research findings related to career counseling and development processes and effectiveness.
4. Knowledge about and ability to apply principles of proposal writing.
5. Knowledge about major evaluation models and methods.
6. Ability to design, conduct, and use the results of evaluation programs.
7. Ability to design evaluation programs that take into account the needs of special populations, minorities, the elderly, persons with the AIDS virus, and women.

Visit Your Nearest U.S. Government Bookstore for the Latest in Government Information

The Superintendent of Documents operates 24 bookstores across the nation. Each store carries the most popular titles and can order any item in the 12,000 title inventory. Store locations sometimes change, and hours vary, so call ahead before visiting.[1]

All stores are open Monday through Friday. Kansas City is open 7 days a week. List is current as of May 1995.

U.S. Government Bookstore
First Union Plaza
999 Peachtree Street, NE
Suite 120
Atlanta, GA 30309-3964
(404) 347-1900
FAX: (404) 347-1897

U.S. Government Bookstore
O'Neill Building
2021 Third Ave., North
Birmingham, AL 35203
(205) 731-1056
FAX: (205) 731-3444

U.S. Government Bookstore
Thomas P. O'Neill Building
Room 169
10 Causeway Street
Boston, MA 02222
(617) 720-4180
FAX: (617) 720-5753

U.S. Government Bookstore
One Congress Center
401 South State St., Suite 124
Chicago, IL 60605
(312) 353-5133
FAX: (312) 353-1590

U.S. Government Bookstore
Room 1653, Federal Building
1240 E. 9th Street
Cleveland, OH 44199
(216) 522-4922
FAX: (216) 522-4714

U.S. Government Bookstore
Room 207, Federal Building
200 N. High Street
Columbus, OH 43215
(614) 469-6956
FAX: (614) 469-5374

U.S. Government Bookstore
Room IC50, Federal Building
1100 Commerce Street
Dallas, TX 75242
(214) 767-0076
FAX: (214) 767-3239

U.S. Government Bookstore
Room 117, Federal Building
1961 Stout Street
Denver, CO 80294
(303) 844-3964
FAX: (303) 844-4000

U.S. Government Bookstore
Suite 160, Federal Building
477 Michigan Avenue
Detroit, MI 48226
(313) 226-7816
FAX: (313) 226-4698

U.S. Government Bookstore
Texas Crude Building
801 Travis Street, Suite 120
Houston, TX 77002
(713) 228-1187
FAX: (713) 228-1186

U.S. Government Bookstore
100 West Bay Street
Suite 100
Jacksonville, FL 32202
(904) 353-0569
FAX: (904) 353-1280

U.S. Government Bookstore
120 Bannister Mall
5600 E. Bannister Road
Kansas City, MO 64137
(816) 765-2256
FAX: (816) 767-8233

U.S. Government Bookstore
U.S. Government Printing Office
Warehouse Sales Outlet
8660 Cherry Lane
Laurel, MD 20707
(301) 953-7974
(301) 792-0262
FAX: (301) 498-8995

U.S. Government Bookstore
ARCO Plaza, C-Level
505 South Flower Street
Los Angeles, CA 90071
(213) 239-9844
FAX: (213) 239-9848

U.S. Government Bookstore
Suite 150, Reuss Federal Plaza
310 W. Wisconsin Avenue
Milwaukee, WI 53203
(414) 297-1304
FAX: (414) 297-1300

U.S. Government Bookstore
Room 110, Federal Building
26 Federal Plaza
New York, NY 10278
(212) 264-3825
FAX: (212) 264-9318

U.S. Government Bookstore
Robert Morris Building
100 North 17th Street
Philadelphia, PA 19103
(215) 636-1900
FAX: (215) 636-1903

U.S. Government Bookstore
Room 118, Federal Building
1000 Liberty Avenue
Pittsburgh, PA 15222
(412) 644-2721
FAX: (412) 644-4547

U.S. Government Bookstore
1305 SW First Avenue
Portland, OR 97201-5801
(503) 221-6217
FAX: (503) 225-0563

U.S. Government Bookstore
Norwest Banks Building
201 West 8th Street
Pueblo, CO 81003
(719) 544-3142
FAX: (719) 544-6719

U.S. Government Bookstore
Marathon Plaza, Room 141-S
303 2nd Street
San Francisco, CA 94107
(415) 512-2770
FAX: (415) 512-2776

U.S. Government Bookstore
Room 194, Federal Building
915 Second Avenue
Seattle, WA 98174
(206) 553-4270
FAX: (206) 553-6717

U.S. Government Bookstore
U.S. Government Printing Office
710 N. Capitol Street, NW
Washington, DC 20401
(202) 512-0132
FAX: (202) 512-1355

U.S. Government Bookstore
1510 H Street, NW
Washington, DC 20005
(202) 653-5075
FAX: (202) 376-5055

Career Counseling Videotapes (in alphabetical order)

Title	Overall rating	Instructional effectiveness	Production quality	NOICC A	NOICC B	Page
America's Hospitality Industry-Ours Is a Special World	C− (81/98)	B− (57/98)	C+ (67/98)	0	8	1
Are You Ready?	A (12/98)	A (17/98)	B+ (33/98)	0	1–12	1
Basic Guide to Résumé Writing and Job Interviews, The	B+ (31/98)	B+ (37/98)	B (47/98)	7	2, 6, 12	2
Be Your Best Self: Assertiveness Training	A (10/98)	A+ (9/98)	A (18/98)	2, 9	1, 5	2
Better Jobs: Using the OOH	D+ (91/98)	D+ (94/98)	D+ (90/98)	6	4, 7, 8, 12	3
Between You and Me: Learning to Communicate	A+ (6/63)	A (10/63)	A+ (4/63)	2	0	3
Black College White College: A Matter of Choice	A− (20/98)	B+ (39/98)	A+ (8/98)	9	1–6, 8, 10–12	4
Black, Male and Successful in America	A− (28/98)	B+ (30/98)	A− (28/98)	0	1–5, 10–11	4
Breaking Out of Boxes: Values Clarification Exercises	D+ (58/63)	D+ (62/63)	C− (55/63)	0	0	5
Building Self-Confidence	A− (27/98)	A (19/98)	A (19/98)	1	2–3, 5, 9	5
Career Close-Ups: Women in Science	B (30/63)	B+ (22/63)	B+ (23/63)	0	4, 11	6
Career Exploration for the 90's	C (75/98)	C (75/98)	C− (89/98)	0	1, 3, 6–12	6
Career Information Interviews	C− (55/63)	C− (56/63)	C− (56/63)	0	7, 12	7

Career Counseling Videotapes (in alphabetical order)   *(continued)*

Title	Overall rating	Instructional effectiveness	Production quality	NOICC A	NOICC B	Page
Career Journey, The	C+ (69/98)	C+ (67/98)	B (48/98)	0	4, 6, 8, 10	7
Career Planning: Putting Your Skills to Work, Vol. 1	B (26/63)	B+ (23/63)	B− (36/63)	12	10	8
Career Self-Assessment: Where Do You Fit?	A (10/63)	B+ (20/63)	A (7/63)	4	6, 8, 12	8
Career Tracks	B (42/98)	B− (56/98)	B− (56/98)	0	4–5, 8, 11–12	9
Careers for the 21st Century, Vol. 1, Program 1, Firefighter/Veterinarian	B− (49/98)	A− (22/98)	B+ (30/98)	0	1–12	9
Careers for the 21st Century, Vol. 1, Program 5, Entrepreneur/Coin Dealer, Structural Engineer	A− (26/98)	B− (53/98)	B (45/98)	11	1, 3–6, 8–10, 12	10
Careers in Biotechnology and Genetic Engineering	A− (25/98)	A (11/98)	B− (54/98)	4	6–8, 11–12	10
Careers in Caring (HO-90-2000)	B (45/98)	B (41/98)	B− (52/98)	0	4, 6, 8, 10–12	11
Careers in Health Services: Opportunities For You, Vol. 1	A− (18/63)	B+ (24/63)	A− (17/63)	0	4	11
Careers in Interior Design	A− (19/63)	A− (16/63)	A (12/63)	0	4, 12	12
Careers In Perspective: Nursing	A (12/63)	A+ (6/63)	B+ (22/63)	0	4, 8	12
Careers in Robotics	A (18/98)	A+ (10/98)	A− (25/98)	0	4, 6, 8	13
Careers in Social Sciences	B− (32/63)	B− (37/63)	B− (34/63)	6	4	13
Careers in Transportation and Material Moving	B (47/98)	A− (23/98)	B (41/98)	0	4, 6–8	14
Careers 2000: Where Do I Fit Im?	C+ (68/98)	C− (84/98)	C (79/98)	0	1, 4–6, 9–10, 12	14
Choices in Health	A (11/98)	A+ (8/98)	A (13/98)	6, 8, 10–12	2–5, 7, 9	15

(continued)

Career Counseling Videotapes (in alphabetical order)   (continued)

Title	Overall rating	Instructional effectiveness	Production quality	NOICC A	NOICC B	Page
CHOICES: Nontraditional Jobs for the Nineties	A+ (3/98)	A (13/98)	A− (27/98)	4, 11–12	1, 3, 5–10	15
College Connection, The	A+ (2/63)	A (12/63)	A− (15/63)	4, 9	3, 10	16
Culinary Careers: People, Professionalism, Service	B+ (29/98)	A (15/98)	B+ (31/98)	0	4, 8, 11	16
Dialing for Jobs	B (27/63)	A− (18/63)	B+ (25/63)	7	6	17
Did You Get My Message?	D+ (90/98)	C− (89/98)	C− (80/98)	0	2, 7	17
Does Your Résumé Wear Blue Jeans?	C+ (44/63)	C (50/63)	C+ (43/63)	0	7	18
Dynamic Interviewing	B (46/98)	B+ (31/98)	C− (88/98)	7	2, 12	18
Effective Answers to Interview Questions	C+ (59/98)	C+ (65/98)	C+ (66/98)	0	2, 7	19
Effective Interviewing Skills	C (71/98)	C+ (60/98)	B− (55/98)	0	2, 7	19
Effective Résumés and Job Applications	B− (38/63)	C+ (38/63)	B− (37/63)	0	7	20
Effective Telephone Techniques	D+ (98/98)	D+ (96/98)	D+ (98/98)	0	6–7	20
Employers' Expectations (Or What the Dickens Do Employers Want?)	D+ (59/63)	C− (57/63)	D+ (59/63)	0	0	21
Entrepreneurship: A Vision for Everyone	C+ (65/98)	C (79/98)	C (73/98)	0	1, 3–8, 10, 12	21
Establishing a Child Care Enterprise	A− (17/63)	B (29/63)	A+ (5/63)	10	8	22
Everyone a Problem Solver	B− (36/63)	B (27/63)	B− (35/63)	9	0	22
Feeling Good About Me	B+ (22/63)	B (28/63)	A− (14/63)	1	2	23
Find the Job World	C (45/63)	B− (35/63)	C+ (45/63)	0	7	23

Career Counseling Videotapes (in alphabetical order)   *(continued)*

Title	Overall rating	Instructional effectiveness	Production quality	NOICC A	NOICC B	Page
Finding the Right College	B+ (32/98)	A (20/98)	B (49/98)	0	4, 6, 9, 12	24
Fitting In: A New Look at Peer Pressure	C+ (64/98)	B (47/98)	C+ (64/98)	0	1–2, 9	24
Follow My Directions	C− (54/63)	B− (32/63)	C− (52/63)	0	0	25
Food Service Industry (The): Career Opportunities	B (31/63)	B (31/63)	A− (19/63)	0	0	25
Four Stages of Interviewing, The	C+ (66/98)	B+ (38/98)	B (40/98)	0	2, 7	26
From High School to College: Choice/Transition	A+ (2/98)	A+ (6/98)	A+ (3/98)	0	3–4, 9, 12	26
Get a Job	D+ (62/63)	D+ (60/63)	D+ (60/63)	0	0	27
Getting a Good Start	B (44/98)	B− (51/98)	B+ (35/98)	0	2, 5	27
Go for It! A Career Video for Early Teens	B− (55/98)	B (43/98)	C+ (62/98)	0	3, 6, 9, 12	28
Go for It! Careers in Tooling & Machining	B− (33/63)	A− (17/63)	B (31/63)	0	0	28
Go, Go Goals! How to Get There	A (8/63)	A (11/63)	A (10/63)	9	5	29
Got a Job Interview, Learn the Skills	A− (24/98)	A (16/98)	A+ (9/98)	0	1–12	29
Has Anybody Seen Phil?	A+ (4/98)	A (12/98)	A+ (1/98)	0	1–3, 9–10	30
How to Get Interviews and Organizing Your Time	D+ (63/63)	D+ (63/63)	D+ (63/63)	0	0	30
How to Get the Job You Want	C (50/63)	C− (52/63)	C (49/63)	0	7	31
How to Keep a Job: Self-Management Skills	A (13/98)	A− (27/98)	A (17/98)	2, 5	1, 3, 8–10	31
How to Present a Professional Image, Vol. 1	B− (34/63)	B− (34/63)	B (30/63)	0	1, 2, 5, 11	32
How to Succeed in the Changing Workplace	C+ (43/63)	C (46/63)	C+ (41/63)	3, 8	5	32

(continued)

Career Counseling Videotapes (in alphabetical order) *(continued)*

Title	Overall rating	Instructional effectiveness	Production quality	NOICC A	NOICC B	Page
I Blew It: Learning from Failure	C (78/98)	C+ (71/98)	C (74/98)	0	1–2	33
I Like Being Me: Self-Esteem	A+ (9/98)	A+ (5/98)	A+ (4/98)	1–3	5, 9, 11	33
Identify Your Skills	C– (83/98)	D+ (93/98)	C+ (68/98)	0	7, 12	34
Images of Marketing Education (M-90–100)	C (74/98)	C– (81/98)	C (70/98)	0	4, 8	34
Impact of Single Parenting, The	C+ (60/98)	B (45/98)	C– (86/98)	0	3, 10–11	35
Interviewing Skills	C (48/63)	C– (54/63)	C (48/63)	0	7	35
It Only Takes Once	A (16/98)	A+ (7/98)	A+ (7/98)	9	1–3, 9	36
It's a New World	B+ (34/98)	B– (54/98)	A– (29/98)	8, 11	1, 3–7, 9–10, 12	36
Job Connection: Applying for Work	C (76/98)	C+ (69/98)	C (72/98)	0	7	37
Job Hunt: Staying on Track	B– (54/98)	C+ (66/98)	B (42/98)	0	6–7	37
Job Interviewing	C+ (61/98)	A– (28/98)	B+ (39/98)	0	2, 7	38
Job Search: Locating Potential Employers	C– (80/98)	C– (82/98)	C– (81/98)	0	4, 6–7, 9, 12	38
Job Search Methods that Get Results	C– (85/98)	B– (58/98)	C (76/98)	0	6–7	39
Job Search Strategies	A (11/63)	A– (13/63)	A (11/63)	6, 7, 12	0	39
Job Survival Skills: It's a Jungle Out There	C (72/98)	C+ (59/98)	B– (57/98)	0	2, 5, 7, 10	40
Job World Literacy	D+ (60/63)	D+ (58/63)	D+ (62/63)	0	0	40
Jobs for the 90's	A (13/63)	A (7/63)	A– (13/63)	4, 8, 12	3, 6, 10	41
Kylie's Song	B+ (21/63)	B (30/63)	A– (18/63)	1	3, 9	41

Career Counseling Videotapes (in alphabetical order)   *(continued)*

Title	Overall rating	Instructional effectiveness	Production quality	NOICC A	NOICC B	Page
Let's Go: Success on the Job	B− (48/98)	C+ (70/98)	B− (58/98)	0	2, 5, 7, 10–12	42
Life After High School: Manufacturing Workers	A (17/98)	A− (29/98)	A (12/98)	4	3, 5, 9–12	42
Making Contacts: The Power of Networking	C− (82/98)	C (80/98)	C (77/98)	0	2–3, 7, 12	43
Making It on Your First Job	C+ (39/63)	B− (36/63)	B− (38/63)	0	2, 5	43
Management and Leadership Skills for Women, Vol. 1	C (51/63)	C (51/63)	C (46/63)	11	10	44
Marketing Your Vocational Skills-Competencies	B− (52/98)	B+ (36/98)	C+ (69/98)	0	4–7, 11–12	44
Minou	C (79/98)	D+ (95/98)	B− (53/98)	0	1–3, 5, 8–10	45
Miracle Résumé, The—Creating Effective Résumés	D+ (96/98)	D+ (97/98)	C− (87/98)	0	7	45
Mirror, Mirror	B+ (35/98)	B− (48/98)	C+ (60/98)	4, 11	1, 8–10, 12	46
Moving Up	B+ (38/98)	B+ (32/98)	B+ (32/98)	0	1–4, 7, 9, 12	46
MUSH! Alaskan Grit and the Winning Spirit	A+ (1/63)	A+ (1/63)	A+ (1/63)	0	1, 5, 9, 10	47
Navigating Your Course	C− (52/63)	C− (55/63)	C (51/63)	0	7	47
Negotiating Competitive Salaries and Benefits	A+ (1/98)	A+ (1/98)	A+ (2/98)	6, 8	1–3, 5, 7, 9, 12	48
Nobody Listens	C (47/63)	C (45/63)	C+ (44/63)	0	4	48
Not Just a Job: Career Planning for Women	C+ (58/98)	C (78/98)	B (44/98)	0	1, 3–7, 9–12	49
Not Me! A Drama About Crack Abuse Among Teenagers	A+ (4/63)	A− (15/63)	A+ (3/63)	0	1, 9	49

(continued)

Career Counseling Videotapes (in alphabetical order)   *(continued)*

Title	Overall rating	Instructional effectiveness	Production quality	NOICC A	NOICC B	Page
Only the Good Need Apply	D+ (97/98)	D+ (98/98)	D+ (94/98)	0	7	50
Organize Your Job Search	C− (87/98)	C (72/98)	C− (84/98)	0	6–7	50
Out of a Job	C− (53/63)	C (47/63)	C− (54/63)	0	3, 8	51
Outside	A (15/98)	B −(49/98)	A (11/98)	0	1, 3, 5, 9, 11–12	51
Paper Job Search Tools	C− (86/98)	C− (90/98)	C (75/98)	0	2	52
Personal Goals: Your Path to Success	C− (57/63)	D+ (61/63)	D+ (58/63)	0	9	52
Phonework: Life Skills	B+ (20/63)	C+ (40/63)	C (47/63)	6, 8	3, 4	53
Planning a Successful Job Hunt	A+ (6/98)	A+ (3/98)	A− (21/98)	0	6, 8–9	53
Power of Choice, The—Self-Esteem	A− (19/98)	A− (24/98)	A− (24/98)	1	2–3, 9	54
Preparing for the Jobs of the 1990's: What You Should Know, Vol. 1	C (46/63)	C+ (43/63)	C− (53/63)	0	2	54
Professional Telephone Skills (Vol. 1)	B (29/63)	C+ (42/63)	B− (33/63)	0	0	55
Profiles: People & Jobs Professional Specialty Occupations	C− (84/98)	C (73/98)	C− (82/98)	0	4, 6, 8, 10	55
Proud to Be Me: Developing Self-Esteem	B+ (23/63)	A+ (4/63)	B (26/63)	1	5	56
Putting the Bars Behind You	A+ (3/63)	A− (14/63)	A+ (2/63)	7	1, 2, 3, 5, 11, 12	56
Résumé Experience, The	D+ (95/98)	C− (88/98)	D+ (96/98)	0	0	57
Résumé Remedy	A (9/63)	A (9/63)	B+ (20/63)	0	7, 12	57
Risk-Taking and You	B (41/98)	B+ (34/98)	B+ (36/98)	0	1, 3, 9	58

Career Counseling Videotapes (in alphabetical order)   *(continued)*

Title	Overall rating	Instructional effectiveness	Production quality	NOICC A	NOICC B	Page
Roofing Careers	B+ (37/98)	B (40/98)	B+ (34/98)	0	6, 8, 10–11	58
Self-Defeating Behavior: How to Stop It	B− (56/98)	C+ (61/98)	B− (59/98)	0	1–3, 5, 9	59
Self-Esteem and Peak Performance, Vol. 1	A (7/63)	A− (19/63)	A (9/63)	0	1, 2, 5, 9	59
Self-Esteem—The Personal Development Series	C (70/98)	B− (50/98)	C+ (61/98)	0	1–2, 5	60
Self-Image and Your Career	A+ (8/89)	A− (21/98)	A+ (6/98)	10	1–7, 9, 11–12	60
Setting Goals: The Road to Achievment	B+ (24/63)	B+ (21/63)	B (32/63)	5	2, 3, 4, 9	61
Seven Phases of a Job Interview, The	C− (88/98)	C (74/98)	C (78/98)	0	2, 6–7, 9	61
Seven Secrets to High School, The	D+ (92/98)	C− (83/98)	D+ (95/98)	0	0	62
Shhh! I'm Finding a Job: The Library and Your Self-Directed Job Search	C+ (42/63)	C+ (44/63)	C+ (42/63)	6	7, 12	62
Succeeding in Your Interview	C (49/63)	C (48/63)	C (50/63)	0	7	63
Take This Job and Keep It!	C+ (63/98)	C (77/98)	C− (83/98)	0	2, 5, 8, 10	63
Teenage Parents: Making It Work	D+ (94/98)	D+ (91/98)	D+ (91/98)	0	0	64
Teenage Stress	D+ (93/98)	D+ (92/98)	D+ (97/98)	0	9	64
Ten Fastest Growing Careers: Jobs for the Future Program 1 of 4	A− (22/98)	A (18/98)	A (14/98)	0	3–8, 10–12	65
Tips for a Successful Interview	C+ (67/98)	B+ (35/98)	D+ (92/98)	0	1, 6–8	65

(continued)

Career Counseling Videotapes (in alphabetical order)   *(continued)*

Title	Overall rating	Instructional effectiveness	Production quality	NOICC A	NOICC B	Page
To Be Employed: Ready, Willing & Able	C+ (41/63)	C+ (39/63)	C+ (40/63)	0	5	66
Tonia the Tree	B− (53/98)	C− (86/98)	A− (26/98)	3	1	66
Tooling A Winning Economy	B− (37/63)	C+ (41/63)	B+ (24/63)	0	8	67
Tough New Labor Market, The, and What It Takes to Succeed	B (43/98)	A− (26/98)	B (46/98)	8	3–7, 10–12	67
Tough Times: Finding the Jobs	C+ (40/63)	C (49/63)	B− (39/63)	3, 8	4	68
Trade Secrets—Blue Collar Women Speak Out	A− (16/63)	A+ (5/63)	B (28/63)	11	1, 5, 10	69
Transitions: Choices for Mid Career Changers	B− (57/98)	C+ (62/98)	C− (85/98)	0	1–7, 10, 12	69
Unbridled Opportunities: Careers in the Horse Industry	A+ (5/98)	A+ (2/98)	A+ (5/98)	10	3–9, 11–12	70
Up Close and In Person—The Job Interview	C− (56/63)	C− (53/63)	C− (57/63)	0	7	70
Waiting Room, The	B+ (30/98)	C+ (64/98)	A (16/98)	0	1–2, 5–7	71
Whatcha Gonna Do Now?	B (39/98)	B− (55/98)	B− (51/98)	0	1–2, 4–6, 8–12	71
When The Pressure's On: Groups and You	B+ (25/63)	B+ (25/63)	B (29/63)	0	12, 9	72
Why Work? Six Reasons You Are Better Off Employed	B− (51/98)	B− (52/98)	C+ (65/98)	0	1, 3, 5, 8, 10, 12	72
Winning at Job Hunting in the 90's	A− (23/98)	A (14/98)	A− (23/98)	7, 12	1–2, 6, 8–10	73
Working	A− (21/98)	B (46/98)	A (15/98)	0	1–2, 5, 7, 10	73

Career Counseling Videotapes (in alphabetical order)   (continued)

Title	Overall rating	Instructional effectiveness	Production quality	NOICC A	NOICC B	Page
Working Parents: Balancing Kids and Careers	B− (35/63)	B (26/63)	A− (16/63)	10, 11	8, 12	74
Working Toward a Career	C (77/98)	C (76/98)	D+ (93/98)	0	1, 4–10, 12	74
Working with Your Supervisor	B (40/98)	A− (25/98)	B (43/98)	0	2, 5	75
Would I Work with Me?	B+ (33/98)	C− (87/98)	B+ (37/98)	0	2, 5, 8–10	75
Yes? No? Maybe? Decision-Making Skills	A (14/98)	A+ (4/98)	A− (20/98)	9	1–3, 5, 10	76
Yes! You Can Be a Winner!	A− (15/63)	A (8/63)	B+ (21/63)	1, 5	0	76
You and Your Co-Workers	B− (50/98)	B (42/98)	B+ (38/98)	2	1, 3, 5, 9	77
You Can Choose!—Cooperation	A+ (7/98)	B+ (33/98)	A (10/98)	0	2, 5, 8	77
You Can Say No: Here's How	A+ (5/63)	A+ (3/63)	A+ (6/63)	0	1, 2, 9	78
You're the Pilot	B (28/63)	B− (33/63)	B (27/63)	11	4, 12	78
Your Aptitudes: Related to Learning Job Skills	C− (89/98)	C− (85/98)	C (71/98)	0	6	79
Your Boss and You	A (14/63)	A+ (2/63)	A (8/63)	0	2, 5, 9	79
Your Future: Planning Thru Career Exploration	B+ (36/98)	B (44/98)	A− (22/98)	6	3–5, 9–10, 12	80
Your Interests: Related to Work Activities	C+ (62/98)	C+ (63/98)	C+ (63/98)	0	6, 9–10, 12	80
Your Resume: A Self-Portrait	D+ (61/63)	D+ (59/63)	D+ (61/63)	0	0	81
Your Temperaments: Related to Work Situations	C (73/98)	C+ (68/98)	B− (50/98)	0	1, 4, 9–10	81

SOURCE: From *650 Career Videos: Ratings and Descriptions*, by Richard Feller, Colorado State University. Reprinted by permission. (See p. 238 for complete address and phone number.)

REFERENCES

Aburdene, P., & Naisbitt, J. (1993). *Megatrends for women: From liberation to leadership.* New York: Fawcett Books.

Adkins, D. C. (1947). *Construction and analysis of achievement tests.* Washington, DC: U.S. Government Printing Office.

Alexander, L. C. (1985). *Women in nontraditional careers: A training program manual.* Washington, DC: Women's Bureau, U.S. Government Printing Office.

Amatea, E. S., & Cross, E. G. (1980). Going places: A career guidance program for high school students and their parents. *Vocational Guidance Quarterly, 28*(3), 274–282.

American College Testing Program. (1984). *DISCOVER: A computer-based career development and counselor support system.* Iowa City, IA: Author.

American College Testing Program. (1987). *DISCOVER.* Iowa City, IA: Author.

American College Testing Program. (1996a, Winter). *Activity, 34*(1). Iowa City, IA: Author.

American College Testing Program. (1996b). *The high school profile report, normative data. ACT high school profile report: H.S. graduating class 1995.* Iowa City, IA: Author.

American Psychiatric Association. (1994). *Diagnostic and statistical manual of mental disorders* (4th ed., rev.). Washington, DC: Author.

American Psychological Association. (1985). *Standards for educational and psychological testing.* Washington, DC: Author.

American Psychological Association. (1986). *Guidelines for computer-based tests and interpretations.* Washington, DC: Author.

American Psychological Association. (1990). Ethical principles of psychologists (amended June 2, 1989). *American Psychology,* pp. 453–484. New York: Wiley.

American Psychological Association. (1992). *Ethical guidelines of the American Psychological Association.* Washington, DC: Author.

Anastasi, A. (1954). *Psychological testing.* New York: Macmillan.

Anastasi, A. (1988). *Psychological testing* (6th ed.). New York: Macmillan.

Anderson, T. B., & Olsen, L. C. (1965). Congruence of self and ideal self and occupational choices. *Personnel and Guidance Journal, 44,* 171–176.

Arbeiter, S., Aslanian, C. B., Schmerbeck, F. A., & Brickell, H. M. (1978). *40 million Americans in career transition: The need for information.* New York: College Entrance Examination Board.

Arbona, C. (1995). Theory and research on racial and ethnic minorities: Hispanic Americans. In Frederick T. L. Leong (Ed.), *Career development and vocational behavior of racial and ethnic minorities* (pp. 37–61). Mahwah, NJ: Erlbaum.

Argeropoulous, J. (1981). *Burnout, stress management, and wellness.* Moravia, NY: Chronicle Guidance.

Ashkenas, R., Ulrich, D., Jick, T., & Kerr, St. (1995). *The boundaryless organization: Breaking the chains of organizational structure.* San Francisco: Jossey-Bass.

Astin, A. W. (1984). Student values: Knowing more about where we are today. *Bulletin of the American Association of Higher Education, 36*(9), 10–13.

Axelson, J. A. (1993). *Counseling and development in a multicultural society* (2nd ed.). Pacific Grove, CA: Brooks/Cole.

Bailey, L. J., & Stadt, R. W. (1973). *Career education: New approaches to human development.* Bloomington, IL: McKnight Publishing Company.

Baker, L. J., Dearborn, M., Hastings, J. E., & Hamberger, K. (1988). Type A behavior in women: A review. *Health Psychology, 3,* 477–497.

Bandura, A. (1977). *Social learning theory.* Englewood Cliffs, NJ: Prentice-Hall.

Bandura, A. (1986). *Social foundations of thought and action: A social cognitive theory.* Englewood Cliffs, NJ: Prentice-Hall.

Bandura, A. (1989). Regulation of cognitive processes through perceived self-efficacy. *Developmental Psychology, 25,* 729–735.

Barnet, R. J., & Cavanagh, J. (1994). *Global dreams: Imperial corporations and the new world order.* New York: Simon & Schuster.

Barry, J., & Glick, D. (1992, Nov. 23). Crossing the gay minefield. *Newsweek,* p. 26.

Basow, S. A. (1992). *Gender: Stereotypes and roles* (3rd ed.). Pacific Grove, CA: Brooks/Cole.

Beck, A. T. (1985). Cognitive therapy. In H. J. Kaplan & B. J. Sadock (Eds.), *Comprehensive textbook of psychiatry* (pp. 1432–1438). Baltimore: Williams & Wilkins.

Benin, M. H., & Agostinelli, J. (1988). Husbands' and wives' satisfaction with the division of labor. *Journal of Marriage and the Family, 50,* 349–361.

Bennett, G. K., Seashore, H. G., & Wesman, A. G. (1974). *Differential aptitude test.* San Antonio, TX: The Psychological Corporation.

Bernardo, D. H., Shehan, C. L., & Leslie, G. R. (1987). A residue of tradition: Jobs, careers, and spouses' time in housework. *Journal of Marriage and the Family, 49,* 381–390.

Berry, R. E., & Williams, F. L. (1987). Assessing the relationship between quality of life and marital and income satisfaction: A path analytical approach. *Journal of Marriage and the Family, 49,* 107–116.

Betz, N. E. (1992a). Career assessment: A review of critical issues. In S. D. Brown & R. W. Lent (Eds.), *Handbook of counseling psychology* (pp. 453–484). New York: Wiley.

Betz, N. E. (1992b). Counseling uses of career self-efficacy theory. *The Career Development Quarterly, 41,* 22–26.

Betz, N. E. (1993). Issues of the use of ability and interest measures with women. *Journal of Career Assessment, 1,* 217–232.

Betz, N. E. (1994a). Basic issues and concepts in career counseling for women. In W. B. Walsh & S. H. Osipow (Eds.), *Career counseling for women: Contemporary topics in vocational psychology* (pp. 1–41). Hillsdale, NJ: Erlbaum.

Betz, N. E. (1994b). Self-concept theory in career development and counseling. *Career Development Quarterly, 43*, 32–42.

Betz, N. E., & Fitzgerald, L. F. (1987). *The career psychology of women*. Orlando, FL: Academic Press.

Betz, N. E., & Fitzgerald, L. F. (1995). Career assessment and intervention with racial and ethnic minorities. In Frederick T. L. Leong (Ed.), *Career development and vocational behavior of racial and ethnic minorities* (pp. 263–277). Mahwah, NJ: Erlbaum.

Betz, N. E., & Hackett, G. (1986). Applications of self-efficacy theory to understanding career choice behavior. *Journal of Social and Clinical Psychology, 4*, 279–289.

Biehler, R. F., & Hudson, L. M. (1986). *Developmental psychology*. Boston: Allyn & Bacon.

Blau, P. M., Gustad, J. W., Jessor, R., Parnes, H. S., & Wilcox, R. S. (1956). Occupational choices: A conceptual framework. *Industrial Labor Relations Review, 9*, 531–543.

Bloland, P. A., & Edwards, P. B. (1981). Work and leisure: A counseling synthesis. *Vocational Guidance Quarterly, 30*(2), 101–108.

Blustein, D. L. (1990). An eclectic definition of psychotherapy: A developmental contextual view. In J. K. Zeig & W. M. Munion (Eds.), *What is psychotherapy? Contemporary perspectives* (pp. 244–248). San Francisco: Jossey-Bass.

Bolles, R. N. (1993). *A practical manual for job-hunters and career changers: What color is your parachute?* (9th ed.). Berkeley, CA: Ten Speed Press.

Borow, H. (Ed.). (1964). *Man in the world at work*. Boston: Houghton Mifflin.

Bottoms, J. E., Evans, R. N., Hoyt, K. B., & Willer, J. C. (Eds.). (1972). *Career education resource guide*. Morristown, NJ: General Learning Corporation.

Bowman, S. L. (1995). Career intervention strategies and assessment issues for African Americans. In Frederick T. L. Leong (Ed.), *Career development and vocational behavior of racial and ethnic minorities* (pp. 137–161). Mahwah, NJ: Erlbaum.

Brammer, L. M., & Abrego, P. J. (1981). Intervention strategies for coping with transitions. *The Counseling Psychologist, 9*, 27.

Bretz, R. D., Jr., & Judge, T. A. (1994). Person-organization fit and the theory of work adjustment: Implications for satisfaction, tenure, and career success. *Journal of Vocational Behavior, 44*, 32–54.

Brewer, J. M. (1918). *The vocational guidance movement*. New York: Macmillan.

Brislin, R. (1993). *Understanding culture's influence on behavior*. Fort Worth, TX: Harcourt Brace Jovanovich.

Brolin, D. E., & Gysbers, N. C. (1989). Career education for students with disabilities. *Journal of Counseling and Development, 68*, 155–159.

Brown, B. B., Mounts, N., Lamborn, S. D., & Steinberg, L. (1993). Parenting practices and peer group affiliation in adolescence. *Child Development, 65*, 467–482.

Brown, D. (1980). Life-planning workshop for high school students. *The School Counselor, 29*(1), 77–83.

Brown, D. (1996). Brown's values-based, holistic model of career and life-role choices and satisfaction. In D. Brown, L. Brooks, & Associates (Eds.), *Career choice and development* (3rd ed.) (pp 337–338). San Francisco: Jossey-Bass.

Brown, D., & Brooks, L. (1991). *Career counseling techniques*. Boston: Allyn & Bacon.

Brown, D., Brooks, L., & Associates. (1990). *Career choice and development* (2nd ed.). San Francisco: Jossey-Bass.

Brown, D., Brooks, L., & Associates. (1996). *Career choice and development* (3rd ed.). San Francisco: Jossey-Bass.

Brown, D., & Crace, R. K. (1995). A values-based model of career choice and satisfaction. *Career Development Quarterly, 44*.

Brown, D., & Minor, C. W. (1989). *Working in America: A status report on planning and problems*. Alexandria, VA: National Career Development Association.

Brown, D., Minor, C. W., & Jepsen, D. A. (1991). The opinions of minorities about preparing for work: Report of the second NCDA national survey. *The Career Development Quarterly, 40,* 5–19.

Bureau of Indian Affairs. (1993). *Federally recognized tribes*. Washington, DC: U.S. Department of Interior, Bureau of Indian Affairs.

Burlew, Larry D. (1996). Career counseling is not mental health counseling: More myth than fact. In R. Feller & G. Walz (Eds.), *Career transitions in turbulent times* (pp. 371–379). Greensboro, NC: ERIC Counseling and Student Services Clearinghouse, University of North Carolina.

Burton, M., & Wedemeyer, R. (1991). *In transition*. New York: Harper Business Publications.

California Advisory Council on Vocational Education. (1977). *Barriers and bridges*. Sacramento: California State Department of General Services.

Campbell, R. E., & Heffernan, J. M. (1983). Adult vocational behavior. In W. B. Walsh & S. H. Osipow (Eds.), *Handbook of vocational psychology: Vol. 1.* (pp. 223–262). Hillsdale, NJ: Erlbaum.

Career information center. (1979). *Career education occupational clusters*. Austin, TX: Austin Independent School District.

Carson, A. D., & Mowesian, R. (1993). Moderators of the prediction of job satisfaction from congruence: A test of Holland's theory. *Journal of Career Assessment, 1,* 130–144.

Carter, J. K. (1995, Winter). Applying customer service strategies to career services. *Journal of Career Development, 22*(2).

Cattell, R. B., Eber, H. W., & Tatsuoka, M. M. (1970). *Handbook for the sixteen personality factor questionnaire (16PF)*. Champaign, IL: Institute for Personality and Ability Testing.

Cautela, J., & Wisock, P. (1977). The thought-stopping procedure: Description, application and learning theory interpretations. *The Psychological Record, 2,* 264–266.

Cente for choice. (1980). Dallas: Richland College, Dallas County Community College.

Cetron, M., & Davies, O. (1988). *The great job shake-out*. New York: Simon & Schuster.

Cetron, M., & Gayle, M. (1991). *Educational renaissance*. New York: St. Martin's Press.

Chadwick, B. A., & Heaton, T. B. (1992). *Statistical handbook on the American family*. Phoenix: Oryx Press.

Charting the projections: 1994–2005. (1995, Fall). *Occupational Outlook Quarterly, 39*(2), 2–3.

Chartrand, J. M. (1991). The evolution of trait-and-factor career counseling: A person-environment fit approach. *Journal of Counseling & Development, 69,* 518–524.

Cherniss, C. (1980). *Staff burnout: Job stress in the human services*. Newbury Park, CA: Sage.

Chipping away at the glass ceiling. (1991, May). *Nations Business,* pp. 20–21.

Chodorow, N. J. (1989). *Feminism and psychoanalytic theory*. New Haven, CT: Yale University Press.

Chu, L. (1981, April). *Asian-American women in educational research*. Paper presented at annual conference of the American Educational Research Association, Los Angeles.

Chusmir, L. H. (1983). Characteristics and predictive dimensions of women who make nontraditional vocational choices. *Personnel and Guidance Journal, 62*(1), 43–48.

Chusmir, L. H. (1990). Men who make nontraditional career choices. *Journal of Counseling and Development, 69,* 11–16.

Chusmir, L. H., & Parker, B. (1991). Gender and situational differences in managers' lives: A look at work and home lives. *Journal of Business Research, 23,* 325–335.

Clark-Stewart, A. (1993). *Daycare* (rev. ed.). Cambridge, MA: Harvard University Press.

Clausen, J. S. (1991). Adolescent competence and the shaping of the life course. *American Journal of Sociology, 96,* 805–842.

Cochran, L. (1994). What is a career problem? *Career Development Quarterly, 42,* 204–215.

Cole, M. J. (1963, Sept.). *Our Lutheran heritage.* Address to faculty of Texas Lutheran College, Seguin.

Coleman, M. T. (1988). The division of household labor. *Journal of Family Issues, 9* (1), 132–148.

Collin, A. (1994). Fracture lines for career. *NICEC Bulletin, 42,* 6–11.

Comstock, G. A., with Haejung Paik. (1991). *Television and the American child.* San Diego: Academic Press.

Cook, D. W. (1981). Impact of disability on the individual. In R. M. Parker & C. E. Hansen (Eds.), *Rehabilitation counseling.* Boston: Allyn & Bacon.

Coon-Carty, H. M. (1995). *The relation of work-related abilities, vocational interests, and self-efficacy beliefs: A meta-analytic investigation.* Unpublished master's thesis, Loyola University, Chicago.

Copeland, L., & Griggs, L. (1985). *Going international.* New York: Random House.

Cordes, C. L., & Dougherty, T. W. (1993). A review and integration of research on job burnout. *Academy of Management Review, 18,* 621–656.

Corey, G. (1991). *Theory and practice of counseling and psychotherapy.* Pacific Grove, CA: Brooks/Cole.

Cormier, W., & Cormier, L. S. (1991). *Interviewing strategies for helpers: Fundamental skills and cognitive behavioral interventions* (3rd ed.). Pacific Grove, CA: Brooks/Cole.

Courtenay, B. C. (1994). Are psychological models of adult development still important for the practice of adult education? *Adult Education Quarterly, 44* (3), 145–153.

Cox, M. J., Owen, M. T., Henderson, V. K., & Margand, N. A. (1992). Prediction of infant-father and infant-mother attachment. *Developmental Psychology, 28,* 474–483.

Cozby, P. C. (1973). Self-disclosure: A literature review. *Psychological Bulletin, 79,* 73–91.

Crace, R. K., & Brown, D. (1996). *Life values inventory.* Minneapolis, MN: National Computer Systems.

Craig, R. J. (1989). *Clinical and diagnostic interviewing.* Northvale, NJ: Aronson.

Crites, J. O. (1973). *Theory and research handbook: Career maturity inventory.* Monterey, CA: CTB-MacMillan-McGraw-Hill.

Crites, J. O. (in press). Assessment and counseling for career mastery. In M. L. Savickas & W. B. Walsh (Eds.), *Handbook of career counseling and practice.* Palo Alto, CA: Davies-Black.

Crites, J. O., & Savickas, M. L. (1995). *Career maturity inventory.* Odessa, FL: Psychological Assessment Resources.

Crites, J. O., & Savickas, M. L. (1996). Revision of the career maturity inventory. *Journal of Career Assessment, 4*(2), 131–138.

Cronbach, L. J. (1949). *Essentials of psychological testing.* New York: Harper & Brothers.

Cronbach, L. J. (1984). *Essentials of psychological testing* (4th ed.). New York: Harper & Row.

Cronbach, L. J. (1990). *Essentials of psychological testing* (5th ed.). New York: Harper & Row.

Curnow, T. C. (1989). Vocational development of persons with disability. *The Career Development Quarterly, 37,* 269–277.

Dancer, L. S., & Gilbert, L. A. (1993). Spouses' family work participation and its relation to wives' occupational level. *Sex Roles, 28,* 127–145.

Daniels, J. L. (1981). World of work in disabling conditions. In R. M. Parker & C. E. Hansen (Eds.), *Rehabilitation counseling* (pp. 169–199). Boston: Allyn & Bacon.

Danish, S. J. (1977). Human development and human services. A marriage proposal. In I. Iscoe, B. L. Bloom, & C. D. Spielberger (Eds.), *Community psychology in transition.* New York: Halsted Press.

Danish, S. J., & D'Augelli, A. R. (1983). *Helping skills II: Life-development intervention.* New York: Human Sciences Press.

Davidson, P. E., & Anderson, H. D. (1937). *Occupational mobility in an American community.* Palo Alto, CA: Stanford University Press.

Davis, D. A., Hagan, N., & Strouf, J. (1962). Occupational choice of twelve-year-olds. *Personnel and Guidance Journal, 40,* 628–629.

Davis, D. M. (1990). Portrayals of women in prime-time network television: Some demographic characteristics. *Sex Roles, 23,* 325–332.

Davis, F. B. (1947). *Utilizing human talent.* Washington, DC: American Council on Education.

Dawis, R. V. (1991). Vocational interests, values, and preferences. In M. D. Dunnette & L. M. Hough (Eds.), *Handbook of industrial and organizational psychology: Vol. 2* (2nd ed.) (pp. 833–871). Palo Alto, CA: Consulting Psychologists Press.

Dawis, R. V. (1996). The theory of work adjustment and person-environment-correspondence counseling. In D. Brown, L. Brooks, & Associates (Eds.), *Career choice and development* (3rd ed.) (pp. 75–115). San Francisco: Jossey-Bass.

Dawis, R. V., Dohm, T. E., Lofquist, L. H., Chartrand, J. M., & Due, A. M. (1987). *Minnesota occupational classification system III.* Minneapolis: Vocational Psychology Research, Department of Psychology, University of Minnesota.

Dawis, R. V., & Lofquist, L. H. (1984). *A psychological theory of work adjustment: An individual differences model and its application.* Minneapolis: University of Minnesota.

Defrank, R., & Ivancevich, J. M. (1986). Job loss: An individual-level review and model. *Journal of Vocational Behavior, 19,* 1–20.

de Vaus, D., & McCallister, I. (1991). Gender and work orientation. *Work and Occupations, 18,* 72–93.

Diamond, E. E. (1975). Overview. In E. E. Diamond (Ed.), *Issues of sex bias and sex fairness in career interest movement.* Washington, DC: U.S. Government Printing Office.

Dickson, G. L., & Parmerlee, J. R. (1980). The occupational family tree: A career counseling technique. *The School Counselor, 28*(2).

Dittenhafer, C. A., & Lewis, J. P. (1973). *Guidelines for establishing career resource centers.* Harrisburg: Pennsylvania Department of Education.

Division of Testing Staff, U.S. Employment Service (USES). (1978). Ten years of USES test research on the disadvantaged. *Vocational Guidance Quarterly, 26,* 334–341.

Dosser, D. A. (1982). Male inexpressiveness: Behavioral interventions. In K. Solomon & N. B. Levy (Eds.), *Men in transition* (pp. 343–432). New York: Plenum.

Doyle, J. A. (1983). *The male experience.* Dubuque, IA: Wm. D. Brown.

Doyle, R. E. (1992). *Essential skills and strategies in the helping process.* Pacific Grove, CA: Brooks/Cole.

Drucker, P. F. (1992). *Managing for the future.* New York: Truman Talley Brooks/Dutton.

Dudley, G. A., & Tiedeman, D. V. (1977). *Career development: Exploration and commitment.* Muncie, IN: Accelerated Development.

Eccles, J. S. (1987). Gender roles and women's achievement-related decisions. *Psychology of Women Quarterly, 11,* 135–172.

Eccles, J. S. (1993). School and family effects on the ontogeny of children's interests, self-perceptions, and activity choices. In J. E. Jacobs (Eds.), *Nebraska Symposium on Motivation: 1992, Vol. 40* (pp. 145–208). Lincoln: University of Nebraska Press.

Edelwich, J., & Brodsky, A. (1980). *Burnout: Stages of disillusionment in the helping professionals.* New York: Human Sciences Press.

Eldridge, N. S. (1987). Gender issues in counseling same-sex couples. *Professional Psychology: Research and Practice, 18*(6), 567–572.

Elkind, D. (1968). Cognitive development in adolescence. In J. F. Adams (Ed.), *Understanding adolescence*. Boston: Allyn & Bacon.

Elkind, D. (1981). *A sympathetic understanding of the child from six to sixteen*. Boston: Allyn & Bacon.

Ellis, A. (1962). *Reason and emotion in psychotherapy*. Secaucus, NJ: Lyle Stuart.

Ellis, A. (1971). *Growth through reason*. Hollywood, CA: Wilshire Books.

Ellis, A., & Grieger, R. (1977). *Handbook of rational-emotive therapy*. New York: Springer.

Emener, W. G., & Rubin, S. E. (1980). Rehabilitation counselor roles and functions and sources of role strain. *Journal of Applied Rehabilitation Counseling, 11*(2), 57–69.

Engels, D. W. (Ed.). (1994). *The professional practice of career counseling and consultation: A resource document* (2nd ed.). Alexandria, VA: American Counseling Association.

Englander, M. E. (1960). A psychological analysis of a vocational choice: Teaching. *Journal of Counseling Psychology, 7*, 257–264.

Epstein, C. F. (1980). Institutional barriers: What keeps women out of the executive suite? In M. O. Morgan (Ed.), *Managing career development*. New York: Van Nostrand.

Erikson, E. H. (1950). *Childhood and society*. New York: Norton.

Erikson, E. H. (1963). *Childhood and society* (2nd ed.). New York: Norton.

Etaugh, C., & Liss, M. B. (1992). Home, school, and playroom. Training grounds for adult gender roles. *Sex Roles, 26*, 129–147.

Ettinger, J. M. (Ed.). (1991). *Improved career decision making in a changing world*. Garrett Park, MD: Garrett Park Press.

Evanoski, P. O., & Tse, F. W. (1989). Career awareness program for Chinese and Korean American parents. *Journal of Counseling and Development, 67*, 472–474.

Fagot, B. I., & Leinbach, M. D. (1989). The young child's gender schema: Environmental input, internal organization. *Child Development, 60*, 663–672.

Farber, B. A., & Heifetz, L. J. (1981). The satisfaction and stresses of psychotherapeutic work: A factor analytic study. *Professional Psychology, 12*(5), 621–630.

Feck, V. (1971). *What vocational education teachers and counselors should know about urban disadvantaged youth* (ERIC Clearinghouse, Information Series No. 46). Columbus: Ohio State University, Center for Vocational Technical Education.

Feldman, D. C. (1988). *Managing careers in organizations*. Glenview, IL: Scott, Foresman.

Feller, R. (1994). *650 Career videos: Ratings, reviews and descriptions*. Ft. Collins, CO: Colorado State University.

Feller, R., & Walz, G. (1996). *Career transitions in turbulent times: Exploring work, learning and careers*. Greensboro, NC: ERIC Counseling and Student Services Clearing House, University of North Carolina.

Fernandez, J. P. (1986). *Child care and corporate productivity*. Lexington, MA: Lexington Books.

Fernandez, M. S. (1988). Issues in counseling southeast Asian students. *Journal of Multicultural Counseling and Development, 16*, 157–166.

Ferree, M. M. (1984). Class, housework, and happiness: Women's work and life satisfaction. *Sex Roles, 11*, 1057–1074.

Fine, M., & Asch, A. (1988). Disability beyond stigma: Social interactions, discrimination, and activism. *Journal of Social Issues, 44*(1), 3–21.

Firth, H., & Britton, P. (1989). Burnout: Absence and turnover amongst British nursing staff. *Journal of Occupational Psychology, 62*, 55–59.

Fitzgerald, L. F., & Betz, N. E. (1994). Career development in cultural context: The role of gender, race, class and sexual orientation. In M. Savickas & R. Lent (Eds.), *Convergence in career development theories: Implications for science and practice* (pp. 103–115). Palo Alto, CA: Consulting Psychologists Press, Inc.

Fitzgerald, L. F., & Ormerod, A. J. (1991). Perceptions of sexual harassment: The influence of gender and academic context. *Psychology of Women Quarterly, 15,* 281–294.

Flanders, R. B. (1980). NOICC: A coordinator for occupational information. *Occupational Outlook Quarterly, 24*(4), 22–28.

Flannelly, S. (1995). *A study of values shifts across life roles.* Unpublished dissertation, University of North Carolina, Chapel Hill.

Forney, D. S., Wallace-Schultzman, F., & Wiggens, T. T. (1982). Burnout among career development professionals: Preliminary findings and implications. *Personnel and Guidance Journal, 60,* 435–439.

Fouad, N. A. (1995). Career behavior of Hispanics: Assessment and career intervention. In F. T. L. Leong (Ed.), *Career development and vocational behavior of racial and ethnic minorities* (pp. 165–187). Mahwah, NJ: Erlbaum.

Fouad, N. A., & Spreda, S. L. (1995). Use of interest inventories with special populations. *Journal of Career Assessment, 3,* 453–468.

French, M. (1992). *The war against women.* New York: Summit Books.

Frenza, M. (1982). *Counseling women for life decisions.* Ann Arbor: ERIC Counseling and Personnel Services Clearinghouse, University of Michigan.

Freudenberger, H. J. (1974). Staff burnout. *Journal of Social Issues, 30*(1), 159–165.

Freudenberger, H. J., & Richelson, G. (1980). *Burnout: The high cost of high achievement.* Garden City, NY: Anchor Press.

Friedman, M., & Rosenman, R. (1974). *Type A behavior and your heart.* Greenwich, CT: Fawcett.

Garbarino, J. (1992). The meaning of poverty in the world of children. *American Behavioral Scientist, 35,* 220–237.

Garland, S. B. (1991, Aug. 19). Throwing stones at the glass ceiling. *Business Week,* p. 29.

Garte, S. H., & Rosenblum, M. L. (1978). Lighting fires in burned-out counselors. *Personnel and Guidance Journal, 57*(3), 158–160.

Geary, J. (1972). Forty newspapers forty. In J. E. Bottoms, R. N. Evans, K. B. Hoyt, & J. C. Willers (Eds.), *Career education resource guide.* Morristown, NJ: General Learning Corporation.

Gelatt, H. B. (1989). Positive uncertainty: A new decision-making framework for counseling. *Journal of Counseling Psychology, 36*(2), 252–256.

Gelatt, H. B. (1996). Developing a future sense. In R. Feller & G. Walz (Eds.), *Career transitions in turbulent times* (pp. 387–393). Greensboro, NC: ERIC Counseling and Student Services Clearinghouse, University of North Carolina.

General aptitude test battery. (1970). Washington, DC: U.S. Government Printing Office.

Ghiselli, E. (1966). *The validity of occupational aptitude tests.* New York: Wiley.

Gianakos, I., & Subick, L. M. (1986). The relationship of gender and sex-role orientation to vocational undecidedness. *Journal of Vocational Behavior, 29,* 42–51.

Gibson, R. L., Mitchell, M. H., & Basile, S. K. (1993). *Counseling in the elementary school: A comprehensive approach.* Boston: Allyn & Bacon.

Gilbert, L. A. (1993). *Two careers/one family.* Newbury Park, CA: Sage.

Gillies, P. (1989). A longitudinal study of the hopes and worries of adolescents. *Journal of Adolescence, 12,* 69–81.

Ginzberg, E. (1966). *Lifestyles of educated American women.* New York: Columbia University Press.

Ginzberg, E. (1972). Toward a theory of occupational choice: A restatement. *The Vocational Guidance Quarterly, 20,* 169–176.

Ginzberg, E. (1984). Career development. In D. Brown & L. Brooks (Eds.), *Career choice and development.* San Francisco: Jossey-Bass.

Ginzberg, E., Ginsburg, S. W., Axelrad, S., & Herma, J. L. (1951). *Occupational choice: An approach to general theory.* New York: Columbia University Press.

Goldberg, H. (1983). *The new male-female relationship.* New York: Morrow.

Goldfried, M. R., & Friedman, J. M. (1982). Clinical behavior therapy and the male sex role. In K. Solomon & N. B. Levy (Eds.), *Men in transition.* New York: Plenum.

Golding, J. M. (1989). Role occupancy and role-specific stress and social support as predictors of depression. *Basic and Applied Social Psychology, 10,* 173–195.

Goleman, D. (1990, July 10). Homophobia: Scientists find clues to its roots. *New York Times,* pp. C1, C11.

Goodenough, F. L. (1949). *Mental testing.* New York: Rinehart.

Gordon, L. V. (1967). *Survey of personal values.* Chicago: Science Research Associates.

Gottfredson, G. D., & Holland, J. L. (1989). *Dictionary of Holland occupational codes.* Odessa, FL: Psychological Assessment Resources.

Gottfredson, G. D., & Holland, J. L. (1991). *The position classification inventory: Professional manual.* Odessa, FL: Psychological Assessment Resources.

Gottfredson, G. D., & Holland, J. L. (1994). *The career attitudes and strategies inventory.* Odessa, FL: Psychological Assessment Resources.

Gottfredson, G. D., Jones, E. M., & Holland, J. L. (1993). Personality and vocational interests: The relation of Holland's six interest dimensions to five robust dimensions of personality. *Journal of Counseling Psychology, 40,* 518–524.

Gottfredson, L. S. (1981). Circumscription and compromise: A developmental theory of occupational aspirations. *Journal of Counseling Psychology, 28*(6), 545–579.

Gottfredson, L. S. (1996). Gottfredson's theory of circumscription and compromise. In D. Brown, L. Brooks, & Associates (Eds.), *Career choice and development* (3rd ed.) (pp. 179–228). San Francisco: Jossey-Bass.

Gould, S., & Parzen, J. (Eds.). (1990). *Enterprising women.* Organization for Economic Cooperation and Development. Columbus: ERIC Clearinghouse on Adult, Career, and Vocational Education. (ERIC Report No. ED 335 463)

Green, L. B., & Parker, H. J. (1965). Parental influence upon adolescents' occupational choice: A test of an aspect of Roe's theory. *Journal of Counseling Psychology, 12,* 379–383.

Greenberger, E., & Steinberg, L. (1986). *When teenagers work: The psychological and social costs of adolescent employment.* New York: Basic Books.

Greenglass, E. R. (1991). Type A behavior, career aspirations, and role conflict in professional women. In M. J. Strube (Ed.), *Type A behavior* (pp. 277–292). Newbury Park, CA: Sage.

Grossman, G. M., & Drier, H. N. (1988). *Apprenticeship 2000: The status of and recommendations for improved counseling, guidance, and information processes.* Columbus: National Center for Research in Vocational Education, Ohio State University. (ERIC Report No. ED 298 356)

Grubb, W. N., Davis, G., Lum, J., Plihal, J., & Mograine, C. (1991). *The cunning hand, the cultured mind: Models for integrating vocational and academic education.* Berkeley, CA: National Center for Research in Vocational Education. (ERIC Report No. ED 334 421)

Gulliksen, H. (1950). *Theory of mental tests.* New York: Wiley.

Gysbers, N. C. (1996). Beyond career development—life career development revisited. In R. Feller & G. Walz (Eds.), *Career transitions in turbulent times* (pp. 11–20). Greensboro, NC: ERIC Counseling and Student Services Clearinghouse, University of North Carolina.

Gysbers, N. C., & Henderson, P. (1988). *Developing and managing your school guidance program.* Alexandria, VA: American Association for Counseling and Development.

Gysbers, N. C., & Moore, E. J. (1987). *Career counseling, skills and techniques for practitioners*. Englewood Cliffs, NJ: Prentice-Hall.

Hackett, G. (1995). Self-efficacy in career choice and development. In A. Bandura (Ed.), *Self-efficacy in changing societies* (pp. 232–258). Cambridge, U.K.: Cambridge University Press.

Hackett, G., & Lent, R. W. (1992). Theoretical advances and current inquiry in career psychology. In S. D. Brown & R. W. Lent (Eds.), *Handbook of counseling psychology* (2nd ed.) (pp. 419–451). New York: Wiley.

Hackett, G., Lent, R. W., & Greenhaus, J. H. (1991). Advances in vocational theory and research: A 20-year retrospective. *Journal of Vocational Behavior, 38,* 3–38.

Hackett, J. C., & Lonborg, S. D. (1994). Career assessment and counseling for women. In W. B. Walsh & S. H. Osipow (Eds.), *Career counseling for women: Contemporary topics in vocational psychology* (pp. 43–85). Hillsdale, NJ: Erlbaum.

Hackett, R. D., & Betz, N. E. (1981). A self-efficacy approach to the career development of women. *Journal of Vocational Behavior, 18,* 326–329.

Halaby, C. N., & Weakliem, D. L. (1989). Worker control and attachment to the firm. *American Journal of Sociology, 95,* 549–591.

Hall, D. T. (Ed.). (1986). *Career development in organizations*. San Francisco: Jossey-Bass.

Hall, D. T. (1990). Career development theory in organizations. In D. Brown & L. Brooks (Eds.), *Career choice and development* (2nd ed.) (pp. 422–455). San Francisco: Jossey-Bass.

Hall, D. T. (1996). *The career is dead: Long live the career*. San Francisco: Jossey-Bass.

Halle, E. (1982). The abandoned husband: When wives leave. In K. Solomon & N. B. Levy (Eds.), *Men in transition*. New York: Plenum.

Halpern, A., Raffeld, P., Irvin, L. D., & Link, R. (1975). *Social and prevocational information battery*. Monterey, CA: CTB-MacMillan-McGraw-Hill.

Halpern, T. P. O. (1977). Degree of client disclosure as a function of past disclosure, counselor disclosure, and counselor facilitativeness. *Journal of Counseling Psychology, 24,* 42–47.

Hammer, M., & Champy, J. (1993). *Reengineering the corporation: A manifesto for business revolution*. New York: HarperCollins.

Hansen, J. C., Collins, R. C., Swanson, J. L., & Fouad, N. A. (1993). Gender differences in the structure of interests. *Journal of Vocational Behavior, 42,* 200–211.

Hansen, L. S. (1970). *Career guidance practices in school and community*. Washington, DC: National Vocational Guidance Association.

Hansen, L. S. (1978). *BORN FREE. Training packets to reduce stereotyping in career options*. Minneapolis: University of Minnesota.

Hansen, L. S. (1990). *Integrative life planning: Work, family and community*. Paper presented at International Round Table for the Advancement of Counseling, July 1990. Helsinki, Finland.

Hansen, L. S. (1991). Integrative life planning: Work, family, community. [Special Issue from World Future Society Conference on "Creating the Future: Individual Responsibility," Minneapolis, MN: July 25]. *Futurics, 14* (3 & 4), 80–86.

Hansen, L. S. (1996). ILP: Integrating our lives, shaping our society. In R. Feller & G. Walz (Eds.), *Career transitions in turbulent times* (pp. 21–30). Greensboro, NC: ERIC Counseling and Student Services Clearinghouse, University of North Carolina.

Harmon, L. W., & Meara, N. M. (1994). Contemporary developments in women's career counseling: Themes of the past, puzzles for the future. In W. B. Walsh & S. H. Osipow (Eds.), *Career counseling for women: Contemporary topics in vocational psychology* (pp. 355–367). Hillsdale, NJ: Erlbaum.

Harris, P. R., & Moran, R. T. (1991). *Managing cultural differences* (3rd ed.). Houston: Gulf.

Harway, M. (1980). Sex bias in educational-vocational counseling. *Psychology of Women Quarterly, 4,* 212–214.

Havighurst, R. (1953). *Human development and education.* New York: Longman.

Havighurst, R. (1972). *Developmental tasks and education* (3rd ed.). New York: Longman.

Healy, C. C. (1982). *Career development: Counseling through life stages.* Boston: Allyn & Bacon.

Healy, C. C. (1990). Reforming career appraisals to meet the needs of clients in the 1990s. *The Counseling Psychologist, 18,* 214–226.

Healy, C. C., & Quinn, O. H. (1977). *Project Cadre: A cadre approach to career education infusion.* Unpublished manuscript.

Helwig, A. A. (1992). Book review of career development and services. *Journal of Employment Counseling, 29,* 77–78.

Heppner, M. J., & Johnston, J. A. (1994, Winter). Evaluating elements of career planning centers: Eight critical issues. *Journal of Career Development, 21* (2).

Heppner, P. P., & Krauskopf, C. J. (1987). An information processing approach to problem solving. *The Counseling Psychologist, 15,* 371–447.

Hermans, H. J. M. (1992). Telling and retelling one's self-narrative: A contextual approach to life-span development. *Human Development, 35,* 361–375.

Herr, E. L. (1989). Career development and mental health. *Journal of Career Development, 16*(1), 5–18.

Herr, E. L., & Cramer, S. H. (1996). *Career guidance and counseling through the life span: Systematic approaches* (5th ed.). New York: HarperCollins.

Herring, R. D. (1990). Attacking career myths among Native Americans: Implications for counseling. *The School Counselor, 38,* 13–18.

Hersen, M., & Turner, S. M. (1985). *Diagnostic interviewing.* New York: Plenum Press.

Hetherington, C., Hillerbrand, E., & Etringer, B. (1989). Career counseling with gay men: Issues and recommendations for research. *Journal of Counseling and Development, 67,* 452–454.

Hetherington, C., & Orzek, A. (1989). Career counseling and life planning with lesbian women. *Journal of Counseling and Development, 68,* 52–57.

Hirschorn, M. W. (1988). Students over 25 found to make up 45 pct. of campus enrollments. *The Chronicle of Higher Education, 34,* p. A35.

Hoffman, L. W. (1983). Increased fathering: Effects on the mother. In M. E. Lamb & A. Sagi (Eds.), *Fatherhood and family policy.* Hillsdale, NJ: Erlbaum.

Hoffreth, S. L., & Phillips, D. A. (1987). Child care in the United States: 1970 to 1985. *Journal of Marriage and the Family, 49,* 559–571.

Hofstede, G. (1984). *Culture's consequences: International differences in work-related values.* Newbury Park, CA: Sage.

Holland, J. L. (1966). *The psychology of vocational choice.* Waltham, MA: Blaisdell.

Holland, J. L. (1985a). *Making vocational choices: A theory of careers* (2nd ed.). Englewood Cliffs, NJ: Prentice-Hall.

Holland, J. L. (1985b). *Manual for the vocational preference inventory.* Odessa, FL: Psychological Assessment Resources.

Holland, J. L. (1987a). Current status of Holland's theory of careers: Another perspective. *The Career Development Quarterly, 36,* 31–34.

Holland, J. L. (1987b). *The self-directed search professional manual.* Odessa, FL: Psychological Assessment Resources.

Holland, J. L. (1987c). *The occupations finder.* Odessa, FL: Psychological Assessment Resources.

Holland, J. L. (1992). *Making vocational choices* (2nd ed.). Odessa, FL: Psychological Assessment Resources.

Holland, J. L. (1994a). *Self-directed search (SDS), Form R.* Odessa, FL: Psychological Assessment Resources.

Holland, J. L. (1994b). *You and your career.* Odessa, FL: Psychological Assessment Resources.

Holland, J. L. (1994c). *You and your career booklet.* Odessa, FL: Psychological Assessment Resources.

Holland, J. L. (1996). Exploring careers with a typology: What we have learned and some new directions. *American Psychologist, 51,* 397–406.

Holland, J. L., & Astin, A. W. (1962). The prediction of academic, artistic, scientific and social achievement. *Journal of Educational Psychology, 53,* 132–143.

Holland, J. L., Fritzsche, B. A., & Powell, A. B. (1994). *The SDS technical manual.* Odessa, FL: Psychological Assessment Resources.

Holland, J. L., Daiger, D., & Power, P. G. (1980). *My vocational situation.* Odessa, FL: Psychological Assessment Resources.

Holland, J. L., Johnston, J. H., & Asama, N. (1993). The vocational identity scale: A diagnostic and treatment tool. *Journal of Career Assessment, 1,* 1–12.

Holland, J. L., Powell, A. B., & Fritzsche, B. A. (1994). *The SDS: Professional user's guide.* Odessa, FL: Psychological Assessment Resources.

Hollender, J. (1967). Development of a realistic vocational choice. *Journal of Counseling Psychology, 14,* 314–318.

Holmberg, K., Rosen, D., & Holland, J. L. (1990). *Leisure activities finder.* Odessa, FL: Psychological Assessment Resources.

Hopkinson, K., Cox, A., & Rutter, M. (1981). Psychiatric interviewing techniques III: Naturalistic study: Eliciting feelings. *British Journal of Psychiatry, 138,* 406–415.

Hotchkiss, L., & Borow, H. (1996). Sociological perspective on work and career development. In D. Brown, L. Brooks, & Associates (Eds.), *Career choice and development* (3rd ed.) (pp. 281–326). San Francisco: Jossey-Bass.

Houston, B. K., & Kelly, K. E. (1987). Type A behavior in housewives: Relation to work, marital adjustment, stress, tension, health, fear-of-failure and self esteem. *Journal of Psychosomatic Research, 31,* 55–61.

Hoyt, K. B. (1972). *Career education: What it is and how to do it.* Salt Lake City: Olympus.

Hoyt, K. B., & Lester, J. N. (1995). *Learning to work: The NCDA Gallup survey.* Alexandria, VA: National Career Development Association.

Hsia, J. (1981, April). *Testing and Asian and Pacific Americans.* Paper presented at the National Association for Asian and Pacific American Education, Honolulu.

Hudson, J. S. (1992). *Vocational counseling with dual-career same-sex couples.* Unpublished manuscript, Southwest Texas State University.

Huffine, C. L., & Clausen, J. A. (1979). Madness and work: Short- and long-term effects of mental illness on occupational careers. *Social Forces, 57* (4), 1049–1062.

Humes, C. W., Szymanski, E. M., & Hohenshil, T. H. (1989, Nov./Dec.). Roles of counseling in enabling persons with disabilities. *Journal of Counseling & Development, 68,* 145–149.

Hunter, J. E., & Hunter, R. F. (1984). Validity and utility of alternative predictors of job performance. *Psychological Bulletin, 96,* 72–98.

ISO 9000: Providing the basis for quality. (1992, April 29). *CHEMICALWEEK,* pp. 30–41.

Issacson, L. E. (1985). *Basics of career counseling.* Boston: Allyn & Bacon.

Ivancevich, J. J., & Matteson, M. T. (1980). *Stress and work, a managerial perspective.* Dallas: Scott Foresman.

Ivey, A. E. (1986). *Development therapy*. San Francisco: Jossey-Bass.

Jackson, B. (1975). Black identity development. *Meforum: Journal of Educational Diversity and Innovation, 2,* 19–25.

Jackson, E. L. (1988). Leisure constraints: A survey of past research. *Leisure Sciences, 10,* 203–215.

Jepsen, D. A. (1986). Getting down to cases: Editor's introduction. *Career Development Quarterly, 35* (2), 67–68.

Jiang, W., Babyak, M., Krantz, D. S., Waugh, R. A., Coleman, R. E., Hanson, M. M., Frid, D. J., McNulty, S., Morris, J. J., O'Connor, C. M., & Blumenthal, J. A. (1996). Mental stress-induced myocardial ischemia and cardiac events. *JAMA, 275,* 1651–1656.

JIST. (1993). *Enhanced guide for occupational exploration.* Indianapolis: Author.

Job market for UCLA 1987 graduates. (1988). Los Angeles: University of California at Los Angeles.

Job stress at work around the world. (1993, Spring). *San Antonio Express-News,* p. 1B.

Johnson, G. J. (1990). Underemployment, underpayment, and self-esteem among black men. *Journal of Black Psychology, 16* (2), 23–44.

Johnson, M. J., Swartz, J. L., & Martin, W. E., Jr. (1995). Applications of psychological theories for career development with Native Americans. In F. T. L. Leong (Ed.), *Career development and vocational behavior of racial and ethnic minorities* (pp. 103–129). Mahwah, NJ: Erlbaum.

Jones, M. (1991). Gender stereotyping in advertisements. *Teaching of Psychology, 18,* 231–233.

Jourard, S. M. (1964). *The transparent self.* Princeton, NJ: Van Nostrand.

Judge, T. A., & Bretz, R. D., Jr. (1992). Effects of work values on job choice decisions. *Journal of Applied Psychology, 77,* 261–271.

Kail, R. V., & Cavanaugh, J. C. (1996). *Human development.* Pacific Grove, CA: Brooks/Cole.

Kando, T. M., & Summers, W. C. (1971). The impact of work on leisure: Toward a paradigm and research strategy. *Pacific Sociological Review, 14,* 310–327.

Kaneshige, E. (1979). Cultural factors in group counseling and interaction. In G. Henderson (Ed.), *Understanding and counseling ethnic minorities* (pp. 457–467). Springfield, IL: Charles C Thomas.

Kanter, M. (1989). *When giants learn to dance.* New York: Simon & Schuster.

Kapes. J. T., Borman, C. A., Garcia, G., Jr., & Compton, J. W. (1985, April). *Evaluation of microcomputer based career guidance systems with college students: SIGI and DIS-COVER.* Paper presented at the annual meeting of the American Educational Research Association, Chicago.

Kapes, J. T., Mastie, M. M., & Whitfield, E. A. (1994). *A counselor's guide to career assessment instruments* (3rd ed.). Alexandria, VA: National Career Development Association.

Kaplan, R. M., & Saccuzzo, D. P. (1993). *Psychological testing: Principles, applications, and issues* (3rd ed.). Pacific Grove, CA: Brooks/Cole.

Karasek, R., & Theorell, T. (1990). *Healthy work: Stress, productivity, and the reconstruction of working life.* New York: Basic Books.

Kasl, S. V. (1978). Epidemiological contributions to the study of work stress. In C. L. Cooper & R. Payne (Eds.), *Stress at work.* New York: Wiley.

Katz, M. R. (1975). *SIGI: A computer-based system of interactive guidance and information.* Princeton, NJ: Educational Testing Service.

Kavruck, S. (1956). Thirty-three years of test research: A short history of test development in the U.S. Civil Service Commission. *American Psychologist, 11,* 329–333.

Keating, D. P. (1980). Thinking processes in adolescence. In J. Adelson (Ed.), *Handbook of adolescent psychology.* New York: Wiley.

Keller, L. M., Bouchard, T. J., Jr., Arvey, R. D., Segal, N., & Dawis, R. V. (1992). Work values: Genetic and environmental influences. *Journal of Applied Psychology, 77,* 79–88.

Kelly, J. R. (1981). Leisure interaction and the social dialectic. *Social Forces, 60*(2), 304–322.

Kibrick, A. K., & Tiedeman, D. V. (1961). Conception of self and perception of role in schools of nursing. *Journal of Counseling Psychology, 8,* 26–29.

Kivlighan, D. J., Jr., Johnston, J. A., Hogan, R. S., & Mauer, E. (1994). Who benefits from computerized career counseling? *Journal of Counseling and Development, 72,* 289–292.

Kjos, D. (1996). Linking career counseling to personality disorders. In R. Feller & G. Walls (Eds.), *Career transitions in turbulent times* (pp. 267–273). Greensboro, NC: ERIC Counseling and Student Services Clearinghouse, University of North Carolina.

Kleinfield, N. R. (1996). A new and unnerving workplace. In *New York Times* (et al.), *The downsizing of America* (pp. 37–76). New York: Time Books.

Klinger, G. (1988). *Dual-role model.* Unpublished manuscript, Southwest Texas State University, San Marcos.

Knapp, R. R., & Knapp, L. (1977). *Interest changes and the classification of occupations.* Unpublished manuscript, EDITS, San Diego, CA.

Knapp, R. R., & Knapp, L. (1984). *COPS interest inventory technical manual.* San Diego, CA: EDITS.

Knapp, R. R., & Knapp, L. (1985). *California occupational preference system: Self-interpretation profile and guide.* San Diego, CA: EDITS.

Knowdell, R. L., McDaniels, C., & Walz, G. R. (1983). *Outplacement counseling.* Ann Arbor: ERIC Counseling and Personnel Service Clearinghouse, University of Michigan.

Kohlberg, L. (1973). Continuities in childhood and adult moral development revisited. In P. B. Baltes & K. W. Schase (Eds.), *Lifespan development psychology: Personality and socialization.* New York: Academic Press.

Kotter, J. P. (1984). The psychological contract: Managing the joining-up process. In J. A. Sonnenfeld (Ed.), *Managing career systems* (pp. 499–509). Homewood, IL: Irwin.

Kram, K. E. (1985). Improving the mentoring process. *Training and Development Journal, 39* (4), 40–43.

Kram, K. E. (1988). *Mentoring at work: Developmental relationships in organizational life.* Lanham, MD: University Press of America.

Krannich, R. L., & Krannich, C. R. (1990). *The complete guide to international jobs and careers.* Woodridge, VA: Impact Publishers.

Kriegel, L. (1982). Claiming the self: The cripple as American male. In M. G. Eisenberg, D. Kriggins, & R. J. Duvall (Eds.), *Disabled people as second-class citizens.* New York: Springer.

Kronenberger, G. K. (1991, June). Out of the closet. *Personnel Journal,* 40–44.

Krumboltz, J. D. (1983). *Private rules in career decision making.* Columbus, OH: National Center for Research in Vocational Education.

Krumboltz, J. D. (1991). *Career beliefs inventory.* Palo Alto, CA: Consulting Psychologists Press, Inc.

Krumboltz, J. D. (1992). Thinking about careers. *Contemporary Psychology, 37,* 113.

Krumboltz, J. D. (1993). Integrating career and personal counseling. *Career Development Quarterly, 42,* 143–148.

Krumboltz, J. D., Mitchell, A., & Gelatt, H. G. (1975). Applications of social learning theory of career selection. *Focus on Guidance, 8,* 1–16.

Krumboltz, J., & Nichols, C. (1990). Integrating the social learning theory of career decision making. In W. B. Walsh & S. H. Osipow (Eds.), *Career counseling: Contemporary topics in vocational psychology* (pp. 159–192). Hillsdale, NJ: Erlbaum.

Krumboltz, J. D., & Sorenson, D. L. (1974). *Career decision making*. Madison, WI: Counseling Films, Inc.

Kuder, G. F. (1963). A rationale for evaluating interests. *Educational and Psychological Measurement, 23,* 3–10.

Kuder, G. F. (1964). *Kuder general interest survey: Manual*. Chicago: Science Research Associates.

Kuder, G. F. (1966). *Kuder occupational interest survey: General manual*. Chicago: Science Research Associates.

Kumata, R., & Murata, A. (1980, March). *Employment of Asian/Pacific American women in Chicago*. Report of conference sponsored by the Women's Bureau, U.S. Department of Labor, Chicago.

Kurpius, D., Burello, L., & Rozecki, T. (1990). Strategic planning in human service organizations. *Counseling and Human Development, 22* (9), 1–12.

LaFromboise, T. D., Trimble, J. E., & Mohatt, G. V. (1990). Counseling intervention and American Indian tradition: An integrative approach. *The Counseling Psychologist, 18* (4), 628–654.

Lamb, M. E., Frodi, A. M., Hwang, C., & Frodi, M. (1982). Varying degrees of paternal involvement in infant care: Attitudinal and behavioral correlates. In M. E. Lamb (Ed.), *Nontraditional families: Parenting and child development*. Hillsdale, NJ: Erlbaum.

Lapan, R. T., & Jingeleski, J. (1992). Circumscribing vocational aspirations in junior high school. *Journal of Counseling Psychology, 39,* 81–90.

Lauer, R. H., & Lauer, J. C. (1986). Factors in long-term marriages. *Journal of Family Issues, 7,* 382–390.

Lazarus, A. A. (1989). *The practice of multimodal therapy*. Baltimore: Johns Hopkins University Press.

Lazarus, R. S. (1980). The stress and coping paradigm. In L. A. Bond & J. C. Rosen (Eds.), *Primary prevention of psychopathology: Vol. 4*. Hanover, NH: University Press of New England.

Leahy, R. L., & Shirk, S. R. (1984). The development of classificatory skills; and sex-trait stereotypes in children. *Sex Roles, 10,* 281–292.

Leana, C. R., & Feldman, D. C. (1991). Gender differences in responses to unemployment. *Journal of Vocational Behavior, 38,* 65–77.

Leclair, S. W. (1982). The dignity of leisure. *The School Counselor, 29* (4), 289–296.

Lent, R. W., Brown, S. D., & Hackett, G. (1996). Career development from a social cognitive perspective. In D. Brown, L. Brooks, & Associates (Eds.), *Career choice and development* (3rd ed.) (pp. 373–416). San Francisco: Jossey-Bass.

Leong, F. T. L. (1991). Career development attributes and occupational values of Asian American and white high school students. *Career Development Quarterly, 39,* 221–230.

Leong, F. T. L. (1993). The career counseling process with racial/ethnic minorities: The case of Asian Americans. *Career Development Quarterly, 42,* 26–40.

Leong, F. T. L., & Serafica, F. C. (1995). Career development of Asian Americans: A research area in need of a good theory. In F. T. L. Leong (Ed.), *Career development and vocational behavior of racial and ethnic minorities* (pp. 78–99). Mahwah, NJ: Erlbaum.

Leung, S. A., Conoley, C. W., & Scheel, M. J. (1994). The career and educational aspirations of gifted high school students: A retrospective study. *Journal of Counseling & Development, 72,* 298–303.

Levi, L. (1984). *Preventing work stress*. Reading, MA: Addison-Wesley.

Levinson, D. J. (1980). The mentor relationship. In M. A. Morgan (Ed.), *Managing career development*. New York: Van Nostrand.

Levinson, D. J. (1996). *The seasons of a woman's life*. New York: Knopf.

Levinson, D. J., Darrow, C. N., Klein, E. B., Levinson, M. H., & McKee, B. (1978). *The seasons of a man's life*. New York: Knopf.

Lindsey, L. L. (1990). *Gender roles: A sociological perspective*. Englewood Cliffs, NJ: Prentice-Hall.

Livson, N., & Peskin, H. (1980). Perspectives on adolescence from longitudinal research. In J. Adelson (Ed.), *Handbook of adolescent psychology*. New York: Wiley.

Locke, E. A., & Lathan, G. P. (1990). *A theory of goal setting and task performance*. Englewood Cliffs, NJ: Prentice-Hall.

Lofquist, L. H., & Dawis, R. V. (1984). Research on work adjustment and satisfaction: Implications for career counseling. In S. Brown & R. Lent (Eds.), *Handbook of counseling psychology* (pp. 216–237). New York: Wiley.

Lofquist, L. H., & Dawis, R. V. (1991). *Essentials of person-environment-correspondence counseling*. Minneapolis: University of Minnesota Press.

Lott, B. E. (1994). *Women's lives: Themes and variations in gender* (2nd ed.). Pacific Grove, CA: Brooks/Cole.

Lowman, R. L. (1993). *Counseling and psychotherapy of work dysfunctions*. Washington, DC: American Psychological Association.

Lunnenborg, P. W. (1981). *The vocational interest inventory (VIII) manual*. Los Angeles: Western Psychological Services.

Lunnenborg, P. W. (1984). Practical application of Roe's theory of career development. In D. Brown & L. Brooks (Eds.), *Career choice and development* (pp. 54–61). San Francisco: Jossey-Bass.

Lytton, H., & Romney, D. M. (1991). Parents' differential socialization of boys and girls: A meta-analysis. *Psychological Bulletin, 109,* 267–296.

Magnuson, J. (1990). Stress management. *Journal of Property Management, 55,* 24–28.

Malcolm, S. M. (1990). Reclaiming our past. *Journal of Negro Education, 59*(3), 246–259.

Maley, D. (1975). *Cluster concept in vocational education*. Chicago: American Technical Society.

Manson, N. M. (Ed.). (1982). *Topics in American Indian mental health prevention*. Portland: Oregon Health Sciences University Press.

Marcia, J. E. (1967). Ego identity status: Relationship to change in self-esteem, "general adjustment," and authoritarianism. *Journal of Personality, 35*(1), 119–133.

Marcia, J. E. (1980). Identity in adolescence. In J. Adelson (Ed.), *Handbook of adolescent psychology*. New York: Garland.

Marcia, J. E. (1991). Identity and self-development. In R. M. Lerner, A. C. Petersen, & J. Brooks-Gunn (Eds.), *Encyclopedia of adolescence: Vol. 1*. New York: Garland.

Mariani, M. (1994, Fall). The young and the entrepreneurial. *Occupational Outlook Quarterly, 38,* 2–10.

Mariani, M. (1995-96, Winter). Computers and career guidance: Ride the rising ride. *Occupational Outlook Quarterly, 39,* 16–27.

Marsh, H. W. (1991). Employment during high school: Character building or a subversion of academic goals? *Sociology of Education, 64,* 172–189.

Martin, W. E., Jr. (1995). Career development assessment and intervention strategies with American Indians. In F. T. L. Leong (Ed.), *Career development and vocational behavior of racial and ethnic minorities* (pp. 227–246). Mahwah, NJ: Erlbaum.

Maslach, C. (1976). Burned out. *Human Behavior, 5*(9), 16–22.

Maslach, C. (1981). Burnout: A social psychological analysis. In J. W. Jones (Ed.), *The burnout syndrome: Current research, theory, interventions*. Park Ridge, IL: London House Press.

Maslach, C., & Jackson, J. E. (1981). The measurement of experienced burnout. *Journal of Occupational Behavior, 2,* 99–113.

Matsumoto, David. (1996). *Culture and psychology*. Pacific Grove, CA: Brooks/Cole.

Mauer, E. B., & Gysbers, N. C. (1990). Identifying career concerns of entering university freshmen using *My Vocational Situation. Career Development Quarterly, 39,* 155–165.

Maze, M. (1985). How much should a computerized guidance program cost? *Journal of Career Development, 12* (2), 157–164.

Maze, M., & Cummings, R. (1982). Analysis of DISCOVER. In M. Maze & R. Cummings, *How to select a computer-assisted guidance system* (pp. 97–107). Madison: University of Wisconsin, Wisconsin Vocational Studies Center.

McBay, S. M. (1992). The condition of African American education: Changes and challenges. In B. J. Tidwell (Ed.), *The state of black America 1992* (pp. 141–156). New York: National Urban League.

McBride, A. B. (1990). Mental health effects of women's multiple roles. *American Psychologist, 45,* 381–384.

McBride, M. C. (1990). Autonomy and the struggle for female identity: Implications for counseling women. *Journal of Counseling and Development, 69,* 22–26.

McClelland, D. C. (1961). *The achieving society*. Princeton, NJ: Van Nostrand.

McCormac, M. E. (1988). Information sources and resources. *Journal of Career Development, 16,* 129–138.

McDaniels, C. (1984). Work and leisure in the career span. In N. C. Gysbers & Associates (Eds.), *Designing careers, counseling to enhance education, work and leisure* (Chap. 21). San Francisco: Jossey-Bass.

McDaniels, C. (1990). *The changing workplace: Career counseling strategies for the 1990s and beyond*. San Francisco: Jossey-Bass.

McGowan, B. G. (1984). *Trends in employee counseling programs*. New York: Pergamon Press.

Meir, E. I., Esformes, Y., & Friedland, N. (1994). Congruence and differentiation as predictors of workers' occupational stability and job performance. *Journal of Career Assessment, 2,* 40–54.

Meister, J. C. (1994). *Corporate quality universities: Lessons in building a world-class work force*. New York, NY: Irwin Professional Publishing.

Micro-tower: The group vocational and research center. (1977). New York: ICD Rehabilitation and Research Center.

Military Career Guide. (1989). North Chicago, IL: U.S. Military Processing Command.

Miller, D. C., & Form, W. H. (1951). *Industrial sociology*. New York: Harper & Row.

Miller, J. M., & Springer, T. P. (1986). Perceived satisfaction of a computerized vocational counseling system as a function of monetary investment. *Journal of College Student Personnel, 27,* 142–146.

Miller, M. J. (1986). Usefulness of Gati's hierarchical model of vocational interests for career counselors. *Journal of Employment Counseling, 23,* 57–65.

Miller, N. B. (1982). Social work services to urban Indians. In J. W. Green (Ed.), *Cultural awareness in the human services*. Englewood Cliffs, NJ: Prentice-Hall.

Miller-Tiedeman, A. (1988). *Lifecareer: The quantum leap into a process theory of career*. Vista, CA: LIFECAREER Foundation.

Miller-Tiedeman, A. L., & Tiedeman, D. V. (1982). *Career development: Journey into personal power*. Schenectady, NY: Character Research Press.

Miller-Tiedeman, A. L., & Tiedeman, D. V. (1990). Career decision making: An individualistic perspective. In D. Brown, L. Brooks, & Associates (Eds.), *Career choice and development: Applying contemporary theories to practice* (2nd ed.) (pp. 308–337). San Francisco: Jossey-Bass.

Minority numbers expected to grow. (1993, March 25). *San Antonio Express-News,* p. 12A.

Mitchell, L. K., & Krumboltz, J. D. (1984). Social learning approach to career decision making: Krumboltz's theory. In D. Brown & L. Brooks (Eds.), *Career choice and development*. San Francisco: Jossey-Bass.

Mitchell, L. K., & Krumboltz, J. D. (1987). Cognitive restructuring and decision making training on career indecision. *Journal of Counseling and Development, 66,* 171–174.

Mitchell, L. K., & Krumboltz, J. D. (1990). Social learning approach to career decision making: Krumboltz's theory. In D. Brown & L. Brooks (Eds.), *Career choice and development: Applying contemporary theories to practice* (2nd ed.) (pp. 145–196). San Francisco: Jossey-Bass.

Mitchell, L. K., & Krumboltz, J. D. (1996). Krumboltz's learning theory of career choice and counseling. In D. Brown, L. Brooks, & Associates (Eds.), *Career choice and development* (3rd ed.) (pp. 233–276). San Francisco: Jossey-Bass.

Moir, E. (1981). Career resource center in business and industry. *Training and Development Journal, 35* (2), 54–62.

Money, J. (1982). Introduction. In K. Solomon & N. B. Levy (Eds.), *Men in transition*. New York: Plenum.

Morrow, P. C. (1985). Retirement planning: Rounding out the career process. In D. W. Myers (Ed.), *Employee problem prevention and counseling*. Westport, CT: Quorum Books.

Multon, K. D., Brown, S. D., & Lent, R. W. (1991). Relation of self-efficacy beliefs to academic outcomes: A meta-analytic investigation. *Journal of Counseling Psychology, 38,* 30–38.

Myers, D. W. (1984). *Establishing and building employee assistance programs*. Westport, CT: Quorum Books.

Nadelson, T., & Nadelson, C. (1982). Dual careers and changing role models. In K. Solomon & N. B. Levy (Eds.), *Men in transition*. New York: Plenum.

Naisbitt, J. (1994). *Global paradox: The bigger the world economy, the more powerful its smallest players*. New York, NY: Avon Books.

National Commission on Children. (1993). *Just the facts: A summary of recent information on America's children and their families*. Washington, DC: Author.

National Consortium of State Career Guidance Supervisors. (1996). *Planning for life: 1995 compendium of recognized career planning programs*. Columbus, OH: Center on Education and Training for Employment, Ohio State University.

National Occupational Information Coordinating Committee (NOICC), U.S. Department of Labor. (1989). *National career development guidelines*. Washington, DC: U.S. Department of Labor.

National Occupational Information Coordinating Committee (NOICC), U.S. Department of Labor. (1992). *The national career development guidelines project*. Washington, DC: U.S. Department of Labor.

National Science Foundation. (1989). *Science and engineering indicators—1989*. Washington, DC: National Science Foundation.

Neff, W. S. (1985). *Work and human behavior* (2nd ed.). Chicago: Aldine.

Nelson, C. (1990, March). The beast within Winnie the Pooh reassessed. *Children's Literature in Education, 21,* 17–22.

Nevill, D. D., & Super, D. E. (1986). *The Salience Inventory manual: Theory, application, and research*. Palo Alto, CA: Consulting Psychologists Press.

Nevo, O. (1987). Irrational expectations in career counseling and their confronting arguments. *Career Development Quarterly, 35,* 239–250.

Newman, B. M., & Newman, P. R. (1995). *Development through life: A psychosocial approach*. Pacific Grove, CA: Brooks/Cole.

Nielsen Media Research. (1989). *'89 Nielsen report on television*. Northbrooks, IL: Author.

Nihira, K., Foster, R., Shellhaas, M., & Leland, H. (1975). *AAMD adaptive behavior scale.* Washington, DC: American Association on Mental Deficiency.

Norrell, G., & Grater, H. (1960). Interest awareness as an aspect of self-awareness. *Journal of Counseling Psychology, 7,* 289–292.

O'Driscoll, M. P., Ilgen, D. R., & Hildreth, K. (1992). Time devoted to job and off-job activities, interrole conflict, and affective experiences. *Journal of Applied Psychology, 77,* 272–279.

Office of Technology Assessment, U.S. Congress. (1990). *Worker training: Competing in the new international economy.* Washington, DC: U.S. Government Printing Office.

O'Hara, R. P., & Tiedeman, D. V. (1959). Vocational self-concept in adolescence. *Journal of Counseling Psychology, 6,* 292–301.

O'Neil, J. M. (1982). Gender role conflict and strain in men's lives: Implications for psychiatrists, psychologists, and other human-services providers. In K. Solomon & N. B. Levy (Eds.), *Men in transition.* New York: Plenum.

O'Neil, J. M. (1990). Assessing men's gender role conflict. In D. Moore & F. Leafgren (Eds.), *Men in conflict* (pp. 23–38). Alexandria, VA: American Association of Counseling and Development.

Osipow, S. H. (1983). *Theories of career development* (3rd ed.). New York: Appleton-Century-Crofts.

Osipow, S. H., & Fitzgerald, L. (1996). *Theories of career development* (4th ed.). Needham Heights, MA: Allyn & Bacon.

Othmer, E., & Othmer, S. (1989). *The clinical interview.* Washington, DC: American Psychiatric Press.

O'Toole, J. (1981). *Making America work.* New York: Continuum.

Palkovitz, R. (1984). Parental attitudes and fathers' interactions with their 5-month-old infants. *Developmental Psychology, 20,* 1054–1060.

Parcel, T. L., & Menaghan, E. G. (1994). Early parental work, family, social capital, and early childhood outcomes. *American Journal of Sociology, 9,* 972–1009.

Pardine, P., Higgins, R., Szeglin, A., Beres, J., Kravitz, R., & Fotis, J. (1981). Job stress, worker-strain relationship moderated by off-the-job experience. *Psychological Reports, 48,* 963–970.

Pareles, J. (1990, October 21). The women who talk back in rap. *New York Times,* pp. H33, H36.

Parker, R. M., & Hansen, C. E. (1981). *Rehabilitation counseling.* Boston: Allyn & Bacon.

Parsons, F. (1909). *Choosing a vocation.* Boston: Houghton Mifflin.

Pascarel, E. T., & Terenzi, P. T. (1991). *How college affects students: Findings and insights from twenty years of research.* San Francisco: Jossey-Bass.

Peatling, J. H., & Tiedeman, D. V. (1977). *Career development: Designing self.* Muncie, IN: Accelerated Development.

Peterson, G. W., Ryan-Jones, R. E., Sampson, J. P., Jr., Reardon, R. C., & Shahnasarian, M. (1987). *A comparison of the effectiveness of three computer-assisted career guidance systems on college students' career decision making processes* (Technical Report No. 6). Tallahassee: Florida State University, Center for the Study of Technology in Counseling and Career Development.

Peterson, G. W., Sampson, J. P., & Reardon, R. C. (1991). *Career development and services: A cognitive approach.* Pacific Grove, CA: Brooks/Cole.

Peterson, G. W., Sampson, J. P., Jr., Reardon, R. C., & Lenz, J. G. (1996). A cognitive information processing approach to career problem solving and decision making. In D. Brown, L. Brooks, & Associates (Eds.), *Career choice and development* (3rd ed.) (pp. 423–467). San Francisco: Jossey-Bass.

Peterson, M. (1982). VALPAR component work sample system. In J. T. Kapes & M. M. Mastie (Eds.), *A counselor's guide to vocational guidance instruments.* Falls Church, VA: The National Vocational Guidance Association.

Piaget, J. (1929). *The child's conception of the world.* New York: Harcourt Brace.

Piaget, J., & Inhelder, B. (1969). *The psychology of the child.* New York: Basic Books.

Picchioni, A. P., & Bonk, E. C. (1983). *A comprehensive history of guidance in the United States.* Austin: Texas Personnel and Guidance Association.

Pietrofesa, J. J., & Splete, H. (1975). *Career development: Theory and research.* New York: Grune & Stratton.

Pine, G. J., & Innis, G. (1987). Cultural and individual work values. *Career Development Quarterly, 35* (4), 279–287.

Pines, A., & Aronson, E. (1988). *Career burnout causes and cures.* New York: Free Press.

Pines, A., & Maslach, C. (1979). Characteristics of staff burnout. *Psychiatry, 29,* 233–237.

Pleck, J. H. (1985). *Working wives/working husbands.* Newbury Park, CA: Sage.

Polkinghorne, D. E. (1990). Action theory approaches to career research. In R. A. Young & W. A. Borgen (Eds.), *Methodological approaches to the study of career* (pp. 87–105). New York: Praeger.

Ponterotto, J. G. (1987). Counseling Mexican Americans: A multimodal approach. *Journal of Counseling and Development, 65,* 308–311.

Poole, M. E., & Clooney, G. H. (1985). Careers: Adolescent awareness and exploration of possibilities for self. *Journal of Vocational Behavior, 26,* 251–263.

Porter, T. L. (1981). Extent of disabling conditions. In R. M. Parker & C. E. Hansen (Eds.), *Rehabilitation counseling.* Boston: Allyn & Bacon.

Posner, B. Z. (1992). Person-organization values congruence: No support for individual differences as a moderating influence. *Human Relations, 45,* 351–361.

Powell, A., & Vega, M. (1972). Correlates of adult locus of control. *Psychological Reports, 30,* 455–460.

Powell, D. H. (1957). Careers and family atmosphere: An empirical test of Roe's theory. *Journal of Counseling Psychology, 4,* 212–217.

Prediger, D. J. (1974). The role of assessment in career guidance. In E. L. Herr (Ed.), *Vocational guidance and human development.* Boston: Houghton Mifflin.

Prediger, D. J. (1995). *Assessment in career counseling.* Greensboro, NC: ERIC Counseling and Student Services Clearinghouse, University of North Carolina.

Prediger, D. J., & Swaney, K. B. (1995). Using the UNIACT in a comprehensive approach to assessment for career planning. *Journal of Career Assessment, 3,* 429–452.

Purcell, P., & Stewart, L. (1990). Dick and Jane in 1989. *Sex Roles, 22,* 177–185.

Rabinowitz, F. E., & Cochran, S. V. (1994). *Man alive: A primer of men's issues.* Pacific Grove, CA: Brooks/Cole.

Radin, N. (1983). Primary caregiving and role-sharing fathers. In M. E. Lamb (Ed.), *Nontraditional families: Parenting and child development.* Hillsdale, NJ: Erlbaum.

Ragheb, M. B., & Griffith, C. A. (1982). The contribution of leisure participation and leisure satisfaction to life satisfaction of older persons. *Journal of Leisure Research, 14,* 295–306.

Rapoport, R., & Rapoport, R. (1978). The dual career family. In L. S. Hansen & R. S. Rapoza (Eds.), *Career development and the counseling of women.* Springfield, IL: Charles C Thomas.

Reardon, R. C. (1996a). *Curricular career information service.* Unpublished manuscript, Florida State University, Tallahassee.

Reardon, R. C. (1996b). A program and cost analysis of self-directed career advising services in a university career center. *Journal of Counseling and Development, 74,* 280–285.

Reardon, R. C., & Domkowski, D. (1977). Building instruction into a career information center. *Vocational Guidance Quarterly, 25,* 274–278.

Reich, R. B. (1991). *The work of nations.* New York: Knopf.

Reschke, W., & Knierim, K. H. (1987, Spring). How parents influence career choice. *Journal of Career Planning and Employment,* 54–60.

Reskin, B. F. (1993). Sex segregation in the workplace. *Annual Review of Sociology, 19,* 241–270.

Rich, A. R., & Schroeder, H. E. (1976). Research issues in assertiveness training. *Psychological Bulletin, 83,* 1081–1096.

Richards, M. H., & Larson, R. (1993). Pubertal development and the daily subjective states of young adolescents. *Journal of Research on Adolescence, 3,* 145–169.

Richardson, M. S. (1993). Working people's lives. *Journal of Counseling and Development, 40,* 425–433.

Rimer, S. (1996). The fraying of community. In *New York Times* (et al.), *The downsizing of America* (pp. 111–138). New York: Time Books.

Rodriguez, M., & Blocher, D. (1988). A comparison of two approaches to enhancing career maturity in Puerto Rican college women. *Journal of Counseling Psychology, 35,* 275–280.

Roe, A. (1956). *The psychology of occupations.* New York: Wiley.

Roe, A. (1972). Perspectives on vocational development. In J. M. Whiteley & A. Resnikoff (Eds.), *Perspectives on vocational development.* Washington, DC: American Personnel and Guidance Association.

Roe, A., & Lunneborg, P. W. (1990). Personality development and career choice. In D. Brown & L. Brooks (Eds.), *Career choice and development. Applying contemporary theories to practice* (pp. 68–101). San Francisco: Jossey-Bass.

Roessler, R., & Rubin, E. (1982). *Case management and rehabilitation counseling: Procedures and techniques.* Baltimore: University Park Press.

Rogers, C. R. (1942). *Counseling and psychotherapy.* Boston: Houghton Mifflin.

Rokeach, M. (1973). *The nature of human values.* New York: Free Press.

Roos, P. A., & Jones, K. W. (1993). Women's inroads into academic sociology. *Work and Occupations, 20,* 395–428.

Roselle, B., & Hummel, T. (1988). Intellectual development and interaction effectiveness with DISCOVER. *The Career Development Journal, 35–36,* 241–251.

Rosen, D., Holmberg, K., & Holland, J. L. (1994a). *Dictionary of educational opportunities.* Odessa, FL: Psychology Assessment Resources.

Rosen, D., Holmberg, K., & Holland, J. L. (1994b). *Educational opportunities finder.* Odessa, FL: Psychological Assessment Resources.

Rosenberg, M. (1957). *Occupations and values.* Glencoe, IL: Free Press.

Rosenthal, R. H., & Akiskal, H. S. (1985). Mental status examination. In M. Hersen & S. M. Turner (Eds.), *Diagnostic interviewing.* New York: Plenum.

Rosenwasser, S. M. (1982, April). *Differential socialization processes of males and females.* Paper presented to the Texas Personnel and Guidance Association, Houston.

Rosenwasser, S. M., & Patterson, W. (1984, April). *Nontraditional males: Men with primary childcare/household responsibilities.* Paper presented to the Southwestern Psychological Association, New Orleans.

Roskies, E., & Louis-Guerin, C. (1990). Job insecurity in managers: Antecedents and consequences. *Journal of Organizational Behavior, 11,* 345–359.

Ross, C. C., & Stanley, J. C. (1954). *Measurement in today's schools* (2nd ed.). New York: Prentice-Hall.

Rotter, J. B. (1966). Generalized expectancies for internal versus external control of reinforcement. *Psychological Monographs, 80* (Whole No. 609).

Rounds, J. B. (1990). The comparative and combined utility of work value and interest data in career counseling with adults. *Journal of Vocational Behavior, 37,* 32–45.

Rounds, J. B., & Tracey, T. J. (1990). From trait-and-factor to person-environment fit counseling: Theory and process. In W. B. Walsh & S. J. Osipow (Eds.), *Career coun-*

seling: Contemporary topics in vocational psychology (pp. 1–44). Hillsdale, NJ: Erlbaum.

Rounds, J. B., & Tracy, T. J. (1993). Prediger's dimensional representation of Holland's RIASEC circumplex. *Journal of Applied Psychology, 78,* 875–890.

Rowland, D. T. (1991). Family diversity and the life cycle. *Journal of Comparative Family Studies, 22,* 1–14.

Russell, G. (1982). Shared-caregiving families: An Australian study. In M. E. Lamb (Ed.), *Nontraditional families: Parenting and child development.* Hillsdale, NJ: Erlbaum.

Russo, N. F., Kelly, R. M., & Deacon, M. (1991). Gender and success-related attributions: Beyond individualistic conceptions of achievement. *Sex Roles, 25,* 331–350.

Ryan, L., & Ryan, R. (1982). *Mental health and the urban Indian.* Unpublished manuscript.

Rychlak, J. F. (1993). A suggested principle of complementarity for psychology. *American Psychologist, 48,* 933–942.

Sadker, M., & Sadker, D. (1986, March). Sexism in the classroom: From grade school to graduate school. *Phi Delta Kappan,* pp. 512–515.

Sadri, G., & Robertson, L. T. (1993). Self-efficacy and work-related behavior: A review and meta-analysis. *Applied Psychology: An Internal Review, 42,* 139–152.

Sagi, A. (1982). Antecedents and consequences of various degrees of paternal involvement in child rearing: The Israeli project. In M. E. Lamb (Ed.), *Nontraditional families: Parenting and child development.* Hillsdale, NJ: Erlbaum.

Salomone, P. R. (1996, Spring). Tracing Super's theory of vocational development: A 40-year restrospective. *Journal of Career Development, 22* (3).

Salomone, P. R., & Slaney, R. B. (1978). The applicability of Holland's theory to professional workers. *Journal of Vocational Behavior, 13,* 63–74.

Sampson, J. P. (1983). Computer-assisted testing and assessment: Current status and implications for the future. *Measurement and Evaluation in Guidance, 15* (3), 293–299.

Sampson, J. P. (1994). *Effective computer-assisted career guidance: Occasional paper number 2.* Center for the Study of Technology in Counseling and Career Development, Florida State University.

Sampson, J. P., & Pyle, K. R. (1983). Ethical issues involved with the use of computer-assisted counseling, testing and guidance systems. *Personnel and Guidance Journal, 61*(3), 283–287.

Sampson, J. P., Peterson, G. W., Lenz, J. G., & Reardon, R. C. (1992). *Career Development Quarterly, 41,* 67–73.

Sampson, J. P., Jr., Peterson, G. W., Lenz, J. G., Reardon, R. C., & Saunders, D. E. (1996a). *Career thoughts inventory: Professional manual.* Odessa, FL: Psychological Assessment Resources.

Sampson, J. P., Jr., Peterson, G. W., Lenz, J. G., Reardon, R. C., & Saunders, D. E. (1996b). *Improving your career thoughts: A workbook for the career thoughts inventory.* Odessa, FL: Psychological Assessment Resources.

Samuelson, R. J. (1995). *The good life and its discontents: The American dream in the age of entitlement, 1945–1995.* New York: Time Books.

Sanguiliano, I. (1978). *In her time.* New York: Morrow.

Sastre, M. T. M., & Mullet, E. (1992). Occupational preferences of Spanish adolescents in relation to Gottfredson's theory. *Journal of Vocational Behavior, 40,* 306–317.

Saunders, L. (1995). Relative earnings of black and white men by region, industry. *Monthly Labor Review, 118*(4), 68–73.

Savickas, M. L. (1990). The use of career choice measures in counseling practice. In E. Watkins & V. Campbell (Eds.), *Testing in counseling practice* (pp. 373–417). Hillsdale, NJ: Erlbaum.

Savickas, M. L. (1995). Current theoretical issues in vocational psychology: Convergence, divergence, and schism. In W. B. Walsh & S. H. Osipow (Eds.), *Handbook of vocational psychology* (2nd ed.) (pp. 1–34). Hillsdale, NJ: Erlbaum.

Scarr, S., Phillips, D., & McCartney, K. (1989). Working mothers and their families. *American Psychologist, 44,* 1402–1409.

Schnall, M. (1981). *Limits: A search for new values.* New York: Clarkson N. Potter.

Schunk, D. H. (1995). Education and instruction. In J. E. Maddux (Ed.), *Self-efficacy, adaptation, and adjustment: Theory, research, and application.* New York: Plenum.

Schutz, R. A., & Blocher, D. H. (1961). Self-satisfaction and level of occupational choice. *Personnel and Guidance Journal, 39,* 595–598.

Schwab, R. L. (1981). The relationship of role conflict, role ambiguity, teacher background variables and perceived burnout among teachers. (Doctoral dissertation, University of Connecticut, 1980.) *Dissertation Abstracts International, 41(9),* 3823-A.

Schwartz, E. (1989). The mental status examination. In R. J. Craig (Ed.), *Clinical and diagnostic interviewing.* Northvale, NJ: Aronson.

Scott, K. P. (1981, April). Whatever happened to Jane and Dick? Sexism in texts reexamined. *Peabody Journal of Education,* 135–140.

Sharf, R. S. (1984). Vocational information-seeking behavior: Another view. *Vocational Guidance Quarterly, 33* (2), 120–129.

Sharf, R. S. (1992). *Applying career development theory to counseling.* Pacific Grove, CA: Brooks/Cole.

Sharf, R. S. (1996). *Theories of psychotherapy and counseling: Concepts and cases.* Pacific Grove, CA: Brooks/Cole.

Shelton, B. A., & John, D. (1993). Ethnicity, race, and difference: A comparison of white, black, and Hispanic men's household labor time. In J. C. Hood (Ed.), *Men, work and family* (pp. 131–150). Newbury Park, CA: Sage.

Sheppard, H. L., & Rix, S. E. (1977). *The graying of working America.* New York: Free Press.

Shostak, A. B. (1980). *Blue-collar stress.* Reading, MA: Addison-Wesley.

Shotter, J. (1993). *Conversational realities: Constructing life through language.* Newbury Park, CA: Sage.

Sigelman, C. K., & Shaffer, D. R. (1995). *Life-span human development* (2nd ed.). Pacific Grove, CA: Brooks/Cole.

Signorelli, N., & Lears, M. (1992). Children, television, and conceptions about chores: Attitudes and behaviors. *Sex Roles, 27,* 157–170.

Silberstein, L. R. (1992). *Dual-career marriage: A system in transition.* Hillsdale, NJ: Lawrence Erlbaum Associates, Inc.

Siltanen, J. (1994). *Locating gender: Occupational segregation, wages, and domestic responsibility.* Greensboro, NC: ERIC Counseling and Student Services Clearinghouse, University of North Carolina. (ERIC Report No. ED 377 373)

Simmons, R. G., & Blyth, D. A. (1987). *Moving into adolescence: the impact of pubertal change and school context.* New York: Aldine De Gruyter.

Skovholt, T. M. (1978). Feminism and men's lives. *The Counseling Psychologist, 7(4),* 3–10.

Skovholt, T. M. (1990). Career themes in counseling and psychotherapy with men. In D. Moore & F. Leafgren (Eds.), *Men in conflict* (pp. 39–56). Alexandria, VA: American Association for Counseling and Development.

Smith, A., & Chemers, M. (1981). Perception of motivation of economically disadvantaged employees in a work setting. *Journal of Employment Counseling, 18,* 24–33.

Smith, A. B., & Inder, P. M. (1993). Social interaction in same and cross gender preschool peer groups: A participant observation study. *Educational Psychology, 13,* 29–42.

Smith, C. K., Smith, W. S., Stroup, K. M., & Ballard, B. W. (1982). *Broadening career options for women*. Ann Arbor: ERIC Counseling and Personnel Services Clearing House, University of Michigan.

Smith, E. J. (1983). Issues in racial minorities' career behavior. In W. B. Walsh & J. H. Osipow (Eds.), *Handbook of vocational psychology: Vol. 1.* (pp. 161–222). Hillsdale, NJ: Erlbaum.

Snodgrass, G., & Wheeler, R. W. (1983). A research-based sequential job interview training model. *Journal of College Student Personnel, 24* (5), 449–454.

Solomon, K. (1982). The masculine gender role: Description. In K. Solomon & N. B. Levy (Eds.), *Men in transition.* New York: Plenum.

Sorapuru, J., Theodore, R., & Young, W. (1972a). Financial facts of life. In J. E. Bottoms, R. N. Evans, K. B. Hoyt, & J. C. Willers (Eds.), *Career education resource guide.* Morristown, NJ: General Learning Corporation.

Sorapuru, J., Theodore, R., & Young, W. (1972b). Job hunting. In J. E. Bottoms, R. N. Evans, K. B. Hoyt, & J. C. Willers (Eds.), *Career education resource guide.* Morristown, NJ: General Learning Corporation.

Spencer, A. L. (1982). *Seasons.* New York: Paulist Press.

Spindler, G. (Ed.). (1955). *Education and culture.* Stanford, CA: Stanford University Press.

Splete, H. (1996). Adult career counseling centers train career counselors. In R. Feller and G. Walls (Eds.), *Career transitions in turbulent times* (pp. 405–414). Greensboro, NC: ERIC Counseling and Student Services Clearinghouse, University of North Carolina.

Splete, H., Elliott, B. J., & Borders, L. D. (1985). *Computer-assisted career guidance systems and career counseling services.* Unpublished manuscript, Oakland University, Adult Career Counseling Center, Rochester, MI.

Splete, H., & Stewart, A. (1990). Competency-based career development strategies and the national career development guidelines. (Information Series No. 345). Columbus: ERIC Clearinghouse on Adult, Career, and Vocational Education. (ERIC Report No. ED 327 739)

Spokane, A. R. (1985). A review of research on person-environment congruence in Holland's theory of careers [Monograph]. *Journal of Vocational Behavior, 26,* 306–343.

Spokane, A. R. (1991). *Career intervention.* Englewood Cliffs, NJ: Prentice-Hall.

Spokane, A. R. (1996). Holland's theory. In D. Brown, L. Brooks, & Associates (Eds.), *Career choice and development* (3rd ed.) (pp. 33–69). San Francisco: Jossey-Bass.

Spokane, A. R., & Holland, J. L. (1995). The self-directed search: A family of self-guided career interventions. *Journal of Career Assessment, 3,* 373–390.

St. Peter, S. (1979). Jack went up the hill . . . but where was Jill? *Psychology of Women Quarterly, 4,* 256–260.

Staats, A. W. (1981). Paradigmatic behaviorism, unified theory, unified theory construction methods, and the zeitgeist of separatism. *American Psychologist, 36,* 239–256.

Steidl, R. (1972). Financial facts of life. In J. E. Bottoms, R. N. Evans, K. B. Hout, & J. C. Willers (Eds.), *Career education resource guide.* Morristown, NJ: General Learning Corporation.

Stein, T. S. (1982). Men's groups. In K. Solomon & N. B. Levy (Eds.), *Men in transition* (pp. 275–307). New York: Plenum.

Stephenson, R. R. (1961). Occupational choice as a crystallized self-concept. *Journal of Counseling Psychology, 8,* 211–216.

Stephenson, W. (1949). *Testing school children.* New York: Longmans, Green.

Stimpson, D., Jensen, L., & Neff, W. (1992). Cross-cultural gender differences in preferences for a caring morality. *Journal of Social Psychology, 132,* 317–322.

Stoltz-Loike, M. (1992). *Dual-career couples: New perspectives in counseling.* Alexandria, VA: American Association for Counseling and Development.

Stone, J., & Gregg, C. (1981). Juvenile diabetes and rehabilitation counseling. *Rehabilitation Counseling Bulletin, 24,* 283–291.

Strong, E. K. (1983). *Vocational interest blank for men.* Stanford, CA: Stanford University Press.

Strube, M. J. (Ed.). (1991). *Type A behavior.* Newbury Park, CA: Sage.

Suchet, M., & Barling, J. (1985). Employed mothers: Interrole conflict, spouse support, and marital functioning. *Journal of Occupational Behavior, 7,* 167–178.

Sue, D. W. (1978). Counseling across cultures. *Personnel and Guidance Journal, 56,* 451.

Sue, D. W. (1981). *Counseling the culturally different.* New York: Wiley.

Sue, D. W. (1992). The challenge of multiculturalism: The road less traveled. *American Counselor, 1,* 7–14.

Sue, D. W. (1994). Asian American mental health and help-seeking behavior: Comment on Solberg, et al. (1994), Tata & Leong (1994), and Lin (1994). *Journal of Counseling Psychology, 41,* 292–295.

Sue, D. W., Ivey, A. E., & Pedersen, P. B. (1996). *A theory of multicultural counseling and therapy.* Pacific Grove, CA: Brooks/Cole.

Sue, D. W., & Sue, D. (1990). *Counseling the culturally different: Theory and practice* (2nd ed.). New York: Wiley.

Sue, S., & Abe, J. (1988). *Predictors of academic achievement among Asian American and white students* (Report No. 88-11). New York: College Entrance Examination Board.

Sue, S., & Okazaki, S. (1990). Asian American educational achievements: A phenomenon in search of an explanation. *American Psychologist, 45,* (8), 913–920.

Super, D. E. (1949). *Appraising vocational fitness.* New York: Harper & Brothers.

Super, D. E. (1957). *The psychology of careers.* New York: Harper & Row.

Super, D. E. (1970). *The work values inventory.* Boston: Houghton Mifflin.

Super, D. E. (1972). Vocational development theory: Persons, positions, and processes. In J. M. Whiteley & A. Resnikoff (Eds.), *Perspectives on vocational development.* Washington, DC: American Personnel and Guidance Association.

Super, D. E. (1974). *Measuring vocational maturity for counseling and evaluation.* Washington, DC: National Vocational Guidance Association.

Super, D. E. (1977). Vocational maturity in mid-career. *Vocational Guidance Quarterly, 25,* 297.

Super, D. E. (1980). A life-span, life-space approach to career development. *Journal of Vocational Behavior, 16,* 282–298.

Super, D. E. (1984). Career and life development. In D. Brown & L. Brooks (Eds.), *Career choice and development.* San Francisco: Jossey-Bass.

Super, D. E. (1990). A life-span, life-space approach to career development. In D. Brown, L. Brooks, & Associates (Eds.), *Career choice and development: Applying contemporary theories to practice* (pp. 197–261). San Francisco: Jossey-Bass.

Super, D. E., & Crites, J. O. (1962). *Appraising vocational fitness by means of psychological tests* (rev. ed.). New York: Harper & Row.

Super, D. E., & Overstreet, P. L. (1960). *The vocational maturity of ninth grade boys.* New York: Teachers College, Columbia University.

Super, D. E., Savickas, M. L., & Super, C. M. (1996). The life-span, life-space approach to careers. In D. Brown, L. Brooks, & Associates (Eds.), *Career choice and development* (3rd ed.) (pp. 121–170). San Francisco: Jossey-Bass.

Super, D. E., Starishesky, R., Matlin, N., & Jordaan, J. P. (1963). *Career development: Self-concept theory.* New York: College Entrance Examination Board.

Super, D. E., Thompson, A. S., & Lindeman, R. H. (1988). *Adult career concerns inventory: Manual for research and exploratory use in counseling.* Palo Alto, CA: Consulting Psychologists Press.

Swanson, J. L. (1992). Vocational behavior, 1989-1991: Life-span career development and reciprocal interaction of work and nonwork. *Journal of Vocational Behavior, 41,* 101–161.

Tannen, D. (1990). *You just don't understand.* New York: Ballantine Books.

Tanner, J. M. (1972). Sequence, tempo, and individual variation in growth and development of boys and girls aged twelve to sixteen. In J. Kagan & R. Coles (Eds.), *Twelve to sixteen: Early adolescence.* New York: Norton.

Taylor, R. L. (1990). Black youth: The endangered generation. *Youth and Society, 22* (1), 4–11.

Texas Rehabilitation Commission. (1980). *Prevocational training manual.* Austin: Author.

Texas Rehabilitation Commission. (1984). *Eligibility requirements of rehabilitation.* Austin: Author.

Texas Rehabilitation Commission. (1985). *Career orientation manual.* Austin: Author.

Thase, M., & Page, R. A. (1977). Modeling of self-disclosure in laboratory and nonlaboratory settings. *Journal of Consulting Psychology, 24,* 35–40.

Thomas, J. K. (1973). Adolescent endocrinology for counselors of adolescents. *Adolescence, 8,* 395–406.

Thomas, K. R., & Butler, A. J. (1981). Counseling for personal adjustment. In R. M. Parker & C. E. Hansen (Eds.), *Rehabilitation Counseling.* Boston: Allyn & Bacon.

Thomason, T. C. (1991). Counseling Native Americans: An introduction for non-Native American counselors. *Journal of Counseling & Development, 69,* 321–327.

Thompson, A. S., Lindeman, R. H., Super, D. E., Jordaan, J. P., & Myers, R. A. (1984). *Career development inventory: Technical manual.* Palo Alto, CA: Consulting Psychologists Press.

Thompson, E. H., Grisanti, C., & Pleck, J. H. (1987). Attitudes toward the male role and their correlates. *Sex Roles, 13,* 413–427.

Thorndike, R. L. (1949). *Personnel selection tests, and measurement techniques.* New York: Wiley.

Thorndike, R. L., & Hagen, E. (1959). *10,000 careers.* New York: Wiley.

Thurer, S. (1980). Vocational rehabilitation following coronary bypass surgery: The need of counseling the newly well. *Journal of Applied Rehabilitation Counseling, 11,* 98–99.

Tiedeman, D. V., & O'Hara, R. P. (1963). *Career development: Choice and adjustment.* Princeton, NJ: College Entrance Examination Board.

Tomasko, R. T. (1987). *Downsizing.* New York: American Management Association.

Tracy, D. M. (1990). Toy-playing behavior, sex role orientation, spatial ability, and science achievement. *Journal of Research in Science Teaching, 27,* 637–649.

Triandis, H. C. (1992, February). *Individualism and collectivism as a cultural syndrome.* Paper presented at the Annual Convention of the Society for Cross-Cultural Researchers, Santa Fe, NM.

Trimble, J. E., & LaFromboise, T. (1985). American Indians and the counseling process: Culture, adaptation, and style. In P. Pedersen, *Handbook of cross-cultural counseling and therapy* (pp. 125–134). Westport, CT: Greenwood Press.

Troll, L., Israel, J., & Israel, K. (1977). *Looking ahead.* Englewood Cliffs, NJ: Prentice-Hall.

Trower, P., Casey, A., & Dryden, W. (1988). *Cognitive-behavioral counseling in action.* Newbury Park, CA: Sage.

Tyler, L. E. (1961). Research explorations in the realm of choice. *Journal of Counseling Psychology, 8,* 195–202.

Uchitelle, L., & Kleinfield, N. R. (1996). The price of jobs lost. In *New York Times* (et al.), *The downsizing of America* (pp. 3–36). New York: Time Books.

UCLA placement and career planning center. (1980). Los Angeles: University of California at Los Angeles.

Unger, R. (1979). Toward a redefinition of sex and gender. *American Psychologist, 34,* 1085–1094.

Unger, R., & Crawford, M. (1992). *Women and gender: A feminist psychology.* Philadelphia: Temple University Press.

University of Minnesota. (1984). *Minnesota Importance Questionnaire.* Minneapolis: Author.

U.S. Bureau of the Census. (1990). *Characteristics of American Indians by tribe and selected areas.* Washington, DC: U.S. Government Printing Office.

U.S. Bureau of the Census. (1992). *Statistical abstract of the United States, 1992.* Washington, DC: U.S. Government Printing Office.

U.S. Department of Education. (1990). *Individuals with Disabilities Education Act of 1990.* Washington, DC: U.S. Government Printing Office.

U.S. Department of Education and U.S. Department of Labor. (1996). *School-to-work opportunities.* Washington, DC: National School-to-Work Office.

U.S. Department of Justice. (1991). *Americans with disabilities handbook.* Washington, U.S. Government Printing Office.

U.S. Department of Labor. (1970a). *Career thresholds.* Washington, DC: U.S. Government Printing Office.

U.S. Department of Labor. (1970b). *Manual for the general aptitude test battery.* Washington, DC: U.S. Government Printing Office.

U.S. Department of Labor. (1977). *Dictionary of occupational titles* (4th ed.). Washington, DC: U.S. Government Printing Office.

U.S. Department of Labor. (1979a). *Guide for occupational exploration.* Washington, DC: U.S. Government Printing Office.

U.S. Department of Labor. (1979b). *Manual for the USES general aptitude test battery. Section II: Occupational aptitude pattern structure.* Washington, DC: U.S. Government Printing Office.

U.S. Department of Labor. (1991a). *Dictionary of occupational titles* (4th ed. revised). Washington, DC: U.S. Government Printing Office.

U.S. Department of Labor. (1991b). *What work requires of school: A SCANS report for AMERICA 2000.* Washington, DC: U.S. Department of Labor.

U.S. Department of Labor. (1992–1993). *Occupational Outlook handbook.* Washington, DC: U.S. Government Printing Office.

U.S. Department of Labor. (1994–1996). *Occupational outlook handbook.* Washington, DC: U.S. Government Printing Office.

U.S. Department of Labor, Bureau of Labor Statistics. (1991). *Employment and earnings, February 1991.* Washington, DC: U.S. Government Printing Office.

U.S. Department of Defense. (1978). *Armed Services vocational aptitude test battery.* Washington, DC: Unified States Military Enlistment Processing Command.

U.S. Executive Office of the President (USEOP), Statistical Policy Division. (1977). *Standard occupational classification manual.* Washington, DC: U.S. Government Printing Office.

Valach, L. (1990). A theory of goal-directed action in career analysis. In R. A. Young & W. A. Borgen (Eds.), *Methodological approaches to the study of career* (pp. 107–126). New York: Praeger.

Velasquez, J. S., & Lynch, M. M. (1981). Computerized information systems: A practice orientation. *Administration in Social Work, 5* (3/4), 113–127.

Vetter, B. M. (1989). *Professional women and minorities: A manpower data resource service* (8th ed.). Washington, DC: Commission on Professionals in Science and Technology.

Vocational biographies. (1985). Sauk Centre, MN: Author.

von Cranach, M., & Harre, R. (Eds.). (1982). *The analysis of action: Recent theoretical and empirical advances.* Cambridge, England: Cambridge University Press.

Vontress, C. E. (1979). Cross-cultural counseling: An existential approach. *Personnel and Guidance Journal, 58,* 117–121.

Wall, W. (1984, May). Student values in the workplace. *Bulletin of the American Association of Higher Education,* 2–6.

Walsh, W. B., & Chartrand, J. M. (1994). Person-environment fit: Emerging directions. In M. L. Savickas & R. W. Lent (Eds.), *Convergence in career development theories: Implications for science and practice* (pp. 185–194). Palo Alto, CA: Consulting Psychologists Press.

Walsh, W. B., Craik, K. H., & Price, R. H. (1992). Person-environment psychology: A summary and commentary. In W. B. Walsh, K. H. Craik, & R. H. Price (Eds.), *Person-environment psychology: Models and perspectives* (pp. 243–268). Hillsdale, NJ: Erlbaum.

Walsh, W. B., & Osipow, S. H. (1988). *Career decision making.* Mahwah, NJ: Erlbaum.

Walz, A. (1972). Required courses. In J. E. Bottoms, R. N. Evans, K. B. Hoyt, & J. C. Willers (Eds.), *Career education resource guide.* Morristown, NJ: General Learning Corporation.

Walz, G. R. (1982). The career development diamond: Touching all the bases. In G. R. Walz (Ed.), *Career development in organizations.* Ann Arbor: ERIC Counseling and Personnel Services Clearinghouse, University of Michigan.

Wanous, J. P. (1980). *Organizational entry.* Reading, MA: Addison-Wesley.

Warr, P. (1992). Age and occupational well-being. *Psychology and Aging, 7,* 37–45.

Waterman, J. A. (1992). Career and life planning: A personal gyroscope. In J. Kummerow (Ed.), *New directions in the workplace* (pp. 1–33). Palo Alto, CA: Consulting Psychological Press, Inc.

Watson, M. A., & Ager, C. L. (1991). The impact of role valuation and life satisfaction in old age. *Physical and Occupational Therapy in Geriatrics, 10,* 27–62.

Weinrach, S. G. (1984). Determinants of vocational choice: Holland's theory. In D. Brown & L. Brooks (Eds.), *Career choice and development.* San Francisco: Jossey-Bass.

Weinrach, S. G., & Srebalus, D. J. (1990). Holland's theory of careers. In D. Brown & L. Brooks (Eds.), *Career choice and development: Applying contemporary theories to practice* (2nd ed.) (pp. 37–67). San Francisco: Jossey-Bass.

Wentling, R. M. (1992, Jan./Feb.). Women in middle management: Their career development and aspirations. *Business Horizons,* 48–54.

White, R. W. (1959). Motivation reconsidered: The concept of competence. *Psychological Review, 66,* 297.

Wigglesworth, D. C. (1992). Meeting the needs of the multicultural work force. In J. Kummerow (Ed.), *New directions in career planning and the workplace* (pp. 155–167). Palo Alto, CA: Consulting Psychological Press, Inc.

Wiinamaki, M. K. (1988). *My vocational experience.* Unpublished manuscript, Southwest Texas State University, San Marcos, TX.

Wilcox-Matthew, L., & Minor, C. W. (1989). The dual career couple: Concerns, benefits, and counseling implications. *Journal of Counseling and Development, 68,* 194–198.

Williamson, E. G. (1939). *How to counsel students: A manual of techniques for clinical counselors.* New York: McGraw-Hill.

Williamson, E. G. (1949). *Counseling adolescents.* New York: McGraw-Hill.

Williamson, E. G. (1965). *Vocational counseling: Some historical, philosophical, and theoretical perspectives.* New York: McGraw-Hill.

Wilson, R. N. (1981). The courage to be leisured. *Social Forces, 60* (2), 282–302.

Wolfson, K. T. P. (1972). *Career development of college women.* Unpublished doctoral dissertation. University of Minnesota, Minneapolis.

Wolpe, J. (1958). *Psychotherapy by reciprocal inhibition.* Palo Alto, CA: Stanford University Press.

Wolpe, J. (1973). *The practice of behavior therapy.* New York: Pergamon Press.

Wood, J. T. (1994). *Gendered lives: Communication, gender, and culture.* Belmont, CA: Wadsworth, Inc.

Woodman, S. (1991, May). How super are heroes? *Health,* pp. 40, 49, 82.

Woods, J. F., & Ollis, H. (1996). *Labor market & job information on the Internet.* Submitted for publication in the Winter (March 1996) issue of *Workforce Journal.*

Woody, B. (1992). *Black women in the workplace.* Westport, CT: Greenwood Press.

Wrenn, C. G. (1988). The person in career counseling. *The Career Development Quarterly, 36* (4), 337–343.

Wright, B. A. (1983). *Physical disability—a psychological approach* (2nd ed.). New York: Harper & Row.

Wright, G. N. (1980). *Total rehabilitation.* Boston: Little, Brown.

Yankelovich, D. (1979). Work, values and the new breed. In C. Kerr & J. M. Rosow (Eds.), *Work in America: The decade ahead* (pp. 3–26). New York: Van Nostrand Reinhold.

Yankelovich, D. (1981a). *New rules.* New York: Random House.

Yankelovich, D. (1981b). The meaning of work. In J. O'Toole, J. L. Scheiber, & L. C. Wood (Eds.), *Working: Changes and choices* (pp. 33–34). New York: Human Sciences Press.

Young, R. A., & Valach, L. (1996). Interpretation and action in career counseling. In M. L. Savickas & W. B. Walsh (Eds.), *Handbook of career counseling theory and practice.* Palo Alto, CA: Davies-Black (Consulting Psychologists Press).

Young, R. A., Valach, L., & Collin, A. (1996). A contextual explanation of career. In D. Brown, L. Brooks, & Associates (Eds.), *Career choice and development* (3rd ed.) (pp. 477–508). San Francisco: Jossey-Bass.

Zaccaria, J. (1970). *Theories of occupational choice and vocational development.* Boston: Houghton Mifflin.

Zajonc, E. (1980). Feeling and thinking: Preferences need no influence. *American Psychologist, 35,* 151–175.

Zimmerman, B. J. (1995). Self-efficacy and educational development. In A. Bandura (Ed.), *Self-efficacy in changing societies.* Cambridge, U.K.: Cambridge University Press.

Zunker, V. G. (1987). The life-style and career development standard. *Counselor Education and Supervision, 27,* 110–118.

Zunker, V. G. (1990). *Using assessment results in career counseling.* Pacific Grove, CA: Brooks/Cole.

Zunker, V. G. (1994). *Using assessment results for career development* (4th ed.). Pacific Grove, CA: Brooks/Cole.

Zunker, V. G., Ash, K. A., Evans, D. A., Kight, L. E., Sunbury, R. V., & Walker, A. E. (1979). *Counseling objectives and specific tasks for career decision making.* Unpublished manuscript, Southwest Texas State University, San Marcos.

Zunker, V. G., & Norris, D. (1998). *Using assessment results for career development.* Pacific Grove, CA: Brooks/Cole.

Zytowski, D. G. (1969). Toward a theory of career development for women. *Personnel and Guidance Journal, 47,* 660–664.

Zytowski, D. G. (1994). Tests and counseling: We are still married, and living in discriminant analysis. *Measurement and Evaluation in Counseling and Development, 26,* 219–223.

TO THE OWNER OF THIS BOOK:

I hope that you have enjoyed *Career Counseling: Applied Concepts of Life Planning*, Fifth Edition, as much as I have enjoyed writing it. I'd like to know as much about your experiences with the book as you care to offer. Only through your comments and the comments of others can I learn how to make *Career Counseling* a better book for future readers.

School and address: _____

Department: _____

Instructor's name: _____

1. What did you like most about *Career Counseling*, Fifth Edition? _____

_____

_____

2. What did you like least about the book? _____

_____

_____

3. Were all of the chapters of the book assigned for you to read? _____

   If not, which ones weren't? _____

4. Did you use *Using Assessment Results for Career Development?* _____

5. If so, please tell us what component was most useful? _____

_____

_____

6. In the space below, or on a separate sheet of paper, please let us know any other comments about the book you'd like to make. (For example, were any chapters *or* concepts particularly difficult?) We'd be delighted to hear from you!

_____

_____

_____

_____